William and Henry James

Selected Letters

William and Henry James

Selected Letters

Edited by
Ignas K. Skrupskelis
and
Elizabeth M. Berkeley

with an Introduction by
John J. McDermott

University Press of Virginia
Charlottesville and London

THE UNIVERSITY PRESS OF VIRGINIA
© 1997 by the Rector and Visitors of the University of Virginia

First published 1997
All rights reserved

Printed in the United States of America

Frontispiece: Henry and William James,
early 1900s. (By permission of the
Houghton Library, Harvard University)

The paper used in this publication meets the minimum requirements of the American National Standard for Information Sciences— Permanence of Paper for Printed Library Materials, ANSI Z39.48-1984.

Library of Congress Cataloging-in-Publication Data

James, William, 1842–1910.
    [Correspondence. Selections]
    William and Henry James : selected letters / edited by Ignas K. Skrupskelis and Elizabeth M. Berkeley ; with an introduction by John J. McDermott.
        p. cm.
    ISBN 0-8139-1694-1 (alk. paper)
    1. James, William, 1842–1910—Correspondence.   2. James, Henry, 1843–1916—Correspondence.   3. Philosophers—United States—Correspondence.   4. Psychologists—United States—Correspondence.   5. Authors, American—19th century—Correspondence.   6. Authors, American—20th century—Correspondence.
    I. James, Henry, 1843–1916.   II. Skrupskelis, Ignas K., 1938–   .   III. Berkeley, Elizabeth M.   IV. Title.
    B945.J24A4   1997
    191—dc20
    [B]   96-25921
                                                                      CIP

0-8139-1694-1 (cloth)

Contents

The Letters

Illustrations following page 224

Introduction
JOHN J. McDERMOTT

In an essay on the painter Daumier, Henry James writes of the drawing entitled *Saltimbanques:*

> It exhibits a pair of lean, hungry mountebanks, a clown and a harlequin beating the drum and trying a comic attitude, to attract the crowd at a fair, to a poor booth in front of which a painted canvas, offering to view a simpering fat woman, is suspended. But the crowd does not come, and the battered tumblers, with their furrowed cheeks, go through their pranks in the void. The whole thing is symbolic and full of grimness, imagination, and pity. It is the sense that we shall find in him, mixed with his homelier extravagances, an element prolific in indications of this order that draws us back to Daumier.[1]

And so, too, is it the abiding presence of "imagination" and "homelier extravagances" that draw us to return over and again to the letters written between William and Henry James.[2] The extraordinary correspondence between these celebrated brothers offers a rich kaleidoscopic version of person, places, and events that striate the Euro-American world from 1861 until the death of William James in

---

[1] Henry James, "Honore Daumier," *Picture and Text* (New York: Harper and Brothers, 1893), pp. 143–44.

[2] The selected letters of the present volume have been chosen by the editors from the first three volumes of the Critical Edition of *The Correspondence of William James.* The subsequent nine volumes of the *Correspondence* will feature the epistolary transactions of William James with family, friends, and professional colleagues. The Editors of the *Correspondence* hope that the savoring of the present edition of some 200 letters will encourage the reader to visit the more extensive tapestry of the full correspondence.

August 1910. This veritable feast of personal, social, and cultural insights is indeed "moveable"; not a year goes by that one or both of the brothers James writes from a different place, often from a different country, and especially from France, Germany, Italy, and Switzerland.

The home front for Henry James was England, for the most part a series of apartments, flats, and clubs in and around London. William's home was in Cambridge, Massachusetts, and in later years during the summer at Chocorua, New Hampshire. Reading the letters, one has the impression that London and Cambridge were as much points of departure as they were places of residence. The letters are laced with plans for future travel, reflections on previous travels, and constant complaints about their present whereabouts. On balance, I think it fair to say that they complain more about more than most of us.

William James once wrote of "the restlessness of the theoretic situation." One could add with ample evidence that "restlessness" was a family trait.[3] From their earliest childhood, William and Henry James were on the move. At first this traced to the desire of their father, the redoubtable Henry James, Sr., to provide them with a European education. From the outset the assumption seemed to be that some place, some school, some thing of whatever cast or stripe was better, more promising, than the present situation. Call it what you will, a highly imaginative restiveness, perpetual dissatisfaction, self-pity, or rich veins of creative energy, William and Henry James had a deep belief that all would, or at least could, go better if only this or that

---

[3] For the history of the James family and its literary and philosophical accomplishments I suggest the following works from among a vast repertoire of interpretations and commentaries: Alfred Habegger, *The Father: A Life of Henry James, Sr.* (New York: Farrar, Straus and Giroux, 1995); R. W. B. Lewis, *The Jameses* (New York: Farrar, Straus and Giroux, 1991); Leon Edel, *Henry James: A Life* (New York: Harper and Row, 1985); Fred Kaplan, *Henry James: The Imagination of Genius* (New York: William Morrow and Company, 1992); Ralph Barton Perry, *The Thought and Character of William James*, 2 vols. (Boston: Little Brown, 1935); Gerald Myers, *William James: His Life and Thought* (New Haven: Yale Univ. Press, 1986); Jean Strouse, *Alice James: A Biography* (Boston: Houghton Mifflin, 1980); and Jane Maher, *Biography of Broken Fortunes: Wilkie and Bob, Brothers of William, Henry and Alice James* (Hamden, Conn.: Archon, 1986). See also *The Works of William James*, ed. Frederick Burkhardt, Fredson Bowers, and Ignas K. Skrupskelis, 19 vols. (Cambridge: Harvard Univ. Press, 1975–88) and a collection of major texts in *The Writings of William James*, ed. John J. McDermott (Chicago: Univ. of Chicago Press, 1977).

change would take place. Framing their personal attitudes toward the present was a lifelong interweaving of genuine physical ailments and chronic hypochondriasis. In short, it does not come as a surprise that the brothers were dominated by what we now refer to as future-time prospects.[4]

Each reader of these letters will have his or her impressions of the central themes, dependent, of course, on one's needs, hopes, disappointments, and nostalgic retrospections. For me, these letters have as their internal focus, health, money, work, family, death, and indirectly yet powerfully, personal and moral courage.

My first and lasting overarching impression, however, is the persistence of the *ordinary,* of ordinariness, of lives carried on much like most of us, most of the time. Given this obviousness, why then do we witness such a widespread, continual, and loyal fascination with this correspondence? Yes, William and Henry James are luminaries in their respective accomplishments as writer, psychologist, and philosopher. But then so are many others whose letters do not grip us as these do. Quite simply, it is the prose, the turn of a phrase, the power of description, and the indefatigable literary elegance that clothes even the most mundane of feelings, occurrences, and events.

Take the young Henry James in a letter from Oxford in 1869. He praises his host, Augustus George Vernon Harcourt, for "it is certainly no small favor for a man to trudge about bodily for three hours in the noon-day sun with a creature thus rudely hurled into his existence from over the sea, whom he neither knows nor cares for. His reward will be in heaven." Henry then reports on his lunch with the Rector, obviously a boring affair yet saved for us as he writes:

[4] Perhaps the most telling instance of this family confidence in a better future is found in the letter of 7 August 1910 by William James's wife, Alice Gibbens James, as written to her mother. Penned less than three weeks before William's inevitable death from congestive heart failure, and while preparing for their voyage home from Europe following a series of failed medicinal treatments, Alice writes: "This will be my last letter, and it can be a cheerful one, with a good report. . . . To return to the journey: our heavy baggage can be freighted straight to Irving St. and we shall only take the state-room trunks to Chocorua. It looks so pleasant,—Harry at Quebec, Billy at Intervale and you and Peggy at the house. . . . It seems too good to be true." Too good, indeed! See Gay Wilson Allen, *William James: A Biography* (New York: Viking, 1967), p. 489. See also p. 491 for a description of James's last hours and his death on 26 August 1910. Henry James died similarly. After a period of chronic angina, he had a stroke at the end of 1915 and passed away on 28 February 1916. See F. W. Dupee, *Henry James: His Life and Writings* (Garden City, N.Y.: Doubleday Anchor, 1956), pp. 250–52.

The Rector is a dessicated old scholar, torpid even to incivility with too much learning; but his wife is of quite
another fashion—very young (about 28) very pretty, very
clever, very charming & very conscious of it all. She is I
believe highly "emancipated" & I defy an English-woman
to be emancipated except coldly & wantonly. As a spectacle the thing had its points: the dark rich, scholastic old
dining room in the college court—the languid old rector & his pretty little wife in a riding-habit, talking slang.
Otherwise it was slow. I then went about with Harcourt to
various colleges, halls, & gardens—he doing his duty most
bravely—& I mine for that matter.

On then to the college gardens. "These same gardens are the fairest
things in Oxford. Locked in their own ancient verdure, behind their
own ancient walls, filled with shade & music & perfumes & privacy—
with lounging students & charming children—with the rich old college windows keeping guard from above—they are places to lie down
on the grass in forever, in the happy belief the world is all an English
garden & time a fine old English afternoon" (26 Apr. 1869, pp. 42,
43).
  Almost forty years later William James writes of scenery in New
Hampshire:

The weather was hot indian summer, & early the next
morning I came straight up here to get in a last short
taste of the country's sweetness. No use comparing American scenery with english—they have no common denomi-
nator. So quickly does one take the tune of the english
thing that this N.H. autumn seemed to me almost heartbreaking in its sentimentality. The smoky haze, the windless heat, the litter of the leaves on the ground in their
rich colours, with enough remaining on the trees to
make the whole scene red and yellow, the penury & shab-
biness of everything human, the delicate emaciated morbidness, and feminine secretness of all nature's effects was
so pathetic! No sound, no people, earth & sky both
empty, and almost alarming in their emptiness. The elabo-
rateness of english scenery, the simplicity of American,—
its hard to be torn so both ways by one's admirations,

and the best policy is to think as little as possible about
the contrast. (21 Oct. 1908, pp. 497–98)

In virtually all of the letters, we find a phrase or a line that startles
us, gives us pause, causes us to reflect, or just to admire. Read, for
example, Henry James writing of London: "So does one move all the
while here on identified ground" (29 Mar. 1877, p. 111). From
William James we read his version of two storied hamlets in New
England: "There is a strange naked and lonely poetry about clean
pure little Nantucket under its tender sky. The settlement at Martha's
vineyard, 'oak bluffs' is probably the most audacious paradise of 'caddish'ness which has ever flaunted itself in the eye of day. A flat insipid
sand bank" (5 July 1876, p. 103). Much later in his life, while traveling by train, William writes: "These magnificent railroads & new
settlements bring home to one the fact that all life rests so on the
physical courage of common man. It trims the best of one's conceptions" (22 Sept. 1898, p. 357). Countless other entries in these *Selected
Letters,* attuned to one's personal taste, are sure to enchant the
reader.

Fore and aft, that is the quality of language provided over forty-
nine years for virtually every experience; the jejune, the sad, the irritated, the celebratory, the anticipatory, the failures, the successes,
the worries, and the happenstance. They are intrigued by persons of
every stripe, by visage, by human carriage, by natural light, by
weather, by voices, by topography, and, with virtually everything, by
ambience. Whatever their mood, be it electric or depressed, be it
relieved or worried, their prose sustains a quality of evocation, provocation, and perpetual excellence. In his Introduction to Volume 1 of
The Correspondence of William James, Gerald E. Myers is on the mark
when he writes: "Like their father, William and Henry chose an intellectual life. The sons had been reared on their father's linguistic in-
ventiveness, and they came to believe, as did Socrates in Plato's
Phaedo, that 'to express oneself badly is not only faulty as far as the
language goes, but does some harm to the soul.'"[5]

On occasion, the brothers respond to happenings in their lives, for
example, natural disasters, which have repeated themselves during
the time of our reading their letters, approximately one hundred
years later. It is at once eerie and unsettling to read of their discussion

[5] *Correspondence,* 1:xxix.

of the American intention to effect a blockade of Cuba, when as of today this "strategy" is still under consideration as a foreboding aspect of the Cuban question. William James wrote then as we might now "that our first act should be to exacerbate still more the said sufferings by our blockade is one of those inconsistencies that infest all 'Great' things" (3 May 1898, p. 355).

Despite the extraordinary transformation of both travel and communication technology,[6] it is striking that our present lives and those of the brothers have an abiding sameness to them, limned and penetrated as they are by the petty, the nagging, the insecure, the hoping, the affectionate, and the dreaming as found in everyone's everyday. Certainly the time it takes to travel from New York to London has decreased dramatically. Yet, then as now, and now as then, the person who meets or who fails to meet us, who welcomes or who fails to welcome us, bequeaths to us an experience of caring or of the perilous, and those experiences are identical as undergone in any time and every time.

One thinks here of that old adage which holds that wherever *you* are, there *you* are, complete with bowels, palpitations, financial worries, familial stress, low self-esteem, or conversely, confidence, intentions, aspirations, and perhaps, one hopes, general good feelings. All of these and other equivalent human sensibilities frequent the letters of William and Henry James, although systemic good feelings seemed for them to be a comparatively rare experience.

Upon a closer reading of these letters, just what does occupy them

---

[6] Even when reading the full extant correspondence of William James, it is imperative for the reader to be constantly aware of the time lag in the reception of the letters, no matter how quickly they are answered. Weeks go by before a dispatched letter from America arrives in England or on the Continent. Consequently, subsequent letters often refer to a variety of crises, resolved before the letter arrives, thereby resulting in an impression of constant turmoil. Nowhere is this more graphic than in the letters between the young William James when he was on a scientific expedition in Brazil and his fretful family at home in Cambridge, Massachusetts. Tranquility did exist, but it must have been restricted to the temporal interstices between letters. See the *Correspondence*, vol. 4. Further, although many of the letters are very long by our measure, much remains unsaid. Compare, for example, a transcript of an hour-long telephone conversation! Of special significance here is the aggravating time frame involved in the series of letters that rotate around the deaths of the mother, Mary Robertson Walsh James (1882), the father, Henry James, Sr. (1882), and the sister, Alice James (1892). In none of these deaths were William and Henry in the same place, so the correspondence has a distinctive edge of both urgency and frustration.

in their persistent and seemingly endless effort to stay in touch with each other? An issue that is high on the list of mutual concern, falls under the rubric of personal health. Actually, their discussion of health is better described as a lifelong and sometimes morbid preoccupation with bodily functions, especially those attendant upon the human bowel. Telling also is that the complaint is almost always constipation rather than diarrhea. Should the reader express dubiety about this fixation on the bowel, one need only turn to William's letter of 25 October 1869, where he writes to Henry that "it seems to me you must have somewhere in the gut an accumulation of old faeces wh. block the way."[7] Later, continuing this fraternal quasi-medical diagnosis, William writes to Henry of the helpful result from the use of "sulfuric acid dodge" and proceeds to offer an ameliorative protocol for Henry.

> I have experimented on myself and find it very effica-
> cious. If having started yourself by it, you find symptoms
> of soreness about anus & rectum, slack up; it may then
> be that *small* doses of fluid extract of senna (say a third of
> a teaspoonful 3 times a day[)]—after meals if it will work
> so,—if not, on an empty stomach—(or even a less dose,)
> will keep things open. It is less trouble than the confec-
> tion with figs I wrote you about. Nibbling a little solid
> Rhubarb, 3 times a day may also help. But remember
> that you should in no case get more than a *laxative* effect.
> Real purging is always to be avoided since its after-
> working is in the direction of increased torpor. (5 Dec.
> 1869, p. 57)

The preoccupation with bowel movements led the brothers into the hoary world of Fletcherism, a nostrum that featured complex and aggressive motions for chewing one's food. Early enthusiasm for the curative promise of Fletcherism was slowly replaced by irritation

---

[7] *Correspondence*, 1:112. Although perhaps disconcerting to contemporary readers, discussion of the human bowel connoted depth of feeling to earlier generations. Witness, for example, William James in his discussion of "The Perception of Reality." "The surest warrant for immortality is the yearning of our bowels for our dear ones; for God, the sinking sense it gives us to imagine no such Providence or help" (*The Principles of Psychology* [Cambridge: Harvard Univ. Press, 1981], 2:937).

pertaining to the draconian demands of the method and increased skepticism as to its worth. Finally, Henry James visited the great physician Sir William Osler who led him to believe that Fletcherism had "bedevilled my digestion to within an inch of its life" (15 Mar. 1910, p. 517).

In addition to these alimentary woes, the brothers also detailed worries about headaches, blisters, gout, backaches, insomnia, and acedia, each and all being mainstays of chronic hypochondriasis. Still, none of these personal ailments nor the ongoing worries about worries deterred either of them from writing brilliantly and publishing prodigiously, while moving, traveling, and talking incessantly. The nineteenth-century appellation for this behavior is "neurasthenia."[8] Put simply, neurasthenia is a human state of being that is characterized by affective somatic articulations of inner feelings. In that William and Henry James were both hypersensitive and neurasthenic, it is no wonder that for them bodily affectations were extremely palpable. They were fortunate not to be in the clutches of high-technology medicine for they would have been tested, scoped, medicated, and surgically explored to the point where we would have neither their works nor their letters.

A second theme that resonates throughout the letters is that of finance, that is, money, sometimes very small amounts of money. Henry James writes it straight out: "Like you, with all my heart, I have 'finance on the brain'" (20 Apr. 1898, p. 352). A typical money passage is found in Henry's letter of 24 July 1885.

> My transaction with Osgood's successor has dragged out long, partly through a delay, at the last, of my own; but before you get this he will to all appearance have paid over $4000 to Warner for me. I have instructed Warner immediately, to take $1000 out of this & repay it to you: so that I trust the whole business will have been settled by August 1ˢᵗ.
>
> I shall soon have straightened out completely as regards money, & am now in a position to promise to pay $1000 for the Syracuse building before the bills are due (unless they are to be due unnaturally soon: That is I can

---

[8] See Tom Lutz, *American Nervousness—1903* (Ithaca: Cornell Univ. Press, 1991), especially the sections on neurasthenia and William James (pp. 63–98) and Henry James (pp. 244–75).

easily pay the money by Jan. 1ˢᵗ.) *Therefore,* as this is a perfectly definite engagement, I would rather you did not keep back my share of the rents—but go on paying it to Alice. When I told you to do this I did not clearly understand that $1000 was the maximum I should have to contribute, even covering the advance to Bob. I thought the sum wd. be larger. This sum I now see I can pay out of current income from other sources; &, I repeat, hereby engage to do so if you will, when you next write, tell me the earliest moment at which you will have to settle for the repairs. I could do it *before* January 1ˢᵗ. In this case count upon me for the money & continue to pay my rents to Alice. (p. 175)

Letters of this kind from William and Henry occur frequently and on occasion generate acrimony as, for example, over decisions pertaining to the maintenance of the inherited property in Syracuse, New York, the dispensation of the father's will with regard to shares for the "other" two brothers, Wilkie and Robertson, and most testily, the scrap over the price Henry was to pay for the purchase of Lamb House in Rye, England. In this latter transaction, Henry was so furious with William's meddling as to the question of a fair price for the property that he writes: "My joy has shrivelled under your very lucid warnings, but it will re-bloom" (4 Aug. 1899, p. 384). To this rebuke William replied, "It has filled this home with grief to find that our letters about the purchase 'rubbed you the wrong way.' You took them far too seriously—but I know just how you felt!" (8 Aug. 1899, p. 385).

George Santayana said of William James that he had advantages, namely, the inheritance from the Syracuse properties, which had been the investment of the grandfather, William James of Albany. True, but it was never an advantage capable of liberating the brothers from financial stress. The inheritance was divided among many and the property always seemed to present problems of one sort or another: maintenance, a fire, and the difficulties attendant on absentee ownership. Still, in basic actuarial terms, neither of them was ever impoverished or financially dependent in an awkward, unpleasant way. Given their travel mania and William's large family, they did have to make arrangements for a steady income from a variety of sources. From midlife forward, William had access to his Harvard salary[9] whereas Henry always had to sustain himself by royalties from published writings. As with their physical ailments, the grousing about money did not prevent them from living very well, as witness Henry's lovely Lamb House and William's two spacious homes in New England, each abode ministered by servants!

Thematically, once more, I turn to their discussion of work, that homely, small, yet powerful American word. Work they did! From the beginning of their lives and certainly of their correspondence, they fretted about what they could do, should do, and what would be the upshot of what they had done or were doing. By analogy, they practiced an intellectual Fletcherism, masticating ideas and projects over and over. Despite the long passages about personal health, money, and their living in a staggering variety of domiciles, the vertebral thread in their lives was their work. For Henry, the underlying deposit was his attention to the craft of writing. Quintessentially, he was a writer. His thoughts were absorbed by his plots, his scenes, and, above all, his fictional characters, many of whom have become public figures who have long since outstripped their original literary settings as have Milly Theale and Daisy Miller. For William, the focus was on human behavior, initially in its physiological underpinnings and subsequently its psychological manifestation. In his later work he took up the questions pertaining to moral and religious attitudes and experiences. *En passant* and especially in the last decade of his life, William James developed a highly original and pathbreaking approach to metaphysics and epistemology. Although Ralph Barton Perry, his student and first biographer, understood the importance of William James's rich philosophical contribution, its full significance has been recognized only within the last few decades.

Neither in these *Selected Letters*, nor in the three-volume edition of their *Correspondence*, do we find any trenchant analysis of each other's serious writings. I do not find this surprising, for—the many intelligent and interesting commentaries aside—my position is that neither had a clue to the depth of the other's work. For that matter, William's interpretive responses to literature of any kind, although highly opin-

---

[9] William James was complaining constantly about his Harvard salary and he was not averse to looking elsewhere. For example, he gave consideration to replacing G. Stanley Hall at Johns Hopkins University. His reason for moving strikes a familiar chord in our contemporary professoriate: "But I do believe in keeping the ball rolling, and I know that every man who leaves a college for the sake of higher pay elsewhere helps to reform our system of underpaying intellectual work" (19 Apr. 1888, p. 198).

ionated, are rarely distinctive or unusually enlightening. On several occasions, Henry says just that. For example, in 1878, he writes:

> I was much depressed on reading your letter by your painful reflections on the *Europeans:* but now, an hour having elapsed, I am beginning to hold up my head a little; the more so as I think I myself estimate the book very justly & am aware of its extreme slightness. I think you take these things too rigidly & unimaginatively—too much as if an artistic experiment were a piece of conduct, to which one's life were somehow committed; but I think also that you're quite right in pronouncing the book "thin," & empty. I don't at all despair, yet, of doing something fat. Meanwhile I hope you will continue to give me, when you can, your free impression of my performances. It is a great thing to have some one write to one of one's things as if one were a 3$^{\underline{d}}$ person, & you are the only individual who will do this. I don't think however you are always right, by any means. As for instance in your objection to the closing paragraph of *Daisy Miller,* which seems to me queer & narrow, & as regards which I don't seize your point of view. (14 Nov. 1878, p. 118)

As for William, almost thirty years later, he sends Henry a crusty critique of *The Golden Bowl,* inclusive of his oft-quoted fraternal advice as follows: "But why won't you, just to please Brother, sit down and write a new book, with no twilight or mustiness in the plot, with great vigor and decisiveness in the action, no fencing in the dialogue, no psychological commentaries, and absolute straightness in the style? Publish it in my name, I will acknowledge it, and give you half the proceeds" (22 Oct. 1905, p. 463). This facetious, albeit patronizing, suggestion of William drew an incendiary response from Henry: "I mean (in response to what you write me of your having read the *Golden B.*) to try to produce some uncanny form of thing, in fiction, that will gratify you, as Brother—but let me say, dear William, that I shall greatly be humiliated if you *do* like it, & thereby lump it, in your affection, with things, of the current age, that I have heard you express admiration for & that I would sooner descend to a dishonoured grave than have written" (23 Nov. 1905, pp. 466–67).

Henry James was never as critical of William's work and certainly never as caustic. Rather, the philosophically sophisticated material seemed to just pass by him. In 1884 Henry writes to William that "I have attacked your two Mind articles, with admiration, but been defeated" (21 Apr. 1884, p. 160). One of these pieces was entitled "On Some Omissions of Introspective Psychology" and is regarded as the most important of William James's early essays, for it became the basis of the famous chapter "The Stream of Thought" in his *Principles of Psychology* as well as the foundation position for his subsequent doctrine of radical empiricism and his pragmatic epistemology. This philosophical material as written by William James is very difficult to understand, and I see no reason to expect sibling loyalty to overcome that obstacle. As for sibling rivalry in the assessment of each other's work,[10] that, too, was ongoing, although it abated with the increasing accomplishments of each in turn, distinctively so after the publication of William's monumental *Principles of Psychology* in 1890.

Affectionate and frequent praise was also present. In 1907 Henry writes of William's pragmatism:

> Why the devil I didn't write to you after reading your *Pragmatism*—how I kept from it—I can't now explain save by the very fact of the spell itself (of interest & enthrallment) that the book cast upon me: I simply sank down, under it, into such depths of submission & assimilation that *any* reaction, very nearly, even that of acknowledgement, would have had almost the taint of dissent or escape. Then I was lost in the wonder of the extent to which all my life I have (like M. Jourdain) unconsciously pragmatised. (17 Oct. 1907, p. 489)

Less effusive, but, nonetheless, characterized by enthusiasm, William writes in 1908 that "I read Roderick H. [Hudson] which I hadn't lookt at since it first appeared [1875]. My brain could hardly understand anything, much less *enjoy*, but it bro't back the old charm. What a colossal worker you are, to have gone all over it verbally again! I am not sure either, that in *that* case at all events, it was not labor lost,

---

[10] For an adjudication of the interpretive dispute about the existence and extent of the rivalry between the brothers, see Daniel Mark Fogel's Introduction in *Correspondence*, 2:xliv–xlvi.

or that the simpler and more naive phrasing of the original edition does n't keep a better harmony. But what astounds me is your power of steady *work!*" (4 Feb. 1908, pp. 496–97).

And so it went, sometimes a swap of criticism, sometimes a swap of admiration, other times just an acknowledgment of their respective activity and results. They may not always have cared *for* each other's work, but doubtlessly they cared *about* each other's work. And that continual fraternal jousting forged an ineradicable and enduring bond, easily able to withstand any psychobiographical carping by subsequent critics.

All of the above concerns, notwithstanding, the fulcrum around which this correspondence rotates and the linchpin in their shared lives, however separated by geographical distance, was the family, their family. Rarely, if ever, has a private family been so chronicled with publication of their letters, diaries, autobiographical material as well as extensive biographies and interpretative, critical commentaries. Although we do not possess everything that they wrote, especially letters to and from Henry James, we do have access to an enormous cache of material, both public and private. Everything they wrote seems to be intended some day, for the light of day, that is, for us, generations later, to read. One of William James's students, the philosopher Charles M. Bakewell, once said that James never wrote anything, even a "post card," that he did not intend some day to be published. And so it was to be, for we have published at least one of his postcards with more to come. As early as 1869, William writes to Henry that "your letters from Italy are beyond praise. It is a great pity they should be born to blush unseen by the general public, and that just the matter that they contain, in a little less rambling style should not appear in the columns of the Nation" (5 Dec. 1869, p. 58). And I find it hard to believe that the brilliant, acerbic, and familially controversial *Diary* of Alice James was not intended for the wider audience it now enjoys.

The major family figures in the *Correspondence* are the parents, Henry James, Sr., and Mary Walsh James, the aunt Catharine Walsh (Aunt Kate), the children, William, Henry, Garth Wilkinson (Wilkie), Robertson (Bob), and Alice. Prominent also is Alice Howe Gibbens James, the wife of William James and a powerful figure in the complex relationships of the family.

As one might surmise, the amount, quality, and frankness of the surviving archival materials have given rise to a spate of retrospective

interpretations and judgments, ranging from the hagiographical
to the psychobiographical. The nodal points of these works include
William's relationship to his father, the comparatively unsung life of
the brilliant, psychologically distressed sister, Alice, the latent homo-
sexuality of Henry, and the "broken fortunes" of Wilkie and Bob.[11]
For obvious reasons, each of these works and others in a similar vein
view the family from the experience of one or two of its members.
Consequently, we are enriched by the focus, by the singularity of purpose, but of necessity the understanding of those in the family not in
the focus remains somewhat skewed. I see no way around this difficulty; for every point of departure is in some way constitutive of how
we come to see the other. In this regard George Santayana is wise
when he tells us that "memory is a reconstruction, not a relapse."[12]
And such was the approach of Henry James in his truncated *Autobiography*.

> We were, to my sense, the blest group of us, such a com-
> pany of characters and such a picture of differences, and
> withal so fused and united and interlocked, that each of
> us, to that fond fancy, pleads for preservation, and that
> in respect to what I speak of myself as possessing I think
> I shall be ashamed, as of a cold impiety, to find any ele-
> ment altogether negligible. To which I may add perhaps
> that I struggle under the drawback, innate and inbred,
> of seeing the whole content of memory and affection in
> each enacted and recovered moment, as who should say,
> in the vivid image and the very scene; the light of the
> only terms in which life has treated me to experience.[13]

Herein, the "reconstruction" seems to be cut off from the reality,
for as the James family moved through its own history, "blest" does
not strike us as the appropriate appellation in that at least three of

---

[11] See Howard Feinstein, *Becoming William James* (Ithaca: Cornell Univ. Press, 1984);
the most recent and most forthcoming discussion of Henry James's sexual orientation
is found in Robert Dawidoff's Introduction, *Correspondence*, 3:xxiii–xxxv; see also
Strouse and Maher.

[12] George Santayana, *Scepticism and Animal Faith* (New York: Scribners, 1923), p. 156.

[13] Henry James, *Autobiography* (1913; reprinted New York: Criterion Books, 1952),
p. 4.

Henry's "company of characters," Wilkie, Bob, and Alice, lived profoundly unrequited lives. This judgment is borne out by the family strife reported, diagnosed, and subjected to frequent worry in much of the *Correspondence*.[14]

The present context does not allow for a detailed discussion of this familial montage that makes up the James family or as R. W. B. Lewis calls them, The Jameses. Contrary to received opinion, I do not think that the James family was unusually fraught with mishap or disaster. True, there were problems but as has been famously said, "What family does not have its problems." For those of us who have lived our lives in and on the tumultuous interpersonal matrix of a large family, we know that rarely does a month go by without some fracturing of serenity. Despite obvious skittishness and even denial on the part of William and Henry, the simple fact is that this was a third-generation Irish-American family, with all of the strengths, weaknesses, foibles, and encumbrances so entailed. Only the sister, Alice James, has the personal courage and forbearance to come to grips with the significance of that self-benighted Irish lineage.

This ambivalence about the Irishness of the family is made clear in Henry's response to his reading of Alice's diary, posthumously.[15]

> However, what comes out in the book—as it came out to me in fact—is that she was really an Irishwoman!—transplanted, transfigured—but none the less fundamentally national—in spite of her so much larger & finer than Irish intelligence. She felt the Home Rule question absolutely as only an Irishwoman (not anglicised) could. It was a tremendous emotion with her—inexplicable in any other way—& perfectly explicable by "atavism." What a pity she wasn't born there—& had her health for it. She would have been (if, always, she had not fallen a victim to disgust—a large "if"!) a national glory! (28 May 1894, p. 308)

---

[14] If we were to have access to the correspondence of any large family, assuming there were to be such a correspondence, I believe it to be of significance that those letters would have as their focus virtually identical themes and concerns as found in the James family, namely, health, money, competition, natural disaster, politics, and sickness unto death. Only the quality of the writing would differ, an "only" of paramount importance.

[15] *The Diary of Alice James*, ed. Leon Edel (New York: Dodd, Mead, 1964).

In Irish family parlance, a distinction is made between *problem* and *trouble*. The former can be managed, by patching, punting, or the steadfast waiting it out as time erodes the difficulty in question. *Trouble*, however, is a very different matter. It is the name given to the century-long intransigence within the embattled factions of Northern Ireland. The meaning of *trouble* is that one is at wit's end. Trying is possible and spiritually helpful but seemingly nothing can be done for alleviation. To my mind, William and Henry James had problems. Garth Wilkinson James also had problems, big ones, and his premature death at age thirty-eight prevents us from knowing whether they were intractable.[16] Robertson James and Alice James, however, had *trouble*, were in *trouble*, and caused others in the family to be constantly both distressed and irritated.

Robertson James was an alcoholic and despite the fact that retrospective medical diagnoses are unsure at best, the information we have does point to his being a clinical alcoholic, that is, not simply a person with a drinking problem. At times, he tried valiantly to overcome his malady and even spent several years at the Dansville Asylum in New York State, undergoing hapless and bogus treatment for his addiction.[17] Not having access to a genuine program of recovery, Robertson was doomed, as relapse followed upon relapse, until his death in 1910.

The response of William and Henry James to this lifelong family nightmare is predictable, that is, frustration and dashed hopes, each lamentably understandable, for it is precisely the unpredictability of the alcoholic behavior that causes the most stress and generates some responses unworthy of Robertson's plight.[18] On two occasions William refers to Robertson as a "poor wretch," and at one point hopes for his death. He writes to Henry, "But I wish the poor wretch could die in one of his bad sprees—it would be so much future misery averted for him as well as for his family" (12 Apr. 1887, p. 188). Five months later, William refers to Robertson as "really insane, poor wretch, and grows frantic at any and every minutest practical difficulty or uncer-

---

[16] Henry James refers to the death of Wilkie as a "blessed liberation" (24 Nov. 1883, p. 156).

[17] See Maher, pp. 185–88.

[18] In later years, William James was more perceptive about the "sway of alcohol over mankind," contending that "the drunken consciousness is one bit of the mystic consciousness, and our total opinion of it must find its place in our opinion of that larger whole" (*The Varieties of Religious Experience* [Cambridge: Harvard Univ. Press, 1985], p. 307).

tainty" (22 Sept. 1893, p. 287). In response to William's aggravation, Henry refers to "Bob's fits of madness" and "his present profane state" (28 May 1894, pp. 304, 305).

Similar judgmental phrases about Robertson occur frequently in the *Correspondence*. Henry writes of him as a "volcano," as "impulsive," as a "sad tale" and offers that he waits for the "next explosion." William writes that Robertson is a "bad father." Yet, aspectual of the unpredictability consonant with the disease of alcoholism, William can report in 1890 that Bob "keeps right-side up," in 1898 that he has "tip-top news all the time from Bob," and in 1904 is delighted when he finds Bob sober and making an "excellent impression." It is Henry, however, who puts the entire situation into bold and yet simple relief when he writes that "Bob is ineffable."

If it can be said of Garth Wilkinson and Robertson that the attention paid to their lives is solely due to their presence in the James family, such cannot be said of Alice James, the youngest of the five children and the only female. It is true that the first notice of her importance traces to her relationship with her widely renowned brothers, William and Henry. Nonetheless, if her *Diary* were uncovered independent of that family setting, she would receive encomia as to the quality of mind, her writing, and for the exquisite presentation of her epoch, rendered from a highly original point of view.[19]

It is difficult to know, for sure, just what was the actual medical pathology afflicting Alice James. With each new published commentary, another retrospective diagnosis is offered. Speaking of her, as others did, as an "invalid," Jean Strouse tells us that "like a great many other nineteenth-century women, she was 'delicate,' 'highstrung,' 'nervous,' and given to prostrations. She had her first breakdown at the age of nineteen, and her condition was called, at various points in her life, neurasthenia, hysteria, rheumatic gout, suppressed gout, cardiac complication, spinal neurosis, nervous hyperesthesia, and spiritual crisis."[20]

Obviously, these are diagnoses of symptoms emanating from a penetrating state of depression due either to clinical, neurotransmitter causes or to functional, situational causes. In our time, contexted as we are by the genius and peril of psychopharmacological medicine, it is still extraordinarily difficult to sort out one form of depression

---

[19] The first major intention to take Alice James seriously as a thinker in her own right was F. O. Matthiessen, *The James Family* (New York: Knopf, 1947), pp. 272–85.

[20] Strouse, pp. ix–x.

from another, that is, isolate a biochemical root from that of the frequent sheer burden of our lives.

Whatever all that speculation comes to mean, one version is clear: whatever and no matter how others in the family felt about her, Alice James saw herself as odd person out, estranged and cut off from a calling, a mission. Of the family one could say somewhat ironically, but only somewhat, that William had a father, Henry had a mother, and Wilkie and Robertson chose the Civil War as retroactive parentage. We do know that Robertson on occasion voiced the disturbing assumption that he thought he might be a foundling.

Now where does this leave Alice James? She was in no position to enlist in the Civil War and the overzealous protection of her as the last child and the only female closed off any possibility of her emulating the free-wheeling, traveling, intellectual swashbuckling of her two oldest brothers. So there she was, in the family, with the family, of the family, and by the family. Recipient of letters from faraway places and tales of exotic happenings, she responded from her familial cocoon as powerful events swirled around and about her, yet never to or by her. Depressing? Yes! What was she to do? What could she do? She could have broken out and broken away, which, clearly, would have been scandalous. Alice James was a third-generation Victorian Irish-American female in a nouveau Brahmin family. The odds were against her. Perhaps she once thought, as did William James in 1870, to "frankly throw the moral business overboard" and then, as he, reneged.[21] Whatever the reasons, her genius and her most profound inclinations were suppressed and, unfortunately, festered.

Although those of us who for many decades rummaged in the James family archives knew of the intellectual power and the splendid mind of Alice James, it was not until Leon Edel published the unexpurgated text of *The Diary of Alice James* in 1964 that a wider public become aware of her importance. In 1980 the brilliant and probably definitive biography of Alice James by Jean Strouse assured her of a permanent place in any attempt to understand the cultural texture of the Anglo-American late nineteenth century.

As for the letters herein that contain discussions of Alice James, they bear a remarkable similarity to those shared by the brothers about Robertson James. By this I mean the tone of concern about the unpredictability of the situation. This should not be surprising, for both Robertson and Alice were caught in the clutches of a men-

[21] McDermott, p. 7.

tal pathology, and surprise is one of the hallmarks of that nasty affliction. So, at times, the letters were optimistic, as William wrote in 1869, "Alice *decidedly* improved" (23 Apr. 1869, p. 39). After a European sojourn with Alice, Henry James writes innocently, "I think Alice, in the tranquil leisures of home will find that her mind is richly stocked with delightful pictures and memories" (22 Sept. 1872, p. 82). Tranquility, alas, was never to be the lot of Alice James. Some six years later when Alice was in a very bad state emotionally, Henry writes to William: "Yes, I know that it must be a sad summer in Cambridge, & my thoughts are constantly in Quincy St. But I note what you say about the amelioration of poor Alice's symptoms. She must have been having a tragic time; but I hope most earnestly it is melting away" (23 July 1878, pp. 115–16).

Alice's "attacks" came and they went, but they never "melted away." In fact, Alice did not enjoy a modicum of serenity until she was diagnosed with cancer of the breast and the liver in May 1891. In her *Diary* of that fateful month, she writes:

> To him who waits, all things come! My aspirations may have been eccentric, but I cannot complain now, that they have not been brilliantly fulfilled. Ever since I have been ill, I have longed and longed for some palpable disease, no matter how conventionally dreadful a label it might have, but I was always driven back to stagger alone under the monstrous mass of subjective sensations, which that sympathetic being "the medical man" had no higher inspiration than to assure me I was personally responsible for, washing his hands of me with a graceful complacency under my very nose.[22]

Despite his acute and penetrating understanding of human psychological behavior, William James did not grasp how rich was Alice's awareness of her own life. After receiving the telegram from Henry announcing the death of Alice, William answers, "Poor little Alice! What a life! . . . That is the way her little life, shrunken and rounded in retrospect, has seemed to me to day; and I am sure it is the deepest way in which to regard it from now onward. What a blessed thing to be able to say '*that* task is over!'" (7 Mar. 1892, p. 265).

William James should have known better than to view Alice in

[22] Edel, *Diary,* pp. 206–7.

terms of pathos. After receiving his letter of 6 July 1891, filled with advice to her about how to die, Alice answers with an unsheathed epistolary rapier. Her second paragraph reads: "Your philosophy of the transition is entirely mine and at this remoteness I will venture upon the impertinence of congratulating you upon having arrived 'at nearly fifty' at the point at which I started at fifteen! 'Twas always thus of old, but in time, you usually, as now, caught up."[23]

Lest the length of this Introduction crowd out so much as one of the letters scheduled to be included here, I resist the temptation to continue discussion of the James family, although much remains to be said.[24] Is Robert Dawidoff right when he claims that "Henry was always the sweeter of the two brothers"?[25] I think so. More forebodingly, was Jean Strouse right when she offers that Alice believed "that the people caring for her suffer more than she does," a notion that "reflected her desire to hurt others by hurting herself." Perhaps, and perhaps also, a family trait. Witness the letter of William to Henry following the San Francisco earthquake. Regretting that he did not inform Henry that he was unharmed in the quake although in the vicinity at Palo Alto, William writes, "For *all* the anguish was yours; and in general this experience only rubs in what I have always known, that in battles, sieges & other great calamities, the pathos & agony is in general solely felt by those at a distance, and although physical pain is suffered most by its immediate victims, those at the *scene of action* have no *sentimental* suffering whatever" (9 May 1906, p. 473).

William James's version of the earthquake can be described variously as uninformed, naive, or just insensitive. By all accounts, it was not his finest personal performance. At one point in this letter, William claims that he "didn't hear one pathetic word uttered at the scene of disaster" (9 May 1906, p. 473). He could not have been listening, for a myriad of subsequent reports on that tragedy reveal the experience of utter physical and emotional chaos.[26]

William James knew better than to write as he did with regard to

---

[23] Matthiessen, p. 282. These letters will be published in forthcoming volumes of the *Correspondence*. See also the chapter on "Divine Cessation," in Strouse, pp. 296–317, for a discussion of Alice James's last two years, 1890–92.

[24] For me, despite the comparative brevity of his discussion, I find the most judicious and intelligent treatment of the James family to be that by Gerald Myers in his *Life and Thought* and in his Introduction in *Correspondence*, 1:xvii–1.

[25] *Correspondence*, 3:xxiv.

[26] See *Correspondence*, 3:313n.

the devastation of the earthquake. In 1899 he wrote an essay entitled "On a Certain Blindness in Human Beings" that contained warnings to himself and to us.

> Now the blindness in human beings of which this discourse will treat is the blindness with which we all are afflicted in regard to the feelings of creatures and people different from ourselves. . . .
>
> Hands off: neither the whole of truth, nor the whole of good, is revealed to any single observer, although each observer gains a partial superiority of insight from the peculiar position in which he stands. Even prisons and sick-rooms have their special revelations. It is enough to ask of each of us that he should be faithful to his own opportunities and make the most of his own blessings, without presuming to regulate the rest of the vast field.[27]

And so, upon reflection, it may be that I and other commentators who pick and pore over these letters suffer from some interpretive blindness as well. Be that as it unfortunately may, one upshot of the entire correspondence of the full family is crystal clear; all five James children knew how to die, that is, with equanimity and personal courage. One thinks here of Montaigne, who following the wisdom of Cicero and Lucretius, writes an essay holding "that to philosophize is to learn to die."[28] That, the Jameses did: each of them, William, Henry, Wilkie, Robertson, and Alice, in his or her own way, yet bonded together by acceptance and by dignity.

In the last paragraph of the last essay published before his death, "A Pluralistic Mystic," William James cites an "unknown author of rare quality," Benjamin Paul Blood of Amsterdam, New York. "There is no conclusion. What has concluded, that we might conclude in regard to it? There are no fortunes to be told, and there is no advice to be given.—Farewell!"[29]

---

[27] William James, *Talks to Teachers and to Students on Some of Life's Ideals* (Cambridge: Harvard Univ. Press, 1983), pp. 132, 149.

[28] *The Complete Works of Montaigne*, trans. Donald M. Frame (Stanford: Stanford Univ. Press, 1957), pp. 56–68.

[29] William James, *Essays in Philosophy* (Cambridge: Harvard Univ. Press, 1978), p. 190.

At the risk of violating this wise prescription and proscription of Benjamin Blood and William James, and notwithstanding that we live in an era of instantaneous, albeit frequently ephemeral and un-reflective communication, I do suggest a modest "conclusion" as ema-nating from a reading of this *Correspondence:* it would be salutary if each of us were to take pen in hand—and urge our children, our family, and our friends to do likewise—and write many letters, many long letters to each and all of us.

These *Selected Letters* of William and Henry James now stand as a *festa Jamesiana,* waiting to be appreciatively read. Following William James, I say, "Ring out, ring out my mournful rhymes, but ring the fuller minstrel in."[30]

---

[30] William James, *A Pluralistic Universe* (Cambridge: Harvard Univ. Press, 1977), p. 149.

Editors' Note

The correspondence between William and Henry James extends over nearly fifty years and, judging from letters that are no longer extant but that are mentioned as having been either written or sent, must have amounted to more than forty letters and postcards a year during certain periods. Much of the correspondence has been lost or destroyed, and the 740 letters and postcards that are known probably make up less than half of the original number. The 216 letters in the present volume have been selected from the first three volumes of *The Correspondence of William James,* ed. Ignas K. Skrupskelis and Elizabeth M. Berkeley (Charlottesville: Univ. Press of Virginia, 1992–).

William and Henry rarely wrote routine letters but tended to garnish even the simplest notes with several decorative sentences—a statement truer of Henry, who was capable of writing several pages explaining that he lacked the time to write a proper letter, but one that can also be said of William. Many of their letters were written for the record with the knowledge that they would be preserved in the family archives. A sketch of the history of their preservation is available in the published volumes of the *Correspondence* and need not be repeated here. Inevitably, the reduction of so large a body of correspondence to fit the confines of a single volume means that many good and interesting letters have been omitted. The letters published in the present volume were selected because they more than others illustrate the brothers' responses to each other— responses that spoke at times, as one might expect, of conflicts and rivalries and misunderstandings. But throughout there is a profound bond and in the final years pride in their achievements. While one of the aims of the editors was to show the brothers reacting to each other, the primary intent was to produce enjoyable reading in a volume that the reader can pick up time and time again in moments of leisure.

With one exception all of the letters included in this volume are taken from the James family collections in the Houghton Library of Harvard University. The exception is Henry's letter of 28 December 1882. Six pages of this letter, starting with the beginning of the letter and ending with the word 'unconscious' at 138.10, picking up again at 'I have had' at 139.22 and ending with the closing of the letter, are preserved at Houghton and fit together without any detectable missing text. With no reason to suspect that this letter was incomplete, the editors published it in Volume 1 of the *Correspondence* as a complete letter. We are grateful to William James, grandson of William James, and to Roberta A. Sheehan, member of the Advisory Committee of the *Correspondence* and curator of the James family papers, who made available to us eight pages that Dr. Sheehan found among the family's private papers and recognized as belonging to the letter of 28 December. The letter as published in the present volume unites the two sets of pages. Fitting together the six pages preserved at Houghton with the eight pages found in the family papers made it obvious, however, that the letter is still incomplete with at least four pages, and perhaps more, missing.

The apparatus of scholarship has been kept to a minimum. Many of the notes available in the three volumes of the *Correspondence* are omitted. All persons mentioned in the letters are identified in the Biographical Register. A minimal amount of connecting commentary is supplied in order to make it unnecessary for readers to consult standard biographies. The works of the following authors were used extensively in writing this commentary: Gay Wilson Allen for William James, Leon Edel for Henry James, Jean Strouse for Alice James, and Jane Maher for Garth Wilkinson James and Robertson James. Alfred Habegger's biography of the father, Henry James, appeared too late for this volume but is an informative addition to the roster of James biographies.

In the present volume all of the letters are recipients' copies. A list of the abbreviations used in editing the letters is found on p. 33. The capitalization, punctuation, and spelling of the original letters have been preserved. Although the utmost in readability would suggest the correction of inadvertent errors like *the the*, *sleeplessless* for *sleeplessness*, *thing* for *think*, and *than* for *that* and the expansion of abbreviations like *wh.* to *which* and *A.K.* to *Aunt Kate*, the text will faithfully transcribe these on the theory that they have some interest as representing the writer's haste or else his assumption of informality as against formality. Missing opening or closing quotation marks and parentheses are supplied within inferior brackets, as are characters and words where clarification is needed and where authorial intent is not in question. Errors of commission are commented upon in the notes if clarification is indicated; [*sic*] is not used.

The formal elements of the letters have been standardized. The return address and date are placed at the head and positioned flush right. Missing dates are supplied within inferior brackets by the editors. The salutation is positioned flush left; the closing and signature are positioned flush right. A letterhead imprinted on stationery is represented in print by small capitals. To conserve space, the return address and date are printed on the same line, as are the closing and signature. Vertical lines indicate that the address and date or that the closing and signature were written on separate lines in the original; a vertical line is not used between a printed letterhead and a handwritten date. Underlines, graphic embellishments, and flourishes, whether in the dateline or signature, are not reproduced. Unindented paragraphs are printed with the conventional em indentation.

The parentheses and standard brackets in the letters are the writer's. Inferior brackets [——] enclose editorial interpolation. Descriptions of the state of the manuscript, such as '[*end of letter missing*]', are italic within inferior brackets. Angle brackets < > indicate material that is irrecoverable because the manuscript is torn or otherwise damaged. Text supplied within inferior brackets and angle brackets is obviously the responsibility of the editors.

A series of dots or hyphens, indicating an incomplete thought or transition, is always the writer's. In the body of the letter, words with single underlines are printed in italic; those with double underlines for emphasis are printed in small capitals (or large and small capitals, as the case may be). The writer's capital *A.M.* and *P.M.* are printed in small capitals.

Addresses and postal markings on envelopes (when preserved) are printed immediately below the letter. Enclosures mentioned in letters are to be taken as no longer extant unless commented upon in the notes. A more extensive discussion of the editorial method used in editing the letters is available in each of the first three volumes of the *Correspondence*.

We are indebted to John J. McDermott, Distinguished Professor of Philosophy and Humanities at Texas A&M University and General Editor of the *Correspondence*, for his Introduction to this volume.

Alexander R. James gave permission to use and reproduce materials in the James Collection at Harvard University.

Grateful acknowledgement is offered to the American Council of

Learned Societies, sponsors of the Edition of *The Correspondence of William James,* and to the National Endowment of the Humanities, whose support of that Edition made possible the publication of the first three volumes from which these letters have been selected. The numerous institutions and individuals who provided advice and assistance to the editors in the original publication of these letters in the *Correspondence* are acknowledged in the appropriate volumes in that series.

I.K.S.
E.M.B.

Abbreviations

AGJ	Alice Gibbens James (wife)
AJ	Alice James (sister)
ECR	William James, *Essays, Comments, and Reviews* (Cambridge: Harvard Univ. Press, 1987)
EPR	William James, *Essays in Psychical Research* (Cambridge: Harvard Univ. Press, 1986)
EPs	William James, *Essays in Psychology* (Cambridge: Harvard Univ. Press, 1983)
ERM	William James, *Essays in Religion and Morality* (Cambridge: Harvard Univ. Press, 1982)
GWJ	Garth Wilkinson James (brother)
HJ	Henry James (brother)
HJL	*Henry James Letters*, ed. Leon Edel, 4 vols. (Cambridge: Belknap Press of Harvard Univ. Press, 1974–84)
ML	William James, *Manuscript Lectures* (Cambridge: Harvard Univ. Press, 1988)
NSB	Henry James, *Notes of a Son and Brother* (New York: Charles Scribner's Sons, 1914)
RJ	Robertson James (brother)
VRE	William James, *The Varieties of Religious Experience* (Cambridge: Harvard Univ. Press, 1985)
WJ	William James

William and Henry James

Selected Letters

1861–1868

The arrival of a letter was an important event in the life of a family at the time that the correspondence between the James brothers begins. No matter to whom it was addressed, a letter was read by everyone, passed from hand to hand, discussed at the table. Particularly well-turned or significant phrases were broadcast by proud parents to more distant relatives, neighbors, and friends. Certainly in the James family, a letter was a literary event from the point of view of both the writer and his readers.

William James, the oldest son of Henry James and Mary Robertson Walsh James, was the first to begin the sometimes painful process of gaining independence from the James family circle. In 1861 at age nineteen he abandoned art after a year of studying painting in Newport and enrolled in Harvard's Lawrence Scientific School to study chemistry. He rented a room from Mrs. John Pasco, whose house was on the corner of Linden and Harvard streets in Cambridge, and took his meals at the table of Miss Catharine Upham, who lived near the corner of Oxford and Kirkland streets.

Left behind in Newport, in addition to his parents, were his brothers Henry James, eighteen, the future novelist, Garth Wilkinson James, sixteen, and Robertson James, fifteen; his sister, Alice James, thirteen; and his aunt Catharine Walsh, Mary James's sister who often functioned as a second mother and was known as Aunt Kate. Biographies have been published of all the members of this family circle with the exception of Mary James and Catharine Walsh.

The letter to his brother Henry James—probably the first that William wrote upon his arrival in Cambridge and no doubt anxiously awaited by the family in Newport—records his first impressions of Harvard and of life on his own but is silent about the great event that had begun in April 1861, the Civil War.

To Henry James

Drear & Chill Abode | Cambridge Saturday Eve. [September 7,
1861]

Dear Harry

Sweet was your letter & grateful to my eyes. I had gone in a mechanical way to the P.O. not hoping for anything (though "on espère
alors qu'on désespère toujours") & finding nothing was turning heavily away when a youth modestly tapped me & holding out an envelope
inscribed with your well known characters, said "Mr. James!—this
was in our box!." T'was the young Pasco, the joy of his mother, but
the graphic account I read in the letter he gave me of the sorrow of
my mother almost made me shed tears on the floor of the P.O. Not
that on reflection I should grieve, for reflexion shows me a future
time when she shall regard my vacation visits as "on the whole" rather
troublesome than otherwise; or at least when she shall feel herself as
blessed in the trouble I spare her when absent, as in the glow of pride
and happiness she feels on seeing me, when present. But she need
never fear that *I* can ever think of *her* when absent with such equanimity. I ought not to "joke on such a serious subject" as Bobby
would say, tho', for I have had several pangs since being here at the
thought of all I had left behind at Newport, especially gushes of feeling about the *place*. I have not for one minute had the feeling of
being at home here. Something about the room precludes the possibility of it. I don't suppose I can describe it to you. As I write now
even, writing itself being a cosy cheerful looking amusement, and an
argand gas burner with a neat green shade over it merrily singing
beside me, I still feel unsettled. I write on a round table in the middle of the room with a red and black cloth upon it. In front of me
I see another such-covered table of oblong shape against the wall
capped by a cheap looking glass & flanked by 2 windows, curtainless
and bleak, whose shades of linen flout the air as the sportive wind
impels them. On my left hand are two other such windows with a
horsehair covered sofa between them, at my back a 5th window and
a vast wooden mantel piece with nothing to relieve its nakedness, but
a large cast looking much plumbagoed Franklin. On my right *The
Bookcase*, imposing and respectable with its empty drawers and with
my little array of printed wisdom covering nearly *one* of the shelves.
I hear the people breathing as they go past in the street, and the
roll & jar of the cars is terrific. I have accordingly engaged the other

room from Mrs Pasco, with a little sleeping room up stairs. It looks infinitely more cheerful than this & if I do not find the grate sufficient I can easily have a Franklin put up. She says that the grate will make an oven of it though. The room is on the South side of the house & with the sleeping room costs only 120$ per annum. This just balances the increased expense of Mrs. Upham's table, where I am to start on Monday. I have not made many acquaintances yet. Ropes I met the other eveg. at Quincy's room & was very much pleased with him. Don't fail to send on Will Temples letters to him & Mason, which I left in one of the libraries' mantelpiecejars, to use the Portuguese idiom. Storro Higginson has been very kind to me, making inquiries about tables &c. He is a very nice fellow. We went this morning to the house of the Curator of the Gray collection of engravings who is solemnly to unfold its glories to us to morrow.[1] He is a most serious stately German gentleman, fully sensible to the deep vital importance of the collection of engravings & to the weightiness of a visit to them. Had I though[t] it was to have been such a tremendous formal affair, I hardly think I should have ventured to call. He spoke of Mr Hunt & said he expected to have seen him this summer, as Mr Hunt had promised to put him in the way of getting some photographs. You may as well tell Mr. Hunt if you see him. Jenks seems a nice kind of fellow. Tom Ward pays me a visit almost every evening. Poor Tom seems a cold too.[2] His deafness keeps him from making acquaintances.

Sunday 9 A.M. Splendid morning. The same Tom has just left me having walked home from breakfast with me. Bkfst. at 8 on Sundays. I have not made many acquaintances at the Sc. School. Young Atkinson, nephew of Miss Staiggs friend seems a nice boy. Prof. Eliot is a fine fellow, I suspect, a man who if he resolves to do a thing will do it. I find analysis very interesting *so far* The library has a reading room where th[e]y take the magazines, Rev. des 2 Mondes &c.[3] I shall have plenty of time to myself here I suspect. I am perfectly independent of everyone. Went into the Boston Atheneum Gallery yesterday afternoon. There was not much there worth seeing. Some curious big things of Allston, & the casts.[4] Please tell Father to send me some more money immediately. Neccessary expenses have reduced me to borrowing $2 to pay up my score to night at the boarding house, & don't forget to send the letters of introduction. Heaps of love to all, to poor desolate Niobe of a Mother, to Father, to the noiseless Alice, and last and least (but *multum in parvo*) to Bobby.   Aunt Kate must be home now.   Plenty of love for her. Ask everybody to write often.   I don't feel much like writing now but will write soon again.

I remain with unalterable sentiments of devotion ever my dear Harry, your

Big Brother | Bill

Sunday eveg.   I went to Church in the Chapel of the College this morning, & to Mt. Auburn this afternoon.   Delicious day   I have nothing more to say now.   Pray write soon Harry.   I am going to write to Wilky & then study

Address

Box 575

Cambridge

Mass

[1] The collection of engravings acquired by Francis Calley Gray (1790–1856) is now part of the Fogg Art Museum.   Access to the collection, especially by undergraduates, was severely restricted out of fear that careless viewers might damage the engravings. The curator was Louis Thies.

[2] From *King Lear,* act 3, sc. 4, line 57.

[3] *Revue des Deux Mondes.*

[4] The Boston Athenaeum had an extensive collection of casts of classical sculptures.

In the spring of 1863 William James, suffering from back pain and headaches, withdrew from the Lawrence Scientific School. He returned for the fall term but as a student of anatomy rather than chemistry. In 1864 he entered the Harvard Medical School but interrupted his studies in 1865–66 to go to Brazil as one of Louis Agassiz's unpaid assistants. Before leaving for Brazil, he published two reviews in the North American Review *that marked the beginning of his career as an author. Upon his return he resumed his medical studies and obtained a position as house pupil at the Massachusetts General Hospital for the spring of 1867. But once again he interrupted his studies, resigning suddenly on 21 March 1867 to go to Europe. He set sail for France on 17 April, his plans shrouded in secrecy and mystery. Ostensibly William went to Europe to seek a cure for his painful back and to study physiology. But it is impossible to exclude completely the suspicion that he was engaging in "medical politics," using vague symptoms to obtain financial support from otherwise reluctant parents. Several years*

later, brother Henry was to tour European spas under similar circumstances.

Henry James, who also suffered from back pain as well as constipation, lived at home until 1862–63 when he attended the Harvard Law School. In 1864 he published his first story; by the end
of 1867 he had published forty-five stories and reviews.

In the meantime the James family had abandoned Newport for
Boston and then Cambridge, renting a house there in 1866 at 20
Quincy St. Alice James was at home, suffering from "nerves" and
other obscure ailments but maintaining an extensive social life.
Otherwise, the family circle was breaking up. Garth Wilkinson
James had enlisted in the Union army in September 1862 and
was seriously wounded in the famous assault on Fort Wagner in
July 1863. By 1867 he was living in Florida and, like many
other Union soldiers motivated by a mixture of philanthropy and
greed, had acquired a plantation and was trying to grow cotton,
hoping to provide employment for the former slaves and to become
rich in the process. This enterprise, like all of his later business
ventures, failed, with severe financial losses to the whole family.
Robertson James had also served in the Civil War, enlisting in
May 1863. After working for a railroad in Burlington, Iowa, he
went to Florida to help his brother with the cotton plantation but
returned to Cambridge in the fall of 1867; shortly thereafter he
resumed his railroad position in Iowa.

From Henry James

Cambridge, May 21 [1867]
Dear Will—I drop you a line by the *China*, wh. leaves Boston tomorrow.   We recd. your two letters at once, some 5 or 6 days ago &
with immense satisfaction.   The private one to me was successfully
concealed; & you may imagine that it was the most interesting.   I
groaned in spirit as I thought of your fatigue & your weariness, but
I was glad enough to think it was no worse than when here.   Of
course I could not have expected it to be less.—Heaven protect you!
I hope by this time you have got some permanent repose, & we await
your Dresden letter with great anxiety.   No news.   It seems but yesterday that you left—Father, Mother, & Alice are very well & (apparently) happy.   We hear often from the boys, who are beginning to
suffer from the heat & hard work.   We expect one of them home

before long, & then the other, on his return.   They were equally
surprised & delighted by your departure.   We have sent them your
letter.   I must not forget to say how delighted we were to hear of
your not having been sick!   Bravo!   I remember Pratt well.   Also
Grogan.   What has become of the latter?—Your acct. of Paris was
strange & moving.   I wish indeed I could have been at the theatre
with you.   I had read *Mme Aubray* when your letter came & was
keenly sensible both of its merits & defects.[1]   It's hard to say which
prevail.   Wendell Holmes is gone salmon-fishing in Maine.   The
Spring is well started as to verdure; but the air is cold & the skies
gray.   I have been feeling essentially better since you left; but have
given up the ice as pernicious.[2]   I was of course much interested in
your acct. of the advice you had recd. & wait to hear what are the
results.   I shall proba[b]lly go to N.Y. next week & get a *corset* from
Taylor.   A. Kate is still staying at Dr. Munro's.   Jeff Davis is released
on bail—chiefly that of H. Greely.[3]   I have seen no one and done
nothing—except receive a day or two ago, new overtures from the
Nation.   But I shall not be led into any imprudent promises.   It were
a platitude to say that we miss you.   Nevertheless we do.   But I try
to think that you are feeling very cheerful; instead of, as is probable,
very dismal.   I can only entreat you to watch yourself & do nothing
imprudent (as walking, sightseeing &c)   I am curious to know what
you have heard from T.S.P.—to whom I shall soon write.   But of
course I am more eager still to hear your own personal news, prospects, sensations, impressions of Dresden and so forth.   I sympathise
with you both in your privations & discomforts, and in your hopes
of profit & pleasure whatever they may be.—Have patience & courage and you will manage to keep comfortable.—Farewell.   I envy
you chiefly the Dresden pictures—if you are able to look at any.   I
have been reading Taine's Italy[4]—which made me hungry for works
of art.   Father seems especially well just now.   Alice is extraordinary
sweet.   Adieu.   I shall write often.

Tout à toi—H.J.jr

[1] In Paris while making his way to Germany, WJ attended a performance of *Les Idées
de Madame Aubray* by Alexandre Dumas, *fils*.

[2] HJ was applying ice for medicinal purposes.

[3] Jefferson Davis was released on 13 May 1867.   Horace Greeley was one of ten
signers of the bond.

[4] Hippolyte-Adolphe Taine, *Voyage en Italie* (1866).

To Henry James

12^{III} Mittel Strasse, Berlin | Sept 26. 1867

Beloved Arry

I hope you will not be severely disappointed on opening this fat envelope to find it is not *all letter.* I will first explain to you the nature of the enclosed document and then proceed to personal matters.— The other day as I was sitting alone with my deeply breached letter of credit, beweeping my outcast state, and wondering what I could possibly do for a living, it flashed across me that I might write a "Notice" of H. Grimms novel wh. I had just been reading.[1] To conceive with me is to execute, as you well know. And after sweating fearfully for three days, erasing, tearing my hair, copying, recopying &c, &c, I have just succeeding in finishing the enclosed. I want you to read it, and if after correcting the style & thoughts, with the aid of Mother, Alice & Father, and re-writing it if possible, you judge it to be capable of interesting in any degree any one in the world but H. Grimm himself, to send it to the Nation or the round table.[2] I feel that a living is hardly worth being gained at this price. Style is not my forte, and to strike the mean between pomposity & vulgar familiarity is indeed difficult. Still, an the rich guerdon accrue, an but 10 beauteous dollars lie down on their green and glossy backs within the family treasury in consequence of my exertions, I shall feel glad that I have made them. I have not seen Grimm yet as he is in Switzerland. In his writings he is possessed of real imagination and eloquence, chiefly in an ethical line, and the novel is really *distingué,* somewhat as Cherbuliez's are, only with rather a deficiency on the physical & animal side. He is, to my taste, too idealistic, & father would scout him for his arrant moralism. Goethe seems to have mainly suckled him, and the manner of this book is precisely that of W^{m}. M^{r} or Elect. Aff.[3] There is something not exactly *robust* about him, but per contra, great delicacy, and an extreme belief in the existence and worth of truth, and desire to attain it justly & impartially. In short a rather painstaking liberality and want of careless animal spirits—wh. by the bye seem to be rather characteristics of the rising generation. But enough of him. The notice was mere taskwork. I cd. not get up a spark of interest in it, and I shd. not think it wd. be *d'actualité* for the Nation. Still I cd. think of nothing else to do, and was bound to do something. I was overjoyed yesterday morning to get a mighty & excellent letter from you (Sept 6) with 2 Nations and

a Tribune,[4] and an amusing letter from Elly Van Buren. By the same
mail a fat letter from Charles Atkinson & one from T.S.P. I have in
fact been flooded with letters of late. I can't get over that 4 sheeter
wh. the gentle Babe sent me, and wh. I have not yet answered! You
can't tell how glad I am to hear you are feeling so well. I only hope
it will go on. I am a new man since I have been here, both from the
ruddy hues of health wh. mantle on my back, and from the influence
of this live city on my spirits. Dresden was a place in which it always
seemed afternoon, and as I used to sit in my cool and darksome
room, and see through the ancient window the long dusty sunbeams
slanting past the roof angles opposite down into the deep well of a
street, and hear the distant droning of the market and think of no
reason why it shd. not thus continue *in secula seculoram,* I used to have
the same sort of feeling as that which now comes over me when I
remember days passed in Grandma's old house in Albany. Here on
the other hand, it is just like home. Berlin I suppose is the most
American looking city in Europe. In the quarter which I inhabit,
the streets are all at right angles, very broad, with dusty trees growing
in them, houses all new and flat roofed, covered with stucco, and of
every imaginable irregularity in height, bleak, ugly, unsettled looking,
werdend. Germany is, I find, as a whole, (I hardly think more experience will change my opinion) very nearly related to our country.
And the German nature and ours so akin in fundamental qualities,
that to come here is not much of an experience. There is a general
colorlessness and bleakness about the outside look of life, and in artistic matters a wide spread manifestation of the very same creative
spirit that designs our kerosene lamp models, for instance, at home.
Nothing in short that is worth making a pilgrimage to see. To travel
in Italy, in Egypt, or in the Tropics, may make creation widen to one's
view, but to one of our race all that is *peculiar* in Germany is mental,
and *that* Germany can be brought to us. (thro.' de Vries & others)[5]
If I were you I would consequently not fret much at any delay in
coming here, and even not feel very badly if I never came, but I
would now begin and get accustomed to reading German. It will
hardly take any larger number of hours to acquire a given proficiency
at home, than here, living as you would live, and you will find it
worth while. It seems to me the only gain here wh. is unattainable
by staying home, might be the acquaintance of certain individuals—
but that is precarious, and you are just as likely to meet those you
are in need of in one country as in another.

     (*After dinner.*) I have just been out to dine. I am gradually getting acquainted with all the different restaurants in the neighborhood, of wh. there are an endless number, and will presently choose one for good, certainly not the one where I went to day, where I paid 25 groschen for a soup, chicken & potatoes, and was almost prevented from breathing by the damned condescension of the waiters. I fairly sigh for a home table. I used to find a rather pleasant excitement in dining "'round" but that is long since played out. Could I but find some of the honest florid and ornate ministers that wait on you at the Parker house here, I wd. stick to their establishment no matter what the fare.[6] These indifferent reptiles here, dressed in cast off wedding suits, insolent and disobliging and always trying to cheat you in the change are the plague of my life. After dinner I took quite a long walk under the Linden, and round by the Palace & Museum. There are great numbers of statues, (a great many of them "equestrian") here & you have no idea how they light up the place. What you say about the change of the seasons wakens an echo in my soul. To day is really a harbinger of winter, and felt like an october day at home, with an N.W. wind. Cold and crisp with a white light, and the red leaves falling and blowing everywhere. I expect T. S. Perry in a week. We shall have a very good large parlor & bedroom, *together*, in this house, and steer off in fine style right into the bowels of the winter. I expect it to be a stiff one, as every one speaks of it here with a certain solemnity. We are in the same latitude as london and I believe the sun sets at ½ past 3 P.M. in December, and most of the landladies whose apartments I visited on my arrival assured me that there *never* was any sunshine in winter here. However as they all happened to be living on what would have been the shady side of the street if there were any, I conceived that this was a slight slander devised by their cupidity, and intended to prevent my giving a preference to rooms over the way. Our rooms are on what ought to be the sunny side.

I wish you wd. articulately display to me in your future letters the names of all the books you have been reading. "A great many books, none but good ones" is provokingly vague. On looking back at what *I* have read since I left home it shows exceeding small, owing in great part I suppose to it being in German. I have just got settled down again—after a nearly two months debauch on french fiction, during which time Mrs Sand, the fresh, the bright, the free, the somewhat shrill, but doughty Balzac, who has risen considerably in my esteem or rather in my affection, and Théophile Gautier the good, the golden mouthed, in turn captivated my attention, not to speak of the peerless Erckmann Chatrian who renews one's belief in the succulent harmonies of creation, and a host of others. I lately read Diderot: Oeuvres Choisies, 2 vols. wh. are entertaining to the utmost from their animal spirits and the comic modes of thinking, speaking and behaving of the time. Think of meeting continually such delicious sentences as this—he is speaking of the educability of beasts—"Et peut on savoir jusqu'ou l'usage des mains porterait les singes s'ils avaient le loisir comme la faculté d'inventer, et si la frayeur contin-uelle que leur inspirent les hommes ne les retenait dans l'abrutisse-ment."!!!⁷ But I must pull up, as I have to write to father still. On the other page you will find a rather entertaining extract from Grimm wh. I have copied for you. It relates to young Americans at Berlin. I enclose a photograph of M. Babinet, wh. I weakly bought because it looked so intensely french.

Adieu, lots of love from your aff. Wilhelm.

—All with the intention of getting a european culture, but each with a more or less peculiar method of his own in choosing what best suited him. One, who, without knowing latin or Greek, studied Basque & Sanscrit, and at the same time worked at the model of an original sort of ship; another who drove music, and at the same time attended the mathematical & theological lectures at the University; a 3rd. who gave no utterance of the nature of the direction of his stud-ies but bought masses of engravings of every kind; but *all* distin-guished by this, that altho' they entered upon their subjects for the most part without the preliminary studies wh. seem to *us* neccessary, they notwithstanding advanced rapidly, and always had marked out to themselves distinctly their direction & their end.⁸

I have just been enjoying a 3 days visit from Henry Tuck on his way to Vienna. A rich treat, altho' I suppose you will sneer at the idea

I enclose the letter I got from T.S.P. not because it is particularly good, but it is characteristic & will help you to "realize" our existence here. I wrote him I had the room fm. the 1st instead of the 9th. Your article on Historical novels was very good. I look as yet in vain for the Atlantic with the $200 story.⁹ You must send them.

¹ Herman Grimm, *Unüberwindliche Mächte*, 3 vols. (Berlin: Wilhelm Hertz, 1867), review in *Nation* 5 (28 November 1867): 432–33, reprinted in *ECR*.

² A weekly review of politics, literature, and art published in New York in 1863–69.

³ Johann Wolfgang von Goethe, *Wilhelm Meisters Lehrjahre*, *Wilhelm Meisters Wander-jahre*, and *Die Wahlverwandtschaften*.

⁴ *New York Daily Tribune*.

⁵ De Vries was a publisher in Boston.

⁶ The Parker House was a hotel in Boston, at 60 School St.

[7] Denis Diderot, "Instinct," in *Œuvres choisies de Diderot,* 2 vols. (Paris: Firmin Didot Frères, Fils, et Cie., 1862), 1:267.

[8] Herman Grimm, *Unüberwindliche Mächte,* 2d ed., 2 vols. (Berlin: Wilhelm Hertz, 1870), 1:124. A copy of the first edition (1867) was not available.

[9] HJ, unsigned reviews of Anne E. Manning, *The Household of Sir Thomas More* and *Jacques Bonneval,* in *Nation* 5 (15 August 1867): 126–27; "Poor Richard: A Story in Three Parts," *Atlantic Monthly* 19 (June 1867): 694–706; (July 1867): 32–42; (August 1867): 166–78.

From Henry James

Cambridge, Nov. 22$^{\underline{d}}$ [1867]

Dear Willy—I haven't written to you for some time, because the others seemed to be doing so. We at last got some little news about your health. Praised be the Lord that you are comfortable & in the way of improvement!—I recd. about a fortnight ago—your letter with the review of Grimm's novel—after a delay of nearly a month on the road, occasioned by I know not what. I am very sorry for the delay as it must have kept you in suspense, and even yet I am unable to give you a satisfactory reply. I liked your article very much & was delighted to find you attempting something of the kind. It struck me as neither dull nor flat, but very readable. I copied it forthwith & sent it to the *Nation.* I recd. no answer—which I take to be an affirmative. I expected it to appear in yesterday's paper; but I see it is absent, crowded out I suppose by other matter. I confess to a dismal apprehension that something *may* have happened to it on the road to N.Y. & have just written to Godkin to tell me whether he actually recd. it. But I have little doubt he has done so & that it is waiting, & will appear next week.—Were it not for the steamer I would keep your letter till I get his answer.—I hope you will try your hand again. I assure you it is quite worth your while. I see you scoffing from the top of your arid philosophical dust-heap & commission T.S.P. to tell you (in his own inimitable way) that you are a d——d fool. I very much enjoy your Berlin letters. Don't try to make out that America & Germany are identical & that it is as good to be here as there. It can't be done. Only let me go to Berlin & I will say as much. Life here in Cambridge—or in this house, at least, is about as lively as the inner sepulchre. You have already heard of Wilkie's illness—chills & fever. It finally became so bad that he had to come home. He arrived some 10 days ago & is now much better; but he must have had a fearfully hard time of it. He eats, sleeps &

receives his friends; but still looks very poorly & will not be able to return for some time.   Bob went a few days ago out to his old railroad place at Burlington.   He was very impatient to get something to do, but nothing else turned up, altho' he moved heaven & earth, *more suo.*   I have no news for you.   A. Kate is in N.Y., attending "Em" Walsh's wedding.[1]   The rest of us are as usual—whatever that may be called.   I myself, I am sorry to say, am not so well as I was some time since.   That is I am no worse; but my health has ceased to improve so steadily, as it did during the summer.   It is plain that I shall have a very long row to hoe before I am fit for anything—for either work or play.   I mention this, not to discourage you—for you have no right to be discouraged when I am not myself—but because it occurs to me that I may have given you an exaggerated notion of the extent of my improvement during the past 6 mos.   An important element in my recovery, I believe, is to strike a happy medium between reading &c, & "social relaxation."   The latter is not to be obtained in Cambridge—or only a ghastly simulacrum of it.   There are no "distractions" here.   How in Boston, when the evening arrives, & I am tired of reading & know it would be better to do something else, can I go to the theatre!   I have tried it *ad nauseam.*   Likewise *"calling."*   Upon whom?—Sedgwick's, Nortons, Dixwells, Feltons.   I can't possibly call at such places oftener than 2 or 3 times in 6 months; & they are the best in Cambridge.   Going into town on the winter nights puts a chill on larger enterprizes.   I say this not in a querulous spirit, for in spite of these things I wouldn't for the present leave Cambridge, but in order that you may not let distance falsify your reminiscences of this excellent place.   To night par example, I am going into town to see the French actors, who are there for a week, give Mme. Aubray.[2]   Dickens has arrived for his readings.[3]   It is impossible to get tickets.   At 7 o'clock, A.M. on the 1st day of the sale there were 2 or 3 hundred people at the office, & at 9, when *I* stroled up, nearly a thousand.   So I don't expect to hear him.   Tell Sargy I got his little note, enclosed by you, & am anxiously awaiting his letter.   I *hope* (for his sake<)> he will be able to extend his absence.   If not & he comes in March, I shall be 1st to welcome him.   I haven't a creature to talk to.   Farewell.   I wanted to say more about yourself, personally, but I cant.   I will write next week.

—Je t'embrasse—H.J.jr

[1] Emilie Belden Walsh married Thomas Cochran, Jr., on 28 November 1867.

[2] H. L. Bateman's Parisian Comedy Company, from New York, performed a number of plays at Chickering's Hall, Boston, including *Madame Aubray* on 22 November.

[3] Charles Dickens arrived in Boston on 19 November 1867 and gave his first read-ing on 2 December. Speculators were selling tickets to the first reading for $50.

To Henry James

Berlin Dec. 26. 67

My dear Harry

Another fat pseudo letter. T.S.P. bought the book of Feydeau the other night and after sitting up to read it, it occurred to me that my irrepressible & venal pen might "compliquer" an article out of it wh. shd. be more readable than the other two.[1] So with a mighty sweat and labor I forged the accompanying, wh. I beg you will take care of & smooth if possible the style. I strove to imitate the Saturday Rev., I fear unsuccessfully, but the writing is good practice. I am now more than ever convinced that I was not born for it. Don't read the book, it is as vile and weak as they make 'em. For the last year, I know not why I have found myself growing to despise the french in many ways. Paris seems now to be in a state of moral & intellectual debasement, of wh. it really seems hard to imagine any peaceful issue. Every cord is tightly screwed up, to a hair of the snapping point; every thing *screams* falsetto, the point seems coming when pleasure must be bloody to be felt at all. TS.P. takes the *figaro* daily.[2] It is the most hideous little sheet I ever saw. One part *bons-mots*, personal *cancans*, and bawdy anecdotes, spun out with that infernal grinning flippancy & galvanized gaiety ye wot of, the rest devoted to execu-tions, murders & crimes generally in different countries, and theatri-cal gossip. I seriously think our Police Gazette is a higher paper.[3] It is the organ of naturally coarse & low minds, but this Fig. is that of minds lost & putrefying. Bah!

By the way it may please you to know that your health was drunk here the other night at a tea party by Herr u. Frau Geheimrath some-body, Frl. & Dr. Bornemann, a Miss Adams & Mrs Hopkins aus Amer-ika & myself. Miss Borneman told me she had been read[g] some Atlantic monthlies. I asked to see them, when lo! among them were "Friend Bingham" and no ii of the great $200 story.[4] She had read both & was vexed at not getting the whole of the latter. Imagine the enthusiasm when I announced the author's name. Er lebe hoch!

Christmas has passed quietly. Every house in town whether of old or young has had its tree. The maid-servant said to me last week as she was heating up the stove "Das schöne weihnachtsfest ist bald da," and as I "drew her out" on the subject, she said that every one felt "wehmüthig" before a Xmas tree.   I wish I cd. understand this feeling of theirs.   I dined yesterday with the Fischer family to whom hosmer introduced me.   They belong to the elite, and in politeness to each other *as Fischers* leave the Sedgwicks no where.   I am sorry you were not interested in Hosmer.   I saw him but 2 hours & thought he might prove a "1st class mind."

I sent you about two mos. ago a letter containing photogs. of "Shakespeare's death mask" wh. Grimm gave me.[5]   As you have said nothing about it I fear it may have been lost or detained like the other.   I hope the latter only, for the mask is extremely interesting.

I have been trying blisters on my back and they do undeniable good.   Get a number about the size of a 25 cents piece, or of a copper cent.   Apply one every night on alternate sides of the spine over the diseased muscles.   In the morning prick the bubbles, and cover them with a slip of rag with cerate, fastened down by cross straps of sticking plaster.   Try a dozen in this way at first.   Then wait two weeks and try ½ dozen more,—two weeks, ½ doz more & so on.   If the blistering is done too *continuously* it loses its effect.   Between times sponge back with cold water, (wrung out sponge) twice a day.   I think it does good, the *Ice* is too powerful, the parts can't react against it.

I wrote Alice to send leaf for Frl. Bornemann for Frl. Thies.[6]   It has not come in time.   Too bad.   I find reading slow work especially in German and pine after some special practical work.   I hope next summer to get it.   My attention is much distracted by a no. of stupid mining students (americans) whom T.S.P. has brought to the room, and who lounge all day talking with him about the way their pipes colour.   It is getting to be a serious nuisance.   But I have just made the acquaintance of 2 german physiological students whom I hope to gain s'thing fm.   I hope you are getting on better again.

Ever your loving bro.   Wm. James.

[1] Ernest Aimé Feydeau, *La Comtesse de Chalis* (Paris: Michel Lévy Frères, 1868), WJ, review in *Nation* 6 (23 January 1868): 73–74, reprinted in *ECR*.

[2] French satirical newspaper, a daily from 1866.

[3] *National Police Gazette*, a weekly published in New York from 1845, devoted to covering crime until about 1875, afterwards to reporting anything gory and bizarre.

[4] HJ, "My Friend Bingham," *Atlantic Monthly* 19 (March 1867): 346–581, and "Poor Richard."

[5] The so-called Kesselstadt death mask was discovered in 1849 by Ludwig Becker, a librarian at Darmstadt.

[6] Frl. Bornemann had requested some leaves from the garden with which to surprise Frl. Thies at Christmas.

To Henry James

Teplitz Feby. 1 2. 68

My dear Harry

I rec'd last week your letter of Jany 17, Aunt Kate's fm. Newport of Jany 15, & Mother's of Jany 20. Father's of 10th the week before. Many thanks to you all. Baring has advised me of Father's remittance.[1] I enclose with this another article for Charles Norton.[2] I rec'd while writing it Dr. Holmes's lecture from H. P. Bowditch & appended a few remarks suggested thereby, wh. are "gassy" enough as far as they go. The lecture tickled me to death by the perfection of its style. Have you read it? If not, borrow it from Wendell. I don't know whether the Teplitz medium prevents me from appreciating rightly the relative value of things, but it seems to me one of the best things I know of Dr. Holmes's. The "strange intensity of my feeling" on the subject of article writing, of wh. you speak is to be explained by the novelty of the exercise, & by the enormous difficulty I experience in turning out my clotted thought in a logical & grammatical procession. I find more freedom however in each successive attempt, and hope before long to write straight ahead as you do. What an activity by the bye you are displaying in the nation![3] I like your last articles very much indeed. There is a vein of freedom about them, greater than that which used to obtain in connection with your earlier ones. I don't think ephemeral newspaper articles ought to appear too nice. I was much pleased the other day by receiving from Fräulein Bornemann some old Atlantic Monthlies, in wh. I found parts II & III of your "Poor Richard." I found it good much beyond my expectations, story, characters, & way of telling excellent in fact. And hardly a trace of that too diffuse explanation of the successive psychological steps wh. I remember attacking you for when you read it to me. The Atlantics came in a Box which was sent me apparently fm. a party at the grimm's house, for it contained 3 sheets of allegorical contributions in German manuscript signed by seven or 8 of the grimm crowd. The head-senders however were Mrs Grimm Miss Thies & Frl. Bornemann. The contents varied from a big and bully liver sausage to a bottle of champagne—passing through some pots of the most india rubber like calves foot jelly, chocolate, meringues, cologne water, pin cushion, oranges, plaster statuary &c, forming with the allegory of the manuscript a most German mixture. Luckily the allegory was in Prose, or it wd. have been even more insipid. The sapidity of the sausage made amends—and there is in every phenomenon that takes place in the German female nature the most curious coexistence of sausage & what seems to us cold & moonshiny sentimentality.   It must be felt, for it cannot be analytically exhibited to a foreigner.   Mother's beloved letter contained an appeal couched in terms of that mellifluous persuasiveness with[4] the maternal heart alone can give utterance to, to come home & be nursed instead of remaining alone outcast among the unfeeling foreigners.   I might simply content myself with pointing to the above box as a proof that I am kindly treated (Ay! Alice, well may you blush. When did *you* ever feed me with sausage and jelly?)   But I will say in addition, that I live not only with every comfort I cd. possibly desire—(the "horrid german cookery" she speaks of being a mere myth evolved from the popular american consciousness) but I am convinced that I pass my time here on the whole much more profitably than I could possibly do so at present at home.   In fact I am just beginning to reap the harvest of my months of probation, just beginning to feel at home with the language & the people & to lose the sense of effort and strangeness with wh. the common processes of living have hitherto been conducted.   It wd. accordingly as a mere matter of self indulgence be foolish to go home at this moment.   But in addition to that, if I get enough improvement fm. this Cure this time to get into a laboratory, it will be a matter to affect the prosperity of my whole future life, and turn me from a nondescript loafer, into a respectable working man, with an honorable task before him.   I do not wish to run the risk of being disappointed by having immoderate expectations.   My cure is over at the beginning of next week (30 days) and the improvement will not begin till then.   At present I feel a good deal worse than when I came—but that is a good sign and the normal result of the weakening effect of the baths.   I will let you know without any exaggeration how I am 3 weeks hence.—Life in this village is far more sociable than I expected.   There were actually three young englishmen here for 8 days, Cambridge men & very good fellows, there is now an Irishman at the Hotel with whom I dine every day, besides wh., I visit my doctor (as a friend) and am hand in glove with the teacher of languages of the town, than whom a more absolute rascal never walked in the sun.   He visited me in his quality of an american citizen, & as he is a most entertaining beggar I have cultivated him.   He is a pole, a red-republican, and his hand is against every gov'! in Europe.   He speaks french like a native and (without any exageration on my part) lies worse than any character I ever heard of in a novel or saw in a Farce.   He is a liar *absolute,* and tells a story with admirable dramatic effect. The 43 battles wh. he led in the last polish revolution, the immense hereditary wealth he has lost, his bearding the Czar Nicholas when a mere boy, his unnumerable escapes from death, &c. are as good as a circulating library full of adventures. There is moreover in the house the charming Anna Adamowiz of whom I remember writing to Alice. But the jealous manners of the country, wh. do not permit me to go a walking or a driving with her, but only to way lay her in the entry, wh. is always crowded with children, domestics and workmen, have not allowed me an opportunity of revealing *les feux dont je brûle.* Besides her, there is here for her rheumatism, an actress, a very handsome & agreeable jewess, who speaks german beautifully. I have in fact far more society than last summer.—The workmen mentioned above are re-opening a bath which has been closed for several years, and to wh. hangs a slight tale. The late King of Prussia who came here for the gout, was sent to the Herrenhaus, a bath house below the Fürstenbad, and having inspected (as Kings always do,) all the bath mechanism, he came to the conclusion that the water in wh. he bathed at the Herrenhaus came from a spring wh boiled up in a public charity bath in this Fürstenbad, in wh. 12 rheumatic & paralysed beggars used to sit all day long. This, alltho' exceedingly swell for the beggars, did not please the King at all, and he caused the bath to be sealed up. I have not read anything lately worth recording. The bathing weakens one's brain so as to almost prevent all study. I took up Balzac's "Modeste Mignon" the other day.[5] I don't know whether you know it. It must be one of the very early ones, for the extraordinary research and effort in the style is perfectly *cocasse.* It is consoling to see a man overcome such difficulties. But the story was so monstrously diseased morally that I cd. not finish it, reading novels as I do for the sake of refreshment. It struck me as something inconceivable almost. Lots of love to every one at home. Excuse the egotism of this letter.

Ever yr | Wms.

[1] Baring Brothers & Co., London bankers with offices in Boston and elsewhere, offering travelers checks and telegraphic transfers.

[2] Claude Bernard, *Rapport sur les progrès et la marche de la physiologie générale en France* (Paris: L'Imprimerie Imperiale [Hachette], 1867). WJ, review in *North American Review* 107 (July 1868): 322–28, reprinted in *ECR.* The review contains some remarks about Oliver Wendell Holmes, *Teaching from the Chair and at the Bedside: An Introductory Lecture Delivered before the Medical Class of Harvard University, November 6, 1867* (Boston: David Clapp, 1867).

[3] From October 1867 to January 1868, HJ published six items in the *Nation.* The

last two were "The Huguenots in England," 6 (9 January 1868): 32–33, and "Father Lacordaire," 6 (16 January 1868): 53–55.

[4] A slip for 'which'.

[5] Honoré de Balzac, *Modeste mignon* (1844).

To Henry James

Fürstenbad, Teplitz, Bohemia March 4. 68

My dear H'ry

I rec'd last week a letter fm. Father, and the week before one fm. you & another fm. him.—You will be surprised to see that I am still in this place. I am very sorry to say that the Cure (as they call it here) wh. I finished two weeks ago, has had this time an effect exactly opposite to that of last summer, & has made me decidedly worse. It was a longer & a much more violent course of treatment than the first one, and I can only conceive of the result by supposing that it overstepped the bounds wh. in my case are salutary, & produced a permanent depression. This view seems to be countenanced too by the experience of both of us with the ice, & by what you said of that Irish youth's rubbing of you—at first great benefit and after passing a certain point a contrary effect. It shows that, whatever treatment is applied, there must be a very cautious adjustment of it. Being as I am I have judged it more prudent not to go back to Berlin for some time, as it is impossible for me to keep quiet there. Teplitz is as *safe* a place as there is on the globe. Nothing moves at this season save the heavenly bodies, & as one hardly feels tempted to arise & pursue them around their orbits, one can keep very still. In other respects, it is a singularly blameless place, too. This house is excellently kept and I feel exactly like one of the family, and am on the most affection-ate terms with the domestics male and female, who in sooth are an excellent crowd. The male, der alte Franz, resembles general Wash-ington, both in form & feature & in moral character. He walks at the rate of about ½ a mile an hour, but never sits down and so in the course of the day gets through a fabulous amount of the most heterogeneous work. When spoken to, he always seems to count 25 before answering, and when angry (if that ever occurs) I have no doubt he counts a full hundred. I take my dinner at the one hotel wh. is now open. The bill of fare generally consists of veal in various shapes, but now and then there is beefsteak, & even mutton, on wh. days I lay in a large supply. The liar I wrote you about continues to be attentive to me, but begins as you may imagine, to be a little of a bore.[1] For the last 3 days there has been a roving young Englishman here, named Shepherd, whose gift of the gab, and power of quotation (I wonder if *all* Englishmen have this latter, all I've met have been remarkable for it) were astounding.[2] He left this morning. I was very glad to have seen him, he's traveled in the Holy Land, in Iceland, Egypt &c. &c, & will soon go to the U.S. where you may perhaps see him. He has written a short book on Iceland, & is a capital fellow. I have been admitted to the intimacy of a family here named Glaser, who keep a hotel & restaurant. Immense bulky garrulous kindhearted woman, Father with thick red face, little eyes & snow white hair, two daughters of about twenty. The whole conversation & tea taking there reminded me so exactly of Erckmann Châtrian's stories, that I wanted to get a stenographer & a photographer to take them off. The great thick remarks, all about housekeeping & domestic economy of some sort or other, the jokes, the masses of eatables, fm. the awful swine soup (tasting of nothing I cd. think of but the perspiration of the animal) and wh. the terrible mother forced me to gulp down by accusing me, whenever I grew pale and faltered, of not relishing their food, through the sausages, (liver sausages, blood sausages) & more, to the beer & wine, then the masses of odoriferous cheese, wh. I refused in spite of all attacks, entreaties and accusations, & then heard, oh horrors! with some what the feeling I suppose with which a criminal hears the judge pass sentence of death on him,—then heard an order given for some more sausages to be brought in to me instead, the air of religious earnestness with wh. the eating of the father was talked about, How the mother told the daughter not to give him so much wine, because he never enjoyed his beer so much after it, while he with his silver spectacles on pointing with his pudgy forefinger to the lines, read out of the newspaper half aloud to himself,—the immense long room with walls of dark wood, the big old fashioned china stove at each end of it &c, &c, all brought up the *Taverne du Jambon de Mayence* into my mind. There are lots of picturesque domestic architecture here in T. Nothing at all swell for Germany, but courts broken up into every possible combination by the irregularity of the buildings, stone arches, & stairs and galleries outside the houses, &c, &c, which break the light delightfully. And streets in the town wh. the sun never enters, (so that a deadly chill like that of a humid cellar strikes into your bones,) altho the whole open country in wh. to build lies close at hand. To tell the truth, Harry, I had a dream before the effects of my treatment were known, that if it did me a great deal of good, I shd. send home

to have you sent here at any sacrifice, for it wd. be your only chance
of salvation.   You cd. have 3 spells of bathing by october & spend
the meantimes in Dresden while I shd. be close at hand in Leipsic in
Ludwig's laboratory, and might perhaps go home in the Fall leaving
you heare to enjoy your recovered strength.   Foolish dream! Apart
fm. the hypothetical benefit to your back, I infer fm. the tone of your
letters that even a few months of change of scene wd. do your mind
a great refreshment.   It's a great pity it's fallen through.   I think I
shall stay however and take another course in April, strange as such
logic may at first appear to you.   For if this second course sinned
only in excess, a 3rd. *milder* one wd. be as likely to repair its evil
effects as those of any heterogeneous violence.   It is a slight risk,
perhaps, but its the best chance I see for myself. If I don't get better
then I think I shall start for home, as I can't do anything profitable
here, & its too lonely and expensive. My cost of living at this season
here, without bathing, is but very little, if at all greater than in Berlin.
I wrote you 3 weeks ago enclosing an article on Cl. Bernard for Chas.
Norton.   I was "struck all of a heap" by Chas.'s offering you the
N.A.R.,[3] and though my idea of the duties are rather cloudy, I shd.
think you did wisely in declining. I get the Nations reglar, including
my 2 last articles.[4] Keepasending of them! I regard the Nation as
the sole bulwark of our country's honour.   If I were a rich man I wd.
have 10,000 distributed gratis every week through the land, but I
wd. keep *Godkin* poor & hungry, so that his "vein" might not be
clogged and dulled by the vapours of prosperity.   My schriftsteller-
isches Selbstgefühl was naturally rather mangled by the mutilations
you had inflicted on my keen article about Feydeau, for I had rather
regarded those racy remarks on the french character wh. you left out
as the brightest jewels in my literary coronet & the rest merely as an
illustration of them.   However, if you do not claim any of the money
for your improvements, I shall not complain.   Darwin's book has just
come to me.[5] As it is of course too late for the next N.A.R., I will
send review of it at my leisure.—I have rec'd the 2nd. Galaxy &
Atlantic for Feby. with yr. story of old Clothes.[6] Both stories show a
certain neatness & airy grace of touch wh. is characteristic of your
productions (I suppose you want to hear in an unvarnished manner
what is exactly the impression they make on me) and both show a
greater suppleness & freedom of movement in the composition; altho'
the first was unsympathetic to me fm. being one of those male versus
female subjects you have so often treated, and besides there was
something cold about it, a want of heartiness or unction.   It seems

to me that a story must have rare picturesque elements of some sort, or much action, to compensate for the absence of heartiness, and the elements of yours were those of every day life. It can also escape by the exceeding "keen"ness of its analysis & thoroughness of its treatment as in some of Balzacs, (but even there the result is dis*agreeable,* if valuable) but in yours the moral action was very lightly touched and rather indicated than exhibited. I fancy this rather dainty & disdainful treatment of yours comes fm. a wholesome dread of being sloppy and gushing and over abounding in power of expression like the most of your rivals in the Atlantic,[7] (there was one in the same no. I've forgotten its name) and that is excellent, in fact it is the instinct of truth against humbug & twaddle, and when it governs the treatment of a rich material it produces 1st class works. But the material in your stories (except Poor Richard) has been *thin* (and even in P.R. relatively to its length) so that they give a certain impression of the author clinging to his gentlemanlyness tho' all else be lost, and dying happy provided it be *sans déroger.* That to be sure is expressed rather violently, but you may understand what I mean if I point to an article named Mrs. Johnson (I suppose by Howells) wh. was sent me in the Feby. Atlantic by T.S.P.[8] The quality of its humor is perfectly exquisite, and as far as I noticed never *dérogérs,* but the article left on me (and I suspect on you) a certain feeling of dissatisfaction, as if the author were fit for better things, as if this material were short measure and he had to coax & cook it to make it fill even that sober form, as if it were at bottom a trifling, for him. Well, I feel something of a similar want of blood in your stories, as if you did not fully fit them, and I tell you so because I think the same thing wd. strike you if you read them as the work of another. (For instance Charles Lambs essays are perfect because they are so short, and when De Quincey blames him for his want of continuity & his "refusing openings" continually, he seems quite wrong.[9] Probably if Lamb had expanded his articles into the size of Mrs. Johnson a similar effect of inward dis-harmony wd. have arisen wh. wd. have been painful.) If you see what I mean perhaps it may put you on the track of some useful discovery about yourself wh. is my excuse for talking to you thus unreservedly. So far I think Poor R. the best of your stories because there is warmth in the material, and I shd. have read it and enjoyed it very much indeed had I met it anywhere. The story of O. Clothes is in a different tone fm. any of yours, seems to have been written with the mind more unbent & careless, is very pleasantly done, but is, as the Nation said, "trifling" for you.[10] I have read since

I have been here "4 Neue Novellen" by Paul Heyse, a small book, wh. if the German is not too great an obstacle wd. probably be useful to you.[11]   The *genre* is just what you are engaged in & they are just about the length of magazine stories.   They are very conscientiously and firmly done, and thence satisfactory, tho' to me they had little magic.   But thoroughly respectable and good to have been written. If you get the book, begin with das Mädchen von Treppi, wh. seemed to me the best.   I have uttered this long rigmarole in a dogmatic manner, as one speaks, to himself, but of course you will use it merely as a mass to react against in your own way, so that it may serve you some good purpose.   It must be almost impossible to get anyone's real whole feeling about what one has written.   I wish I cd. say it *viva voce*.   If I were you I'd select some particular problem, literary or historical to study on.   There's no comfort to the mind like having some special task, and then you cd. write stories by the way for pleasure & profit.   I dont suppose *your* literarisches Selbstgefühl suffers fm. what I have said; for I really think my taste is rather incompetent in these matters, and as beforesaid, only *offer* these remarks as the impressions of an individual for you to philosophize upon yourself———

What will Cambridge do without the Nortons?   I have no time for more—my veal-time is long foreby.   But give lots of love to all, including Alice & Aunt Kate.   Send my love to the boys   Can't you send me occ.ᵞ one of Bob's letters.

Ever yours affect.ˡʸ | Wm. James

I found tinct. of Iodine sovran against the european chilblain or frostboil as the G.'s call it,[12] wh. s'evi———d[13] on my toes early this winter.   Paint on 2 times daily till skin begins to loosen.

Direct communications *here* till further orders.

[1] The Polish teacher described in the previous letter.

[2] Charles William Shepherd, *The North-West Peninsula of Iceland: Being the Journal of a Tour in Iceland in the Spring and Summer of 1862* (1867).

[3] The *North American Review*.

[4] WJ, reviews of Feydeau and Armand Quatrefages de Bréau.

[5] Charles Darwin, *The Variation of Animals and Plants under Domestication* (1868).

[6] HJ, "The Romance of Certain Old Clothes," *Atlantic Monthly* 21 (February 1868): 209–20; "The Story of a Masterpiece," *Galaxy* 5 (January 1868): 5–21; (February 1868): 133–43.

[7] The description fits Harriet Elizabeth Prescott Spofford, "Flotsam and Jetsam," pt. 2, *Atlantic Monthly* 21 (February 1868): 186–98.

[8] William Dean Howells, "Mrs. Johnson," *Atlantic Monthly* 21 (January 1868): 97–106.

[9] Thomas De Quincey, "Charles Lamb" (1848), *The Collected Writings of Thomas De Quincey*, ed. David Masson, vol. 5 (London: A. & C. Black, 1897), 234.

[10] "A tantalizing story which, when the end turns out trivial, is seen to be trivial altogether," *Nation* 6 (30 January 1868): 94.

[11] Paul Johann Ludwig von Heyse, "Das Mädchen von Treppi," in *Neue Novellen* (1858).

[12] Die Frostbeule in German.

[13] Evidenced itself. WJ was comfortable in French and enjoyed playing with words. In this instance, he combined the French reflexive with the English 'evidenced'.

To Henry James

Dresden Apl. 5. 68

My dear Harry

Since writing I have rec'd a letter fm. Aunt Kate (Mch. 4) fm. you (12th) & fm. Father (18th) the 2 latter came yesterday in Co. with one fm. M. Temple. Much obliged to all concerned.—You see I am still in Dresden. I have picked up a good deal in a dorsal point of view since leaving Teplitz & am rather better than I was at Berlin— I know I shd. be more so still if the uneasiness of my blood did not drive me to do so much running about—I have been more restless this time at Dresden than at all yet—I have been a number of times in the Gallery, you may imagine with what pleasure—like a bath from Heaven—for last summer when I was here I was only able to thrust my nose into it twice and look for a few minutes at some ½ dozen pictures. I'd give a good deal to import you and hear how some of the things strike you. I have been more absorbed this time in the general mental conception of the different schools & pictures than in their purely artistic qualities. When you see together a nomber of different schools, each so evidently looking on the world with entirely different eyes, the result is very striking. I have come to no conclusions of any sort, and see that to do so would require a study of all the galleries & antiquity cabinets of europe, & then you wd. very likely be unintelligible to any one but yourself. Still the problems are fascinating. One thing is certain, that the German blood is almost without a sense or a want of the beautiful. The decadence of all schools shows in the same way a neglect of the beautiful, and a sea[r]ch of expression, spiciness, startling effects instead. Some such pictures here by Ribera, Guido Reni, Rubens, & a lot of others whose names I cannot now think of show talent and ability wh. really *strike* you more than in the purer masters, but they are cold and heartless, and to one who stands out side of the race course of school-competition in wh. they were painted by men half unconscious of the peculiarity of their work, it seems a wonder how any one cd. have taken pleasure in such industry. (Rubens is a bad example above, but I've not been for 10 days to the Gallery, & some other names escape me. Rubens has a warmth & heat of his own—and the torrents of fat & rosy fleshed women wh. he pours out, the inexhaustible *verve* of the critter gives one a sympathy with him—though I think he is only to be classed with such men as Gustave Doré.) I've no doubt that the present school of novel-writing, I mean the french realistic school, will strike people hereafter just as the later Roman & Bolognese pictures strike us. The painters were real strong men and their work was to them earnest, but they missed the one thing needful, & so do these novelists. The old Germans seem nevertheless to have caught the beautiful very often, but I fancy it has been mostly incidentally. They seem to have striven mainly after mere fact, truth of detail without choice in genre subjects, which are consequently generally really vulgar & hideous; and in religious subjects, truth of *ideal* detail, that is dressess ideally handsome, cheeks ideally smooth, light ideally pure, &c, &c, wh. of course makes the ensemble pleasing and accidentally carries many parts over into the territory of what other races call beautiful. I think the real charm in nature which they *sought* to render will be found to be the *agreeable i.e.* that by wh. each separate sense is affected pleasantly, such as brightness, velvetiness; and not at all that higher and more intellectual harmony, (consistent with far duller & inferior separate sensations) wh. leaps at once to ones eyes out of the beginnings of the Italian schools, (*e.g* Bellini &c) With all this there is yet in the old Germans a repose, wh. is analogous in some measure to that of the Greeks &c, inasmuch as both seem to have conceived their subjects as simply *being,* and degenerate schools need to have the Being determined in some picturesque & expressive manner. But the general mode of looking at the Universe was as wide as East fm. West between the Greeks & Germans; and I fancy their agreeing in this point may possibly arise fm. the fact that German *art* (and the repose I speak of is strongest in ideal subjects) may have expressed only a small holy corner of what the Germans call their "Weltanschauung," while to the Greek it expressed every thing. The real brothers of the Greeks are the glorious Venetians—in both does the means of expression the artist is able to dispose of seem to cover all he wants to say—the Artist is adequate to his universe.

Finiteness & serenity & perfection—tho' out of the finiteness in both cases there steals a grace, wh. pierces the moral hide of the observer, and lays hold of the "infinite" in some mysterious way.—It is a touching thing in Titian & Paul Veronese, who paint scenes wh. are a perfect charivari of splendor & luxury; and manifold sensations as far removed fm. what we call simplicity as anything well can be, that they preserve a tone of sober innocence, of instinctive single heartedness, as natural as the breathing of a child. The "blondness" of some Venetian things here!, as if the picture were breathed on the canvass. (That head "Isaac of York" by Allston[1] in the Boston Atheneum will give you an idea of the kind of thing I mean—only with Allston, you feel that the purity & unity comes through a pretty deliberate choice & sacrifice, while it looks in the Venetians as if it were effortless and instinctive[)]—I hope you will excuse this vague tirade, of unripe & probably false impressions—tho' by the blindness of the language in wh. I have expressed them, their falsity or truth will probably neither strike you very plainly.—Besides the Gallery, I have been enjoying that imperturbable old heathen, Homus lately, and have read XX books of the Odyssey. There are ½ doz. Germ. translations, all of wh. are esteemed to be far ahead of Voss, and in verity the thing reads just like a german poem—no trace of an inversion or an awkward forced sentence such as abound in translations generally, but a divine old marrowy homely concrete unconscious-seeming language & narrative. For my part, I've no doubt its just as good as reading the original!? The Odyssey strikes me as very different in spirit from the Iliad, though whether such difference neccessarily implies a diff. of time of production I am too ignorant to have any idea. My S. Am indians keep rising before me now as I read the O., just as the Iliad rose before me as I went with the Indians.—But the health! the brightness, & the freshness! and yet "combined with a total absence" of almost all that we consider peculiarly valuable in ourselves. The very persons who wd. most writhe & wail at their surroundings if transported back into early Greece wd. I think be the neo-pagans, & Hellas worshippers of to day—The cool acceptance by the bloody old heathens of every thing that happened around them, their indifference to evil in the abstract, their want of what we call sympathy, the essentially definite character of their joys, or at any rate of their sorrows (for their joy was perhaps coextensive with life itself,) wd. all make their society perfectly hateful to these over cultivated and vaguely sick complainers. But I don't blame them for being dazzled by the luminous harmony of the Greek productions.

The Homeric Greeks "accepted the Universe"[2]—their only notion of evil was its perishability—We say the world in its very existence is evil—they say the only evil is that every thing in it in turn ceases to exist. To them existence was its own justification and the imperturbable tone of delight & admiration with wh. Homer speaks of every fact, is not in the least abated when the fact becomes to *our* eyes perfectly atrocious in character. As long as Ulysses is in the hands of the Cyclop, he abhors him, but when he is once out of danger, the chronic feeling of admiration or at least indifferent tolerance gains the upper hand. To the Greek a thing was evil only transiently & accidentally and with respect to those particular unfortunates whose bad luck happened to bring them under it. Bystanders cd. remain careless & untouched—no after-brooding, no disinterested hatred of it *in se*, & questioning of its right to darken the world, such as now prevail. No *vague* discontent—Are you free?—exult! Are you fettered or have you lost anything?—Lament your impediment or your loss, and that alone!—Or if a hero, accept it with sober sadness, and without making a fuss, for it is *ultimate*. There is no "reason" behind it, as our modern consciousness restlessly insists. This sad heroic acceptance (sans arrière pensée) of death seems to me the great tragic wind that blows through the Iliad, and comes out especially strong in Achilles. See a beautiful example in Il. XXI. 103 & following.[3] (Read the whole Book in Voss, it's worth the trouble.) It strikes us with a terrible impression of unapproachable greatness of character; but I can't help thinking that its *peculiarity* in our sight lies rather in an intellectual limitation than in any extraordinary moral tremendousness on the part of the hero. Take a modern man of vigorous will & great pride, and *give him the same conception of the world as Achilles had,*—a warm earth where every thing is good, a brazen Fate wh. is *really* inscrutable, and wh. is ever striking her big licks into the pleasant earth and finally cutting us off from it,—and I have no doubt he wd. live like Achilles, (firmly enjoying his earth & as firmly looking at the face of Fate,) without needing the introduction of any new & peculiar moral element of strength into his character. The trouble with the modern man wd. be intellectual; he wd. always be trying to get behind Fate, and discover some point of view fm wh. to reconcile his reason to it—either by denying the good of the world,—or inventing a better one on t'other side,—or something else. But this wd. neccessarily introduce a subtlety into his conception wh. wd be fatal to simplicity; and the seemingly super-human grandeur of Achilleus is due merely to the simplicity of the 2 elements wh. he seems

to hold together by pure brute force of character.—9.30 P.M. At
this pint I was interrupted by the thick-set-but-beaming-with moral-
excellence-wench who said "Bitte Kommen Sie zu Tische!" So I
went & devoured my portion of Kalbsbraten with the greater zest for
having done you so much writing. I hope it boreth you not to read
it. I write off my reflexions to you as they arise because it is the
nearest intercourse of that pensive nature that I can have with my
kind, & it is a satisfaction to make some definitions, however provisional, when you are reading. I don't know that I have anything
more to say about the irrepressible Ulysses, at any rate on paper, but
I advise you to try a Book or two in Voss's Iliad—I am pretty sure
you'll get a bigger impression than from anything english. I am just
in fm. the Theatre where has been a sacred concert to inaugurate
passion week and the tones of Beethoven's 9th Symphony & Schiller's
Hymn to Joy are ringing in my alas! too profane ears; and after a
bowl of chocolate imbibed, and another mass of the Veal, very wet &
cold as is the wont of the animal the first day in this country, en-
gulphed, I sit down again in your society. I am enjoying here in
Dresden the very best society of decayed gentlewomen which the city
affords. All have a *von* to their name, some are widowed some not
yet married, but all agree in having lost their money, and receiving
pensions of 100 or 200 Thlrs. fm. the King or Queen. They are of
course, all old Friends of Frau Spangenberg and every day some one
of them dines with us or spends the evening in the Parlor. They are
in general a lacklustre set, but I am getting more german out of them
than ever before out of any one else. Frau Sp. herself is a darling
old lady, full of life and interest in every thing, with a great big warm
heart and a great & good talker. Most of her young boarders have
been in the habit of calling her "Gross mutter" but altho' I have as
yet evaded that form, I really have a filial feeling towards her, and
shall be sorry to part with her. There is another lady in the house,
also of noble birth, Fräulein von Kracht over whose blond head some
30 summers may have flown—but she has all the wayward ways of
(and speaks of herself as) a naughty child. She has hands of wondrous length & exquisite tenuity, to match her general frame, and a
mode of speaking German so rich and beautiful that I cd. sit mute
for hours (by spells) just to hear her. Really with many little vain
weaknesses, she is a very agreeable companion & I can't help feeling
sorry for her. Without a penny, too proud of her birth &c to do any
work, and in fact too weak in health to do much, she has got an
appointment from the queen to a sort of genteel asylum for 6 spin-

sters of quality founded by someone in his will.   She gets a good room & 200 Thlrs a year, and is engaged to do nothing in return but wear clothes wh. shall be black or silver grey.   But her only friends that I can hear of seem to be these old tottering dowagers, and her path down life seems without any brighter spot ahead.   Poor girl, she was engaged 2 years ago to a Prussian officer who for unknown reasons shot himself during the campaign in Bohemia.[4]   I insert these details to interest alice.   Your last letters tell me she has been keeping her bed. I have had no idea of her being so sick and it makes me feel very badly.   Give her my true love, and a solid hug.   I think I may before long be home and then she'll get well.   She little knows what imaginary dialogues I keep having here with her, things to be said when we are once more together under the one roof, Bless her excellent little Soul!—I am very glad to hear fm. you my dear Harry that you are doing well.   The news of your sudden backsliding in the winter was very painful to me.   You have no idea how my sympathy with you has increased since I have had the same.   I am glad you can go out so much.   Keep it up.   I wrote you fm. Teplitz a long letter relative to your writings.   Exactly what escaped me in the ardor of composition I cannot now remember, but I have the impression I assumed a rather law-giving tone.   I hope it did not hurt you in any way, or mislead you as to the opinion I may have of you as a whole, for I feel as if you were one of the 2 or 3 sole intellectual & moral companions I have.   If you cd. have known how I have ached at times to have you by and hear your opinion on different matters or see how things wd. strike you, you wd. not think I thought lightly of the evolutions of your mind.   But I have no doubt you understood rightly all I may have said.—One of the most fearful features of my being abroad it[5] this terrible fluency wh. is growing on me of writing letters—Last week I wrote 5 *sheets* to Arthur Sedgwick, de Populo americano, wh. I wd. like you to read, so ask him for it.[6]   My organ of perception-of-national-differences happened to be in a super-excited state that week and that letter was the consequence.   I don't know whether the "pints" raised, will seem to you just.—I was very much amused by Father's account of Emerson[7]—but I think Emerson probably has other "intellectual offspring" than those wretched imitators, and has truly stirred up honest men who are far fm. advertizing it by their mode of talking.—Good night! my dear old boy.   Once more, impress in some forcible way or other upon Alice the fact of my devotion to her—at any rate, smother her with kisses fm. me.

Thank A.K. heartily for her excellent letter—Give my love to F., M., Wilky & Bob, & believe me

Yours. W.J.

Address until told not to: 2 Dohna Platz, Parterro

Dresden

Sachsen

I go in a week to Teplitz again for a month & Fr. Spangenb. will take care of my correspondence.

[1] For the painting see *A Man of Genius: The Art of Washington Allston (1779–1843),* ed. William H. Gerdts and Theodore E. Stebbins, Jr. (Boston: Museum of Fine Arts, 1979), 79.

[2] The phrase "I accept the universe" was reportedly a favorite of Sarah Margaret Fuller, Marchioness Ossoli (1810–1850), American critic and reformer; see *VRE,* 41.

[3] The slaying of Lycaon, whose pleas for mercy are rebuffed by Achilles to the effect that the same fate awaits everyone.

[4] Apparently, during the Austro-Prussian War in the summer of 1866.

[5] A slip for 'is'.

[6] For the letter to Arthur George Sedgwick see *Correspondence,* 4:269–76.

[7] In his prefatory note to Henry James, "Emerson," *Atlantic Monthly* 94 (December 1904): 740–45, WJ writes that the essay was written in about 1868 and read to private audiences. His father, WJ adds, was working off his "mingled enchantment and irritation" with Emerson.

To Henry James

Dresden April 13. 68

My dear Harry

I am just in from the theatre and feel like dropping you a line to tell you I have got your last Atlantic story (Extraord? Case) and read it with much satisfaction.[1] It makes me think I may have partly misunderstood your aim heretofore, and that one of the objects you have had in view has been to give an impression like that we often get of people in life: Their orbits come out of space and lay themselves for a short time along of ours, and then off they whirl again into the unknown, leaving us with little more than an impression of their reality and a feeling of baffled curiosity as to the mystery of the beginning and end of their being, and of the intimate character of that segment of it wh. we have seen. Am I right in guessing that you had a conscious intention of this sort here? I think if so, you have succeeded quite well with the girl, who gave me an impression of having roots spreading somewhere beyond your pages, and not failed with the

men, though somehow they are thinner.[2]   Some expressions of feeling from the sick one did however "fetch," and had to me the mark
of being drawn from experience.   Of course the average reader feels
at the end as if he had had a practical joke played upon him—and
I myself after being let down suddenly from the pitch of curiosity
excited by the title and the progress of the narrative felt rather as if
you'd gone off sticking your thumb to your nose at my feelings.   I
chuckled fiendishly at the sell.   But soon justified it on esthetic principles—You seem to acknowledge that you can't exhaust any character's feelings or thoughts by an articulate displaying of them—You
shrink from the attempt to drag them all reeking and dripping &
raw upon the stage, which most writers make and fail in,   You ex-
pressly restrict yourself accordingly to showing a few external acts
and speeches, and by the magic of your art making the reader *feel*
back of these the existence of a body of being of which these are
casual features.   You wish to suggest a mysterious fullness which you
do not lead the reader through.   It seems to me this is a very legitimate method and has a great effect when it succeeds.   (I only think
at this moment of Mérimée as an example—I read a story of his:
"Arsène Guillot," last summer that struck me much by it.)[3]   Only it
must succeed.   The gushing system is better to fail in, since that
admits of a warmth of feeling, and generosity of intention that may
reconcile the reader.   I think in much of your previous productions
you have failed through selecting characters uninteresting *per se,* and
secondly in not indicating enough of them to make them stand out
mysteriously.   (I except from all this Poor Richard wh. seems to belong to another type) e.g. The husband in your old clothes story[4]
both the husband and the painter & the old lady in your Masterpiece
story[5] under the first head.   Your young women seem to me all along
to have been done in a very clean manner—they feel like women to
me, and have always that atmosphere of loveliness and unapproach-
ability, which the civilized women wears into the world, without seeming any the less fleshly for it.   This last one, although she is indicated
by so few touches seems to me to stand out vividly.   I think a few
plastically conceived situations help this effect very much: e.g where
she smiles & takes a bite from her cake.   (Great oaks fm. little acorns
grow!) Your style grows easier, firmer & more concise as you go on
writing.   The tendency to return on an idea and over-refine it becomes obsolete—you hit it, the first lick now.   The face of the whole
story is bright & sparkling, no dead places, and on the whole the
skepticism and as some people wd. say impudence implied in your

giving a story which is no story at all is not only a rather *gentlemanly* thing, but has a deep justification in nature, for we know the beginning and end of nothing. Still, while granting your success here, I must say that I think the thorough and passionate conception of a story is the highest, as of course you think yourself. I haste to send you these remarks as I fancy in my previous ones I got exagerating in the unfavorable sense.—I have been hearing Devrient play in Hamlet. He was the 1st german actor—I believe Dawison is considered to have got ahead of him now—is an old man but no one wd. believe it of him on the stage. His hamlet is of the same Class as Booth's, and interesting in the same way, tho' by my recollection Booth goes ahead of him greatly in variety & subtlety. What a thing the human voice is though! The endless fullness of the play never struck me so before—It bursts & cracks at every seam—I may feel it the more for having been thinking of classical things lately—I was in the Cast collection again yesterday.[6] The question what is the difference between the Classical conception of life & art & that of wh. Hamlet is an example besets me more & more, and I think by a long enough soaking in presence of examples of each, some light might dawn—And then the still bigger question is: what is the warrant for each? Is our present only a half way stage to another Classical era with a more complete conception of the Universe than the Greek, or is the difference between Classic & Romantic not one of intellect but of race & *temperament*. I was only thinking yesterday of the difference between the modern flower-on-a-dung hill (e.g. Victor Hugo *passim*) poetry, where often the dirtier the dung the more touching the poetry of the flower, and the Greek idea, wh. cd. not possibly have conceived such a thing, but wd. have either made the flower leaven the heap or turned back on it altogether—harmony being the sine qua non; and here comes to add to my "realizing sense" of the chasm between them this awful Hamlet, which groans & aches so with the mystery of things, with the ineffable, that the *attempt* to express it is abandoned, one form of words seeming as irrelevant as another, and crazy conceits & counter senses slip and "whirl" around the vastness of the subject, as if the tongue were mocking itself. So too, action seems idle and to have nothing to do with the point; just as in a moral point of view it must have seemed vain to the author's of the Fantine-poetry & to so many Christian sects.[7] While the Greeks were far greater "Positivists" than any now.—But I fear you begin ere now to be in the same doubt about *my* sanity as most people are about Hamlets. Excuse the bosh wh. my pen has lately got into the habit of writing. In this matter I am prevented from expressing myself clearly by reason of the fogginess of my ideas—I think I could reach some analysis by keeping works of both sorts long enough before my eyes, but opportunity and skill are both lacking. And perhaps after all, such analyses are made by everyone more or less for himself and understood by no one else—witness all the german treatises on Aesthetiks; every one has written one here, just as every one has kept school once, in Mass.—I saw by the bye t'other day a German theory: Shakspere a homeopath! It waxes very late. Good night! Letter fm. mother (25 Mch.) rec'd. I'm very sorry Alice is so unwell. Heaps of love to her, I sent you two notices of Darwin last week. I see by 2 Nations rec'd yesterday that I am forestalled there—Perhaps the Round Table might pay for it, or the Atlantic. Do you know who wrote the Nation article?[8] Good night & my blessings to all

Yrs. W.J.

T.S.P. having asked me my opinion of your story I, to save trouble send him this to read and Post, at wh. I hope you will not be offended.[9]

[1] HJ, "A Most Extraordinary Case," *Atlantic Monthly* 21 (April 1868): 461–85.

[2] In the story Ferdinand Mason, a Union officer wounded in the Civil War, falls in love with Caroline Hofman. He becomes inexplicably ill and dies after Caroline becomes engaged to someone else. Her real feelings are never disclosed.

[3] Prosper Mérimée, *Arsène Guillot* (1844).

[4] Arthur Lloyd in HJ, "The Romance of Certain Old Clothes."

[5] John Lennox, Mrs. Denbigh, and Stephen Baxter in HJ, "The Story of a Masterpiece."

[6] Casts of classical sculptures in the Zwinger Museum.

[7] Perhaps a reference to Fantine, the heroine of Victor Hugo, *Les Misérables* (1862), who in spite of her total degradation has the possibility of redemption.

[8] Asa Gray, in *Nation* 6 (19 March 1868): 234–36.

[9] Thomas Sergeant Perry added the following note: 'Read approved & respectfully forwarded. By the next steamer a letter fm. me. Yrs. recd'.

To Henry James

Dresden July 10 [1868]

My dear H'ry

Your letter of the 21 is just to hand—also a galaxy with the story entitled Osbornes Revenge, the which on a full stomach, and comfortably reclining on the sofa I have degustated with great satisfaction.[1] You grow in the variety of elements which you wield and the previous somewhat too great daintiness of your style is giving way to a mere

"chastened"ness<.> The richness of coloring of your story in the Atlantic (De Grey) is quite remarkable, altho the "human<">< interest of
the story is small.[2] In both stories the reader's curiosity to know what
is coming is kept greatly stretched. Go on—I trust your boarding
house life this summer will enlarge your sphere of observation and
give you some new characters. I wish you could have seen a so-
called Russian princess whom I travelled with lately & who told me
all about her conjugal troubles. Her husband (the great Hanoverian
statesman, Graf Münster) procured a divorce fm. her and married
one Lady Harriet Sinclair (who wrote the book called dainty dishes
wh. I believe mother has.)[3] Learning that I was a Doctor this lady
gave me various interesting details about her divers *accouchements* (—
or "enfantillages"—Mme. Grymes told me of a German who spoke
French with great severity & precision, saying that his wife "est morte
dans son second enfantillage") Your article about Ste. Beuve was
recognized by me immediately.[4] I like your notice of Trolloppe's
Novel as well as anything you have done in that line.[5] The Galaxy
containing "The Problem" has not turned up.[6] I formally request it
to be sent. How much money have you made in the past year? Answer this question.—About my sleep article I am sorry, (as far as so
trifling a matter admits of sorrow,) that you shd. have sent it to the
Nation.[7] Even if Hammond's Quarterly did not pay (wh. is doubtful,
for it has started with great charivari, and costs a big price each number) I shd. rather have had it there, for the article dealt with a matter
still in doubt and only fit for physicians to handle, and I wanted
moreover to bring myself under Dr. Hammond's notice as one ready
to do that kind of work for him, if neccessary. It seems to me that
the Nation has no concern with an article of that kind. However, no
harm is done.—I am very glad to hear of your "lifting cure."[8] It is
strange that when the contracting of those muscles in walking &c.
should be deleterious, it should be advantageous in this other motion. What a dark business it all is, nit wahr? I saw T.S.P. in Berlin
in excellent condition & replete with German. As he goes home in
a month he will give you the latest news of me. He is as good in
quality as one need desire but it is a pity he so hates to take trouble
of any sort. It will keep him back all his life. I suppose you are
now somewhere in the mountains &, I hope, enjoying it there. Macte
virtute, valetudine, librorum notitiis, articulis fabulisque in magazin-
ibus &c &c. I have just read Tourguénieff "Smoke" and another
short novelet "Faust."[9] They are exceedingly brilliant and masterly,
showing the artistic excellence of the French *school* with a wider range

of ideas and a less provincial culture of the whole mind.   But, subjectively speaking, I have a sort of dislike to these lurid & suffocating love stories of which I have read so many which prevents the artistic excellence of them from receiving sympathetic justice at my hands.

Much love fm yours ever   W.J.

I wrote you June 4.   I suppose the letter has turned up sometime since your writing

[1] HJ, "Osborne's Revenge," *Galaxy* 6 (July 1868): 5–31.

[2] HJ, "De Grey: A Romance," *Atlantic Monthly* 22 (July 1868): 57–78.

[3] Harriet Elizabeth (St. Clair-Erskine), Gräfin zu Münster-Ledenburg, *Dainty Dishes. Receipts Collected by Lady Harriett St. Clair.*

[4] HJ, review of Charles-Augustin Sainte-Beuve, *Portraits of Celebrated Women*, in *Nation* 6 (4 June 1868): 454–55.

[5] HJ, review of Anthony Trollope, *Linda Tressel*, in *Nation* 6 (18 June 1868): 494–95.

[6] HJ, "A Problem," *Galaxy* 5 (June 1868): 697–707.

[7] WJ, "Moral Medication," a review of Ambroise Auguste Liébeault, *Du sommeil et des états analogues*, *Nation* 7 (16 July 1868): 50–52, reprinted in *ECR.*

[8] At various times both HJ and WJ lifted weights.

[9] Ivan Sergeevich Turgenev, *Fumée* (French translation 1867); *Smoke, or Life at Baden* (English translation 1868).   The French translation of "Faust" appeared in *Scènes de la vie russe* (1858).

1869–1870

For both brothers, the years 1869 and 1870 were a period of literary quiet. After returning from his European tour in November 1868, William managed to publish two reviews in 1869 but nothing else until August 1872. He spent the spring of 1869 preparing for his medical examinations, passing them on 21 June 1869. Then followed several years of drifting, depression, and introspective brooding by a William unable to decide how best to spend his life. He recorded his inner struggles in a diary that is marked by sudden shifts from conceptual analyses of Goethe and art to outbursts of disgust with the "dead drifting" of his own life. Little of his inner agony is reflected in the letters to Henry, which deal largely with external events, family and neighborhood gossip, medical symptoms and possible cures, books and literary reflections. Throughout, William continued to read massively. It is during this period that he read the works of the French philosopher Charles Renouvier, a reading culminating in the famous diary entry for 30 April 1870 that his "first act of free will shall be to believe in free will."

Henry James, too, was publishing at what for him was a very slow rate. Only three tales appeared in 1869 and seven reviews in 1870. On 27 February 1869 he arrived at Liverpool, the beginning of what Leon Edel calls the "passionate pilgrimage." As far as stated reasons are concerned, he was traveling in search of a cure for back pains and constipation. Leaving his real reasons for psychobiographers to uncover, readers of these letters can enjoy with envy and wonder a time when constipation was accepted as a good reason for spending fifteen months visiting spas and museums. In Europe, Henry spent his time absorbing impressions and recording them in letters to his family, making certain that they noticed the aristocratic world into which he was moving.

On 9 March 1870, Minny Temple, the favorite cousin of both William and Henry, died of tuberculosis. In his diary, William sketched the outlines of a tombstone with the date and the initials MT and on 22 March wrote: "By that big part of me that's in the tomb with you, may I realize and believe in the immediacy of death!" It is strange that Henry learned of the death not from his brother but from their mother. Strange also is William's failure to reply to Henry's reflections on Minny contained in his letter of 29 March 1870, other than remarking that he had received the letter "about M.T." Whether William was in love with Minny, as some have argued, remains unknown.

Of the remaining members of the family circle, Garth Wilkinson James was still in Florida struggling with his failing cotton plantation. The year 1869 was especially difficult for him; while resting in Cambridge, he learned that his crops had been ravaged by caterpillars. Robertson James was working as a clerk for the railroad in Milwaukee, where he had transferred in the fall of 1868. Alice James was still at home in Cambridge, but Aunt Kate traveled to Europe where she remained from May 1869 until the following summer.

From Henry James

London March 19ᵗʰ [1869] | 7 Half-Moon St W.

Dear Bill—

As I have written three very long letters home without as yet anything like a sufficient equivalent, I wont trouble you this time with more than a few lines. You must be very much startled, by the way, by my charming prolixity; I suppose my impressions have been too many for me & that I shall gradually acquire greater self-control. You see I'm still in London but without a great deal of news beyond that simple fact—if simple it can in any sense be called. Or rather I have a piece of news which ought to interest you very nearly as much as myself—which is two words that my experiment is turning out a perfect success & taking in all essentials the course that I had counted upon. I go thro' everything that comes up, feeling the better and better for it; I feel every day less & less fatigue. I made these long recitals of my adventures in my former letters only that you might appreciate how much I am able to do with impunity. You mustn't think of course that I am literally on the gallop from morning till night: far from it. I mentioned all the people & things I saw, without speaking of the corresponding intervals of rest, which of course have been numerous & salutary. But I may say that I can do all that I care to—all I should care to, if I were in perfect order. I wouldn't go in if I could, for perpetual & promiscuous pleasure. It cheapens & vulgarizes enjoyment. But when a man is able to breakfast out, to spend a couple of hours at the British Museum & then to dine out & go to the play, & feel none the worse for it, he may cease to be oppressed by a sense of his physical wretchedness. Such is my programme for to day—the first item of which has been executed. (You can interpolate this letter, by the way, into the list of my achievements.) I have been breakfasting with my neighbor Rutson, of whom I have spoken, who seems to take a most magnanimous view of his obligations towards me. He entertained me this morning with a certain Hon George Broderick (a son of Lord Middleton, you know)—an extremely pleasant & intelligent man. (Rutson has just stopped in to ask me again for Sunday. He is indeed as my landlord describes him—"wrapped up in goodness & kindness.["]) The dinner this evening is to be at the Stephen's. It will have been however, except at the Nortons & Wilkinsons, the only house at wh. I've dined. I've really of course seen no people on my own basis. I breakfasted yesterday at the Nortons along with Frederic Harrison & Professor Beesly—the politico-economists of the Fortnightly Review. It's very pleasant meeting people at the N.'s as thanks to their large numbers, you are lost in the crowd & can see & hear them without having to talk yourself. The gents in question were very agreeable—altho' I felt of course no special vocation for "meeting" political economists. I shall have gone off without seeing any literary folk, I suppose, save Leslie Stephen—who in spite of his good nature seems mortally untalkative. I was asked to dine to day at the N.'s with Ruskin & John Morley, editor of the Fortnightly, but this dinner prevents. Also to go with C.N. to Lord Houghton's to see his collection of Blakes, but for various reasons I have declined. I spent a very pleasant morning the other day by going out to Ruskin's at Denmark Hill, near Sydenham, with C.N. I didn't see the grand homme in person as he was shut up with some very urgent writing; but I saw what was as good, his pictures—a splendid lot of Turners (the famous *Slaver* among others) a beautiful Tintoret & an ineffably handsome Titian—a portrait. I enjoyed very much too the sight of a quiet opulent long-established suburban English home. Tell Alice the house was (fundamentally) just like Miss Austen's novels. I shall perhaps (or probably) dine there next week. I went out the other morning, by rail, to Dulwich to see the gallery & spent an hour there very pleasantly.[1] One long gallery, lit from an old fashioned ceiling, paved with brick tiles & lined with very fair specimens of most of the great masters. A pale English light from the rainy sky—a cold half-musty atmosphere & solitude complete save for a red nosed spinster at the end of the vista copying a Gainsborough—the scene had quite a flavor of its own.   Only these indifferent Rubenses & Rembrandts make me long for the good ones.   The National Gallery is still closed.—I dined yesterday with the Wilkinson's.   Mary is away.   Madame is agreeable & the Doctor excellent.   He is a great admirer of Swinburne & said some very good things about him.   In fact he said nothing but good things.   Father will know what I mean by his peculiar broad rich felicity of diction.   I doubt whether I should see in England a better talker in a certain way.   But my "few lines" are losing their fewness.   I leave as usual to the end to say that on Monday I received father's little note of March 2 enclosing Nelly's, wh. I have answered.[2]   I was thankful for this small favor, but wofully disappointed at getting nothing else.   I live in the expectation of the next mail.   Next week I will have matured & will communicate my plans ahead.   I shall not outstay April 1st in this place.   Of course I shall go to Malvern, as I intended.   I needn't say how much I hope to get from you as good news as I have given.   I am in the most superior spirits—& very anxious to get some news fr. the boys or, at least, of them.

Beaucoup d'amour!   H.J.jr

[1] The gallery at Dulwich, a district of London, was noted for its collection of Dutch paintings.

[2] Nelly was Mary Helen James Grymes.

To Henry James

Cambr. Apr. 23. 69

Dear H'ry,   Yours of Malvern Apr 8 just got and read at bkfst. table. I will try concisely to give you advice, writing in pencil because it is Friday mng. and Ellen is revelling in my room in a carnaval of blood and dust, and Father is using the ink stand down here.   I'm sorry you keep so plugged up, and sorry that Malvern hills are unfavorable to the right kind of exercise.   You ask if the "douche rectale" of Divonne makes it worth while to go there.   It did me no good.[1]   But it does good in some cases, and I shd. think that for walking &c, Divonne wd. be better for you than Malvern.   It sounds strange for you to say the baths are "weakening"; to me they were unspeakably invigorating.   But you cant expect much *solid* benefit fm. them in less than 2 months.—We are all alarmed at what you write of spending £60, in 2–3 weeks in a tour in England. Father tells me to suggest that it seems a pity to let such a sum go bang in a single escapade when hereafter on the continent you may need it so much more. I know if *I* were abroad now I shd. feel uncomfortable about staying a day in a land so expensive, without some definite sanitary hope such as Malvern affords. I wd. postpone the enjoyment of E. to my back trip, when you hope to be better and perhaps to be in writing trim. A pound with exchange & gold is worth now abt. 8 dols., and you can get so much more for it on the continent that it seems a pity not to. If you shd. make pretty straight for Divonne now and stay there 6 weeks I can't help thinking it would be worth while. You cd. spend the rest of the summer (until you got tired) in Switzerland and then make up your mind where to settle for the winter. If after Switzerland were done up, you still had inclination, a month at Wildbad in Wurtemberg *might* do yr. back much good. - - - - I have found myself realizing of late very intensely how much I had gained by the knowledge of German, more than I ever appreciated at the time. It is a really classical & cosmopolitan literature, compared to which French & Engl. both seem in very important respects provincial. I take back all I ever said to you about it being no matter if you never shd. learn it. I wd. give a good deal if I cd. have learned it 10 years ago—it wd. have saved me a great many lost steps and waste hours. The common currency of german thought is of a so much higher denomination than that of Engl. and Fr. that a mind of equal power playing the game of life with that coin for counters accomplishes far more with an equal exertion. So that if after Switzerland you feel like going Eastward instead of to Paris, you will be sure not to repent it in the End, however dull it may seem at the time.—With these contributions to your resolution I close. We are all well at home, Bob has a vacation in a day or two and is com^g back. Alice *decidedly* improved. Since March 11, I seem to have gone to Pot rather as to the back, and have been lying still and not making any applications to it. Strange to say, I feel quite indifferent to the damned thing— and have (any how for a time) cast off that slavish clinging to the hope of *doing* s'thing wh. has been the torment of my life hitherto, with a mental exhilaration I have been devoid of for a long time. Adieu,

Yours in haste | Wm. James

[1] WJ had tried the treatment at Divonne in September and October 1868.

From Henry James

Oxford April 26ᵗʰ [1869] | Randolph Hotel.

Dearest Bill—

I found here to day on my arrival your letter of April 9ᵗʰ which I was mighty glad to get. It seemed strange, foul & unnatural to have heard from you only once in all these weeks. What you say of yourself & your prospects & humor interested me deeply & half pleased, half distressed me. I thoroughly agree with you that to exonerate your mind in the manner you speak of will of itself conduce to your recovery, & I fancy that the result of such a decision will be to smooth the way to convalescence in such a manner that much sooner than you seem inclined to believe you will be able to redeem your pledges & find that you had been even too much reconciled. For heaven's sake don't doubt of your recovery. It would seem that on this point I ought to need to say nothing. My example is proof enough of what a man can get over. Whenever you feel downish, think of me & my present adventures & spurn the azure demon from your side.—At all events I am heartily glad that your reflections have cleared up your spirits & determined you to take things easy. *A la bonne heure!*—Altho' it lacks some days of mail-time I can't resist putting pen to paper for a few minutes this evening & getting the start of any possible pressure of engagements or fatigue later in the week. I feel as if I should like to make a note of certain recent impressions before they quite fade out of my mind. You know, by the way, that I must economise & concentrate my scribblements & write my diary & letters all in one. You must take the evil with the good. These same impressions date from no earlier than this evening & from an hour & ½ stroll which I took before dinner thro the streets of this incomparable town. I came hither from Leamington early this morng., after a decidedly dull 3 days in the latter place. I know not why—probably in a measure from a sort of reaction against the constant delight—the tension of perception—during my 3 days run from Malvern—but the Leamington lions were decidedly tame. I visited them all faithfully. Warwick Castle is simply a showy modern house with nothing to interest save a lot of admirable portraits, wh. I couldn't look at, owing to my being dragged about by a hard alcoholic old housekeeper, in the train of a dozen poking, prying, dowdy female visitants. Kenilworth, for situation & grandeur, reminded me forcibly of the old stone-mill, & at Stratford, too, my enthusiasm hung fire in the most humiliating manner. Yesterday afternoon I drove over to Coventry. I enjoyed the drive but the place disappointed me. It would seem decidedly older if it didn't seem quite so new. But I investigated a beautiful old church, alone worth the price of the drive. These English abbeys have quite gone to my head. They are quite the greatest works of art I've ever seen. I little knew what meaning & suggestion could reside in the curve of an arch or the spring of a column—in proportions & relative sizes. The Warwickshire scenery is incredibly rich & pastoral. The land is one teeming garden. It is in fact too monotonously sweet & smooth—too comfortable, too ovine, too bovine, too English, in a word. But in its way its the last word of human toil. It seems like a vast show region kept up at the expense of the poor.—You know, as you pass along, you feel, that it's not poor man's property, but rich man's. *Apropos* of Leamington, tell Alice that I found at the hotel her friend the late Julia Bryant & family.[1] I called & had a pleasant visit. I don't find in myself as yet any tendency to flee the society of Americans. I never had enough of it in America to have been satiated & indeed, from appearance, the only society I shall get here will be theirs.—

27ᵗʰ a.m. I turned in last evening without arriving at the famous "impressions." Mrs. Norton gave me a letter to A. Vernon Harcourt esq. fellow of Christ-Church & at about five p.m. I strolled forth to deliver it. Having left it at his college with my card I walked along, thro' the lovely Christ Church meadow, by the river side & back through the town. It was a perfect evening & in the interminable British twilight the beauty of the whole place came forth with magical power. There are no words for these colleges. As I stood last eveg. within the precincts of mighty Magdalen, gazed at its great serene tower and uncapped my throbbing brow in the wild dimness of its courts, I thought that the heart of me would crack with the fulness of satisfied desire. It is, as I say, satisfied desire that you feel here; it is your tribute to the place. You ask nothing more; you have imagined only a quarter as much. The whole place gives me a deeper sense of English life than anything yet. As I walked along the river I saw hundreds of the mighty lads of England, clad in white flannel & blue, immense, fair-haired, magnificent in their youth, lounging down the stream in their punts or pulling in straining crews & rejoicing in their godlike strength. When along with this you think of their haunts in the grey-green quadrangles, you esteem them as elect among men. I recd. last eveg. when I came in a note from Harcourt, telling me he would call this morg. & asking me to dine at his college commons in the eveg. I have also from Jane Norton a note to Mrs.

Pattison, rectoress of Lincoln College wh. may shew me something good. As this letter promises to become long, I will here interpolate a word about my physics, *en attendant* Harcourt, whose hour is up. I gave you at Leamington, a list of my *haut faits* in Monmouthshire. What I then said about my unblighted vigor is more true than ever. I felt my improvement in the midst of my fatigue; I feel it doubly now. There is no humbug nor illusion about it & no word for it but good honest *better.* If my doings at Oxford have the same result I shall feel as if I have quite established a precedent.

29th Harcourt turns out to be simply angel no. 2. He is tutor of chemistry in Ch.-Ch.[2] & a very modest pleasant & thoroughly obliging fellow. He came for me the other morning & we started together on our rounds.   It is certainly no small favor for a man to trudge about bodily for three hours in the noon-day sun with a creature thus rudely hurled into his existence from over the sea, whom he neither knows nor cares for.   His reward will be in heaven.   He took me first to Convocation—a lot of grizzled & toga'd old dons, debating of University matters in an ancient hall and concluding with much Latin from one of them.   Thence to lunch with the rector of Lincoln's— Harcourt having kindly arranged with Mrs. Pattison before hand to bring me there.   The Rector is a dessicated old scholar, torpid even to incivility with too much learning; but his wife is of quite another fashion—very young (about 28) very pretty, very clever, very charming & very conscious of it all.   She is I believe highly emancipated & I defy an English-woman to be emancipated except coldly & wantonly.   As a spectacle the thing had its points: the dark rich, scholastic old dining room in the college court—the languid old rector & his pretty little wife in a riding-habit, talking slang.   Otherwise it was slow.   I then went about with Harcourt to various colleges, halls, & gardens—he doing his duty most bravely—& I mine for that matter. At four I parted from him & at 6 rejoined him & dined with him in Hall at Ch.-Ch.   This was a great adventure.   The hall is magnificent: an immense area, a great timbered & vaulted roof & a 100 former worthies looking down from the walls, between the high stained windows.   I sat at the tutors' table on a platform, at the upper end of the Hall, in the place of honor, at the right of the Carver. The students poured in; I sat amid learned chat & quaffed strong ale from a silver tankard.   The dinner & the service, by the way, were quite elaborate & elegant.   On rising *we tutors* adjourned to the Common-room across the court, to desert & precious wines.   In the eveg I went to a debating club, & to a soirée at Dr. Acland's (I've quite forgotten who & what he is) where I saw your physiological friend Mr. Charles Robin. 'Twas mortal flat. All this was well enough for one day. Yesterday I kindly left Harcourt alone & drove in the morng. out to Blenheim,[3] which was highly satisfactory. The palace is vast cold & pretentious but the park is truly ducal. As far as you can see, it encircles & fills the horizon—"immense, ombreux, seigneurial." (T. Gautier) Enfin, I could talk a week about the park. But the great matter is the pictures. It was with the imperfect view at Warwick, the other day, my 1st glimpse (save Ruskin's Titian & the poorish things at Dulwich) of the great masters: thank the Lord it is not to be the last. There is a single magnificent Raphael & two great Rembrandts, but the strength of the collection is in the Rubenses & Vandyks. Seeing a mass of Rubenses together commands you to believe that he was the 1st of painters—of *painters,* in fact, I believe he was. A lot of his pictures together is a most healthy spectacle—fit to cure one of any woes. And then the noble, admirable modern Vandyk! His great portrait of Chas. I on horse-back is a thing of infinite beauty.—I strolled slowly away thro' the park, watching the great groves & avenues murmuring & trembling in the sunny breeze & feeling very serious with it all. On my return I went out alone & spent the afternoon in various college gardens. These same gardens are the fairest things in Oxford. Locked in their own ancient verdure, behind their own ancient walls, filled with shade & music & perfumes & privacy—with lounging students & charming children— with the rich old college windows keeping guard from above—they are places to lie down on the grass in forever, in the happy belief the world is all an English garden & time a fine old English afternoon. At 6 o'clock, I dined in Hall at Oriel with Mr. Pearson (the author of the early English History who was in America while you were away.) It was Ch.-Ch. over again on a reduced scale. I stole away betimes to get a little walk in Magdalen Gardens—where by way of doing things handsomely they have, in the heart of the city—an immense old park or chase filled with deer—with deer, *pas davantage. Ce détail,* it seems to me, gives, as well as anything, a notion of the scale of things here. To day I am to lunch with Harcourt but shall take things quietly. To morrow I shall depart. I rec'd. yesterday a note fr. Frank Washburn saying he had just arrived in England *en route* for home, May 11th. We shall probably meet. If I feel as well to morrow as to day I shall satisfy my desire for seeing a little more in the Cathedral line by going to London (roundabout) *via* Salisbury & Winchester. My present notion is to stay a fortnight in London in lodgings & then make for Geneva. There is much in & about London that I want still to see. My letter has been long & I fear, boresome.—Do in writing give more details gossip &c. I'm glad you've been seeing Howells: give him my love & tell him to expect a letter. Tell T.S.P. *I* expect one. Do tell me something about Wendell Holmes. One would think he was dead. Give him my compliments & tell him I'm sadly afraid that one of these days I shall have to write to him.—I suppose all is well within doors, fr. your silence. What demon prompts Father to direct the letters he doesn't write? It is really cruel. If he only would write a few lines I'd as lief Isabella should direct them.[4] You must have rec'd. my message about the *Nation:* I miss it sadly. I repeat I heartily applaud your resolution to lie at your length & abolish study. As one who has sounded the *replis* of the human back, I apprise that with such a course you cannot fail to amend. Love to Mother & Alice, to Wilk & Bob. Aunt Kate will have sailed. Regards to Ellen & Isabella. Is Eliza's successor a success?—Another piece of mine will have appeared in the *Galaxy*[5]— probably very ill printed. You will of course have sent it. Howells will send father a proof to correct. I am haunted with the impression that it contains an imperfect quotation of a scripture text to the effect that out of the lips of babes & sucklings cometh knowledge.[6] If there is such a text or anything like it ask him to establish it; if not suppress it. But farewell

—Your's H.J.jr.

[1] Not identified. Apparently HJ means that she has recently been married.

[2] Christ Church.

[3] Blenheim House, an 18th-century mansion near Oxford, noted for its art collection. The two paintings by Rembrandt were *The Woman Taken in Adultery* and *Isaac Blessing Jacob*.

[4] Isabella, Ellen, and Eliza were servants employed by the Jameses.

[5] HJ, "Pyramus and Thisbe."

[6] HJ, "Gabrielle de Bergerac," *Atlantic Monthly* 24 (July 1869): 55–71; (August 1869): 231–41; (September 1869): 352–61. The quotation from Psalms 8:3 is found in "Gabrielle de Bergerac," *The Complete Tales of Henry James,* ed. Leon Edel (Philadelphia: Lippincott, 1962), 2:117.

To Henry James

[Cambridge] Saturday mng. June 12. 69

My dear H'ry

    O call my brother back to me,

    I cannot play alone

The summer comes with flower & bee
Where is my brother gone?[1]

Your 2nd letter fm. Geneva (May 29) having just arrived has intensified the above familiar sentiment to the point of making me incontinently sit down & write ye a line. To hear you call life at Geneva dull does not surprize me. It used to amuse me to hear you say after I got home that you felt a kind of yearning to get there again. The life of Geneva seems to differ from that of most continental towns in being shut up within doors almost as much as our life here at home. The stranger is out in the cold. But is there not a grand sort of *style* about the respectable old city up a top the hill, and don't you get a proud sort of municipal flavor from the place, encamped as it were in the middle of all the newfangledness of its outskirts but superior to them like this grand Peace Jubilee "Coliseum" they are just building in Boston in the midst of the thousands of shanties & booths that have grown up about it.[2] I recollect being struck by a big placard last time I was in Geneva: "Bouffes Genevois." The incongruity was at its maximum, but the term bouffes did not seem to get any hold on the term Genevois and was absolutely killed by it. - - What you wrote of your walks to Fernex and the Salève was the best thing I have heard from you yet. The condition of your back is totally incomprehensible to me, and I have no opinion on the subject anyway. My diagnosis of it now wd. be simply "dorsal insanity."—It wd. *seem* however that the general tonic effect of all this exercise and sight seeing you are now able to go through with must be gradually to revolutionize the old thing and through sympathy with the rest of your system bring it back to sanity. So go ahead, but don't *over* fatigue yourself—The temptations thereto in Switzerland must be very great.—I should thing that by loafing around at central places such as Interlaken etc. you could pass the 3 months very well and scrape a great many at least american acquaintances. It seems to me that *the* way to become well acquainted with americans is to go to Europe. Don't mind ennui, you've got to have it everywhere, I'm sure I had enough of it in Europe, but I now see that those heaviest days were full of instruction to me.

At any rate dont yield to homesickness.—I have seen Frank Washburn a couple of times. He gives a good account of you but looks pretty shaky himself.—Next friday my clinical examination at the dispensary (wh. I tried to get exempted from but failed) takes place and the following monday the big examination. The tho't becomes more grisly every day, and I wish the thing were over. My thesis was decent, and I suppose Dr. Holmes will veto my being plucked no matter how bad my examination may be, but the truth is I feel unprepared.   I've no doubt I'll éprouver a distinct bodily improvement when it's all over.   My feeling of unpreparedness has, so far from exciting me to study, given me a disgust for the subject—and this I account lucky for my head &c.   I made a discovery in sending in my credentials to the Dean which gratified me.   It was that adding in conscientiously every week in which I have had anything to do with medecine, I can't sum up more than 3 years and 2 or 3 months.   3 years is the minimum with wh. one can go up for examination; but as I began away back in '63 I have been considering myself as having studied about 5 years, and have felt much humiliated by the greater readiness of so many younger men, to answer questions and understand cases.   My physical status is *quo;* but, as I say, I suppose the summer will make some difference.   Meanwhile I am perfectly contented that the power which gave me these faculties should recall them partially or totally when and in what order it sees fit.   I don't think I should "give a single damn" now if I were struck blind.— Tom Ward was here a few days ago—unpleasantly egotistical and ostentatious of his excentricity.   If this be not in him a transient humor, I am sorry for him.   He always had the germ of it, but a modesty and intellectual earnestness always kept it under.   I have read nothing of late but Turgueneff's Nouv. scènes de la vie Russe[3] and your Onéguine of Pouchkine.[4]   The latter even in its stiff french garb is charming, and in the pliant Russ, lapped in the magic of metre it must be *delirant.*   I have glanced at Cherbuliez's Ladislas Bolski.[5] Quelle fougue! quel esprit!   But it seems to me that as he becomes more astonishingly clever he becomes vulgar like the frenchmen, and less winningly interesting and distingué

Boston is to have her olympic games in the shape of the "jubilee" of which I dare say some news has been wafted to your ear.   *Streng musikalisch genommen,* it may be poor enough, but as a grand imposing spectacle I feel sure it will be really worth having.   I wd. give a good deal to get in to it.   The outside of the building alone which is down opposite the institute of technology is very striking from its mere brute size.[6]   You have of course heard from mother of our going to Pomfret *Conn.*   I believe Minny Temple is going there also for the month of July—Poor Aunt Kate & Cousin Helen!   We have as yet had no letter from them since landing, but uncle R.[7] writes this morning that A.K. has written to him that they have decided to stay out their year.[8]   We all feel delighted at Hel[e]ns showing so much sense.—John La f. wrote to ask for our different Taine works the other day. He is writing a review of him, for what periodical, I know not. Your story is advertized in the July Atlantic and will be sent to you as soon as got.[9]—Henry Bowditch writes me fm. Bonn where he is to spend the summer, and hopes you may come there. He is an honest man.—You say you mean to write me about what I wrote to you of Germany. I wrote another letter on the same subject a few days ago. (care of Barings.) I hope the legislative tone of my advice don't offend you—it is for the sake of concision.—I shd. think, your physical state being of the kind it is, you wd. feel tempted to try *this* winter in Italy, where I suppose more & cheaper winter loafing is possible than elsewhere—*Whatever* time you spent in Italy wd. have to contain more of the loafing element in it than that spent elsewhere, and this year being peculiarly adapted for loafing for you, it wd. be the most economical division of time.

Alice, father, mother & Wilky all well. I blush to say that detailed bulletins of your bowels, stomach &c as well as back are of the most enthralling interest to me. A good plan is for you to write such on separate slips of paper marked private, so that I may then give freely the rest of the letter to Alice to carry about & re-read and wear in her bosom as she is wont to. If you put it in the midst of other matter it prevents the whole letter from circulation. Sur ce, Dieu vous garde.

Ever yrs aff? | Wm. James

Charles Ritter, professeur a Morges or rue de la Machine, (en l'Ile) 5, Geneva wd. I know like to see you and is most *coulant* to meet. I wrote him but he has not answered me yet.

[1] Felicia Dorothea Hemans (1793–1835), British poet, "The Child's First Grief."

[2] The first concert in the new coliseum, built in Boston for the National Peace Jubilee to mark the return of peace after the Civil War, was held on 15 June 1869. Newspaper reports claim that the orchestra and chorus consisted of 10,000 performers.

[3] Ivan Sergeevich Turgenev, *Scènes de la vie russe*, French trans. by Xavier Marmier (Paris: L. Hachette, 1858).

[4] Aleksandr Sergeevich Pushkin, *Eugène Onéguine*, French trans. by Paul Béesau (Paris: Franck, 1868).

[5] Victor Cherbuliez, *L'Aventure de Ladislas Bolski* (Paris: L. Hachette, 1869).

[6] The Massachusetts Institute of Technology.

[7] Alexander Robertson Walsh.

[8] The list of first-class passengers on the *Siberia*, which left New York for Liverpool on 5 May 1869, includes Henry A. Wyckoff, Mr. and Mrs. L. Perkins (Helen Wyckoff and her husband), and Miss Helen Ripley. Aunt Kate is not listed. Since it is un-

likely that she would have traveled second class, either her name was left off in error or she joined the group in Europe.

[9] HJ, "Gabrielle de Bergerac."

From Henry James

Florence—Hotel de l'Europe | Thursday October 7$\underline{\text{th}}$ [1869]
Dear W$\underline{\text{m}}$.—

In writing to you some ten days since from Venice I mentioned intending to write shortly again on another topic; & as in a letter to Alice yesterday I threw out a hint on this topic, I had better come to the point without delay. I hoped to find here yesterday a letter from you, speaking of the receipt of a little note I sent you just before leaving Switzerland; it had not come however; but tho' it is probably not far distant I shall not wait for it. I feel too strongly the need of emitting some cry from the depths of my discomfort. I am sorry to have to put things so darkly; but truth compels me to state that I have none but the very worst news with regard to my old enemy no. 2—by which of course I mean *my* unhappy bowels. Things have reached that pass when I feel that *something must be done*—what I know not, but I have a vague hope that you may be able to throw some light on the subject. To begin with, it is of my *constipation* almost solely that I speak: those old attacks of pain have almost completely disappeared—tho' a very small error in diet is sufficient to start them up again. In spite of this I suffer so perpetually & so keenly from this hideous repletion of my belly that I feel as if my gain had been but small. That immense improvement which I felt in England ceased as soon as I touched the continent & tho' I have had fleeting moments of relief since the summer, my whole tendency, considering my uninterrupted & vehement efforts to combat it seems to have been to aggravation. When I reflect that after seven months of the active, wholesome open-air life I have been leading, I have no better tale to tell, I feel extremely miserable. During this last month in Italy my sufferings seem to have come to a climax. At Venice they came as near as possible to quite defeating the pleasure of my stay, & the week of busy sightseeing that I spent in the journey to this place has brought no amelioration. I had great hopes of Italy in this matter—I fancied I should get plenty of fruit & vegetables & that this effect would be highly laxative. Fruit is abundant but I can eat it only in small quantities; otherwise it produces pain. As for vegetables, *haricots verts* & spinach are obtainable, but invariably *fried in grease*—which quite robs them of their virtue. I have managed on the whole to feed reasonably enough, however,—which is only the more discouraging. I am compelled to eat a good amount of meat. Leading the life I do, this is essential—& meat is more nourishing & less crowding than other things. So I always breakfast on a beef-steak. At dinner I have more meat & a vegetable, which with a little fruit in the middle of the day is my regular diet. Potatoes I long since forswore, & I am now on the way to suppressing bread as nearly altogether as I can. Wine I never touch—the common sorts are too bad & the better too dear. At dinner I drink Vienna beer & at breakfast chocolate made with water. You must have been in Italy to appreciate the repugnance that one acquires for the *water* of the country as a beverage. Heaven knows what it passes thro' before it reaches you. My bowels yearn for the *cuisine* of my own happy land—& I think I should faint with joy at the sight [of] a leg of plain boiled mutton—a great mess of fresh vegetables—or a basin of cracked wheat, flanked by a loaf of stale brown bread. As regards diet however I might be worse off. The régime I follow would be kindly enough for a case less cruelly stubborn than mine. I may actually say that I *can't get a passage.* My "little squirt" has ceased to have more than a nominal use. The water either remains altogether or comes out as innocent as it entered. For the past ten days I have become quite demoralized & have been frantically dosing myself with pills. But they too are almost useless & I may take a dozen & hardly hear of them. In fact, I don't pretend to understand how I get on. When I reflect upon the utterly insignificant relation of what I get rid of to what I imbibe, I wonder that flesh & blood can stand it. I find it in every way a grievous trial & my wretched state alone prompts these outpourings. My condition affects alike my mind & my body: it tells upon my spirits & takes all the lightness & freedom out of them; & more & more as time goes by I feel what a drag it is upon my back. If I could get a daily passage, I am sure my back would improve as rapidly again, to say the least, as at present. To go about with this heavy burden weighing down my loins is the worst thing in the world for it. But this is quite a long enough recital of my miseries; I have made it only as a preliminary to the question of practical remedies. Somehow or other I *must* take the thing in hand. I have regretted very much of late (how wisely I know not) that I didn't get the opinion of some eminent London physician—or some big Paris Authority. The memory of my happy condition during my last month in England makes me feel as there I might again find

some relief. It was Malvern that started me up & English cookery &
English air that helped me along afterwards. It may surprise you to
hear it—but here in this distant Italy I find myself hankering after
Malvern. If I should return there I should submit to no treatment
for my back, but simply take the running sitzbaths. As I think of it
(as I have done many times) the idea assumes an enormous attraction—& the vision of the beef & mutton & the watery cauliflower
of the Malvern table & of great walks across the Malvern hills causes
my heart to beat & throb. I have good reason to believe that I
should suffer very much less now than I did last spring from the
monotony & dullness of the life. I can walk more & read more.—
On the other hand it would break my heart to leave Italy a moment
before I have had my fill. I fancy nevertheless that I shall be obliged
to make a very much shorter stay here than I originally intended.
If my condition remains as it is I shall go thro' the country rapidly &
be ready to leave it about three months hence, instead of six. Long
before then I hope to have heard from you & if you suggest nothing
more practicable I shall think seriously of making straight for Malvern. Mention if you are able to the names of a couple of the great
Paris & London doctors. In the latter place I know of Sir Wm Ferguson & Mr. Paget; but you may tell me something more to the purpose.—Beloved brother, I hope you'll not let this dreary effusion
weigh upon your spirits. I thought it best to be frank & copious.
My petty miseries seem but small when I think I have such a guide &
friend as you, to slap over to—& am so divinely blessed with means
that I can freely consider of remedies & methods. I have written
not in passion but in patience. Speak to father & mother of all this
in such terms as you think best. I expect a letter from you tomorrow & shall keep this over, so that I may add a word. I say nothing
of Florence nor of yourself. You can both wait.—*Friday.* A letter
from mother & one from B. Temple (a most amusing one) but *none,*
oh, my brother, from you. Mother, however, gives me your message—that you want awfully to write, but that you've so much to say
you don't *dare* to begin. Allons, du courage! She says nothing more
about your visits to Newport & Lenox—from wh. I infer that they
were given up. I was extremely interested, as you may suppose, in
her mention of Dr. Wilkinson's diagnosis & prescription for you. I
palpitate to hear more & invoke the next mail with tears in my eyes.
Cut out & send me your articles in the N.A.R.[1] *À propos,* I again
receive the *Nation.* It comes apparently from the office & always
thro' Lombard & Odier & thence thro' my subsequent bankers. As

it is not well to have it pass thro' so many hands & yet difficult to keep making them change my address at the office, you had better make them send my copy thence to you, so that you may mail it weekly, just as you do your letters. *Pray act upon this.*—I have been reading over what I wrote yesterday & am half-dismayed at its dismal aspect. But I shall not change it, as it reflects fairly the facts of the case.—To day the Malvern plan seems wild & unnatural: tomorrow it will again seem judicious. So oscillates the morbid human spirit.— Florence looks so promising & pleasant that I feel as if it would be a delightful thing to settle down here for a winter & pass the time with pictures & books. I mustn't think of the books, in any serious way, but I hope during whatever stay I make, to plunge deeply into the pictures. I had a most interesting journey here from Venice, tho' I have written Alice an extremely stupid letter on the subject. To tell the truth for some days past my peculiar affliction has developed the faculty of giving me an out & out *headache* & it was under this influence that I wrote. But this is probably but temporary, "considering," my head has always been remarkably easy. True, I have used it so little. I hope to write you something satisfactory about the things here. B. Cellini's *Perseus,* in the great square, quite deserves the fuss he makes about it in his book.[2] It kills M. Angelo's *David.* But I must knock off. Answer my question about the physicians & above all don't let this nasty effusion prey upon your spirits.

Tout à toi   H.Jjr

Address: Wm James esq | Quincy St. | Cambridge | Mass | Etats Unis d'Amerique
Postmarks: FIRENZE 9 OTT 69   MILANO STAZ. 10 OTT 69.   A third postmark is illegible.

[1] WJ, review of Horace Bushnell, *Women's Suffrage; The Reform against Nature* (New York: Charles Scribner, 1869), and John Stuart Mill, *The Subjection of Women* (New York: D. Appleton, 1869), in *North American Review* 109 (October 1869): 556–65; reprinted in *ECR*.

[2] Benvenuto Cellini's sculpture *Perseus with the Head of Medusa* in the Loggia dei Lanzi, Florence, is described in *The Life of Benvenuto Cellini,* trans. John Addington Symonds, 5th ed. (London: Macmillan, 1901), 409–11. The sculpture is pictured on p. 416.

From Henry James

Rome Hotel d'Angleterre, Oct. 30th [1869]

My dearest W^m—

Some four days since I despatched to you & father respectively, from Florence, two very doleful epistles, which you will in course of time receive. No sooner had I posted them however than my spirits were revived by the arrival of a most blessed brotherly letter from you of October 8th, which had been detained either by my banker or the porter of the hotel & a little scrap from father of a later date, enclosing your review of Mill & a paper of Howells—as well as a couple of *Nations.* Verily, it is worthwhile pining for letters for 3 weeks to know the exquisite joy of final relief. I took yours with me to the theatre whither I went to see a comedy of Goldoni most delightfully played & read & re-read it between the acts.—But of this anon.—I went as I proposed down to Pisa & spent two very pleasant days with the Nortons. It is a very fine dull old town—& the great square with its four big treasures is quite the biggest thing I have seen in Italy—or rather was, until my arrival at this well-known locality.—I went about a whole morning with Chas. N. & profited vastly by his excellent knowledge of Italian history & art. I wish I had a small fraction of it. But my visit wouldn't have been complete unless I had got a ramble *solus,* which I did in perfection. On my return to Florence I determined to start immediately for Rome. The afternoon after I had posted those two letters I took a walk out of Florence to an enchanting old Chartreuse—an ancient monastery, perched up on top of a hill & turreted with little cells like a feudal castle.[1] I attacked it & carried it by storm—*i.e.* obtained admission & went over it. On coming out I swore to myself that while I had life in my body I wouldn't leave a country where adventures of that complexion are the common incidents of your daily constitutional: but that I would hurl myself upon Rome & fight it out on this line at the peril of my existence. Here I am then in the Eternal city. It was easy to leave Florence; the cold had become intolerable & the rain perpetual. I started last night & at 10 & ½ o'clock & after a bleak & fatiguing journey of 12 hours found myself here with the morning light. There are several places on the *route* I should have been glad to see; but the weather & my own condition made a direct journey imperative. I rushed to this hotel (a very slow & obstructed rush it was I confess, thanks to the longueurs & lenteurs of the Papal dispensation) & after a wash & a breakfast let myself loose on the city. From midday to dusk I have been roaming the streets. Que vous en dirai-je?—At last—for the 1st time—I live! It beats everything: it leaves the Rome of your fancy—your education—nowhere. It makes Venice—Florence—Oxford—London—seem like little cities of pasteboard. I went reeling & moaning thro' the streets, in a fever of enjoyment. In the course of four or five hours I traversed almost the whole of Rome & got a glimpse of everything—the Forum, the Coliseum (stupendissimo!) the Pantheon—the Capitol—St. Peter's— the Column of Trajan—the Castle of St. Angelo—all the Piazzas & ruins & monuments. The effect is something indescribable. For the 1ˢᵗ time I know what the picturesque is.—In St. Peter's I staid some time. It's even beyond it's reputation. It was filled with foreign ecclesiastics—great armies encamped in prayer on the marble plains of its pavement—an inexhaustible physiognomical study. To crown my day, on my way home, I met his Holiness in person—driving in prodigious purple state—sitting dim within the shadows of his coach with two uplifted benedictory fingers—like some dusky Hindoo idol in the depths of its shrine.[2] Even if I should leave Rome to night I should feel that I have caught the key-note of its operation on the senses. I have looked along the grassy vista of the Appian Way & seen the topmost stonework of the Coliseum sitting shrouded in the light of heaven, like the edge of an Alpine chain. I've trod the Forum & I have scaled the Capitol. I've seen the Tiber hurrying along, as swift & dirty as history! From the high tribune of a great chapel of St. Peter's I have heard in the papal choir a strange old man sing in a shrill unpleasant soprano. I've seen troops of little tonsured neophytes clad in scarlet, marching & countermarching & ducking & flopping, like poor little raw recruits for the heavenly host.—In fine I've seen Rome, & I shall go to bed a wiser man than I last rose— yesterday morning.—It was a great relief to me to have you at last give me some news of your health. Thank the Lord it's no worse. With all my I[3] heart I rejoice that you're going to try loafing & visiting. I discern the "inexorable logic" of the affair; courage, & you'll work out your redemption. I'm delighted with your good report of J.L.F.'s pictures. I've seen them all save the sleeping woman. I have given up expecting him here. If he does come, tant mieux. Your notice of Mill & Bushnell seemed to me (save the opening lines which savored faintly of Eugene Benson) very well & fluently written. Thank Father for his ten lines: may they increase & multiply!—Of course I don't know how long I shall be here. I would give my head to be able to remain 3 months: it would be a liberal education. As it is, I shall stay, if possible, simply from week to week. My "condition" remains the same. I am living on some medicine (aloes & sulphuric acid) given me by my Florentine doctor. I shall write again very shortly. Kisses to Alice & Mother. Blessings on yourself. Ad-

dress me *Spada, Flamini* & Cie, Banquiers, Rome.   Heaven grant I
may be here when your letters come.   Love to father.

À toi   H.J.jr.

[1] The visit to the monastery is described by HJ in "Florentine Notes," *Transatlantic Sketches* (Boston: James R. Osgood, 1875).

[2] Pope Pius IX (1792–1878), pope in 1846–78, ruler of the Papal States to 1870.

[3] It is not clear why HJ wrote 'I' after 'my', but he may have been anticipating the 'I' after 'heart'.

To Henry James

[Cambridge] Tuesday, Nov. 1. 69.[1]

My dearest Harry—I answered your constipation letter last monday
immediately on its reception.   I hope you will have got it and put
yourself in the hands of a Doctor before you get this.   I pity you
from the bottom of my heart.   I divined all along from the tone of
your letters that something was wrong with you though the rest of
the family did not notice it.   It was more from what you did not say
than from anything you did.   I have no doubt this bowel trouble lies
at the root of your sleeplessless, which I imagine (also fm. what you
don't say) still to continue; and of your inability to do any study, which
I suppose (from your saying nothing to the contrary) to be as bad or
worse than ever.   It must also as you say pull down your back.   If it
continues 3 months longer in spite of what Doctors can do for you
in Italy and of the experiment (for 'tis nothing else) of galvanism, I
would post for Malvern again and see what England can do for me.
You have of course atony of the bowels, but that seems to me to be
consecutive to some old stoppage which must first be *déblayé* and the
place *kept déblayé*'d till the bowel acquire a healthy habit.   That, thank
heaven, is in man's power.   It is *possible* on the other hand that your
repeated colics may have produced inflammatory adhesions in parts
of the bowel & narrowed the passage so that the whole difficulty is
mechanical   But that seems to me counter indicated by the fact of
your having relief at times—A mechanical difficulty is of course absolutely permanent, and if your open condition in Malvern & summer
before last in the M^{ts} here was not the result of diarrhoea, producing
liquid stools, you may conclude pretty reasonably that the difficulty,
not being organic, is curable.   Anyhow the thing demands active
medical interference and you must not let it go any longer.   What
you say of the difficulty of feeding well in Italy grieves me very much,
especially in that it debars you from a "pension" and so keeps up

your loneliness. You can eat but little fruit—you know of course that before bkfst is the most potent time for such grapes and figs as you *can* command. *Fried* oil don't agree with you. If butter, and fat generally, agree with your *stomach,* the more of them you can take, the better for your bowels, and eke for your nervous system. At the risk of *rabachering* and repeating what your D.ʳ tells you I will press these maxims once more. Go through the formality of a regular hour— *but never ignore an impulse to stool at any other hour.* If you *have* to depend on purgatives it is better to take small doses daily than to run a number of days and then take a large dose. Aloes in small quantities. A small piece of rhubarb taken repeatedly during the day is often efficacious. (though not to me) D.ʳ Flint says he has found cases where a few drops of tincture of colchicum after each meal answered perfectly.[2] Aloes (of which doses of 8 grains do all that can be done by any dose, and repeated doses of 1 or two are the best) are said to produce or aggravate *piles* when they do not succeed in evacuating the rectum. So if you are troubled with tenesmus after any pills that may be ordered you, and yet do not get relief, you may suspect that you have had too much aloes. Most of these purgatives irritate the stomach which makes it impossible for *me* to use them the remedy being worse than the disease. The "peristalt. loz." you wot of, work on my bowels perfectly if taken not 2 at night but one before each meal and one at night, but they play the deuce with my stomach. You must determine such things as this for yourself experimentally. One last maxim. "If more than one small dose of purgative is required, it is better to divide it into 3 small doses to be taken through the day.["] Less of it is needed than if given all at once. Aloes and rhubarb may be given with meals, everything else so far as I know is better on an empty stch. I hope you will get the better of this thing, for life is a burden till you do. I don't wonder at your feeling gloomy—for that trouble goes to the root of things and attacks first of all the mind. I suspect more of your inability to do head work depends on it than you have considered hitherto. I wish by the way you wd. write me exactly how your back is. I hear of your doing all this walking—but not that your *consciousness* of your back has a whit diminished.—If after all, you go back to England after a couple of months, I don't know that it shd. be considered by you in the light of a collapse, even if you shd. *never* see Germany. One's powers of absorbing material are limited at best—and I don't see how you could hope in any event to do *justice* to England and Germany too. We all learn sooner or later that we must gather our selves up and more or less arbitrarily concentrate our interests, throw much overboard to save *any*.   You have made a favorable start with England moreover, and will get more thorough cultivation fm. "living yourself still further *hinein*" (German idiom) than by doing both it and Germany superficially.   Only what we truly appropriate helps us really, and England is evidently "sympathique" to you.   *My* enthusiasm for Germany has been entirely on the basis of letting England slide. Your better plan wd. probably be the opposite; the more so as your business is to write English & the study of english writers can best help you therein.   German wd, perhaps even hurt you.   I came t'other day across an anecdote of Schiller—(by the bye 'twas in Crabb Robinson)   Crabb saw a German Shakespeare in his library and asked him whether he did not read him in Engl.   S. said he could, but did not, as his business was writing German and the habit of other tongues he thought hurt the delicacy of his feeling for what was good German.   You could not get even *started* in German fairly in less than 15 months.   All this to be seriously thought of by you, not only as consolation after, but in deliberation before, your return to England.   I wish now you'd write about your back, power of reading, and sleep.   *I* sleep like a top.   My "power of reading" however is gone to the dogs.   I regret it the more now, as my mind was never in a more active, i.e. earnestly inquiring state and problems define themselves more sharply to me.   I read lately Lecky's Hist. of Morals which is a fascinating work, though with a strange effect of amiability.[3]   I was much satisfied by a new vol. of "Nouvelles Moscovites" of our old friend Turgeneff.[4]   His mind is morbid but he is an artist through & through.   His work is solid and will bear reading over and over.   In other words *style* is there,—that mystery.   I have been reading Moralism & X^{ty} and Lect. & Miscel.[5]   Father is a genius certainly—a religious genius.   I feel it continually to be unfortunate that his discordance fm. me on other points in wh. I think the fault is really his—his want or indeed absence of *intellectual* sympathies of any sort—makes it so hard for me to make him feel how warmly I respond to the positive sides of him.—Minny has postponed her trip to Calif. for a month & we expect her here Thursday to say good bye to us.[6]   T.S.P. femine to the last degree, but very good at bottom. Wendle Holmes ambitious and hard working.   He took your Venice letter home to read last week.   Alice first rate.   Mother & father ditto.   Clear frosty weather.

  Adieu.   Gute Besserung!

Yours ever   W.J.

[1] 1 November 1869 was a Monday.

[2] Either Austin Flint or his son Austin Flint, Jr.

[3] William Edward Hartpole Lecky, *History of European Morals from Augustus to Charlemagne* (1869).

[4] Ivan Sergeevich Turgenev, *Nouvelles moscovites*, trans. Prosper Mérimée (1869).

[5] Henry James, *Moralism and Christianity* (New York: Redfield, 1850); *Lectures and Miscellanies* (New York: Redfield, 1852).

[6] There was a change of plans and Mary Temple went to Cambridge several weeks later on 19 November 1869.

To Henry James

Cambr. Dec 5. 69[1]

Dear Harry   You can with difficulty conceive of the joy with which I received in your enclosed sheet from Rome of Nov 8 with the sulf. acid & aloes prescription the news of the temporary end of your moving intestinal drama.   If I could believe it to be the beginning of *the* end, the happiness wd. be almost *too* great; it may be even that; but even if only a temporary respite, it comes at a moment which is important for your whole future, in deciding perhaps, whether you shall or shall not have Rome to furnish your consciousness with.   Don't be too sanguine, nor count on escaping definitively the bore of Malvern. The trouble with an habitual use of Aloes is that it tends to produce piles.   I spoke rather slightingly in one of my late letters (I have written you 2 long & one brief one, by the way since your first *complainte,* and hope you'll get them all) of your florence D.—but it seems you fell into good hands as this Sulfuric acid dodge is either a very late one not yet generally known or an ancestral secret of his.   Stillé's materia med. says nothing of it,[2] and I find Tuck & Dwight never heard of it.   I have experimented on myself and find it very efficacious.   If having started yourself by it, you find symptoms of soreness about anus & rectum, slack up; it may then be that *small* doses of fluid extract of senna (say a third of a teaspoonful 3 times a day[)]— after meals if it will work so,—if not, on an empty stomach—(or even a less dose,) will keep things open.   It is less trouble than the confection with figs I wrote you about.   Nibbling a little solid Rhubarb, 3 times a day may also help.   But remember that you should in no case get more than a *laxative* effect.   Real purging is always to be avoided since its after-working is in the direction of increased torpor. The minimum with which you can get a stool at all, is what you must aim at, and a steady consumption of minute quantities of medecine

is far better than a rarer large dose.   I do hope you'll get on well
after this, as "something tells me" as it were, that it is your main
trouble at present.   But if you get bad again dont delay too long in
Italy—and above all don't be shy of consulting a Doctor again.   Remember that there are purgatives & purgatives, and the undiscrimi-
nating advice of druggists may be fatal.———I dare say you'll thank
me at last for dropping the subject.   Your letters from Italy are beyond praise.   It is a great pity they should be born to blush unseen
by the general public, and that just the matter that they contain, in
a little less rambling style should not appear in the columns of the
Nation.   They are read partially to appreciative visitors and seem to
cause "unfeigned delight." Father took some to Emerson at Concord
the other day.   He pleaded hard to keep them for study, but F. refused.   Meeting Edward in the Athenaeum the next day, the latter
said his father was doing nothing but talk of your letters.   That sample ought to be enough for you.   As for my more humble self, your
admirably discriminating remarks on Art matters go to the right spot.
I can well sympathize with what must be the turmoil of your feeling
before all this wealth—that strange impulse to exorcise it by extracting the soul of it and throwing it off *in words*—which translation
is in the nature of things impossible—but each attempt to storm its
inaccessible heights, produces, with the pang of failure, a keener
sense of the reality of the ineffable subject, and a more welcome submission to its yoke.   I had a touch of the fever at little Dresden; and
I can't help hoping that with your larger opportunities, there will be
a distinct intellectual precipitate from your experience, which may
be communicable to others.   I'm sorry that your letter to me at Florence anent these matters should have been stifled ere its birth.   It
does not do to trust to the matter remaining in the mind—Nothing
can take the place of notes struck off with the animal heat of the
fever upon them, and I hope you are making some for your own use
all this time.—What you say of the antique & of architecture touches
a kindred chord in me.   It seems as if the difference of classical &
romantic had some metaphysic parallel—and was but a symbol.
Soak yourself in the symbol and perhaps the meaning will suddenly
dawn upon you.   You can't tell how *satisfied* I feel at your being
able at last to see these things, or how I pray that you may finally
attain the power to lead a working life and let your faculties bear
their legitimate fruit.   After all, even if you be cut short in
Italy—what I said in a recent letter remains true, that one must have
(nor try to escape it) but one intellectual *home*—if one tries to escape

specialty, one misses being anything at all; and the more you get of England the better for you. I was struck yesterday in reading Sainte-Beuve's notice of Leopardi (Port. Contemp. t. iii) to find him asserting this so well of himself as critic. He apologizes for treating of a foreigner, persuaded as he is "que la critique litteraire n'a toute sa valeur et son originalité que lorsqu'elle s'applique à des sujets dont on possède de près & de longue main les fonds, les alentours, & toutes les circonstances."[3] In other words, we possess nothing well till we possess it to its remotest radicles. I sympathize fully with your wishing to spend some months in Paris. What I doubted was the propriety of your giving a year to it.———What can I tell you of our common home? M. Temple was here for a week a fortnight since. She was delightful in all respects, and although very thin, very cheerful. I am conscious of having done her a good deal of injustice for some years past, in nourishing a sort of unsympathetic hostility to her. She is after all a most honest little phenomenon, and there is a true respectability in the courage with which she keeps "true to her own instincts"—I mean it has a certain religious side with her. Moreover she is more devoid of "meanness," of anything petty in her character than any one I know, perhaps either male or female. *Je tiens à* telling you this, as I recollect last winter abusing her to you rather virulently. She sails this bright cold day for Californy. I trust the voyage won't be too hard upon her. The thermom. fell to twelve last night, and to day the sky is brilliantissimo & the shadows blue on the thin snow. Jno l. f. has been contributing a chapter on Japanese art to a book of travels by one Pumpelly professor in the mining school here.[4] Excellent in matter, but I think fm. want of literary practice, without the important *points* being accented enough for the cursory reader.— T.S.P. seems to have genuinely buckled down to the study of philology, and is very well & happy. Its a pleasure to see him. O.W.H.jr. whom I've not seen for 3 weeks has accepted the $2000 (but 2 years of hard work) job, of annotating Kent's Commentaries.[5] C. S. Peirce gets now a salary of 2,500$ at the Observatory,—Bob Temple after a career of debauchery, has reenlisted at Savanna, and writes to father yesterday begging him to pawn out his chest from the hotel keeper who holds it for debt, and announcing that he will hereafter keep a silence of 5 years, "the world forgetting, by the world forgot."[6] He says he rec'd your letter, which I forwarded to him there.—Indoors everything is lovely. Our servants are a first class set—stylish in fact. The no. of periodicals taken has been swelled by the "Academy," and "Nature." The A. is really worth taking, giving a thoroughly businesslike conspectus of the *whole* literature of the month, instead of the accidental fragments one gets elsewhere. I find in my present condition that these periodicals are less odious than they have been. I have been reading Max Müller's "Chips" lately with much pleasure[7]—likewise a little of Leopardi, the italian of which is by no means insurmountable, and the matter & manner of wh. strangely attract me. The extracts from a persion poet wh. C.E.N. sent to the last N.A.R. are mighty things.[8] Borrow the book from him if you have a chance. I have been galvanizing my back of late but so far ineffectually; or rather I suspect with a bad effect, the left side, which for the sake of comparison I have alone treated, being now more sensitive than the right. Nevertheless I have been quite active the past 3 weeks or more, and though I dont assert anything on the subject, should not feel surprized if 3 months hence I realized that I had been gradually working into a more active condition—there seem so many days now on which my state surprizes me at not being as bad as I should from past experience have anticipated. But as yet these days are sporadic, and among them abound days of equally unexpected collapse. So I bide my time and even to my own heart say nothing encouraging. Time passes with me like a whirlwind, however, and I am beginning to go regularly into the evening visit business.—To prove to you how well Alice is I may tell you that to day (Saturday) she started before eleven for town, where she is to go to the lifting cure, thence to lunch at a restaurant alone, then to be caught up by Mother & Annie Ashburner and to go to the Boston theatre to hear Maggie Mitchell in the Pearl of Savoy and then home to dinner. Last night she was at her bee. They hoped to hear M.M. in her great new play "Lorlie, the tiny belle of the Canton" but the play has been changed.[9] Such words as tiny, dainty, winsome, booklet, &c, &c, are growing ever more prevalent in our native literature.———Mother just bustles in with some clean shirts, and says I'd better tell "the dear boy" that we have every reason to suppose our offer of 20,000 for the house will be taken.[10] You may be with A.K. when this gets you. If so, give her lots of love say I got her letter & she may count on another fm. me soon. Sunday 6th. Letter fm. Minny to Alice yest. saying Temple Emmet had telegraphed her not to come to Cal. as he was coming East in December. Alice not tired a bit by her theatre. I spent yest^y eve^g at the Child's and am as well as ever this mng. Billy Washburn's story "Fair Harvard" is anonymously published. Characters & action absolutely *nil*. All his old jokes embalmed there without exception. Much coarseness of allusion &c. Nothing but drinking & "going to Parker's" which are spoken of as if they were the highest flights human freedom cd. soar to—in fact the tone of the 1st freshman month throughout. A strange objectivity of treatment wh. is almost "weird," in that you hear and see the figures move & speak but are furnished by the Author with no clue as to their motives or reasons; and half the time are uncertain whether he himself is writing of them sarcastically or admiringly. A style however almost classical in its clearness and "terseness." Write good news of yrself to your

W.

[1] The letter may be misdated since WJ says he is writing on Saturday; 5 December 1869 was a Sunday.

[2] Alfred Stillé, *Therapeutics and Materia Medica* (1860).

[3] Charles-Augustin Sainte-Beuve, *Portraits contemporains*, 3 vols. (Paris: Didier, 1855), 3:72.

[4] Raphael Pumpelly, *Across America and Asia* (1870). Chapter 14, "An Essay on Japanese Art" is by John La Farge.

[5] James Kent, *Commentaries on American Law* (1826–30). The 12th edition (1873) was edited by Holmes.

[6] From Alexander Pope, "Eloisa to Abelard" (1717).

[7] Friedrich Max Müller, *Chips from a German Workshop*, 5 vols. (1867–75).

[8] Charles Eliot Norton, review of *Les Quatrains de Khèyam*, trans. J. B. Nicolas (1867), and *Rubáiyát of Omar Khayyám, the Astronomer-Poet of Persia*, 2d ed. (1868), in *North American Review* 109 (October 1869): 565–84. Numerous verses are quoted. The latter translation is by Edward FitzGerald.

[9] WJ is confused about either the day or the play. *The Pearl of Savoy* was performed at the Boston Theater on Monday, 6 December 1869, while other plays with Maggie Mitchell were performed on other nights. *Linda, the Pearl of Savoy: A Domestic Drama* is an adaptation from the French by Charles Zachary Barnett. *Lorlie* is not identified.

[10] The house at 20 Quincy St., Cambridge, which the Jameses were renting from the Thies family.

To Henry James

[Cambridge] Jany 19. 70

Dear Harry, Your letter from Naples 21 Dec & Rome 23rd, arrove yesterday mng. We were all heartily glad to have a tolerably cheerful report of your health, though it did not descend into details. There was as usual the jaunty promise of a letter to me "in a day or two," which will as usual be kept I suppose in 3 or 4 weeks. A letter was sent you by [*blank space for name*] three or 4 days ago to Fenzi & Co. I write now a few words only (being impeded these days by an inflammation of the eyelids, produced in a remarkable way by an

overdose of chloral (a new hypnotic remedy) which I took for the fun
of it as an experiment, but whose effects are already on the wane).
I write mainly to undo the impression my last letter written about
Christmas tide must have made on you.   Those days marked the
turning point, and the unaccountable symptoms which have been
bothering me for many months began to combine themselves about
the new year in a way which gives me the strongest suspicion that
they have formed but the transition to a second stage of the complaint.   The pain in the shoulders has abated of late although my
exercise has been steadily increasing, and the days certainly are more
frequent on which exercise does me more good than harm.   For the
past week, to be sure I have been laid up, and without cause, but I
have come to regard that as a periodical neccessity.   Had I the somewhat mystical faith of a Hosmer, I suppose I should feel an inward
conviction that I was from henceforth to rise; as it is, I only strongly
suspect that it *may* be so.   It will need another month or two to make
me feel sure; and meanwhile failure will not hurt my feelings as much
as if my hopes had been more confident.—What a pity that the
weather, which is I suppose the mainspring of Naples's power to
charm, failed you when there.   Your wanderings and sight seeings
are beginning to foot up to quite a respectable sum, and the tolerably
simple conception that it has been possible to frame of your life since
you were reft from us, is fading to a many hued chaos with a gradually widening gulf between it and the grasping-power of our imagination.   But it doeth my very gizzard good to think of you being able
to lay all those meaty experiences to your soul.   Pourvu seulement
que tes sacrés boyaux s'arrangent!   I have nothing new to tell you of
home matters, or of myself, except the above.   Alice will have told
you of our fandango a week or 10 days ago, which though hardly a
success in point of livelyness, escaped failure.   Father has been writing a couple of articles on "woman" & marriage in the Atlantic.[1]   I
can't think he shows himself to most advantage in this kind of speculation.   I will send you to Bowle the Jany. no of the Atlantic, with a long
and good poem by Lowell,[2] and also the other no. when it appears.   I
won't send any nations to Paris, as you can see them at the Bankers,
and they are so uninteresting of late.—I enjoyed last week the great
pleasure of reading the "House of 7 Gables."[3]   I little expected so
great a work.   It's like a great symphony, with no touch alterable without injury to the harmony.   It made a deep impression on me and I
thank heaven that H. was an American.   It also tickled my national
feeling not a little to note the resemble of H's style to yours & How-

ell's, even as I had earlier noted the converse.   That you & Howells with all the models in English literature to follow, should needs involuntarily have imitated (as it were) this American, seems to point to the existence of some real American mental quality.   But I must spare my eyes & stop.

Ever your devoted Wms.

—It's a burning shame that all the while you were in Italy you should not have been able to write any "notes" for the Nation.   Is it now too late? and how is your brain power on the whole?   It is rather discouraging to think of it lagging behind so.

[1] Henry James, "'The Woman Thou Gavest with Me,'" *Atlantic Monthly* 25 (January 1870): 66–72; "Is Marriage Holy?" *Atlantic Monthly* 25 (March 1870): 360–68; "The Logic of Marriage and Murder," *Atlantic Monthly* 25 (June 1870): 744–49.

[2] The word seems to be 'Bowle', but no such place was found.   James Russell Lowell, "The Cathedral," *Atlantic Monthly* 25 (January 1870): 1–15.

[3] Nathaniel Hawthorne, *The House of the Seven Gables* (1851).

From Henry James

Great Malvern. | Sunday—February 13th, '70. Beloved Brother—I have before me two letters from you—one of Dec. 27th of that dead & gone old year which will have been so heavily weighted a one in my mortal career (to say nothing of yours)—the other of the 19th January in this lusty young '70.   They were both received in Paris in those all too rich & rapid days that I tarried there on that memorable—that tragical—pilgrimage from Florence—from Naples, I may say—across the breadth of Europe, to this actual British Malvern.   A week ago I wrote to mother from London & on the following day, Monday last, came up to this place.   Here I am, then, up to my neck in cold water & the old scenes & sensations of ten months ago.   It's a horrible afternoon—a piercing blast, a driving snow storm & my spirits *à l'avenant*.   I have had a cheery British fire made up in my dingy British bedroom & have thus sate me down to this ghastly mockery of a fraternal talk.   My heart reverts across the awful leagues of wintry ocean to that blessed library in Quincy Street & to the image of the gathering dusk the assembled family, the possible guest, the impending—oh the impending American *tea!*   In fine, if I wanted I could be as homesick as you please.   All the conditions are present: *rien n'y manque*.   But I'll steep myself in action lest I perish with despair.   I'll drive the heavy footed pen & brush away the importunate tear.—Your last letter was a real blessing & a most indispensable supplement to the previous one. It contained, in your statement of your slowly dawning capacity for increased action, just the news that I had been expecting—that I had counted on as on the rising of tomorrow's sun. I have no doubt whatever that you have really entered upon the "2$\underline{d}$ stage." You'll find it a happier one than the first. Perhaps when I get home, six mos. hence (heaven forbid that at the present moment I should entertain any other hypothesis) I shall be able gently to usher you into the 3$\underline{d}$ & ultimate period of the malady. It does me good to think of you no longer leading that dreary lonely prison-life. Before long I hope to hear of your trying Dr. Butler.[1] I can assure you, it will be a great day when, having lifted, you find you're no worse, & then, having lifted again, you find you are visibly better. This experience sets the seal, in the very sanctity of truth, to your still timid & shrinking assumption that you *can* afford—that you must attempt, to indulge in action: & I almost think (as I look back hence on those blessed two months that I practised it) that the trouble is almost worth having for the joy of hugging to your heart that deep & solid conviction which you wring from those iron weights. Yet, just as I did, possibly, you may find that having brought you to a certain point the lifting will take you no further. What I gained I gained in two mos. But the gain was immense. God speed you! I see you booked indelibly for the ringing grooves of change.—I believe that I haven't written to you since my last days in Rome, & any reflections on my subsequent adventures will have reached you thro' father, mother & Alice. Nevertheless I have had many a fancy & feeling in the course of that extraordinary achievement—the deliberate cold-blooded conscious turning of my back on Italy—the gradual fatal relentless progression from Florence to Malvern—many a keen emotion & many a deep impression which I should have been glad to submit to your genial appreciation. Altogether, it has been a rather serious matter. I mean simply that you feel the interest of Italy with redoubled force when you begin to turn away from it & seek for the rare & beautiful in other lands. Brave old bonny England of ten short months ago—where are you now?— Where are the old thrills of fancy—the old heart-beats, the loving lingering gaze—the charm, the fever, the desire of those innocent days? Oh but I'll find them again. They lie nestling away with the blossoms of the hedges—they sit waiting in the lap of the longer twilights, & they'll burst forth once more in the green explosion of April. This I firmly count upon. Meanwhile I sit shuddering up to my chin in a "running sitz" & think of the olive groves at San Remo—

of the view of Florence from San Miniato—of the Nortons at the Villa d'Elsi—of Aunt Kate looking across the Neapolitan bay to Capri. I got a letter from her yesterday. I haven't read it properly—I'm afraid to. I only know that it tells of a drive to Sorrento—of a drive to Baise—of a projected day at Perugia on the way to Florence. When Aunt Kate gets back make much of her! She's not the common clay you parted with. She has trod the perfumed meadows of Elysium—she has tasted of the magic of the South & listened to the echoes of the past!—I was very much disappointed in not being able to write to you at Florence, about which I fancied I had a good deal to say. Perhaps however that this was an illusion & that of definite statements I should not have found many rise to my pen. One definite statement however I do feel warranted in making—viz: that I became interested in the place & attached to it to a degree that makes me feel that it has really entered into my life & is destined to operate there as a motive, a prompter an inspirer of some sort.—By which I suppose I mean nothing more pregnant or sapient than that one of these days I shall be very glad to return there & spend a couple of years. I doubt that I shall ever undertake—shall ever care—to study Italian art—Italian history—for themselves or with a view to discoveries or contributions—or otherwise than as an irradiating focus of light on some other matter. *Ecco!* that I hope is sapient enough for one sitting!—I hope you managed to wring from my torpid pages some living hint of the luminous warmth & glory of my two days at Genoa & the following three days' journey to Nice. These latter were not surpassed by anything in my whole Italian record; for beside their own essential divineness of beauty & purity they borrowed a fine spiritual glow from the needful heroics of the occasion. They're a precious possession of memory, at all events & even Malvern douches can't wash them out. At Nice the charm of that happy journey began to fade: at Marseilles I found it dead in my bosom—dead of cold & inanition. I tried to stop & do a little sight-seeing in the South of France: but between being half paralysed by the *mistral* & half-sickened by the base insufficiency of the spectacle I was glad enough to push rapidly on to Paris.

At a first glance I found Paris strangely hollow & vulgar: but after the lapse of a few days, as soon as I had placed myself on a clean fresh basis I began to enjoy it—to admire it—& lo! before I left, to esteem it. I should be sorry to think that for a little paltry prettiness that confounded Italy had left me with a warped & shrunken mind. Let us be just to all men! (I'm coming to England presently.) From

Nice to Boulogne I was deeply struck with the magnificent order &
method & decency & prosperity of France—of the felicity of *manner*
in all things—the completeness of form.   There was a certain *table
d'hôte* breakfast at Dijon where the whole cargo of the express train
piled out & fed leisurely, comfortably, to perfection, *qui en disait* on
the subject more than I can repeat.   And the excellence of the little
hotel de l'Amirauté where I spent a week—& the universal merit &
sagacity of the cookery—& above all the splendors of arrangement—
quite apart from the splendors of material—in the Louvre!   The latter by the way are wondrous—a glorious synthesis of Italy. Altogether,
as I say, I enjoyed Paris deeply.   Beautiful weather came to my aid.
A fortnight ago this afternoon—amazing thought!—I climbed the
towers of Nôtre Dame.   She is really great.   Great too is the Théâtre
Français where I saw Molière & Emile Augier most rarely played.
En voilà, de l'Art!   We talk about it & write about it & criticize &
dogmatize & analyse to the end of time: but those brave players stand
forth & exemplify it & *act*—create—produce!

It's a most quickening & health giving spectacle!—with a strange
expression of simplicity & breadth & dignity which I wouldn't have
gone there to find.   I also went to the Palais Royal to see a famous
four act Farce of the latest fashion: but I confess seeing Got as Sganarelle had spoiled me for it.[2]   Molière is every inch as droll & so much
more beside!   I saw little else.   I needn't tell you how one feels &[3]
leaving Paris half-seen, half-felt.   You have only to remember how
you left it a year & ½ ago.   I have now been some ten days in England.   In one of your last letters you very wisely assure me that England like every other place would seem very flat on a second visit.
For this contingency I made the most ample & providential preparation & in this way I have eluded serious disappointments.   But on
the whole I don't much pretend or expect now, at best, to be ravished & charmed.   I've been to my rope's length & had my great
sensations.   In spite of decidedly unpropitious circumstances I find
I like England still & I expect her (if I get better) to yield me many
an hour of profit and many a visible delight.   I have come upon very
fierce hard weather & of course I feel it keenly for this plunge into
cold water.   We have had a week of grim winter that would do honor
to Boston.   I find this house all that I remembered it—most comfortable—most admirably & irreproachably conducted.   There are some
eighteen persons here at present—from whom however (without mis-
anthropy) I expect little & gain less—such a group of worthy second
rate Britons as invests with new meaning & illuminates with a super-

natural glow—the term common-place. But as if we Americans were any better! I can't affirm it to my knowledge! I find in Malvern itself even at this dark season all the promise of that beauty which delighted me last spring. The winter indeed here strips the land-scape far less than with us or in the South. Literally (save for the orange trees) the country hereabouts looks less naked & out of season than that about Naples. The fields are all vivid with their rain-deep-ened green—the hedges all dark & dense & damp with immediate possibilities of verdure—the trees so multitudinously twigged that as they rise against the watery sky a field's length away, you can fancy them touched with early leafage. And ah! that watery sky—greatest of England's glories!—so high & vast & various, so many lighted & many-shadowed, so full of poetry & motion & of a strange affinity with the swarming detail of scenery beneath. Indeed what I have most enjoyed in England since my return—what has most struck me—is the light—or rather, if you please, the darkness: that of Du Maurier's drawings. Elsewhere 'tis but a garish world. If I can only get started to feeling better (of wh. I have good hopes) I shall get my fill of old England yet. I have had a long walk every day of the past week. The *detail* of the scenery is the great point. Beside it even Italy is vague & general. I walked this morning six miles—half of them in the teeth of the snow sharpened blast—down this Newlands to Maddersfield Court—a most delightful old moated manor-house, the seat of Earl Beauchamp. In spite of the snow it was still gentle England. English mutton was grazing in the lee of the hedges & English smoke rolling from the chimneys in low-latticed, steep-thatched cottages. *À propos* of mutton I wish I could enclose here-with one of those unutterable joints which daily figure on our board. You don't *eat* it—you devoutly ecstatically appropriate it: you put a bit into your mouth & for the moment *il n'y a que ça*. It beats the beef. The beef varies—it has degrees, but the mutton is absolute, infallible, impeccable. With plenty of mutton & a good many walks & a few books I hope to thrive & prosper. I am able both to walk & read much more than when I was here before & I am quite amused at having then objected to the place on the ground of its giving you so much up-hill. I shall probably do no very serious read-ing, but I hope at least to win back the habit. I rec'd. your *Atlantic* with Lowell's poem, which I enjoyed largely, tho' it seems to me lack-ing in the real poetic element thro' excess of cleverness—the old story. I enjoyed unmitigatedly Howells' little paper.[4] I have en-joyed all his things more even since being abroad than at home.

They are really American.   I'm glad you've been liking Hawthorne.
But I mean to write as good a novel one of these days (perhaps) as
the H. of the 7 G.s.   *Monday 14ᵗʰ*.   With the above thrilling prophecy
I last night laid down my pen.   I see nothing left but to close my
letter.   When I began I had a vague intention of treating you to a
grand summing up on the subject of Italy.   But it won't be summed
up, happily for you.   I'm much obliged to you for your regret that
I didn't achieve any notes for the *Nation*.   I have a vague dream, if
I get started towards a cure, of attempting a few retrospective ones
here.   Oh, no words can tell of the delicious romantic look it now
suits my Italian journey to put on!—I have my heart constantly burdened with messages to all my friends at home which I never manage
to discharge.   Keep me in the memories of my brothers.   Give my
love to T.S.P. to whom I have the best will to write.   I wrote lately to
A.G.S.⁵   Tell me anything that comes up about J.L.F. & O.W.H.   I
am in daily hope of a letter from Howells.   A. Kate mentions that
Mrs. Post has asked Minny to go abroad with her.   Is it even so?
But I must be getting up a "pre-action" for that d——d running sitz.
I calculate while here to walk from 8 to 10—or from 10 to 12 miles
daily.   Farewell.   Think of me as most comfortable hopeful & happy.
I *may* not write for a fortnight, until I have some results to announce.
But I'll not promise silence. Farewell.   Love to all—

Yours most fraternally | H James jr.

P.S.   An Anecdote.   You spoke recently of having read with pleasure Lecky's *Hist. of Morals*.   I found at Florence that for a fortnight
at Rome I had been sitting at breakfast opposite or next to the elegant
author.   We never spoke.   He is very young & lanky & blond & soft-
looking—but most pleasant of face: with quite the look of a better-
class Cambridge Divinity student.   I have been sorry ever since that
I never addressed him: but he always came in to his breakfast about
as I was finishing.—*À propos*—one of these days I'll tell you my little
tale of "The Little Frenchman of Padua"—just such a one as F. J.
Child likes to tell.

¹ Dr. Butler was not identified.
² Sganarelle is a farcical character in Molière's *Dom Juan*.
³ A slip for 'at'.
⁴ William Dean Howells, "By Horse-Car to Boston," *Atlantic Monthly* 25 (January
1870): 114–22.
⁵ Arthur George Sedgwick.

From Henry James

Malvern March 29th [1870]

Dear Willy—

My mind is so full of poor Minny's death that altho' I immediately wrote in answer to mother's letter, I find it easier to take up my pen again than to leave it alone. A few short hours have amply sufficed to more than reconcile me to the event & to make it seem the most natural—the happiest, fact, almost in her whole career. So it seems, at least, on reflection: to the eye of feeling there is something immensely moving in the sudden & complete extinction of a vitality so exquisite & so apparently infinite as Minny's. But what most occupies me, as it will have done all of you at home, is the thought of how her whole life seemed to tend & hasten, visibly, audibly, sensibly, to this consummation. Her character may be almost literally said to have been without practical application to life. She seems a sort of experiment of nature—an attempt, a specimen or example—a mere subject without an object. She was at any rate the helpless victim & toy of her own intelligence—so that there is positive relief in thinking of her being removed from her own heroic treatment & placed in kinder hands. What a vast amount of truth appears now in all the common-places that she used to provoke—that she was restless—that she was helpless—that she was unpractical. How far she may have been considered up to the time of her illness to have achieved a tolerable happiness, I don't know: hardly at all, I should say, for her happiness like her unhappiness remained wholly incomplete: but what strikes me above all is how great & rare a benefit her life has been to those with whom she was associated. I feel as if a very fair portion of my sense of the reach & quality & capacity of human nature rested upon my experience of her character: certainly a large portion of my admiration of it. She was a case of pure generosity—she had more even than she ever had use for—inasmuch as she could hardly have suffered at the hands of others nearly as keenly as she did at her own. Upon her limitations, now, it seems idle to dwell; the list of her virtues is so much longer than her life. My own personal relations with her were always of the happiest. Every one was supposed I believe to be more or less in love with her: others may answer for themselves: I never was, & yet I had the great satisfaction that I enjoyed *pleasing* her almost as much as if I had been. I cared more to please her perhaps than she ever cared to be pleased. Looking back upon the past half-dozen years, it seems as if she *represented*, in a

manner, in my life several of the elements or phases of life at large—
her own sex, to begin with, but even more *Youth*, with which ow\<in\>g
to my invalidism, I always fel\<t\> in rather indirect relation.　Poor
Minny—what a cold thankless part it seems for her to have played—
an actor & setter-forth of things in which she had so little permanent
interest!　Among the sad reflections that her death provokes, for me,
there is none sadder than this view of the gradual change & reversal
of our relations: I slowly crawling from weakness & inaction & suffering into strength & health & hope: she sinking out of brightness &
youth into decline & death.　It's almost as if she had passed away—
as far as I am concerned,—from having served her purpose—that of
standing well within the world, inviting & inviting me onward by all
the bright intensity of her example.　She never knew how sick &
disordered a creature I was & I always felt that she knew me at my
worst.　I always looked forward with a certain eagerness to the day
when I should have regained my natural lead, and our friendship on
my part, at least might become more active & masculine.　This I
have especially felt during the powerful experience of the past year.
In a measure I had worked away from the old ground of my relations
with her, without having quite taken possession of the new: but I had
it constantly in my eyes.　But here I am, plucking all the sweetest
fruits of this Europe which was a dream among her many dreams—
while she has "gone abroad" in another sense!　Every thought of her
is a singular mixture of pleasure and pain.　The thought of what
either she has lost or we, comes to one as if only to enforce the idea
of *her* gain in eternal freedom & rest & our's in the sense of it.　Freedom & rest! one must have known poor Minny to feel their value—
to know what they may contain—if one can measure, that is, the balm
by the ache.—I have been hearing all my life of the sense of loss wh.
death leaves behind it:—now for the first time I have a chance to
learn what it amounts to.　The whole past—all times & places—
seems full of her.　Newport especially—to my mind—she seems the
very genius of the place.　I could shed tears of joy far more copious
than any tears of sorrow when I think of her feverish earthly lot
exchanged for this serene promotion into pure fellowship with our
memories, thoughts and fancies.　I had imagined many a happy talk
with her in years to come—many a cunning device for cheering &
consoling her illness, & many a feast on the ripened fruits of our
friendship: but this on the whole surpasses anything I had conceived.
You will all have felt by this time the novel delight of thinking of
Minny without the lurking impulse of fond regret & uneasy conjec-

ture so familiar to the minds of her friends. She has gone where there is neither marrying nor giving in marriage! no illusions & no disillusions—no sleepless nights & no ebbing strength. The more I think of her the more perfectly satisfied I am to have her translated from this changing realm of fact to the steady realm of thought. There she may bloom into a beauty more radiant than our dull eyes will avail to contemplate.—My first feeling was an immense regret that I had been separated from her last days by so great a distance of time & space; but this has been of brief duration. I'm really not sorry not to have seen her materially changed & thoroughly thankful to have been spared the sight of her suffering. Of this you must all have had a keen realization. There is nevertheless something so appealing in the pathos of her final weakness and decline that my heart keeps returning again & again to the scene, regardless of its pain. When I went to bid Minny farewell at Pelham before I sailed I asked her about her sleep. "Sleep," she said: "Oh, I don't sleep. *I've given it up.*" And I well remember the laugh with which she made this sad attempt at humor. And so she went on, sleeping less & less, waking wider & wider, until she awaked absolutely! I asked mother to tell me what she could about her last weeks & to repeat me any of her talk or any chance incidents, no matter how trivial. This is a request easier to make than to comply with, & really to talk about Minny we must wait till we meet. But I *should* like one of her last photos., if you can get one. You will have felt for yourself I suppose how little is the utmost one can *do,* in a positive sense, as regards her memory. Her presence was so much, so intent—so strenuous—so full of human exaction: her absence is so modest, content with so little. A little decent passionless grief—a little rummage in our little store of wisdom—a sigh of relief—and we begin to live for ourselves again. If we can imagine the departed spirit cognizant of our action in the matter, we may suppose it much better pleased by our perfect acceptance of the void it has left than by our quarreling with it and wishing it filled up again. What once was life is always life, in one form or another, & speaking simply of this world I feel as if in effect and influence Minny had lost very little by her change of state. She lives as a steady unfaltering luminary in the mind rather than as a flickering wasting earth-stifled lamp. Among all my thoughts & conceptions I am sure I shall never have one of greater sereneness & purity: her image will preside in my intellect, in fact, as a sort of measure and standard of brightness and repose. But I have scribbled enough. While I sit spinning my sentences she is *dead:* and

I suppose it is partly to defend myself from too direct a sense of her death that I indulge in this fruitless attempt to transmute it from a hard fact into a soft idea.   Time of course will bring almost even-handedly the inevitable pain & the inexorable cure.   I am willing to leave life to answer for life: but meanwhile, thinking how small at greatest, is our change as compared with her change & how vast an apathy goes to our little murmur of sympathy, I take a certain satisfaction in having simply written twelve pages.—I have been reading over the three or four letters I have got from her since I have been abroad: they are full of herself—or at least of a fraction of herself: they would say little to strangers.   Poor living Minny!   No letters would hold you.   It's the *living* ones that die; the writing ones that survive.—One thought there is that moves me much—that I should be here delving into this alien England in which it was one of her fancies that she had a kind of property.   It was not, I think one of the happiest.   Every time that I have been out during the last three days, the aspect of things has perpetually seemed to enforce her im-age by simple contrast & difference.   The landscape assents stolidly enough to her death: it would have ministered but scantily to her life.   She was a breathing protest against English grossness, English compromises & conventions—a plant of pure American growth. None the less, tho', I had a dream of telling her of England & of her immensely enjoying my stories.   But it's only a half change: instead of my discoursing to her I shall have her forever talking to me. Amen, Amen to all she may say!   Farewell to all that she was!   How much this was, & how sweet it was!   How it comes back to one, the charm & essential grace of her early years.   We shall all have known something!   How it teaches, absolutely, tenderness & wonder to the mind.—But it's all locked away, incorruptibly, within the crystal walls of the past.   And there is my youth—& anything of yours you please & welcome!—turning to gold in her bright keeping.   In ex-change, for you, dearest Minny we'll all keep your future.   Don't fancy that your task is done.   Twenty years hence we shall be loving with your love & longing with your eagerness—suffering with your patience.

30th p.m.   So much I wrote last evening; but it has left me little to add, incomplete as it is.   In fact it is too soon to talk of Minny's death or to pretend to feel it.   This I shall not do till I get home.   Every now & then the thought of it stops me short but it's from the life of home that I shall really miss her.   With this European world of associations & art & studies, she has nothing to do: she belongs to the deep domestic moral affectional realm.   I can't put away the thought that just as I am beginning life she has ended it.   But her very death is an answer to all the regrets it provokes.   You remember how largely she dealt in the future—how she considered & planned & arranged.   Now it's to haunt & trouble her no longer—she has her present & future in one.—To you I suppose her death must have been an unmitigated relief—you must have suffered keenly from the knowledge of her suffer<ings.>   Thank heaven they lasted n<o> longer.   When I first hear<d of> her death I could think <only> of them: now I can't think of them even when I try.————I have not heard from you for a long time: I am impatiently expecting a letter from you.   With this long effusion you will all have been getting of late an ample share *de mes nouvelles.*   From Alice too I daily expect to hear.   Yesterday came to me a very welcome & pleasantly turned note from Mr. Boott.—I hope I haven't hitherto expressed myself in a way to leave room for excursive disappointment when I say that after now nearly 8 weeks of this place, I have made materially less progress than I hoped.   I shall be here about ten days longer.   In town, I shall immediately go <to s>ee a couple of as good & *special* <physi>cians as I can hear of.   Unhappily <my sou>rces of knowledge are few. [*end of letter missing*]

To Henry James

Cambr. May 7. 70

Dear Harry,   T'is Saturday eve⸢ 10 minutes past 6 of the clock and a cold & rainy day (Indian winter as T.S.P. calls such)   I had a fire lighted in my grate this afternoon.   There is nevertheless a broken blue spot in the Eastern clouds as I look out, and the grass and buds have started visibly since the morning.   The trees are about ½ way out—(you of course have long had them in full leaf)—and the early green is like a bath to the eye.   Father is gone to Newport for a day & is expected back within the hour.   My jaw is aching badly in consequence of a tooth I had out 2 days ago the which refused to be pulled, was broken but finally extracted, and has left its neighbors prone to ache since.   I hope it won't last much longer.   I spent the morning—part of it at least—in fishing the revues germaniques up fm. cellar, looking over their contents, and placing them volume wise, and flat, in the two top shelves of the big library bookcase, *vice* Thies's good old books, just removed; the shelves being too low to take any

of our books upright. I feel melancholy as a whip-poor-will and took
up pen and paper to sigh melodiously to you.   But sighs are hard
to express in words. We have been three weeks now without hearing
from you, and if a letter don't come to morrow or Monday, I dont
know what will become of us.   Howells' bro't a week ago a long letter
you had written to him on the eve of leaving Malvern so our next
will be from London and I hope will contain a word to me of definite
news about your health & plans.   It's a mean business this constipation of yours.   In fact I dont feel as if I knew anything about your
health at all, not from any reticence of yours, but from the want of
my own eyes' testimony.   That you should not yet be able to work
shows you still to be pretty badly off, in spite of your activity.   And
apropos of that, haven't you perhaps overdone walking &c?   You
speak to howells' of nightly exhaustion—and your habit is you know
to know no bounds in anything of that sort wh. you undertake.   If
you go to switzerland this summer I conjure you to bear that possibility in mind, you may *drain* all strength from yourselfe.   Certainly for
the bowels after 6 miles a day, I should suppose nothing would tell.
And probably any amount of walking which led to general physical
exhaustion & fatigue wd. tend rather to paralyse than to stimulate
them. Sedentary life is bad, but it does not follow that the *more* exercise the better, absolutely, any more than if an ounce of salts are a
purge, a pound is a better one.   Mother wrote advising your return
in September.   I am impatient to hear your answer.   Of course if
you should be able to stay and work there, one wd. gladly think of
your staying; but if not, my sympathies too will be with your return.
My! how I long to see you and feel of you & talk things over.—I have
I think at last begun to rise out of the slough of the past 3 months,
and I mean to try not to fall back again.   I think I at last see a certain
order in the state I'm in.   I'm better now than at the same date last
year, and I don't despair consequently of getting even more good out
of this summer than I did out of that.   The difficulty will be to regu-
late my exercise, but I'll bend all my energies to it.   I intend to be
almost absolutely idle—no easy work as you know.   In a fortnight I
hope to go to the lifting cure.   What a blessing this change of seasons
is, as you used to say especially the spring.   The winter is man's enemy he must exert himself against it to live, or it will squeeze him in
one night out of existence.   So it is hateful to a sick man—and all
the greater is the peace of the latter when it yields to a time when
nature seems to cooperate with life & float one passively on.   But I
hear father arriving & must go down to hear his usual compte rendu

(Sunday 3. P.M) No letter fm you this mng but one fm. A.K. just after her arrival in London speaking of a violent pain in your back and a reference of it to your kidneys by Dr Reynolds, moving a load off your mind. What new horror is this? and is the catalogue to be absolutely endless? She speaks of a letter you wrote me "a fortnight ago." The last letter we have got fm. you was one to me about M.T., but written 3½ weeks before aunt Kate's, so a subsequent one may have been lost. I am more than ever anxious to see Aunt Kate and hear some full account of your condition. Perhaps the kidney trouble, whatever it is, may be a winding up crisis, one likes until forced not to, to indulge in such poetical interpretations.—It seems to me that all a man has to depend on in this world, is in the last resort, mere brute power of resistance. I can't bring myself as so many men seem able to, to blink the evil out of sight, and gloss it over. It's as real as the good, and if it is denied, good must be denied too. It must be accepted and hated and resisted while there's breath in our bodies I will write no more now. There's no news to tell you that I think of except poor Salter's death on board the steamer going to Europe, fm. heart disease.[1] It was wholly unexpected. He was a manly fellow. I hope to God this new trouble of yours wont amount to anything. You don't know what a good inspiration it was for you to write those letters about Minny to me—I can say—they were a solid gift—

Yours aff^{ty} Wm. James.

Monday morn. Your letter of Apl. 24th lay on my plate this mng. The letter fm. Oxford you speak of in it has never come—a providential occurrence as it must needs have given us great anxiety. Probably it was in the Siberia which put back. It seems queer you should be so out of order after your weeks of Water Cure, but it may be a crisis bro't on by the Water Cure. Low spirits is a concomitant of oxaluria—so remember that, if you feel too blue, and pick up heart. Wilkinsons advice about Karlsbad is doubtless good; but I'd rather have the advice of some German D^r—unless indeed W. have specially studied the subject of bath places in Germany. Each of them fills some special indications, and to prescribe the right one is quite a German specialty. However Karlsbad is perhaps the most *potent* of all in abdominal disorders—and is a delightful abode, they say.—But it is quite a long journey to get there. If I were in your place I would consult some good physician in one of the nearest large German towns—perhaps you can hear of such a one in London—as to the best waters for my case. Very likely he too will say Karlsbad; but its best to make sure. I believe 30 days is the term of sojourn there. I shall be glad to think of your having enjoyed a spell of German watering place life 'ere your return. I cant help thinking you'll find it delightful.

And I hope to God it will do you good. You've had by this time your fair share of earth's misery. As to your coming home—there is one advantage about bremen besides the cheapness, namely that the stoppage at southampton gives the stomach time to recover itself and start afresh wh. must be, judging by my St. Thomas experience, a considerable advantage. We are all counting the hours until Aunt Kate's arrival. I hope her passage will have been an easy one. The last 4 days here have been drearily cold and rainy, but with little wind. If you go to Karlsbad, you will be near Teplitz. You may feel like going there for a day for my sake. If so go to the "Stadt London" hotel, and try to get a bath in the Fürstenbad in remembrance of me, and take the drive to Doppelburg. In passing through Dresden, Frau Spangenberg's new address is "Walpurgis Strasse 8, parterre." We have just decided to go to pomfret again with the bootts, for 4 weeks in July, father & A.K. staying at home together. I have nothing else to tell you. Never say die

Ever your loving | Wm. James

Mother tells me to add that they heartily agree to this new plan of yours—viz. Karlsbad &c.

[1] Charles Christie Salter.

1872–1873

The flurry of letters occasioned by Henry James's "passionate pilgrimage" ends with his return to Cambridge in the spring of 1870. Having tasted the Old World, with men and landscapes shaped by centuries of human labor, he was no longer comfortable in the raw and vacant land of his birth. American society, he frequently complained, offered him only boredom and "slender profit." It was at this time that Henry James began his evolution into an Englishman, crowned many years later by the surrender of his American passport in 1915 and by his oath of allegiance to King George V. While in Cambridge, he wrote his first novel, Watch and Ward *(1871). During 1871 and the first six months of 1872, he published in addition to the novel seventeen tales, reviews, and notes on art.*

By the summer of 1872 William James was beginning to emerge from his years of brooding. In August he resumed his literary career by publishing a review in the Nation, *followed several months later by a review in the* Atlantic Monthly. *This period in his life is very sparsely documented. For example, only two letters by him and no diary entries are known for the year 1871. The outward stimulus toward recovery at this time was the suggestion made by Henry Pickering Bowditch in July 1872 that William replace him and teach the physiology course—fifty hours of instruction for $300—in the 1873 spring term. Charles William Eliot accepted the suggestion, probably in late July, and at the age of thirty, William James was settled on his path in life.*

Robertson James was still living in Milwaukee where on 18 November 1872 he married Mary Lucinda Holton. Although the youngest of the brothers, he was the first to enter married life—a life that was to prove difficult as it would be interrupted by periods of drinking sprees and estrangement from his wife and family. Garth Wilkinson James abandoned the Florida plantation in early 1871 and spent the summer traveling to San Francisco with a party that included Ralph Waldo Emerson. In the fall, he established residence in Milwaukee and obtained work with a railroad.

In May 1872 Alice James and Aunt Kate, escorted by Henry, sailed for Europe. Alice returned in October, but Henry stayed

*behind, traveling in Europe until his return to Cambridge in
August 1874.*

To Henry James

                    Atlantic House, Scarboro | Saturday Aug. 24. 72
Beloved H'ry
    I got yʳ letter fm. Grindelwald and Meyringen some 10 days ago
just as I was starting for the second time for Mᵗ Desert. I meant to
have written you immediately fm. there, but circumstances prevented, and in the interests of local color, 'tis as well I should be here.
I drove down here yesterday evening from Portland where I arrived
with Grace Ashburner after 24 hours on the Steamboat. She went on
to Boston. I could not resist the temptation of stopping and getting
3 sea baths. I shall return on Monday. The beach shines as of
yore—it is really superb, and the wood is delightful even after Mᵗ
D. None of the Canⁱaⁱdians, not even the MꞈDonalds, of last year have
been here, but the first man I saw was old Uncle Hartshorne writing
a letter in the office. Mrs. H. is bulkier, and has a coating more of
sunburn than she had. Mrs. Clifford is here—her accomplished
spouse being off stumping the state in favor of Greeley![1] The Gen-
nets are here, the Toffies, Mᵗ Smith, &c. The Clarks, Mrs. C. fatter,
whiter & more sonorous than ever, Mr. Guanison is the same, and
his graceless & mysterious sister seems to be as fond as ever of mrs
hartshorne, and as determined as ever to die without having been in
bathing.[2] Freedom is still in the stable, having dyed his moustache,
to keep up with the progress of the age, Ida & Jenny in the dining
room. But the other "personnel" is changed. Every one has been
cordial in questions about you all, & about Wilky, and Mrs. Gennett
confided to me that she and several other ladies had always tho't Aunt
Kate "the fāinest lady" they had ever had in the house here. Don't
tell A.K. if you think it will make her arrogant. I write in the little
parlor opposite the Office—4.30 P.M—the steady heavy roaring of
the surf comes through the open window borne by the delicious salt
breeze over the great bank of stooping willows, field and fence. The
little horse chestnut trees are as big, the cow with the board face still
crops the grass. The broad sky & sea are whanging with the mellow
light. All is as it was & will be. Alice's words in a late letter, "What
a joke poor dear scarboro' seems from here!" (grindelwald) words
which I keenly enjoyed as having felicitously come to her pen to ex-

press all the distance fm. Europe & Cathay, rise again in my memory—but I spurn. Scarboro, which I myself despised at m! Desert,
is real, and in such glorious weather as this capable of yielding solid
and lasting joy even to a European. My lounge in the wood this AM.
and my bath this noon were in their kind perfect—So now conjure
up one last picture of the place—and say good bye to it.—Your own
letters, especially Alice's[—]Aunt Kate has written not so often—have
given me great delight. I have tried feebly to imagine the scenes
you have lived through. Alice must be tired ere now of the epithet
of Mme de Sevigné, so I won't repeat it. I expect to find her on her
return sprung into full possession & exercise of faculties of mind and
I trust heart, hitherto undreamt of by any of us, & only drempt of
by herself. She will be the lioness of the next season. I will sniff up
some of the incense, and live on that, her photograph book, and the
300 dollars a year of my instructorship. I do envy you very much
what you are going to see in Italy, and a good deal what you are and
have been seeing in Switzerland. Though Nature as to its *essence* is
the same anywhere, and many nervous puckers which were in my
mind when I left Cambridge in July have been smoothed out gently &
fairly by the sweet influences of many a lie on a hill top at mt. Desert
with sky & sea & Islands before me, by many a row, and a couple of
sails, and by my bath and siesta on the blazing sand this morn. But
I envy ye the world of Art. Away from it, as we live, we sink into a
flatter blanker kind of consciousness, and indulge in an ostrichlike
forgetfulness of all our richest potentialities—and they startle us now
and then when by accident some rich human product, pictorial, literary, or architectural slaps us with its tail. I feel more and more as if
I ought to try to learn to sketch in water-colours, but am too lazy to
begin. Perhaps I will at Mrs. Tappans. Your letters to the Nation
of wh. I have as yet seen three, have been very exquisite, & both I
and others especially Sara Sedgwick have got great refreshment
fm. them.[3] But as one gets more appreciative one's self for fineness
of perception & fineness of literary touch either in poetry or prose,
one also finds how few there are to sympathize with one. I suppose
moreover that descriptive writing is on the whole not a popular kind.
Your own tendency is more and more to over-refinement, and elaboration. Recollect that for Newspaporial purposes, a broader treatment hits a broader mark; and keep bearing that way as much as
you can with comfort. I suppose traits of human nature & character
wd. also agreeably speckle the columns.

(24th.[4] After Episcopal service in the old parlor, wh. is un-

changed—& still has "they're saved! they're saved!" upon the wall.)—
I have passed a summer on the whole profitable at M.ʳ Desert and
certainly pleasant, tho' it was somewhat marred by wakeful nights.
The society there is *too* numerous & good for creatures no tougher
in nerve than myself, but the last time I managed to confine myself
to the inmates of the house—(except Miss Minturn) & got on better.[5]
I am absolutely ashamed of not falling in love with Sara Sedgwick—
so fully does my judgment commend her.   Tell Alice this to offset
certain remonstrances I erst made against her engouement, but don't
let it be repeated.   Poor Theodora fell sick & spoilt her fun.   She is
very ladylike, both in her propensities and aversions, but has too few
of the former, and rolls her eyes so interrogatively upon you whenever your glances meet, that you don't know what to do for her.   But
she's a very amiable girl.   Grace Ashburner's *ways* have a good deal
of the catlike stealthiness which I suppose old maidhood breeds—I
mean her way of eating, of silent suffering & the like—but she's a
charming companion, & was I think a great social success.   Miss Minturn is a regular phoenix and no mistake, her acquirements wd. be
extraordinary in a man of her age—and she is full of feminine timid-
ity & sensibility beside.   But one suspects a certain dryness to accompany so firm & hard an understanding.   She condescended to say
she liked *you*, about the only creature or institution in favor of wh.
she made a like confession.   But my chief delig[h]t in the way of
human nature was Miss Greene, who was chock full of it, & whom I
hope Alice may get to know sometime.   The Sedgwicks have warmly
taken her up.   She is the only woman I have met who can be classi-
fied with Minny Temple, for originality and inexhaustible good nature.   Her interests too are mainly moral, but her temperament is
very different, being singularly devoid of the coquettish impulse.   I
like her extremely and am the better for having known her.   My first
impression, which I think I communicated to alice, was very wrong,
Let it never be repeated.   Arthur arrived at M.ʳ D, the day before I
left, well & in good spirits, & fond of his work.

    You will like an account of my own condition.   My eyes serve fm
3 to 4 hrs. daily.   I dont wish in this vacation to use them more—
seldom as much, but feel sure they will respond whenever I make
the demand.   My other symptoms are gradually modifying themselves—I can hardly say for the better, except that all change is of
good omen, and suggests a possible turn of the wheel into the track
of soundness.   The fits of languor have become somewhat rarer, but
what were the healthy intervals have been assuming since your depar-

ture more and more of a morbid character, namely just the opposite, nervousness, wakefulness, uneasiness. Perhaps the whole thing will soon smooth itself out. The appointment to teach physiology is a perfect godsend to me just now. An external motive to work, which yet does not strain me—a dealing with men instead of my own mind, & a diversion from those introspective studies which had bred a sort of philosophical hypochondria in me of late & which it will certainly do me good to drop for a year.—I have just read Babolain— so unsatisfactory in its ability—but the rascal is growing more & more into a serious writer.[6] I should like to hear you talk about it. McCobb and Looney, two names I saw in Portland, are good for Novills.[7] It is one o'clock—I now go down to take a plunge in the surf, & close this epistle with lots of love to you, Alice & dear old Aunt Kate. Good bye

ever y.ʳ W.J.

Home, Monday Aug. 27.[8] I find Camb.ʳ not looking at all wan or seedy, as it has looked to me in past years, and F. & M. perfectly comfortable & happy. F. says it is the pleasantest summer he ever spent—and mother has experienced no ennui, tho' she confesses to an occasional pant for the sea wind, or a wider foliage than Quincy St. affords. I write before bkfst in our study with the crickets filling the air with their stridulation and the sky muffled in mist. I hear Maria setting the table mother has read me your three letters (one apiece) the last yrs. of Aug 4. from the entrance to Via Mala. What a gorgeous time you must be having, and how I envy you. I see y.ʳ 4th letter in the Nation & shall read it after bkfst. Anderson told me a good hawthornian plot for a story. It is the property of Billy Everett, so you may not use it, but it may suggest s'thing to you. A man while murdering some one perceives the flash of a dark lantern thrown upon him—no more; and ever through life is accompanied by the dread uncertainty thence arising. Adieu once more. Heaps of love to Alice, Aunt Kate & yrself fm. your ever affect.ᶦᵒⁿᵃᵗᵉ

W.J.

I go now to the P.O.

[1] Horace Greeley was a candidate for president of the Liberal Republican party in 1872.

[2] Summer friends are usually too much out of context for purposes of identification and none in this group has been identified.

[3] HJ's seven pieces titled "A European Summer" appeared in the *Nation* in 1872 and 1873; for a list see *Correspondence*, 1:164n. They were included in *Transatlantic Sketches* (1875).

[4] Probably 25 August, which was a Sunday.

[5] Miss Minturn was not identified.

[6] Gustave Droz, *Babolain* (1872).

[7] McCobb and Looney appear to be names that struck WJ as useful for literary purposes.

[8] Monday was 26 August.

From Henry James

Paris, Hotel Rastadt | Rue Nue. St. Augustin. | Sept 22[d] [1872]
Dear W[m].

I found awaiting me at Munroe's a couple of days since your delightful & excellent letter of Aug. 24th from Scarboro;[1] & I must let my usual Sunday letter, to day, serve as an answer to it. It found us arriving in Paris rather sated with travel & pleased at the prospect of a three weeks' rest. These weeks will slip rapidly by & then I shall find myself turning away from the ship's side, at Liverpool and (if I remain of the same mind that I am of now) leaving my companions to take home such account of me as may seem to them veracious. The five months that we were looking forward to such a short time since, now lie behind us, having changed their blank vacuity for the rich complexion of a mingled experience. They have done more for us, I suppose, than we yet can measure, & I have gathered impressions which tho' now wofully scattered & confused by incessant travel, I hope never altogether to lose. We have really seen a great deal; & I think Alice, in the tranquil leisures of home will find that her mind is richly stocked with delightful pictures and memories. As regards her health, I don't see how the journey could have been a more distinct success; but it is needless to talk of this now, for you will soon see her & make the same judgment. *Sept. 28th* I wrote the above a week ago, was interrupted, & have lacked time since to resume— having devoted my mornings to doing something for the *Nation* about our Italian journey[2]—which there was no chance for at the time & yet is a sort of thing very difficult after the immediate glow of experience is past.—The week has gone pleasantly albeit for Paris, quietly. I already feel so much at home here that I lack the spur of curiosity to drive me into the streets. Alice & A.K., even with their moderate demands, find plenty of occupation with milliners & dressmakers—& have even now sallied forth on an expedition to the Bon Marché. A.K's energy & capacity in this as in everything else, shine forth most powerfully. A letter has just come in from father, enclosing a piece from the Tribune about my new story.[3] The critic is very polite &

makes me curious to see the piece, which I have rather forgotten, so
long ago was it written. Father also says that you have not come
back with J. Gray from Conway & leaves me wondering how you
found it there & what you did. It was just then, last year, that I was
there & somehow wasn't charmed with it. I hope at any rate you
have found some impetus to your physique—& may perhaps have
sounded the mysteries of J. Gray's *morale.* You, too, will have had a
somewhat diversified summer & will have seen more of human nature, at any rate, than we, who have seen none worth mentioning.
Lately we have been spectators of the familiar virtues & vices of the
Tweedies, who live here below us & dine with us every day. The
Nortons too are here, & J. R. Lowell & wife, & Chauncey Wright &
Rowse. C.W. seems in Paris just as he did in Cambridge—serenely
purpurine. He lives at the Grand Hotel, & I frequently see him
trundling on tip-toes along the Boulevard, as he did at home along
the Main Street. The Nortons are excellent, but I feel less & less at
home with them, owing to a high moral *je ne sais quoi* which passes
quite above my head. I went with Charles the other day to the
Louvre, where he made some exellent criticisms, but he takes art
altogether too hard for me to follow him—if not in his likings, at
least in his dislikes. I daily pray *not* to grow in discrimination & to
be suffered to aim at superficial pleasure. Otherwise, I shudder to
think of my state of mind ten years hence. Paris continues to seem
very pleasant, but doesn't become interesting. You get tired of a
place which you can call nothing but *charmant.* Besides, I read the
Figaro every day, religiously & it leaves a bad taste in my mouth.
Hereabouts, moreover, the place is totally americanized—the Boulevard des Capucines & the Rue de la Paix are a perfect reproduction
of Broadway. The want of comprehension of the real moral situation
of France leaves one unsatisfied, too. Beneath all this neatness &
coquetry, you seem to smell the Commune suppressed, but seething.[4]
Alice, Grace Norton & I went the other night to the Comédie Fran-
caise to see Musset's *Il ne faut pas badiner* &c. Perdican was beautifully
played, but the piece is too exquisite not to suffer by acting.[5] The
only other noteworthy things I have seen were two pictures of Henri
Regnault, yesterday, at the Luxembourg, the *Exécution Mauresque* &
the Portrait of General Prim. They are very juvenile works, but they
make one feel that their author if he had lived & kept his promise,
would have been the first of all modern painters, with much of the
easy power which marks the great Italians. He seems to have
thought, so to speak, in color. You have learned, by my recent let-

ters, that I mean to try my luck at remaining abroad.   I have little doubt that I shall be able to pull through.   I want to spend a quiet winter, with a chance to read a good deal & to write enough.   I shall be able to write enough & well enough, I think: my only question is how to dispose of my wares.   But in this, too, I shall not fail.   Your criticism of my *Nation* letters was welcome & just: their tendency is certainly to over-refinement.   Howells wrote to me to the same effect & you are both right.   But I am not afraid of not being able, on the whole, & in so far as this is deeply desirable, to work it off with practise.   Beyond a certain point, this would not be desirable I think—for me at least, who must give up the ambition of ever being a free-going & light-paced enough writer to please the multitude. The multitude, I am more & more convinced, has absolutely no taste—none at least that a thinking man is bound to defer to.   To write for the few who have is doubtless to lose money—but I am not afraid of starving.   *Au point où nous en sommes* all writing not really leavened with thought—of some sort or other—is terribly unprofitable, and to try & work one's material closely is the only way to form a manner on which one can keep afloat—without intellectual bankruptcy at least.   I have a mortal horror of seeming to write thin—& if I ever feel my pen beginning to scratch, shall consider that my death-knell has rung.   I should prefer to spend the winter in Florence or Rome—rather the latter, in spite of its being, I imagine, pretty distracting.   But it would pay me best, I think, & the *Nation* would value letters thence.   But enough of my own affairs.   All we hear of Wilk & Bob & their prospective mates is very interesting— especially father's mention this morning of Bob's possible marriage in November.   I hope he knows what he is about.   If so 'tis excellent. I read your Taine & admired, thought[6] but imperfectly understood it.[7]   Charles Norton praised it to me the other day.—Proceed, & all blessings attend you!   Howells lately wrote me that there was a chance of T.S.P. getting, subordinately, the *N.A.R.* Good luck to him? From allusions in letters, he seems to be still in Camb[ri]dge.   Is he then keeping his place?[8]   Give him my love & tell him that I have a constant design of writing to him.   You sometimes see Wendell H., I suppose, of whose matrimonial fate I should be glad to hear something.[9]   Farewell.   I have another letter to write & the morning is ebbing.   Alice & A.K. are counting the days.—It seemed to me that I had much more to say—& I have: but I must keep it for another day.—

Yours ever—H. James jr

[1] John Munroe and Co., bankers in Paris, often used by travelers as a mailing address.

[2] HJ, "From Chambéry to Milan," final segment of "A European Summer"; see letter of 24 August 1872, note 3.

[3] Nothing in HJ's bibliography fits the description "new story," unless the *New York Tribune* reviewer obtained an advance copy of "Guest's Confession," *Atlantic Monthly* 30 (October 1872): 385–403; (November 1872): 566–83.

[4] The Commune of Paris was suppressed in May 1871.

[5] Perdican is a character in Alfred de Musset, *On ne badine pas avec l'amour.* HJ appears to have combined this title and that of another play, *Il ne faut jurer de rien.*

[6] A slip for 'though'.

[7] WJ, review of Hippolyte-Adolphe Taine, *On Intelligence,* in *Nation* 15 (29 August 1872): 139–41, reprinted in *ECR.*

[8] Perry had been appointed a tutor at Harvard in 1868; he resigned his position in 1872.

[9] The engagement of Holmes and Fanny Dixwell was announced on 13 March 1872; the wedding took place on 17 June 1872.

To Henry James

Cambr Nov 24. 72

Dear H'ry

On this saintly Sabbath morn I take up my long unwonted pen to make you a report of progress at home ensheathed in other gossip. I sit at your old table facing the Lowell's empty house which has grown to look more tumble down than ever during the absence of the family in the country—(they are still there, old Mrs L. being sick)—the double sashes just put up in front and a sickly mist-swathed November sunshine pouring through the back window on the right. Thermometer 32°. Frm. the library comes the din of cheerful voices, those of Bob & Mary Holton among them. Mary has won the hearts of all of us by her combination of prettiness, amiability, vivacity, & modesty with a certain dash of pluckiness wh. is very charming—and even the fastidious Alice is loud in praise of her native "refinement." Bob's good fortune is certainly great. There is not much to be said of him save that he seems in very good condition mentally, and his physique has become even broader & stronger looking than it was. Alice seems perfectly delighted with Mary. They spend a good part of the day rapt in each other's arms or with arms round waists and cheek to cheek &c &c. Father also is very lively with her and I fancy the rather trying ordeal of coming to us will pass off very pleasantly to her. Alice's condition we found of course greatly changed for the better both in "flesh" and in spirit. She has

shown no languor since her return, and evidently is in every respect
more elastic and toned up.   Her journey was a great thing for her
in every way and her talk about things & people seen has been very
abundant & good.   Mother will have told you of A.K's visit to Derby
who reassured her about the cataract & told her to wear glasses &
use her eyes.   Her irritation continuing I found this morning a
rough growth inside of her upper eyelid wh. D. did not see and wh.
she will have to consult him about to morrow.   her spirits seem excellent, and it's a great shame she did not consult an oculist abroad
immediately.   I send you to day the last Nation with your letter about
Chambiery &c &c, a very delightful light bit of work, and perhaps
the best of all for commercial newspaporial purposes.[1]   I must however still protest against your constant use of french phrases.   There
is an order of taste—and certainly a respectable one—to which they
are simply maddening.   I have said nothing to you about Guest's
Confession(!) which I read and enjoyed, admiring its cleverness
though not loving it exactly.   I noted at the time a couple of blem-
ishes, one the french phrase "*les indifférents*" at the end of one of her
sentences which suddenly chills one's very marrow.   The other the
expression: "to whom I had dedicated a sentiment," earlier in the
story—I cannot well look up the page, but you will doubtless identify
it.[2]   Of the people who experience a personal dislike so to speak of
your stories, the most I think will be repelled by the element wh.
gets expression in these two phrases, something cold, thin blooded &
priggish suddenly popping in and freezing the genial current.   And
I think that is the principal defect you have now to guard against.
In flexibility, ease, & light power of style you clearly continue to gain,
Guest's Conf. & this last letter in the Nation are proofs of it, but I
think you shd. fight shy of that note of literary reminiscence in the
midst of what ought to be pure imagination absorbed in the Object,
which keeps every now & then betraying itself as in these french
phrases.   I criticize you so much as perhaps to seem a mere caviller,
but I think it ought to be of use to you to have any detailed criticism
fm even a wrong judge, and you don't get much fm. any one else.   I
meanwhile say nothing of the great delight which all your pieces give
me by their insight into the shades of being, and their exquisite diction & sense of beauty and expression in the sights of the world.   I
still believe in your greatness as a critic and hope you will send home
s'thing good of that kind.   Alice said you were going to do Middlemarch.[3]   If you spread yrself on it, I've no doubt, either Howells
or T.S.P. will be glad to print it in the "Body" part of their respective

periodicals. I have been reading with deep pleasure though not *pure* pleasure, 3 chaps. fm. Morley's forthcoming life of Rousseau wh. have appeared in the Fortnightly.[4] I shd. advise you by all means to get it & read it, paying for it by a notice for the N.A.R. wh. I will now bespeak with Perry, subject to your ulterior refusal. I think I'll try to sling a notice of it for Howells', and keep the book.[5] I gave him a rather ill-considered notice of M's Voltaire contrasting M. favorably with Tyndall & Huxley & in the heat of composition calling T. a coxcomb wh. Howells did not alter and wh. seemed rather uncourteous as T. & the magazine made their appearance at the same moment, and the Boston Globe said it made one despair of the future of American letters to find such criticisms in the Atlantic.[6] But Morley is I think a very great moralist, and if he wd. only be less redundant a very great writer. Your letter describing yr. intimacy with J. R. Lowell and your dinner with the irascible frenchmen at the Hotel de Lorraine was rec'd a few days ago & was very entertaining. But can't you find out a way of knowing any good french people? It seems preposterous that a man like you shd be condemned to the society of washer women and café waiters. I envy you however even the sight of such.

Massive & teeming Paris with its sights sounds & smells is so huge & real in the world that fm. this insubstantial america one longs occasionally for it with a mighty yearn. Just about nightfall at this season with drizzle above & mud paste beneath and gas blazing streets and restaurants is the time that particularly appeals to me with thick wafted associations—Poor Shaler, who, with a little less bombast about him wd. be about the most charming man I know, has had a sort of break down with his head. I trust & think it is superficial but he knocks off work & with his family starts now for the Malvern water cure. Wendell H. spent an eveᵍ here this week. He grows more & more concentrated upon his law. His mind resembles a stiff spring, which has to be abducted violently from it, and which every instant it is left to itself flies tight back. He works less since his marriage and feels the better for it. His wife is getting well and he seems now quite cheerful about her. Chas. Peirce & wife are going to washington again for the winter and perhaps for good. He says he is appreciated there, & only tolerated here and wd. be a fool not to go there. He read us an admirable introductory chapter to his book on logic the other day. I go in to the Med. Sch. nearly every morn. to hear Bowditch lecture or paddle round in his labᵞ It is a noble thing for one's spirits to have some responsible work to do.

I enjoy my revived physiological reading greatly, and have in a corporeal sense been better for the past 4 or 5 weeks than I have been at all since you left.—You may be surprized that I have as yet not mentioned the fire.[7]   But it was so snug & circumscribed an affair that one has felt no *horror* at all about it.   Rich men suffered, but upon the community at large I shd. say its effect had been rather exhilarating than otherwise.   Boston feels rather proud that the fire of youth & prodigality yet smoulders in her.   Harvard Col. has lost nearly ¼ million but last night the subscriptions to aid her footed 80 odd thousand so that she may lose nothing in the end.   And I am convinced now that each occasion for giving in charity strenghthens the habit and makes it easier.   No one that we know intimately seems to have lost much.   But mother will have told you already the "personalities" connected with the affair, so I hush up. Adieu. adieu!   I am glad to hear that you are so well, and hope it will last.   I have found a homeopathic remedy, *hydrastis,* to be of decided efficacy for constip⁺. and will send you a bottle.   If you have chilblains Iodine ointment is better than the tincture, & is *the* thing.   The coat you sent me is very satisfactory.   Ditto the cravats of wh. I have one on now.   Sedgwicks and Anderson dined here yest.ᵈʸ   I go there now— i.e. to Sedgw.⁵   Arthur is writing on N.Y.   His daily Nation scheme depends now on one capitalist who is in N.Y.   But I mistrust Godkin as editor.   Howells says he wd have no difficulty at all in getting more articles for the weekly N.   The length of time your letters are kept unprinted and the fact that they have kept a book notice of mine back nearly 3 mos. shows I think that the poverty of the paper is due to the editors and not to their resources.   The Evening Post wd. I know be glad to print any letter fm. you   I don't know how they pay.   Once more farewell.   Write more now about what you read and think.   You will be able to, now that you have no bulletins to write about Alice.

Ever yr. affec⁺ | W.J.

Mrs R. James modestly refuses my proposal that she shd. add a P.S. to this letter, but "wishes to be affectionatly remembered to you"

[1] See letter of 24 August 1872, note 3.   HJ's sixth piece in the series was titled "From Chambéry to Milan."

[2] Laura Guest, the heroine of "Guest's Confession," concludes one of her remarks with "*les indifférents*" (*Atlantic Monthly* 17 [November 1872]: 571); the objectionable phrase occurs in the first installment, 17 (October 1872): 397.

[3] HJ, review of George Eliot, *Middlemarch,* in *Galaxy* 15 (March 1873): 424–28.

[4] John Morley, *Rousseau,* 2 vols. (London: Chapman and Hall, 1873); excerpts ap-

peared in *Fortnightly Review* 18 (1 September 1872): 287–308; (1 October 1872): 438–57; (1 November 1872): 572–94.

⁵Neither brother reviewed the book.

⁶John Morley, *Voltaire*, 2d ed. (London: Chapman and Hall, 1872), review in *Atlantic Monthly* 30 (November 1872): 624–25, reprinted in *ECR*.

⁷On 9 November 1872 a fire in Boston destroyed some sixty-seven acres of the city.

To Henry James

Cambr. Feb. 13. 73

Dear Harry.

Your letter to me fm. Rome of Jany(?) came to hand some 3 or 4 days agone, & most welcome it was. I have been prevented fm. writing you the many letters lately I have felt like emitting, by having my hands too full of other business. To hear of your dolce far niente under a summer sky, and enthroned among such high sounding, yet familiar names, both of places and of women, is like unto a dream, in white skied Cambridge. That you speak so soundly of health and capacity for work is indeed a subject for rejoicing. And I hope that Roman impressions will some day surprise you by summating themselves suddenly into conscious increment of wisdom, as such things do surely enough, whether you worry about them or not. To day Advertizer & Tribune are out with notices of your tale, which I clip out & enclose. Father decided to squeeze it into one no. by docking its two episodes, I think with advantage, tho' the first one might have had its sense preserved, with the loss of its some what cold & repulsive details had anyone here had the art to abridge it into a short and poetically vague statement that he had once broken with an iconoclastic love. On a 3rd reading I quite agreed with Howells that the story was transparent enough without the 2nd episode, which then became an excrescence. Altogether the story is a masterpiece.¹ Your Bethnal green article, notice of Regnault & Paris theatres, were all admirably easy in touch.² What a slow and mysterious thing the growth of skill is, and how it must cheer one to be convinced that it still takes place in him! Osgood sent $60 for Bethnal Green.³ T.S.P. said he thought you might make better terms for yourself now by asking, and ought to look out for yourself with them, as they are a mean house. The nation is quite the reverse of mean, sending me e.g. $5.00 for a "*note*" on Renouvier's philosophy in last week's no, for wh. I never expected a cent.⁴ T'is a great pity they have crowded

out your things so.   I hope your last Summer in Europe letter may
be used again or elsewhere, but have heard nothing of its Fate.
Perry dined here yesterday, saying he had got your Gautier and wd
put it into the April no.[5]   He liked it.   He is growing to have the
calm breadth and sanguineness of middle life.   His Editorial work
agrees with him very well, and I should think he probably did it
pretty well, altho his original writing seems pretty ineffectual, at least
he gave me a very lame abstract of a notice he had written of Middlemarch.[6]   He was very sorry Dennett had sent yours to the Galaxy
instead of to him.[7]   What a blasted artistic failure Middlemarch is
but what a well of wisdom.   It may be a case of not seeing the forest
for the trees, it may be that her "purpose" did not work out clear in
her own mind, but the obscurity of the ending disappoints everybody.
Her perpetual tendency to criticise and preach a propos of every
detail make you expect some rather distinct doctrine or conclusion
to emerge from the ensemble, and its being sandwiched between
those two St. Theresa covers, still further stimulates you to look for
it.[8]   Unsheathe the Lydgate-Rosamund episode fm. the rest, and you
have in it a pure artistic study, perfectly successful and being an end
in itself, but Ladislaw-Dorothea suggest too much & solve too little.
And again the cold blooded construction and firm working out of
that miserable old mechanical *ficelle* of Bulstrode-Ladislaw-Raffles-
Casaubon—which she adopted fm. the common novelists property-
room but which was never born in her private imagination, and
which she can't possibly have had any glow about—her crafty skill in
the use of this old rubbish, I say, forbids one to excuse her constructive short comings where there *is* a moral matter involved, on the
plea of an innate incapacity for plan and *use* of material.

Feb. 14.   My pen rushed headlong into this diatribe on middlemarch yesterday without the least premeditation, leaving me just time
to dress for a dinner party at the Morses in town.   Alice was seized in
the midst of her toilet by an intensely acute colic (caused no doubt
by inhaling sewer gas wh. came pouring out of all our waste pipes
this mng. esp[ly] in the pantry where she in the lack of a "parlor girl"
was washing the bkfst. things.) and cd. not go, wh. was a pity, as the
party was given in her name.   I packed off in a carriage with Mr. &
Mrs Child, thermometer at 10°, they going to a dinner at the
Bangs's,[9] & Child cursing and swearing all the way in.   At the Morses
sat between Mrs M. & the beauteous and adorably naive miss Mary
M.   Opposite were Jim Putnam Miss Bessie Lee & Edw[d] Emerson
who has returned more charming than ever,[10] and beyond me Chas.

Jackson, & Theodora Sedgwick while Mr. Morse sat silently blushing, squinting & showing his dazzling teeth in a lady like manner at the head of the table. I enjoyed it extremely, as it was my first & probably last dinner party of the season. Coming home found that Alice had soon been relieved "copieusement" (proving cause of trouble) and was all right. This morning arose went to Brewer's to get two partridge's to garnish our cod fish dinner.[11] Bought at Richardson's an Appleton's Journal containing part i of "Bressant" a novel by Julian Hawthorne to send Bob Temple.[12] At 10.30 arrived your letter of Jany. 26th wh. was a very pleasant continuation of your Aufenthalt in Rome. At 12.30 after reading an hour in Flints physiology,[13] I went to town paid a bill of Randidge's[14] looked in to the Atheneum reading room, got 1 doz. raw oysters at Higgins's saloon in Court Street, came out again, thermometer having risen to near thawing point, dozed ½ an hour before the fire, and am now writing this to you.—I am enjoying a two weeks respite from tuition the boys being condemned to pass examinations, in which I luckily take no part at present. I find the work very interesting and stimulating. It presents two problems, the intellectual one—how best to state your matter to them, and the practical one, how to govern them, stir them up, not bore them, yet make them work &c. I should think it not unpleasant as a permanent thing. The authority is at first rather flattering to one. So far, I seem to have succeeded in interesting them, for they are admirably attentive, and I hear of expressions of satisfaction on their part. Whether it will go on next year cant at this hour, for many reasons, be decided. I have done almost absolutely no visiting this winter, and seen hardly any one or heard any thing till last week when a sort of frenzy took possession of me and I went to a symphony concert & thrice to the theatre. A most lovely English actress, young, innocent, refined, has been playing Juliet, which play I enjoyed most intensley, tho' it was at the Boston theatre and her support almost as poor as it could have been. Neilson is she hight. I ne'er heard of her before. A rival american beauty has been playing a stinking thing of Sardou's (Agnes) at the Globe, which disgusted me with cleverness. Her name is Miss Ethel, and she is a lady like but depressing phenomenon, all made up of nerves & american insubstantiality.[15] I have read hardly anything of late, some of the immortal Wordsworth's excursion having been the best.[16] I have simply shaken hands with Gray since his engagement, and have only seen holmes 2ce this winter. I fear he is at last feeling the effects of his overwork. I wish he and his wife wd. go abroad for 6 mos. after he gets his Kent out in the Spring.   It might be the salvation of him physically and of her mentally.—Freund returned to Breslau this week with wife & brats.   Letter fm. Wilky this A.M. saying he may take a new place on the R.R. at "Watertown," lonely but active & more instructive than his present office.   Carrie can't leave her Father or Milwaukie.

Poor Mr. Tweedy.   I'm very glad to hear of his definitive recovery. He must have had a dismal time of it when sick.   But I envied you your run of the house, and your drives in the Coupé.—I enclose one of Bob's recent notes.

—No jokes, no anything to tell you.   My own spirits are very good, as I have got some things rather straitened out in my mind lately, and this external responsibility and college work agree with human nature better than lonely self culture.

Adieu! Adieu! Enjoy & produce.   If you are still with Tweedies & Bootts when you get this give them my love.   I got a week ago a letter & some photogs. fm. Miss Lizzie Boott wh. I will soon reply to. She seems to have missed one letter I wrote her.

Yrs.   W.J.

[1] WJ is describing the editing of "The Madonna of the Future," *Atlantic Monthly* 31 (March 1873): 276–97.

[2] HJ, "The Bethnal Green Museum," *Atlantic Monthly* 31 (January 1873): 69–75; "Henri Regnault," *Nation* 16 (2 January 1873): 13–15; "The Parisian Stage," *Nation* 16 (9 January 1873): 23–24.

[3] James R. Osgood & Co., publishers of the *Atlantic Monthly.*

[4] WJ, note on Renouvier's Contribution to *La Critique Philosophique*, in *Nation* 31 (6 February 1873): 94, reprinted in *ECR.*

[5] HJ, "Théâtre de Théophile Gautier," *North American Review* 106 (April 1873): 310–29.

[6] Thomas Sergeant Perry, review of George Eliot, *Middlemarch*, in *North American Review* 116 (April 1873): 432–40.

[7] See letter of 24 November 1872.

[8] *Middlemarch* begins and ends with allusions to St. Theresa, while Dorothea, the heroine, is described as a later-born Theresa.

[9] The Bangs were not identified.

[10] Edward Emerson, his sister Ellen Tucker Emerson, and their father were in Europe in the fall of 1872.   Edward returned home, while the other two traveled to Egypt, returning to Concord in May 1873.

[11] There were two provision dealers with that name on Brattle St., Cambridge.

[12] Julian Hawthorne, *Bressant* (New York: D. Appleton, 1873).   Benjamin Richardson sold books and stationery at 5 Harvard Square, Cambridge.

[13] Austin Flint, Jr., *The Physiology of Man*, 5 vols. (1866–75).

[14] George L. Randidge, a tailor located at 6 Tremont St., Boston.

[15] Agnes Ethel appeared in *Agnes* at the Globe Theater.

[16] William Wordsworth, *The Excursion* (1814).

1874–1875

William James's first semester of teaching was a success, and he was offered the course in anatomy and physiology for a full year at $600. But still his doubts and feelings of invalidism persisted. Finally, after much hesitation he decided to spend the academic year of 1873–74 in Italy where Henry James was working on his novel Roderick Hudson.

William sailed from New York on 11 October 1873 and reached Florence late at night on 29 October. In Florence he was restless. Writing to Alice James on 23 November, he complained that his mind was being opened like an "unwilling oyster" by a "dead civilization" forcing him to digest masses of disconnected "empirical materials," and "even art comes before one here much more as a problem" and not as a "refreshment & edification." He wanted nothing else but to cultivate the "patch of ground" which was his and hoped in a few weeks to be able to disregard his surroundings and to read the physiology books he had brought from home. It is not surprising that he did not linger in Florence but returned to Cambridge in the middle of March 1874.

Meanwhile the James family circle was widening. On 12 November 1873 Garth Wilkinson James married Caroline Eames Cary, a woman whom the Jameses disliked from the very beginning. And on 18 November 1873, William became an uncle for the first time when Mary Holton James, Robertson's wife, gave birth to a son, Edward Holton James.

To Henry James

Cambr. April 18. 74

Dear H.

Yours of the 22nd to me cum to hand about a week ago and much pleasure did it give by its good news of your health.   May it last! I'm sorry you should have struck on a "morbid" vein in Gryz'—sky —its too bad.   It's also too bad you shd. have "conversed long with Miss Whitwell, *not* about me."   Where's the messages I charged you to give her about my wanting to take her to that restored castle?   Is

it true she's not coming home for another year?   Alack the day!   Any
gossip about florence you can still communicate will be greedily
sucked in by me, who feel towards it as I do towards the old Albany
of our childhood with afternoon shadows of trees &c. &c.—Not but
that I am happy here—more so than I ever was there because I'm
in a permanent path, and it shows me how for our type of character
the thought of the *whole* dominates the particular moments.   All my
moments here are inferior to those in Italy, but they are parts of a
long plan which is good, so they content me more than the Italian
ones wh. only existed for themselves.   I have been feeling uncommonly strong for almost three weeks, (having been pretty miserable
for the six preceding) and done a good deal of work in Bowditch's
laboratory.   I am engaged to go to spend this Saturday night & to
morrow with him at Jamaica Plains.[1]   He is worthy—Yesterday was
a cold NEster, which left two good inches of snow on the ground for
to day's glittering sun to clear away.   A different spring from yours—
but on the whole not intolerable to me for you know that each day
may be the last.   Terrible weather at sea.   I'm glad our joint voyage
in April fell through.   No news yet of the trunk.—I went yesterday
to dine with mrs Tappan & did not get out till midnight through the
snow storm   She lives on Beacon St. looking down Dartmouth, and
Emerson & Ellen D.ʳ Holmes, and Miss Georgina Putnam were the
guests.   None oped the mouth save holmes at table.   Emerson looks
in magnificent health, but the refined idiocy of his manner seems as
if it must be affectation.   After dinner I had a long and drastic dose
of Miss Putnam then was relieved by the incoming of Miss Bessie Lee
who is very "nice."   The Tappan girls are improved.   Ellen longs for
Europe, Boston being so "tame"(!) and they probably will go next
fall.   After all Mrs Tappans eagerness for intellectual sensations, her
passion, more than atone for all her crimes, and make her the most
nutritious person I have yet struck here.   I confess that we seem a
poor lot on the whole.   My short stay abroad has given me quite a
new sense of what you used to call the provinciality of Boston, but
that is no harm.   What displeases me is the want of stoutness &
squareness in the people, their ultra quietness, prudence, slyness, in-
tellectualness of gait.   Not that their intellects amount to anything,
either.   You will be discouraged, I remain happy! but this brings me
to the subject of your return, of which I have thought much.   It is
evident that you will have to eat your bread in sorrow for a time
here—it is equally evident that time (but it may take years) will prove

a remedy for a great deal of the trouble and you will attune your at present coarse senses to snatch a fearful joy from wooden fences and commercial faces,[2] a joy the more thrilling for being so subtly extracted. Are you ready to make the heroic effort? It is a fork in the path of your life and upon your decision hangs your whole future. If you are not persuaded enough of the importance of living at home to wade through perhaps three years slough of despond, I see no particular reason why you should come at all just now—and its extravagance is against it. This is your dilemma: The congeniality of europe on the one hand + the difficulty of making an entire living out of original writing, and its abnormality as a matter of mental hygiene, on the one hand;—the dreariness of american conditions of life + a mechanical routine occupation possibly to be obtained, which from day to day is *done* when 'tis done, mixed up with the writing into which you distil your essence. Alice tells me that since you have been away she has received but $1800 for your writing (this week 25 for your '93, and 20 for your excellent Merimée have come in)[3] You see to *live* by the pen is what very few people can do unless they "prostitute" themselves like [*blank space for name*]

As for better health at home I'm not sure we did not exagerate that. My bowels were very lively till I sailed from Bremen. I hardly passed anything the two weeks I was on board, and they have been very tight ever since in spite of home diet. In short don't come unless with a *resolute* intention. If you come, your worst years will be the first, If you stay, the bad years may be the later ones, when moreover you *cant* change. And I have a suspicion that if you come too and *can* get once acclimated the quality of what you write will be higher than it wd. be in Europe. The rest of the family concur in thinking that if it is probable that you are to return in a year, you had better for economy's sake not come. Of course you can correct proofs of your books by mail, without any trouble. It seems to me a very critical moment in your history. But you have several months to decide.

Goodbye. Bill of lading & key of trunk have just come.

[1] Bowditch lived in Jamaica Plain, an area of Boston.

[2] The phrase "snatch a fearful joy" is from Thomas Gray's "Ode on a Distant Prospect of Eton College," line 38.

[3] HJ, "Ninety-Three," review of Victor Hugo, *Quatrevingt-treize* and its English translation, in *Nation* 18 (9 April 1874): 238–39; "The Letters of Prosper Mérimée," in *Independent* (9 April 1874): 9–10. HJ also published a review of Mérimée's *Dernières nouvelles*, in *Nation* 18 (12 February 1874): 111.

From Henry James

Baden Baden July 6ᵗʰ [1874] | Hotel Royal

Beloved Brother:

I wrote some ten days ago, while I was still waiting for your letters to be sent from Florence: They came a day or two later—one from you of June 1ˢᵗ, one from father of the 11ᵗʰ, & one forwarded from Wilky.   Also a number of the Independent.[1]   The time has come round again for a new arrival, but I won't wait to acknowledge it. Your letter was most welcome & satisfactory, but I am afraid I can give you nothing of equal value in return.   I am sorry your eyes had been bothering you, but I trust you have worked them up by this time to their normal level.   What chiefly pre-occupies me is my wonderment as to what your are going to do with the summer.   I saw in one of the papers an allusion to some late terrific heat in New-Y<or>k. I hope it was not as bad as reported or that if so, it stopped mercifully short of Cambridge.   Alice & A.K. are of course by this time packed off to the Green Mountains & I hope you have salubrious retreat in prospect, for at least a part of the summer.—Writing from out of these shady blue forests of Baden, I feel as if it shamed me even to allude to your possibilities of discomfort.   Heaven bless you (or rather *fan* you, all!)   My last letter will have told you of my coming here straight from Italy, of my having lost my heart my heart to the loveliness of the place & fixed myself here for an indefinite period. I shall probably remain undisturbedly till Sept. 1ˢᵗ, unless induced to adjourn to Homburg about Aug. 1ˢᵗ by the Tweedies, who are probably coming back from England to go there.   But I hope, for a little conversation's sake, to make them c<ome> here.—I have been <here> passing a very tranquil & uneventful ten days.   I scribble in the morning, walk in the woods in the afternoon & sit listening to the music on the promenade & eating an ice in the evening.   Baden is a wonderfully pretty place & exactly arranged by nature for its rôle. It is embowered in Forests & these are singularly handsome; I never knew to the same extent the fascination of trees.   The walks & strolls are multitudinous & wherever you go you want to lie down on the grass in verden shade and look at the blue hills.   Socially, the beaux jours of Baden are over & the life of the place is very dull.   I have seen no one I know, & converse with nature more than with man. Turgenieff, alas, has just sold his villa & departed.   I am told that in former years he was constantly "round."—You will have learned by this time by my late lett<er my> intentions as to coming home, promulgated in reply to your letter received in Florence. You will have observed that I don't consider my return now equivalent to the design of fixing myself there for ever, as you seemed to imply. But we can talk of this when I arrive, which will probably be in October *via* England. I regret that I cannot echo your satisfaction on leaving Italy for Germany. I don't think a residence of years would modify materially my joyless attitude toward this people, their physiognomy, & and their manners. I didn't know, until coming back here now, how wedded I was to my preference for a life in Italy to any other, & indeed if I couldn't live there I think I would rather not live in Europe at all. Either Italy or downright Yankeedom! The hitch in the matter is that I'm wrong in not caring for the horrible G.'s, as Mrs. Lombard <woul>d say, more: but when I <want> a justification, I find it in their atrocious passion for foul air. Reserve your opinion until you have had to sit down with fifteen persons to a 1 o'clock dinner in a low-ceiled dining room, on a July day, with the thermometer at 86° & every crack & cranny hermetically sealed. We have been having very great heat & I'm afraid Baden isn't particularly cool. The nights however, have been delicious. I don't know what to tell you. I note your injunction if I stay in Europe to "get married" & if I write you that I have changed my mind & mean to pass the winter, you may expect to hear of my *matrimonio* by the next steamer. Perhaps the chambermaid here, the large-waisted Anna, will have me. I got, apropos, a letter from Wilky in which, speaking of his marriage, he says *more suo:* "The former condition is as happy a one as any I ever made for myself!" Father's letter contained an extract from Bob, about his baby <which> made me feel unmi<s>t<a>kably the bowels of an uncle. It was a charming sketch and must make mother and Alice hanker terribly after the babe. Tell Alice & A.K. that they must write me about their inn. Do you see Lowell, if as, I suppose, he has returned? I parted from him in Florence most affectionately & promised him to dine with him at home, every Sunday: but I confess I don't look forward with absolute enthusiasm to a life in which the chief recreation should be a weekly dinner with L. I wish you had given me more gossip about certain people at home. How is T.S.P. in matrimony? Do you see La Farge, & what was the history, and what the results of his time abroad? The result, I see by the *Nation,* was his getting his pictures refused at the academy.[2] I have written to W.H.[3] but hear nothing from him: I trust he will come here. Are there any more facts about the Nortons? I heard from A. M. Tweedy lately, from England, that they thought of coming to

Homburg for August & wanted me to meet them there: but this I
have mentioned. I also shortly since heard from Mrs. Lombard, very
desperate for a refuge in Switzerland & wanting to come here.   I
wrote her a report of prices, & as they are not high, she may arrive.
I received *one* Independent, with a notice of the Pitti P<alace>.[4] Father speaks as if two had been sent<. I sent> the Indpt. the other
day a sketch of my journey out of Italy: but of meagre value, as the
subject was not rich.[5]   Farewell, dear Bill: excuse this insipid scrawl.
It is the best I have just now.   Thank father for his letter & blessings
on him & mother.   Peace & comfort to you all—

Yours ever   H. James jr

[1] The *Independent* was publishing a piece by HJ on Italy or Italian art nearly every
week.   These were reprinted in *Transatlantic Sketches*.

[2] *Nation* 18 (4 June 1874): 363, a note on the policies of the picture-hanging committee of the National Academy of Design.   The committee rejected La Farge, hung
a landscape by James Abbott McNeill Whistler where it could not be seen, and used
the space gained for works by members of the committee.

[3] Oliver Wendell Holmes, Jr.

[4] HJ, "Florentine Notes," *Independent* (21 May 1874): 1–2, reprinted in *Transatlantic Sketches*.

[5] HJ, "A Northward Journey," *Independent* (20 August 1874): 6; (27 August 1874): 4.

---

*Henry James returned to Cambridge from Europe in September
1874. Having hinted repeatedly that he did not intend to make
Cambridge his permanent home, he went to New York City in January 1875, where he spent six months in a trial period to see whether
he could make that city the center of his literary activity. But the
call of the Old World was too strong and by November 1875 he
was back in Europe and had established residence in Paris. His
literary productivity during 1874 and 1875 was more than astonishing. In addition to his first novel in book form,* Roderick Hudson *(1875), his first collection of tales,* A Passionate Pilgrim
(1875), and a collection of travel notes, Transatlantic Sketches
*(1875), he published 112 reviews, tales, and notes. William
James, who thought of himself as the more practical of the two,
issued repeated warnings that it was impossible to make a living
from royalties, but Henry was well on his way to proving his older
brother wrong.*

*During these years William also established himself on a perma-
nent path. As an instructor at Harvard in 1874–75, he taught*

Natural History 3: Comparative Anatomy and Physiology of Verte-brates. In 1875–76 he repeated the natural history course and offered Graduate Course 18: The Relations between Physiology and Psychology. The latter course represents the formal introduc-tion of modern psychology in America. His literary productivity, while no match for Henry's, was considerable, consisting of a total of twenty-three published reviews and short notes, all unsigned.

Alice James, still living at home, became associated through her friend Katharine Peabody Loring with the Society to Encourage Studies at Home, a group offering courses by correspondence to women. While there were a few tentative signs that Alice too had found her path in life, her association with the society produced no long-term results.

In Wisconsin the Jameses were multiplying. Robertson James's second child, Mary Walsh James, was born on 18 August 1875. Garth Wilkinson James's first child, Joseph Cary James, was born on 4 October 1874; his second, Alice James, on 24 December 1875. Both brothers changed employment and residences numerous times, but it is impossible to trace these changes because the docu-mentary evidence is lacking.

To Henry James

Cambr. Dec 12. 75

My dear Harry

We have rec'd your first letter from Paris and last night the Tribune arrived with your first official one blazoned forth as you will no doubt see before you get this.[1] I am amused that you should have fallen into the arms of C. S. Peirce, whom I imagine you find a rather un-comfortable bedfellow, thorny & spinous, but the way to treat him is after the fabled "nettle" receipt: grasp firmly, contradict, push hard, make fun of him, and he is as pleasant as any one; but be overawed by his sententious manner and his paradoxical & obscure statements, wait upon them as it were, for light to dawn, and you will never get a feeling of ease with him any more than I did for years, until I changed my course & treated him more or less chaffingly. I confess I like him very much in spite of all his peculiarities, for he is a man of genius and there's always something in that to compel one's sympa-thy. I got a letter from him about Chauncey Wright in which he said he had just seen you. Miss Ammy fay paid me a long visit the other

night—Alice, father & mother having gone to hear Mr Thaxter read
a translation of the Agamennon by Fitzgerald (of Omar Khayam no-
toriety) at the Thayers[2]—she being chaperoned by here[3] bro' in law,
one stone, who sat speechless one hour & a half listening to our gab-
ble—and said that you were C. S. Peirce's particular admiration.
How long does he stay in Paris & when does he return?   I may feel
like asking him to bring me back an instrument or two when he
comes.   Please tell him I got his letter, and enjoyed it, and that a
subscription paper is now passing round to defray the cost of publishing Wright's remains—40 names at $20 each are what is hoped for.[4]
Norton will be editor, & if it is decided to have any extended introductory notice, I will tell him that Peirce is willing to write an account of
his philosophical ideas.   Norton did intend giving it to Fiske, who
wd. make a very inferior thing of it.

Roderick Hudson seems to be a very common theme of conversation, to be in fact a great success, though I can give you no saying
about which is memorable for its matter or its source.   Every one
praises the end, including myself.   You have seen the excellent review in the world, wh. father sent you.[5]   In looking through the volume it seems to me even better than it did, but I must tell you that
I am again struck unfavorably by the tendency of the personages to
reflect on themselves and give an acute critical scientific introspective
classification of their own natures & states of mind, à la G. Sand.
Take warning once more!

Yesterday Howells & wife & Godkin & aunt dined here.   Plenty of
laughter, but not much else.   2 nights ago I took the Adirondack
M.D.'s to see Caste at the Globe.   Mr G. Honey a very broad & able
but not delicate comedian in the chief part.[6]   A few nights previous
to that our club at the Union Club.   6 men—a rather pot bellied
conservative affair—decidedly the price must come down, or some
men of genius get put in, or something or other.   The last parker
house bill was $7.00 which is simply ridiculous.   The only other
thing I have done except mind my anatomy is the Squib in the Nation
which I enclose.   In the interval between sending it and seeing it
appear in print, I have dipped into B., & am reluctantly obliged to
confess that Schérer is quite as wrong as Saintsbury.   It is a pity that
every writer in france is bound to do injustice to the opposite "camp."
B. is really in his fleurs du mal original & in a certain sense elevated, & on the whole I can bear no rancor against him, altho at
times he writes like a person half awake & groping for words.   The

most amusing thing about it all is the impression one gets of the innocence of a generation in wh. the fleurs du mal should have made a *scandal*. It is a mild & spiritualistic book to day. Get it and write about it in the Nation or atlantic if you like, and esp. read a letter of Ste Beuve's at the end of it, which is the ne plus ultra of his diabolic subtlety & *malice*.[7]

I had an interview with C. W. Eliot the other day, who smiles on me & lets me expect $1200 this year and possibly hope for $2000 next, which will be a sweet boon if it occurs. As the term advances I become sensible that I am really better than I was last year in almost every way; which gives me still better prospects for the future. Alice has got her historical professorship which will no doubt be an immense thing for her.[8] Bob writes must[9] contentedly about his farm, Wilky sanguinely about his business, so that altogether the family has not for a long time been in so flourishing a condition.[10]

We have been having a perfectly steady thermometer fm. 25° to 34 degrees for 10 days past and you can imagine how I've enjoyed it—altogether the season has been must humane so far. I called on T.S.P. a few days ago but he was out. I saw a recent envelope fm. you on his table. I am told that he has resumed his work for the Nation. I'm glad of it. His wife has had I believe a relapse, poor thing. Good bye! Heaven bless you—get as much society as you can. Your first letter was a very good beginning, tho' one sees that you are to a certain extent fishing for the proper tone or level. I shd like to accompany you to some of the theatres.

Adieu! | W.J

Latest american humor, quoted last night by Godkin: Child lost at a fair. "Where's my mother? I told the darned thing she'd lose me.["]

[1] HJ, "Paris Revisited," *New York Tribune*, 11 December 1875 (dated 22 November), reprinted in *Parisian Sketches* (1957).

[2] No translation of the *Agamemnon* by Edward FitzGerald (1809–1883), English writer, published at the time of the reading was found. Thaxter could be Levi Lincoln Thaxter, husband of Celia Laighton Thaxter (1835–1894), American author. Stone was not identified.

[3] A slip for 'her'.

[4] Chauncey Wright died on 12 September 1875. His papers were published, *Philosophical Discussions*, ed. Charles Eliot Norton (New York: Henry Holt, 1877).

[5] Apparently the *New York World*.

[6] George Honey appeared at the Globe Theater as Old Eccles in *Caste* by Thomas William Robertson (1829–1871), American-born playwright.

[7] WJ, "The Neo-Pagans and an Editorial Reply," *Nation* 21 (2 December 1875): 355, reprinted in *ECR*, is a discussion of the conflicting views of Baudelaire offered

by George Edward Bateman Saintsbury and Edmond-Henri-Adolphe Scherer.   No edition of Baudelaire's *Les Fleurs du mal* (1857) appeared with comments by Sainte-Beuve.

[8] AJ had agreed to teach a correspondence course on history for the Society to Encourage Studies at Home.

[9] Here and in the next paragraph WJ wrote 'must' for 'most'.

[10] RJ had acquired a farm in Whitewater, Wis., shortly before this letter was written.

1876

During the early months of 1876, William James made further advances in the direction of stability. In February, Harvard officially approved his appointment as an assistant professor of physiology, and at the age of thirty-four, William found himself approaching his first year of full-time employment. At about the same time, he met his future wife, Alice Howe Gibbens, at a meeting of the Radical Club, an informal association that had as its focus the discussion of religious questions from a liberal point of view. On 14 March 1876 he wrote his first letter to Alice, a formal, unromantic note explaining that he was returning to her a satirical poem about the Radical Club. There is nothing of these events in his letters to Henry, who was still in Paris enjoying an unusually rich social life. Henry James's letters for this period read much like a social register of dukes and countesses, literary greats and famous hostesses. But in spite of social distractions, he was writing extensively, his main literary achievement being The American, *the first installment of which appeared in the* Atlantic Monthly *in June 1876.*

William's letters to Henry between the letters of 5 July 1876 and 2 August 1880 are lost, and their contents can only be guessed at from Henry's replies.

To Henry James

Cambr. July 5. [1876]

My dear H.   Your letters breathe more and more a spirit of domestication in the modern Babylon, which is very pleasant to me to receive. I suppose from your gilded & snobbish heights you think of us here with great pity, but for my part I hurl it back at you, being on the whole contented with my outward lot.   I got back last night from a week on the South Shore, including Nantucket, Martha's Vineyard & Wendell Holmes' at Mattapoisett.   There is a strange naked and lonely poetry about clean pure little Nantucket under its tender sky. The settlement at Martha's vineyard, "oak bluffs" is probably the most audacious paradise of "caddish"ness which has ever flaunted itself in the eye of day.   A flat insipid sand bank.   The building company in advertising it perpetrates the most charming instance of the american defiant style of advertisement I ever met. "No vegetation to breed disease by its decay"—!!! I wish Renan & Matt. Arnold might be confined there for a season. They would write s'thing worth reading afterwards. *July 7th.* I was interrupted by a visitor and resume after 2 days during which your letter to me of June 22nd has arrived. Alice also had one from Lizzie Boott (enclosed characteristically in one to the Greenough's) in which she speaks of your blooming appearance. You say nothing of your bodily condition lately & I let myself suppose that it is good. Your spiritual condition is evidently felicitous, with your Tourguenieffs, your de Broglies, your Montargis & your Longchamps.[1] Long may you enjoy them, only keep watch and ward lest in your style you become too Parisian and lose your hold on the pulse of the great american public to which after all you must pander for support. In your last Tribune letter (about the Doudan letters,) there were too many traces of gallicism in manner.[2] It will be a good thing for you to resolve never to use the word "supreme," and to get great care not to use "delicate" in the french sense of a "cultured & fastidious" person. I hear several persons speak well of your letters in the Trib. & I suppose there can be little doubt of their being a success. The two on the Salon I enjoyed very much.[3] I wish you were home to do the Centennial pictures, for, well as Shin writes, he lacks a certain discretion, heats himself & becomes too emphatic. They ought never again in a universal Exhibition to make the mistake they have made in Phila. of admitting such a lot of trashy works of art.[4] They spoil your eye & mind for the enjoyment of the good things. France has nothing good to show. The Makart decorative pieces Shin has written about, *struck* me more than anything. And an unexpected thing that much pleased me was the high average of the american pieces. It is obvious that we are a people of artistic sensibility—Not that there were there any very great american works, but there was almost nothing vile, such as every foreign school gives you in its degenerate pupils who without a grain of inward decency or cleverness of their own, manufacture a far off echo of some one else's chic or ability. An immense preponderance of the american work was landscape, and in almost every case the animus was a perfectly sincere effort to reproduce a natural aspect which had affected in some particular way the painter's sensibility. There was little schooling through it all, but genuine native refinement and speaking in a broad way, intelligence of purpose. The English school was a most curious study, being so good in its best works, but so utterly preposterous and inartistic in some of its worst things of 30 or 40 years ago; the *saugrenu* comic shakespeare scenes, the platitude of the book of beauty portraits, and a general tendency to go wholly off the track, showing a real want of artistic intelligence in the race, which we, with all our present feebleness, do not approach. Lafarges Paradise landscape looked admirably well   The Saint Paul was ruined by indecision of drawing.   Lizzie Boott will have told you of his last landscape.   It is now at Doll's, and is, it seems to me, as distingué a work as has *ever* been produced.[5]   Unfortunately the subject is really arid, so the picture remains somewhat of a *tour de force*, which is always a matter for regret.—Your second instalment of the American is prime.   The morbid little clergyman is worthy of Ivan Sergeitch.[6]   I was not a little amused to find some of my own attributes in him—I think you found my "moral reaction" excessive when I was abroad.   But I do detest the monthly part way of publication except in Geo. Eliot.[7]   The feminine gush and weakness she has begun to show in D.D. are adorable after her big show of cynicism hitherto.   Daniel's preaching is so schoolgirl like that [one] has a sort of tender pity for the inconsistency of the authoress.   I hope in addition to what you say of G. Sand in the Tribune you'll set to and give us a good long N.A.R. article, with lots of short extracts.[8]   I read at Nantucket the Dilemma, by Col. Chesney, a novel of the Indian Mutiny just published which I strongly urge you to read.[9]   It left a impression of reality on me which I can't shake off—it is a strange, gloomy, manly book, and intensely english.   I have also read "Cometh up as a flower" with deep pleasure for its heavy english atmosphere, the wh. I more & more grow attached to in imagination.[10]— I spent three very pleasant days with the Holmes', at Mattappoissett. I fell quite in love with she; & he exemplified in the most ridiculous way Michelet's "marriage de l'homme et de la terre."[11]   I told him that he looked like Millets peasant figures as he stooped over his little plants in his flannel shirt & trowsers.   He is a powerful battery, formed like a planing machine to gouge a deep self-beneficial groove through life, & his virtues and faults were thrown into singular relief by the lonesomeness of the shore, which as it makes every object rock or shrub, stand out so vividly, seemed also to put him and his wife under a sort of lens for you. (Excuse the uncouthness of my epistolary style, I find I don't outgrow it.[)]   Poor father is very feeble and his improvement is latterly almost insensible.   To day he has added to his troubles an attack of lumbago, not bad but very disagreeable, and this afternoon I sit and write in the big green chair in the N.W.

bedroom while A.K. is polishing his bed ridden back with a towel. Alice, thank heaven, has consented to go to Gloucester for a week, where she is with the Childs. Otherwise no news. You ask about Hayes. There is no doubt that both his & Tilden's candidacies are victories for the reform cause.[12] Hayes seems to be a "high toned" man, and the catch words of the election (which are the stepping stones of the people's political education) will lie in virtuousness with each other. There is no doubt there will be progress effected, whoever gets in.—You have again failed to let me know the cost of the lenses you supplied.[13] Send the third one as soon as you conveniently can & I will remit as soon as I know how much. Farewell. Mother is more virtuous than ever since father's illness, & aunt Kate and Alice are considerateness incarnate. Next week I go for a couple of days to the Morses, later to Bowditchs, but I shall be here off and on till August 15 when I shall probably start for a month to the Adirondacks.

Yours ever | W.J

Send Joukowsky's Portrait.

[1] In his letter of 22 June 1876 HJ had reported viewing the annual review at Longchamps and visiting the Childes at Montargis.

[2] Ximénès Doudan, *Mélanges et lettres,* noticed by HJ in "Parisian Topics," *New York Tribune,* 1 July 1876.

[3] HJ, two notes on the Paris salon of 1876 in *Nation* 22 (22 June 1876): 397–98; (29 June 1876): 415–16.

[4] In June 1876 WJ viewed the Centenary of American Independence Exposition in Philadelphia.

[5] Doll & Richards, an art gallery on Park St., Boston.

[6] The second installment of HJ's *American* appeared in the *Atlantic Monthly* in July 1876. WJ is refering to Ivan Sergeevich Turgenev.

[7] George Eliot's *Daniel Deronda* appeared in eight parts beginning in February 1876.

[8] HJ, "George Sand," *New York Tribune,* 22 July 1876.

[9] George Tomkyns Chesney, *The Dilemma: A Tale of the Mutiny* (1876).

[10] Rhoda Broughton, *Cometh Up as a Flower: An Autobiography* (1867).

[11] Jules Michelet, *Le Peuple* (1846). "Marriage de l'homme et de la terre" is the title of the first section of chapter 1, "Servitudes de paysan."

[12] WJ is referring to the presidential election of 1876.

[13] HJ bought some optical instruments for WJ.

From Henry James

Etretat. July 29th. [1876]

Dear Wm. Your long & charming letter of July 5th came to me just before I left Paris—some ten days since. Since then, directly after my arrival here, I wrote a few words to Alice by which you will know where I am "located." Your letter, with its superior criticism of so many things, the Philadelphia Exhibition especially, interested me extremely & quickened my frequent desire to converse with you. What you said of the good effect of the American pictures there gave me great pleasure; & I have no doubt you are right about our artistic spontaneity & sensibility. My chief impression of the Salon was that $4/5^{ths}$ of it were purely mechanical, & *de plus*, vile. I bolted from Paris on the 20th, feeling a real need of a change of air. I found it with a vengeance here, where as I write I have just had to shut my window, for the cold. I made a mistake in not getting a room with sun, strange, & even loathsome, as it may appear to you! The quality of the air is delicious—the only trouble is indeed that it has too shipboard & midocean a savor. The little place is picturesque, with noble cliffs, a little Casino, & your French bathing going on all day long on the little pebbly beach. But as I am to do it in the Tribune, I won't steal my own thunder.[1] The company is rather low, & I know no one save Edward Boit & his wife (of Boston & Rome) who have taken a most charming old country house for the Summer. Before I left Paris, I spent an afternoon with the Bootts, who are in Paradise—though with Ernest Longfellow & lady as fellow-seraphs. They have a delightful old villa, with immense garden & all sorts of picturesque qualities, & their place is (as I found by taking a walk with Boott) much prettier than I supposed—in fact very charming, & with the air of being 500 miles from Paris. Lizzie & Longfellow are working with *acharnement*, & both, I ween, much improving. I have little to tell you of myself. I shall be here till August 15–20, & shall then go & spend the rest of the month with the Childes, near Orléans (an ugly country I believe,) & after that try & devise some frugal scheme for keeping out of Paris till as late as possible in the Autumn. The winter there always begins soon enough. I am much obliged to you for your literary encouragement & advice—glad especially you like my novel. I can't judge it. Your remarks on my French tricks in my letters are doubtless most just, & shall be heeded. But it's an odd thing that such tricks should grow at a time when my last layer of resistance to a long-encroaching weariness & satiety with the French mind & its utterance has fallen from me like a garment. I have done with 'em, forever, & am turning English all over. I desire only to feed on English life & the contact of English minds—I wish greatly I knew some. Easy & smooth-flowing as life is in Paris, I would throw it over to morrow for an even very small chance to plant myself for a while in England. If I had but a single good friend in London I would go thither. I have got nothing important out of P. nor am likely to. My life there makes a much more succulent figure in your letters, as my mention of its thin ingredients comes back to me than in my own consciousness. A good deal of Boulevard & 3ᵈ rate Americanism: few retributive relations otherwise. I know the Théatre Francais by heart!—Daniel Deronda (Dan'l. himself) is indeed a dead, though amiable failure. But the book is a large affair; I shall write an article of some sort about it.² All desire is dead within me to produce something on George Sand; though perhaps I shall, all the same, mercenarily & mechanically—though only if I am forced.³ *Please make a point of mentioning,* by the way, whether a letter of mine, upon her, exclusively, *did* appear lately in the Tribune. I don't see the T. regularly & have missed it. They misprint sadly. I never said, e.g., in announcing her death, that she was *"fearfully* shy": I used no such vile adverb, but another—I forget which.⁴—I am hoping, from day to day for another letter from home, as the period has come round. I hope father is getting on smoothly & growing able to enjoy life a little more. I am afraid the extreme heat does not help him and I fear also that your common sufferings from it have been great—though you, in your letter didn't speak of it. I hope Alice will have invented some plan of going out of town. Is there any one left in Cambridge whom the family sees?—I am glad you went to Mattapoisett, which I remember kindly, tho' its meagre nature seems in memory doubly meagre beside the rich picturesqueness of this fine old Normandy. What you say of nature putting Wendell H. & his wife under a lens there is very true. I see no one here; a common & lowish lot; & the American institution of "ringing in" is as regards the French impossible. I hope your own plans for the summer will prosper, & health & happiness be your portion. Give much love to father, & to the ladies.

—Yours always—H. James jr.

¹ HJ, "A French Watering Place," *New York Tribune,* 26 August 1876.

² HJ, "Daniel Deronda: A Conversation," *Atlantic Monthly* 38 (December 1876): 684–94.

³ HJ, "George Sand," *Galaxy* 24 (July 1877): 45–61.

⁴ See letter of 5 July 1876, note 8. HJ mentioned the death of George Sand in "Parisian Topics," *New York Tribune,* 1 July 1876.

1877

Clearly, London rather than Paris was the place for "turning English all over" and in December 1876, after saying farewell to Parisian society, Henry James took up residence at 3 Bolton Street, Piccadilly, London. Writing to Alice James on 13 December he described his "excellent lodging in this excellent quarter" and his first English breakfast of "tea, eggs, bacon, and the exquisite English loaf," which left him with a "voluptuous glow." His letters to William from the spring of 1877 suggest Henry's sense of having found a home at long last.

In 1876–77, William James was at Harvard teaching his course on natural history, his graduate course in psychology, and a new course, Natural History 2: Physiological Psychology, using Spencer's Principles of Psychology *as a text. This new course was met with objections from those who thought that undergraduates should not be exposed to Spencer, whom they considered suspect from a religious point of view.*

The fall of 1876 marked the beginning of William's turbulent courtship of Alice Howe Gibbens. It was probably in September, while vacationing in the Adirondack Mountains, that he declared his love for the first time and told her of his determination to win her hand. Most likely, William did not write his brother Henry about the courtship. What hints and allusions there may have been cannot be established because, as has been noted, William's letters to Henry for this period are lost.

From Henry James

ATHENÆUM CLUB | PALL MALL March 29th [1877]

Dear W^m—I will write you a few lines before I leave this place this evening. I thanked you for your last letter thro' mother a few days since—a letter of wh. I forget the exact date; (you described your brain-lecture &c.) I have been dining here, & then sitting awhile to read the last no of the 19th Cent'y. (I won't send it you as I send it to Mrs. Lockwood, who can't afford to buy it & would never see it otherwise.) Vide in the same Prof. Clifford's thing at the end.[1]—

London life jogs along with me, pausing every now & then at some more or less succulent patch of herbage. I was almost ashamed to tell you thro' mother that I, unworthy, was seeing a bit of Huxley. I went to his house again last Sunday evening—a pleasant easy, no-dress-coat sort of house (in our old Marlboro' Place, by the ·way.)[2] Huxley is a very genial, comfortable being—yet with none of the noisy & windy geniality of some folks here, whom you find with their backs turned when you are responding to the remarks that they have very offensively made you. But of course my talk with him is mere amiable generalities. These, however, he likes to cultivate for recreation's sake, of a Sunday evening. (The slumbering Spencer I have not lately seen here: I am told he is terribly "nervous.")[3] Some mornings since, I breakfasted with Lord Houghton again—he invites me most dotingly. Present: John Morley, Goldwin Smith (pleasanter than my prejudice agt. him) Henry Cowper, Frederick Wedmore & a monstrous cleverly & agreeably-talking M.P., Mr. Otway. John Morley has a most agreeable face, but he hardly opened his mouth. (He is, like so many of the men who have done much here, very young looking.) Yesterday I dined with Lord Houghton—with Gladstone, Tennyson, Dr. Schliemann (the excavator of old Mycenae &c) & half a dozen other men of "high culture." I sat next but one to the Bard, & heard most of his talk which was all about port-wine & tobacco: he seems to know much about them, & can drink a whole bottle of port at a sitting with no incommodity. He is very swarthy & scraggy & strikes one at first as much less handsome than his photos.: but gradually you see that it's a face of genius. He had I know not what simplicity, speaks with a strange rustic accent & seemed altogether like a creature of some primordial English stock, a 1000 miles away from American manufacture.—Behold me after dinner conversing affably with Mr. Gladstone—not by my own seeking, but by the almost importunate affection of Lord H. But I was glad of a chance to feel the "personality" of a great political leader—or as G. is now thought here even, I think, by his partisans, ex-leader. That of Gladstone is very fascinating—his urbanity extreme—his eye that of a man of genius—& his apparent self surrender to what he is talking of, without a flaw. He made a great impression on me— greater than any one I have seen here: tho' 'tis perhaps owing to my naïveté, & unfamiliarity with statesmen. Dr. Schliemann told me 2 or 3 curious things. 1° he is an American citizen having lived some years in America in business. 2° though he is now a great Hellenist he knew no word of Greek till he was 34 years old, when he learned it in 6 weeks(!!) at St. Petersburg. *Ce que c'est d'être Allemand!* The other men at Houghton's dinner were all special notabilities. Next me sat a very amiable Lord Zouche—noted as the unhappy young peer who a short time since married a young wife who three or four months after her marriage eloped *bel et bien* with a guardsman.—Did I tell you that I some time since spent an evening with F. T. Palgrave? Strictly between ourselves—i.e. as regards H. Adams, & every one else,—I don't particularly like him: but he is evidently very respectable. He is a tremendous case of culture, & a "beggar for talk" such as you never faintly dreamed of. But *all* his talk is kicks & thrusts at every one going, & I suspect that, in the last, analysis, "invidious mediocrity" would be the scientific appellation of his temper. His absence of the *simpatico* is only surpassed by that of his wife. (This sounds pretty scornful: & I hasten to add that I imagine he very much improves on acquaintance. I shall take a chance to see.) Did I tell you too that I had been to the Oxford & Cam. boat-race? But I have paragraphed it in the *Nation,* to wh. I refer you.[4] It was for about 2 minutes a supremely beautiful sight; but for those 2 minutes I had to wait a horribly bleak hour & a ½, shivering, in mid-Thames, the sour March-wind. I can't think of any other adventures: save that I dined 2 or 3 days since at Mrs. Godfrey Lushington's (they are very nice, *blushing* people) with a parcel of quiet folk: but next to a divine little Miss Lushington (so pretty English girls can be!) who told me that she lived in the depths of the City, at Guy's Hospital, whereof her father is administrator. Guy's Hospital, of which I have read in all old English novels. So does one move all the while here on identified ground. This is the eve. of Good Friday, a most lugubrious day here—& all the world (save 4000,000 or so) are out of London for the 10 day's Easter holiday. I think of making two or three excursions of a few hours apiece, to places near London whence I can come back to sleep: Canterbury, Chichester &c (but as I shall commemorate them for lucre I won't talk of them thus.) Farewell dear brother, I won't prattle further. Thank father for the 2 cuts from the *Galaxy*—tho' I wish he had sent a line with them. I enclose $2.00 I accidentally possess. Add them to that $12.00 & expend them for any cost I may put you to. Have you rec'd. your *Maudsley?*[5] Don't you think very well of Hayes, & are not things in a brightening way? Encourage Alice to write to me.

My blessings on yourself from your fraternal H.J.jr.

Ask Alice to keep these London scrawls of mine: I may be glad to refer to them later.

[1] William Kingdon Clifford, his share of "A Modern Symposium," on "The Influence upon Morality of a Decline in Religious Belief," *Nineteenth Century* 1 (April 1877): 353–58.

[2] In 1855–56 the Jameses lived at 10 Marlborough Place, St. John's Wood, London.

[3] Writing to WJ on 28 February 1877, HJ reported that he sometimes took an afternoon nap beside Spencer at the Athenaeum Club and felt that he was "robbing" WJ of the privilege.

[4] HJ, note on the Oxford-Cambridge Boat Race, *Nation* 24 (12 April 1877): 221–22.

[5] A book by Henry Maudsley.

1878

Alice Gibbens at last said yes to William's proposal, and their engagement was announced on 10 May 1878. William informed his brother Henry of his approaching marriage in a letter that is now lost. Henry James's letter of 29 May was the first step in his friendship with the new Alice James, a deep friendship that was to survive William's death. The wedding took place on 10 July 1878, and immediately afterwards the young couple departed for their honeymoon in the Adirondacks. Meanwhile the sister, Alice James, had taken to her bed in April with a severe nervous breakdown in response, many scholars think, to the approaching engagement. The relationship between the two Alices was destined to remain a cool one.

The year 1878 was pivotal in William James's life, not only because of his marriage, but also because in January of that year he published his first signed essay, "Remarks on Spencer's Definition of Mind as Correspondence" in the Journal of Speculative Philosophy. This and several other essays published in 1878 provided him with an entry into European intellectual circles, an opportunity of which he made extensive use several years later. In February he lectured at Johns Hopkins University on "The Senses and the Brain and Their Relation to Thought" in an effort either to win a philosophical position at Johns Hopkins or to force the Harvard authorities to provide a permanent place for him. In June he signed the fateful contract with Henry Holt and began his twelve-year struggle to write The Principles of Psychology. By the end of 1878 William James had emerged as a philosopher and psychologist who could not be ignored.

Henry James continued to write and publish at a great rate. After publishing The Americans in book form in 1877, he published The Europeans and Daisy Miller in 1878, as well as two other books in addition to his usual stream of reviews and notes.

From Henry James

THE REFORM CLUB May 29<u>th</u> [1878]

Dear W<u>m</u>.

You have my blessing indeed, & Miss Gibbens also; or rather Miss Gibbens particularly, as she will need it most. (I wish to pay her a compliment at your expense & to intimate that she gives more than she receives; yet I wish not to sacrifice you too much.) Your letter came to me yesterday, giving me great joy, but less surprise than you might think. In fact, I was not surprised at all, for I had been expecting to get some such news as this from you. And yet of Miss Gibbens & your attentions I had heard almost nothing—a slight mention a year ago, in a letter of mother's, which had never been repeated. The wish, perhaps, was father to the thought. I had long wished to see you married; I believe almost as much in matrimony for most other people as I believe in it little for myself—which is saying a good deal. What you say of Miss Gibbens (even after I have made due allowance for natural partiality) inflames my imagination & crowns my wishes. I have great faith in the wisdom of your choice & am prepared to believe everything good & delightful of its object. I am sure she has neither flaw nor failing. Give her then my cordial— my already fraternal—benediction. I look forward to knowing her as to one of the consolations of the future. Very soon I will write to her—in a few days. Her photograph is indispensable to me—please remember this; & also that a sketch of her from another hand than your's—father's, mother's & Alice's—would be eminently satisfactory. This must be a very pleasant moment to you—& I envy you your actualities & futurities. May they all minister to your prosperity & nourish your genius! I don't believe you capable of making a marriage of which one must expect less than this. Farewell, dear brother, I will write before long again, & meanwhile I shall welcome all contributions to an image of Miss Gibbens.

Always yours   H.J.jr

From Henry James

REFORM CLUB, | PALL MALL. S.W. July 15<u>th</u> [1878]

Dear William:

I have just heard from mother that you had decided to be married on the 10<u>th</u> ult; & as I was divorced from you by an untimely fate on this unique occasion, let me at least repair the injury by giving you, in the most earnest words that my clumsy pen can shape, a tender bridal benediction. I am very glad indeed to hear that you have ceased to find occasion for delay, & that you were to repair to the happy Adirondacks under hymeneal influences. I should think you would look look forward, in effect, to next winter's work more freely & fruitfully by getting your matrimonial start thus much earlier. May you keep along at a pace of steady felicity! The abruptness of your union has prevented me from a becoming punctuality in sending Alice a small material emblem of my good wishes; & now I shall wait till next autumn & the beginning of your winter life. I thank her meanwhile extremely for the little note—the charming note—that she sent me in answer to my own—& I feel most agreeably conscious of my intensification of kinship. I envy you your mountains & lakes—your deep, free nature. May it do you both—weary workers—all the good you deserve.

Ever your fond & faithful brother   H.J.jr

From Henry James

REFORM CLUB, | PALL MALL. S.W. July 23ᵈ [1878]

Dear Wᵐ.

I just find your letter of July 8ᵗʰ, enclosing your wife's lovely photograph (which, having carefully, & as Ruskin says, "reverently," studied it, I re-enclose here, with a 1000 thanks.) You tell me that you were to be married 2 days later, but you are painfully silent as to details— saying not a word as to the hour, or place, or manner of the ceremony—the officiating functionary, or any of those things which in such a case one likes to be told of. I should not forgive you for this if it were not that I count upon mother, after the event, writing to me in a manner to supply deficiencies. I wrote you briefly the other day, on 1ˢᵗ hearing that your marriage was coming off immediately— so that you know my sentiments about it. I can best repeat them by saying that I rejoice in it as if it were my own; or rather much more. I wish I could pay you a visit in your romantic shanty, among those mountains with which you must now be so familiar & which I have never seen. It will surely be the beginning of a beautiful era for you. You have only to go about your work, & health & happiness will take care of themselves.—Yes, I know that it must be a sad summer in Cambridge, & my thoughts are constantly in Quincy St. But I note what you say about the amelioration of poor Alice's symptoms. She must have been having a tragic time; but I hope most earnestly it is melting away. I am much interested in the prospect of the Baltimore professorship, of which you speak, & surely hope that, since you desire it, you will quietly come into it. But I shall regret, on grounds of "general culture," &c that you should detach yourself from Harvard College. It must, however, conduce to "general culture" to have Baltimore winters instead of Massachusetts ones. Bravo also for the Holt psychology & its coincidence with your labors. May it go along triumphantly. I am very glad indeed that you were pleased with "Daisy Miller," who appears (*literally*) to have made a great hit here. "Every one is talking about it" &c, & it has been much noticed in the papers. Its success has encouraged me as regards the faculty of appreciation of the English public; for the thing is sufficiently subtle, yet people appear to have comprehended it. It has given me a capital start here, & in future I shall publish all my things in English magazines (at least all the *good* ones) & sell advance sheets in America; thereby doubling my profits. I am much obliged to you for your economical advice; such advice is never amiss, but I don't think I specifically need it. I think I am decently careful, & have no fear but that, after a little, I shall be able at once to live very comfortably, to "put by," & to make an allowance to each member of the family. This is my dream. I am very impatient to get at work writing for the stage—a project I have long had. I am morally certain I should succeed, & it would be an open gate to money-making. The "great novel" you ask about is only begun; I am doing other things just now. It is the history of an *Americana*—a female counterpart to Newman.[1] I have the option of publishing it in *Macmillan* or in the *Cornhill* (with preference given to the former), & I hope to be able to get at work upon it this autumn; though I am not sure.—As regards the *Europeans* I am very sorry, & it is a great injustice to it, that it should have been advertised or talked of as a *novel*. It is only a sketch—very brief & with no space for much action; in fact it is a "study," like Daisy Miller. (I am just completing, by the way, a counterpart to *D.M.*, for the *Cornhill*.)[2] I have no personal news of any value. It is very hot indeed, at last—though not so terrible as I see by the papers it has been at home, as I am afraid F. & M. & Alice & A.K. must have felt to their cost. I shall be in London all summer, as I have plenty of occupation here. I have rec'd. several invitations to pay short visits, but have declined them all, save one for a week at Wenlock Abbey (Charles Gaskell's) on August 10ᵗʰ. I have just telegraphed a refusal to Wm Spottiswoode, the new Presdt. of the Royal Society, who has a very charming place down in Kent. I shall, however, probably go to spend next Sunday with Sara Darwin. I rejoice in your rejoicings in my fat, & would gladly cut off fifty lbs. or so and send them to you as a wedding-gift. I am extremely well, & though London heat is rather a vile compound, I, strange to say, like it. I was sure I had acknowledged the P.O. order for 15$: a thousand pardons. I sent home the toothbrushes and cravats by Theodora S.,³ & took the liberty of joining to them the present of a pair of hair brushes, for travelling, in a leather case. I got only six cravats; & could not get them of the maker you designated. But I will send another six by a near opportunity. Read all this to Alice: it is a great pleasure to me to be writing to her too, as I always shall in writing to you. Here I sit with the uproar of Charing X. in my ears, & envy you your strange woodland life. May it be excellent for you this summer. You had better forward this to Cambridge; it will eke out my correspondence there. Farewell; all my love to your wife. Seeing her photo. & getting an image of her beautiful face has made all the difference.

Yours, H.J.jr

¹ Christopher Newman is the central character of *The American*.

² HJ, *An International Episode*, published in the *Cornhill Magazine* 38 (December 1878): 687–713; 39 (January 1879): 61–90.

³ Theodora Sedgwick.

From Henry James

DEVONSHIRE CLUB | ST. JAMES'S, S.W. Nov. 14th [1878]

My dear William—

I have only just now—by an extraordinary accident—rec'd. your note, from Keene Valley, of Sept. 12th. (The Reform Club is closed for repairs & meanwhile the members come here, where the servants, not knowing them & getting confused, play all kinds of devilish tricks with the letters.) This incident is perhaps all the pleasanter for the long delay; but I fear I must have seemed brutal in not acknowledging your letter & not mentioning in writing to the others. I can't do more than simply acknowledge it now—I can't write you a worthy reply. With it were handed me three other (English) notes, equally delayed, to which I have had to write answers, apologies & explanations (one of them was from Wm Spottiswoode the President of the Royal Society asking me to go down—a month ago—& stay at his place in Kent!) & as I have been working all the morning, particularly

long, I am too tired for a regular letter.   But I must congratulate
you on your interesting & delightful remarks upon an "inside view"
of matrimony.   They fill me with satisfaction, & I would declare, if
it were not superfluous, that I hope you may never take it into your
head to take another tone.   You evidently won't!   I am as well
pleased as if I had made your match & protected your courtship.
I am hardly less gratified by your statement of your psychological
development & prospects.   May they daily expand & brighten & may
your book, for Henry Holt, sweep through many an edition.   (You
had better have it published also here.   I will put this through for
you, if you like, when the time comes, with ardor.)   With your letter
was handed me the Journal of Spec. Science with your article on the
brain in animals & man, which I shall read;[1] & this a.m. came a letter
from mother telling me how well you were going through your Lowell lectures.[2]   Please tell mother I have rec'd. her letter (it's of October 30th) & that I will very soon write to her.   Give them this, meanwhile, to read, in Quincy St., as a stopgap.   I am delighted with the
manner in which mother speaks of Alice's continued improvement—
what a blessing it must be!   I will say nothing of father's loss of
money, of which I have written, & will again write, to mother.—I was
much depressed on reading your letter by your painful reflections
on the *Europeans:* but now, an hour having elapsed, I am beginning
to hold up my head a little; the more so as I think I myself estimate
the book very justly & am aware of its extreme slightness.   I think
you take these things too rigidly & unimaginatively—too much as if
an artistic experiment were a piece of conduct, to which one's life
were somehow committed; but I think also that you're quite right in
pronouncing the book "thin," & empty.   I don't at all despair, yet, of
doing something fat.   Meanwhile I hope you will continue to give
me, when you can, your free impression of my performances.   It is
a great thing to have some one write to one of one's things as if one
were a 3d person, & you are the only individual who will do this.   I
don't think however you are always right, by any means.   As for instance in your objection to the closing paragraph of *Daisy Miller,*
which seems to me queer & narrow, & as regards which I don't seize
your point of view.   J'en appelle to the sentiment of any other story-
teller whomsoever; I am sure none such would wish the paragraph
away.   You may say—"Ah, but other *readers* would."   But that is the
same; for the teller is but a more developed reader.   I don't trust
your judgment altogether (if you will permit me to say so) about
details; but I think you are altogether right in returning always to the

importance of subject.   I hold to this, strongly; & if I don't as yet, seem to proceed upon it more, it is because being "very artistic" I have a constant impulse to try experiments of form, in which I wish to not run the risk of wasting or gratuitously using big situations. But to these I am coming now. It is something to have learned how to write, & when I look round me & see how few people (doing my sort of work) know how, (to my sense) I don't regret my step by step evolution.   I don't advise you however to read the 2 last things I have written—one a thing in the Dec. & Jan *Cornhill,* which I will send home;[3] & the other, a piece I am just sending to Howells.[4]   They are each quite in the same manner as the *Europeans.*—I *have* written you a letter, after all.   I am tired & must stop.   I went into the country the other day to stay with a friend a couple of days (Mrs. Greville)[5] & went with her to lunch with Tennyson, who, after lunch, read us Locksley Hall.[6]   The next day went to Geo. Eliot's.   Blessings on Alice.

Ever your   H.J.jr

[1] WJ, "Brute and Human Intellect," *Journal of Speculative Philosophy* 12 (July 1878): 236–76.

[2] WJ lectured before the Lowell Institute, Boston, on "The Brain and the Mind" from 15 October to 1 November 1878; for the lectures see *ML.*

[3] See letter of 23 July 1878.

[4] HJ, "The Pension Beaurepas," *Atlantic Monthly* 43 (April 1879): 388–92.

[5] There are two well-known diarists of that name, brothers, Charles Cavendish Fulke Greville (1794–1865) and Henry William Greville (1801–1872). Mrs. Greville was probably related to them.

[6] Alfred, Lord Tennyson, "Locksley Hall" (1842).

1879

The major event of 1879 for the Jameses was the birth on 18 May 1879 of Alice and William's first son, the third Henry James in three generations. William, in part driven by considerations of publish or perish, published a number of minor pieces and two major essays in Mind, *"Are We Automata?" and "The Sentiment of Rationality." Apart from their content these two essays were important because they established his reputation among English psychologists and philosophers. But William's publication rate was no match for that of Henry's, who having forsworn matrimony had settled ever more comfortably into his London life. In 1879 Henry published four books,* An International Episode, The Madonna of the Future, Confidence, *and* Hawthorne, *the last of these in the series* English Men of Letters.

But while the two older brothers were firmly establishing themselves, the fortunes of the younger brothers in Milwaukee were taking another turn for the worse. In response to some crisis, perhaps the loss of a job by Robertson James, William rushed to Milwaukee in early April 1879. William's letters for this period contain hints but no hard information about Robertson's lack of business success, his trials with his nervous system, and the outspoken words William used during his visit.

The friendship between sister Alice James and Katharine Peabody Loring, begun some years earlier, had deepened and by 1879 Katharine was assuming most of the responsibility for Alice's care. In July the two spent several weeks together in the Adirondack Mountains, leading Alice to declare that she would never again imitate her brother William and resort to the wilderness as a cure for her ills.

From Henry James

3, BOLTON STREET, | PICCADILLY. W. June 15th [1879]

Dear William—I have been balancing for some moments between addressing this letter to our common (or rather, uncommon) mother, or to you; I have decided for you on the general ground of having long intended & desired to write to you,—as well as the special one of having received a letter from you (accompanying one from your Alice) some fortnight ago. But please give mother very tenderly to understand that I adore her none the less, & that I have before me now two good letters from her—one received some ten days since, & the other last night, the latter enclosing a most charming letter from Bob, & also an extract from the Springfield Republican which in its crude & brutal vulgarity strikes me as anything but charming.[1] The American newspaper tone strikes one over here, where certain reticences & ménagements, a certain varnish of good manners & respectful way of saying things, still hold their own, as of too glaring, too scorching, an indecency. But never mind that.—I wrote to Alice just a week ago—much more briefly than I could have desired, but I hope my letter will have reached her safely, as it contained a little document which constituted its only value. I gather from father's *p.s.* to mother's letter of last night that your wife is so well on the way to her normal condition again that you have no longer any cause for anxiety. I delight in the image, indiscinctly as I yet perceive it, of your infantine Henry & cordially hope he will be a fund of comfort & entertainment to you. He will be for many a day the flower of Quincy St. & I hope he will bloom with dazzling brilliancy. I can fancy the interest you will take (as a psychologist) in watching. his growth, & can trust you to give him a superior education.—Let me say before I go any further that I have *not* yet heard definitely from Knowles about your MS.[2]—He told me the other day that he was *greatly* crowded with philosophic & psychologic papers (I don't know whose) but that he shld. (though he thought on this ground the presumption was against yours) be sorry to decide not to take it till he had looked at it more closely. He is keeping it for this purpose, but I hope soon to hear from him. If he doesn't take it I have hopes of being able to get it printed somewhere—I will try everything I can.— Mother has lately given me a good deal of information about you— e.g. with regard to your plan of building a house upon father's "grounds."[3] It seems a bright particular idea, & I deeply regret that delays & difficulties interpose themselves. It is an odious thought that you should have so small an income, & I am very sorry to hear that the inconsiderate Bowen shows the reverse of a tendency to resign. But patience will see any game out, & yours I trust will brighten materially before your supply of this commodity is exhausted. A curse indeed must your deficient eye-sight be!—I wonder greatly at the work you manage to do.——Bob's letter, enclosed

by mother, was very delightful, & has helped to dispel the impression
of the rather dark account of him & of his possible future contained
in your letter.   It is strange that with his intelligence & ability—as
one seems to perceive it in his letters—he shouldn't arrive at more
successful occupations.   I am very sorry for him, & I wish I were
nearer to him & able to see him sometimes & perhaps help him along
a little.   His account of Wilkie's *manière d'être* is quite to the life &
is on the whole favorable as regards the amenity of existence for poor
W.   But into what a queer, social *milieu* he must have planted himself.
Some months ago he sent me a friend of his from Milwaukee, with
a letter of introduction, describing him as his most beloved intimate
& requesting me to make him *mine!*   The friend was a French-
teacher—an old Frenchman who appeared to have been in Milwaukee for many years & to have quite unlearned his native tongue,
which he pronounced & spoke in the most barbaric & incomprehensible fashion.   He seemed very stupid & common & had nothing at
all to say (even about Wilkie) but that he desired I should try to find
him *pupils* for the few weeks that he was to remain in London—or
failing this, that I should do the same in Edinburgh, whither, I believe, he afterwards betook himself.   He was in every way a most
curious apparition (he appeared to speak no English, & his French
was atrocious) & not an encouraging specimen of the social resources
of Milwaukee.   Wilkie wrote—"Show him London, & above all show
him yourself!"   I was as tender as possible with him, but I was not
sorry when he vanished.   (N.B.   Never report this to Wilky—who
had evidently been very kind & humane to the poor old man.)—I feel
at moments as if I could write you 50 pages of general & particular
reflections upon my own manner of life, occupations, observations,
impressions &c—but when it comes to the point, in giving my account
of London days & London doings, one hardly knows where to begin.
I suppose this is a proof that such days are full, such doings numerous, & that if one could, by a strong effort detach one's self from
them & look at them as objectively as a person living quite out of it &
far away from it, (like yourself) would do—there would be many
more things worth dwelling upon than one falls here into the way of
seeing.   To dwell on *nothing*, indeed, comes to be here one's desire
as well as one's habit—& half the facts of London life are tolerable
only because they exist to you just for the moment of your personal
contact with them.   Heaven have mercy on you if you were obliged
to drag them about in memory or, in esteem!   I am sinking also rapidly into that condition of accepted & accepting Londonism when

impressions lose their sharpness & the idiosyncrasies of the place cease to be salient. To see them, to feel them, I have to lash my flanks & assume a point of view. The confession is doubtless a low one, but I have certainly become a hopeless, helpless, shameless (and you will add, a *bloated,*) cockney. No, I am not bloated—morally; I am philosophic to lean-ness—to stringiness. Physically, it's another affair, & I am bloated *tout que vous voudrez.* I am as broad as I am long, as fat as a butter-tub & as red as a British materfamilias. On the other hand, as a compensation, I am excellently well! I am working along very quietly & steadily, & consider no reasonable share of fame & no decent literary competence out of my reach. Apropos of such matters, mother expresses in her last night's letter the hope that I have derived much gold from the large sale (upwards of 20000 copies) of my two little Harper stories. I am sorry to say I have done nothing of the sort. Having in advance no prevision of their success I made a very poor bargain. The *Episode* I sold outright (copyright & all!) for a very moderate sum of ready money—so I have had no percentage at all on its sale![4] For Daisy Miller I have rec'd. simply the usual 10%—which, as it sells for twenty cents, brings me but 2 cents a copy. This has a beggarly sound, but the Harpers sent me the other day a cheque for 200$. This represents but meanly so great a vogue—but you may be sure that I shall clinch the Harpers in future; as having now taught them my value I shall be able to do. A man's 1ˢᵗ successes are those, always, by which he makes least. I am not a grasping business-man—on the contrary, and I sometimes—or rather, often—strike myself as gaining wofully less money than fame. My reputation in England seems (considering what it is based on) ludicrously larger than any cash payments that I have yet received for it. The Macmillans are everything that's friendly—caressing— old Macmillan physically *hugs* me; but the delicious ring of the sovereign is conspicuous in our intercourse by its absence. However, I am sure of the future—that is the great thing—& it is something to behave like a gentleman even when other people don't. I shall have made by the end of this year very much more money than I have ever made before; & next year I shall make as much as that again. As for the years after that,—nous verrons bien. The other night, at a "literary gathering," the excellent Cotter Morison came at the "urgent request" of *celui-ci* to introduce me to Edmond About, who is here in a sort of 2ᵈ rate "International Literary Congress" which appears to have made a foolish *fiasco.*[5] About seized me by both hands & told me that what he wished of me (beyond the pleasure of making my acquaintance) was that I should promise to give him a translation of my next novel for the feuilleton of his paper, the XIXe Siècle. "Voyons, cher Monsieur James, je tiens à cela très-seriousement—je tiens à ce [que] vous me donnez la parole. Mettez la main sur un traducteur qui vous satisfasse—envoyez moi le manuscrit—je vous donne ma parole qu'il n'attendra pas. Je sais que vous êtes tres-puissant, très-original que vous êtes en train de vous poser ici comme personne: etc, etc." I gave him my promise, & I shall probably send him "Confidence"; but what strikes me in everything of this kind is the absurd, the grotesque, facility of success. What have I done, juste ciel? It humiliates me to the earth, & I can only right myself by thinking of all the excellent things I mean to do in the future.— The other night John Fiske rose, moon-like, above my horizon—apparently very well & happy, & I immediately invited him to dine with me to meet Turgenieff next week—the latter coming over by invitation to receive the D.C.L. degree at Oxford—a very pretty attention to pay him (to which I imagine James Bryce chiefly put them up.) He has promised solemnly (by letter from Paris) to dine with me on the 20th; & it is quite on the cards that he shld. play me false; but I trust he wont. I wish you were here to share & adorn the feast— Fiske on his return will tell you about it.—Henry Adams & his wife arrived a few days since & are staying at the Milnes Gaskell's. I have seen them but once or twice & find them rather compressed & depressed by being kept from getting into quarters of their own. Gaskell has taken a great house in London on purpose to entertain them, & this seems to weigh upon their spirits. Henry A. can never be in the nature of things a very gracious or sympathetic companion, & Mrs. A. strikes me as toned down & bedimmed from her ancient brilliancy; but they are both very pleasant, & doubtless when they get into lodgings will be more animated. I have had as yet very little talk with them.—I have scrawled you a great many pages—but it seems to me I have told you none the things I meant to in sitting down. But I must pause—I have already written two letters before this. I hope you will get all possible good of your vacation—that your eyes will heal—and that your bride & babe will flourish in emulation.—Every now & then (irrelevantly) I meet Mallock & have a little talk with him.[6] He has promised to come & see me; but he never does—to my regret. I think he wants to, but is defeated by a mixture of English shamefacedness & London accidents. I regret it much for I have a strong impression I should like him & we should get on. But I shall probably see more of him some time—his face expresses his intelligence.   Farewell.   My blessings on mother, father, sister, &—if she is there, God bless her!, as they say here,—upon the aunt.   Many greetings to your Alice—I suppose you will get into the country with her and the infant.   I take much interest in the latter, & if ever you shld. get tired of him, shall be very glad to adopt him.

Fraternally yrs. | H. James jr

I enclose to Alice (single) a very pleasant letter from Lowell, which I beg her to keep for me.—

[1] A newspaper published in Springfield, Mass.

[2] Probably WJ's "Rationality, Activity, and Faith," *Princeton Review* 2 (July 1882): 58–86, reprinted in *The Will to Believe* (1897).

[3] WJ considered several possibilities until 1889 when the house at 95 Irving St. was built.   The plan mentioned involved a lot owned by his father on Quincy St.

[4] HJ, *An International Episode* (1879).

[5] The first session of the Congrès Littéraire International was held at the Paris Universal Exposition; the second session in London, beginning on 9 June 1879.   Edmond About presided.

[6] William Hurrell Mallock (1849–1923), British author, published *Is Life Worth Living?* (1879).

1880–1881

In early June 1880, William James departed for Europe. He wrote to his wife of his "great sense of consecration" to make his vacation fruitful "for him and his." During a month's stay in London at 3 Bolton Street, he spent his time visiting the theater, making social calls, and meeting a number of English philosophers. While there, he realized that his brother Henry was completely at home in England, preferring it to America.

In the middle of July, William made his way to Switzerland by way of Amsterdam and Heidelberg, spending most of August hiking and viewing scenery in Switzerland. Back in America in early September, he moved to rooms at 15 Louisburg Square, Boston, where he lived until December when he returned to Cambridge and for a time lived at 10 Oxford Street. But his return to America did not excite him and he must have expressed his disappointment with American life to Henry, judging from Henry's response of 13 November 1880 to a letter written by William in September and now lost.

Henry found William too much given to talking about his nerves and physical condition. "I wish he had a little more of this quiet British stoutness," he wrote their parents (HJL, 2:292). Having already published two books in 1880 and with a third, Washington Square *to appear in December, Henry was hard at work on his "long novel,"* The Portrait of a Lady, *for which he expected to receive $6,000. This work forced him to postpone his return to America, planned for late August 1880.*

From Henry James

3, BOLTON STREET, | PICCADILLY. W. Nov. 13th. [1880]

Dear William.

I have a short letter of yours long unanswered—it is of the date of Sept. 30th. I have not written to you partly because the tone of your letter was rather low & I didn't know in what fashion to respond. You appear not to have been exhilarated on your return by renewed contact with American life, or by the aspect of the American individual, & I am obviously not in a situation to reassure you on these points. Doubtless the feeling you expressed has melted down a good deal since you have got into your work again & ceased to see Boston & London in immediate juxtaposition. I hope you are physically comfortable, & that Louisburg Square stands the test of time. Of me there is little to tell you. The weeks that have elapsed since you left me have been very quiet ones; but profitable; inasmuch as I have both written & read a good deal. I am afraid that if you found me basely naturalised here when you came out, I am not less so these few months later. I feel more & more at home here, & find London more & more, on the whole, the best point of view. Though one gets sick of it at times & tired to death of the flatness of much—though, fortunately, by no means of *all*—of one's social life, yet there is a daily sustenance in the huge, multitudinous place. It has been a very fine autumn—clear, bright & american-like; & is only now turning to soft darkness & mild moisture—an element I like. The fogs are as yet (after a false alarm early in the season) mercifully absent. The town is still quiet & society not reconstituted; so I have seen but few people—though I dined yesterday at Andrew Lang's (the vaguely-glancing,) in company with Lionel Tennyson (the much-stammering) & his wife.—I got a letter a few days since from Alice (sister)—long, bright & delightful, which I beg you to thank her for while I wait to acknowledge it. I hope your own wife & babe do not languish in the air of the town, & send a tender remembrance to each. I dined a few days ago (on the 9th) with the Lord Mayor—the big banquet which he gives annually at the Guildhall to the Cabinet Ministers & a couple of 1000 others, & at which the head of the Government usually makes a more or less sensational speech. It is a huge, scrambling, pompous & picturesque affair, well to see once; but I should care little to go again—even to hear Gladstone speak—as the rank & file of the guests are squeezed to death & fed only (or almost only) with aldermanic Turtle.[1] I dont know what else I can tell you. Edwin Booth is acting here, with but indifferent success; people find him very inferior to Irving. To me they are both so bad there is little to choose. I embrace them in Quincy St, & also in Louisburg Square. God bless & sustain you.

Ever yours | H. James jr

P.S. Your article in the Atlantic a couple of months ago, gave me extreme pleasure.[2]

[1] Sir William McArthur (1809–1887), newly elected Lord Mayor of London, held his inaugural banquet on 9 November 1880.   Gladstone, the prime minister, was present and spoke.   The report in the *Times* says nothing about the menu and it is not clear whether "aldermanic Turtle" is meant to describe the fare or the speeches.

[2] WJ, "Great Men, Great Thoughts, and the Environment," *Atlantic Monthly* 46 (October 1880): 441–59; reprinted in *The Will to Believe* (1897).

From Henry James

REFORM CLUB, | PALL MALL. S.W. Nov. 27th [1880]

Dear William.

I sent you last p.m. the two vols. of Rosmini, done up separately & registered; & I hope they will arrive safely.[1]   Don't talk of refunding.—A few days before, I had received a very welcome letter from you, in Alice's hand; & should have addressed this answer to her if I had not begun merely with the intention of notifying you about the book.   As it is, I can now hardly do more.   This is a Saturday afternoon, & I go very presently down to spend Sunday at Lord Rosebery's—so I have only a moment.   (If the party at Mentmore proves interesting I will write of it to Quincy St., whence I received, the same day as your, a dear letter from mother.)[2]   It gives me great pleasure to hear that your work this year leaves you leisure for reading & study, which must be a great satisfaction.   It is the position I desire more & more to arrive at—which I am happy to say I tend to do.   Thank you for what you say about my two novels.   The young man in *Washington Square* is not a portrait—he is sketched from the outside merely & not *fouillé*.   The only good thing in the story is the girl.   The other book increases, I think, in merit & interest as it goes on, & being told in a more spacious, expansive way than its predecessors, is inevitably more human, more sociable.[3]   It was the constant effort at *condensation* (which you used always to drum into my head—àpropos of Mérimée &c—when I was young & you bullied me,) that has deprived my former things of these qualities.   I shall read what G. Allen & Fiske reply to you in the *Atlantic,* but shall be sure not to enter into what they say as I did into your article, which I greatly appreciated.[4]—I spent last Sunday at Wm Darwin's, very pleasantly, owing to beautiful cold, crisp weather & to Sara seeming very well & happy.   I am very sorry your lodgings smell of soup, especially as I have lately wholly abjured it by the advice of Dr. Andrew Clark, whom I had to consult for matutinal nausea, which has vanished by the suppression for[5] the pottage.   Tell them in Quincy St. that I will speedily respond to Mother's letter.   Say to Alice (sister) that I send her a new hat a week or two hence by Mrs. Mason, who has kindly offered (taking a great interest in the episode) to carry it.   It came home this a.m. & is much superior to the other.   Love to your own Alice & baby.   I will send them some benefits the 1st chance I get.

Tout à toi   H. James jr

[1] Antonio Rosmini-Serbati (1797–1855), Italian philosopher.

[2] Mentmore was Lord Rosebery's estate.

[3] HJ's *Portrait of a Lady* was serialized in *Macmillan's Magazine*, October 1880–November 1881 (vols. 42–45) and in *Atlantic Monthly*, November 1880–December 1881 (vols. 46–48).

[4] Charles Grant Blairfindie Allen, "The Genesis of Genius," *Atlantic Monthly* 47 (March 1881): 371–81; John Fiske, "Sociology and Hero-Worship: An Evolutionist's Reply to Dr. James," *Atlantic Monthly* 47 (January 1881): 75–84. Both papers are responses to criticisms made by WJ in "Great Men, Great Thoughts, and the Environment."

[5] A slip for 'of'.

In December 1880 the Harvard authorities approved William James's appointment as assistant professor of philosophy for five years. He was hoping for a leave of absence and a winter in Europe with his family, but in April 1881 he learned that he was not eligible for leave until the following year. In early April 1881 he traveled to Baltimore where he met Daniel Coit Gilman and discussed the possibility of an appointment at Johns Hopkins University. Shortly after returning to Cambridge he learned, probably with relief, that the Hopkins trustees were not going to offer him a position, preferring instead a religiously orthodox scholar from Europe.

Having completed The Portrait of a Lady *in 1881, Henry James suffered something of a dry spell. Besides the novel, which was published both in serial and book form, he published only one review. He traveled to Paris in early February, staying there a few weeks before proceeding to Italy in March, where he spent the spring and early summer, returning to London in July.*

From Henry James

                    Milan. Hotel de la Ville. | March. 21ˢᵗ, 1881.
Dear William.

    Your letter of the 3ᵈ ult. dictated to Bob,[1] has (after an apparently long voyage) just reached me here, & I lose no time in replying to it.———I am very glad to hear you have the prospect of being able to come abroad for a year's study, but I confess that I don't feel able to "advise" you very definitely. What strikes me first is that from the point of view of economy, the *nearest* place (the one reached with least frais de voyage) ought to have most to recommend it.   This would put a residence in England first on the list.   A winter in Florence would have many charms, but there would be within a few months the journey there & back to be paid for, & from the moment one begins with hotels & railways . . . . ! It might be that you would live there cheaply enough to make up for this, but of that I can't judge, having no experience of Florence from the house-keeping point of view. As regards London, I don't at all know the price of lodgings in Bloomsbury &c; I only know that they are considerably cheaper than in my part of the town.   If I were in London I would immediately make inquiries for you—but you see I am far away.   It is my belief that you could get good lodgings in the neighborhood of the British Museum or in some other unfashionable but respectable part of London, for a sum within your means.   I pay 2½ guineas a week for my second floor in Bolton St.; which, however, has always struck me as, for the situation, cheap.   On the other hand the extra-expenses of living in London are larger than they would be in some other places; the single item of cab fares is in itself a thing to be considered.   It is useless to say you wouldn't use cabs.   In fact, you would, & Alice would have to: that is, more or less.   You would need human intercourse after your work (as you say;) & human intercourse in a *big* place inevitably entails certain expenses—especially when a woman is concerned.   In Paris you would perhaps have a cheaper rent—but I can't think Paris would be really cheap for you unless at the price of too sordid efforts.   You would have little chance for human intercourse there, & there would be nothing left for you, in the way of recreation, but venal pleasures—i.e. the theatres, dining at restaurants &c.   These are all more or less costly, & the general situation of living in a city like Paris *for economy,* sums me to a contradiction & a discomfort.   There are temptations at every turn to spend money, & it is better to be where there are fewer.   Paris strikes me in a word as having the drawbacks of London without the compensations—the same scale of prices (about) & none of the social advantages.   In London you might see some interesting men (those you already know, & others;) whereas in Paris you would see none; (for I put the American colony out of the question.)   (You would have nothing to do with it.)   Your suggestion of *Cambridge* seems to me the best in your letter; though I should need to know more about the place to venture to *recommend* you to go there.   If I were in England I would make inquiries for you—but now can only offer to do so when I go back.   It must be cheaper than London, & I have no doubt that you could get good rooms there, & be decently nourished, on terms that from the American point of view would appear moderate.   My own disposition is to urge you to choose *England,* as being so much more filling at the price than any foreign land.   Your impressions there would sink into you, & nourish you more, than any you would have in Paris or Florence; & besides, you would know some people.   In Florence there is no one but Hillebrand.   Assuming that England is the best country, Cambridge appears better than London as having a sufficient life of its own & yet being smaller, more concentrated & easy to deal with.   It is true that if you come abroad this summer I shouldn't recommend you to begin with Cambridge then, or before October.   Your summer would therefore have to be spent somewhere, & you suggest Wales.   Wales would probably do beautifully if you knew (or I knew) before hand just the sequestered nook to go to: but Wales, roughly speaking, means crowds of tourists, dear hotels, &c.   Scotland the same.   Nevertheless, if you don't insist on the *fine fleur* of scenery, I think you would have no trouble in finding reasonable & wholesome (also pleasant) country lodgings *somewhere* in England for the summer—especially in the North. Behold then the general contention of my letter.   1$\underline{°}$ That England is intrinsically the best residence for you, as a year there would enrich your mind humanly &c; & extrinsically as being the nearest.   2$\underline{°}$ That if you come abroad for the summer you may pass it comfortably if you will be content to go to some small & quiet (unfashionable) English watering place, & STICK THERE.   3$\underline{°}$ That for the winter (or the part of it you speak of especially—October to February) Cambridge would be decidedly worth trying & has presumptions in its favour.   4$\underline{°}$ That Paris & Florence are, one too dear & superfluously rich; & the other too far away to go to *except for a long stay.*—I may add that I assume with regard to an English residence that your having your wife & child with you makes all the difference; & that you can support the "insularity" &c. of English life infinitely better with them than you could alone—in which latter case I shld. never recommend it.—I won't add more, except to hope very much that your plans won't take such a form as that   I shall miss you both here & in the U.S., to which I return as you know, either in the late summer or in October. That is, I hope you will either arrive some little time before I leave or some little time after.   I won't write about myself—I am on my way to Rome, & wrote to Mother very few days since.   Love & blessing to Alice & the Babe.   Shouldn't she like to try England?

Ever yours | H James jr

[1] RJ was from time to time estranged from his wife and living in Cambridge.

1882–1883

In 1882 the Jameses suffered the first deaths in the immediate family circle: Mary Robertson Walsh James died on 29 January and the elder Henry James on 18 December.

His mother's death is not recorded in William James's surviving correspondence. At the time of her death, he was returning by train from a Harvard alumni banquet in Chicago. Henry James was in Washington, D.C., where he was seeing a great deal of the Henry Adamses. He returned to Cambridge on 31 January and in several letters expressed his sense of loss for the mother to whom he was "passionately attached." Garth Wilkinson James arrived from Milwaukee on 1 February. Robertson James, estranged from his wife, was in Cambridge where he had been living since December 1881. Alice James, still living at home, was present at her mother's death, and it was upon her that the responsibility fell for the care of her widowed father. Early in the spring of 1882, she and the elder Henry James moved from Cambridge to 131 Mt. Vernon Street in Boston.

Henry had arrived in Cambridge on 1 November 1881 for his often-postponed visit home. From there he had gone to New York for a visit and then to Washington, where his stay was cut short by his mother's illness. In late May 1882, he returned to London and 3 Bolton Street. From a literary point of view the year was not a productive one for him, the most noteworthy event being the private printing of Daisy Miller *in an adaptation for the stage, the first of his several unsuccessful ventures into the theater.*

William James became a father for the second time with the birth of a son, named William, on 17 June 1882. He was now eligible for leave from Harvard and spent 1882–83 in Europe. In one respect, this was an important trip since he renewed his friendships with the English philosophers and psychologists and made a number of important new contacts on the Continent. But he failed with respect to the main purpose of his leave, which was to make headway in his writing of The Principles of Psychology. *In his baggage he carried a caligraph, a heavy typewriter capable of producing only capital letters. The machine was damaged during the trip and William, an unskilled typist at best, spent more time tinkering with it than using it. He was at 3 Bolton Street on 10 December when the telegram arrived from his wife announcing that the elder Henry James had suffered a "softening" of the brain. Alice urged him not to return and it was decided that Henry alone should go. The younger Henry James reached Cambridge on the night of 21 December, after the funeral, which had been held that morning. At the Boston station, he met Robertson James who had arrived for the funeral and was returning to Milwaukee.*

Prominent in the letters of these years are two themes, the underlying meaning of which has given much trouble to scholars of the Jameses. First, it is clear that the Jameses in Cambridge, and especially his wife, did not want William to return. Did they fear that his interference would make it more difficult to settle his father's affairs? Or that a premature return and failure to write his book would be embarrassing? Or were there other and deeper reasons? Second, there is the disagreement over the will—a common event in this and other families—in which Garth Wilkinson James was singled out and slighted. Perhaps not enough is known about Garth Wilkinson's financial dealings with his father to enable scholars to establish with any certainty the motives of the various parties involved. In a hitherto unpublished portion of Henry James's letter of 28 December 1882, Henry makes the significant claim that Garth Wilkinson himself asked to be treated differently in the will. (For the provenance of this letter, see Editors' Note, pp. xxix–xxx.)

A third topic is absent from this segment of the correspondence between the two brothers. Henry James writes little about the condition of their sister. At this time, Alice Gibbens James was reporting to her husband in Bolton Street that the sister had almost broken the heart of Aunt Kate and that Katharine Loring was becoming "painfully" prominent in the family. In her view, Henry James faced a difficult task in soothing the troubled waters.

To Henry James

Bolton St | Wdsdy. Dec 20. 82 | 8 P.M.

My dear Harry

All is over! as I learn by the Standard this P.M.[1] Poor Father! It saddens me more, much more than I expected. I wish I had been there, & I cannot cease to regret that you should be arriving, perhaps even *now,* too late. I wrote to Alice. You will write me a full account of everything. Were Wilky & Bob there?[2] My last news is only to Dec. 4th, when alice says he was "decidedly recovering." I feel like leaving for home—not for any definite reason—but because when such changes are happening it seems the place. But I will of course wait a fortnight till I hear more of how the details are going. Pray write fully & promptly. Best of love to A, A.K. & the boys. I have been lapped in comfort here in your quarters—I feel in fact too much at home & wish it were more foreign.

Yours | W.J.

[1] The *Standard,* a London newspaper.
[2] RJ was present.

From Henry James

131 Mount Vernon St. | Dec. 26th [1882]

My dear William.

You will already have heard the circumstances under which I arrived at New York on Thursday 21st, at noon, after a very rapid & prosperous, but painful passage. Letters from Alice & Katherine L. were awaiting me at the dock, telling me that dear Father was to be buried that morning. I reached Boston at 11 that night; there was so much delay in getting up-town. I found Bob at the station here; he had come on for the funeral only, & returned to Milwaukee the next morning. Alice, who was in bed, was very quiet & A.K. was perfect. They told me everything—or at least they told me a great deal—before we parted that night, & what they told me was deeply touching, & yet not at all literally painful. Father had been so tranquil, so painless, had died so easily &, as it were, deliberately, & there had been none—not the least—of that anguish & confusion which we imagined in London.—The next morning Alice was ill, & went to Beverly—for complete change, absence from the house &c.—with Miss Loring. Meanwhile I had become conscious of a very bad head, which was rapidly getting worse. I had disembarked with it, & hoped it would pass away, but on Friday p.m. I had to take to my bed, after having seen your Alice in the afternoon & definitely learned from her that you had *not* been telegraphed to. This had been judged best, but I regretted it so much that on Saturday a.m. which was the earliest time possible, I got A.K. to go out & do it. Alice's letters will however already [have] explained to you this episode. Their not telegraphing you was not neglect, but simply a mis-calculation of the advisable. My head got much worse, I sent for Dr. Beach, & have been for 3 days in bed, with one of the sharpest attacks of that damnable sort that I have ever had. To-day, however, I am much better, but my still seedy condition must explain the poverty of this letter. Alice is still absent, & I have spent these days wholly with A.K., who quite unexhausted by her devotion to Father, has been, as always, the perfection of a nurse. She has now told me much about all his last days—about everything that followed that news which was the last to come before I sailed. Your wife tells me that since then she has written to you every day or two—so that you will have had, by the time this reaches you, a sort of history, in detail, of his illness. It appears to have been most strange, most characteristic, above all, & as full of beauty as it was void of suffering. There was none of what we feared—no paralysis, no dementia, no violence. He simply after the "improvement" of which we were written before I sailed, had a sudden relapse—a series of swoons—after which he took to his bed not to rise again. He had no visible malady—strange as it may seem. The "softening of the brain" was simply a gradual refusal of food, because he *wished* to die. There was no dementia except a sort of exaltation of belief that he had entered into "the spiritual life." Nothing could persuade him to eat, & yet he never suffered, or gave the least sign of suffering, from inanition. All this will seem strange & incredible to you—but told with all the details, as Aunt Kate has told it to me, it becomes real—taking father as he was—almost natural. He prayed & longed to die. He ebbed & faded away—though in spite of his strength becoming continually less, he was able to see people & to talk. He wished to see as many people as he could, & he talked with them without effort. He saw F. Boott, & talked much 2 or 3 days before he died. Alice says he said the most picturesque & humorous things! He knew I was coming & was glad, but not impatient. He was delighted when he was told that you would stay in my rooms in my absence, & seemed much interested in the idea. He had no belief apparently that he should live to see me, but was perfectly cheerful about it. He slept a great deal, &, as A.K. says there was "so little of the sick-room" about him. He lay facing the windows, which he would never have darkened— never pained by the light. I sit writing this in his room upstairs, & a cast which Alice had taken from his head but which is very unsatisfactory & represents him as terribly emaciated, stands behind me on that high chest of drawers. It is late in the evening, & I have been down into the parlour—I broke off ½ an hour ago—to talk again with Aunt Kate, who sits there alone. She & the nurse alone were with him at the last—Alice was in her room with your Alice & K. Loring, & had not seen him since the night before. She saw him very little for a good many days before his death—she was too ill, & K.L. looked after her entirely. This left Father to Aunt Kate & the nurse, & the quiet simple character of his illness made them perfectly able to do everything—so that, as I said just now, there was no confusion, no embarrassment. He spoke of everything—the disposition of his things, made all his arrangements of every kind. Aunt Kate repeats again & again, that he *yearned unspeakably* to die. I am too tired to write more, & my head is beginning to ache; I must either finish this in the morning, or send it as it is. In the latter case I will write again immediately, as I have many more things to say. The house is so *empty*—I scarcely know myself. Yesterday was such a Xmas as you may imagine—with Alice at K. Loring's, me ill in bed here, & A.K. sitting alone downstairs, not only without a Xmas dinner but without any dinner, as she doesn't eat according to her wont!— 27ᵗʰ a.m. Will send this now & write again tonight. All our wish here is that you should remain abroad the next six months.

Ever your   H. James jr

From Henry James

131 Mount Vernon St. | Dec. 28ᵗʰ [1882]

Dear William.

I was not able yesterday to write you a second letter, as I hoped, as I was still suffering rather too much from my head; but this evening I am pretty well myself again, & shall endeavour to go on with my story. I have seen your wife yesterday & to-day, & she tells me again that she wrote you so minutely & so constantly during the progress of Father's illness that my very imperfect record gathered from hearsay will have little value for you.[1] Mainly, I can only repeat that the whole thing was tranquil & happy—almost, as it were, comfortable. The wanderings of his mind which were never great, were always of a joyous description, & his determination not to eat was cheerful & reasonable. That is, he was always prepared to explain why he wouldn't eat—i.e. because he had entered upon the "spiritual life,["] & didn't wish to keep up the mere form of living in the body. During the last 10 or 15 hours only his speech became thick & inarticulate: he had an accumulation of phlegm in his throat which he was too weak to get rid of. The doctor gave him a little opium, to help him, as I understand A.K., to clear his larynx, which had to some extent this effect, but which also made him sink into a gentle unconsciousness, in which, however, he still continued vaguely to talk. He spoke then several times of mother—uttering (intelligibly) her name: "Mary—my Mary." Somewhat before this A.K. says he murmured—"Oh, I have such good boys—*such* good boys!" The efforts that he made to speak toward the last were, the Dr. (Ahlborn) assured A.K., quite mechanical & unconscious. Aunt Kate was with him uninterruptedly from midnight on Sunday to 3 p.m. Monday, when he died. She had left him late Sunday evening with the nurse, but the nurse presently called her back & the two sat with him till the end, alone, save while the Doctor, at intervals, was there. Bob arrived on Wednesday—there was no question of Wilky's coming—it is too difficult for him to travel. Alice will have told you about the funeral. Dr. Toy read simply the Kings Chapel Service; there were three carriages to the grave. Bob & George Higginson, F. J. Child & Joe Warner lowered the coffin into the grave. I am going out tomorrow afternoon to see where he lies beside Mother; it has been impossible for me to go, up to to-day. So it is all over & poor Father has become absent for ever! You may imagine how one feels his absence—how, personally, we *miss* him—how strange & empty the house is without him. I sit here at his table, I sleep in his bed, I am surrounded with everything that belonged to him in life, & it seems to me that I still hear his voice, & that if I go down-stairs, I shall find him. But he is already a memory, & every hour makes him more so—he is tremendously & unspeakably absent. It doesn't seem so much, however, that he is dead, as that a strange deadness has fallen upon *us*, who have lost his living, moving, pervasive presence. This *missing* will last a long time, & you will feel it for yourself when you come back. Alice has returned from Beverly very much better—so much better that my spirits, which were low about her when I saw her on my arrival, have considerably risen. *Dec. 29ᵗʰ a.m.* I had to stop writing again last night, but I am really, I think all right to-day, and Alice seems better still than yesterday. This morning your letter of the 14ᵗʰ to Father has come in, & I have read it, dear William & been touched to the heart by it. Reading it to myself here, in his room, at his table, it seemed as if your last farewell reached him, & it were not all lost & wasted. It will seem so still more if I take it out to Mount Auburn to-day & hold it in my hand as I stand beside his grave. You have spoken for me, as well as for yourself. I am not sure that I should have opened your letter (not returned it to you unopened) if I had not thought, from the cover, that it was addressed to me. It was so thinking that I broke the envelope, & then I couldn't help reading it. You must let me keep it now.—I have had by this time to give my attention to the fact that Father has made me his executor—to read his will & make arrangements to have it proved, the property appraised &c. Money must be drawn to carry on the house &c; & to this end I had a conference yesterday with J. B. Warner. Before giving him up the will, I took a copy of it, & I accordingly enclose you this copy without more delay. I shall do the same to Wilky (poor Wilky!) & Bob. I won't go into the matter now, but write you again in as few days as possible. You will see that the most striking feature of the will is the omission of Wilky. Father determined upon this omission at the earnest request of W. himself. This request, made in the past, was reiterated & confirmed by Wilky during his visit here this autumn, & Aunt Kate & Alice tell me that Father told them that it was with a perfect understanding of his intention that Wilky returned to Milwaukee. I think, therefore, that the will cannot at any rate come to W. as a surprise. When all the facts are considered— the magnitude of [*pages missing*] I have had (with as little delay, myself, as possible) to learn as executor. Father's property is roughly estimated at $95000; of which $75000 are in the three Syracuse houses, the rest in railway (B.C. & Q.) bonds & shares.[2]—I wish I could be assured that you have banished all thoughts of coming home, & that you find London habitable & profitable. If not, go back to Paris, but stay abroad & get all possible good, so long as I stay here, which will be till the summer. This is what we all wish. (Don't tell this to people in London, however,—or to Miss Balls, to whom I shall soon be writing.) (If you are asked about my stay, say you don't know— it is uncertain.) Alice was here yesterday with the two children, whom she had been having photographed—all very lovely. Farewell, dear William.

Ever yours   H James

[1] Many of AGJ's letters describing Henry James's final illness have survived and are published in volume 5 of *The Correspondence of William James*.

[2] The railway referred to may be the Chicago, Burlington & Quincy Line. But during this period there were many mergers of lines and numerous small railway companies with similar names.

From Henry James

131 Mt. Vernon St. | Jan 1st 1883.

Dear William

I receive this a.m. your note of the 20th, written after you had seen the news of Father's death in the *Standard*. I can imagine how sadly it must have presented itself, as you sit alone in those dark, far-away rooms of mine. But it would have been sadder still if you also had arrived only to hear that after those miserable eight days at sea he was lost forever & forever to our eyes. Thank God we haven't another parent to lose; though all Aunt Kate's sweetness & devotion makes me feel, in advance, that it will be scarcely less a pang when *she* goes! Such is the consequence of cherishing our "natural ties!" After a little, Father's departure will begin to seem a simple & natural fact, however, as it has begun to appear to us here. I went out yesterday (Sunday) morning, to the Cambridge cemetery (I had not been able to start early enough on Saturday afternoon, as I wrote you I meant to do)—& stood beside his grave a long time & read him your letter of farewell—which I am sure he heard somewhere out of the depths of the still, bright winter air.[1] He lies extraordinarily close to Mother, & as I stood there and looked at this last expression of so many years of mortal union, it was difficult not to believe that they were not united again in some consciousness of my belief. On my way back I stopped to see Alice & sat with her for an hour & admired the lovely babe, who is a most loving little mortal. Then I went to see F. J. Child, because I had been told that he has been beyond every one full of kindness & sympathy since the first of father's illness, & had appeared to feel his death more than any one outside the family. Every one, however, has been full of kindness—absolutely *tender* does this good old Boston appear to have shown itself. Among others Wendell Holmes (who is now a Judge of the Supreme Court) has shone—perhaps a little unexpectedly,[2] in this respect. Alice has been ill this last 24 hours—but not with any nervousness; only from nausea produced apparently from the doses of salvic soda that Beach has been giving her. She is at present much better Your letter makes me nervous in regard to your dispositions of coming home. *Don't for the world think of this, I beseech you*—it would be a very idle step. There is *nothing* here for you to do, not a place even for you to live, & there is every reason why you should remain abroad till the summer. Your wishing to come is a mere vague, uneasy sentiment, not unnatural under the circumstances, but corresponding to no real fitness.   Let it subside as soon as possible, we all beg you.   I wrote you two days ago everything that there is to be told you as yet as regards Father's will.   Wait quietly till you hear more from me.   I am going as soon as I can get away, to Milwaukee, & I will write you more as soon as I have been there.   A.K. is still here.   Make the most of London.

Ever yours   H. James jr

I receive all your enclosures.

[1] WJ's farewell letter of 14 December 1882 is published in volume 5 of the *Correspondence.*

[2] Oliver Wendell Holmes, Jr., served as a justice on the Supreme Judicial Court of Massachusetts from 1883 to 1902, when he was appointed to the United States Supreme Court.

To Henry James

Bolton St. Jan. 9th. '83

My dear Harry,

Your eagerly awaited letter came yesterday.   I was truly grieved to hear of your tumbling immediately into such a bad headache.   But I hope it may have cleared you up & left you all the better for a time. Your details of the illness were very touching, but in no essential points altered the impression Alice's letters have given me.   I still regret extremely that you could not have got there in time.   What would I not give myself if I could have seen the dear old man lying there as you describe him, culminating his life by this drama of complete detachment from it.   I must now make amends for my rather hard non-receptivity of his doctrines as he urged them so absolutely during his life, by trying to get a little more public justice done them now.   As life closes, all a man has done seems like one cry or sentence. Father's cry was the single one that religion is real.   The thing is so to "voice" it that other ears shall hear,—no easy task, but a worthy one, which in some shape I shall attempt.[1]

I should have written you earlier, but knowing you would get my news, I concluded to wait till I should receive your letter.   You speak of a "prosperous but *painful*" voyage, a singular epithet, whose significance awakens my curiosity, as it hardly seems to betoken seasickness.   Alice writes no details about the will, but implies that Wilky has been cut off, to my great regret.

His diminutions of the estate in Florida were done when he was a mere boy, doing the best he knew how, too, & father was as much

responsible for them as he, &c. His sickness now will make him need
more money than ever, & the Cary estate, whatever its potential value
may be, does not, as far as I know, bring in any considerable revenue
at present.[2]   I wait for more details; but my present impression is
that, however it may be with the principal, I shall make over to Wilky
whatever turns out to be his natural portion of the income of my
share. With Bob & Alice the case may be somewhat different. I hope
I shall hear from you in a few days just what the details of the will are.

Of course I am anxious to know how Alice's plans & yours are
shaping themselves; but that will probably be a gradual thing. Tell
her to count on my co-operation & help in any thing she thinks best
for herself.

And now I suppose you would like to hear a little about the life of
me in this habitat of yours. It has been dull decidedly; & more than
once I have found myself tempted to cut it all & run back to Paris
where I was feeling so well, & beginning so to enjoy the expressiveness of the place.   There has been no bad fog since the week you
left, but almost steady mildness & darkness, so that my eyes have got
quite used up, & of late I have hired a reader for a couple of hours
a day.   I found the difference of light between the two floors so in-
considerable that I have stuck to the lower one as the most luxurious.
The service runs like clock-work, of course, & I feel as if I had never
lived anywhere else all my life. That is one objection to London, that
its sights & sounds so soon fail to call out your observing faculties.
My social existence has been rather languid too The rhythm of London life is so slow that I see that if one wishes to lay social "siege" to
the place he must be prepared to spend many patient months of
waiting till his turn come round.   Hodgson & Robertson are good
friends, with whom I am always at home.   Leslie Stephen has
called & asked me to dinner twice, so that is all right.   Fred. Pollock
asked me to dinner one Sunday noon, but has shown no subsequent
thirst for my acquaintance, not calling or speaking to me in the club,
&c.   Of course I have done my duty in the way of calling on the
ladies of all the houses that have fed me. I went to the Smalleys, but
S. hasn't even left a card.   I've called twice on Lady Rose, & found
her friendly enough, but no further notice.   Mrs. Stanley Clark the
same.   Hodgson has been out of town, & so has Sully.   Gurney,
whom I should most have liked to know, has taken no notice of me,
&c, &c, &c.[3]   Dont think for heaven's sake that I enumerate all this
by way of complaint!   I know perfectly well that were I to stay here
long enough I should get as familiar with all these people as I am

with my friends at home. But meanwhile, with intense homesickness gnawing at my vitals, with no literary work being accomplished, with the darkness & with bad sleep, it need not surprise you to hear that I sometimes felt as if what I wanted to gain in London were hardly likely to be worth, when it should come, the time spent in earning it.

What is the difference of outward *expressiveness* between our Anglo-Saxon civilizations & those of the continent? The complete absence of any aggregate & outward expression of pure & direct intelligence is what is so striking here. After Paris, London seems like a mediaeval village, with nothing but its blanket of golden dirt to take the place of style, beauty, & rationality. At times one feels as if the former were a poor substitute. & then one does grow impatient at times with the universal expression of aggregate stupidity, stupidity heavy & massive with a sort of voluntary self corroboration, the like whereof exist nowhere else under the sun. Germany is the abode of the purest grace & lucency compared with this life, clogged with every kind of senseless unneccessariness, & moving down the centuries under its thick swathings, all unconscious of its load. It appeals to me as a physical image,—with which doubtless the meteorological conditions of my stay here have s'thing to do,—England under a filthy, smeary, smoky, fog, lusty & happy, hale & hearty, with the eternal sunlit ether outside, & she not suspecting, or not caring, to think that with a puff of her breath she might rend the veil & be there. You ought to have seen the Rossetti exhibition,—the work of a boarding school girl, no color, no drawing, no cleverness of any sort, nothing but feebleness incarnate, & a sort of refined intention of an extremely narrow sort, with no technical power to carry it out. Yet such expressions of admiration as I heard from the bystanders! Then the theatres & the hippopotamus-like satisfaction of their audiences! Bad as our theatres are, they are not so massively hopeless as that. It makes Paris seem like a sort of Athens. Then the determination on the part of all who write not to do it as amateurs, & never to use the airs & language of a professional, to be first of all a layman & a gentleman, & to pretend that your ideas came to you accidentally as it were, & are things you care nothing about. As I said, it makes one impatient at times; & one finds himself wondering whether England can afford forever, when her rivals are living by the light of pure rationality to so great an extent, to go blundering thus unsystematically along, & trusting to mere luck to help her to find what is good, a fragment at a time. It's a queer mystery! She never *has* failed to find it hitherto in perhaps richer measure than they, by her method of blundering into it.   But will it always last? & can she *always* fight without stripping?   Won't the general clearness & keen- ness of a rational age force her to throw some of her nonsense away, or to fall behind the rest?   I thus vomit out my bile into your prob- ably in part sympathizing, in part indifferent ear.

But I must now stop.   I have faithfully sent all letters.   Give my warmest love to Aunt Kate, & to Alice, who of course is ere this back in Mount Vernon Street.

Ever your affectionate brother | Wm James

You might, after letting my Alice see this, send it to Wilky, to whom however I will write in a day or two.

Your "Siege of London" begins capitally.[4]

[1] WJ edited *The Literary Remains of the Late Henry James* (Boston: James R. Osgood, 1884).

[2] GWJ's father-in-law, Joseph Cary, was a wealthy merchant who owned a clothing store in Milwaukee.

[3] Edmund Gurney.

[4] HJ, "The Siege of London," *Cornhill Magazine* 47 (January 1883): 1–34; (February 1883): 225–56.

From Henry James

131 Mt. Vernon St. | Jan. 11th [1883]

Dear William.

I wrote you two letters within these last days, & I telegraphed you to day—so that you will not have been without news of me.   My telegram was the result of Alice sending me your last from London this a.m. & of my going out to see her & talking with her of your apparent plans of return.   These plans were so definitely announced in the letter she had sent me, (I forget of what date,) that I was moved on my return to town to go straight to the telegraph office & send you the despatch which you will almost have received as I write this. You speak of being "determined to sail at latest in Servia of Feb. 11th." This determination makes me really so sad—& Alice as well, I think—that I must do what I can to keep you from breaking loose from Europe & giving up your stay there as a failure, prematurely. The *pity* of it almost brings tears to my eyes; & when I look upon the barren scene (bating your wife & babes) that awaits you here, I feel as if I were justified in doing almost anything to keep you on the other side.   I left you so comfortably established in London, with such promise of improvement & stability (as far as the fundamentals or rather, materials of life could give it) that it seems a kind of "irony of fate" that will bring you back, in the midst of this harsh & rasping winter, to narrow &, as it were, accidental accommodation in Mrs. Gibbons's[1] small house, where I think that for these coming months you would greatly lack space & quiet. For you to return before the summer seems a melancholy confession of failure (as regards your projects of absence,) & sort of proclamation of want of continuity of purpose. I am afraid my three last letters (in relation to Father's will) will have ministered to your unrest & anxiety, & therefore have made it more difficult to persuade you to remain. But I wish I could convince you how entirely such emotions are "subjective" & without foundation in any necessities or opportunities that exist here. I am assuming that you will agree to a redivision of the estate, & once that is agreed to everything will go on as simply smoothly & easily as possible. I go to Milwaukee on the 15th. Our Alice is improving every day, & fills me with the conviction that in six months time she will have reached a comparatively normal level. There is every prospect of her being able to (afford to) keep this house.[2] We have it (the estate has it) for the next two years & ½, & she has almost made up her mind to take it to herself; so that she will have no anxiety, fatigue or general trouble of change. Your wife strikes me as distinctly *distressed* at the prospect of your return, & she could not restrain her tears as she spoke of it to me today. She sees you back here by the end of February (if not before) in a house where no provision has been made for having you & where you cannot live as it will be well for you to live; & with a long stretch of time to be provided for before the end of next summer; the whole question of *what to do* forced upon her early in the season (or as soon as you return indeed) while she hoped it would sleep on for some months to come. It is of course very disappointing that you have not been able to get well at work—that you continue to feel seedy—that the London winter should not be more helpful. But there is the general fact that your being in Europe is a valuable thing & that your undertaking there oughtn't to be abandoned—to set against these things. It *is a long, long change for you* & as that, even as that alone, it seems to me you would do well to hold on to it. It is a chance, an opportunity, which may not come to you again for years. All this came over me much as this morning I went out to poor nudified & staring Cambridge & thought that *that* & your life there is what you are in such a hurry to get back to! At furthest you will take up that life soon enough—*interpose* therefore as much as you can before that day—

continue to interpose the Europe that you are already in possession of.   Do this even at the cost of sacrifices.   You thought it well to make a great point of going there, & you were surely not altogether wrong.   You don't know when it will be possible for you to go again— therefore don't drop the occasion from your grasp.   Even if you don't do your psychology, you will do something else that it is good (being there & with strong reasons at any rate against your return) to do; & you will escape the depressing effect of seeing yourself (& being seen by others) simply *retomber* here, to domestic worries & interruptions & into circumstances from which you had undertaken to abstract your-self.   It seems to Alice of course (as well as to me) that your idea of going to live in some other house (i.e. take a room somewhere in Garden St.) would give a dreary & tragic completeness to such a col-lapse & have the air of your having committed yourselves to incon-stant & accidental (not to say shiftless) ways.   Therefore I say, stick to Europe till the summer, in spite of everything, in the faith that you are getting a great deal out of it & that it is a good & valuable thing.   My rooms shall you have for an *indefinite period,* without *the cost of a penny.*   After Feb 1ˢᵗ your circumstances will improve—the air will be much more fogless, the days longer, the light abundant. If you are lonely, I will send you as many introductions as you can desire.   Take the money that is necessary, for the reason that you are doing a thing that you will not do again for a long time.   As soon as the estate is settled you will begin to receive your share of the income from the houses in Syracuse, which (if the redivision takes place,) will then be owned by you, Wilky, Bob, & me; Alice's share residing wholly in the railway securities into which the money of the Quincy St. house was put.   These houses are of the value of \$75000, & Mr. Munroe writes a very favourable account of the property.   It yields *ten percent,* which however is reduced to *seven* by taxes, repairs & other expenses (his salary, which he has now begun to take.)   The houses in question are to be greatly improved by the creation, close to them, of the new public offices of the city—post-office, city hall, court house, &c. There is nothing to be done, that I know of, to delay the settlement of the estate after the re-distribution (to include Wilky) is made.   The more promptly therefore as well as the more definitely, I hear from you about this the sooner the whole business will be brought to a conclusion.   Of course on your assent being given to the re-division, a document, which we are all to sign, must be sent out to you; so that there will be delay to that extent.   My last three letters must have seemed to you very dry & sordid—especially the first, in which I enclosed you a copy of Father's Will; but the whole subject is one I have had to *aborder* without loss of time. I think it very possible that you wrote to Wilky after you had got that first letter of mine & if so, told him that you desired, in your degree, to make up to him for his having been excluded by Father. In this case you will have done what the rest of us have done. Don't judge that exclusion of Wilky harshly, as regards Father; *don't judge at all,* in fact, for the present. Eventually when you have been home & we have talked about it, & you know the circumstances, you will see it all in a just light. I wish to warn you once for all, in advance, most solemnly, against letting anything I may write to you, by accident or necessity, add in any degree to your restlessness, foster your anxiety or your homesickness or make you believe in the least that there is a reason for your being here. There is & can be no such reason, & it is only the agitation of sentiment (very natural, of course) that will make you feel so. I must close my letter, lest you think I say too much. Excuse me if I have been indiscreet or violent; I have only tried to translate the impression that is strong within me—the fear that after you should get back, finding yourself face to face with the long stretch of time which you would have to dispose of in uncomfortable ways before begining your college work next autumn, you would curse your folly in having let go of your simpler existence in Europe. Send postcards to the people (e.g. Miss Hilliard) who write to you, telling them that you can't answer them at length. Alice tells me that she has spoken to you of a plan of going out to you for the summer, to spend it in some quiet place in England. I think it would be feasible, for, as she says, you & she have no present home & you must arrange yourselves somewhere & somehow, from June to September. Ask Mrs Leslie Stephen about St. Ives, Cornwall, where she & her husband have a house & go every summer. I should think that would suit you—& you would have the Stephens' society. I told Alice I would write you a "strong" letter on the subject of your return; she gave her full assent, & you will probably think I have succeeded.—Aunt Kate who has been ten days in Newport, will by this time have returned to N.Y. Poor old Tweedy appears to be failing. Father's absence has become a natural fact—it seems (to me at least) as if he had been gone for a long time. But that comes of course partly from my own absence. I write this in the parlour, late in the evening, after Alice has gone to bed; Duveneck's picture, which is opposite to me, grows unexpect-

edly in value. It seems so odd that *he* should have translated, perpet-
uated Father! There has been a week of snowstorms, & the earth is
buried deep. Does the Athenaeum comfort you?

Ever your brother   H. James jr

P.S. Much as I have said I feel as I had not said enough: expressed
my sense of the (as it were) painful want of *form* there would be in
your coming back—a few weeks after Father's death—after having
been away at that time, & through all his illness—to live in a homeless & nondescript way in Cambridge, where you have ceded your
place—and where, for the time, you would be neither in the college
nor out of it. And I can't bear to see you *lâcher* Europe! Lastly, I
think it would be a great disappointment to your wife!—

[1] Eliza Gibbens.
[2] The house at 131 Mount Vernon St., Boston.

To Henry James

Bolton St. Jan 23 [1883]

My dear Harry,

On my return from a little dinner party at Hodgsons half an hour
ago, I found your long letter of the day of the "stay" telegram (Jan.
11) waiting for me. I shall owe you the price of that telegram, plus
I dont know what for literary work spent on me. It makes my heart
bleed that the relation of brother should entail such sacrifices. & I
know now just how one's half-crazy relations feel when they get letters
of good counsel. Your solicitude is natural enough, but it certainly
flows from a great misconception of all the premisses that are operative in the case,—it is true that you are not to blame for that, since
I alone can know them. In the first place, I hesitated long whether
to take my leave of absence at all; doubting whether anything material
was to be gained by it. What decided me was the Psychology alone.
Then I long doubted whether the better way would not be to finish
that in Cambridge, & not come away; & finally decided that the
chance of hygienic benefit & refreshment for me, & undisturbed possession of its mother by the baby, spoke in favor of departure. But
as far as the opinion of outsiders & their exclamations of "failure"
(which you seem so much to dread,) go, I took great pains to say to
every one that I did not think I could stay the winter, & I heard
many, President Eliot among the rest, echo that they should not think
I could, away from my wife. The horror you seem to feel at Cam-

bridge is something with which I have no sympathy, preferring it as I do to any place in the known world. Quite as little do I feel the infinite blessing of simply being in London, or in Europe ueberhaupt. The truth is, we each of us speak from the point of view of his own work; the place where a man's work is best done seems & ought to seem the place of places to him. I feel tempted to go back now just to show you how happy a man can be in the wretched circumstances that so distress your imagination. A room outside of my wife's house, with the privilege of seeing her twice a day, is luxury itself compared with *this* mode of being outside of her house. A quiet evening with sleep at ten, is heaven, to this obligatory Punchinello-existence every night in the week, a thing I never could stand at home & which threatens completely to undo my sleep here. Of course, feeling as I did about my possible return, it was a terrible practical mistake to have let my house to Toy. I did it in a moment of economic impulsiveness & hope, repented it loudly the next instant, and every instant afterwards,—last summer hardly less than now. But it is folly because you can't have everything to take nothing. If Cambridge out of my wife's house appears better for work & sleep than Europe, I ought to go there; even tho Cambridge *in* my wife's house would be better still. I have already gained much from Europe in the way of seeing philosophers & races of men; but all that is secondary to my main purpose. I have *apparently* gained nothing at this date in the way of health, but that can't be fully known till next winter when I shall see if I bear the year's strain better for this rest. I certainly believe, since I have *begun* the experiment, in prolonging it as long as possible, short of the point of absolutely losing the year, which would happen if if the non-psychologising weeks of hitherto extend into the future. I also believe in leaving Alice as long as possible to the baby undisturbed. When I decided on returning, a few weeks ago, things seemed less hopeful here than they do now. The stress of my correspondence is now over, not to be renewed. (To poor Miss Hillard I have not even sent the post-card you recommend). The last two days I have written some psychology; & since yesterday noon a dry east wind & cold air has made me feel like a different man,— I should not have supposed that change of weather could effect such a revolution. Dr. Ferreir told me last night he had never seen such weather as that of the last month for aggravating nervous diseases, all his patients, & himself, worse than they ever had been. Having a reader occasionally helps matters very much too, & I accordingly thought this morning it would be safe to write to Alice that it would not be neccessary for me to return on the 10th.   The fact is that although from a moral point of view your sympathy commands my warmest thanks; from the intellectual point of view, it seems first to suppose that I am a bachelor, & second that I am one who suffers intensely from the skinniness & aridity of America.   I should perhaps suffer were I not at work there, but as it is I dont; & being a married man, any place near *her* is a good bit better than any place where she is not.

If the Psychology only keeps on as it has now started, & more than all, if the air either of Paris or of an improved London,—they tell me that never in the memory of man has there been so uninterruptedly depressing a winter here,—starts up my eyes & sleep again, I certainly shall not think of coming home for a good many weeks to come.

I suppose you will be sorry to get so elaborate a self "vindication." I might have simply sent you a line of light reassurance.   But really there was something distressing about so painful a solicitude on your part, resulting from so imperfect an apprehension of the facts of my *status* in Cambridge.   There is not a man in the College who knows me, to whom my return now would not seem the most natural & proper of acts.   I should only have to make the best of the joke of having let my house to Toy, surely a very easy thing to do.   (24th A.M.)   I have half a mind to tear up this over solemn reply & write you a single page.   But I can't do any more writing on the subject. It was drawn from me in the first flush of indignation at being treated like a small child who didn't know what his own motives or interests were.   Your feeling evidently comes from comparing Cambridge at large with Europe at large, & then supposing that any given human being must be worse off in the one than in the other.   Whereas it all depends on which place the human being has *business* in.   I'm sure I've heard you complain enough of having to live where all your time went in futilities and your serious affairs went irreparably lost.   Your working power is about three times mine; & what is lost this year on my psychology can perhaps never, or not for 8 years to come, be made up.   *All* that I see & do here is futility compared to that.—I'm glad you intimate that the Syracuse property is not to be sold yet.   I must go out & see it, as soon as I return.   I'm especially glad that you give so encouraging an account of Alice.   Please give her my best love & with many thanks to yourself for your sympathy and trouble believe me always your loving bro.

Wm.

My Alice can tell you all about our doubts relative to Europe. Just the things we realized as dangers beforehand are what have come to pass,—and the remedy of return was always present to our minds<.> Of course if Syracuse is not to be sold, division by simple fifths is by far better than my proposal.

What is our Alices glove number   I'll send her some from Paris.

To Henry James

Bolton St. Feb. 6th 1883

My dear Harry,

Two letters from you, one from Syracuse, & the other of the 25th from Boston just after your return.   Your account of poor Wilky is pathetic enough; I hope the plan of his spending some weeks or months in Boston will prove a feasible one.   What you say of the Syracuse property is good to hear,—I had thought it might be a good thing to get rid of it, having heard nothing for years past but delays of rent, & taxes & repairs eating up so much of what came at last. You say you enjoyed the outpouring of my bile upon England: you will ere this have learned from my other letters that I see "the other side" as well.   They are a delectable brood, & only the slow consider-ings of a Goethe could do them plenary justice.   The great point about them seems their good-humour & *cheerfulness;* but their civiliza-tion is *stuffy.*   In spite of that, *it* is, & their whole nature is, one of the most exquisite *Kunstwerke* that the womb of time has ever brought forth.   It might have failed to ripen so smoothly, but fortune sec-onded them without a break, & they grew into the set of customs & traditions & balancing of rights that now rolls so elastically along.

However, I can't write a proper letter & must refer you to my bride for gossip.   Your allusions to my return, continue by their solemn tone to amuse me extremely.   Especially are the expressions "confes-sion of failure" & "appearance of vacillation" comical.   The only pos-sible "failure" would be to stay here longer than the refreshment, which was the only motive, either tacit or avowed, of my coming, lasted.   & there can be no appearance of vacillation where there was no plan announced beyond that of staying on from week to week as long as I found it to pay.   However, my reply to your first letter will have opened your eyes to all that; meanwhile the strength of your sympathy does equal credit to your head & heart.   For some reason

or other London does thoroughly disagree with me.   I am in a state
of acute brain-fag, although I've done a mere minimum of work.   I
am only staying out the week on account of a philosophical dinner
which takes place on Friday, this being Monday.[1]   I feel as if the darkness of your quarters must have something to do with it; & I can't
bear to think of you yourself being permanently here.   I'm sure any
man of your temperament needs the direct light of the sky, if not of
the sun, in his rooms, bed-room as well as sitting room.   I am glad
to hear from my wife that Alice is doing well. This letter is for her
as well as for you.   Give her lots of affection & sympathy, & believe
me ever yours,

Wm. James

How your letter writing must destroy you.   Don't feel any call to
write to me when inconvenient.   You know my Alice tells me everything, & will tell me any messages you send.

[1] Monday was 5 February 1883.   The dinner was that of an informal philosophical
group called the Scratch Eight, with Edmund Gurney, George Croom Robertson,
Frederick Pollock, Leslie Stephen, James Sully, Shadworth Hodgson, and Frederic
William Maitland (1850–1906), British legal historian, as members.   The talk WJ
gave that evening became "On Some Omissions of Introspective Psychology."

From Henry James

131 Mt. Vernon St. | Feb. 7th [1883]

Dear William.

I receive this a.m. your letter of Jan 23^{d} written on the receipt of
my letter (accompanying telegram) urging you to remain in Europe.
I quite expected that you would be irritated by my long argument
on the subject of your not coming home, & you may imagine how
much I wished to put it before you that I should have written to you
in the face of this conviction—& have also recurred to the matter
more than once in writing to you since—with touches which will have
revived your irritation.   Of course I didn't pretend or attempt to
treat of the reasons that presented themselves to you on behalf of
your coming back—for you could be amply trusted to look after these
yourself.   Such reasons there were, I know—but all I could afford
to do was to talk of the opposite ones.   It *did* seem a part of my
duty to put these latter before you as they presented themselves here,
especially as I saw that Alice was so full of them; & I even thought
you might after all be glad to know how your return would look—
superficially at least from the point of view of standing here.   I have

no doubt that you *have* been glad, since you wrote.　But all this is over & done with by this time, & I only write to acknowledge your letter though I wrote you yesterday　(Don't of course answer my letters any more than is absolutely necessary).　There has also come this a.m. your other note of Jan. 23$^{\underline{d}}$, making it all right about the equal re-division—which, if I had waited till to-day, would have spared me my letter of yesterday.—I enter fully into all your reasons for coming back, as set forth in your to-day's letter—but I *still* hope you will have gone to Paris, & will be better enough for the change to remain there some weeks.　I am bound to say, however, that I still don't see how in your lonely life in London (for though you speak now of seeing more people) you had written me at the time I telegraphed that your social solitude was complete, your time is not more your own than in Cambridge, surrounded by so many relatives, & so much family, all in so little room.　You speak of a "Punchinello-life" in the evenings—but I don't know what you mean by this—& you must allude to something quite different from the state you were in a month ago.　Different, & if you survive it, I venture to believe better!　I stick to the doctrine of the "skinniness" of Cambridge, even for you, enough to be sure that [there] is nothing Punchinello-like that may have happened to you in London, even at the cost of your sleep, that you will not be glad of after you get back here.　Let me add that so far from writing to you as a bachelor, my letter was the direct product of much talk with your wife about your return & much sympathy with the distress that the prospect caused her—distress I mean, on acct. of your homeless condition & the failure of your attempt.　Now, I shall be equally satisfied, whichever you do.　Don't use your eyes upon me, any more than simple business may require.

Ever your　H. James

From Henry James

131 Mt. Vernon St. | Feb. 11$^{\underline{th}}$ [1883]

Dear W$^{\underline{m}}$

I feel as if I ought to write to you again to-day on acct. of your letter of Jan. 22$^{\underline{d}}$ (just rec'd.) although I have written you so much of late.　My last, two or three days since, was a rather (perhaps) heated reply to the letter in which you acknowledge the arrival of mine (sent at the same time as the telegram) urging you not to return home.　If this has seemed to you nasty or ill-tempered, please don't mind it.   It *was* rather meddlesom in me to have so much to say about the question of your coming back—but I repeat that it was a case in which to meddle seemed the *safest* thing, & to trot out all the reasons against your return (leaving you to do justice to the others) seemed the only way to treat the subject from this side (if treated at all.)   I even persist in meddling, so far as to be glad that you have not yet come & that according to your last (of the 25th Jan.) to Alice you are probably now in Paris.   (Alice reads me & sends me everything possible.)   I write this with a clear understanding that you won't answer it, & that you will write to me after this as little, & as briefly, as possible.   This is only to return, very briefly on my side, to the question of the redivision of the estate with regard to Wilky, as to which I have already written you so much & to which you again return yourself, in this letter of Jan 22^{d} (I have just been for three days to Newport, & I find it on my return.)   I agree in all you say as to the *principle* of Father's holding Wilky responsible for the $5000 advanced to him before his failure, & I can only repeat that if the circumstances were now more favourable to our cutting down his allowance it should certainly be done. But they are as little so as possible.   I have now decided to assent to his *own* request to except $5000 from the amount I am to put into trust for him (*i.e.* the rest of his equal share,) to enable him to pay his debt to Bob & two or three other "debts of honour."   (His debt to Bob, it now appears, amounts, not as I told you last, to $1000 but to about $1500)   To cut off more than this would be rather grievous—& his state of mind & of health together are such that I shrink from carrying out such a plan. Just now both his children are ill with scarlet fever (it appears to be light) & in the midst of this addition to his other troubles I feel like letting him off easily.   You may think that I am rather weak about this; & I am, I admit.   But I put it all on the ground of Wilky's generally collapsed condition.   If it were a palpable injury to any of us, I should not urge my own project in preference to yours.   But as the difference between the two is so small, in favour of yourself, of Alice & of me, & as Bob moreover is to be paid in this way, as well as in yours, I think we had better abide by the fact that having Wilky equal with us & not insisting on the forfeit in order to justify Father, will be the thing which satisfies most of the proprieties of the case. The will was unfortunate, in its wholesale character, & the best way to justify Father is simply to assume that he expected us, (as he *did* expect us) to rearrange equally.   No need to go over all this though, as I believe that I said in my last, you will have assented to my way of doing the thing, before this reaches you.   What I have, after all, mainly wished to tell you is that I have judged it best *not* to forward him your letters recommending this modification of my proposal.   I shall let him suppose that you have simply assented to it, & shall leave it to your confidence that I am acting for the best as the circumstances appear to me here, to justify me.

Yours ever | H. James

Our Alice gets on very well.

In the spring of 1883, William James was using the "pendulum method of reaching a decision," to use a phrase from one of his wife's letters. When the caligraph worked, he was inclined to stay in London; when it needed tinkering, Cambridge appeared more suitable for writing the psychology. From the middle of February he was in Paris but was back in England in March. After suggesting in a letter to his wife that she meet him in New York City for a "spree," he sailed for America, reaching New York on 26 March. It is not clear whether Alice was there to meet him. In Cambridge he had nothing to do but spend his mornings in writing and studying, except for the chore of sending his photograph to his new European friends. He assumed the responsibility of looking after the family estate in Syracuse, keeping Henry James informed about profit, taxes, repairs, and prospects. Henry, who immediately after his father's death dropped the "junior" from his signature, returned to 3 Bolton Street in early September. A collected edition of his novels and tales in fourteen volumes was published in November.

Alice James spent several months in an asylum seeking a cure for her nervous disorder. She settled in at 131 Mount Vernon Street in November 1883. Robertson James, for a time reconciled with his wife, was in Milwaukee from where he reported to William that he was working five hours a day on his painting. The Milwaukee city directory for 1884 lists Robertson James, artist, living on the corner of 35th and State streets. He was the only member of the family present during Garth Wilkinson's last illness and subsequent death at age thirty-eight on 15 November 1883 from Bright's disease. The Milwaukee city directory for 1882 lists Garth Wilkinson James as a collector for the custom house, living at 473 Jefferson

Street. The 1883 directory lists him with no occupation. His death initiated another dispute over inheritance, not reflected in these selected letters. His widow and children, never close to the James family, became even more estranged from them after his death, continuing a process that began with his marriage to a woman whom the Jameses disliked.

From Henry James

3 Bolton St. W. | Nov. 24th [1883]

Dear William.

I return without delay Bob's letter enclosed to me this a.m. I rejoice in his apparently reasonable state of mind, & hope the trusteeship can be settled satisfactorily. It seems to me a hundred times better that you shldn't. be saddled with it. At the same time it must be also arranged that *you* do not have to send elaborate monthly reports—a burden under which you will perish if it be kept up. Never, I again beg you, take the trouble to tell ME anything at all about my Syracuse dividend. I have made my income entirely over to Alice & take no further interest in it.———A telegram from Carrie about poor Wilkie's blessed liberation came to me two hours before yours, which arrived at 2.30 a.m. I instantly wrote to Carrie, & afterwards to Alice, who will have forwarded you my letter. It is a great weight off my spirit—not to see him lying there in that interminable suffering. Meanwhile your letter comes to me, forwarding Carrie's & Bob's notes & speaking of the days before his death—just as they came to you here, last winter, after you had heard that Father had gone. You will, I hope, have had news to send me about his last hours. May they have been easy—I suppose they were unconscious. I like to think that somewhere in the mysterious infinite of the universe, Father & Mother may exist together as pure, individual spirits—& that poor Wilkie, lightened of all his woes, may come to them & tell them of us, their poor *empêtrés* children on earth.—This post brings me also a letter from Katherine Loring from which I gather, though she tries to dissimulate it, that on the whole, since I have been away, Alice has been pretty poorly. I try to hope, however, that now she is in her own house, independent & surrounded with her own arrangements, she may pull herself together, if she doesn't languish from loneliness. I am very sorry to hear of Miss Webb's condition—& fear it must make a sad house in Garden St. Much love to your Alice.—You will have rec'd. my letter expressing my anxious hope for an *early* execution of the division.

Ever your Henry

P.S.—As I must always worry about something, I worry now, as regards Wilkie, about his burial-place. It will be a great regret to me if he doesn't lie beside Father & Mother, where we must all lie.[1] I hope, at any rate, you have had no trouble—that is no discussion & no excessive correspondence or fatigue about it—& above all no expense. I have sent Carry £42, to contribute to Wilkie's funeral (& other last expenses.)

Yours ever | H.J.

[1] GWJ was buried in Milwaukee.

1884–1885

On 31 January 1884 Alice Gibbens James gave birth to a third son. The birth provoked a series of earnest letters from Henry James on the subject of naming children. The name finally chosen by Alice and William was Herman, in honor of a German friend.

Alice James, still seeking a cure, was in New York City in the spring of 1884, trying a new course of treatment involving electricity and exercise.

From Henry James

3 Bolton St W. | March 26ᵗʰ [1884]

My dear William.

I wrote to you a few days ago, but since then I have another missive from you; enclosing a couple of notes from A.K., & another one from Stickney about the La Farge portrait. I must let this pass, as I haven't £60 now to expend upon it—especially as I don't think it very valuable—as I recollect it;—though if I *could* I would buy it simply for the sake of auld lang syne. I enclose the £5 note I promised you the other day, to help you to meet the next demand from Josephine.[1] You can easily get it changed the next time you go into State St.—I confess, also to gladness that your helpless babe is not for the (possibly) 80 years of his life to be made a Tweedy!—a cruel little label to tie to him for all the long future. I don't like *Hagen* (it will eventually be pronounced Haygan & mistaken for the Irish Hagan) much better.[2] I hold in the matter of names to my dislike to the idea of giving children the *whole* names of others. If one wishes to name a babe after a friend it seems to me enough to give it the friends Christian name—e.g. Edmund or Hermann. If I wished to gratify certain friends, I shld. name my child after each of them, as they do abroad—Edmund Hermann Francis. The first would be name he would go by (I put the above in *any* order) & the two others would be dormant save when he signed his name in full—in legal documents &c. They would however always be a part of him. Hermann James strikes me as a very pretty name: Hermann H. James (that it will virtually be) as no name at all. The second[3] is so pretty that it is a pity to spoil it by the second. I repeat, too, that to give a child the *surname* of a strange family whom he has had had no contact with save the temporary relation of his progenitors to *one* member of it, is to saddle him with an awkward element of which he may easily feel the inanity in future years, especially if confronted with the family who rightfully bear it and who may view him with all kinds of obliquity. Such are my sentiments on the subject of infant nomenclature—crudely & hastily stated. I attach great importance to it—& think the appellation of a child cannot be too much considered: it affects his life forever! I confess that I breathe a sigh of relief that we are not to have a "Tweedy" among us (*Edmund* James I think a very nice name)—affiliated to all the rest of the Tweedy brood for upwards of a century after poor E.T. of Newport has descended to his rest. I rejoice too that *our* kind parents didn't make us (for the most part) William P., Henry W., & Robertson F. & urge you to follow their example!—The communications in regard to Alice in New York of course interest me much: & I have a letter from her by the same post as yours. She appears to have such a long road to travel that I sometimes lose courage for her—but she doesn't seem to lose it for herself, & so long as she isn't nervous I can think of her with some equanimity. I fear your wife returns slowly to active life. I embrace her tenderly.

Ever yours—Henry (P.) James

[1] Howard James was the husband of Josephine Worth James. According to family letters, at one time he was destitute and in an inebriate asylum; Josephine sometimes appealed to relatives for support.

[2] Why WJ would consider naming his son after Hagen is not clear, yet the coincidence of names leaves little doubt that they are thinking of Hermann Hagen.

[3] HJ meant 'first'.

From Henry James

3 Bolton St. W. | April 21ˢᵗ [1884]

Dear William

I receive a note from you of 9ᵗʰ, to which, though it doesn't demand any particular answer I will dash off a few lines of response before taking up the pen of imagination. You enclose an extract from a newspaper purporting to be an article of Matt. Arnold's about Chicago society, & seem to have believe[d] it is his! It doesn't, I must confess, appear to me even a good hoax—full of phrases ("intelligent gentleman," "cultured people," "owner of a large grocery-business,"

&c), which he is incapable of using.   Nor would he talk about "Chicago-society." It seems to me poor as a parody—& it marks the (geographical) gulf that separates Appian Way[1] from—Bolton St!— that this writer should have appeared to you to catch the tone in which a London man of M.A.'s stamp would express himself.   The thing, of course, never appeared in the P.M.G.[2] Excuse the invidious style of my acceptance of your offering.—I too am "excited" about the prospect of your getting into John Gray's house.[3] It is a charm- ing idea, but I shld. fear you would find it an expensive place to live in; as you would have to have a man for the grounds.—But I shall hear with great interest of the sequel.   As you don't dwell on the character of Aunt Kate's convalescence, besides saying it is slow, I suppose there is nothing particular to hope or fear in regard to it, & nothing to be done for the poor dear woman but to write to her when one can, which I do.—I got your enclosure of Bob's note, a few days since, with news of his curatorship.   I hope he may keep it & make it grow.   Have you any idea that he has himself this winter advanced in the practice of art?[4] As regards your child's name I am glad the appendage has not yet been fastened.   I am afraid *all* "selected" names appear to you "tawdry." If I had a child I would call him (very probably) *Roland!* "Roland James" is very good.   If this doesn't suit you—nor Godfrey, nor Gautier, nor any name of chivalry, take some- thing out of Shakspeare: a capital source to name a child from: Sebas- tian, Prosper, Valentine (I like Valentine though not sure I'd give it;) Adrian, *Lancelot,* Bernard, *Justin,* Benedick, or Benedict, *Bertram,* Conrad, Felix, Leonard, &c. Putting Hagen apart, I like *Herman.* But I don't exactly understand the obligation you seem to feel under to provide Dr. Hagen with a namesake—"because he was never in America"—& has failed to make the provision himself.[5] Did I tell you in my last that I spent at Easter nearly 3 days at the Durdans (Roseberys') with Gladstone, & only two or three others?[6] Haec olim meminisse juvabit,[7] I suppose; but in the present Gladstone's mind doesn't interest me much: it appears to have no preferences, to care equally for all subjects—which is tiresome!   Look in the *Academy* of April 19th for a notice of your last article in *Mind.*[8] I would send you the paper, were it not so difficult, & out-of-the-way (time-taking,) to buy.   I have attacked your two Mind articles, with admiration, but been defeated.[9] I can't give them just now the *necessary* time.   I lunched the other day with Arthur Balfour, & lunch tomorrow (else- where) to meet Pasteur, returning from the Edinburgh tricentenary.

I am anxious to hear your impression of Alice on her return from N.Y. Love to your own.

Ever, H. James

[1] WJ was then living at 15 Appian Way, Cambridge.

[2] *Pall Mall Gazette.*

[3] Until he established himself at 95 Irving St. in the fall of 1889, WJ made frequent plans for a permanent home. The plan to buy John Gray's house was not carried out.

[4] RJ was appointed curator of the Milwaukee Art Museum in March 1884. The museum was located in the rear of "Poposkey's" store.

[5] If the reference is to the Hagen who was teaching at Harvard, the remark about America cannot be taken literally.

[6] The Durdans is Lord Rosebery's residence at Epsom, used primarily for raising horses and for entertaining friends.

[7] From Virgil's *Aeneid,* 1:203.

[8] *The Academy: A Weekly Review of Literature, Science, and Art,* 19 April 1884, p. 278, commenting on WJ's "What Is an Emotion?" called it a "brilliant, dashing article," suggesting, however, that the author was more interested in literary effect than in a sober search for truth.

[9] WJ, "On Some Omissions of Introspective Psychology," *Mind* 9 (January 1884): 1–26; "What Is an Emotion?" *Mind* 9 (April 1884): 188–205; both reprinted in *EPs*.

A number of events and changes occurred in 1884. Henry James's literary projects included work on two major novels, **The Bostonians** *and* The Princess Casamassima, *both published in 1886 in book form after serialization. Alice James was planning a trip to England. She sailed on 1 November 1884, never to return to the United States. Robertson James had another rupture with his wife and was for a time in Cambridge, performing secretarial chores for his brother. Within several months, however, he had moved to Concord, Mass., where he established residence and was eventually joined by his wife and children. In the winter of 1884–85, William James was busy attending meetings and dealing with the correspondence of the American Society for Psychical Research, which was being organized at that time with William as its leading figure.*

To Henry James

Dictated

15 Appian Way | Cambridge | Oct 18th '84

Dear Harry,

Your letter of 5th was very welcome this A.M. I am glad you have had six weeks of the country which I think you must have sorely needed, and specially glad that you speak so hopefully, of your forthcoming novel. Osgood sent me yesterday your Tour in France and Three Cities in their usual spring back binding. I read part of the Tour in France in the Atlantic & shall reserve the book for next vacation. Of the "Tales" you already know my opinion[1] The last two are exquisite though of course they will be taken by people of both nationalities as *attacks*.

Things have moved rapidly since my last. You see Bob is my emanuensis. All we can say of him in his presence is that he seems in better condition than for a long time back & I should be tempted to say nothing else in his absence. You speak of Alice's prosperity abroad being contingent upon her willingness to be more sociable than heretofore. She has already turned over an entirely new leaf this summer in that way, as the record of her life will have shown you. There is nothing like neccessity to bring us out. If Alice only stays the first year I can hardly conceive of her not permanently preferring Europe to America. She can get many more comforts there for her money, and see just as many friends. However we must leave that all to her. The progressive simplification of my life by the loss of relatives outside the house is made up in part by the growth of the sweet children of whom the youngest is so far, decidedly the most of a success, a creature of imperturbable good nature & fatness.

Mr Munroe suddenly died a while ago in Syracuse with two months rent in his possession which he had kept back to pay taxes—but I imagine there will only be a slight delay in our extracting. If we can renew the two long leases, now falling in at $800 advance which I have asked the tenants & have no doubt of their accepting I shall be in no hurry to get a new agent, as the business is very simple and a biennial visit to Syracuse will cost at the outside $50 whereas an agent costs 400$ per annum. If we find inconvenience from correspondance &c we can get a resident Agent at any time.

You ask about fathers book.—My introduction will be about 120 pages, more than ½ of it being extracts   I worked hard at it for two or three weeks during the summer and felt as if I had never been as intimate with father before. The Book ought to [be] out by middle of November. I let Scudder have the little autobiography for the Atlantic.[2] I thought it would advertise somewhat the book and in this age of publication would on the whole be no sacrifice of dignity.—I trust you feel so likewise.

College work has begun never for me with so little strain. Only six hours a week so far, and subjects I have been over before I hope this will permit me to do something toward my psychology My working day is sadly short however,—do what I will with my eyes I cant get them to do any thing by lamplight without having to pay the piper for it afterwards & the hunger that arises in me for reading in the evening is sometimes most poignantly severe Our housekeeping is running very smoothly—the little house looking charming. Herbert Pratt spent two delightful evenings with us lately. Arthur King is expected at supper to night.

I am glad you have seen Paul Bourget. What was he doing at Dover. His essays de P.C. are a direfully disappointing book.[3] The man has so much ability as a writer and such perceptions that it seems a ten fold shame that he should be poisoned by the contemptible & pedantic Parisian ideal of materialism and of being scientific. How can men so deep in one way be so shallow in another, as if to turn living flesh & blood into abstract formula's were to be scientific St. Beuve's method of giving you the whole of an individual is far more scientific than this dissecting-out of his abstract essence, which turns out after all only a couple of his bones. What strikes me in all this side of Bourgets School is its essential debility—But this is enough for all 3 of us. I look eagerly forward to your a/c of Alice on the other side. Judging by my experience a winter in London will be bad for her.

Affect^{ly} yours Wm. James

[1] HJ, *A Little Tour in France* (Boston: James R. Osgood and Co., 1885); *Tales of Three Cities* (Boston: James R. Osgood and Co., 1884). The former appeared as *En Provence* in *Atlantic Monthly*, July 1883–May 1884 (vols. 52–53).

[2] Henry James, "Stephen Dewhurst's Autobiography," *Atlantic Monthly* 54 (November 1884): 649–62, reprinted in *The Literary Remains of the Late Henry James*.

[3] Paul Bourget, *Essais de psychologie contemporaine* (1883).

From Henry James

3 Bolton St. Piccadilly | Jan. 2ᵈ 1885.

Dear William.

I must give some response, however brief, to your letter of Dec. 21ˢᵗ, enclosing the project of your house & the long letter from R. Temple.   Three days ago, too, came the two copies of Father's (& your) book, which have given me great filial & fraternal joy.[1]   All I have had time to read as yet is the introduction—your part of which seems to me admirable, perfect.   It must have been very difficult to do, & you couldn't have done it better.   And how beautiful & extraordinarily individual (some of them magnificent) are the extracts from Father's writings which you have selected so happily.   It comes over me as I read them (more than ever before,) how intensely original & personal his whole system was, & how indispensable it is that those who go in for religion should take some heed of it.   I can't enter into it (much) myself—I can't be so theological, nor grant his extraordinary premises, nor through[2] myself into conceptions of heavens & hells, nor be sure that the keynote of nature is humanity &c.   But I can enjoy greatly the spirit, the feeling & the manner of the whole thing (full as this last is of things that *dis*please me too,) & feel really that poor Father, struggling so alone all his life, & so destitute of every worldly or literary ambition, was yet a great writer.   At any rate your task is beautifully & honourably done—may it be as great—or even half as great—a service as it deserves to be, to his memory!   The book came at a bad time for Alice, as she has had an upset which I will tell you of; but though she has been able to have it in her hand but for a moment it evidently gives her great pleasure.   She burst into tears when I gave it to her, exclaiming "how beautiful it is that William should have done it! isn't it, isn't it, beautiful?   And how good William is, how good, how good!"   And we talked of poor Father's fading away into silence & darkness, the waves of the world closing over this system which he tried to offer it, & of how we were touched by this act of yours which will (I am sure) do so much to rescue him from oblivion.   I have received no notice from Trübner of the arrival of the other volumes, & shall write to him in a day or two if I don't hear.[3]   But I am rather embarrassed as to what to do with so many—wishing only to dispose of them in a manner which will entail some prospect of decent consideration & courtesy.   I can give away five or six copies to persons who will probably have some attention & care for them (e.g. Fredk Harrison, Stopford Brooke,

Burne Jones, Mrs. Orr, &c.) But the newspapers & reviews are so gross & philistine & impenetrable, & stupid that I can scarcely think of any to which it isn't almost an act of untenderness to send it. But I will go into the matter with Trübner.—Alice's upset was a sudden illness on Sunday night last (this is Friday) which gave her great distress of *heart* &c, & made her think she was dying. I needn't go into the details of it as she is already much better, & will be quite so, probably, a fortnight hence. The thing was so strange & unaccountable in its nature that Garrod looked for some special & extraordinary cause, & found it (apparently to his complete satisfaction) in the fact that she had, [(]the last thing before going to bed,) with her maid's help, applied Galvanism (to relieve a headache) to the base of her neck, behind—top of her spine. He says she had struck the pneumo-gastric(?) nerve, & what she had induced was an *approach* to a paralytic stroke! He has seen just the same effect from the same cause, has treated her beautifully & she is now another creature. K. Loring came to her from Bournemouth on Tuesday, & will stay till the 5th or 6th. Of course she will never touch Galvanism, at least in that way, again; but never, surely, was a creature born to worse luck or more grievous accidents. She had been remarkably well for 10 days before this sudden catastrophe, out of a clear sky. Don't do more than allude to it in the lightest way, if you write, for by the time your letter comes it will belong quite to the past, and of course don't breathe the word *paralysis!* Garrod has now seen her several times, she likes him extremely & finds his thoroughness minuteness & general 1st rateness superior to anything (medical) she has ever known. He has not gratified her very much in her theory of *gout*, & thinks that her trouble in her legs comes from a functional weakness of the lower part of the spine which is perfectly treatable & not permanently dangerous. The treatment he was giving her had already helped her much when this accident occurred; but he regards the way in which she has already thrown off the attack (most serious) of Sunday night as a sign that there is in her condition nothing profoundly bad. I have had 2 talks with him, & he gives on the whole a distinctly favourable account of Alice. He says she has no organic malady of any kind, & that there is no reason why a person in so many respects so sound should not get very much better, & at last really well. He is a charming little old man, of a gentlemanly-Punchinello type, very polite & conscientious & Alice (fortunately) quite adores him!—I have read the letter from B.T. which you enclose & I return, & have received various very similar ones from him myself. He now begs *me*

to pay the $250 to get him out of prison, entreats me very hard &
even piteously. As he makes no acknowledgment of any kind of, &
no allusion to, the $35 including the $10 from you on my behalf, I
sent him in November, he is not encouraging, though possibly he
had not had time to receive these when he wrote. I am much perplexed, & at any rate find it impossible to hand out £50 to him on
the spot, as he appears to expect. It goes hard, when one has so
many poor relations, to give one's earnings to a being so degraded,
worthless & shameless. I have just sent a Xmas (or rather New
Year's) present to Carrie, & have all my 1st Jan. annual bills to pay;
But I will think of the matter (his definite appeal came only last
night) & answer him in two or three days. The project for your
house is charming—very big, it looks, & of a most pleasant type.
Love to all.

Ever yours   Henry

[1] *The Literary Remains of the Late Henry James.*

[2] A slip for 'throw'.

[3] No copies of the *Literary Remains* with a Trübner & Co. imprint are known, but it
was common practice for American publishers to use British publishers as agents and
send them copies for European distribution.

The first installment of The Bostonians *appeared in the* Century
Magazine *for February 1885, giving rise immediately to the outcry that in the character of Miss Birdseye, Henry James intended
to caricature Elizabeth Palmer Peabody, a respected New England
reformer and friend of the transcendentalists at Concord. Most
critics suspect the intensity of Henry's protest and believe that the
caricature, beginning with the name, was intentional.*

From Henry James

3 Bolton St. W. | Feb. 14th [1885]

Dear William

I am quite appalled by your note of the 2^{d}, in which you assault
me on the subject of my having painted a "portrait from life" of Miss
Peabody! I was in some measure prepared for it by Lowell's (as I
found the other day) taking for granted that she had been my
model, & an allusion to the same effect in a note from Aunt Kate.

Still, I didn't expect the charge to come from you. I hold that I have done nothing to deserve it, & think your tone on the subject singularly harsh & unfair. I care not a straw what people in general may say about Miss Birdseye—they can say nothing more idiotic & insulting than they have already said about all my books in which there has been any attempt to represent things or persons in America; but I should be very sorry—in fact deadly sick, or fatally ill—if I thought Miss Peabody *herself* supposed I intended to represent her. I absolutely had no shadow of such an intention. I have not seen Miss Peabody for 20 years, I never had but the most casual observation of her, I didn't know whether she was alive or dead, & she was not in the smallest degree my starting point or example. Miss Birdseye was evolved entirely from my moral consciousness, like every person I have ever drawn, & originated in my desire to make a figure who should embody in a sympathetic, pathetic, picturesque & at the same time grotesque way, the humanitary & *ci-devant* transcendental tendencies which I thought it highly probable I should be accused of treating in a contemptuous manner in so far as they were otherwise represented in the tale. I wished to make this figure a woman, because so it would be more touching, & an old, weary battered & simple-minded woman because that deepened the same effect. I elaborated her in my mind's eye—& after I had got going reminded myself that my creation would perhaps be identified with Miss Peabody—*that* I freely admit. So I bore in mind the need of being careful, at the same time that I didn't see what I could do but go my way, according to my own fancy, and make my image as living as I saw it. The one definite thing about which I had a scruple was some touch about Miss Birdseye's spectacles—I remembered that Miss P.'s were always in the wrong place; but I didn't see, really, why I should deprive myself of an effect (as regards this point,) which is common to a thousand old people. So I thought no more about Miss Peabody *at all*, but simply strove to realize my vision. If I have made my old woman *live* it is my misfortune, & the thing is doubtless a rendering—a vivid rendering, of my idea. If it is at the same time a rendering of Miss Peabody I am absolutely irresponsible—& extremely sorry for the accident. If there is any chance of its being represented to *her* that I have undertaken to reproduce her in a novel I will immediately write to her, in the most respectful manner, to say that I have done nothing of the kind, that an old survivor of the New England Reform period was an indispensable personage in my story, that my paucity of data & not my repletion is the faulty side of the whole picture, that, as I went, I had no sight or thought of her, but only of an imaginary figure which was much nearer to me, and that in short I have the vanity to claim that Miss Birdseye is a creation. You may think I protest too much: but I am alarmed by the sentence in your letter "—It is really a pretty bad business," & haunted by the idea that this may apply to some rumour you have heard of Miss Peabody's feeling *atteinte*. I can imagine no other reason why you should call the picture of Miss Birdseye a "bad business" or indeed any business at all. I would write to Miss P. on the chance—only I don't like to *assume* that she feels touched, when it is possible that she may not, & know nothing about the matter. If you can ascertain whether or no she does & will let me know, I will, should there be need or fitness, immediately write to her.   Miss Birdseye is a subordinate figure in the *Bostonians*, & after appearing in the 1$^{\underline{st}}$ & 2$^{\underline{d}}$ numbers, vanishes till toward the end, when she re-enters, briefly, & pathetically & honourably dies. But though subordinate, she is I think, the best figure in the book, she is treated with respect throughout, & every virtue of heroism & disinterestedness is attributed to her. She is represented as the embodiment of pure the purest philanthropy. The story is, I think, the best fiction I have written, & I expected you, if you said any thing about it, would intimate that you thought as much—so that I find this charge on the subject of Miss P. a very cold douche indeed.———

I shall be very willing to let little Howard James have $25, to be taken by you out the money you say you owe me—by which I think you mean the money you had *prélevé* (or borrowed) from my share of the Syracuse rents to pay for Father's book (that is, for your half of the costs.)   In writing to B. Temple to tell him I withheld the $100, I enclosed him a ten dollar greenback.———About Alice I have written to AK. two or three times quite lately, & there ought to be an agreement between you that she always forwards you my notes.   I sent her a word this a.m. with a very short note of Alice's, & one of K. Loring's, both just received by me from Bournemouth enclosed. Alice is evidently now rather stationary, but not *bad*. She has been a month at Bournemouth but has not yet left her room.   Her *legs* seem always a serious question.   K. Loring & Louisa will probably remain at B. till the end of April, & then go elsewhere. I shall then go to Alice, who, however, may subsequently rejoin the Lorings in the place they go to.   They spend the summer in Europe.   I don't think the climate has anything at all to do with Alice's state. She isn't in the least in touch with it, always in doors, with the same profuse fires, never reached by the outer air.   I am sorry—very—for your botherations about your house.

Ever yours   H. James.

From Henry James

3 Bolton St. W. | Feb. 15$\underline{th}$ [1885]

Dear William.

Let me say as a p.s. to my letter of yesterday that I was wrong in telling you to take the $25 for Howard James from the Syracuse money you owe me, as I have assigned this as you know altogether to Alice, to whom of course you continue to pay it, & I want it to go to her intact.   She appears scarcely to touch it, & her idea is to "save it up" for me, but I wish her to have it, all the same.   The subtraction of the money to pay for my ½ of Father's book was an exceptional case, arranged between us.   Therefore I will send you one of these very next days a postal order or a £5 note, for the $25.   To day is a Sunday, & I can do nothing.———I have been thinking over the rest of my novel, in relation to Miss Birdseye, & it seems to me that even if Miss Peabody *should* think I meant to portray her (which, however, heaven forfend!) she cannot on the whole feel that what I had in mind is not something very fine & is not tenderly & sympathetically expressed.   The later apparition & death of Miss B. is the prettiest thing in the book, & even should it be resentfully insisted that the picture is a portrait (I am told, on all sides, here, that my *Author of Beltraffio* is a living & scandalous portrait of J. A. Symonds & his wife, whom I have never seen)[1] I believe the story will remain longer than poor Miss P.'s name or fame, & I don't hold that it will be an obloquy or ground of complaint for her, to be handed down as having suggested anything so touching & striking.   In a word, after you have read the book I don't think it will seem to you any more wounding for her to be known as Miss Birdseye than to be known as Miss P. But probably, later, if the episode *does* strike people as I think it will, they will deny *then* that I *did* have Miss P. in my mind or that they ever said so; they will never give me the credit of having wished to represent her gracefully!—As I told you yesterday I never wished or attempted to represent her *at all,* or dreamed of it, & to be accused of doing so is a poor reward for having laboriously bodied forth out of the vague of imagination, & with absolute independence of any model that my own wits did not afford me, a creature who is (as I think) interesting & picturesque.   If you think it so bad a business now, perhaps you will think that the sequel does *not* better it—but I can do nothing more than I have done, at this last hour—except, as I say, write a letter of absolute protest to Miss Peabody.—You don't tell me whether you had any rejoinder from Godkin to the letter you wrote about the review of your book.[2]   When I had read the article it was absolutely impossible for me not to write to him on my own account, & as I told him that the notice was "contemptible, &, under the circumstances, barbarous," he may see fit to terminate our acquaintance.   Melancholy, after 20 years!

Ever yours | H. James

[1] HJ, "The Author of Beltraffio" (1884), reprinted in *The Author of Beltraffio* (1885). The story concerns an author whose wife, detesting his writings and fearing his influence upon their son, allows the child to die.

[2] WJ wrote Godkin on 16 January 1885 protesting what he viewed as an unfair review of the *Literary Remains* in the *Nation* 40 (15 January 1885): 60–61.

On 2 May 1885 James Ripley Osgood, to whom Henry James had sold the copyright of The Bostonians, *notified his creditors that Osgood & Co. was unable to meet its obligations. Reading the news in the London newspapers, Henry immediately started looking for ways to salvage something of the £1,000 Osgood owed him. Henry had sold both serial and book rights to Osgood, who in turn had sold the serial rights to the* Century Magazine. *In the end, Osgood's liabilities and assets were taken over by the new firm of Ticknor & Co. Henry regained the copyright of* The Bostonians *and sold it to Macmillan who eventually published the book.*

To Henry James

Cambr. Thursday May 21 '85

Dear H.   Your letter about Osgood's failure arrived Sunday A.M.   I waited till the meeting of the creditors should have taken place, on Tuesday, & on Wednesday went to see Osgood, who informed me that Warner had already been entrusted by you with your interests. I did n't succeed in seeing him finally till this A.M., hence my delay. He will have explained to you the status.   It's a godsend you've still got your own end of the story to hang on to—as that practically puts the game into your own hands. Your alternative seems to be, 1) to get Osgood to cancel the agreement, in which case you lose apparently all proceeds from him & gain only such as you may extort from the Century for the end of the novel, leaving them to sue him for damages, and owning your own copyright; or 2) to extort etc from them *without* cancelling, and still get your 50 cents on the dollar or whatever Osgood pays if he is put through bankruptcy. In either case you ought not to lose. I should think the latter course would be the more dignified on the whole. I doubt whether Osgood will be willing to cancel. He said he hoped the creditors would allow them to continue business, but I imagine they will not. At the meeting on Tuesday the committee of them cut down the firm's estimate of its assets from about $270,000 to $100,000 dollars. Its indebtedness is about $220,000. Osgood said yours was the hardest case of all, and seemed to feel pretty badly about it. Your various copyright contracts revert to you if arrears are not paid in full, and Osgood cannot sell his right in them to anyone who does not pay you all arrears. The money due by you to the firm for copies furnished to you is not put into the general pot of "assets" but counted as an offset to their indebtedness on your special account. Altogether you will probably lose little, if anything, and will be only inconvenienced by delay. How great that inconvenience may be I dont know. Osgood said that if they were allowed to go on, payments would begin in a couple of months. I will gladly lend you anything you want. I owe you, as it is, $128.50 advanced on father's book. I am not likely to lose more than 25 dollars of what they owe me on that. Aunt Kate insisted on paying $150.00 of the publication expenses. I will send you the $128.00 to morrow, & am glad to get the debt off my hands so quickly.

Very glad Alice is begining to look up again. God bless you both! Very busy. Haven't read last number of Bostonians.

W.J.

Bob is in Petersham—rather doleful.

In February 1885 the Harvard authorities approved William James's appointment as professor of philosophy. For the coming academic year he had to prepare a new course of an introduction to philosophy that included a segment on formal logic, a subject that he claimed to detest. He was also to repeat a course on British philosophy and an advanced course of experimental research in psychology. Most Harvard courses at that time lasted the full year.

The summer of 1885 was a time of confusion for the Jameses. According to William, it was during that summer that he came to understand the ferocity of the "summer problem." Two servants left them unexpectedly. William was called suddenly to Syracuse, where he discovered that repairs to the James property would cost $2,500. His mother-in-law went to Europe for reasons of health, and he and Alice and the children moved from 15 Appian Way to the Gibbens house at 18 Garden Street. With Alice still recovering from six weeks of scarlet fever, William was forced to spend the summer vacation in New Hampshire looking after the two older boys with the help of his sister-in-law. The youngest son, Herman, was sick with whooping cough and was left behind. When Herman's condition worsened in late June, James returned to Cambridge. Herman died on 9 July 1885.

To Henry James

Cambridge, July 11. 85

Dear Harry,

Your letter from Bolton St. of the 28th ult. has just arrived as I was about to write to you to tell you of the painful death of the flower of our little flock, Herman, night before last.   Whooping cough, complication with broncho-pneumonia of a very severe sort, and finally four separate attacks of convulsions closed his little career, in which never till the last fortnight or so had he excited in us a moment of solicitude, he seemed so uncommonly hearty and strong and able to take care of himself, now & hereafter.   A fortnight ago his case began to look alarming,—nine days ago he had his first convulsions, since then he has just walked a tight rope, ready to fall off on either side, and surprising the doctors at each successive visit that he should be still alive.   He was a broad generous patient little nature; and as I now look back it seems to me as if I had hardly known him or seen him at all—I left him so to his mother, thinking he would *keep*.   We buried him three or four hours ago under the little pine tree at the corner of the ancestral lot, with a space between him and father's side, and our little family circle now seems remarkably contracted and bare. The great part of it to me has been the spectacle of Alice through it all. The old word Motherhood, like so many other old words, suddenly gets and unsuspected meaning. For six weeks not a night of adequate sleep—for 9 days & nights never as much as three hours in the whole 24, and yet every day as fresh and passionate and eager to do and work as if it were the first. Of course there will now be a collapse. But she is so essentially mellow & free from morbidness, that with all her sensibility, I fear nothing bad. Well, *finis* for little Humster, whom nobody will ever know but ourselves.

I am excessively glad to hear better news from Alice, and especially of the cottage being got.[1] The change, & Katherine's presence, will, I hope accelerate recuperation. I may be wrong about the bracing air business, but as soon as she *can* move again I think the experiment should be tried in a distinct way. I judge from my own experience in that matter—which may not prove hers, but the probability is that it will. What a spirit she shows—it is hard to believe, with the weeks and months so full of varied life for us, that that for her they can have been so monotonous and unrelieved.

Our furniture is almost all moved into the Gibbens house, and much of Mrs. G.'s is stored. Alice and I will go away in a day or two to Jaffrey N.H. where Margaret G. has been keeping little Billy, but the high air seems to disagree with him so we shall have to cast about for some other resort for 6 weeks. Bob keeps quiet at Petersham— but I'm afraid it is the old ornière, with an explosion at the end of it. He can't keep in the middle path. It is either desoeuvrement & seclusion, or a violent plunge into excitement.—As for what you say about pay[ing] Bob's share of the Syracuse repairs with your money, it is quite unneccessary. He would never consent, and 'tis best he should pay himself out of his surplus. He seems to be the only one of the family whose income exceeds his needs, and paying surplus into Syracuse is better that getting rid of it by the hundred at a time in a spree as soon as it begins to accumulate. As for the £200 I sent you, don't trouble yourself at all about it till your coffers overflow. It is no inconvenience *whatever* to me—being part of my capital that lies in Higginson's hands. I will retain your rents from Syracuse until your share is paid. But as the bills will be due before the sum is made up by rents I shall probably have to raise some money also, which I can easily do, and which you can repay when you come into funds again. As I wrote, we shall probably owe something like $700 apiece, and as you and I between us advance Bob's share, *we* shall need a thousand in cash apiece.   He consents to the arrangement and in less than two years will have paid up.

I write very little to Alice directly, not because I forget her or don't feel like it, but because I don't know how she is about letters now.

Ever affect^{ly}. yours | Wm. James

She will see this or as much of it as K. deems best.

¹AJ and Katharine Loring rented a cottage at Hampstead Heath for the summer of 1885. At the time AJ was unable to walk and was wheeled about in a "bath chair" by Katharine.

From Henry James

3 Bolton St. W | July 24th [1885]

Dearest William.

Your letter has just come, with the news of your dear little boy's death.   I had begun to fear some such news, as you had been silent for some time, following the tidings of the first appearance of the whooping cough.   You have my full sympathy, & above all Alice has it—in the loss of a little tender innocent clinging belonging like that. Poor little mortal, with his small toddling promenade here below, one wonders whence he came & whither he is gone.   But babies are soft memories & Alice will always throb to the vision of his little being. Give my very affectionate love to her, & tell her how much I hope she is rested & refreshed now—with recovered sleep & contact with her other children.   I am very sorry to be able to have come no nearer to the little Herman than to see his small earthly mound nestling near father's.   But that I shall some day see.   Requiescat!—I wrote to A.K directly after Alice's successful move on the 13th ult.   It was effected much more easily than I feared, & for a day or two afterwards she seemed to have borne it very well.   Then came a big collapse, which, however, was brief & not at all excessive, & from which (save that her *legs* seem absolutely lifeless,) she has already almost entirely emerged.   The state of her legs varies, & they will probably soon be again at the point they were when she left Bournemouth—permitting her to walk about her room for several minutes at a time.   They fluctuate & recuperate.   The cottage at Hampstead is exceedingly diminutive—but she & Katherine fit into it & it is very salubrious & *gay*.   You appear to underestimate the quality of the Hampstead air.   The heath to which Alice is close, or *on*, is only

40 feet lower than Malvern, & the atmosphere is exceedingly fresh & tonic. It is thought the most bracing air in this part of England & people come to it from a distance. What Alice needs is to *take* it, to breathe it, such as it is, & to get out of the close sick room, with windows forever shut & fire, on the hottest days, forever burning, in which she has been immured for so many months. This she will probably do during the next month.—My transaction with Osgood's successor has dragged out long, partly through a delay, at the last, of my own; but before you get this he will to all appearance have paid over $4000 to Warner for me. I have instructed Warner immediately, to take $1000 out of this & repay it to you: so that I trust the whole business will have been settled by August 1ˢᵗ.

I shall soon have straightened out completely as regards money, & am now in a position to promise to pay $1000 for the Syracuse building before the bills are due (unless they are to be due unnaturally soon: That is I can easily pay the money by Jan. 1ˢᵗ.) *Therefore,* as this is a perfectly definite engagement, I would rather you did not keep back my share of the rents—but go on paying it to Alice. When I told you to do this I did not clearly understand that $1000 was the maximum I should have to contribute, even covering the advance to Bob. I thought the sum wd. be larger. This sum I now see I can pay out of current income from other sources; &, I repeat, hereby engage to do so if you will, when you next write, tell me the earliest moment at which you will have to settle for the repairs. I could do it *before* January 1ˢᵗ. In this case count upon me for the money & continue to pay my rents to Alice. I shall probably go on August 1ˢᵗ to Dover, for that month, to my rooms of last summer, & to such peace & control of one's time as one can simply *never* get in London.

I read in the papers here of long & intense heat in the U.S., & fear you have been much roasted. I hope at any rate you are now in some cool & calm country. I embrace you both, & Alice twice over, & am ever yours

Hy. James

Other members of the James family were also experiencing a summer of difficulties and confusion. Robertson James, who was still living in Concord, was increasingly a problem. Fearing that he would either sell or squander away his property, William arranged that he and Joseph Warner become Robertson's trustees. Although he thought that Robertson was producing some fine paintings, William's accounts of Robertson during this period are pessimistic. In his view his brother was deteriorating mentally and morally because he lived in constant excitement and had no regular occupation. William thought that a divorce from Mary would simplify Robertson's life. In England, Alice James faced the problem of finding a more permanent residence. In the fall of 1885 she and Katharine Loring moved to 7 Bolton Row, five minutes away from Henry James in Bolton Street.

From Henry James

29 Rue Cambon. | Oct. 9ᵗʰ 1885

Dear William.

This must be a very short effusion, mainly to enclose you another draft of $250, & to thank you for 2 letters, both received during the month that I have been spending in Paris. The 1ˢᵗ was from Cambridge & was about Bob's having made you his trustee &c; the 2ᵈ from Keene Valley—acknowledging my former draft, the power of attorney &c, & containing several pages of advice & warning *àpropos* of the "Bostonians."[1] For these last I thank you heartily & think it very nice of you to have taken the trouble to write them. I concur absolutely in all you say, & am more conscious than any reader can be of the redundancy of the book in the way of descriptive psychology &c. There is far too much of the sort of thing you animadvert upon—though there is in the public mind at the same time a truly ignoble levity & puerility & aversion to any attempt on the part of a novelist to establish his people solidly. All the same I have overdone it—for reasons I won't take time to explain   It would have been much less the case if I had ever seen a proof of the *Bostonians;* but not a page have I had before me till the magazine was out. It is the same with the *Princess Casamassima;* though that story will be found probably less tedious, owing to my having made to myself all the reflections your letter contains, several months ago, & never ceased to make them since. The *Princess* will, I trust, appear more "popular." I fear the *Bostonians* will be, as a finished work, a fiasco, as not a word, echo or comment on the serial (save your remarks,) have come to me (since the row about the 1ˢᵗ 2 numbers) from any quarter whatever. This deathly silence seems to indicate that it has fallen flat.

I hoped much of it, & shall be disappointed—having got no money for it I hoped for a little glory. (What do you mean, by the way by saying—"now that I am to lose nothing by Osgood!" I lose every penny—not a stiver shall I have had for the serial, for which he received a large sum from the *Century*.) But how can one murmur at one's success not being what one would like when one thinks of the pathetic, tragic ineffectualness of poor Father's lifelong effort, & the silence & oblivion that seems to have swallowed it up? Not a person to whom I sent a copy of your book, in London, has given me a sign or sound in consequence, & not a periodical appears to have taken the smallest notice of it. It is terribly touching &—when I think of the evolution of his productions & ideas, fills me with tears. Edmund Gurney spoke to me with extreme enthusiasm of your preface, but said he considered it dispensed him from reading the rest.—I have been all this month (from Sept 10th,) in a perfectly empty, & very dull & provincial Paris, which however I have enjoyed very much. I have had my time to myself, worked, gone to the theatre &c. I shall stay another 2 or 3 weeks, as some of my friends are coming back—including Bourget, who, to my great regret, has been wholly absent. The Bootts come next week. I can't give you any impressions of Paris—partly because they aren't much worth it, & partly because I must catch the train to go & dine at Versailles with poor Charlotte King. Alice is settled at 7 Bolton Row, & Katherine will *probably* be with her another month. I won't write about her now—I shall be sure to do it so much, later. Thank your wife for a sweet note, acknowledging my photographs. I am delighted that Keene Valley poured so much satisfaction into you. May it remain. I tremble to ask about Bob.

Ever, in haste, your affectionate   Henry.

[1] The pages of WJ's letter of 17 September 1885 containing advice about *The Bostonians* are lost and their content can only be guessed at.

To Henry James

Cambr. Oct. 23 85

My dear Harry

Your letter from Paris in reply to my "strictures" on the Bostonians showed you in such an attitude of angelic humility that I wished I had ne'er been born rather than have written such things. The best advice I can give you as an author, and the last I shall now ever give you, is to imitate your own method in your shorter stories, and in the American & Roderick H.[1] No better models are possible. I see in a list of subjects *excluded* from "forensics" during this current year the following: "Critical estimate of the writings of Henry James."[2] The exclusion must come from the business being overdone. I wish you could see some of those past forensics!—You say no notice has been taken of fathers book. *Doch!* in the Spectator, one of the last September numbers or 1st October ones, I think, was a page-long article, respectful enough, but completely common place, and not worth looking up.[3]

I thank you for the $250 check, and trust you will not feel pressed for the remainder. It makes little or no difference to me now when that is paid. I have been executing the mortgage papers in your name to day and by the middle of next week these tedious repairs will be all paid for & the accounts squared & balanced.

The only news is Jim Putnam's engagement to Miss Marion Cabot,[4] 2nd cousin to Lilla Perry. Alice will be amused. She is plain, very good humoured & intelligent, and might just as well be his sister, exactly the same type. He ought to have run off with a ballet girl.

Bob & Mary seem to get on swimmingly so far. She has prevailed on him to join a painting class in Boston instead of keeping by himself, and they will live at Concord—until the next explosion!

I long to hear all about Alice. Write soon & let me know. A.K. has got letters from Katherine but has not sent them, as she usually does.

Much love & good wishes. Wm James

[1] HJ, *The American* (1877); *Roderick Hudson* (1875).

[2] Harvard juniors and seniors were required to take "forensics," courses in which they had to write argumentative papers on topics selected from a list supplied by the instructor.

[3] The review of *Literary Remains* in *Spectator* 58 (19 September 1885): 1237–39 was favorable in tone but did mention Henry James's "mystical and unsound theology."

[4] James Jackson Putnam married Marion Cabot (1857–1932) on 15 February 1886.

1886

Omitted from the present selection is Henry James's letter of 9 March 1886 in which he announced his move to his "chaste & secluded Kensington quatrième" at 34 De Vere Gardens. His enjoyment of his new lodgings was great: the rooms were "very pretty," "flooded with light," and there were many new furnishings to fuss about. While Henry was visiting Robert Louis Stevenson at Bournemouth in February, a riot broke out at Trafalgar Square. Had he been at home in Bolton Street, Henry could have seen the "roughs & thieves" from his balcony. It was his view that the real unemployed took little part in the rioting and looting; rather, it was others who seized the opportunity for a "day of license." In his letter of 9 May, William, in turn, comments on the labor problems in America, writing to Henry that the "anarchist" Haymarket Riot in Chicago was the work of "a lot of pathological germans & poles."

Henry makes extensive observations in the letter of 9 March on the conditions in his ancestral Ireland, a country populated by a "poor lot, with great intrinsic sources of weakness." He favored limited home rule but opposed the "disruption of the British Empire."

Giving William news of their sister, Henry remarks that in spite of the weather that kept her indoors and contributed to the weakness in her legs Alice was going through one of her better periods, maintaining a "saloon" and receiving many visitors. She was determined to spend the summer at Leamington, an English watering place, and was hoping that Katharine Loring would return to help with the move.

To Henry James

Cambr. May 9. 86 | Sunday A.M.

My dear Harry,

I seize my pen the first leisure moment I have had for a week to tell you that I have read the Bostonians in the full flamingness of its bulk, and consider it an exquisite production. My growling letter was written to you before the end of Book I had appeared in the atlantic;[1] and the suspense of narrative in that region, to let the relation of Olive and Verena grow,[2] was enlarged by the vacant months between the numbers of the magazine, so that it seemed to me so slow a thing had ne'er been writ.   Never again shall I attack one of your novels in the magazine.   I've only read one number of the princess Casamassima—tho' I hear all the people about me saying it is the best thing you've done yet.   To return to the Bostonians, the two last books are simply sweet.   There is n't a hair wrong in Verena, you've made her neither too little nor too much—but absolutely *liebenswürdig.*   It would have been so easy to spoil her picture by some little excess or false note.   Her moral situation,—between Woman's rights' and Ransom,—is of course deep and her discovery of the truth on the Central Park day etc inimitably given.[3]   Ransom's character which at first did not become alive to me, does so, handsomely, at last. In Washington, Hay told me that Secretary Lamar was delighted with it, Hay himself ditto, but especially with Casamassima.   I enclose a sheet from a letter of Gurney's but just received.[4]   You see how seriously he takes it.   And I suppose he's right from a profoundly serious point of view—i.e. he would be right if the characters were real— but as the story stands, I don't feel his objection.   The *fancy* is more tickled by R.'s victory being complete.   I hear very little said of the book and I imagine it is being less read than its predecessors.   The truth about it, combining what I said in my previous letter with what I had just now written, seems to be this, that it is superlatively well done, provided one admit that method of doing such a thing at all. Really the *datum* seems to me to belong rather to the region of fancy, but the treatment to that of the most elaborate realism.   One can easily imagine the story cut out and made into a bright short sparkling thing of a hundred pages, which would have been an absolute success.   But you have worked it up by dint of descriptions and psychologic commentaries into near 500,—charmingly done for those who have the leisure and the peculiar mood to enjoy that amount of miniature work,—but perilously near to turning away the great majority of readers who crave more matter & less art.[5]   I can truly say however that as I have lain on my back after dinner each day for ten days past reading it to myself my enjoyment has been complete.   I imagine that inhabitants of other parts of the country have read it more than natives of these parts.   They have bought it for the sake of the information.   The way you have touched off the bits of american nature, central park, the cape, etc, is exquisitely true & calls up just the feeling. Knowing you had done such a good thing makes the meekness of your reply to me last summer all the more wonderful.

I cannot write more—being much overloaded and in bad condition. The spring is opening deliciously—all the trees half out, and the white bright afternoon east winds beginning. Our household is well. Poor Richardson, as you will have heard, is gone just as he had reached complete consciousness of his purposes and possession of his powers, a most real loss to the country, I can hardly imagine a greater in the purely intellectual way—Gurney is quite broken down.[6] Edward Hooper ditto and goes abroad this month. I gave poor Geo. P. Bradford Alices address the other day. Henry Adams goes to Japan.[7]

Your letter about father's portrait etc, Alice, & your lodgings, duly arrived a couple of weeks since. Give my best love to Alice and show her this. I hope her summer problem will somehow straighten out and that it may be through Katherine's ability to be with her. I will send you the chest weights soon, they are getting out an improvement in them, and the new ones are not quite ready yet.

I enclose a couple of bits of local colour. The photog. is the abode of Alice's Cousin Susie Webb who has been teaching indian girls for 3 or 4 years there and thoroughly enjoys it. When London palls upon your jaded and palsied heart turn to that photograph and think where your lot might be cast. The other clipping was sent me by the subject thereof, in a letter relating to some business.

Don't be alarmed about the labor troubles here. I am quite sure they are a most healthy phase of evolution, a little costly, but normal and sure to do lots of good to all hands in the end. I don't speak of the senseless "anarchist" riot in Chicago, which has nothing to do with knights of labor, but is the work of a lot of pathological germans & poles. I'm amused at the anti gladstonian capital which the english papers are telegraphed to be making of it. All the irish names are among the killed and wounded policemen. Almost every anarchist name is continental.[8]

Affect[ly], W.J.

[1] See letter of 9 October 1885, note 1.

[2] Olive Chancellor and Verena Tarrant are the major female characters in *The Bostonians*, and the novel revolves around the development of their friendship. Olive Chancellor is a feminist and perhaps a lesbian. Verena's hand is sought by Basil Ransom, who in the end persuades her to marry him.

[3] In chapter 34 of *The Bostonians*, Verena Tarrant and Basil Ransom spend several hours in Central Park in New York City discussing the woman question. Ransom

maintains that the business of women is to be pleasing to men.   Verena realizes that Ransom is on the wrong side and seeks comfort from Olive Chancellor, her feminist companion.

[4]A page is missing from Edmund Gurney's letter to WJ of 16 April 1886. Just before the missing page, Gurney wrote "Talking of books, what a joy."   Probably the missing page is the one that WJ sent to HJ.

[5]Shakespeare, *Hamlet,* act 2, sc. 2, line 95.

[6]Ephraim Whitman Gurney.

[7]Following the suicide of his wife, Marian (Clover) Hooper Adams, on 6 December 1885, Henry Adams spent the summer of 1886 in Japan.

[8]WJ is referring to the Haymarket Riot of 4 May 1886 in Chicago in which seven policemen and several strikers were killed.   Most of the anarchist leaders who addressed the rally were of German background.   Four of them were eventually hanged.

From Henry James

OSTERLEY PARK, | SOUTHALL, | W. June 13th 1886

Dear William.

As I have just written to Aunt Kate & asked her to forward you the letter it is bad economy, no doubt, to give you at the same moment, a letter for your self.   But on the other hand I have a moment of leisure & the sharp consciousness of having since I last gave you of my direct news heard copiously & liberally from you.   So I will just seize this fleeting occasion to thank you for your letter received I think nearly a month ago, on the subject of the *Bostonians.*   Everything you said in it gratified me extremely—& very superfluous was your retractation of what you wrote before (last autumn, while the thing was going on in the magazine & before you had more than dipped into it.)   I myself subscribe just as much to those strictures now as I did then—& find 'em very just.   All the middle part is too diffuse & insistent—far too describing & explaining & expatiating.   The whole thing is too long & dawdling.   This came from the fact (partly) that I had the sense of knowing terribly little about the kind of life I had attempted to describe—& felt a constant pressure to make the picture substantial by thinking it out—pencilling & "shading."   I was afraid of the reproach (having *seen* so little of the whole business treated of,) of being superficial & cheap—& in short I should have been much more rapid, & had a lighter hand, with a subject concerned with people & things of a nature more near to my experience.   Let me also say that if I have displeased people, as I hear, by calling the book the Bostonians—this was done wholly without invidious intention. I hadn't a dream of generalizing—but thought the title simple & handy, & meant only to designate Olive & Verena by it, as they appeared to the mind of Ransom, the southerner & outsider, looking at them from New York. I didnt even *mean* it to cover Miss Birdseye & the others; though it might very well. I shall write another: "The other Bostonians." However, this only by the way; for after one of my productions is finished & cast upon the waters it has, for me, quite sunk beneath the surface—I cease to care for it & transfer my interest to the one I am next trying to float. If Aunt Kate sends you the letter I have just written to her you will receive it almost as soon as you do this one. It will tell you that Katherine L. came over about three weeks ago (she has left Louisa at Ems, with W$^{\underline{m}}$ Loring & his wife,) & a few days later conveyed Alice to Leamington. Alice appears to have been greatly—too greatly, & somewhat disappointingly fatigued by the journey; but she is now emerging from this bad sequel—& at any rate has suffered *less* than from any similar effort she has made since she came to England. K.L. will stay with her 3 weeks longer, & very possibly come back to her later in the Summer. I have no doubt that during the next three months Alice will form *habits* of going out (in her chair) & that will be the beginning of a much better order of things. Katherine, who had not seen her for 7 months, finds her, in spite of the knock-up of the journey, wonderfully better.—I am spending this Whitsunday down at this fine old place, (close to London) of which Lord Jersey is the happy proprietor. Lowell is in the house, & a few others, of no particular importance. Lowell, who has returned to England on a visit, as a private individual, is no less happy than when he was here as Minister;[1] rather, indeed, I think, more so, as he has no cares nor responsibilities—& his "social position" is (bating precedence, as to which they let him off easily,) quite as good. They are making, in London, an extraordinary lion of Dr. Holmes, who strikes me as rather superannuated & extinct (though he flickers up at moments) & is moreover dazed & bewildered by the row. He is handicapped, unfortunately by having with him his singularly, inexplicably common daughter Amelia—who throws a kind of lurid light of consanguinity on some of *Wendell's* less felicitous idiosyncrasies.[2]—Of course you are hearing all about Gladstone's defeat a week ago; which I don't deplore, for though it seems to me that Home Rule must come, his whole conduct in forcing it upon a house of Commons not in the least elected to pronounce for it—so that it might be done by *him* & him only—has been a piece of high political egotism. I don't know how the G.O.M. looks at the distance of across the seas, but seen on this spot he appears to me to have become rather baleful & demagogic.[3]   His talk about the "people's heart" the "classes" &c, is unworthy of a man having his responsibilities; & his influence, or rather his boundless authority, is demoralizing—his name is a kind of fetich with so many millions & the renunciation of personal judgment, before him, so complete. But the whole drama is very interesting.   There are to be new elections next month exclusively on the Home Rule issue, & it will be momentous to see what they bring forth.   All the England one doesn't see may be for it—certainly the England one does is not.   It seems highly probable that whatever happens here, there will be civil war in Ireland—they will stew, in a lively enough manner, in their own juice.—Edward Hooper, who is out here, lunched with me the other day & I pumped him vigorously for information about Cambridge & Boston.   He would scarcely talk, however, of anything but poor Richardson—whose departure I much deplore.   I hope the approach of the long vacation lifts you up.   I am about to be called to lunch & can only squeeze in my love to Alice & many fraternal & avuncular assurances from yours ever affectionately

Henry James

P.S   You had better send this to A.K. in exchange for hers

[1] James Russell Lowell served as the American minister to Great Britain in 1880–85.
[2] Amelia Jackson Holmes Sargent was traveling in Europe with her father.
[3] Gladsone, often referred to as the Grand Old Man, introduced the Irish Home Rule Bill.   The bill was rejected by Parliament on 7 June 1886, resulting in the fall of Gladstone's government.

By the time of his move to De Vere Gardens, Henry James was in all probability an Englishman beyond recall. Alice James was also settling into her English life. In September, still at Leamington, she wrote to William describing an invasion of cockroaches in her bedroom. She urged William and Alice to use whatever they wanted from the furniture she had stored in Cambridge, as she was too ill to attempt a voyage to Boston for the next several years. Although doctors assured her that she would get better when she reached "middle life," her health continued to deteriorate, and she returned to London for the winter of 1886–87.

In the fall of 1886 William James bought a farm of seventy-five acres in Chocorua, N.H. The land was by the shore of Cho-

corua Lake, with a view of Mount Chocorua, named, according
to legend, for an Indian chief who was killed on its peak by bounty
hunters from Massachusetts. Chocorua became the Jameses' sum-
mer home.

Margaret Gibbens and her mother were returning from an ex-
tended European tour when their ship, the Pavonia, *hit a sandbar*
near Boston on 29 October 1886. The passengers had to climb
down rope ladders and board lifeboats. The accident is the subject
of Henry James's letter.

From Henry James

34, DE VERE GARDENS, | W. November 13ᵗʰ 1886

Dear William.

Yesterday came your post card about Mrs. Gibbens & Margaret, startling & shocking me by its apparent indication that the disaster to the Pavonia was a more serious one than the mention of it in these newspapers prompts me to suppose. And what you say is tormenting in its brevity, & greatly makes one desire details—as to how Margaret "fell into the sea," & whether the alarm & suspense were great, & whether she & Mrs. Gibbens were very seriously shaken. Please assure them both of my (& Alice's) affectionate interest & sympathy—& my deep lamentation over their meeting such a vile catastrophe at the very last moment of what apparently had been a happy & prosperous year. I saw much of them while they were here & we became very intimate. All the more do I grieve for them, for the bad hour they must have passed, & the "2 trunks probably spoiled"—if spoiled they prove to have been. I feel in particular the disgustingness of this, as I almost saw their trunks filled! I hope before long to hear details from you—& meanwhile I hope the agony is in a way to be forgotten & the damage has been minimised. But I am haunted by the figure of "Margaret in the sea," even though she was "held up." Meanwhile who was holding up her mother?—I am happy to say that, from here, I have nothing so bad as all this to tell you. Alice is in excellent condition, distinctly better than she has been at any time since she came abroad. Her return to town has had no bad effects whatever—none but conspicuously good ones. She is extremely pleased with her quarters, which turn out excellent, so that (if they continue to be as satisfactory,) she will cling to them for next winter also. The state she has been in since her return, adds to her

conviction that she is better in London than any where else—a fortunate circumstance in many ways, particularly in relation to my looking after her.   Her powers of conversation increase daily, & she is the
best company in the place.   I only wish she could shine in a wider
circle.   Her circle, at present, however, is wide enough for her
strength.   Katherine & Louisa Loring have been in London, through
many postponements of departure (for the Riviera) until today,—that
is, if they have, in fact, left today, which was their intention yesterday.
I imagine that as the day is fine they have really at last moved.   At
any rate Alice will have had the benefit of a particularly long piece
of K.P.L.'s society—I sometimes questioned this benefit of old, but I
don't at all now.   I myself have a plan of going down to Florence for
three or four weeks, about Dec. 1$^{\underline{st}}$.   Alice only wants to push me off
(she has so little fear, or prospect, of loneliness,) & as I haven't been
to Italy for six years I am well disposed.   K.P.L. expects to rejoin
Alice for a month later in the winter—Louisa being much enamoured
of a nurse-companion whom she has.   Look out, in Boston, for Frank
Hall's portrait of Mr. Loring, just painted here, which (I haven't seen
it,) is said to be superior.—We figure you & Alice, with infinite compassion, overwhelmed by your Harvard jubilee—bewildered, exhausted, perhaps ruined.   My ideas about its nature & duration are
too vague for me to pity you in detail—but I hope your prostration
won't prevent your being able to write us some detail.   I pray you
may not have had much obligatory hospitality.—We are sickened, unspeakably, by the infamous trick played upon Lowell by Julian Hawthorne, who must have become the basest cad unflogged.   I have
heard it said here—once—that Lowell "can never return"—but that
is nonsense.   His protest, however, ought to have been sharper.[1]
Much love to Alice, & no end of sympathy to the Gibbenses.

Ever. H. James

[1] Julian Hawthorne published what he claimed was an interview with James Russell
Lowell, "Lowell in Chatty Mood," *World,* 24 October 1886, in which he quoted Lowell
as saying that the Prince of Wales was fat and that there were many fools in the House
of Lords.   In his response Lowell denied many of the comments attributed to him
and claimed that his conversation with Hawthorne had been off the record.

1887

To obtain the quieter mornings he needed for work, Henry James spent the winter of 1886–87 in Italy, spending part of the time at the Florentine villa of a friend, the novelist Constance Fenimore Woolson, writing mostly short pieces to appear here and there. During his absence Alice James suffered a crisis and in the spring of 1887 was staying in Henry's London apartment. Her presence there prevented Henry from returning home after his planned short vacation.

William James's second son, William, spent the winter in Aiken, S.C., with his grandmother and his Aunt Margaret. William was suffering from asthma, and the resort boasted the "driest climate east of the Rocky Mountains." On 24 March 1887 Alice Gibbens James gave birth to a daughter, Margaret Mary, an event that, according to sister Alice, improved her sister-in-law's chances against three males.

To Henry James

Cambridge April 12. 87 | 6.30 A.M.

My dear Harry,—Your letter from Venice (of March ?th) came duly a fortnight or more ago. I am glad you are going for once to escape the London season, and with such a good result, too, as that of letting Alice stay in your flat. I should think it would become a weariness both to spirit & flesh, and taste a good deal better next year for this year's intermission.—I got back yesterday from five days spent at my sylvan home at Lake Chocorua, whither I had gone to see about getting the buildings in order for the summer. The winter has been an exceptionally snowy one back of the coast, & I found, when I arrived, 4 feet of snow on a level and 8 feet where it had drifted. The day before yesterday the heat became summer like, and I took a long walk in my shirt sleeves, going through the snow the whole length of my leg when the crust broke. It was a queer combination—not exactly agreeable. The snow-blanket keeps the ground from freezing deep; so that very few days after the snow is gone, the soil is dry, and spring begins in good earnest. I tried snow-shoes but found them clumsy. They were making the maple sugar in the woods, I had excellent comfort at the hotel hard by, with whose good landlord and still better landlady I am good friends, I rested off the fumes of my lore-crammed brain, and altogether I smile at the pride of Greece and Rome—from the height of my New Hampshire home. I'm afraid it will cost nearer 2000 than $800 to finish all the work. But we shall have 10 large rooms (2 of them 24 x 24), & three small ones—not counting kitchen, pantries etc, and if you want some real roomy rustic happiness, you had better come over and spend all your summers with us. I can see that the thought makes you sick, so I'll say no more about it—but my permanent vision of your future is that your pen will fail you as a means of support, and that, having laid up no income, you will return like the prodigal son, to my roof. You will then find that, with a woodpile as large as an ordinary house, a hearth 4 feet wide, and the American sun flooding the floor, even a new Hampshire winter is not so bad a thing. With house provided, 2 or 3 hundred dollars a year will support a man comfortably enough at Tamworth Iron Works, which is the name of our township. But enough—my vulgarity makes you shudder.

I find Alice well, though still white & weak. She is always slow it[1] getting strength after these shocks. The daughter is a queer little thing with a long nose—quite unlike any of the boys except that her complexion resembles Harry's. You can't tell what they are going to look like at this age. The strange thing is that you *can* tell so well what their character & moral disposition is. It is a perfectly distinct and positive thing in each, when two days old. Little Billy is still at Aiken with his grandmother, and well enough.

I got a letter from Annie Emerson yesterday telling me about Bob.[2] I have heard nothing directly, because he is sulking with me and Mary, it seems, has been afraid to irritate him by writing. He has been drinking a good deal & quarreling with her, and I imagine she will soon have to go back to Milwaukee. His case is incurable because the drinking comes from his pathological mental condition which is part of his very nature. He has *no* affection. And yet in his crises he goes through the emotional expressions of an angel. Now that his property is in trust, one great danger is averted. But I wish the poor wretch could die in one of his bad sprees—it would be so much future misery averted for him as well as for his family. College begins to morrow, and there are seven weeks more of lectures. I never did my work so easily as this year, and hope to write two more chapters of psychology ere the vacation. That immortal work is now more than two-thirds done. To you, who throw off two vols. a year, I must seem despicable for my slowness. But the truth is that (leaving other impediments out of account) the "science" is in such a confused and imperfect state that every paragraph presents some unforeseen snag, and I often spend many weeks on a point that I did n't foresee as a difficulty at all. American scholarship is looking up in that line. Three first-class works, in point both of originality and of learning, have appeared here within 4 months. Stanley Hall's and mine will make five.³ Meanwhile in England they are doing little or nothing. The ["]Psychical Researchers" seem to be the only active investigators. My colleagues Barrett Wendell and Royce have just pub'ᵈ novels, & our librarian Justin Winsor is about to do the same!⁴ Wendell's is excellent. Royce's, (who dedicates it to me) has first rate material and is strong in the passionate passages—but elsewhere is very crude and ineffectual. He wrote it too fast, to see if he could turn a penny.—You've seen, I suppose, Howells's note on your Princess, in the April Harper's.⁵ He and Perry are to leave together in July. Mrs. P. to study Painting in Paris!⁶ Who would have expected T.S.P. to turn out the model slave of a husband that he is. I imagine he needs all his virtue. His evolution of the snob is the best of his books—and really reads very well indeed.⁷ Addio!

God bless you. W.J.

If you want to make me a present, as you come through Paris, send me a couple of my favorite blue silk foulard cravats with a white spot—smallish. Impossible to buy 'em here.

¹A slip for 'at'.

²RJ was living in Concord and took part in social activities with the Emersons.

³George Trumbull Ladd, *Elements of Physiological Psychology* (1887); John Dewey (1859–1952), American philosopher, *Psychology* (1887); Borden Parker Bowne (1847–1910), American philosopher, *Introduction to Psychological Theory* (1887). Granville Stanley Hall did not publish a book on psychology during this period.

⁴Barrett Wendell, *Rankell's Remains: An American Novel* (1887); Josiah Royce, *The Feud of Oakfield Creek* (1887). No novel by Justin Winsor was found.

⁵A note on *The Princess Casamassima* appeared as part of "The Editor's Study," *Harper's New Monthly Magazine* 74 (April 1887): 829.

⁶While in Paris, Lilla Cabot Perry established friendships with some of the leading impressionist painters, especially Claude Monet and Camille Pissarro.

⁷Thomas Sergeant Perry, *The Evolution of the Snob* (1887).

From Henry James

34, DE VERE GARDENS, | W. October 1$\underline{st}$. 1887

My dear Brother.

Your good & copious letter of September 20$\underline{th}$, travelling swiftly, came in to me yesterday & gave me great joy—our communications had so long been cut. I have written of late certain letters to Aunt Kate which I have always asked her to hand on to you (one only four days ago,) but it's an age since I had any direct speech with you. I have an idea, however, that I wrote to you somewhile between the 25$\underline{th}$ July & the 1$\underline{st}$ August, just after my return from abroad. It was a great pleasure to me that your letter breathes a spirit of respectable well-being—though also alas, of "over-pressure" & tells of too many things perpetually to do. But that seems the universal law to-day, & if I feel it who have neither wife nor wean, I sometimes wonder that you don't faint by the wayside. But I suppose a wife simplifies as well as complicates—tell Alice I don't wish to seem to take too dark a view of *her!* I have always supposed that such a one (especially such a one as she) transacts for her husband some of the business of life & some of those relations with the world, that the lone bachelor has to transact for himself. My excellent but wooden-faced cook (who has exactly the same shy, frightened manner to-day that she had the 1$\underline{st}$ hour she was in my service,) has just presented herself as usual (with a large, clean, wh<ite> respectful apron,) to ask fo<r> the "orders for the day." It is at these moments that I feel the want of assistance, especially as the lady in question is so reverent that she never presumes to suggest. On the other hand she & her spouse buy everything for me (I never have to go into a shop,) & don't cheat me.[1] They are on board-wages (i.e. have to provide their own food,) & every bone that leaves my table comes back with a persistency that makes me say "Is your master a dog that you should treat him thus?" But this is parenthetic. I take this morning to write to you because I am too much under the shadow of impending departure to concentrate on sterner work. My departure is only for the purpose of spending tomorrow (Sunday) & perhaps also Monday in the country. I am going down to the Frank Millets, who with the genial & gifted little Abbey form (there are usually two or three others, especially Sargent, but he has just gone to America to paint a portrait—I wrote about him, by the way, in the October *Harper,*)[2] a very friendly & entertaining small summer- & autumn colony at the wonderfully picturesque old village of Broadway in Worcestershire.

Here they paint & walk & play lawn tennis & receive their friends, & the whole region is a delight to me—mainly on account of the interest of its magnificent monumental villages. I always get a couple of good walks while I am there—one of them usually over to Chipping Camden, which is a place of rapture especially when its wide long, wandering, grassy yet wonderfully architectural high-street is seen at the twilight hour. I have paid them a couple of days' visit for three years running, and I don't care to interrupt the tradition as it's American & fraternizing & does something to keep me "in touch" as they say here, with the land of my birth. Moreover, Millet is an excellent fellow who has ended by painting very well indeed (he didn't at all at first,) as a consequence of mere hard Yankee "faculty"—& Abbey is a pure genius, with the biggest kind of Philadelphia twang & an inspired vision of all old time English aspects & figures. Apart from this I shouldn't care to go away again for many a week—it chaws up one's time so fatally. I have done a good deal of it since I returned— in brief but repeated dashes—which were more or less inevitable after a long absence from those friends with whom one keeps up some sort of visiting habits, & more or less irresistible from the influence of this splendid season. It has been the most glorious summer, not an hour that wasn't pleasant, & all the weather pure gold—one of the summers of one's childhood, as one remembers them, thinking they have left the world, come to life again. Even yet it doesn't break—all these last days have been magnificent. I went, the last of August, among other things, to spend three days with Lowell, at Whitby, on the Yorkshire coast, where he was spending a month. The place is delightful, & he is ever the same; wonderfully simple & genial, at the same time as "clever," & expressively kind to me. I get on with him well, though he belongs to a more primitive generation (essentially) & in spite of all his ambassadorial accretions, & the experience & fame that have come to him of late years, he is not a "man of the world." Du Maurier was also there, whom I like very much & who is, &[3] a very charming & intelligent fellow & companion (one of the most so I know,) into the bargain. We are excellent friends. The other day I spent a week with the Roseberys (to make up for not having been near them for a year, thank heaven!) but Mentmore is always a peculiar experience, half pleasant & half insupportable, into which it would take too long to enter. Rosebery is a gifted being & has, in the opinion of all the world, a great future before him, & yet the conditions in which he has grown up & lives are such as to make it difficult for me to take him in some ways seriously—which no doubt

is a proof o[f] scoffing shallowness on my part. At any rate now that
the autumn is closing in and one's fireside begins to glow I only long
to settle down to work & gilded halls are a simple nuisance. They
have been beco[m]ing so to me, more & more, for a long time past, &
I begin to perceive, with delight, the fair fruit of a policy of letting
them almost severely alone. I have tried for a good while now to
get *out* of society, as hard as certain people are supposed to try to get
"into" it; & I am happy to say I am perceptibly succeeding. I have
very large accumulations (of "observation of the world" &c) & I now
simply want elbow-room for the exercise, as it were, of my art. I
hope during the next ten years to do some things of a certain importance; if I don't, it wont be that I haven't tried hard or that I am
wanting in an extreme ambition. I am able to work better, & more,
than I have ever been in my life before; it isn't much, but it's
enough, & at any rate it is so much more than has been the case in
former years that I look back with wonder & pity to the wretchedly
bad basis I have always been on. It makes me think rather well of
myself to have done anything at all. Little by little I have grown less
sick, especially as regards the relation of such sickness to the act of
reading & writing. Now I can do the essential—it's not too much to
say that hitherto (I am particularly changed for the better within a
year,) I couldn't. I *ought* therefore to produce better stuff than ever
before, especially as I have many more ideas & am not in the least
tired of work—on the contrary. The damnation still is that I can't
read a quarter as much as I should like. Indeed while my writing is
going on I can read very little—the writing unsubstantial as it may
appear to some, so empties the measure of what I can do. So I can
only read to speak of, in *intervals*. But as I say, the whole case
mends & may mend more. *Unberufen*, after all this swagger! I am
glad you desire the sight of more of my prose, & very sorry that the
mysterious ways of editors keep me apparently silent for so long.
But I *am* productive, & in the course of this autumn shall have sent
off the 8$\underline{th}$ or 9$\underline{th}$ fiction of about the length of "Daisy Miller" since I
quitted England on the 1$\underline{st}$ December last. These things will finally
appear, I suppose, very much together, so that you will have a good
deal of me at once. I haven't all this time said a word about Alice,
but that is because I only the other day gave Aunt Kate a pretty full
account of her, which you will receive. Her determination to remain
at Leamington for the winter rests on all sorts of good reasons, & at
any rate it is fixed. Her isolation there combined with her weakness
seems rather pitiful but mainly to *us*—she doesn't think it so. She

gave me, on Monday last, a very good account of herself, & her appearance bore it out.   She misses Katharine but elle en a pris son
parti.   That she has been able to do it is a proof of strength.   But
of that sort of strength she has much.   She is also very strong about
home-rule, & in various other ways.[4]   I miss her greatly here, as a
communicant & talker.   I *understand* her condition no better than I
did 2 years ago, but I am more of the impression that eventually
better years are in store for her.   However, she lives from month to
month—& in that sense I live with her.   I should be very sorry to
pretend to any views that she hasn't herself—her capacity for views
is so large and excellent.   Her patience is equally inexhaustible &
admirable, & the coming months portend good to her much more
than ill.   I shall go to her, for a day at a time, with all possible frequency.—I mentioned Edith James in my recent letter to Aunt Kate,
so as to let you know that I had given her (in one way or another—
from 3 to 4 of them were for an ulster which I purchased & even
fitted myself,) £16—in order that you might feel easier as to dona-
tions.   Poor girl, I didn't like her much, but I consoled her to the
best of my ability when she mourned her father's removal as the loss
of every good.   OCTOBER 5ᵗᴴ   I had to stop the other day & keep
over my letter.   I paid my little visit at Broadway & came back yesterday.   It shall be the last (I mean the last I shall pay there, tho' it was
pleasant enough) as there is a limit, after all, to what one ought to
do for people because they are Americans.   I grudged the time so
much that I didn't enjoy myself—but I won't add to the loss by talking
about it.   I'm afraid I must close up my letter.   Your plan is very
interesting—the plan of your house in the country—& your existence
there sounds very attractive from the loafing-out-of-doors point a
view—an element of which my life is terribly destitute.   It can't be
got here save by "shooting"—& I don't shoot.   Besides which if one
shoots the loafing is the least part of it.   Fishing costs £10 a bite.
Switzerland is the only thing—& it is crammed with cockneys, & I
never go there.   But I mean to try & manage it next summer.   I *did*
spend one day there (on foot, on the Simplon) crossing from Italy
the end of July, which was a rapture of wild flowers & mountain
streams—but it was over in a flash.   I am full of sorrow for the little
girl's bad ear—but surely it will become a good one with time?   And
won't the other be all right?   I just receive a letter from Grace Norton, which I shall probably, though not certainly answer this a.m.   If
I don't I'm afraid I shan't for a long time.   Her letters breathe a kind
of desolation—or rather a "thinness" of life, which I trust her sure

existence doesn't so much express.   This however, is entirely unin-
tentional on her part.   Eliot (Norton) was here this summer &
lunched with me twice.   He struck me as the most portentous reproduction, in aspect, tone & manner, of his Father (whom he however
seemed to dislike very much) & as—moreover—appallingly aged.   I
have rarely been made to feel so much like a frivolous little boy.
Other Americans I haven't seen: fewer this summer I think than ever
before.   Sometimes they have been too numerous—for what they
were.   I found Boott's card yesterday (on his way back from the U.S.
where you perhaps saw him?) & I have written to him to return to
day.   I saw him of course last winter frequently in Florence, & found
him very shrunken & contracted, not that he was ever very capacious.
But he is a mere pinch of his old smallness.   In reading over the last
two or three pages it strikes me that I will strike you as ill-natured.
But I can't help it, &, besides, I don't think I am.   At any rate it won't
prevent me from saying that as to T. S. Perry, for instance (concerning
whom you inquire,) I have neither seen nor heard anything whatever
of him, & don't want to.   He wrote me a most offensive & impertinent letter about a year ago—about what, I could scarcely make out,
except that he disapproved of my living in London.   It was too idiotic
to notice & it was almost impertinent enough to return, & it set the
seal upon the conviction I have always privately had that he is a singularly poor creature.   I had never failed, for years, for auld acquaintance sake, to pay him little occasional attentions—writing to him,
sending him my books punctually &c—under the empire, somehow
of that superstition which he has to a certain extent managed to im-
pose upon people in regard to his singularly helpless mediocrity—
but it is really a relief to have nothing more to do with him.   The
letter, from him (it was but a short note,) that I speak of, made me
feel as if I had been "giving myself away" for 30 years, & as one has
only one life—! I'm afraid you won't see Louis Stevenson, who is a
most moribund but fascinating being, of whom I am very fond.   If
he were in health he would have too much "side," as they say here,
but his existence hangs but by a thread & his almost squalid invalidism tones down the "Ercles vein" in him, as well as any irritation that
one may feel from it.   He has a most gallant spirit & an exquisite
literary talent; but don't read the verses to me in his new little volume
of poems, as they happen, especially the 1st, to be the poorest things
in the book.   The 2^{d} was occasioned by my giving his wife the little
mirror he commemorates. Both were scribbled off at the moment—
the 1st put on my plate one day I went to dine with him at Bourne-

mouth—& I never dreamed that he had kept copies of them & wd. publish them.[5] Four or five other pieces in the thin volume are perfect & destined I think to live.   He & Howells are the only English imaginative writers to day whom I can look at.   I hadn't seen the latter's "tribute" in the September *Harper,* but I have just looked it up.   It gives me pleasure, but doesn't make me cease to deplore the figure that Howells makes every month in his critical department of *Harper.*   He seems to me as little as possible of a critic & exposes himself so that I wish he would "quit," & content himself with writing the novel as he thinks it should be and not talking about it: he does the one so much better than the other.   He talks from too small a point of view and his examples (barring the bore he makes of Tolstoi,) are smaller still.[6]   There is, it seems to me, far too much talk around & about the novel in proportion to what is done.   Any *genre* is good which has life—which of course is perfectly consistent with the fact that there are some that find it mighty hard to have it and others that one very much prefers to some.   But I am sprawling into quires and reams.   I hope indeed you may finish your Psychology by the date you desire.   It will be a tough morsel for me to chew, but I don't despair of nibbling it slowly up.   What you tell me of poor Father's book would make me weep if it weren't somehow outside & beyond weeping.   After that who shall be confident or believe that one's inner conviction is a voucher?   I send no end of love to Alice & return (in another envelope) the queer, tragic Chicago letter.[7]

Ever your   Henry James

[1] HJ is referring to the Smiths.

[2] HJ, "John S. Sargent," *Harper's New Monthly Magazine* 75 (October 1887): 683–91; reprinted in *Picture and Text* (1893).

[3] The comma after 'is' and the '&' are an undeleted false start.

[4] AJ had great sympathy for the Irish cause and commented on the subject frequently in her diary.

[5] The two poems by Stevenson are "Henry James" and "The Mirror Speaks," published in *Underwoods* (1887).

[6] Howells's criticism for *Harper's New Monthly Magazine* has been reprinted in the *Editor's Study,* ed. James W. Simpson (Troy, N.Y.: Whitston, 1983).   Tolstoi was discussed extensively.

[7] The letter mentioned in WJ's letter of 1 September 1887 probably concerns William Francis Barnard, author of several collections of poems published in Chicago.

1888

In January 1888, with his wife and three children in Aiken, S.C., William James found himself a bachelor for several months. Margaret Mary, the baby, was suffering from an "obstinate bronchitis" when she was bundled up in six inches of wool and taken to the Boston station for the day-and-a-half train ride to South Carolina. They reached Aiken on the morning of 21 January after a difficult journey during which Alice and son Henry suffered from motion sickness. William's social schedule that winter was very heavy, an endless round of teas, receptions, dinners, and calls, sometimes as many as three or four a day. On 27 January he was in New York, returning from a trip to Syracuse where he had sold one of their stores. In Cambridge on the twenty-ninth, he found the house "swept & garnished" and three smiling servants asking for news. The next day he was in Concord, spending the evening with his brother Robertson and others who were performing spiritualistic experiments with a planchette. It was, he informed his wife on the thirty-first, a pleasant party because "one beautiful girl is enough to make a party pleasant, & one was there raven hair, coal black eyes." But he worried about Robertson's condition. On 2 February he received a telegram from Robertson's wife saying that Robertson had gone on a spree, cut and bruised his face, and was begging to be confined. On 4 February, after leaving Robertson in an asylum in Hartford, Conn., he ate a supper of "Bass's ale, oysters, Rye bread & Sweitzerkäse" and then stretched out on a bench at the Hartford depot to wait for the 2:17 A.M. train to Boston.

Henry James spent the winter of 1887–88 in London. On 3 March 1888 he agreed to produce a serial in twelve parts for the Atlantic Monthly. *Each part was to be approximately twenty pages, for which he would receive fifteen dollars a page. The work, conceived in this businesslike fashion, was* The Tragic Muse, *published in book form in 1890.*

To Henry James

Cambridge April 19. 88

My dear Harry, It is a perfect age since I have written to either you or Alice; but as life advances, that seems the natural tendency. Your last letter was extremely interesting—about Balfour etc. For B's & Morley's portraits, many thanks, B's is a disappointing face—not manly or generous in any way. Alice also has sent a staving letter to my Alice since I wrote, Church of England Irish question, trepidations of stomach etc etc—all *most* interesting and as Mr. Pater would say "most curious." You'll want to know the news. There isn't much of a stateable sort. Frank James's death, Mrs. Channing's death, Tudy Masons death, Kitty van Buren's separation from Peyton etc etc. Miss C. has left her property to Helen,[1] I don't know how much, Mrs Gurney left them $6000, and the college owing to a Gurney bequest of something like $150000 has relieved Child of ½ his work.[2] So their lot is being alleviated. The Masons have had 800000 left to Henry M. by one eccentric old Joshua —— - - ? It is to be hoped that if the patriarch of the house doesn't return home from Paris to enjoy it, he will at least send some of it to his wife and deserving & lovely daughter Serena. What sort of a creature is Carnes. They say in N.Y. that Serena never speaks of their separation as if it were due to anything but pecuniary reasons, but I suppose it must be incompatibility. Their son Mason is I fancy a very promising youngster, going through the "College of the City of N.Y." formerly "free Academy." I spent 4 days a week or more ago at Aunt Kate's. *What* a situation for a Labiche farce! Henry, 72 years old, with the plasticity of nature of a box tortoise, so deaf that you must now *write* to him half the time, with his irreproachable correctness and essential goodness, his dense obstinacy and dislike to obey suggestions from others ("Now that's *telling*, that *roils* me, that gives me a *shock*, a *cotch*") his five-cent ideas, and his $40000 dollar income, and quarter of a million of disposable capital, is of course the nucleus of the situation. Around it, you can imagine the atmosphere of mercenary and pecuniary speculation and worriment that condenses itself, and never clears away, in his presence or out of it. Poor Aunt Kate is acting with the greatest dignity, and is grown singularly gentle and mellow, as it seems to me, in her ways. She has a very happy home there with all these young cousins as attentive to her as they are. My own family is doing very well at Aiken, all in exuberant health according to my "advices," and to return about the 1st of May. The balm &

the blessing of feeling all this time that I have a country place of my own to go to is unspeakable.   I am well and plodding away in my slow fashion, with incessant interruptions from "bad days" at my work—a little stirred up just now by the appointment of G. Stanley Hall of the Johns Hopkins to the presidency of a grand newly endowed University ("Clark U.") in Worcester Mass.[3]   It would be a natural thing for me to be invited to the J.H.U. to fill Hall's place, and a rather hard thing to decline, [I perceive I have not a sheet more of the sort of paper I began upon] so I can only hope that I shan't be invited, as I hate to leave this place, for the children's sake, if for no other.   But I do believe in keeping the ball rolling, and I know that every man who leaves a college for the sake of higher pay elsewhere helps to reform our system of underpaying intellectual work.   I have followed your advice & not looked at the Aspern papers.   But I have taken great satisfaction in the Stevenson & Maupassant articles.[4]   The only fault I find with the Stevenson is that having said as much as you do about the pains he takes to polish his english, you omit to say anything of the *results,* which are surely about as successful as results in that line can possibly be.   I think his Lantern Bearers one of the most beautiful things every written, you read his sentences over & over again, for everything about them is just *right,* — classic.[5]   In your Maupassant article you used that author's own directness more than is your wont, and I think with great good effect. If you keep on writing like that I'll never utter another cavil as long as I live.   Did you work over it more than over other things, or did it couler de source in that form?   Alice's letter from Aiken this A.M. happens to contain the following: "Miss Russell [poor little bent Lucy Russell, Ellen Jackson's friend][6] has been reading aloud Harry's 'guy. de Maupassant.'   I can well read it again to you for she made parts of it almost unintelligible—the dear little woman.   Sally Norton withdrew, in the rôle of *jeune fille.*   Dear me!   She must be 24 years old, and she acts like 18, with frequent allusions to her ["]tender years."

I rejoice in your obesity & your fencing.   As for me chest weights are as high as I can fly.   Pray send this to Alice—it is as much for her as for you, & believe me, your ever affectionate

Wm James

P.S.   Poor Matthew Arnold.   I suppose they'll be asking you for articles about him.   His last paper on America was very sensible and good and artistically composed, in his peculiar way.[7]   The papers here, so far as I know, have behaved pretty decently about it, nothing worse than a little chaff have I seen.   Smalley sent a most asinine telegram, however, to the tribune about it.[8]   A whole column about Matthews lamentable change of front due to personal spleen & peevishness etc.   The trouble about Matthew which sets so many against him is the entirely needless priggishness of his *tone*.   If he had talked straightforwardly about the high things no one would have ever objected, but the everlasting little snickering about the vulgarities which they are *not,* is not the high style of treating them.   His ultimate heads of classification, too, are lamentable.   Think of the "interesting" used as an absolute term!!   I believe that the great gross popular plebeian mind always rightly catches the weak side of a public *character*—and when Matthew passes for a fantastic personage among the people, and naught else, it is that (although he is much else) he is most vulnerably that as well.   They are right in feeling that way about Lowell here too—as a political teacher and wiseacre he surely ought not to be very seriously taken.   Doesn't "think straight" etc. Charles Norton ditto! with his "culture" never forgetting that it is not vulgarity ———— ————

But lord how I
do run on!

Pray tell Alice I've read her Philippe Daryl with the greatest interest and recommended it to others.[9]   It has engendered in me a fierce desire to start of[f] the summer after next with my wife (& her if she'll join us!) and get off at Queenstown & peregrinate through the Emerald isle, keeping an eye open to the fine purchasable "sites" which will be thrown upon the market when the final *débacle* arrives!

[1] The legatee was Helen Child Sargent.   Her benefactor was not identified.

[2] Ellen Hooper Gurney bequeathed money and property to endow "higher instruction."   The Gurney Fund was to be used to make teaching responsibilities of professors "sufficiently moderate" and give them leisure to contribute to the advancement of knowledge.

[3] Clark University opened as a graduate school in 1889 with Hall serving as its first president.

[4] HJ, *The Aspern Papers* (1888); "Robert Louis Stevenson," *Century Magazine* 35 (April 1888): 868–79; "Guy de Maupassant," *Fortnightly Review* 49 (March 1888): 364–86 (both reprinted in *Partial Portraits* [1888]).

[5] Robert Louis Stevenson, "The Lantern-Bearers," *Scribner's Magazine* 3 (February 1888): 251–56; reprinted in *Across the Plains* (1892).

[6] Neither Ellen Jackson nor Lucy Russell was identified.

[7] Matthew Arnold died on 15 April 1888.   His "Civilisation in the United States" appeared in the *Nineteenth Century* 23 (April 1888): 481–96.

[8] Smalley's criticism of Arnold, which appeared in the *New York Tribune*, 1 April 1888, described Arnold's essay as an "elaborate lampoon on America."

[9] Paschal Grousset, writing under the pseudonym Phillipe Daryl, *Ireland's Disease; Notes and Impressions* (1888).

It was probably his wife who pushed William James to study spiritualism and to spend tedious hours with mediums, most of whom were frauds and charlatans. For theories and methods of psychical research, however, he looked to the English psychical researchers, especially Edmund Gurney. Historians of psychical research often contrast Gurney, an honest inquirer, with Frederic Myers, a more sinister figure obsessed with dreams of immortality whom James himself did not like on first acquaintance. Gurney's death on the night of 22 June or in the early hours of 23 June 1888 was thus a great blow. In his letter of 26 June informing William of the death, Henry mentioned the possibility of suicide, only to dismiss it. While nothing is known with certainty, there are reasons for suspecting that Henry's first thoughts were correct. It is at least likely that Gurney, upon learning that he had been tricked by some of his associates in psychical research, killed himself and that the English researchers led by Myers conspired to hush up the affair. It is impossible to say how much William knew and suspected. The absence of documents, where there should have been many, is itself a suspicious circumstance suggesting that much was destroyed. Edmund Gurney and his wife were part of Alice James's social circle, and it is significant that more than a year later, on 5 August 1889, Alice wrote in her diary: "They say that there is little doubt that Mr. Edmund Gurney committed suicide."

To Henry James

        Address: | Tamworth Iron Works, N.H. | July 11. 88
My dear Harry

   Your note announcing E. Gurney's death came yesterday, and was a most shocking surprise. It seems one of Death's stupidest strokes, for I know of no one whose life-task was begun on a more far-reaching scale, or from whom one expected with greater certainty richer fruit in the ripeness of time. I pity his lovely wife, to whom I wrote a note yesterday; and also a brief notice for the Nation.[1] To me it will be a cruel loss; for he recognized me more than any one, and in all my tho'ts of returning to England he was the Englishman from whom I awaited the most nourishing communion. We ran along on very similar lines of interest. He was very profound, subtle, &

voluminous, and bound for an intellectual synthesis of things much solider and completer than any one I know, except perhaps Royce. Well! such is life! all these deaths make what remains here seem strangely insignificant and ephemeral, as if the weight of things, as well as the numbers, was all on the other side.

I have to thank you for a previous letter 3 or 4 weeks old, which, having sent to Aunt Kate, I cannot now date. I must also thank for Partial Portraits & the Reverberator. The former I of course knew (except the peculiarly happy Woolson one) but have read several of 'em again with keen pleasure, especially the Turguenieff.[2] The Reverberator is masterly and exquisite. I quite squealed through it, & all the household has amazingly enjoyed it. It shows the technical ease you have attained, that you can handle so delicate and difficult a fancy so lightly. It is simply delicious. I hope your other magazine things which I am following your advice and not reading, are only ½ as good. How you can keep up such a productivity and live, I don't see. All your time is your own, however, barring dinner parties, and that makes a great different. Most of my time seems to disappear in college duties, not to speak of domestic interruptions. Our summer starts promisingly. How with my lazy temperament I managed to start all the things we put through last summer, now makes me wonder. The place has yet a good deal to be done with it, but it can be taken slowly, and Alice is a most *vaillante* partner. We have a trump of a hired man, a South Carolina darkey of 23 whom Alice brought up, and who is superior in intelligence industry ability and conscience to all the yankees of the region put together. "Shiftlessness" seems now a days to be the great New Hampshire characteristic. Some day I'll send you a photog. of the little place. Please send this to Alice, for whose letters I'm duly grateful. I only hope she'll keep decently well for a little while.

Yrs ever. | W.J.

P.S. I have just been down stairs to get an envelope, and there on the lawn saw a part of the family which I will describe, for you to insert in one of your novels as a picture of domestic happiness. On the newly made lawn in the angle of the house & kitchen ell, in the shadow of the hot afternoon sun lies the mattress that was once on Aunt Kates bed in Quincy St, taken out of our spare-room for an airing against Richard Hodgson's arrival to morrow. On it, the madonna and child—the latter sewing in a nice blue print dress, and smiling at the former (named Peggy),[3] immensely big and fat for her years, & who, with quite a vocabulary of adjectives and proper names, and a mouthfull of teeth, shows as yet, although in her sixteenth month, no disposition to walk. She is rolling and prattling to herself, now on mattress & now on grass, and is an exceedingly good natured, happy, and intelligent child. It conduces to her happiness to have a hard cracker in her fist, at which she mumbles more or less all day, and of which she is never known to let go, even taking it into her bath with her and holding it immersed till that ceremony is o'er. A man is papering & painting one of our parlors, a carpenter putting up a mantel piece in another. Margaret & Harry's tutor are off on the backs of the two horses to the Village 7 miles off to have 'em shod. I, with naught on but gray flannel shirt, breeches, belt, stockings & shoes, shall no[w] proceed across the Lake in the boat and up the hill to get & carry the mail. Harry will probably ride along the shore on the pony which Aunt Kate has given—him, and where Billy and Fraulein are, Heaven only knows. Returning I shall have a bath either in Lake or brook—does n't it sound nice. On the whole it is nice, but very hot.

[1] WJ's untitled note on Gurney's death appeared in *Nation* 47 (19 July 1888): 53; reprinted in *ECR*.

[2] HJ, *The Reverberator* (1888); *Partial Portraits* includes the essays "Miss Constance Fenimore Woolson" (1887) and "Ivan Turgénieff" (1884).

[3] WJ confused the order in which he had mentioned his wife and daughter.

To Henry James

Tamworth I. W. Oct 14. 88

Dear Harry & Alice,

(For I don't know to which of you a letter is due, or to which of you I last wrote) I take my pen in hand on this snowy New Hampshire morning to keep you *au fait* of all our fortunes. I am just up for the Sabbath to see the family, and go down again to morrow. Another visit a fortnight hence & we all go down together. We are moving the barn from the front of the house, so as to open the view a little more, down to the flat meadow below, with its margin of trees behind which the brook flows. Most people buy a site and then put a house on it. I have bought a house and am now creating a site round about it, lowering the level of the landscape, in order to make the house appear on a little higher ground. I now know what people mean when they say you always spend more than you expect on a place. The low price of mine was what tempted me—$750. I didn't foresee that extending the house would oblige me to grade up to it, and move the road farther away. That obliged the stone walls to be moved. Now the barn, which looked all in keeping at first, has to be moved. Presently a collossal amount of grading, about its old emplacement will be absolutely neccessary, and so on and so on, ad libitum for several years to come I suppose. We're in great clover this fall, for Aunt Kate presented us with $500 after her visit, which will amply cover all. Papering painting, and wood staining, ploughing harrowing and fencing, carpentering and barn-moving together make up a sum-total which it is very hard to imagine in advance, but which result in smoothing off one's place amazingly. I suppose Aunt Kate will have told you of her impressions of its prettiness or ugliness, whichever it is, so I will say naught. Alice has been magnificent all summer, hardly sitting down at all, so busy has she kept, and for the last three or 4 weeks she has had constantly six men, sometimes ten, at work under her eagle eye, and kept on good terms with all of them without allowing them to shirk. Men & oxen, and the brown earth, and the new chopped wood, are goodly things to dwell among; and if one had plenty of money, I can imagine no more fascinating way of throwing it away than in owning a lot of land and playing the "gentleman farmer." Having put so much into this place, we now wish it were in a more fertile region, and a warmer winter clime, for future possible contingencies.—Enough of what, this morning, has been filling my attention! We have had hardly a dry day for a month past—a migration hitherwards of your English summer, apparently. It is now lightly snowing and the trees & bushes green, yellow, purple, crimson, all mixed together, look exquisite, powdered all over with feathery white. But it melts as it touches the warmer ground. The Cambridge year begins with much vehemence—I with a big class in Ethics, and seven graduates from other Colleges in advanced Psychology, giving me a good deal of work.[1] But I feel uncommonly hearty, & shall no doubt come out of it all in good shape. There will probably be no migration to the South neccessary, and we shall have a dull and steady time at home. Mrs. G. & her mother will spend most of the winter in Chicago, near the Salters.[2] So much for our domestic history. The political campaign is the best we've ever had. No personalities whatever, but an immense amount of economic reasoning adapted to every grade of intelligence. It seems impossible that Cleveland shouldn't be elected, but the tariff-issue is so new, and his poor civil-service record will alienate so many of the 'independents' who voted last time, that I doubt if any one feels confident.[3]— The College has not perceptibly grown this year, whilst other Colleges, Yale, Cornell etc have. I'm afraid we have about reached our limits for the present. It makes a difference in respect of income whether we have a hundred students more or less, & the possibility of raising salaries hinges on it. But in other ways the Corporation grows richer, so there may be some relief ere long. My leave of absence falls due next year, but for various reasons beside the economical one it will be unwise to take it again so soon. Two years hence, it may be best to do so, it is impossible now to foresee.—I ask everyone, Alice, who has seen you whether you are *homesick,* and can't make out how it is, either from their replies or from your letters. You being caught over there is the strangest fate, and might well make a person feel homesick, who, if she *could* come home mightn't care to do so. Mary Watson was in the cars last evening, and told me of her visit to you last summer, praising (like every one else) your charm, brilliancy and beauty. Why don't you have your photog. sold as a professional? There would also be an american market. Your trunks and packing cases are on the way hither to be stored for the winter, and the indefinite future. It is absurd to keep paying $4.00 a month for them. I should have paid steadily hitherto, since you've given me the use of all your other things, and did pay part of the time, but a couple of bills I hadn't literally the cash for, and so sent them to Warner. The pictures are all in Garden St. So that henceforward the things will be kept in good condition without anyone paying anything at all. I keep all insured. Your letter of a month ago, about E. Gurney etc. was very interesting.[4] Keep a writing of 'em as much as you can!—As for Harry, when is his next volume coming over? I hunger and thirst for some more of these short stories which I have purposely avoided reading in their periodical shape. The Reverberator is immortal. Aldrich told me that you had a splendid serial for next year's Atlantic.[5] I don't see how you can produce at such a rate, or how you find time for a line of reading or anything else. I should think you'd feel all hollowed out inwardly, and absolutely need to fill up. I am to have lots of reading and no writing to speak of this year, and expect to enjoy it hugely. It does do one good to read classic books. For a month past I've done nothing else, in behalf of my ethics class—Plato, Aristotle, Adam Smith, Butler, Paley, Spinoza, etc etc—no book is celebrated without deserving it for some quality, and recenter books, certain never to be celebrated, have an awfully squashy texture.—Aldrich got into the Saturday Club in the accidental absence of at least three (including myself) who would have black-balled him. What is it about the little cuss that's so caddish?   He writes like a man who oughtn't to look like that.   Lowell and Holmes were bent on having him in.[6]   I go dutifully to that Club—but it is n't genial—the old and the (relatively) young together at half past two in the afternoon.—The other Club is good enough.   Plenty of talk weighty and light, and passing from the one to the other without an effort.   Wendell Holmes is going to vote for Harrison, God knows why, except to show the shady side of himself—he couldn't give an articulate reason for it the other night. He made a flying trip to California with his wife, seeing no end of country and being elated thereby, and then he spend two months at the Clifton House at Niagara Falls, very happily as he always does. He's just been reading the Bible through, and as John Gray says, its a great thing to have a virgin mind turned on to so trite a book—as odd as G. Doré's illustrations.   I don't see how his judgeship gives him so much leisure.[7]   Speaking of Judges, Judge Gray was at the last Saturday Club next to me, and spoke of you with much affection and of your novels with much anger, that you should n't *risk* anything with your personages in the way of making them plunge into action! The poor man does n't know, I suppose, that one can't deal with one's personages so at will.   Well! this is as good a place to pull up as any.   Good bye to both of you.   Receive a brother's blessing from your affectionate

Wm. James

P.S   What a hideous thing this recrimination is between Mackenzie and the German Doctors!   Our little governess is *wüthend* after Mack.'s life.[8]   I make no comment on Bismark and the Empress concerning the Emperor's Diary,[9] nor on the Whitechapel murders which I hope haven't given Alice a bad turn.[10]   I haven't read the Diary yet, tho I've just got it.

[1] WJ is referring to Philosophy 4: Recent English Contributions to Theistic Ethics and to Philosophy 20a: Questions in Psychology.

[2] WJ's sister-in-law, Mary Gibbens, married William Mackintire Salter in December 1885 and moved to Chicago, where Salter was leading a congregation of the Society for Ethical Culture.   Mrs. Gibbens's mother was not identified.

[3] Grover Cleveland, who favored lower tariffs, won a popular majority in the 1888 elections but lost in the electoral college.

[4] WJ probably means AJ's letter of 21 August 1888 in which she presented her version of Gurney in some detail, describing some of his pathological mental traits and arguing that he should never have married.

[5] WJ is referring to HJ's *Tragic Muse*.

[6] When Thomas Bailey Aldrich moved from New York to Boston, James Russell Lowell and Oliver Wendell Holmes, Sr., became his patrons.   WJ was elected a mem-

ber in 1881. The Saturday Club was a group of leading men in Boston and vicinity who met for a "long lunch" on the last Saturday of each month.

[7] Oliver Wendell Holmes, Jr., was at the time a justice on the Massachusetts Supreme Court.

[8] Sir Morrell Mackenzie (1837–1892), British physician, treated Frederick III, emperor of Germany. When Frederick died, Mackenzie's German colleagues publicly questioned his competence. Mackenzie replied in kind in *The Fatal Illness of Frederic the Noble* (1888). The Jameses' governess was German.

[9] Victoria (1840–1901), empress of Germany, and wife of Frederick III (1831–14 June 1888), emperor of Germany, was the daughter of Queen Victoria and was suspected by Bismarck of favoring England and trying to break up the German empire. In September 1888 several German periodicals published extracts from the war diaries of Frederick III in which he emphasized his own role in German conquests and minimized that of Bismarck. Bismarck accused the empress of arranging the publication of the diary.

[10] From 7 August to 10 November 1888 at least seven women were mutilated and killed in the Whitechapel section of London. Letters claiming responsibility for the murders and signed Jack the Ripper were sent to the police.

From Henry James

Hotel de l'Ecu: Geneva.[1] | October 29th 1888.

My dear William.

Your beautiful & delightful letter of the 14th, from your country home, descended upon me two days ago, & after penetrating myself with it for 24 hours I sent it back to England, to Alice, on whom it will confer equal beatitude; not only because so copious, but because so "cheerful in tone" & appearing to show that the essentials of health & happiness are with you. I wish to delay no hour longer to write to you, though I am at this moment rather exhausted with the effort of a long letter, completed 5 minutes since, to Louis Stevenson, in answer to one I lately received from his wife, from some undecipherable cannibal-island in the Pacific.[2] They are such far-away, fantastic, bewildering people—that there is a certain fatigue in the achievement of putting one's self in relation with them. I may mention in this connection that I have had in my hands the earlier sheets of the *Master of Ballantrae,* the new novel he is about to contribute to Scribner, & have been reading them with breathless admiration.[3] They are wonderfully fine & perfect—he is a rare, delightful genius.—I am sitting in our old family *salon* in this place & have sat here much of the time for the last fortnight, in sociable converse with family ghosts—father & mother & Aunt Kate & our juvenile selves. I became conscious, suddenly, about Oct. 10th, that I wanted very

much to get away from the stale dingy London, which I had not
quitted, to speak of, for 15 months & notably not all summer—a
detestable summer in England, of wet & cold.   Alice, whom I went
to see, on arriving at this conclusion assured me she could perfectly
dispense for a few weeks with my presence on English soil; so I came
straight here, where I have a sufficient, though not importunate sense
of being in a foreign country, with a desired quietness for getting on
with work.[4]   I have had 16 days of extraordinarily beautiful weather,
full of autumn colour as vivid as yours at Chocorua, & with the Mt.
Blanc range, perpetually visible, literally hanging, day after day, over
the blue lake.   I have treated myself, as I say, to the apartments, or
a portion of them, in which we spent the winter of 59–60, & in which
nothing is changed save that the hotel seems to have gone down in
the world a little, before the multiplication of rivals—a descent, however, which has the *agrément* of unimpaired cleanliness & applies apparently to the prices as well.   It is very good & not at all dear.   Geneva seems both duller & smarter—a good deal bigger, yet emptier
too.   The Academy is now the University—a large, winged building
in the old public garden below the Treille.   But all the old smells &
tastes are here, & the sensation is pleasant.   I expect, in three or
four days, to go to Paris for about three weeks—& back to London
after that.   I shall be very busy for the next three or four months
with the long thing I am doing for the *Atlantic* & which is to run no
less than 15—though in shorter instalments than my previous fictions;[5] so that I have no time for wanton travelling.   But I enjoy the
easier, lighter feeling of being out of England.   I suppose if one lived
in one of these countries one would take its problems to one's self
also, & be oppressed & darkened by them—even as I am, more or
less, by those which hang over me in London.   But as it is, the Continent gives one a refreshing sense of getting *away*—away from
Whitechapel & Parnell & a hundred other constantly thickening
heavinesses.[6]   Apropos of which I may say, in response to your speculation about Alice's homesickness (leaving her to answer the question
directly for herself,) that she doesn't strike me as made *unhappy*, nos-
talgically, so much as occupied & stimulated, healthily irritated.   She
is homesick, but not nearly so much so as if she had a definite, concrete nest to revert to—a home of her own; & as if she had *not* a
habitation which, materially & economically, happens to suit her very
well in England.   I don't think she *likes* England or the English very
much—the people, their mind, their tone, their "hypocrisy" &c.
This is owing partly to the confined life she leads & the partial, pas-

sive, fragmentary, unreacting way in which she sees them. Also to her seeing so many more women than men; or rather *only* women, so far as she now sees any one—& no men at all. Also to her being such a tremendously convinced home ruler. She *does* take a great interest in English affairs—& that is an occupation & a source of well-being (in the country) to her. It is always a great misfortune, I think, when one has reached a certain age, that if one is living in a country not ones own & one is of anything of an ironic or critical disposition, one mistakes the inevitable reflections & criticisms that one makes, more & more as one grows older, upon life & human nature &c, for a judgment of that particular country, its natives, peculiarities &c, to which, really, one has grown exceedingly accustomed. For myself, at any rate I am deadly weary of the whole "international" state of mind—so that I *ache,* at times, with fatigue at the way it is constantly forced upon one as a sort of virtue or obligation. I can't look at the English & American worlds, or feel about them, any more, save as a big AngloSaxon total, destined to such an amount of melting together that an insistence on their differences becomes more & more idle & pedantic & that that melting together will come the faster the more one takes it for granted & treats the life of the 2 countries as continuous & more or less convertible, or at any rate as simply different chapters of the same general subject. Literature, fiction in particular, affords a magnificent arm for such taking for granted, & one may so do an excellent work with it. I have not the least hesitation in saying that I aspire to write in such a way that it wd. be impossible to an outsider to say whether I am, at a given moment, an American writing about England or an Englishman writing about America (dealing as I do with both countries,) & so far from being ashamed of such an ambiguity I should be exceedingly proud of it, for it would be highly civilized. You are right in surmising that it must often be a grief to me not to get more time for reading—though not in supposing that I am "hollowed out inside" by the limitations my existence has too obstinately attached to that exercise, combined with the fact that I produce a great deal. At times I do read almost as much as my wretched little *stomach* for it (literally[)] will allow, & on the whole I get much more time for it as the months & years go by. I touched bottom, in the way of missing time, during the 1st half of my long residence in London—having traversed then a sandy desert, in that respect—where however I took on board such an amount of human & social information that if the same necessary alternatives were presented to me again I should make the same choice. One can read when one is middle-aged or old; but one can mingle in the world with fresh perceptions only when one is young. The great thing is to be *saturated,* with something—that is, in one way or another, with life; & I chose the form of my saturation. Moreover you exaggerate the degree to which my writing takes it out of my mind, for I try to spend only the interest of my capital.—I haven't told you how I found Alice when I last saw her. She is now in very good form—still going out, I hear from her, in the mild moments, & feeling very easy & even jolly about her Leamington winter. My being away is a sign of her really good symptoms. She was *wüthend* after the London police in connection with the Whitechapel murders, to a degree that almost constituted robust health. I have seen a great many (that is, more than usual) Frenchmen in London this year; they bring me notes of introduction—& the other day, the night before coming away, I "entertained" at dinner (at a club,) the French Ambassador at Madrid (Paul Cambon,) Xavier Charmes of the French Foreign Office, G. du Maurier, & the wonderful little Jusserand, the chargé d'affaires in London, who is a great friend of mine, & to oblige & relieve whom it was that I invited the 2 other diplomatists, his friends, whom he had, rather helplessly, on his hands. THERE is the *real* difference— a gulf, from the English (or the American) to the Frenchman, & vice-versa (still more;) & not from the Englishman to the American. The Frenchmen I see all seem to me wonderful the 1st time—but not so much, at all, the 2^{d}. But I must finish this without having touched any of the sympathetic things I meant to say to you about your place, your work on it, Alice's prowesses as a country lady, the childrens' *vie champêtre* &c. Aunt Kate, after her visit to you, praised all these things to us with profusion and evident sincerity. I wish I could see them—but the day seems far. I haven't lain on the ground for so many years that I feel as if I had spent them up in a balloon. Next summer I shall come here—I mean to Switzerland, for which my taste has revived. I am full of gratulation on your enlarged classes, chances of reading &c; & on your prospect of keeping the invalid child this winter.[7] Give my tender love to Alice. You are entering the period of keen suspense about Cleveland, & I share it even here. I have lately begun to receive & read the *Nation* after a long inter-val—& it seems to me very rough. Was it *ever* so? I wonder about Bob.

Ever your affectionate Henry James

[1] The James family stayed in the Hôtel de l'Écu in 1859.

[2] The Stevensons were on their way to Samoa.   The letter was probably written from one of the Marquesas Islands.

[3] Robert Louis Stevenson, *The Master of Ballantrae* (New York: Charles Scribner's Sons, 1889).

[4] According to HJ's letter to Francis Boott, 29 October 1888, Constance Fenimore Woolson was staying in a nearby hotel and HJ was seeing her regularly.

[5] HJ, "The Tragic Muse," *Atlantic Monthly,* January 1889–May 1890 (vols. 63–65).

[6] On 6 May 1882 several British officials were killed in Dublin.   This episode became known as the Phoenix Park murders.   The London *Times,* 18 April 1887, published a letter supposedly written by Parnell excusing the killings. A special commission, formed to investigate the *Times* allegations, began its inquiry on 17 September 1888.   The commission concluded that Parnell was innocent and that the *Times* letter was a forgery.

[7] HJ is replying to WJ's remark in his letter of 14 October 1888 that the James children will not go south for the winter of 1888–89.

To Henry James

                                              Cambr. Nov. 18. [1888]
My dear Harry
    A delightful letter from you from the Hotel de l'Ecu is hereby acknowledged.   It has given me a great yearning to skip over and gossip with you a while, and see the old haunts.   I am working hard and feeling well and overcome every now and then by the strangest desire to travel, E., W. or S.—anything but farther north by sea.   The funds however are not forthcoming and my next sabbatical year in Europe is a long way off.   Why shouldn't it be, however, since I don't need it for rest.   The Aspern Papers came duly and have been read. The A.P. themselves are a lovely story, all in tone and keeping.   The suicide of the American bride in the modern warning was rather abrupt & shocking to the reader, a piece of wanton tragedy as it seems.[1]   I am eager for all the other stories, Liar, London Life etc, of which I hear such accounts.[2]   I suppose they are to appear *incessament* and hope you'll send 'em without delay.   I wish you say what you mean by the greatness of the chasm between us and the french. Of course I say amen to all you write about the needlessness of one between us and the English.   I have much admired Brownell's article in the Nov. Scribner about french manners.[3]   He is over subtle in[4] often hard to understand, but I don't know any such delicate national psychologist, unless you should become one—some day you must write both on France and on England as substantive subjects.—Poor

Mrs. Lodge may be in a bad way though she is as affectionate and cheery as ever. She had a tumor cut out in the spring (from what organ I know not) and it may be cancerous. She *does n't know or suspect this!* So dont reveal it. But write to her if you can, often. She seems to hang upon you.

We are all well. No news except that poor Harry who is a model of health and vigor & goodness other wise, seems afflicted with head aches too frequently.—Mrs. Tappan is dead. I suppose you know. Good bye! this is no letter. Only an acknowledgement of yours.

W.J.

[1] HJ, "The Modern Warning," one of the stories in *The Aspern Papers*, tells of an American woman, Agatha Grice, who commits suicide after marrying Sir Rufus Chasemore, a Britisher writing an anti-American book. Her husband blames her anti-British brother, who in turn blames her anti-American husband.

[2] HJ, "The Liar," *Century Magazine* 36 (May 1888): 123–35; (June 1888): 213–23; "A London Life," *Scribner's Magazine* 3 (June 1888): 671–88; 4 (July 1888): 64–82; (August 1888): 238–49; (September 1888): 319–30; both reprinted in *A London Life* (1889).

[3] William Crary Brownell, "French Traits—Manners," *Scribner's Magazine* 4 (November 1888): 619–30; included in *French Traits: An Essay in Comparative Criticism* (1896).

[4] A slip for 'and'.

1889

For most of her life, Catharine Walsh was a member of her sister's household, acting at times, in the words of the elder Henry James, as both father and mother to the James children. Sometime around Christmas—no record of the trip is known—William James hurried to New York City, called there by Aunt Kate's illness. A few months later, probably on 2 March 1889, he again rushed to New York to get a "last smile of recognition" but was too late since she no longer recognized anyone. In New York he discovered that Henry James's letter of farewell had also arrived too late. Catharine Walsh died at midnight on 6 March, after William's return to Cambridge. Meanwhile, on 6 March, Robertson James and Alice Gibbens James had a sitting in Boston with Leonora Piper, in which the spirits told them of Aunt Kate's death. When they returned home, they found a telegram announcing the death, just as the spirits had told them they would.

During this period Alice James was living in Leamington, having moved there in late June 1887 to escape the stimulating effects of London upon her nerves. Aunt Kate's death precipitated a sad and ugly situation for Alice. Her regret that she had "failed" her aunt after the death of the elder Henry James turned to indignation when she learned that the provisions in Aunt Kate's will left her only a "life-interest" in a shawl and some silver. Some of her angriest letters to William date from this time.

From Henry James

34 De Vere Gardens W. | January 19ᵗʰ 1889.

Dear William.

I have been wishing and striving—for the past two or three weeks (ever since my return from abroad,) to write to you about Aunt Kate, dearest woman, but have vainly struggled with the aggregation of present importunities   Yesterday arrived, forwarded from Leamington, your interesting, moving & agitating letter, written after your return from N.Y. & accompanied by the 2 from Lilla Walsh (how lucidly & well she writes!) from whom, as well as from Helen Ripley,

Alice had already received tolerably definite reports.   Your letter makes me snatch this passing hour at any cost.   We have been won- dering at your silence about Aunt Kate—as we had begun to perceive, through her letters, a great change in her, beginning suddenly, from one letter to another, some three months ago.   But very likely you were more unperceiving through being in less constant correspon- dence with her: for she has continued to write to Alice, shortly & with visible feebleness, though by no means incoherently, till three or four weeks when she stopped—I sadly fear, beloved old aunt, almost forever.   I spent eight days near Alice, at Leamington, at the New Year & while there I wrote to her at some length & also wrote to Lilla Walsh.   I fear my letter to the former may have been a little too long & complicated—but I hope she was able to receive pleasure from it.   I shall write to her now *often,* very briefly & simply, till I hear that letters don't, mentally, reach her.   Your picture of her *fall,* as you so well say, is infinitely touching: & the idea of her talking helplessly about her helplessness.   She must, at present, suffer much from her inability to write to us—I can imagine nothing that would distress her more than to feel herself sinking away, as it were, from Alice.   One morning, in Leamington (the other day,) sitting by Alice's bed, I had a long talk with her about Aunt Kate & about all the past, which relieved somewhat a good deal of emotion & distress that she feels about being so far away from her & so cut off from her natural part of befriending her now.   I feel the same pain—& I would go over to her if I were free.   But I am, in my way, as helpless as poor Alice; that is, it would be madness for me to cross the ocean & leave Alice, in her state, alone in this country.   I did so lately, when I went to the continent: but I was already within telegraphic call in 30 hours. I found myself indeed the subject of telegraphic call a few days after my return; rushing down to learn that she had a very bad attack of the *heart*—alarming, for some hours, as if from one moment to an- other it might be fatal, produced, however, wholly by an external accident & following upon a period of several months of marked im- provement.   It is odd how, in this country, & in her extreme seclu- sion, she is liable to assaults of chance from the outside—the results of an "old civilization" & all more or less illustrative, fortunately, of English life.   This contretemps was a complicated story, not worth going into; the essence of which was simply that the other set of rooms in her house was unguardedly let to a young couple who proved to have taken them, concealing their situation, for the woman to be surely confined: which she was, offhand, with complications of

a dead child, not born dead, a young man drunken, noisy & inso-
lent & a nurse, brought in for them, who proved to be the same thing
in a still worse degree; all of which threw poor A. into such a state of
nervous terror that I had to remain with her a week—till the house
could be cleared of the people—a consummation delayed of course
through the condition of the mysterious mother. Their co[m]ing in
was a real accident (a momentary inadvertence of the landlady, who
is devoted to A. & wd. make any sacrifice for her,) the like of which
need *never*, with a little common care, occur again. For the present moreover, Alice has taken the rest of the house for herself. Her
nervous agitation (it is always *dread* & fear) brought on her violence
of the heart; but she was excellently attended by the shy Eardley-
Wilmot, & the thing passed away with a promptness & success which
was in itself a proof of her increase of strength. She is certainly
greatly better—I don't mean only of this particular access, but than
she was even 6 months ago. But it all makes me feel that it is impossible I should be really far from her. My coming cured her immediately (I mean the simple reassurance of my presence, as against the
idea of some assault on her by the terrible other nurse—*her's* is a real
pearl—& the cad of a man, whom I had a satisfactory scene with.)
Without it I think she might have passed away. Don't mention this
episode, please: she doesn't wish it spoken of: being, naturally, struck
with its sounding very "squalid." It wasn't, for *her;* but only agitating; & she has risen from it so promptly that I only tell it you for
your, as it were, amusement. I am full of the thought of how Aunt
Kate is to be cared for—& take consolation from your saying that she
will accept a paid caretaker as soon as that is necessary. I wrote on
purpose to thank Lilla for all *her* attention; & will do so again. Please
give us a word about her, so far as you know, when you can. Alice &
I are full of darkness, that is, of wonderment as to where, how &c he
is—about Bob. You haven't mentioned him for months. I hope
there have been no cataclysms that are unknown to us, & that you
have been thru no bad hours with him.—Alice tells me she has
received from your A., to whom I send much love, some "lovely"
photographs of your children, & as I probably shan't go back to
Leamington again for three or four weeks I shall ask her to *lend* me
a sight of them, so impatient am I to behold their loveliness. Your
remarks about A.'s *documentary* position here are excellent & cogent.
I wish something might come of it. Only *I* don't see her letters. I
wish I did. When I returned from abroad at Xmas, London seemed

all foul fog, sordid mud, vile low black brick, impenetrable English density & irrecoverably brutal & miserable lower classes!   But *I* am now better—if London isn't!

Ever your affectionate   Henry

To Henry James

Cambridge May 12. 89

My dear Harry

I have been feeling so dead-tired all this spring that I believe a long break from my usual scenes is neccessary.   It is like the fagged state that drove me abroad the last two times.   I have been pretty steadily busy for 6 years and the result isn't wonderful, considering what a miserable nervous system I have anyhow.   The upshot of it is that I have pretty much made up my mind to invest $1000 (if neccessary) of Aunt Kate's legacy in my constitution, and spend the summer abroad.   This will give me the long wished opportunity of seeing you & Alice, and enable me to go to an international congress of "physiological psychologists" which I have had the honour of an invitation to attend in the capacity of "honorary committee"man for the U.S.[1]   It will be instructive & inspiring, no doubt, and won't last long, and give me an opportunity to meet a number of eminent men.   But for these three reasons I think I should start for the Pacific Coast as being more novel.   I confess I find myself caring more for landscapes than for men—strange to say, and doubtless shameful, so my stay in London will probably be short.   I learn from Godkin that he is to be with you about the same time that I shall be in London.   I don't suppose you have room for both of us, but pray don't let that trouble you.   I can easily find a lodging somewhere for a few days, which are all that I shall stay.   I am heartily glad Godkin is about to go abroad, I know of no one who so richly deserves a vacation.   My heart is warming up again to the Nation, as it hasn't for many years. I long to have a good long talk with you about yourself, Alice, and 10000 old things.   Alice used to be so perturbed at *expecting* things that in my ignorance of her present condition I don't venture to announce to her my arrival.   But do you use your discretion as to when & how she shall be informed.   Send her this, if it is the best way.—It's a bad summer for me to be gone, with the house-building here, the Chocorua place unfinished, and the crowds set in motion by the Paris exhibition;[2] and *perhaps,* if I find myself unexpectedly hearty when lectures end 2 weeks hence, I may not go after all.   But I can't help feeling in my bones that I *ought* to go, so I probably shall. It will then be the Cephalonia, sailing June 22, and I shall get off at Queenstown, as I am on the whole more curious to see the Emerald Isle than any other part of Europe, except Scotland, which I probably shan't see at all.   The "Congress" in Paris begins Aug 5.

How good it will be to see poor Alice again, and to hear you discourse.

Ever affect^{ly}. yours | W.J.

[1] The International Congress of Experimental Psychology was held in Paris in August 1889.

[2] The Paris International Exposition was held in 1889.

Alice James's distress over her treatment in Aunt Kate's will resulted in an angry and sarcastic letter of 7 April 1889 to William. William's reply, in a letter now lost, was in Henry's view "not fortunate."

From Henry James

34, DE VERE GARDENS. W. June 13th 1889

My dear William.

I have just received your letter of the 4th, & I lose no time in answering it.   I thought it very likely I should hear from you in some such terms—for I knew, after the letter had gone, that Alice's Nurse had written to you; & I have been thinking more or less what I should tell you.   The 1st thing is to tell you that you must not let this episode exercise the *smallest* weight in the question of your coming out this summer; but decide it wholly on independent grounds.   You must not let it interfere on *any* ground—& least of all on the idea of Alice's not wanting to see you—or on that of any benefit to her in not seeing you.   I can imagine nothing worse for her than to learn, or suspect, afterwards, that you had given it up from any motive connected with your relations with her.   This would distress her more than anything else could do—& be much the *least* simplifying course.   For myself I greatly hope you will be able to come—for heaven knows when I

shall see you if you don't.   I long to talk with you—of, as you say, a
100 things; & so will Alice, as soon as her late *maladive* nervousness
has passed away.   She *delights,* in general, in your letters, & a *happy*
interview with you, which will come off of itself with perfect facility
when you are here, will do her more good than anything could do.
I think, when you see her, that you will find that all complications
will *of themselves* drop out.   She *was,* in fact, much upset by the letter
which led to her nurse's writing to you; & I may as well say, frankly,
that I myself thought it not fortunate, under the circumstances, &
tolerably irritated in tone—possessed as I necessarily am with the
sense that the extremity of her hapless condition makes it of *prime*
importance to allow her a large margin of sensibility.   In consequence
of what I heard I went down to Leamington the day after she got
your letter, & she talked much about it.   Of course as I hadn't seen
hers, to which it was an answer, I couldn't appreciate the case fully:
but I could see that, given hers (though she said she scarcely remembered it in detail,) she found your reply unexpected & angry.   The
fact is she was full of participation in *your* situation under Aunt Kate's
will (communicated to me all along,) & anything she wrote to you
was at bottom produced by a fermentation of feeling connected with
that.   She was keenly & I think not unjustly wounded by the *exceptional* provision, in the will, by which she was made, by law, the recipient of a life-interest in certain objects, with the determination of what
was to become of them afterwards.   In two or three other cases Aunt
Kate simply expressed a general suggestion as to how the legatee is
to leave the things; and Alice felt "singled out" where she least deserved it, &, as she said to me, publicly humiliated.   I say "least deserved it," because I think, really, that half her time in her lonely life
is spent in thinking over & planning what she can do with her little
property, at the end of that life, which she doesn't believe destined
to be long, for our benefit & especially for yours & your children's,
which is most upon her mind.   She animadverted to me, crying bitterly, on the cruelty or at least the infelicity of Aunt Kate's taking
from her, in her miserably limited little helpless life, passed in one
dreary room in a far-off country, the small luxury of devising *for herself* the disposal of the objects in question—to *you* as a perfect foregone conclusion—& of anticipating the pleasure she shld. thereby
give.   As I say, she told me she didn't remember definitely how she
had written to you, but that her letter proceeded really from a sense
that she had been snubbed in her innermost & most *reflective* preoccu-

pation with your affairs & your future—in their relation to what *she* can ultimately do; and I think that she honestly felt, on receipt of *your* letter, that she had been still more snubbed. This feeling was quite enough to overturn her—for the pity of her condition is that one can't without danger (a danger *great,* when one has seen her in one of her dreadfully bad states,) make any sort of retort or repartee to her. One must forego that otherwise natural right in consideration of the terrible nervousness that preys upon her, & as to which she is perfectly conscious that it makes her unreasonable. She is absolutely far from wishing to *se prévaloir* of this condition, and to me is perpetually—sometimes even in a kind of *terror,* which is most touching to me—asking for mercy for it and throwing herself on one's indulgence. Your mistake was, I take it, that you wrote to her too much as a well woman—the case being, as it often seems to me, that as regards any fitness for the contacts & accidents of life in general she is as little well as it is *possible* to be. Then, too, your letter came upon her when she was particularly agitated by all the general disquiet of the whole episode of A.K.'s illness death, will &c, & the suspense produced by Henry's condition & what might come of it. You say she had showed nothing of this in writing to you—but I think this was largely from a not unnatural fear that if she did so you would think she felt some *personal* disappointment in regard to what Aunt Kate had done with her money. I should do her great injustice if I seemed to suggest to you that she felt an *iota.* She spoke to me once, by accident, about the matter a year ago, & I was even surprised at the little that she took for granted. I had some difference with her about it—she telling me that she thought A.K. would leave her simply her *things*—clothes, few personal possessions &c—& *no* money: though this was perhaps partly because she believed she had so much less money than she really left. *This,* the amount of the estate, was a surprise to her; for she has spoken to me often of the misery she felt, at home, before coming away, about the extreme smallness of means of which A.K. often almost despairingly spoke to her, & about the question of whether she oughtn't, as a duty, to give her some of her own, so that she might not seem to be leaving her in poverty, in addition to the *fact* of leaving her. The last weeks she was at home she tells me she was quite tortured by this—& only did nothing because she felt, herself, so ill, so uncertain of the future, so *afraid* of it &c. I think she *was* a good deal staggered at finding Aunt Kate had a good deal more money than she herself, whereas she supposed she had a good deal less. The 1ˢᵗ thing she said to me when A.K.'s illness became apparent was that she & I must contribute to the wages of a caretaker for her, as she would be unable to pay them herself; & this we immediately wrote to Lilla. For the rest her discomposure at the will was wholly *un*personal & vicarious, as it were, & was largely communicated to her by mine. I am afraid you will only deride & think it grotesque when I tell you that mine was really "vicarious" too & was the result of a different preconception of what A.K. would do or rather what she would *not* do. I took for granted she would *not* leave the bulk of her money to the Stamford Walshes & *would* leave it to us, mother's children with whom her life had been spent & who would more naturally expect it—& with *us* I thought she would as a matter of course include Lilla. The 1st criticism Alice made, when she sent me your letter telling in a few words what the will was, was a regret that it didn't do *more* for Lilla & for you. You will probably think it *invraisemblable* if I tell you that *I* had expected A.K. would leave *you*, in view of your 3 children & their absence of moneyed relations from [whom] anything (considerable) more would come, about $20,000; & that my disappointment was largely owing to her not having done so. The 3 Walsh girls are unmarried & form a *combined* household in a house of their own, to which the gift of a smaller sum counts far more than when people are alone & houseless: therefore I thought she would leave them simply 3 or 4 thousand dollars apiece. Emmy Cochrane is married to a rich man—so I thought she would leave *her* nothing! In short I saw it all, in good faith, differently. I hate saying anything which seems to day a reflection on the judgment of the dear old Aunt, & I recognise that her view was a very possible & perfectly conscientious one. Only it took, when it came, considerable readjustment to embrace it. I had no idea at all *what* A.K.'s property was; but I was pretty sure it was more than Alice supposed.—I tell you all this because it helps to account for our not being in our *assiette* even quite yet in regard to the whole business—& Alice, as I say, largely *through* me.—Otherwise it seems a vain chewing over of dead trifles. And in reading over what I have written I seem to myself rather to have had the effect of magnifying the delicacy of Alice's condition than of reassuring you about it—which was what I intended. In a word she has no conscious resentment & not a bit of general unreasonableness of intention—She has only a chronic physical precariousness as to which, if you were to see her after so long an interval, you would probably agree that in dealing with her it can't well be too much considered. EVERYthing goes to her *legs*—helpless shrunken members whose condition seems to me the darkest spot of her future—though they definitely improve whenever she has a "let up."   Only pass over, in writing to her, everything as to which there is the least doubt; don't be literal or hold her—unless jocularly—to a normal account, & everything will be passing well.   I hope you will keep the silver, saying nothing about it for the present: indeed I feel tempted, as a favour, to beseech you to do so: & then, *later,* write her a friendly note about it.   And it would be an act of rare beneficence if you would write *me* a note that I could *send on to her* expressing your regret at the consequences of your letter, saying it was all a miscalculation of means—& professing in short an affectionate & even (if you don't mind it!) an exaggerated remorse.   She is wonderfully open to that sort expression—& it would clear up everything.   You might even then say you are coming out *because you want to see her*—& that would be the best & simplest way for her to learn it.—I feel as if I had still a lot more to say; but this is enough—& I am pushed with other writing.   Godkin is with me—tho' in the country today—& he takes me inevitably a goodish bit off my work.   I will only repeat that you must not for the world modify your coming on Alice's acct., but come *straight,* if you can arrange it.   And I think very well indeed of the idea that you should in a letter to me that I can show her express regret at her overturn & say that it is your desire to express it further that, taken with your other reasons, is sending you forth.   Also that you wrote to *me* on purpose.   This would have a boundless efficacity; & make everything all right—make her want to see you—though not to humiliate you.   Much love to your Alice—whom I thank tenderly for her tribute to my "tact".   May it never be wanting!   We have had some lovely warm days & Alice has been out in her chair & is much the better for it.—I am almost startled by a quite affectionate note from Wendell Holmes telling me he is coming out next month—the only manifestation I have had from him for years. Godkin is less light than of yore—but good company.

Ever your   Henry.

P.S.   The *Venice* &c, as to which you sent a postcard some time ago, saying it had started or was to start, thro' Sherlock's agent, has never yet arrived—with Lizzie B.'s little landscape, the clock(!) &c.   Grandmother Walsh's picture *has,* on the other hand, & is a very pleasant, beautifying possession to me.[1]   Do you know exactly *how* the Venice was to come?

[1] AJ left various possessions in WJ's care when she moved to England and in letters to him often returned to the question of their disposition.   The items listed are appar-

ently those that AJ had requested. The *Venice* was probably a painting owned by AJ; the "little landscape" is by Elizabeth Boott Duveneck. The grandmother was Elizabeth Robertson Walsh (1781–1847).

The unpleasantness over Aunt Kate's will prevented William James from informing his sister in advance about his European tour. He sailed from Boston on the Cephalonia, *reaching Queenstown in Ireland on 1 July 1889 and disembarking there to visit his ancestral homeland and Scotland before proceeding to Liverpool. On 18 July he and Henry arrived in Leamington for the dreaded meeting with Alice. According to her diary, Henry went into the house first to get some sense of how Alice might behave, leaving William outside to watch for a signal—a handkerchief tied to the balcony. According to Alice's diary, Henry looked "as white as a ghost" from anxiety while William had not changed much in the last five years. All "that there is to be said of him, of course, is that he is simply himself" and "would lend life and charm to a treadmill," she wrote in her diary for 4 August. While in England, William tried unsuccessfully to persuade Henry to buy some land at Chocorua.*

In early August, William was in Paris for the International Congress of Experimental Psychology, having spent two "very pleasant" days at Boulogne walking on the beaches that he remembered from childhood. At the congress one of his concerns was to win support for the census of hallucinations, an extensive statistical study of hallucinations corresponding with actual events that had been initiated by Edmund Gurney. William became the collector for the census in America, receiving and writing several thousand letters in connection with it. On 15 August he sailed for Boston on the Cephalonia.

Meanwhile, work was progressing on the Jameses' permanent home at 95 Irving Street in Cambridge. Until they were able to partially move into the new house in October, Alice and the children stayed in Chocorua, William at Grace Norton's at 43 Kirkland Street. In a letter of 4 September 1889, now lost but mentioned by Henry in his letter below, William apparently described himself looking out the window at his future home.

To Henry James

Chocorua N.H. | Aug 30. 89

Dear Harry,

I have now been at home 4 days and am quite settling into my old ruts of desk-work in the A.M. and out of door work or expatiation in the afternoon.   I find the family in splendid condition, the baby a real beauty, and Billy looking particularly well.   Alice has had a rather dull summer, having badly sprained her ancle, and kept it concealed from me, and being I think, rather tired with her monotonous pursuance of household duties for so many years.   I wish we had come abroad together—but its too late for regrets, and her turn will come ere long.   I don't myself at all repent of coming home, as I shall have a good month of work (and consequent worry saved from next year) and my expedition was a perfect success as it stands.   Of the two farms I spoke of, the one adjoining our own on top of the hill was sold to Mr. John Albee the day before I arrived, much to Alices chagrin who supposed herself to have the refusal of it.   I don't regret it, nor does she now.   The other place is much the finer of the two.   I will go over it as soon as possible and report.   As an investment it is perfectly *secure,* to say the very least—and it will lock up some of your money if you take it.   Two other places have been sold here this summer.—Adieu for the "nonce."   Travelling makes the world seem smaller—and sadder in a fashion.   The pleasantest part of my trip to look back on was my leisurely stay with you which gave us a chance to become intimate again as in old times.   I much enjoyed it.   The voyage home was so good that a few more like it would almost corrupt one into reconciliation with the Ocean.—Send this to Alice, to whom much love.   I hope that she is swimming in a sea of felicity with Katherine L.—My Alice sends much love, and thanks for portfolio and book.

Fare well.   W.J.

From Henry James

Lord Warden Hotel | Dover Sept. 21st [1889]

My dear William.

Comfortable news of you has come to me through a good note from you of Aug. 30th, accompanying a still better one of your wife's; & more lately through my receiving from Leamington, after Alice had read it, your delightful letter of September 4ᵗʰ. They all give me the idea that you presented yourself aux vôtres—& to yourself—in good shape when you returned. A flash, as you say your visit was—so much so that it seems to me now to have been rather projected & written & telegraphed about than actually performed. However it was a flash which lights up—or leaves less dark—one's sense of your general situation. I am delighted that even at the end of some days of relapsed existence your rush abroad appeared to have served a practical purpose. My heart bleeds that that purpose should not have included Alice, since it was a possibility that it might. Tell her with my love & many thanks for her sweet note, that I know exactly how she feels & feel, myself, almost guilty, at not having had a hand in alleviating her this summer. Your allusions to your beautiful rustic home & your swimming, riding & rowing children, seem to transport you already to fabulous distances: my own life has jogged along so much on the brick & mortar since we parted. I have rescued the last three weeks, however, from the too prosaic London. I remained there till Aug. 31ˢᵗ, when I went up to Whitby, on the Yorkshire coast, & spent 4 days with the eternally juvenile & most sociable & hospitable Lowell. I am very fond of the picturesque place, lying between an equal grandeur of coast & "purple" moors, & enjoyed a (to me) exciting amount of out of doors. Then I came & spent three days at York, in whose grey old minster & city walls I delight; after which I returned rather vaguely to London; which however, then, seemed so stale & close that I quickly fled from it & made for the blue sea at this convenient place, which I like & where I have spent the last ten days. We are having the finest, brightest September. Paris hasn't yet come off—I have been working too continuously. The exhibition, however, is to be continued through November, & I have the time.[1] I remain here till the 25ᵗʰ, when I go to spend 3 days with Lord Coleridge in Devonshire—with probabilities of being through October in London, which I then shan't object to. Katherine Loring's stay with Alice makes me communicate with Leamington much less—& this intermission is a change & a rest all round. But I surmise that her presence there is very beneficent & salutary—to herself as well—& it seems to proceed without interruptions—unberufen! I am interested in what you tell me about the farm near you that is not sold; & shall probably assent to any rerecommendation that you make—if the purchase-money is really little—in regard to my becoming the owner of it.   In this case I shall probably tell you take some of the Syracuse money for the purpose; but please let me understand about it 1$\underline{\text{st}}$ & I will reply definitely.   There may be some other way of arranging it.   I note gratefully the episode of your station in your nightshirt at Grace Norton's window—gazing at your house in the August dawn—it must have seemed queer indeed, with all the dead past putting in such an appearance at the same time.   May the house have a happier future than any past.

Ever your affectionate—& Alices—Henry

¹ Paris International Exposition.

William James, ca. 1869.
(By permission of the Hough-
ton Library, Harvard Uni-
versity)

William James, ca. 1873.
(By permission of the Hough-
ton Library, Harvard Uni-
versity)

William James. *(From the*
Edward Bok Collection
[# 6779], by permission of the
Clifton Waller Barrett Li-
brary, Special Collections De-
partment, University of Vir-
ginia Library)

Henry James at Geneva,
1859–60. *(By permission
of the Houghton Library,
Harvard University)*

Henry James, 1882. *(By
permission of the Houghton
Library, Harvard University)*

A sketch of Henry James
by John Singer Sargent.
(From the Yellow Book, *July
1894)*

Henry James in the New York studio of Alice Broughton, 1906. *(From Harry T. Moore,* Henry James and His World)

Henry James. *(By permission of Mrs. Francis L. Pell)*

Henry James, Sr. *(By permission of the Houghton Library, Harvard University)*

Mary Temple. *(By permission of the Houghton Library, Harvard University)*

Garth Wilkinson James, December 1868. *(By permission of the Houghton Library, Harvard University)*

Robertson James at Mil-
waukee, ca. 1872. *(By permission of the Houghton Library, Harvard University)*

Alice James, June 1870.
*(By permission of the Hough-
ton Library, Harvard Uni-
versity)*

Alice Howe Gibbens
James, ca. mid-1870s. *(By
permission of the Houghton
Library, Harvard University)*

HOUSE FOR PROFESSOR WILLIAM JAMES ON IRVING STREET.

From the *Cambridge Tribune,* 27 July 1889.

The James house at Chocorua, N.H. *(By permission of Jacques Barzun)*

William James (*right*) at Chocorua, with Paul Ross, the Jameses' handyman. *(By permission of the Houghton Library, Harvard University)*

The Robert Gould Shaw Memorial, Boston. *(From a 1906 postcard)*

1890

In November 1889 William James's title at Harvard was changed from professor of philosophy to professor of psychology, a somewhat ironic development since he was approaching the end of his career as a contributor to psychology. His new salary was $4,000 a year. The contract with Henry Holt for The Principles of Psychology *had set 12 June 1880 as the deadline for completion of the manuscript. Now, some ten years later, he was finally to finish the job. Thus, the academic year of 1889–90 had to be one of feverish activity with James facing a 1 May 1890 deadline. The manuscript of* Principles, *which he estimated at 460,000 words, was finished at last on 19 May, and he spent the summer of 1890 reading proof and working on the index. With his wife and children at Chocorua, he spent most of the day working, then took the car to Boston, posted the completed pages to Holt, and about nine in the evening took his meal in a Boston restaurant. On 26 September he received printed copies of the book.*

One of Henry James's longest novels, The Tragic Muse, *estimated at about 200,000 words, was published in June 1890. That spring he was alive with schemes for making a fortune in the theater and in his letter of 9 March alludes to his plan to dramatize* The American.

From Henry James

34, DE VERE GARDENS, | W. March 9ᵗʰ 1890

My dear William

Your stereotype plates, in compliance with your last letter, went to you by an express agency more than a week ago.[1] I *pre*paid them—it was very little—so you ought to have no charge to meet. But you *will*—one always has—but it ought to be very trifling. Your letter had the scent of a hospital on it, so overcharged was it with the sad ailments of your house. I hope poor dear little Billy's bad head was less gruesome than it sounded—though certainly it must have sounded enough if he was "shouting with pain." I hope a healthy stillness has overtaken all these troubles & that Alice has been able to rest from such a burden of woe. Give my very best love to her & tell her that the next time things get so tight she must just quickly ship herself over to me till the squall (& the squalling) is past. I shall be delighted to lodge her here in my quiet spare room, alongside of me, & nurse & soothe & watch over her. I can assure her the maximum of refreshment with the minimum of responsibility & all the brilliancies of London with none of its troubles. What's the good of having a good healthy foreign spare-room in the family without ever using it?—for your scant inhabitancy last year is not worth speaking of. The dark pestilence hung over London for weeks & weeks—& has scarcely gone yet—but I am afraid I rather inhumanly liked it— it made one's life here so quiet. I had it very lightly, & at Leamington Alice hasn't had it at all—though her house (nurse, landlady, &c) was full of it. She has had a better winter than ever since she came to this country—that is very evident. Her bad moments have been fewer & shorter. I go down to see her tomorrow—1ˢᵗ time for 6 or 7 weeks, & shall add a word to this when I come back—keeping it over for the purpose. I am in better heart about her than I have been for a long time. Thanks to the bad state of London—which has kept its importunities *down,* I have had a very good winter of work. I am trying with great energy & conviction, great confidence, or at any rate great resolution, as I may say, some new ventures which I won't talk of now, but which you will know & judge by their results—as I hope essentially to do myself, inasmuch as these results are intended to be profoundly pecuniary. MARCH 13ᵗʰ. I had to stop off on Sunday, & on Monday (this is Wednesday,)[2] I went down to see Alice & spent my usual five hours with her. Seeing her again confirmed my aforesaid impression of her good winter—though it confirmed also, I am sorry to say, my sense of what a very relative matter that implication of "strength" is confined to being; &, further, revived the depressing vision of her almost absolute solitude. Her meagre tabby cat little society there is too poor to be "kept up," or to keep itself up, & for all practical purposes she is wholly alone. Not that she admits for a moment that she suffers from it—she regards it as an advantage & in many ways it is. But the advantage is overdone. However it will all ["]work out"—& meanwhile her interest in politics & in the Irish question &c, almost constitutes a roomful for her. This A.M. she sends me Lilla Walsh's two letters to you, & your own note, announcing poor Henry's death.[3] It lifts a black weight off one's chronic consciousness—but I fear that "theres more to come" which will deposit there in his stead a burden of worry for some time. I can only think Mrs. A.W. will be very shameless to contest (rich, largely benefitted & childless as she is,) & very lucky if she contests successfully—sane & *un*eccentric as the will is. But she may be both shameless & lucky—we shall see.[4] Meanwhile the uncertainty will disagree with many persons—& be especially flatting out to poor Alice.—Mrs. Stanley Clarke goes to America in a few days to spend only 6, one of them—or even less than 24 hours—of course at the Tweedies. Her brother Charles Rose takes her; & *she* takes to you, to post in N.Y. an interesting little volume sent you by its author, through me, he being much interested in your work, & especially in your introduction to Father's *Remains*. He brought me a letter of introduction from France this winter, & is a very "fine mind" & interesting nature. He is a Connecticutt American by birth but has lived in Europe all his life, was educated in France from his infancy (so that he looks & speaks like a Frenchman;) is married to a German, is evidently well-off, & lives at Geneva, Florence & such places. He is working seriously at philosophy & writing another book. The one I send you "Theories of Anarchy and Law: a Midnight Debate," strikes me—I have read it—as rather exquisite & remarkable. Acknowledge it in some way *if you can*, to *Henry B. Brewster, Union Bank, Geneva*.[5] I have seen him a number of times during three months he has just spent in London, & found him an esprit bien distingué. I am very sorry to hear of your miscarried dinner party, mentioned in your letter to Alice, & which I doubt not you too luridly paint. I wish I cld. ship you my servants. I "entertain" in my small way without the least difficulty, & could do it in a much larger one with just as little. But I seem to mock at you. I have been fascinated by the *Hidden Self,* in *Scribner*—& I quite yearn for your book.[6] The prime motive—or almost—of the mysterious artistico-financial schemes above mentioned is to obtain more time for reading—for I shall lose my reason unless I do. I leave town on May 1ˢᵗ for May, June, July, & if I can, August; but don't know yet where I go. Much love to Alice & all round. I am today also writing to Grace Norton for news of Lowell.[7]

Ever your affectionate   Henry

[1] WJ had requested plates of an article in *Mind* for use in connection with *Principles*.

[2] Wednesday was 12 March.

[3] Henry Albert Wyckoff died on 23 February 1890.

[4] The will was contested and the case dragged on until the fall of 1894. Mrs. Albert Wyckoff was Sarah J. Wyckoff, wife of Henry Albert Wyckoff's nephew.

[5] Henry Bennet Brewster, *The Theories of Anarchy and the Law: A Midnight Debate* (1887).

[6] WJ, "The Hidden Self," *Scribner's Magazine* 7 (March 1890): 361–73; reprinted in *EPs*.

[7] Lowell was fatally sick.

To Henry James

Newport | April 2nd. 90

Dear Harry

I got the electrotype blocks duly and your letter shortly thereafter. I am much obliged to you for prepaying them which of course I never dreamed of your doing; and can only say that it will be one more of the things which will make it the easier to support you in your old age. I have just dictated and written a letter to Alice which she will of course send on to you, and which contains a certain amount of gossip that I needn't here repeat.[1] I am heartily glad both for your sake and Alice's of the plan you announce of spending the 'season' abroad. I[t] ought to refresh both of you very much. How is the Smith difficulty to be regulated? I suppose the fortune making plan to which you so mysteriously allude is the dramatization of the American, and possibly something additional thereto. I have long been curious to know how that business was ripening, & wish that you would let me know something definite. I am eager to read the Tragic Muse. But it seems quite interminable—I suppose it will be out soon however. My own book gets on steadily, and August will see it published, at this rate. I have no other news to communicate or remarks to make beyond what Alice's letter contains

So good bye.—We are just about starting for a walk, on the blowing sunny cliffs with Daisy Waring, whose portrait of Tweedy is really good,—Brother Bob keeps right side up very steadily. Is much pre-occupied with spirit rappings etc, *one* of which he swears he indubitably got by himself alone lately. I will write again ere long.

Affect[ly] yours   Wm James

[1] WJ's letter to AJ of 2 April 1890 includes information about the will of Henry Albert Wyckoff from which they hoped to benefit but which was being disputed.

To Henry James

Tamworth Iron Works (no longer "Chocorua") N.H. June 4. 90
My dear Harry, Your delightful long letter from Milan came four
days ago whilst I was still at home all by myself trying to tie up the
loose ends of the College year. I am now in this peaceful abode
joined to the rest of the family for a few days, ere I have to descend
upon Cambridge again for an examination. I am thoroughly glad
to hear of you away for the London season which by this time must
be pretty hollow and innutritious as well as exhausting. In the original form in which I heard that you were going, Alice was to take your
place in De Vere Gardens, but as you say nothing about that, I suppose it has fallen through, for which I feel very sorry, as I imagine
that the change of scene would refresh her, whatever incidental damage might come of the fatigue etc. The newspapers speak of the
great H.M.S. being at 34 de Vere Gardens,[1] but I suppose you would
have mentioned the fact had he become your tenant. The colossal
magnitude of all popularities nowadays spoils everything. I should
think that Stanley would wish to be back in the African forest among
his dwarfs. It makes all literary and scientific successes greater also
than they ever were before. The competition gets harder and
harder because the rivals are more numerous, but the *top*-man has
an audience the like of which never existed on earth before. This
is to encourage you still more about your mysterious fortune making
plans, which I assume to be of a theatrical sort—the formation of an
international "trust" to produce your plays simultaneously in all the
capitals of the earth, or something of that kind. You ought to know
enough critically about the qualities that the stage requires, if you
can only cold bloodedly throw in enough *action* to please the people.
Last week the climax seemed reached in the modern development
of the drama, when I read on a street poster the advertisement of a
play called the Fakir, the words NO PLOT—ALL FUN! as its crowning attraction. What a relief to the intellect to have *no* plot! I trust
that whatever the mystery is to be, I shall learn it the first day it is
"out."—The Tragic Muse is not yet received, I am ready and hungry
for it. I heard great things of it at first* but of late never a word—
it may have kept a going too long. The *only* way for me to read a
novel is to read it straight through myself. I can't tell what deadness
and disillusion steal in from too interrupted an ingestion in doses
that are too small. I have just been reading with great delight Hall
Caine's "Bondman"—not exactly in your style, but a noble and mas-

terly thing all the same.[2] Who is the cuss? How old? a Scotchman,
I suppose! I rejoice at your praise of the good Howells's last book—
The print has been too small for me to read and it has been too
long to read aloud, but Alice has been enthusiastic over it.[3] Barring
Howells's queer spasmodic moralism which I confess that I cannot at
all understand, I think he is always delectable.

And now for home news! I wrote to Alice a week ago a very con-
densed abstract of a lot of it, which she will, I suppose, have forwarded to you duly so that you will have got it ere you get this. The
Syracuse fire is being repaired fast, and the prospects are that we
shall even make a little off the insurance rather than lose anything.[4]—
Poor Kitty Prince has been very badly, and a week ago was supposed
to be dying, but she has revived some what, and I fear may continue
to live. But I imagine that after this attack the end cannot be much
delayed.—The great event for me is the completion at last of my
tedious book. I have been at my desk with it every day since I got
back from Europe, and up at 4 in the morning with it for many a
day of the last month. I have written every page 4 or 5 times over,
and carried it "on my mind" for 9 years past, so you may imagine
the relief. Besides I am glad to appear at last as a man who has
done something more than make phrases and projects. I will send
you a copy, in the Fall I trust, though H. Holt is so inert about starting
the proofs that we may not get through till midwinter or later. *As
Psychologies go,* it is a good one, but psychology is in such an ante-
scientific condition that the whole present generation of them is pre-
destined to become unreadable old mediaeval lumber, as soon [as]
the first genuine tracks of insight are made. The sooner the better,
for me!—On the evening of May 31st the new Club was opened in
our old Quincy St. house.[5] All freshly papered painted carpeted and
decorated, the old house looked quite grand, and bright. The upper
rooms will be kept as bedrooms for transient guests. Father's and
Mothers room and the old picture gallery are thrown into one, with
the hall made smaller in consequence, and a wide central door opening into the picture gallery part. Altogether the impression was as
pleasing as it had been depressing a few months previous when I had
gone through the house and tasted the bitter sweets of memory, with
it all so shrunken, dark and shabby before my eyes.—Of personal
gossip I have none to communicate, since I see so little of the
world.—Grace Norton remains the same. Charles ditto. The
Child's, except Susy who is temporarily down, are rosier and smil-
inger and better than ever. I have only seen Lowell once since his

illness—too busy every moment of the time to get there. But I will try it again next week when I return. Poor dear young Gemma Timmins is dead—God rest her soul—the most *delightful* young woman in Boston. Her loss is a sad blow to the Brimmer's and is universally mourned.[6] Mr. Boott, the Lothrops, and Edward Hooper and his girls all sail on Saturday the 7th in the Cephalonia. E.H. sent me 400 volumes of the Gurney's books a week ago, which make a good deal of difference in the look of my shelves.[7] Altogether I feel stout and middle aged and prosperous. I find that the size and comfort of the Cambridge house has made this little place seem cheaper. Tis ever thus. But it is an admirable place for the family as a whole. The children are getting more and more delightful as they get older, and enjoy the garden horses cows etc as ducks enjoy water. They have a first rate riding pony, and I have invested $150 + 40 dolla[r]s in an excellent saddle horse which our darkey Andrew bro't up from S.C. I mean to keep in the saddle as much as possible this summer and see the effect of it. It may prove very salubrious. I shall need all my health next year, for my college work will be harder than anything I have ever had before. After that, a year of absence, with the whole family abroad!—I am forgetting to mention that I got a short note from Lilla yesterday saying that Albert & consort were going to contest the will. I am very sorry, especially for Alices sake. Lilla said that she had written her details, so I believe I didn't send her note, which was very short. I am writing to her now to find out what pecuniary liabilities the heirs by the will are exposed to. Pray send this letter (which is written in the first breathing space of the year) to Alice to whom I wrote most telegraphically last week. This is for her as much as for you. Alice sends her "feelingest" love to both of you; and I hope you'll have the most prosperous of summers whilst the Tory party in England moves slowly and the republican party here dances enthusiastically to its doom!

Ever thy | Wm. J.

*I have already reported to you Howells's & Lowell's praise.

[1] Nothing was found linking Henry Morton Stanley and 34 De Vere Gardens.

[2] Sir Hall Caine, *The Bondman: A New Saga* (1889).

[3] William Dean Howells, *A Hazard of New Fortunes* (1890).

[4] The fire of 24 April 1890 affected only the James property. Newspaper reports placed the total loss at $60,000 and noted that most of the tenants were underinsured (Clippings at the Onondaga Historical Society).

[5] The Colonial Club, which opened at 20 Quincy St., Cambridge, maintained card rooms, a bowling alley, a library, and other facilities for encouraging "social intercourse." The address is now that of the Harvard Faculty Club.

[6] Mary Ann Timmins Brimmer was an aunt of Gemma Timmins. The Brimmers were responsible for Gemma's upbringing after the death of her father.

[7] Many books from WJ's library are preserved at Houghton and some are signed by Ephraim Whitman Gurney. E.H. is Edward William Hooper.

To Henry James

TAMWORTH IRON WORKS, | N.H. June 26. [1890]

My dear Harry

At last you've done it and no mistake. The Tragic Muse caps the climax. It is a most original, wonderful, delightful and admirable production. It must make you feel jolly to have so masterfully and effortlessly answered the accusation that you could do nothing but the international and cosmopolitan business; for cosmopolitan as the whole atmosphere of the book is, yet the people and setting are most easily and naturally english, and the perfect air of good society which reigns through the book is one of its most salient characteristics. It leaves a good taste in ones mouth, everyone in it is human and good, and although the final winding up is, as usual with you, rather a losing of the story in the sand, yet that is the way in which things lose themselves in real life. The only thing I positively find to object to in the book is the length of the chapter on Mr. Nash's portrait, which is a little too much in the Hawthornian allegorizing vein for you.[1]—I have nothing to say in detail. The whole thing hangs together most intimately and well; and it is truly a spectacle for rejoicing to see that by the sort of practice a man gives himself he attains the plenitude and richness which you have at last got. Your sentences are straighter and simpler than before, and your felicities of observation are on every page. I wish you had managed to bring in a little more business with Julia ere the end; her love making scene was exquisite; but it must be a difficult task to tread the crack between her charms and femininity and her hardness and politicicality.[2] The whole thing is an exquisite mirage which remains afloat in the air of one's mind. I imagine that that sort of thing is extremely educative to a certain "section" of the community. As for the question of the size of your public, I tremble. The work is too refined, too elaborate and minute, and requires to be read with too much leisure to appeal to any but the select few. But you mustn't mind that. It will *always* have its audience. No reason however for not doing less elaborate things for wider audiences; which I hope ere long to have direct testimony that you have done.

I've been up here 10 days, very lazy and contented as usual after the end of the College year. The family is extremely well, and I have again a good young tutor in the house. I'm afraid we're on the road to financial ruin, but these years are the planting of a certain capital of health & experience in the boys and in fact to some degree in all of us, of which the fruits will be reaped when we're older & the place is sold. Our darkey bro't up a first-rate new saddle horse for me from Aiken—I wanted to test thoroughly the sanatory effect of riding.—Our baby is the prettiest and most charming little 3-year old flirt. The boys are already good riders, harry a first rate fearless swimmer, and both of them great insect-collectors, and (now) poppers away at birds with their air-guns. The place is getting more and more into shape and a relatively passive life is more and more possible. The success of it so far is all due to Alice's really remarkable practical energy and good sense, which seems to take hold of rural affairs with particular success. I confess that the care of the fields and the garden weigh heavily on *my* contemplative disposition.—I just got a note from Leslie Stephen who is staying in Cambridge, declining to come up here. I'm glad I asked him and glad on the whole that he couldn't come. We shall have few guests this year. My proofs have only just begun coming in; but they promise to come thick and fast. I take little pride or pleasure in the accursed book, which has clung to me so long, but I shall be glad to have it out, just to show that I *can* write one book.—Send this to Alice, whom I have treated shabbily of late in the way of letters; but that is due to the mere external accident of *your* having written the Tragic Muse. Tell her that J.B.W. informs me that the courts make a handsome "allowance" out of the *estate* for the defence of a will; so we need not neccessarily be impoverished even if Mrs. Albert gains her cause,[3] which I devoutly hope she won't.

Yrs ever   W.J.

[1] Gabriel Nash is the well-educated and talkative friend of several of the central characters in *The Tragic Muse*.

[2] In *The Tragic Muse*, Julia Dallow, a widow, is in love with Nicholas Dormer, the hero of the novel. Julia breaks off their engagement because she prefers politics while he prefers the life of a painter.

[3] Sarah J. Wyckoff.

From Henry James

Paradisino, | Vallombrosa, | Tuscany. | July 23ᵈ 1890.
My dear Brother:

I had from you some 10 days ago a most delightful letter written just after the heroic perusal of my interminable novel—which, according to your request, I sent off, almost too precipitately, to Alice, so that I haven't it here to refer to. But I don't need to "refer" to it, inasmuch as it plunged me into a glow of satisfaction which is far, as yet, from having faded. I can only thank you tenderly for seeing so much good in the clumsy thing—as I thanked your Alice, who wrote me a most lovely letter, a week or two ago. I have no illusions of any kind about the book, & least of all about its circulation & "popularity." From these things I am quite divorced & never was happier than since the dissolution has been consecrated by (what seems to me) the highest authorities. One must go one's way & know what one's about & have a general plan & a private religion—in short have made up one's mind as to *ce qui en est* with a public the draggling after which simply leads one in the gutter. One has always a "public" enough if one has an audible vibration—even if it shld. only come for one's self. I shall never make my fortune—nor anything like it; but—I know what I shall do, and it won't be bad.—I am lingering on late in Italy, as you see, so as to keep away from London till August 1ˢᵗ or thereabouts. (I stay in this exquisite spot till that date.) I shall then, returning to my normal occupations, have had the best & clearest & pleasantest holiday, of 3 months, that I have had for many a day. I have been accompanied on this occasion by a literary irresponsibility which has caused me to enjoy Italy perhaps more than ever before: let alone that I have never before been perched (more than three thousand feet in the air) in so perfect a paradise as this unspeakable Vallombrosa. It is Milton's Vallombrosa, the original of his famous line, the site of the old mountain-monastery which he visited & which stands still a few hundred feet below me as I write, "suppressed" & appropriated some time ago by the Italian Government, who have converted it into a State school of "Forestry."[1] This little inn—the Paradisino, as it is called, on a pedestal of rock overhanging the violet abysses like the prow of a ship, is the Hermitage (a very comfortable one,) of the old convent. The place is extraordinarily beautiful & "sympathetic"—the most romantic mountains & most admirable woods—chestnut & beech & magnificent pine-forests, the densest, coolest shade, the freshest, sweetest air & the most enchanting views.   It is full 20 years since I have done anything like so much wandering through dusky woods & lying with a book on warm, breezy hillsides.   It has given me a sense of summer which I had lost in so many London Julys; given me almost the summer of one's childhood back again.   I shall certainly come back here for other Julys & other Augusts—& I hate to go away now.   May you, & all of you, these weeks, have as sweet, or ½ as sweet an impression of the natural universe as yours affectionately

Henry James

¹ Vallombrosa, a well-known resort near Florence, is the site of an old Benedictine abbey.   HJ is alluding to Milton's *Paradise Lost*, bk. 1, lines 302–3: "Thick as autumnal leaves that strow the brooks in Vallombrosa."

On 2 August 1890 Alice James suffered a serious breakdown in Leamington and sent a telegram recalling Henry from his "paradise" at Vallombrosa. Shortly thereafter Henry telegraphed for Katharine Loring and the two moved Alice to the South Kensington Hotel in London. Alice, who described her symptoms as "squalid indigestions," was diagnosed less than a year later as having breast cancer and was suspected of having cancer of the liver. In her diary for 12 September 1890, she found "cheering to all parties" a doctor's remark that patients in her condition "sometimes" die, her only regret being that she who had been "denied all dramatic episodes" would most likely die in her sleep and would not be a member of the audience as "the curtain rolls down on this jocose humbuggery."

To Henry James

TAMWORTH IRON WORKS, | N.H. Aug 22. 90

My dear Harry,

It gave me great pleasure to get your letter from Vallombrosa about a fortnight ago, but still greater pain to hear from K.P.L. a week later of your being summoned to Alice, and of that poor girl having to call Katherine again to her side.   If only something could be *done* for her, but my mind wanders among the possibilities in vain.   I await anxiously your account of the whole thing, and as speculation is idle I will say no more until it comes, but tell you of our own news.—You see now why I have been urging you all these years to take more of your vacation in the face of nature.   Your last two letters have breathed a spirit of youth, a sort of Lebenslust, which has long been absent from them, and which nothing but mother earth can give. Alternation between her and the gas-lit life of corrupt capitals is the optimum for man here below.   Ne[i]ther element alone will do, but both must be there.   I'm glad you've had such a vacation from writing.   I don't see how either you or Howells can keep it up at such a rate.   I am just now in the middle of his Hazard of N.F. which is an extraordinarily vigorous production, quite up to Dickens I should say, in humour, detail of observation and geniality, with flexible human beings on the stage instead of puppets.   With that work, your tragic muse, and last, *but by no means least,* my psychology, all appearing in it, the year 1890 will be known as the great epocal year in American literature.   I finished and post my index yesterday, so my mind is free to turn to the Universe receptively again.   A wondrous boon.   I have been six weeks in Cambridge all alone in the house, until the last week when Alice came down, and cooked and helped, and corrected 1400 pp. of proofs, much of them in small type.   I almost never got away from my writing-table till 9 P.M. and then used in a starving condition, to go booming along through the sultry night on the front seat of an electric car, the finest locomotion in the world, to get my dinner between 9 & 10 at Young's or Parker's after mailing the proofs in the Boston P.O. to catch the late N.Y. mail. It was hard on the digestive organs, but it has left no bad effects, and I look back to the month and a half of it as a most delightful period of time—only one thing to thing about, and great strides of progress in that every day—so different from the College year, with 50 things to think about and no sensible progress made at all.   But it is the sort of life to which you have been long accustomed, so it will make you smile to hear me making such a fuss.   I took my breakfast, *or* lunches, in the Club house in Quincy St in our old dining room, which like the whole house, with its new paint and paper, hardly reminded me at all of old times, save for the outlook rather more umbrageous than of yore, from the windows.—I have just raised $4000—500 I hope, of them from Tweedy—for a psychological Laboratory and fixings, so with that and other things I expect to have a hardworking year of it next year.[1]   We ought to get abroad for 1891–2 if it be possible to afford it, but nothing will be known about

it until next spring.—Alice wears well, and is in good condition morally and intellectually this summer, although suffering for 10 days
past with a tremendous cold—"Mamma's Nase is ganz *abgenutzt*"
(worn-out), said the infant Margaret Mary this A.M.   Good bye!
Heaven bless you!   Send this to Alice whom Heaven bless also, if it
can bless.

Yrs W.J.

I spent a night at Wendell's Holmes's (who is with his father at
Beverly) lately   He said he would have crossed the atlantic for no
other purpose than to have seen *you* last summer.   Also a couple of
nights at Mrs. Whitman's who has become the most admirable
woman.   Ditto at the Merriman's at North Conway, 3 days since—I
hardly know whether you know them—she was Miss Helen Bigelow,
also admirable.

Edith James arrived last night and is down on the piazza with Alice
and Margaret.[2]

Address Cambridge after receipt of this—we go back earlier this
year.

Address: Henry James Esq | 34 De Vere Gardens | London W. | England
Postmarks: TAMWORTH IRON WORKS, N.H. AUG 23 1890   LONDON. W. SP 4 90

[1] Harvard *Treasurer's Report* for 1891, p. 17, indicates that $4,300 were raised for
"fitting up" the psychological laboratory, including $500 from "a friend."

[2] Margaret is probably Margaret Merrill Gibbens Gregor.

———————————————

*Over the years there has been a great deal of controversy concern-
ing the founding of the first American psychological laboratory.
Claims have been made that William James was the founder, but
much depends upon deciding exactly what constitutes a psychological laboratory. When William was still an instructor in physiology,
Harvard appropriated small amounts of money for his use in the
physiological laboratory. In the academic year 1885–86 and afterwards, his graduate course in psychology usually included laboratory work among its formal requirements. During this period of his
Harvard career, William was busy as an organizer and fund raiser
in support of laboratory psychology. Thus, the fund-raising efforts
mentioned in the preceding letter represent a continuation of efforts
begun some fifteen years earlier.*

*Meanwhile, William was also active as a psychical researcher
and supporter of psychical research, much of his research involving*

Leonora Piper, whom he met in late 1885. Mrs. Piper, a trance medium controlled at the time by a spirit calling himself Dr. Phinuit, appeared to have a great deal of information about sitters, including members of the James family, that she had not acquired in ordinary ways. Hundreds of hours were spent recording her words and testing them against the recollections of witnesses to see whether she was a fraud or whether she was endowed with mysterious psychic powers that allowed the dead to communicate through her. Alice James, the sister, was amused by "the dreadful Mrs. Piper" and hoped that she would not be let loose upon her "defenseless soul." In 1885 William asked Alice for a lock of her hair for a psychic reading by Mrs. Piper. Wickedly and without letting her brother in on the prank, Alice sent the lock of hair of a friend who had died some years earlier. Henry James, who did not know Mrs. Piper but who had a "general aversion to her species," delivered William's report, mentioned in the following letter, before the Society for Psychical Research. Years later he was greatly moved by communications from his dead mother received through Mrs. Piper.

To Henry James

CAMBRIDGE Oct 20. [1890]

Dear Harry

I only mailed last night a letter to Alice urging more frequent news on your part, and this A.M. your letter came, telling of Alice's being so much better in consequence of her change, than worse in consequence of the fatigue etc. Thank God!

Warner wrote to you a while since asking about the silver left to Alice in A.K.'s will, of which I knew nothing. Alice in the country told me where it was. I wrote him to tell you forthwith. He didn't do it, and I fear you may have troubled Alice about it. To day I went to the safety vaults & verified it, and he has already doubtless sent the receipt required to Jae, and the dozen teaspoons which I gave him to Louisa who by the will was to receive them.[1]

I think your reading my Piper letter (of which this very A.M. proof came to me from Myers) is the most comical thing I ever heard of.[2] It shows how first rate a business man Myers is: He wants to bring variety & éclat into the meeting. I will *think of you* on the 31st at about 11 A.M. to make up for difference of longitude. I enclose a couple of letters lately rec'd from Elly Temple, & will give her your message.   More love to Alice—and also to Katherine.   I wish I could run over & visit you again, your avuncular allusions to our children &[3] very winsome to both Alice's heart & mine.

Good night.   W.J.

I sat up till 4 last night reading Stanley's book.[4]   What a jolly book it is.

Alice says I have not *melted* enough over your reading of my paper. I *do* melt to perfect liquefaction.   Tis the most beautiful and devoted brotherly act I ever knew, and I hope it may be the beginning of a new career on your part of psychic apostolicism.   Heaven bless you for it.

Write short and often.

[1] Louisa Corrin Walsh.

[2] WJ, "A Record of Observations of Certain Phenomena of Trance," reprinted in *EPR*.   HJ read the report before the Society for Psychical Research in London on 31 October 1890.

[3] A slip for 'are'.

[4] Henry Morton Stanley, *In Darkest Africa* (1890).

From Henry James

34, DE VERE GARDENS, | W. November 7th 1890

My dear William.

Both Alice & I have fresh bounties—recent letters—to thank you for.   Katherine, I know, will already have written you that it has been definitely settled that Alice is for the present—that is, for the winter— to remain just where she is, instead of embarking on the somewhat bleak & precarious experiment of Tunbridge Wells.   She is not fit for *any* experiment, or any journey; especially now that the winter (or what is winter to her,) has definitely begun.   Fortunately she is in excellent quarters—better rooms than she has ever had, since she has been in England—an excellent, quiet modern hotel, close to me. The "improvement" that took place in her on 1st coming up to down[1] has, unfortunately, been much interrupted—she has relapsed & collapsed a good deal.   Still, she has sometimes better days.   At any rate K.P.L. will not leave her while she is in the present condition.   She told me the other day that she shld. consider it "inhuman"—& this is a vast relief to me.   Alice *is*, really, too ill to be left; & the difficult question of doctors (owing to A.'s extreme dread of them, & her absolute inability, which they can't understand, to *take* tonic doses, drugs &c—they put her into a fearful nervous state,) may loom up again.

On the other hand, she *may* re-"improve": though her extreme, her really intense weakness is against that. At all events, & in any case, she is at present in the least bad place to encounter either contingency. Her little "improvements"—where she emerges out of a bad period—discourage her, really, more than her relapses: she wants so to have done with it all—to sink *continuously*. But her great vitality prevents her doing that. Don't, however, worry about her: she is "fixed," & on a good extrinsic basis, for the winter. Her not being away is a great simplification to me.—It was a week ago today that I read you at the S.P.R., with great éclat—enhanced by my being introduced by Pearsall Smith as "a Bostonian of Bostonians." You were very easy & interesting to read, & were altogether the "feature" of the entertainment. It was a full house—& Myers was rayonnant. I will be thus brief today because I am in a very busy phase, which however will not prevent me from writing soon again. That is I have I have to keep dashing off into the country (I came back only last night from 2 days at Portsmouth) for the hard *énervant* work of rehearsing—something that as yet, for a few weeks longer, I absolutely don't speak of—so PLEASE DON'T YOU. It consumes much time & infinite "nerve power"; especially if taken as seriously (all & *only* for the dream of gold—MUCH GOLD) as I take it, immersing myself in it practically up to the eyes, & really *doing* it myself, to the smallest detail. It is all for preliminary "country production"—to be followed later by the London.[2] I spent upwards of 5 hours yesterday on the deadly cold stage of the Portsmouth theatre (the "ladies" had *such* red-noses!) going at them tooth & nail, without pause; & then 2 more with my *grand* 1er *rôle* at his lodgings, coaching him with truly psychical intensity, *acting*, intonating everything *for* him & showing him simply *how!* The authorship (in any sense worthy of the name) of a play only *begins* when it is written, & I see that one's creation of it doesn't terminate till one has gone with it every inch of the way to the rise of the curtain on the 1st night. (I will tell you *when* to pray for me then.) I go to Brighton next week for another bout, & the next to Northampton &c; for my company is "on tour" with the rest of its repertory. It is fatiguing, largely owing to the terrible want of plasticity of one's British material; but if I have, from the experiment, & from other adventures of the same kind that are closing round me, the results that are perfectly *possible*, I shall be superabundantly rewarded. The conditions (of the Ang[l]oSaxon stage) are really so base that one would be unpardonable for going to meet them if one's inspiration were *not* exclusively mercenary. But to provide for one's old age one is *capable de tout*—& it is a revelation to me to find how "capable" I am, in the whole matter.—Meanwhile, to compare great things with small, your Psychology has never turned up—though you told me you had ordered an early copy sent. Has there been some error or non-compliance? Will you kindly see? I yearn for the book—to lift me out of histrionics.

Love all round—ever your   Henry.

P.S.   Please be utterly *dumb* about my histrionics

What gorgeous Democratic returns![3]   The news just came!

[1] A slip for 'town'.

[2] Edward Compton's Comedy Company was rehearsing the dramatization of HJ's *American* in preparation for its "country" opening at Southport on 3 January 1891.

[3] The London *Times,* 6 November 1890, announced the results of the congressional elections in the United States under the headline, "Great Democratic Victory."

William James was approaching fifty when he completed and published the Principles. *He never completed another book, contenting himself with the publication of collections of essays and courses of lectures. On 22 December 1890 the Jameses' last child was born, a son, "vigorous looking" and weighing eleven pounds. When after much discussion, they decided to name the infant Francis Tweedy and informed Henry James of their choice, Henry objected with passion, as if the whole business had stirred up unpleasant memories. Years later, Francis Tweedy renamed himself Alexander Robertson, choosing a name used by several of his ancestors.*

Meanwhile Henry was occupied with his own "delivery." His dramatization of The American *opened on 3 January 1891 at Southport, near Liverpool, with Edward Compton and his wife, Virginia Frances Bateman, in leading roles. The play had been written at the suggestion of Edward Compton and was produced by the Compton Comedy Company. According to Alice, who described the opening night in her diary entry for 7 January 1891, Henry was so nervous that afternoon that "his knees began almost to knock together." Unable to eat dinner, he went to the theater and straightened out the vases and rugs upon the stage, "after his usual manner in my apartments." In her view, "the dear being" deserved the three rounds of ovations and curtain calls and the prospects of the play were very good.*

From Henry James

Prince of Wales Hotel | Southport. | Saturday, Jan. 3ᵈ. [1891]
My dear William.

Yesterday came to me here your note (with photograph of your charming house) announcing the birth of your third son. I am delighted that he has come easily & smoothly into the world & that dear Alice was, as they say here, at the moment you wrote, in good form. I ardently pray that she may have remained so, & that the little boy, as yet pretty indefinite I judge, may find a spare corner in the crowded world.   We shall be now very anxious for later & more "evolved" news.   The anecdote of Margaret Mary & her babe most delightful.   It seems trivial at such a time to trouble you with *my* deliveries, but by the time this reaches you, you & Alice will have got a little used to yours.   However, you are to receive news of the coming into the world of *my* dramatic 1$^{\underline{st}}$-born (which takes place here tonight,) some time tomorrow, through Alice, from London, as I am to wire her early in the morning the upshot of the dread episode (tomorrow unfortunately is Sunday,) & she expressed to me before I left town day before yesterday the ardent wish that *she* might be allowed to cable you; as from herself, my report of the verdict that I am so oddly (till my complicated but valid material reasons are explained,) seeking of this Philistine provincial public.   The omens & auspices are good—the theatre is bad but big & every seat in it has been taken for a week.   The principal London critic, W$^{\underline{m}}$ Archer, of the weekly *World* (I will send you his pronouncement,) is coming down & can scarcely get one.   The play will owe nothing whatever to brilliancy of interpretation, & the mounting is of the meagrest— it will all, if the thing isn't damned, be a success of intrinsic vitality. We are resting & quaking today—but we had yesterday a supreme, complete, exhaustive rehearsal, during which I sat in the stalls watching & listening as to the work of another: the result of which (I boldly say it—on the untried eve,) was a kind of mystic confidence in the ultimate life of the piece—& even in the immediate.   God grant that tonight—between 8 & 11 (spend *you* the terrible hours in fasting, silence & supplication!) I don't get the lie in my teeth.   Still, I *am*, at present, in a state of abject, lonely fear—sufficient to make me say in retort to my purpose of trying again, again & yet again,—"What, a repetition of *this* horrid & quite peculiar preliminary?"   I am *too* nervous to write more—& yet it's only 3 o'clk. & I've got to wait till eight.—But I shall finish, either with triumph or resignation, tomorrow.—Thursday, Jan 8$^{\underline{th}}$; 34 D. V. Gdns.   I haven't had a moment to add a word since I wrote the foregoing last Saturday. But meanwhile I knew Alice had cabled you, & I asked her to send you off immediately the letter I wrote *her* the a.m. after my 1$^{\underline{ère}}$.   I paid a country visit after leaving Southport & my leisure has undergone complete extinction till this moment.   At present I shall only scribble a few lines to catch the steamer & say that my ordeal *did* blossom into a complete & delightful success—limited only by the instrinsic limitations of a place like Southport in the matter of conferring success. But that circumstance works in 2 ways: I mean that if the *cachet* of a biggish provincial town isn't authoritative on the other hand the play had to suffer from the want of adventitious aid conferred by provincial production—ill-mounted, meagrely interpreted &c—& yet quite overcame that drawback. I *think* it has a strong life & will surmount the more formidable tests in store for it. At any rate there was no drawback to our felicity on Saturday & the Comptons are delighted. He, will I, surmise, make a "big" creation (with more time to live into it,) of the principal character—I mean for the English public. Only an American can do it for the Americans. Only these raw words today—I want to write you properly by the next mail—or the next.

Ever your affectionate Henry.

P.S. Quantities of love to Alice & the Babe.

To Henry James

CAMBRIDGE Jan 4, 1891

Dear Old Harry,

A telegram from Alice this A.M. announces "unqualified triumph—great future author—ovation." I am almost as glad as you are, and hope that it is only the beginning of a sort of Sardou or Dumas career. It will of course inspire you with the 9 or 90 other plays which you have in mind. I long for details which of course you will send duly.—I should have written anyhow to day, but probably this time to Katherine L., in return for a most excellent letter from here[1] which came a week ago. Thank her very much, & say that in virtue of the telegram you seemed this time the person to whom to write. I fear it is a horrid dark and cold winter for all of you—here it is crystalline & beautiful, if it *is* rather cold. Our baby is an entirely "new departure" in that line, for us. Never whimpers; sleeps almost all night; and Alice is proportionally serene and well. I feel rather jaded by my Xmas vacation, not having finished the work I had set myself to do therein, but such is life. I did some sociability the last few days—dined with Brimmers, lunched with la Whitman, dined with Lowell. He is rather disconsolate, eats and drinks nothing, but makes no complaint and always inquires most earnestly about *you*. I will send him the telegram—it will please him. No other news to tell. Bless Alice, poor girl, and bless Katherine Loring for all she does to us.

Farewell | W.J.

[1] A slip for 'her'.

From Henry James

34, DE VERE GARDENS, | W. February 12ᵗʰ [1891]

My dear William.

I wrote to you at some length the other day—but your letter to Katherine, from Newport, which she has just showed me, makes me want to add a belated postscript. You make a hopeful inquiry about the great question of one's theatrical profits—& though I think—but am not sure—I touched on the matter to you the other day, I have à coeur to dot, briefly the i's of the question, lest you shouldn't be living, as it were, in a fool's paradise in relation [to] my *actual* unearned increment. It is only from the moment a play is produced in *London* & thereby played nightly, & during a *long run,* that profits begin to figure up to great heights, whether for manager or author. I fear I didn't make it clear to you that the *American* isn't played by the Comptons *every night* of their provincial tour—or anything like it. No play *can* be, in the smaller towns—the company stays a week & *must* give (the public is too small else,) a nightly change of bill. My play is therefore acted only on Fridays—the "fashionable" night. It will thus be given only about some 25 times at the most between now & the late summer vacation; & as country prices are very low— the stalls usually only 4/—my royalty is proportionately scant. Moreover I have already had it, in a lump—£250 paid down as soon as my contract was signed. I never expected to make money in the country—it's impossible; but London is the reverse of the medal, as later the U.S. (*and* the country there,) & would make the story totally different. If my play succeeds here I can't get *less* than a hundred pounds a week from it and I may easily get more. (There is now a great success here, at the Haymarket, called *The Dancing Girl,* by one Henry Arthur Jones—the clumsiest trash, alas, of a play—& the said Henry Arthur, with a largeish theatre & full houses derives £180 a week—and will evidently go on doing it for months: which will make him, by the end of six months, £5000, &, at the end of a year, during which the play may perfectly run, £10,000—not counting his American or Australian profits, or the eventual country-tours of his play *by itself,* played every night, (not as one of a repertory, which is the only thing that can be done, as is being done with mine, *before* London production.) It is the American proceeds of a play that are much the biggest now; so that Henry Arthur, if the *Dancing Girl* is a success in the U.S., may easily, with that help, at the end of a year, double his £10,000. You see all this is worth waiting for; and it was inevitable that, beginning late, I should be a longish while getting *en train;* especially with the peculiar complication that I agreed at the outset to wait for Compton, as he so took me by the hand, to finish his 10 years (ghastly thought,) of "Touring" & settle down deliberately & preparedly with a London Theatre of his own. I think I told you that he has taken one on a long lease—a very good one, in spite of its awkward name, the Opera Comique: it is where all Gilbert & Sullivan's earlier productions were performed. There is every present appearance that as soon as the London run, whatever it may prove to be, of the *American* is over, he will produce there an admirable three-act comedy by the same author. I go into these vulgarities (which *please* keep utterly to yourself—there was a phrase in your letter to Katherine about the "Irving St & Kirkland St. Circle" which makes me shiver![1]—with a sense as of extreme ventilation of one's privatest affairs,) I say I bore you with these details simply that you may not for the present look to me to ship over nuggets for investment under your eye. Later I do expect to give your eye plenty to do.—I am afraid that in writing last week, I seemed to overstate a little Alice's weakness—inasmuch as she has "stayed up" to her dinner (I mean got out of bed at about 6, for perhaps the 2$^{\underline{d}}$ time & had it, with much assistance, on the sofa) several times lately—though these very last days have been bad with her. However, all the same, her feebleness is extreme, & if a somewhat extreme description of it is not true one day, it is another; so that the above rectification is more for "form" than anything else.————I take the greatest interest in your new Babe's name; but frankly, I am rather unhappy about the one you mention as virtually settled upon—so much so as to feel strongly moved—even to tears—to supplicate you to *un*settle it. I have thought over your combination, wondering much at your reasons for it—& reflecting, at any rate, on the whole thing deeply. *Francis* is very good, & I suppose is a friendliness—certainly most just & grateful to F. J. Child. Besides I like the name in itself. *Tweedy* I hate in itself—I think it wofully ugly—but accept willingly enough for its associations—though, as to this, they are essentially yours, not the child's, who will carry the name through life wondering, rather, why he was *affublé* with it. It is for *Temple* that I reserve all the horror that an uncle & a brother may be judged by you to have a right to express. I don't understand it—I don't like it—I can't away with it anyhow. That it may be a sign, on your part of attachment to Aunt Mary's maiden name, to the far-off dead Minny's or to the very near (me) living Elly's (whom as I wrote you, I *suspect* of an intention to *change* hers—for the 2ᵈ time—to Hunter!)—these things seem to me to count for nothing, in favour of it, as compared with the *odiousness* of the false air it has of *our*—I mean of any of us—trying to connect ourselves so with the T. family—hook ourselves on to the name or make use of it because it is "aristocratic." It doesn't matter that you are so sublimely incapable of any such motive—& that it will dawn upon you in these words for the 1ˢᵗ time. It is enough that there is a *fatal* air of elastic snobbishness about it—from the moment we have cousins of the name—cousins too who have always made so much of it, & under circumstances which would, had they been wiser, made them keep silent or even drop it. They come by it through illegitimacy & through an individual who was horribly dishonoured. Aunt Mary's father was a *bastard* son of Sir John Temple, the "founder" of the family in America, & he hanged himself, after burning the public office of which he was in charge, to cover the tracks of his peculations. This doesn't prevent the Roses, here, from taking a great stand on the name (so that Sir Wᵐ. the late Sir John's eldest son has bought Moor Park, Sir William Temple's old place!) & one hates to be connected, even by implication, & in spite of all the good faith possible on one's own part, with all the general American & Canadian swagger about it.[2] Nothing would induce me to let it appear to a "Temple" that I wished to make my child seem to be connected with them by THAT strain in his blood; which is what any Temple wd. inevitably assume! If the word is a tribute to Aunt Mary T., isn't this surely, for one child, covered by the *Tweedy?* Why give the boy so much of it? I, moreover, hate all surnames given to children when they are not own *family*-names. The boy grows up to find himself nominally & thereby hollowly & uncomfortably connected with people who are nothing to him, or he to them, ten to one, & yet whom he seems to hook himself on to. For instance I am m<o>re glad than I can say today that it was not *me* who<m> father named "Garth Wilkinson"— dangling on to Wilkinsons here who are no Wilkinsons of mine. The Wilkinson who was *his,* father's, would have been long departed, when I shld. be still in that false position with his children. If *I* were the Father of children I shld. say: "Go to, let us use what we *have,* when, to simplify an always difficult problem, we *can*"; & I wd. give one of my boys the name or one of the names, of Mother's maternal grandfather,* the worthy Alexander Robertson, who came from Scotland to the U.S. in the middle of the last century & was a good & solid burgess of New York. That's an association worth perpetuating— it means something, preserves the continuity one likes to preserve, connects itself with something which is *of* us—& not of other people. Our Bob, as having the Robertson, needn't be a stumbling block, with a proper Christian name <befo>re it. I, for my part, think Alexander Robertson James a very good name—though I shld. think Francis R. J. almost equally good—& can't help wishing your New Boy, who I hope won't be a Newsboy, had either of them. At any rate think better of the "Temple"—do, *do,* DO! Alice feels as intensely on the subject as I do < he>r feelings I am < >t my own. <Excus>e the warmth of them, dear William, & dearest Alice—<c'>est plus fort que moi. I am sure, moreover, that *you,* dearest Alice, are not eager to contend for the luckless idea. But I have deluged you.—I take Minnie Emmet, who dines with me tonight to the theatre. Elly is still in Scot<land>—& < > Paris < > 17th I shan't see her, I fear, before she returns to the US (the end of this month,) unless Scotland does for her on the spot.

Ever both of your affectionate   Henry James
*or even "Hugh Walsh["] (James) her Newburgh *pa*ternal grandfather.[3]

[1] Grace Norton and Francis James Child lived on Kirkland St.

[2] The Temples were a large family and the relation of the American Temples to their noble namesakes in Britain is unclear. HJ probably had in mind Sir William Temple (1628–1699), British statesman and author, who in about 1680 built Moor Park. It is virtually impossible for HJ's relatives to be descendants of this Sir William Temple, but they could have descended from other Sir Williams. John Temple (1731–1798) was born in Boston, served as a British customs agent, and married Elizabeth Bowdoin, with whom he had two sons. There are references to him in the papers of Benjamin Franklin and Samuel Adams, but these concern his public life. He later became Sir John, although his claims to the dignity of eighth baronet have been challenged. Mary Tweedy's father was Robert Temple (1783–1834), said by some genealogists to be a son of the William Temple who was a brother of Sir John Temple. Robert Temple, a lawyer, collected pensions in the names of Revolutionary War veterans but failed to send the money to the pensioners. He shot himself after burning his papers. The "Sir Wm." is Sir William Rose, son of Sir John and Charlotte Temple Rose.

[3] Hugh Walsh (d. 1817), born in Ireland, was one of the first inhabitants of Newburgh, N.Y.

William spent the summer of 1891 preparing an abridgment of The Principles of Psychology, *published as* Psychology: Briefer Course *(1892). He omitted many of the quotations and references, rewrote some chapters, and rearranged others. The book was intended for use as a textbook, and soon after its publication he had to revise several sentences that in the view of protesting parents were unsuitable for young readers because the text was sexually explicit. In the objectionable passages, James contrasted "brainless frogs," which embrace anything placed between their arms, with frogs who have lost their cerebral hemispheres and postpone "this reflex until a female" of their own "species is provided." The same sentences survived intact in numerous printings of the larger book, which was used primarily by graduate students.*

But this controversy receded into the background in the face of the approaching death of Alice James. Alice was living in a "little house on Camden Hill" in Kensington with her companion, Katharine Loring, when she learned in late May 1891 that she had cancer and had only a short time to live. She received the news that she was nearing that "supremely interesting moment in life" in a triumphant mood. Writing to her on 6 July 1891 William expressed the thought that he believed her to be "reconciled to the prospect with all its pluses and minuses," especially as he knew that she had never cared for life. He himself had come to realize at the age of fifty how close death was to all of us and "life a mere farce of frustration." In her letter of 30 July, Alice congratulated him on at "nearly fifty" having reached the point where she had started at fifteen. On 12 September, having arranged for someone to take over his classes, William departed for England for a farewell meeting with Alice. While there, he attended the London opening of The American *on 26 September.*

To Henry James

BATTERY PARK HOTEL, | ASHEVILLE, N.C., Aug 20. 1891

My dear Harry—This date will doubtless surprise you—I came here a few days ago in search of novelty, being to that degree elaborately tired in my insides after preparing a "briefer course" of my psychology straight on top of the year's work that I felt like going where I should be reminded of nothing that I had ever seen or heard or smelt or tasted before. It does n't take many days, however, to get ones "bearings" rested, and I shall return home, a healed man, within a week. This Asheville is a charming cosmopolitan place, 2000 odd feet above the sea, and only about 10 years old in its present estate

of boom.   I came here to compare the mountains with our northern
ones, and got back last evening from a two days trip to the top of
Mount Mitchell the highest peak, and about 500 feet higher than M!
Washington.   The most exquisite forest, an easy walk of 5 hours to
the top, and the most buxom air when there.   To day I am kept by
rain from going to Roan mountain, 6300 ft high, with a hotel on
top.   I long for the high air—it is too warm here.   The Hotel is
unexceptionable, filled with quiet southerners, the only peculiar class
of whom are the young girls, who abound, and who have a very sweet
and innocent air, and at the same time a gay and playful tone of
conversation, as I hear their soft broad accents—all ôs— with each
other & with their beaux, who on their pôt seem very cô-teous.—I
have gone on to finish what I should have to say about myself before
entering on the subject of Alice and of your last letter which came to
me from Kingstown just a week ago.   I had had a full account from
Katherine of D! Baldwin's visits together with a letter from him to
you, and on top of all a very remarkable and reassuring letter dictated by poor Alice herself.   She is certainly the most remarkable
member of the family, though I say this at the risk of flattering her,
in view of the probability that this letter will meet her eyes!   How
one feels that the definiteness and comparative stability of her outlook rests and steadies her.   It gives one an idea of how the state of
suspense, agitation, trepidation, and uncertainty in which she has
lived for so many years is the hardest thing of all to bear.   Poor dear
girl! poor dear girl!   But the back has been fitted to the burden as
few "backs" have; and, in some hidden way or other, I am as sure as
I am of anything that her life has been bearing its fruit, fruit not only
for her, I mean, but for life at large.   I only hope that with morphia
etc, she may be spared physical suffering in the weeks that are to
come.   You may well thank Providence for giving to her and to us
a K.P.L.

    Of poor Lowell's death you heard.   I left Cambridge the evening
of the funeral, for which I had waited over, and meant to write to
you about it that very afternoon.   But as it turned out, I did n't get
a moment of time.   The autopsy revealed a most extensive cancerous trouble, right kidney entirely gone, liver largely affected, spots
in lungs etc.   Death came much sooner than was supposed, and his
last weeks were painless.   He was unconscious a good deal for the
past fortnight, and flighty in his mind at times when awake.   He
looked well to the last, and had nothing of the cancer-complexion.

I think he had little or no curiosity about the pathology of his case, & only wondered at his various symptoms as they arose. He had never been ill in his life till two years ago, and did n't seem to understand or realize the fact as most people do. I doubt if he dreamed that his end was approaching until it was close at hand. Few images in my memory are more touching than the picture of his attitude in the last visits I paid him. He was always up and dressed, in his library, with his velvet coat & tobacco pipes, & ready to talk and be talked to, alluding to his illness with a sort of apologetic and whimsical plaintiveness that had no querulousness in it, though he coughed incessantly, and the last time I was there (the last day of June I think), he was strongly narcotized by opium for a sciatica which had lately supervened. Looking back at him what strikes one most was his singularly boyish cheerfulness and robustness of temperament. He was a sort of a boy to the end, and makes most others seem like premature old men.* He was always very full of questions about you and your minutest concerns, which I was only sorry to be able to reveal to him so little. Your dramatic prospects and achievements in particular seemed to fill him with curiosity.—And this reminds me that although you gave in your last so exhilarating a fore*cast* of the American at the Opera Comique, you didn't breathe a word concerning the other plays in process of gestation. Pray tip us a word concerning them. If you knew how well I had kept the secret of the American, you would have no fear. I hope and pray that they may none of them be inferior to that. Your story of the Marriages was one of the most perfect little things you ever did—a chef d'oeuvre. It seems to be generally regarded as such, but, strange to say, Howells says that it gave rise at the Intervale House to a great casuistical controversy about lying.[1] H. Scudder, who is our neighbor at Chocorua, tells me that he is immediately going to print another story by you in three parts.[2] How you keep it up.—My psychology seems to be a great success so-far, and I am quite sure that the "briefer course" will practically be *the* book used in the colleges. I am much amused at your and Alice's indignation over the Nation's review, which was a simply excentric production, probably read by no one. The second instalment was utterly unintelligible. I know that Garrison took pains to get it worthily reviewed and sent it to some old fogy whom he considered an authority. It shows how at the mercy of accidental reputation these editors are who try to get "experts" to do their reviewing, men who "do not ordinarily write for the newspapers" as the Nation's advertisement says. I did n't care a single straw for the matter one way or the other, not even enough to find out who wrote it.[3] Well! Good bye and God bless and keep you both.

Yours ever W.J.

*Lowell's funeral was in the College Chapel, densely packed, although at noon of a fearfully hot day, with everyone out of town. Eliot, Norton, Child, D!̱ Holmes & John Holmes, Cranch, Howells, and one other whom I can't remember made quite an impressive group as pall bearers, though I dare say that the enumeration does n't strike you so.

[1] HJ, "The Marriages," *Atlantic Monthly* 68 (August 1891): 233–52; reprinted in *The Lesson of the Master* (1892). In the story Adela Chart lies about her father to his fiancée to prevent him from remarrying.

[2] HJ's story was probably "The Chaperon," *Atlantic Monthly* 68 (November 1891): 659–70; (December 1891): 721–35; reprinted in *The Real Thing* (1893).

[3] Charles Sanders Peirce, unsigned review of *The Principles of Psychology* in *Nation* 53 (2 July 1891) 15; (9 July 1891): 32–33.

From Henry James

34, DE VERE GARDENS. W. September 1ˢᵗ [1891]

My dear William.

Coming home last night from 3 days in the Isle of Wight I find your good letter from Asheville, N.C. It is delightful to hear of you from such a place—after the execution of your big job, with such a sense of holiday earned. I was in very truth on the point of writing to you, & as you see, I don't lose an hour. I have wished to tell you how I found Alice on my return from five weeks in Ireland—but I came back to occupations immediately pressing. She is of course *more* ill, weaker, & her state more precarious; but she is also, thank heaven—& Baldwin, easier. She has less pain, with constant morphia. It acts quite as it's desired to, & makes all the difference. I haven't seen her for several days (she was too ill for 2 days before I left town, & since last evening I have had no time to go round,) & in general she is able to see me much less & for shorter moments: only between 5 & 7, & many days not at all. This shows a great increase of feebleness. I am not going out of town, however, even for a day, for some weeks to come. My rehearsals begin in a few days—the scenery has had the very last touches; the furniture (or portions of it,) is just (as it is all French,) arriving from Paris, & the

dresses have had my personal superintendance.   These things will
all be of prime perfection; & oh, if the success can only be to match!
I haven't spoken of my *other* theatrical preoccupations, because they
are anxious & bothering & somewhat confused—& I would rather
not do so till after the *American* has been played in London.   *That*, if
it is the success I hope, will have a direct & immediate action on
everything else; & consecrate & fix my theatrical position—the terms
on which I may deal with the barbarous, the ignorant, the sickening
race of managers, &c.   The great stumbling-block in the whole business is the question of *time*—the slowness, the waiting, the delays
which are a large part of the very essence of managerial production.
They talk of years as we talk of months.   I am handicapped by having
begun too late—being too old: I ought to have done it 10 years ago.
But I shall vanquish, all the same.   The only thing I *do* care to speak
of now (and ONLY to you,) is the drama in three acts, *Mrs. Vibert*,
which John Hare is to produce at the Garrick some time this season.[1]
But here there are irrepressible delays—produced largely indeed almost wholly—by the intense difficulty of casting.   One tries to write
as simple & feasible a thing as possible, & still—with the ignoble
poverty of the English-speaking stage—the people capable of *beginning* to attempt to do it are not findable.   *There's* a career for talent—
to act my plays!   *Mrs. Vibert* is blocked largely by the difficulty of
putting one's hand on a young man who can *touch* an important little
part of a boy of 20—who must be a *character*, a touching one.   But,
as I say, if the *American* prospers it will clear up many things.—Very
interesting, very touching is your description of dear old Lowell—
your last impressions of him.   Yes indeed he was an extraordinary
boy—I was as much struck with it the year before his fatal illness as
I ever was.   All my relations with him were of the most affectionate
character, & I shall infinitely miss him.—Grace Norton has just given
up her pretty cottage & gone to Windermere till she sails, Oct 1.   I
have seen her when I could & so far as the drawback of her strange
domestication of the boresome & incongruous Bôchers has permitted.   They seem practically to live with her.   We have had the vilest,
coldest, wettest summer of all the vile, cold, wet ones I have known
here—they disagree with me more & more as I grow older—far more
than the winters.   A tempest rages as I write.   Your *warm* rusticity
is a balmy image.

Ever your faithful   Henry.

[1] HJ's *Mrs. Vibert,* later called *Tenants,* was not produced.

*Returning from England, William reached New York on 7 Octo-
ber. The season in the North Atlantic was a stormy one, and
Henry was concerned for his safety. In fact, some passengers on
the steamer that William had originally intended to board suffered
injuries during the rough voyage.*

From Henry James

34, DE VERE GARDENS. W. Oct 10th [1891]

My dear William

It was an unspeakable relief to me to hear, from the office, of your
safe restoration to *les vôtres*—so conscious was I of the heavy price
you so heroically paid for your visit to us. I thought it a tremendous
tribute while you were here—but now I think a still greater one; &
I feel as if worried & worrying, preoccupied & detached as I was
during those days, I had given you a very meagre & unamiable hospitality. I should think you would have a shuddering recollection of
your visit—& I heartily forgive you if you have. I hope your homeward course was comfortable—as comfortable as any such misery can
be. But I won't waste conjecture & curiosity, but simply wait to hear
from you. Alice has undergone no particular change since you were
here—though the last couple of days she has been too ill to see me.
Yesterday she had a bad condition of the heart—great distress, with,
however, too much weakness to allow of the violent agitations of it
then in such moments she used to have. The remedy that Baldwin
sent her as a substitute for morphia appears very beneficent & operative—I forget its name. The other invalid—the illstarred play—is
having a difficult infancy—a very difficult one—owing to the still extreme emptiness of the town (as to its stall-taking population) & to
the injury done it first by the newspapers & 2^d by the 4 bad actors—
which is too terrible a number for any play to carry. We shall probably fight it through this month & then the fates must decide. Unfortunately their decision appears already only too clear. Dont, however, *say* this in America—& say simply that it's too soon to determine
how it's going. The strain is great & was at first intolerable; but I am
getting a little used to it. Meanwhile, every night, the thing *appears*
to succeed admirably, afresh—it is listened to with an absolute *tension*
of stillness & interest—it plays closer & shorter—judicious excisions

have improved it—Claire is better[1] & Compton continues excellent. But my friends—mostly—shun the subject like a dishonour.   The thing has been a revelation to me of how queerly & ungracefully friends can behave.   I shall only live, henceforth, for my *revanche*. This is all today—save to express the tenderest sentiments to Alice. I hope the house is sound & still.

Ever your   Henry

P.S.   Will you kindly say to Grace Norton that I throw myself—for my silence—on her indulgence.   I shall speedily write to her.   Please give her my particular love.

[1] The role of Claire de Centré, the heroine of *The American*, was performed by Elizabeth Robins.

From Henry James

34, DE VERE GARDENS. W. November 15th [1891]

My dear William.

Many thanks for the note with which you addressed me your last to Alice—in which you gave news of Carrie &c.   This news—of Carrie's increase of means—has given her great comfort,[1] & Katherine has probably answered your letter.   I have seen Alice myself comparatively [little] these 10 days—she has so often been too weak & ill to see me.   She has had some very bad—nervously bad—days of late—& when I saw her, 48 hours ago, after an interval of several, I was instantly struck with her great increase of emaciation.—She looks far more wasted—especially severe in the face, at present than she has ever done.   She is a mere anatomy   On the other hand the pain from her breast has ceased very much—& she can take less morphia, which has begun to have a bad nervous effect.   Katherine has brought her (she will have written you) Doctor Tuckey, of 14 Green St. Park Lane, the author of an article on Hypnotism in the December *Fortnightly*, who has given her hypnotic treatment—to soothe her nerves & make her sleep—three successive times with very promising results.[2]   She likes him—he appears to be a very sane, "pure" personage & a gentleman, & I have hopes of some good from it.   Her weakness is absolute now.   But, as I say, Baldwin's forecast that the tumour would *become* painless has been justified—unless the pain comes back.———*The American* is in its 8th week, & has celebrated its 50th night.   It "goes" so much better than the 1st nights that it is now quite a different thing; & I have altered the whole last part of the 3^d

act so that I have converted it from the least successful (with the applausive audience,) to the most successful. And whatever may happen now, I have had an honourable run—& it may become more honourable yet. Whatever *shall* happen, I am utterly launched in the drama, resolutely & deeply committed to it, & shall go at it tooth & nail. The American has distinctly done me good. I wish you could see it in its present maturity. A tempestuous autumn preys upon us—but rather fogless—& the part of the London year I like best. I long to do something to rescue your Alice from her servitude. I wish I could send her my Smiths. But they are always ill. I can only send her the tender love of yours & hers ever & always

Henry James.

[1] Caroline Eames Cary James had received an inheritance from her brother.

[2] Charles Lloyd Tuckey, "The Applications of Hypnotism," *Contemporary Review* 60 (November 1891): 672–86. HJ was in error about the *Fortnightly*.

From Henry James

34, DE VERE GARDENS. W. March 5th 1892.

My dear William

I wrote to you on the 2^d & this morning I despatched you dear Alice's touching cable-message—her last word, as it will probably be, of farewell.[1] It will probably startle you a good deal, as our last (previous) news will not have prepared you for so sudden a fall. In a few days, however, you will receive my letter which is now on its way & one from Katherine written on the same 2^d. Nothing particular has happened (since I wrote) save an accelerated increase of weakness. Katherine, & I think the Doctor too, judge that she cannot live more than three or four days—yet she *may* linger (I can't help believing,) some little time at the very last—I mean, however, only counting by days. Yet when I saw her this a.m. (K. had sent round for me quickly,—& I hadn't seen her—she couldn't—yesterday) I was struck with the great change—a supreme deathlike emaciation—that had come over her in 48 hours. Her lung, her heart, her breast are all a great distress, & she has constant fever, which rises and falls. She has a most distressing, choking retching cough, which tries her strength terribly—BUT since last, evening, thank heaven, there are symptoms that she has become too weak to be actively nervous. She slept not a moment all night—yet she remained *quiet*, with it, Katherine tells me: which is a very new phenomenon. Therefore we greatly hope *that* condition will be every day less & less a feature of this last period. It will greatly simplify—though hypnotism does hold the nervousness in arrest. Only the heroic, the colossal Katherine has to go at it every twenty minutes—when it is bad. We *haven't* said much, as you remind me, of the local tumour because there has not been much to say—it has only been one feature among several, & though it has greatly increased in size & hardness its painfulness does not seem to have *proportionately* increased. Morphia has always checked the feeling of it—& though the distress of it has been constant it has seemed as if she felt it more by reason of her great weakness than by that of its own increased intensity. But it has been a constant element in all her recent suffering. She fainted away, quite painlessly, last night & felt as if she were dying—& hopes that that is the way she *will* pass away. K. was just sending for me when she came to. She is perfectly clear & humorous & would talk if doing so didn't bring on spasms of coughing. But she does speak in a whisper—& gave me, in my ear, very distinctly, three words to cable to you. I will of course cable instantly whenever the end comes, & write you meanwhile by next post. Thanks for your last letter & all your Syracuse trouble.[2] I bless you for this.

Ever your   Henry

[1] On 5 March 1892 AJ telegraphed WJ, "Tenderest love to all farewell   Am going soon." She died the next day.

[2] There were difficulties with the James property in Syracuse because one of the tenants was unable to pay rent.

From Henry James

London [March 6, 1892]

RECEIVED AT Cambridge Mass Mch 6 1892
James, 95 Irving St
Cambridge Mass
  Alice just passed away painless   Wire Bob

Henry

To Henry James

Cambr. March 7. 92

My dear Harry
   Saturday evening came Alice's pathetic little telegram, & yesterday evening yours, announcing the end.

What a relief! and yet long as we had thought of it and wished it, it seems too strangely sudden to have it despatched in the twinkling of a telegram as it has been for us. Poor little Alice! What a life! I can't believe that that imperious will and piercing judgment are snuffed out with the breath. Now that her outwardly so frustrated life is over, one sees that in the deepest sense it was a triumph. In her relations to her disease, her mind did not succumb. She never whined or complained or did anything but spurn it. She thus kept it from invading the tone of her soul. It made her doubtless despotic to others, but it did n't make her weak. And if one regards the work-ing out of that problem as the particular burden that was laid on her, one can only say that it was well done, and that her life was anything but a failure. So much of her mysterious debt to this universe safely finished and paid off! That is the way her little life, shrunken and rounded in retrospect, has seemed to me to day; and I am sure it is the deepest way in which to regard it from now onward. What a blessed thing to be able to say "*that* task is over!"

Of course we all live in the expectation of your letters telling the details. I had expected no slow agony but rather some sudden syn-cope. I telegraphed you this A.M. to make sure the death was not merely apparent, because her neurotic temperament & chronically reduced vitality are just the field for trance-tricks to play themselves upon, and she might possibly [*end of letter missing*]

From Henry James

34, DE VERE GARDENS, | W. March 19ᵗʰ 1892

My dear William.

Alice's death has brought me, here, such a deluge of notes & letters, from friends of mine, mainly of course, as her own were few in num-ber, that I can only answer, briefly, the one just received from you, written after the receipt of my telegram. By Monday next, 21ˢᵗ, I hope, you will have received all my letters & all Katherine's, and have learned the whole history of her last days. You will see, among other things, how little your fears about a fake appearance of death were justified.[1] Nothing could have been of a process more step-by-step or more transparent. Yes indeed, I echo all your reflections on the meaning, as it were, of her frustrated life & the consistency, as it were, of her character. Even more than before (though I was particularly conscious of it during all the last year,) I feel that her character was rare & remarkable. How it would have got on with the world if she had had to live in the world I know not; but I think she never *could* have lived in the world. The temper & nature of her spirit made the particular life & experience she had the only possible ones. To this experience she lent herself with extraordinary courage & superiority—it is this last word, somehow, that expresses to me—vague as it is—most of what she was. Strange & rare was the force that she exercised in all her prostration & weakness—& strange enough it seems—in the little house that is now so senseless & void—that this force has, in an hour, been quenched. I go to see Katherine there every day—she has still plenty to do in closing and cleaning it & making her preparations for departure. She goes sometime between the 2$^{\underline{d}}$ & 9$^{\underline{th}}$ April—probably on the 9$^{\underline{th}}$. I don't exactly know what you mean by "getting Alice's will from Warner & sending it to me"— inasmuch as her late & final will (the one I spoke to you of in September,) is here and will be taken home by Katherine—or rather, I think, has just been sent by her to Warner or one of the executors—so that he may begin the proceedings for proving it. I wrote to you, on the 8$^{\underline{th}}$ or 9$^{\underline{th}}$, what the provisions of this last will are—just as I spoke to you of what I believe to be her intentions, in a general way, when you were here in September, & wrote you, more definitely, about them when you wrote to me, later in the autumn, about Carries increase of fortune, Bob, &c. Her will seems to me singularly wise & enlightened—I don't see *how* she neglects to take acct. in some degree of the fact that Bob has a rich father-in-law. I think he will understand this—I mean I hope he will; & that there is no source whatever from which you or I can inherit any money. I shall wait for your next letter before writing more—I am overdone with much writing.

Ever your Henry James

P.S. I thought I had written on this page before crossing over to the edges of the other sheet—but it serves instead of the new scrap I was on the point of taking to add a word of rejoicing at the news of your having taken your passage. I am delighted at the prospect of so soon seeing you all—& only impatient, now, for your plans of detail. I trust Alice & you, after planting your children, are soon to come—I mean *very* soon—to England: I mean during the rest of the summer. I can put you *both* up BEAUTIFULLY & will hear of your taking no other asylum.—I have lately written nearly 50 answers to notes here. Dont let anyone you can prevent write me from the U.S.

[1] A possibility WJ had raised in his letter of 7 March 1892.

The estate of Alice James amounted to about $80,000. Her will divided it into four parts, with William, Henry, and Katharine Loring receiving full shares, and Robertson getting half of the remaining share. The other half was distributed to various friends and relatives. This time it was Robertson's turn to feel discriminated against, and several of the following letters discuss ways of soothing his hurt feelings. Similar situations had followed the deaths of the elder Henry James, when Garth Wilkinson felt slighted, and of Catharine Walsh, when Alice found herself with only a life interest in a shawl and some silver.

The academic year 1892–93 was William's year to take a sabbatical. On 25 May 1892 he sailed with his wife and four children from New York for Antwerp. After a summer in Switzerland, the family spent the winter in Florence. William found himself much perplexed about schools for the children, just as his father had been many years before. In the end, he realized that it was much easier to travel without small children.

To Henry James

Cambridge, March 22. 92

My dear Harry,

Your three pathetic letters written Tuesday and wednesday after the fatal Sunday arrived on Sunday morning. How beautiful a picture of the last 24 hours—but what a week of torture to precede! If there is any personal immortality, I declare that Alice's experience in getting free from her sick room life must be a curiously exciting one. I can't imagine a more intense situation. I can readily feel how deep a hollowness her going will have made round about *you!* But of course, like all things earthly, that also will cease. Poor old Boott showed me your beautiful letter to him.

It seems probable now that we may get off by the 25th of May!—a consummation devoutly to be wished, as the month of June in Cambridge is always pure fag with no refreshment at all so long as one stays. Since Warner is executor I hope K. will have sent the will immediately to him, so that things may be finished whilst I am still here.

I suppose that on account of the inferior "expectations" of my children the discrimination against Bob was fair enough.   Of course I wrote to him that, although I could n't equalize the principal, I considered that I ought to set aside the income of my third of the difference for his use.   To which I get the enclosed reply as his first reaction.[1]   I think it would be a good thing if we both made him the same offer in due and definite form again.   If either one of us deserves a little feeling of ease in money matters it is surely he, with his intense anxiety about them.   I imagine his present income to be $3000 or a little over, and he is so frugal that of this he always lays something by.   At the same time he is magnanimous and disinterested where his dignity is touched.   I do hope that you won't suffer one cent of Alice's *capital* to be invaded by you[r]self.   You will need a good deal more than you are likely to have when your writing powers are cut short, as in the nature of things they must be some day if you live.

Your last book came duly.[2]   No time even to look at it as yet!

Ever affectionately   W.J.

The Punches & Speaker came this A.M.   Queer emotion of her being there—yet gone.

[1] Neither of the letters was found.
[2] HJ, *The Lesson of the Master* (1892).

From Henry James

34, DE VERE GARDENS, | W. April 1st [1892]

My dear William.

I just receive your letter of the 22d, enclosing Bob's note in answer to yours about Alice's will.   The latter (B.'s note,) touches me with an unspeakable horror of any analogy with the sickening time I went through after father's death—in regard to the "discriminations" of *his* will.   Alice's decision was the result of the most earnest & troubled & conscientious consideration & balancing, as I wrote you last winter. She was moved (mainly by hearing that Holton had left $75,000 to a western college,) to remember that Mary might have sources of inheritance that would more than make up for any difference *she* would establish between him (Bob) & you & me.   She regarded Bob's wife's father's wealth as an element, in other words, which it would be wrong *not* to consider—to treat, in the question, as non-existent. She treated it therefore in the way her will shows—but I am accessible to the fact that Bob does not view the matter in the same light (as I gather from his note to you.)   If he judges that, practically there is a want of *foundation* in the reasons that governed her, (& I perfectly, I am bound to say, trust his fairness to appreciate it,) he knows it better than anyone else. If in short he *feels* unfairly treated, that, I think, represents, on his part a reality, & I have written to him that if this *is* his view of the case I shall be quite ready to give him $5,000 of my share. In that way we shall each have, he and I, $15,000, &, I think substantial justice will be done. I should be much indisposed to offer him the *income* of a part of my capital coming from Alice, as you suggest—& shouldn't expect from him to such an offer as that any reply but the one you enclose. The arrangement I speak of is much the best & the simplest way to correct in so far as it is urgent to correct it, the inequality which he resents. K.P.L.'s share is absolutely *inattackable,* I needn't say, Alice's desire to do *this* for her was over-whelming, & except Alice I am the person to realise best how abso-lutely fit a recognition it forms of years of (as it were) slavish (save that it was so spontaneous) heroically devoted person labour & sacrifice in her behalf. If it was a "reward" for the history of this last winter alone it would be none too much. She must keep her share intact, & you must keep yours. You have 4 children—& Bob has only two. I have none—& the above mentioned rectification is designated by every finger of circumstance as coming most fitly from me. And it enables the will to be quickly put through—as I shall simply have to make him over the money afterwards.—It is thrilling to know that I may see you a month sooner—or that you are perhaps coming, then, whether I see you or not. But this is exactly what I want to ask you, or to ask Alice to give me some definite information in relation to— I mean in relation to your 1ˢᵗ whereabouts & movements after you get here. I should *greatly* like to have it in advance & as what I do for the next three or four months (& I must arrange in advance,) will greatly depend on what you expect to do. Dear Alice, will you kindly answer these questions? 1/ *Where* are you thinking of going after your arrival at Antwerp(?) where are you going—or thinking of go-ing—to "plant" the children &c?

2/ *When* are you & William *thinking* of coming to England? Soon, I hope—soon, I mean, after you *have* planted the children?—though I don't absolutely & utterly invoke your presence in the feverish hu-man London July. You will of course stay with me—I can put you both up *perfectly*—as I have 3 bedrooms & 3 sitting-rooms. And I will reward you with *not* staying with you when I go to see you on the continent. I am planning to get away from London for some weeks the last of April. The earliest light you can throw for me on your *general* plan of movements will be a real convenience to me. Katherine sails on the 9ᵗʰ on the *Etruria*. Excuse this sickly scrawl— I am overdone, as to hand & head, with the deluge of notes & letters I have had to answer in relation to Alice. I have done little else but write them, ever since.

Ever yours   Henry James

To Henry James

Cambr. April 11. 92

My dear Harry,

Your letter of the 1st. *in rê* Alice's will & Bob, has just come. I was going to write to you anyhow this evening, it being the last of the "April recess," and I having just returned from a trip to Manchester to take a look at the little house where I last saw Father alive.[1] It seemed very small and poor, with its scanty bareness, all the windows boarded or blinded up so that for the most part I had to use two candles, and the simple wildness of the original "Smith's Point" corrupted with the weight of the lot of overgrown houses that have been superimposed upon it. The day was cold, a strong NW wind blowing and a sky full of gray clouds with gleams of sunshine making a hard light. I shall never go there again, whatever becomes of the house!

As for Bob, I am sorry I have started you to propose a sacrifice that I never meant you should. He will probably decline to take either your offer or mine, though I think it would be a perfectly fair thing for us to press upon him the equalization of income, *that* being what he most feels the need of—feels it, I dare say, morbidly. *You* ought not to alienate one dollar of any principal of which you may become possessed,—for reasons which I have expressed too often to wish to express them again. Alice of course made the will very deliberately—it was a very difficult task which she had to perform. As things stand, Bob was discriminated *against*, out of four; that is always humiliating; and considering that from the pecuniary point of view he has been the one entirely praiseworthy member of the family it is natural (even apart from his chronic morbidness) that he should feel sore. I trust that he will refuse both our offers; and that our having given him the chance to do so will be some sort of a balm to his wounded pride. *Practically,* he can do without the money better than we can, for if our earning power stops, as it may any day, we experience a terrible tumble, whereas he can't possibly tumble any lower than he now is, having ceased earning many years ago, and his wants being in equilibrium with his receipts. You say K's share is "inattackable". I trust you don't suspect me of a desire to attack it, or to propose anything to her about Bob. I hope, though, that in some way she will hear of your offer to Bob. I can well sympathize with Alice's desire to leave her something handsome; but I must say that her own consent (being apparently privy to the will) to receive more than Alice's bodily brother strikes me as *tant soit peu* lacking in delicacy. Surely no one of us would like to be in such a position in her family or in any other.* But now for Heaven's sake let things take their course, and say no more about such unpleasantness. It's enough to disgust one with the name of "will" that such evil passions should inevitably follow in their train. Even if Bob accepts your offer (which he wont) he will surely refund the amount again in case you ever come to grief.

Alice is writing you what we know of our plans at this date. Children & adults have opposite needs, and those of the children will probably have to be heavily taken into account. The worst of it is that the whole thing may shatter if my colleague Palmer accepts an invitation which they are making him & his wife at the new University which one of the Rockefellers of the Standard Oil Company has founded at Chicago on a handsome and very modern scale. If Palmer goes, and neither of our houses are rented (so far no serious nibble!) we may have to stay after all. In that case I must take one of my ruinously expensive vacations again to be ready for next year. Palmer's decision wont be known for three weeks yet.[2]

I have been seething in a fever of politics about the future of our philosophy dep! Harvard must lead in Psychology; and I, having founded her laboratory, am not the man to carry on the practical work. I have *almost* succeeded, however, in clinching a bargain whereby Münsterberg the ablest experimental psychologist in Germany, allowance made for his being only 28 years old—he is in fact the Rudyard Kipling of psychology—is to come here. When he does he will scoop out all the other Universities as far as that line of work goes. We have also had another scheme at the various stages of which you, Balzac or Howells ought to have been present, to work up for a novel or the stage. There's a great comedy yet to be made out of the University newly founded by the American millionaire. In this case the millionaire had announced his desire to found a professorship of psychology applied to education.[3] The thing was to get it for Harvard, which he mistrusted. I went at him tooth & nail, trying to persuade him that Royce was the man.   Letters, pourparlers, visits (he lives in N.Y.) finally a 2 days visit at this house, and a dinner for him.   He is a real Balzackian figure—a regular porker—coarse, vulgar, vain, cunning, mendacious etc etc.   The worst of it is that he will probably give us nothing—having got all the attention and flattery from us at which he aimed—so that we have our labor for our pains, and the gods laugh as they say "served them right."

I have long been meaning to write of my intense enjoyment of Du Maurier's Peter Ibbetson which I verily believe will be one of the classics of the English tongue.[4]   The *beauty* of it goes beyond ever[y]thing—and the light and happy touch—the rapid style!   Please tell him if you see him that we are all on our knees.   Your last book fell into Margaret G.'s hands, and I have barely seen it.[5]   I shan't have time to read it till the voyage.   I read "P.I." during the Xmas vacation.—What do you mean by talking of your *3* bed rooms and *3* sitting rooms?—In a couple of days I shall send you a quarterly Syracuse dividend of 342 dollars.

Ever affectionately yours, | Wm James

[*]If she had Bob's share & Bob hers, all would have been ideally proper.

[1] WJ had spent the summer of 1882 traveling and visiting friends and relatives. In early July he had visited his father, who was staying with AJ in her cottage in Manchester, Mass.

[2] Palmer declined the Chicago offer while Alice Palmer accepted an appointment as dean of women and served from 1892 to 1895.   Special arrangements were made that allowed her to continue to live in Cambridge.

[3] The target of WJ's fund raising was Marcus Dwight Larrowe, who wrote on mnemonics under the pen name of Alphonse Loisette.

[4] George Du Maurier, *Peter Ibbetson* (1891).

[5] HJ, *The Lesson of the Master* (1892).

To Henry James

Vers. chez. les. Blanc | Sept 1. 92

Dear H.

A letter from Baldwin who is at S! Moritz, arrived last night & gave a satisfactory account of the english school.   At any rate, I have thrown responsibility for the boys' education to the winds and breathe happy in consequence.   We leave here to morrow for Château d'Oex I think, or somewhere in that neighborhood.   Will write you the address when we know it.   A servant was carried away from this pension ill a week ago, and turns out to have typhoid fever, which of course casts a doubt on the water supply etc. It's a pity for the Cruchon's—but there is no other course for us.[1] The Flournoys went last night.

Both Loring[2] & Baldwin say that Oct 1. is late for a good choice of rooms in Florence, so we shall go by Sept. 20th. School doesn't begin till Oct 25. I look forward with great cheerfulness to the prospect of a winter there.

I got yesterday your vol of Daisy Miller in the Tauchnitz Edition. They seem to have *estropie'd* your four meetings (which I never read before) and which surely can't have ended in the original in that place—"unsatisfactory" as your endings are accused of being! If this is so, it is an outrage and they ought to know it. It ends after the *third* meeting, at Grimwinter with the french woman in possession. The last words are "her presentiment that she should still see something of that dear old Europe."[3]

Yrs aff[ly] W.J.

[1] WJ was staying at the Pension Cruchon.
[2] Francis William Loring.
[3] HJ, "Four Meetings" (1877), included in *Daisy Miller: A Study; An International Episode; Four Meetings*, 2 vols. (London: Macmillan, 1879). The volume was also published in the Collection of British Authors by Bernhardt Tauchnitz in Leipzig. In the several editions examined, "Four Meetings" ends with the words quoted by WJ. HJ's reply was not found.

From Henry James

34, DE VERE GARDENS. W. Nov. 15th '92

My dear William.

Your pale-green postcard follows your letter in pencil from Venice. I have taken the greatest satisfaction in your week at Padua & Venice—& especially in the words (contained in one of your notes to Alice from Padua, which she enclosed to me) "I surrender to Italy." I rejoice to hear it—for it is what I did 23 years ago—once for all— when it was revealed to me in September 1869. And with all the lapse of life, & the changes of sensibility & even exhaustion of the same, the place is still to me one of the greatest of comforts. I will try and clear up the question of the D.N. responsibility[1]—but don't worry about it, for what I paid (for only 3 months,) was the merest of trifles. I have no personal news for you at all—unless it be that I came back yesterday from a day at Bath, whither I went to carry

Compton a completely rewritten & reconstructed (in a *comedy-sense*—heaven forgive me!) 4th act of the American. The actual 4th act (the old,) militates markedly by its grimness &c against the *remaining* of the play in his repertory. He has now played it every Friday for several months & had time to feel country audiences, *very* friendly indeed up to the end of 3^{d}, *regimber* & droop over the 4th. So the 4th is now *another* 4th, which will basely gratify their artless instincts & British thick-wittedness, & thanks to it the poor old play will completely save one's *honour* (which is all I care for,) as a *permanent* & regular thing. It will be much for it to "keep the stage." The Comptons are delighted with the new act (a feat of unspeakable difficulty,) & it is played for the 1st time at Bristol next week (without, of course, the smallest reference to any change. Please never *make* any.) I am expecting to hear this week from Daly exactly *when* he is to produce my comedy in New York.[2] There are various indications that it will be very soon—perhaps immediately. I shall at any rate know definitely in a few days.—We are living in horrors of foul black fog—an atmospheric misery (lamplight from early morn every day for a week,) that makes me almost frantic when I think there are Florences and Romes. I cherish more and more the dream of getting away in January. If I *can* manage it I will go down, then, through France. The Bourgets are to be at San Remo & have appealed to me strongly to spend another month near them. I shall not spend so much—but I shall see them, unless the whole thing fails. Mrs. Cuyler Mary's sister, writes to ask me to come & see her here—where she has come to see her daughter's prospective mother-in-law.[3] I hate to be even *so* much mixed up with their affairs. A very contented (save with her niece's marriage!) letter from Mary herself at Dresden.

Yours & Alice's always   Henry.

[1] *Daily News.*

[2] Augustin Daly did not produce HJ's *Mrs. Jasper,* later called *Disengaged.*

[3] The daughter of Alice Millard Holton Cuyler was to marry Sir Philip Henry Brian Grey-Egerton.

Established with his family in an apartment in Florence, William missed the conveniences of Irving Street. But even with all the problems encountered in living abroad—the temperature below freezing, no water in the house for most of the day, sick servants and children, one room serving both as his study and as a playroom for the boys, and having to "diaperize" the baby—he still enjoyed the luxury of reading without interruptions by students and informed Henry on 17 January 1893 that "all goes well" but that they will be happy when the weather improves. The American colony in Florence provided many opportunities for society. Samuel Clemens was there occupying a "delightful" villa and writing much more than he could have at home, as he informed the Jameses in the course of a pleasant dinner. Also in Florence was Mary Holton James, Robertson's wife, with her mother and daughter. Her father's death in 1892 had left Mary James financially independent and she spent much of her time traveling.

Violet Paget, who wrote criticism and stories under the pseudonym of Vernon Lee, was also in Florence. William's first response to her, as he reported to Henry on 17 January, was enthusiastic. He found in her a "divine spark" that few critics have. Her writings, in his view, were "magnificent for perception, style constructive criticism." Henry, who had been on friendly terms with her for some time, heard reports in January 1893 that in her Vanitas: Polite Stories *(1892) he had been caricatured in a "saucy" manner. Thus, when William informed him that he was about to make a social visit to her, Henry responded with strong warnings.*

From Henry James

34, DE VERE GARDENS. W. Jan. 20th [1893]

My dear William.

I wrote you a few days since a letter which you will have got by this time—but meanwhile comes in your own of the 17th, (inclosing Katie Rodgers's—poor, poor Katie!)[1] and picturing the sad [state] of things in casa tua—with which this is designed as a hasty word of sympathy. May the acuteness, or at any rate the simultaneity of those *disgrazie* already have waned. Keep up a good heart. You will soon have had the last kick of winter & the divine Italian spring, breaking out intermittently but early, will have begun to throb & *gazonner* around you. Then you will be in for a long stretch of clear joy of life; part of which I shall share with you. My letter will have told you of my interrupting attack of gout. It is a fortnight yesterday since it began; but I have only, for a 2ᵈ time, to-day put on a shoe— & a shoe gashed excised, alas, to allow me to go to Mrs. Kemble's funeral. You will have seen her death in the *Daily News*. She died— at the last, happily—in a *second,* with only time to give a faint little "oh!"   (She was letting her maid quietly put her to bed.)   But she had failed & changed so for two or three years that it was [as] if she had gone a good while ago. Don't be disgusted with my procrastina- tion when I tell you that as Bentley, (her publisher for 20 years past & a great personal friend,) has asked me to write 25 pages on her mem- ory for the earliest number possible of *Temple Bar,* I shall probably hang on her[e] long enough to do it—to get it off my hands before starting abroad: wait in other words to about Feb. 7ᵗʰ.[2] It will all be a gain for the time that I shall be abroad—I mean giving me the lengthening days & the milder weeks. I have 1ˢᵗ to finish an article on G. Flaubert's lately completed *Correspondence* for *Macmillan*[3]—oth- erwise I could do the paper on Mrs. K. more immediately. And I shall be able to stay away till *May*—as Daly's advent is delayed by the impossibility of finishing his theatre so soon as he 1ˢᵗ announced.— *Afternoon.* I am back from Mrs. Kemble's funeral at dreary Kemsal Green—a small knot of old friends by her grave in the centre of a rabble of pushing, staring indelicate populace, with the British fe- male of the lower orders as insufferable as on such occasions she always is.—Poor great & extraordinary woman!———Receive from me (àpropos of extraordinary women,) a word of warning about Ver- non Lee. I hope you won't throw yourselves into her arms—& I am sorry you offered to go & see her (after she wrote to you) *first.* My reasons are several, & too complicated some of them to go into; but one of them is that she has lately, as I am told (in a volume of tales called *Vanitas* which I haven't read,) directed a kind of satire of a flagrant & markedly "saucy" kind at me(!!) exactly the sort of thing she has repeatedly done to others (her books—fiction—are a tissue of personalities of the hideous roman-à-clef kind,) & particularly im- pudent & blackguardly sort of thing to do to a friend & one who has

treated her with such particular consideration as I have.   For God's
sake don't betray that I have *spoken* to you of the matter or betrayed
the faintest knowledge of it: I haven't read these tales & never mean
to.   They are moreover[,] the others, excessively, to my sense, brutal & bad. But *don't* caress her—not only on this ground but because
she is as dangerous & uncanny as she is intelligent—which is saying
a great deal.   Her vigour & sweep of interest are most rare & her
talk superior altogether; but I don't agree with you at all about her
"style," which I find *insupportable*, & I find also that she breaks down
in her books.   There is a great second-rate element in her 1ˢᵗ rateness. At any rate draw it mild with her on the question of friendship.
She's a tiger-cat!—You will of course, no doubt, all the same, as I'm
your brother, find the bad taste of her putting me *en scène* (& the
whole treachery to private relations of the *procédé*) a thing to be
judged as, on her part, *deserving*—or at any rate with a hundred
attenuations. *But,* at any rate, show *her* no glimpse of knowing anything about it—*I* know only by hearsay—& I should be glad if
(though I am quite conscious of the loss of good talk entailed on you
by it—as she is far-away the most able mind in Florence,) you could
oblige yourself not to respond to her any further than mere civility
requires.   Ask Mᵐᵉ Villari some day about her!———What a terribly
sad image of poor Katie Rodgers—& what courage & cheerfulness—
to be dragging herself about Europe in such a state & living in the
contraction of cheap hotels & pensions!   I shall of course go to see
her in Paris—but what can one do for her?   But I must draw breath.
I hope Alice gets some leisure—that it isn't all baby & all Peggy—&
cook!   Much love to her—& many assurances in the course of next
month she will begin to be glad to live—in Florence.

Your always | Henry

Address: William James esq. | 16 Piazza dell' Indipendenza 1º pº | Florence Italy.
Postmarks: PARIS 2* 21 93   <FI>RENZE 23 1 93   The part of the envelope containing the originating postmark is missing.

¹ Katharine Rodgers was thought to have a uterine tumor.
² HJ, "Frances Anne Kemble," *Temple Bar* 97 (April 1893): 503–25; reprinted in *Essays in London and Elsewhere* (1893).
³ HJ's review of *Correspondance de Gustave Flaubert* (4th series) appeared in *Macmillan's
Magazine* 67 (March 1893): 332–43; reprinted in *Essays in London and Elsewhere* (1893).

To Henry James

16 P. d. Indip. Feb. 3. 93
Dear Henry

A letter from you to Alice arrived yesterday relative to Miss Paget etc. She has gone off somewhere to find a warm climate for a fortnight or so, and I doubt if we see her much again. Pray *don't send* Euphorion or anything else. When I first wrote I had only read the first vol. thereof and was delighted with her quality, but vol. II and "Baldwin" have made me see her defects, or rather excesses, uncontrollable flux of ideas—*pro rê nata*, adjectives etc.[1] She has the temperament of genius as few have it. But how rare is *effective* genius! The Lord, in loosening her from all inhibitions, has forfeited all permanently interesting quality in her. I have been laid up with a "gastric attack" for 24 hrs., the result of riotous living prompted by my feeling of invulnerability of late, for truly I have been gradually growing extremely "well" in the way of sleep, nerves etc. generally, as a result of the continued holiday. We are beginning to take thought about next year already. Corresponding with the Weimar Gymnasium etc—a distracting problem again.

Peg, at my elbow, sends you her love.

Yours ever | Wm James

We see Baldwin a good deal—lately for Tweedy who has been off his feed. He has an apartment ready to receive you when you come, and is in general so busy that if lodging there you wd. probably be very free.

I[n] writing of Flaubert, his pessimism, haine du bourgeois etc, are not treated as they should be, as distinctly pathological obsessions, by the critics whom I have seen. My conception of him is first, a mental invalid, then a good and true human being, "bon bougre" & finally a man of genius.

[1] Violet Paget, *Baldwin: Being Dialogues on Views and Aspirations* (1886), a critique of religion; *Euphorion: Being Studies of the Antique and the Mediæval in the Renaissance* (1884).

In late February, William went to Munich with his thirteen-year-old son, Henry, to visit art museums, to see where the family might go in the spring, and to give William a chance to meet some colleagues. From Munich he wrote Alice that he had drunk three liters of beer with Albert von Schrenck-Notzing, a German physician interested in psychical research and later famous for his studies of sexual pathology.

Once again in Florence, he sketched a design of an urn for their sister's ashes. After Alice's cremation, Katharine Loring had taken the ashes to Cambridge for burial in the Cambridge cemetery beside the graves of Alice's parents.

To Henry James

Flo. Mch. 10. 93

Dear Harry,   How I wish you were here to take council with about certain matters—many matters in fact.   The burden of the babies weighs us down and planning for the summer is hard.   Peg has been ill in bed for a week, with a mysterious liver trouble.   She kept *noth*-ing on her stch. for 4 days, vomiting bile all that time, every couple of hours.   Now she is convalescent, but Tweedy is equally mysteriously ill, much as he was a month ago.   It weighs on poor Alice.

What I write about now is to get your consent to a design for Alice's tomb which I am making.   It is based on the roman ash-caskets, some thing like this in front.   It is a conventional thing essentially, but carried out with modern refinement of detail, and both rich and beautiful looking.   On front just: "Here lie the ashes of A, daughter of H. & M. J. who di[e]d at London ——— – 1892 in the 43rd year of her age."   Can you supply date of birth & exact age?   On the sides the emblems from Father's seal, jar with butterfly escaping, on one, and on the other serpent with tail in mouth.   On the back I tho't this from Dante would fit very well: "Ed essa da martiro et da esiglio venne a questa pace."[1]   Please give your sanction before I go ahead.   I have seen a workman to whom mead introduced me as honest & capable, and he can do it easily.   Mead says it shouldn't cost more than 50 dollars.

Your Flaubert article came this AM. many thanks.[2]   I have been able just to glance at it, and it looks *very spirited indeed*.   But why not give some specimens?

Great haste.   Answer instantly about the tomb.   I have postponed so long, thinking you wd. be here, and wishing to consult you on the spot.

Leb' wohl. | W.J.

¹ From *The Divine Comedy, Paradiso,* canto 10, line 128: "To soar from martyrdom and exile to this peace."
² See letter of 20 January 1893.

From Henry James

34, DE VERE GARDENS. W. March 13ᵗʰ [1893]

My dear William.

I wrote to you yesterday. This a.m. comes your letter of the 10ᵗʰ about Alice's monument &c. It gives me the heartache—for your burdens & bothers; & makes me want immensely to start straight for Florence for the sake of a talk with you. However, I won't do this—without taking time to turn round, in Paris (whither I go day-after-tomorrow,) & get perhaps better news from you. If it continues to seem probable that you *are* near your time of starting northward it will be better for me to be with you on your arrival at what ever place you do arrive at—where I can *stay*. But if as seems to me the *most* likely effect of the prospect of the Italian May &c—you do remain on in Florence week after week, I won't answer for it that I shall not suddenly bolt down to converse with you. Weary & worn must Alice indeed be with the younger children's ills. She has all my sympathy. May this trouble be speedily lightened.—Is it out of the question or not worth thinking of, that you should come to *England* for the rest of the time (after leaving Italy,) till you sail? Wouldn't it be more paying than Switzerland & more feasible than Germany? I could help you here & it would be interesting to Alice & salubrious for the children. Lodgings, furnished houses &c, are findable by the million. Think of it, and of how I might assist you in it. Might it not (since it appears probable that you do go home in the summer?) be the best way to spend the time till you sail? There may be objections to it—but there are probably objections also to anything else you may be thinking of.*—I assent entirely to your idea for Alice's tomb—& am very glad you have had the inspiration of designing it & finding an executant. I shall of course be delighted to bear ½ the expense, whatever it is. I like all the details you speak of—the design from father's seal & find the words from Dante perfect for the purpose. But I should like the English inscription a little different. She said something before her death which indicated that she would like the word *Kensington* on her grave—so much so that K.P.L. & I spoke of it together afterwards. What I should propose would be what I have written on the accompanying (enclosed) sheet. She surely was born in *1849*. I remember that she was 7 years old in August (I think 4ᵗʰ, but I am not certain as you will remember we never "kept" birthdays) of the summer of 1855 that we spent, near Geneva, at Madame Buscarlet's, "Campagne Gerebsoff." Strangely enough I *forget* her speaking definitely of her age (& any speaking of it with Katherine) at the time of her death—but it *was* 43: I am morally certain. Her birthday was either Aug. 4ᵗʰ or Aug 7ᵗʰ—the former I am *almost* sure. But I don't think it desirable to put this or the *day* of her death (March 6ᵗʰ) on the stone. The two different *years* alone seem to me to say all that is needed about her age and to be simpler, graver and more monumental. "Kensington" is such a definite locality in itself & is so much more human & localised than the vast vagueness of "London" (of which she knew nothing—whereas her Kensington existence was conscious & interested,) that I hope you will prefer it. It will be *particularly* grateful to me. Nothing could be happier than the Dantean line-Vale. I hope that Tweedy (with all my heart,) is being but briefly ill and that Peg is wholly re-established. Courage! The best weeks are at hand.

Ever your   Henry.

*Wouldn't it especially do if you were to remain longer in Italy?— i.e. *through* May—after which you cld. come up for a *straight* stay here.

To Henry James

16. P.d.I. Florence, March 17. [1893]
My dear Harry, Your two letters, one yesterday, the other today, in reference to my tomb-design have arrived. Of all human beings, you are the one I have most wanted to see in these latter days. So much is up concerning we want counsel etc. etc. But it will all straighten out. Your proposal this A.M that we should go straight to England comes in the nick of time to corroborate a scheme which we formed 2 days ago of making tracks as straight as possible from here to Albion's shore, and I was on the point of asking you for topographical advice. Alice ought to have a dose of England, and I am utterly ignorant of the country there so the sooner we get there the better. Harry is settled for 3 mos. in Germany, we can put Billy on the lake of Genève for ditto, and be by so much the less complicated. Then when July comes I can return for the boys, spend that month, or most of it, in walking with them through the Mᵗˢ and by Aug 1st be

in England for a month with them, sailing for home about Sept. 1 or earlier. Of course we will stop at Paris on the way, or wherever you may be, long enough to have big talks with you. I don't wonder that it seems strange to you that we should be leaving here just in the glory of the year. *Your* view of Italy is that of the tourist; and that is really the only way to *enjoy* any place. Ours is that of the resident in whom the sweet decay breathed in for six months has produced a sort of physiological craving for a change to robuster air. One ends by craving one's own more permanent attitude, and a country whose language I can speak and where I can settle into my own neccessary work (which has been awfully prevented here of late), without a guilty sense that I am neglecting the claims of pictures and monuments, is the better environment now. In short Italy has well served its purpose by us and we shall be eternally grateful. But we have no farther *use* for it, and the spring is also beautiful in lands that will [be] fresher to our senses. There are moments when the florentine debility becomes really *hateful* to one, and I don't see how the Lorings and others can come and make their home with it. You have done the best thing, in putting yourself in the strongest *milieu* to be found on earth. But Italy is incomparable as a refreshing refuge, and I am sorry that you are likely to lose it this year. We therefore shall in all probability leave here by the middle of April, proceeding to Geneva by M! Cenis, and settling Billy, thence straight to Paris. Our trip will cost us a bigger slice of poor Alice's legacy than was foreseen when we left home, but *le vin est versé et il faut le boire*, it would be foolish, being here, to let the thing fail out of parsimony. Of course you can give us some hints as to the best region to go towards in the country the first 3 weeks or so, I want to show Alice London a bit. How, by the way, does the matter stand with your Daly play? You have written nothing about it. You will be back there, of course, and we ought to have free orders for the first night! I pity, but admire you with all those proofs. The Flaubert article was a *very* good one. He is the only one of those frenchmen who interests me *personally*, because, in spite of his pathological irritability, he is a real *man*, & absolutely honest. But his whole anti bourgeouis business, Bouvard et Pécuchet etc,[1] are pure reactions against a pathological obsession, altogether analogous to the other pathological obsessions that are enumerated in the recent books about the class of beings called by the fashionable name of degénérés héréditaires. A man, a fine romantic artist, with the obsession of the banal and vulgar grafted on to his nervous system in such a way that he could only work it off by writing on subjects that he felt as an external constraint, and [*two pages missing*] the drawings were of something really charming. The proportions of everything were something over which I *swat*. I think Kensington much better than London, but am not so sure as to the form of your inscription which is more cold and abstract. Mine, of "died at Kensington March 6th in the 43rd year of her age" also permits a running inscription without breaks, filling all the lines in the style of the inscriptions on the old roman tablets. But these are small matters which will gradually settle themselves.

The children are all well again, and you need [not] be concerned about us. My usual spring seediness has thoroughly set in, to my great disappointment, since at home I always console myself by ascribing it to the hard winter's work. But a change of climate will take that away. There is something profoundly inadequate to my constitutional needs in this insignificant italian air.

Alice sends love and rejoicings that you also should propose the english plan, which is to her a great relief from the thought of the mountains. [*end of letter missing*]

[1] Gustave Flaubert, *Bouvard et Pécuchet* (1881). An English translation is subtitled *A Tragi-Comic Novel of Bourgeois Life.*

From Henry James

Hotel Westminster | rue de la Paix. | March 21. [1893]
Dear William & dear Alice.

Your two letters—of the 16th & 17th, gratify me *outre mesure*. I am delighted that you recognise the essential propriety of your coming to England; so much the simplest, yet richest, solution of the question of your remainder. I would have *wailed* at the thought of Alice's departing from Europe without a substantial British impression. It would have been at once a crime & a *bêtise*. It seems to me that the question of *where* is one that may be sufficiently left for future discussion. So that as I am to see you *here*—an idea with which I am also delighted—there is no need of our going into it yet. I congratulate both of you on your sagesse. I needn't add that my house, my person, my experience & everything I have (reserving only a certain quantity of my *time,*) will be at your service. I am very sorry you react so against the lax & lovely Italy. But I can understand it—& your circumstances. So much the better that there is a stodgy Albion to strike such a different variety of notes. I see every reason to believe, then, that I shall hang on here till you come. Paris is at present wonderfully mild & bright—blond & fair.   The air is full of "décadence" (to my sense,) but the light is vernal & the spectacle beguiling.—I am partly amused & partly disconcerted by the William-Paget correspondence: though much gratified indeed at his having felt the throb of resentment on my behalf and acted upon it—for which I thank him.[1] I desired however that the thing (as to which I am utterly in the dark save as my very vivid sense—& other experience—of Violet's possibilities enlightens me,) should not have been "noticed," directly, at all.   However, 'tis doubtless well as it is.   I don't find her note at all convincing;—she is doubtless sorry to be disapproved of in high quarters; but her procédé was absolutely deliberate, & her humility, which is easy & inexpensive, after the fact, doesn't alter her absolutely impertinent nature.   Basta—basta!—I am very happy about William's design for the tomb—& I don't *hold* to my shorter inscription: all I hold to is the "Kensington."   I rejoice that it is in artistic hands. I hope everything will go well with you till you again get into movement.   I have this a.m. a perfect mountain of forwarded letters & proofs—from London—so I break off.   Please notify me, as you see your way—about what sort of *dates* you tend to. It will be useful to have a general sense of them in advance.   Many caresses to the infants.

Yours, dear Alice, dear William, always | Henry James

[1] In his letter of 11 March 1893, WJ scolded Violet Paget for her caricature of HJ (Colby College).   Paget replied in a lost letter to the effect that she had burst into tears upon receipt of WJ's letter.   WJ replied on 18 March 1893 (Colby College).

Sometime in April 1893, Alfred Hodder, a Harvard graduate student in philosophy, and Jessie Donaldson Hodder reached Florence where in the James apartment she gave birth to their first child. Unbeknownst to the Jameses, the Hodders were not married. About ten years later, Alfred Hodder married someone else and Jessie Donaldson found comfort and support in the James family. With their help she became a social worker and prison reformer.

William left Florence on 15 April 1893 for Geneva, where he deposited his son William at a boarding school and spent two hours gossiping with Katherine Rodgers and her sister, finding them in good spirits in spite of Katherine's uterine tumor. Alice joined him

*at Meggen, near Luzern, where in May Henry arrived for a visit
of some three weeks. In June they left the children in the care of a
Swiss pastor and traveled to London where they occupied Henry's
apartment. For most of this time Henry was at the resort of Rams-
gate working on his next theatrical venture,* Guy Domville.

William and his family departed for home on the Cephalonia
*on 24 August 1893 from Liverpool and were in Boston on 2
September. His academic politicking had resulted in the arrival of
Hugo Münsterberg at Harvard to take charge of the psychological
laboratory, leaving William free to undertake a new graduate
course, a seminar on questions of mental pathology, in which he
could combine his interests in psychical research with developments
in the new field of abnormal psychology.*

To Henry James

　　　　　　Salter's Place, Silver Lake near Chocorua Sept 22 93.
Dear Henry,

We have been at home for nearly three weeks, but everything so
unsettled that I have waited to write till there should be something
more definitive to tell.　It has taken a long time to get the house in
order with the contents of our 28 trunks & boxes to store away, and
all the things that we put away to clear the house for a possible tenant
to get into their right places again.　With but two servants, and one
of them with an ankle sprained on the stairs three days after her
arrival, so that she had to lie three days in bed and do very little
walking about since, you may imagine that Alice herself has been
working like a charwoman almost all the time.　The women are
splendid creatures personally, and very happy so far (tho' alice writes
me that she took one to the dentist's the day before yesterday and
had *8* of her teeth extracted), but I rather doubt their cleverness at
their work.　We long for the third who *may* come.　I have hardly
done a stroke of work with all the preparations there have been and
people to see.　We had the great Helmholtz & his wife with us one
afternoon, gave them tea and invited some people to meet them, she
a charming woman of the world, bro't up by her aunt, Madame Mohl
in Paris, he the most monumental example of benign calm and
speechlessness that I ever saw.[1]　He is growing old, and somewhat
weary, I think, and makes no effort beyond that of smiling & inclining
his head to remarks that are made.　I least[2] he made no response to

remarks of mine, but Royce Charles Norton, John Fiske and D.ʳ Walcott who surrounded him at a little table where he sat with tea and beer, said that he spoke. Such power of calm is a great possession. I have been twice to Mrs. Whitman's once to a lunch & reception to the Bourget's a fortnight ago. Mrs Jack Gardner, it would seem, has kept them like caged birds (probably because they wanted it so); Mrs. B. was charming and easy, he ill at ease, refusing to try English unless compelled, and turning to *me* at the table as a drowning man to a "hencoop," as if there were safety in the presence of anyone connected with you. I could do nothing towards inviting them, in the existent state of our ménage, but when later they come back for a month in Boston, I shall be glad to bring them into the house for a few days. I feel quite a fellow feeling for him, he seems a very human creature, and it was a real pleasure to me to see a frenchman of B.'s celebrity *look* as ill at ease as I myself have often *felt* in fashionable society. They are I believe in Canada, and have only too much society. I shan't go to Chicago, for economy's sake—besides I *must* get to work. But *every one* says one ought to sell all one has and mortgage one's soul to go there, it is esteemed such a revelation of beauty.[3] People cast away all sin and baseness, burst into tears and grow religious etc., under the influence!! *Some* people evidently. The people about home are very pleasant to meet—the poor Ashburners wasted to skeletons, but yet alive; Child a good deal older, Grace Norton rheumatic but still as cordial & hearty as ever etc. [Will you by the way, send the prescription of your new gout remedy to me for Child—he is a martyr to it & rheumatism.—Dont forget!] I am up here for a few days with Billy, to close our house for the winter, and get a sniff of the place. The Salter's have a noble hill with such an outlook, & a very decent little house and barn.[4] But oh! the difference from Switzerland, the thin grass and ragged waysides, the poverty stricken land, and sad American sunlight over all—sad because so empty. There is a strange thinness and femininity hovering over all America, so different from the stoutness and masculinity of land and air and everything in Switzerland and England, that the coming back makes one feel strangely sad, and hardens one in the resolution never to go away again unless one can go to end one's days. Such a divided soul is very bad. To you, who now have real practical relations and a place in the old world, I should think there was no neccessity of ever coming back again. But Europe has been made what it is by men staying in their homes and fighting stubbornly generation after generation for all the beauty comfort and order that they have got—we must abide and do the same. As England struck me newly and differently last time, so America now—force and directness in the people, but a terrible grimness, more ugliness than I ever realized in *things*, and a greater weakness in Nature's beauty, such as it is. One must pitch one's whole sensibility first in a different key—then gradually the quantum of personal happiness of which one is susceptible fills the cup—but the moment of change of key is lonesome. Henry Higginson has, I imagine, been through a fearfully anxious time—I feel for him, he is such a noble minded-fellow with half of his friends & acquaintances to carry on his back pecuniarily. Things are better now, and he is off to Chicago. Bob has been attacking me insanely on pecuniary grounds, and Warner is to negotiate with him relative to a possible withdrawal on his part from Syracuse. If you and Mrs. Gibbens and I would combine we could easily buy out his share and I should lead a quieter life than now with his incessant worry. He ought to be mixed with no one else. On the other hand, however, Syracuse is so good an investment for him, with a prospect of becoming even more valuable, that I cannot abet his leaving unless it seems perfectly clear to him that he can reinvest in as good a way. He is really insane, poor wretch, and grows frantic at any and every minutest practical difficulty or uncertainty. He accuses me of spoliation of him in rê Alice's will, and in rê taking Clary's note for two months rent instead of turning him instantly out of doors, he having been our tenant for nine years, during which he had paid us over twenty thousand dollars without a month's delay, and having at last paid up his note all but 200 dollars. Bob says he will never forgive me the loss of that 50 dollars due to him "in this world or the next"— etc etc. He claims a thousand dollars from me for having handed over some Syracuse money to Higginson to invest in bonds for a sinking fund, the bonds having much depreciated in value since they were bought etc. I didn't mean to write any details of this to you, but my pen has run on. I can't have meetings with Bob again, they are so painful, so Warner will have to deal with him. The Salters are going to arrive in London about the middle of October—he to give six Sunday lectures before the "Ethical" Society there, and then return. If you will see them once, speak to them kindly, and lend them the use of your number at the "stores," you will be doing a humane thing and it will be remembered by many in your favor.[5] Mary is a very fine earnest warm hearted character, the most affectionate person I have ever known except her mother, and Salter is a saint. I hope the dramatic career is thickening and that health and happiness are strong.   Every soul here asks after you, & I give a favorable account. Kitty Temple arrived with her 3rd boy Grenville in Cambridge 3 days ago, to put him into the freshman class, although he is only sixteen.   She is very stout, but has a nice low voice and quiet manner and I was glad to see her again.   I fear from what she let drop that Elly's prospects are not very brilliant.   They are on Staten Island, and Hunter has begun business in N.Y.   All her daughters with her.   John Dwight is dead.   Also Fred⸢k⸣ Ames the richest man in Mass., one of the Corporation of the College from whom great moneys were expected.   He was as *giver* a very public spirited man, but in his will leaves *no* public bequests—a bad business.

Yours ever affect⸢ly⸣,   Wm James

I had to pay $145.00 duties—The clock bo't at the stores finds a first-rate place on the library mantel-piece and gives more companionship & comfort than I ever supposed such a thing could.

I have seen Howells, now at Chicago. I saw D⸢r⸣ Holmes & fanny at bkfst.   Wendell was on circuit.   He is threatened with appendicitis, and goes nowhere, but is in consequence better than ever before in his life, is reported to be *fat*, and fanny says is perfectly happy and devoted to playing *solitaire!!*

The D⸢r⸣ is more shamelessly self satisfied and absorbed with the delights of the process of growing old, than any man ever was.   He talks as well as ever and said that the process was one of denudation, but as things were washed away there came to light "crystals of tho't" sharp and beautiful which would other wise never have appeared, etc.

Our Harry's name was printed in the Cephalonia arrivals, and I am told that the reporters have been after you all up and down the Coast and as far as Chicago.[6]

[1] Helmholtz was in the United States for the World's Columbian Exposition in Chicago and stopped in Boston on his way back to Germany.   His wife was Olga von Velten Helmholtz, niece of Julius Mohl.

[2] WJ clearly wrote 'I least', an error for 'At least'.

[3] WJ did not visit the World's Columbian Exposition in Chicago.

[4] Silver Lake, where the Salters had their summer home, is about five miles from Chocorua.

[5] The cooperative stores in London were available only to members and the Salters needed the use of HJ's membership.

[6] Part of WJ's letter is on the back of a letter to HJ from a *Boston Herald* reporter, 12 September 1893.   The reporter was probably named Benjamin H. Rounseville, but the signature is not clear.   He was not identified.

From Henry James

34, DE VERE GARDENS. W. October 19th 1893

My dear William.

I shall probably hear from you soon about the matter I lately wrote you about—my full adhesion to Bob's proposal that we shall take over his share of Syracuse; but I won't delay longer to thank you for the two letters I have had from you since then. I have only delayed till now by reason of the hope that I might—from one day to the other—have news, which I shall be so glad to have, of the whereabouts of the Salters—with whose coming here your second letter mainly concerns itself. I shall be delighted to do anything in my power to make their case easier—& as soon as I hear from them will actively take the field. Did they perhaps think that you were to give me their general London address—so that I would look them up? I have an inkling of this address—but shall doubtless soon hear from them. Then I will put Salter down at the Athenaeum (unless he's already there,) & give them as many "meals" as they will take.—The other feature of this 2^d letter was your mention of having offered your house to let. I am very sorry indeed that you've had to resort to such an extremity to pay the piper. I say "extremity," because it sounds so horrid to think of poor Alice's having, as a sequence of a winter in Florence, to betake herself to the snow-solitudes of Chocorua. I can't help hoping—piper or no piper—that this doom will be averted from her by some slipperiness of your tenant. What will become, in this case, of the foreign maids?—Most interesting, even if most melancholy, were the vivid reflections in your previous letter (the one written while staying at Chocorua,) on the effect on your returning & alienated eye of the scraggy American aspects. I tasted of that intensity once & forever when I returned from Europe (after my 1st independent 15 months there,) in May 1870—& determined, in the deadly days, on my future life. I felt then, as I felt after subsequent returns, that the only way to live in America was to turn one's back on Europe; that the attempt to *mix* them is a terribly comfortless business. You express the lonesome want of "temperament" of it all in a way that brings back so intensely past episodes & histories. I have been supremely fortunate in being able to do what I wanted—i.e. make my election for the older world; & the only way to make use of my fortune is to accept it frankly & consistently. This sounds chill enough for such intercourse as remains to us if you hereafter enlightenedly forbear from Europe; and I would say I would come back (for 3 months—some year,) if you hadn't enclosed me that note from the interviews.[1]   If *he* awaits me on the shining shore I shall never, never go.   The autumn here is very fine & very quiet & my work goes on very well.   I shall, I think, presently be able to write you that I have still another play triumphantly arranged for.   I still don't know my Alexander *date*—I shan't till next month; but meanwhile please *taire* the whole matter in the U.S.—there are particular reasons—bearing on this question of time of production—for temporary silence.   I don't come on at Daly's till January: very tiresome, but very advisable, from the point of view of the theatre-going public—I mean of its presence in London.   Meantime I am so pressed (with the effort to carry out a certain masterly general plan!) that my letter writing must suffer.   I am delighted that it seems good to you to feel over your head the wind of the big University wings.   Also that the great Munsterberg doesn't make you blush for anything—or the clock on the library mantel either.   Grey, delicate, pearl coloured ashes are all that are left, as it were, of your fiery passage here—the ashes of the dead summer.   I think of various things I might have tried for, for you— but let them pass.   Much love to Alice & the babes—I hope with all my heart she isn't to be exiled.

Ever your   Henry.

[1] See letter of 22 September 1893, note 6.

To Henry James

Dictated

Irving St. Cambridge | Oct 29. 1893

Dear Henry,

   I have been trying to write to you for a fortnight but the pace of life has been too hard.   Today comes relief, in the shape of a mild tonsilitis with doctor, bedroom, and excuse for stopping work.   So my chance arrives.   I got your letter duely about buying out Bob's share but I don't think anything is likely to be done in that direction. The idea was prompted by a hasty fit of temper on his part which has blown over, leaving things on the old basis with probably an increased liability to rouse in the future.   He now corresponds with the agent and is, I think, entirely trustworthy.   So give yourself no more concern about that matter.   We are aching to know whether your play-rehearsals have begun and how they are going on and also what new developements may have occurred in your dramatic career since last August. As I dictate this word a most exquisite vision arises of that morning-departure with the brilliant weather, the charming leisure at the station, the friendliness of everyone, the cleanliness of everything with you as ministering uncle to cap it all! With the ideal voyage after it, it seems framed like some bit in a work of art. Why must a thing always be framed in pastness before it gains full aesthetic worth? The present here has been agreeable enough in one way. Our eyes got back from the solid European effects to the loose American ones in a few weeks, and the weather and climate have afforded an uninterrupted spectacle of beauty & mildness until now. We have lighted a fire on only two occasions, and then to please the eye, and the glorious multicoloured foliage has hung on the trees for weeks. But after our 15 months of softness the work goes hard. Alice has too much to attend to in the house and I feel as if I had lost all my memories and other equipments for teaching. I find on comparing notes that this is a common case and expect that it will fade away as far as I am concerned. Our heroic aspiration to rent the house and too scatter came to nought. Two tenants kept us dangling for about 3 weeks when one decided not to come to Cambridge and the other took another house—immensely to our relief. The other thing would have been very disconsolate and, saving Alice's presence, I had not much confidence that her calculations would come out in fact as on paper. People have been having a real hell of a time of it financially. The silver party in the Senate has been acting with a pertinacity worthy of a better cause. Nothing but the certainty of Cleveland's veto has brought things to a square vote there for repeal.[1] Henry Higginson looks as if he had grown 5 years older. I got an idea the first time I saw him of what the strain must have been. Through it all come so strangely, like Aeolian Strains filling the universal air the unbroken murmur of wonder and awe at the beauty of Chicago. Everyone seems uplifted by it and it appears actually to have been a purely ideal conception ideally carried out. Charles Norton has been quoted as always having used "Chicago" in his lectures as the name of all that is ignobly vile in modern civilization. He came back the other day saying, of course only half seriously but with real feeling, that his only regret was that he was too old to have been born a citizen thereof. "I have seen" he says "a real communal spirit like that of ancient Athens where men feel as if they did not own themselves but held their life in fee for their city's service" &c &c.[2] This gives you an idea of the emotional effect produced on everyone. They aimed at pure *beauty* of ensemble as distinguished from picturesqueness & interestingness of detail, and they got it on a very large scale.   The whole aim was so novel in our place and generation that it acted like a unexpected revelation, and the fruits of it on American culture will no doubt be great.   It seems already quite religious in its character.—I have stayed in my big bedroom all day and received visits—Geo Putnam, Charley Atkinson, Mr. Child (much aged alas!) etc.   Of your friends, Grace N. seems hearty and well;—addicted to the society of Bocher as much as ever.   I hardly ever cast my eye over at 9 in the morning without seeing him waddling up to her door. I imagine it a very wholesome and improving relation for both. Maude Fiske told me the other day that she read & re-read your little tour in France.[3]   I have just read your Real Thing book, which I find most capital stuff—all of it.[4]   But what we most want to know about is the playwright business.   Love of the warmest from both of us!

Yours ever | W.J.

I know nothing of the Bourget's save a note from Mrs. Jack at Chicago last week, saying they were there with her, were going presently on an "exploring" expedition with her to the west, thence to Canada (without her) and in mid november were to spend their month with her in Boston.   They seem pretty thoroughly introduced.   I only hope Mrs. G. won't sow discord between B. & his charming bride.

30th.   Your good letter of the 19th with the sequel containing the prescription has just come.   Thanks etc!

Address: Henry James Esq | 34 De Vere Gardens | London W | England
Postmark: CAMBRID<GE> STA BOSTON MAS<S> OCT <3>0

[1] The Sherman Silver Purchase Act of 1890 required the United States government to purchase large quantities of silver and to increase the money supply.   The expanded production of silver led to a drop in the price and a drain on American gold reserves. A special session of Congress was called after the silver panic in the summer of 1893, and on 30 October, following the lead of the House, the Senate voted for the repeal of the Sherman Act.

[2] Charles Eliot Norton visited the World's Columbian Exposition in Chicago in October 1893.   The visit changed his mind concerning Chicago; see *Letters of Charles Eliot Norton*, 2 vols. (Boston: Houghton Mifflin, 1913), 2:217–18.

[3] HJ, *A Little Tour in France* (1884).

[4] HJ, *The Real Thing and Other Tales* (1893).

From Henry James

34, DE VERE GARDENS. W. Nov. 15th 1893.

My dear William; (& my dear enhancing scribe of an Alice:) I have rejoiced in your dictated letter of October 30th—though the part about your being shut up in your room with tonsillitis was not the one I rejoiced most in. I hope that is all over—& that you are in all ways in tune once more with your environment. My compassion for your pathological episodes is tempered always by the sense of the ministering angel at your side, which makes them appear different to me from *my* lonely sufferings. Fortunately I have no particular sufferings to mention—I have been robust in a robust & splendid autumn—all rainless & fogless like the months that preceded it. Your genial questions about my dreary theatricalities are of a sort to make all answers seem poor and humiliated. There is nothing changed in the situation I last mentioned to you: things don't change so quickly—I wish indeed they did. Daly produces me in January *early* (he very publicly announces,) & rehearsals don't therefore begin till next month.[1] Alexander has definitely announced to me that I am to follow the "2^d Mrs. Tanqueray," which is now running.[2] But that is indefinite & must remain so till I see how long the play in question is destined to run. As only 2 months of London were taken out of it before the holidays, there is probably a great deal of duration in it yet. I daresay rehearsals (unless there is some quite unexpected collapse,) won't begin till February. I have almost finished (since you were here,) another 3-act play, which Comyns Carr (who has taken the pretty "comedy" theatre) has under consideration. He is waiting, to decide, for the 3^d act. Daly has been having a very bad season, owing to the losses of his company & the blunders of his repertory— so bad that I see myself *en perspective,* converted from a creature propped (by his *prestige*—which I supposed I was,) into a creature *propping.* My play, inconceivable as it appears, is the only "novelty" with which he seems to have armed himself for his campaign in his new & beautiful theatre. I can only hope in trembling that it may prove indeed a weapon of defense against his very (hitherto) adverse fortune. If I "save" him it will be so much wind in my sails—& if I don't, the explanation will be, largely, not dishonourable to me. But I long for the reality, the ingenuity, & the combined amusement & disgust of rehearsals; especially as the composition of unacted-"unproduced" plays continues to be a most impoverishing pastime. It is work unremunerated which wholly prevents the remunerated.

Please enshroud all these confidences with impenetrable silence. And please forgive me if in these weeks of constant & extreme pressure (for the tension and fatigue of the job's devilish difficulty are extreme,) I am of a very abbreviated speech. (Just what I am working for is spacious eventual *margin*—in which I shall be able to be tremendously sociable in letters.) I grieve to say I have seen very little of the Salters; only *once*—when they came to lunch. I regret it much—but they seem inevitably taken up. Mrs. Mary is *almost* as handsome & benignant as Alice—& Salter is like some pictured saint—or rather some old Testament "personality"—on a painted panel. I haven't heard him lecture—it is too much out of my beat. I try to catch them once more before they go—& hope they may even consent to lunch again. But I doubt it. After all, I am unable to get him down at the Atheneum (through non-meeting of the Committee,) in time to be of any use to him. A whole month was lost before I saw him. But he is probably too busy to miss it. I have just been reading Lowell's letters—with a great sense of beauty & of recreation.[3] The nature they reveal is admirable and the expression they achieve such as to make them *lone* in the the department to which they belong. They are an extraordinary mixture of simplicity and accomplishment—in the "culture" sense. But they are quite touchingly beautiful & human. I should make some reserves of approval, however, as to the lines on which C.E.N. has edited them. There was one sentence in your letter which almost broke my heart— I mean the one about Alice's having "too much to do at home." I seem to feel the strain that lies beneath it. She has all my sympathy—I wish she could have my Smiths. The latter are more & more congested with respect. Mrs. Salter tells me Billy is Captain of his school football-team. Tell him I am so glad that I would almost give myself to be booted by him. But I give myself, dear William, to everything that concerns you all, & embracing you tenderly, am yours evermore

Henry.

P.S. Amen to poor Bob's reconcilement.

[1] Augustin Daly did not produce HJ's *Mrs. Jasper,* later titled *Disengaged.*

[2] *The Second Mrs. Tanqueray* by Arthur Wing Pinero (1855–1934), British playwright, opened at the St. James's Theatre on 27 May 1893. HJ was in the audience. HJ's play was *Guy Domville.*

[3] *Letters of James Russell Lowell,* ed. Charles Eliot Norton (1893).

To Henry James

Cambr. Dec 17. 93

Dear H.

At last I have a Sunday morning on which I can despatch some correspondence, and first of all, to thee. It was hard not to write immediately on getting your letter of a short month ago, but it is best to wait & let the news accumulate between one's efforts, and the result is that now there is a considerable deal to tell. But first let me say how both our hearts were moved by the affectionate tone of your words—as the ranks grow thinner, the survivors draw nearer, and I confess now that I "realize" you in your loneliness, having reached the equilibrium in which you will probably remain more or less for the rest of your days, I feel as if we formed part of a unity, more than I ever did before. "And the width of the waters, the hush . . . may strike peace to the soul of the man on its breast, As the pale waste widens around him, As the banks fade dimmer away, As the stars come out, and the night-wind Brings up the stream Murmurs and scents of the infinite sea,"[1]—that's one of M.A.'s best! Poor little grace Ashburner died a fortnight since. It was so queer to see a little brown centenarian to all appearance, lying all withered and wrinkled away in her bed, yet to feel towards the spiritual wraith inside of her as one does to a little child. Chas. N., Theodora, Lily N., Helen Child, and I, went to Stockbridge to see her buried in the circular Sedgwick lot in the cemetery, populous with members of the family. It was a delicious soft gray day and the country looked beautifully peaceful and inviting. The region is filling with enormously expensive houses. I drove to Lenox and spent the night with Geo. Hig. & Lylie, discoursing family gossip all the time. Geo. is *impayable* in that line.———The Bourgets have come, and to morrow, they say, they go to New York. Short of asking them to stay with us we did for them all that could be asked. A dinner party, a club dinner two lunch parties, and two family teas, many dollars and many hours, for neither of which do I imagine them to be grateful, in any real sense of the word. He is a wonderfully vitalized creature in his queer unnatural way, & when with him I undergo the charm of his expansiveness and talk, but the moment I leave him I have a sort of revulsion of indignation against his whole manière d'être, rotten as it is. He sees everything so clearly and feels his own disease, or at least knows in what terms of feeling to express his perception of it, but such complete inner *zerrissenheit* and incoherence I never saw, nor did I ever get such a complete impression of the spiritual gangrene involved in french education, as in seeing how impossible it is for a man like him to love anything and act in accordance with that impulse. The *last* reaction towards everything is the ferocious parisian blague, and the discontent which this leaves in the mouth is got over by the *don't-care* mood which is the last and only consolation. Of course these are only superficial impressions, and to you who know him intimately they may seem wrong. But never since seeing Bob Temple have I got so strong an impression of a man deliberately & permanently surrendering himself to a life which he knows to be bad, for the lack of just that grain of reality-feeling and will which in common men at a given moment can say *stop!* I can't say that I *gained* anything from the details of his talk, though it was entertaining enough. He listens to nothing and has very unconventi[on]al and bad manners. They hate this junketing, yet he can't live without it, and off they go to New York. He speaks english quite well and readily by this time, and has observed and picked up a lot of odd & picturesque things about America, so that I imagine the book will write itself with no very great degree of trouble.[2] But what strikes me most in these lions and foreigners is the sponging attitude which you say characterizes the nobility. The B's demanded, accepted, and never thanked. They have been loaded with expensive civilities by everyone in Boston, and not a sympathetic word for a soul. The Nortons have had a russian prince and princess staying with them week after week, who act in the same way. Egoists all. Give me the freshness of heart that goes with the scientific character. Münsterberg, *e.g.*, his attitude towards America, so innocent, self-forgetting and really fruitbringing, so diff! from B.'s. I think *you* must first and last have been victimized by B.—he has got more out of you than you have ever got out of him. The little wife is exquisite and I love her english. Her admiration of him is touching, but she has a temper, and the future of the pair will be interesting to follow.— But enough! When one has *paid,* one has the right to talk, however.

I have emerged from the really awful melancholy that held me in October, and am well—sleeping in particular as I haven't slept for years. It may be due to the mind-curer Miss Clarke whom I have visited. She seems to have benefitted half-a-dozen people whose cases I know of who have been visiting her this fall, and what the d——l it all signifies I can't say.—The Salters trip abroad was very successful, though they had a bad voyage home. We haven't seen them.—*Our* great interest this year consists in trying to see whether we can live within our income. It is harder with the Gibbenses out of the house to make both ends meet.[3] Last year, terrible to say, seems to have wiped away ⅔ of Alices legacy, the stocks that had to be sold on account of my letter of credit having to be sacrificed in a panic-market. If we *don't* fetch it, we shall at the end of the year make a radical change of some sort, probably look for a smaller and cheaper house. I hope that *you* will live within *your* income! I sympathize with your theatrical impatience, but those first representations will also, on a certain day drop into the past.—Alice is most devoted to me, the children and the house. In short, she does her full duty and more besides. Oh! the difference of trouble between this and florence last winter, but the difference of comfort too. Our two Vaudoises are treasures, and Julie has developed into the best cook we ever had.

Good bye, and all the blessings of the season upon you. Everybody seems to be reading your books, especially the essays in London.[4]

Affectionately your brother | Wm

I sent you a pamphlet contributed by M'berg to the College "exhibit" at Chicago, for the sake of the pictures which bring the scenes of my life, more my past than my actual life, before you.[5]

There was a review of you in the Nation a couple of weeks ago.[6]

[1] From the last stanza of Matthew Arnold, "The Future."

[2] Paul Bourget published *Outre-Mer: Impressions of America* (1895).

[3] Eliza Putnam Webb Gibbens moved to 105 Irving St. in 1891.

[4] HJ, *Essays in London and Elsewhere* (1893).

[5] An illustrated catalogue, *Psychological Laboratory of Harvard University* (Cambridge, 1893), prepared by Hugo Münsterberg for the Harvard exhibit at the World's Columbian Exposition.

[6] Annie Robertson Macfarlane Logan, review of *Essays in London and Elsewhere* (1893), *The Private Life* (1893), and *The Wheel of Time* (1893), in *Nation* 57 (30 November 1893): 416–17.

From Henry James

34, DE VERE GARDENS. W. Dec. 29th 1893

My dear brother & my dear sister: The most gratifying incident that has befallen me this quiet Christmastide has been the arrival of your two deeply interesting letters, each of Dec 18th. They have crowned with felicity the exceptionally quiet and comfortable manner in which the dread Season has passed away. London has been very still, very empty and of an air extraordinarily soft & clear. I have passed no more selfishly complacent Xmas—in the cheerful void left by the almost universal social flight to the country. The autumn has been wholly fogless, and even the mists which have now at last gathered are harmless & silvery—though I *am* writing to you with the aid of a not absolutely indispensable lamp. Very interesting & thrilling to me is your vivid combined chapter about the Bourgets; &, frankly speaking, confirmatory, altogether, of impressions more or less forced upon me by all my late observation of them, & especially by that of the five days which they spent near me here last August, on their way to embark for the U.S. (confirmatory, that is, of everything but the idea of "Minnie's" bad temper. That is something of a surprise to me; though I saw enough, at Siena, of her terrible nerves and constant *crises*.) About Bourget himself I never had *any* delusions. He has, I think, a distinctly charming and affectionate side, but it loses itself in an abyss of *corruption* & in a sort of personal avidity, a habit of inconsiderate manners, over which his unmistakeable absence of "early training" (as Aunt Kate used to say,) never established a control. Hélas, with all his brilliancy, all his literary *mondanité* &c, he isnt a gentleman. They both "took for granted" when they were here in August to a degree that startled me & which it was that determined me (so fruitlessly alas!) not to give them a letter to you. (My systematic withholding of letters never avails, it appears, to save you, after all, from victimization. I gave them introductions only to 3 or 4 whom I thought it would *please*—Mrs. Jack, Mrs. Whitman & the 2 Nortons: the pleasing of the Bourgets themselves, in the matter, I had already renounced, or was in the act of renouncing as a motive; for I have done, in proportion, enough of that.) Oh yes, you are right in saying that in a manner he has got much more out of me than I out of him—and yet you are wrong. I have got out of him that I know him as if I had made him—his nature, his culture, his race, his type, his *moeurs* his mixture—whereas he knows (as a consequence of his own attitude) next to nothing about me. An individual so capable as I am of the uncanniest self-effacement in the active exercise of the passion of observation, always exposes himself a little to *looking* like a dupe—and he doesn't care a hang! And yet I *like* Bourget and have an affection for him; he has a great deal of individual charm, sensibility, generosity; and the sides by which he *dis*pleases are those of his race and the in so many ways abominable *milieu* in which his life has mainly been passed. Your remarks (William's)

about the putrefactions of the French character are admirable—and
oh, how Bourget lights them up! He can *talk* of them better than
any one! His wife is a strange little mystery to me—and the end of
her revelation is not yet. It strikes me indeed that they have complicated possibilities ahead of them. Their *matrimonio* has hitherto gone
on on the basis of the most complete & cautious absence from Paris;
but he has had (the comparative failure of *Cosmopolis* admonishes him,
and Zola spoke of the matter to me very strongly in September)[1] to
recognize that his literary security now demands his again taking up
his life there or re-entering into "touch"; so that when they are
steeped together into that absolutely seething caldron, the latent elements of lively times will, I fear rise to the surface. They both have
a strange terror of it in advance—a terror which, when I have heard
him speak of it, has seemed to me to *en dire long* on the subject of
their whole view of life & fate & character & conduct—their whole
innermost "tone," as it were. To me, let me add (and I have 3 letters
from him—3 weeks ago quite a long one, almost fatally illegible,) he
has not dwelt on the "horribleness" of the U.S., but spoken of the
interest & imposingness of *ce colossal a[r]bre de vie*, &c. On the other
hand he has spoken with no detail of his impressions. I am intensely
grateful to you for what you did for them—I *dreaded* their invasion
of you. And as for the wasted & unacknowledged courtesey of it all,
don't regard that as squandered, for the luminosity of your remarks
about him show a valued accession of experience. Please bury in
secresy my own foregoing candid observation!—I rejoice greatly in
Alice's announcement (which you, William, coyly don't mention,) of
the presidency of the S.P.R. I hope it's all honour & kudos and pleasantness, without a tax of botherations.[2]—I wish I could give you some
corresponding good tidings of my own ascensory movement; but I
had a fall—or rather took a jump, the other day (a month ago,) of
which the direction was not vulgarly—I mean theatrically and financially, upward. You are so sympathetic about the whole sordid development that I make a point of mentioning the incident. It consisted
simply of the abrupt & disgusted termination of my really quite unnatural connection with that hopeless cad of a Daly. I *withdrew* my
play from him after a single (absolutely humbugging) rehearsal, & in
consequence of an attitude on his part of unmistakeable provocation
to do so. The whole manoeuvre & whole situation were as plain as
day. He has so blundered & muddled away his whole season here
that he has lost money appallingly—has not had a *single* success—
pursuing with a third rate company an utterly 3^{d} rate policy, which

has landed him on the verge of ruin.   Under these circumstances I became for him simply an author to whom he had the dreadful prospect of having "royalties" to pay—and he addressed himself crudely and odiously to getting rid of.   Pledged to me these 14 months & wholly by his own initiative he could only do so circuitously—that is could only make *me* stop the production.   This he did—I wont go into details—by reading & pretendedly rehearsing the play in secret once or twice (in defiance of the rigid and only decent usage in such cases between author & manager,) and then admitting me to one ghastly make-believe, to the end that I might be disgusted.   I *was,* at his bad faith, and at Miss Rehan's singular artistic (and social!) baseness, and I walked straight out of the theatre with the play as it were in my pocket.   On the other hand my whole sense of his discredited & compromised situation, of his theatre, of his company, of his *procédés* and of the "mean" person to deal with that he is—to say nothing of my vision, "close-to", of Ada Rehan's unmistakeable unintelligence: all this gave me a sense of relief & escape—escape as from a sinking ship.   It was none the less for a while a lively disgust & disappointment—a waste of patient & ingenious labour and a sacrifice of coin much counted on.   But à la guerre comme à la guerre. I mean to wage this war ferociously for one year more—1894—& then (unless the victory and the spoils have not by that become more proportionate than hitherto to the humiliations and vulgarities and disgusts, all the dishonour & chronic insult incurred,) to "chuck" the whole intolerable experiment and return to more elevated and more independent courses.   The whole odiousness of the thing lies in the connection between the drama and the theatre.   The one is admirable in its interest and difficulty, the other loathsome in its conditions. If the drama could only be theoretically or hypothetically acted, the fascination resident in its all but unconquerable (*circumspice!*) form would be unimpaired, and one would be able to have the exquisite exercise without the horrid sacrifice.   However, Alexander's preparations of my other play are going on sedulously, as to which situation and circumstances are all essentialy different.   He will produce me, at no distant date, infallibly (his joy in his own part is a guarantee of that,) but the managerial policy at a given moment is an abyss, and he *may* put into rehearsal first something that he is also simultaneously preparing.   As this something is, I believe, a play of the celebrated Jones, nothing is more possible than that it may be a failure.[3]   In that case I am pretty sure I shld. come on with a rush—and after a delay not substantially greater than if I follow *Mrs. Tanqueray* straight.

If it's a success, of course I shall have to wait longer. But meanwhile I am working heroically—though it every month becomes more difficult to give time to things of which the pecuniary fruit is remote. Excuse these vulgar confidences—I have come to *hate* the whole theatrical subject. Only let me add that the rehearsal at Daly's was a mere mumbled *reading* of their parts, book in hand, by actors whom I beheld at that moment (in private, as it were,) for the 1ˢᵗ time, to whom I hadn't been allowed, & wasn't then allowed, an instant's access, & whose proceedings constituted no more a tentative or experimental *expression* of my play than a closed piano constitutes a sonata. Ada Rehan, white, haggard, ill, really with the effort of her bad faith, was too ashamed of what she was doing—of the farce to which she had lent herself—to come near me or to look me in the face. It was a horrid experience—& an interesting illustration of what may happen, in the vulgar theatrical world, to one who is not yet cased in the only success there recognized—the success *not* of the Book. When once one is cased in that success however, one's position wholly changes, and I think the *revanche* must be great & sweet.—There, I have written you 20 pages about these misères and have left myself no more time and space. I am giving up this little remnant of the year's end to terrific arrears of letters; and still day follows day without my having worked through my list. Therefore I will only express very briefly my sympathies with your better & your worse. I am horrified at that loss of money that you speak of—through the sacrificed sale of bonds &c while you were away. Such things are very dreadful—& your year in Europe was a devouring maw. However— you have got much & you feel much, to show for it. But be hospitable & be adventurous no more! They are the saddest but the clearest lessons, & I have learnt them, in general, for myself. Solitude is more and more my portion—but nothing fine was ever done without a large measure of it. You have my tenderest compassion for your late horrible friction with Bob. I lately had a letter from him which I couldn't accept as *sane;* and in consequence of my rejoinder to it— though I didn't say so to him, I am quite prepared that he will cast me off. When the drama becomes successful Harry must come out and pay me a visit. Poor little Miss Grace Ashburner's disposition must leave Miss Anne standing there more and more like a gnarled and blasted tree. Katherine P. L. wrote to me the other day that your arrived sepulchral stone for Alice seemed to her very beautiful—by which I judge that it is in place. How I wish I might have a photograph of it! Embrace for me your 2 Vaudoises, and each other, &

all the young. Don't write to condole with me about the Daly business—I don't in the least "require" it. May the new year not have too
many twists and turns for you; but lie straight & smooth before you.

Evermore your Henry.

[1] Paul Bourget, *Cosmopolis* (1893). HJ met Zola several times.

[2] WJ served as president of the English Society for Psychical Research in 1894–95.
His major responsibility was to deliver the presidential address.

[3] HJ's *Guy Domville* had to wait for the completion of the run of *The Masqueraders,*
by Henry Arthur Jones.

From Henry James

34, DE VERE GARDENS. W. Jan. 24th [1894]

My dear William.

It has made my heart heavy to hear of your being—or having
been—so wearisomely afflicted with grippe.   What a long bout &
what a bother!—and with Alice ill too.   I bleed for you—but hope
that, already some days since, you have found yourself well on your
feet.   Give Alice all my tenderest condolence—as well as receiving
your share.   Don't worry about the "weakness"—it goes as it comes.
With me, the year I went to Ireland, it lingered & lingered—but
then, quite quickly, grew beautifully less.   This isn't a letter, but only
a responsive sigh.   It's also to say, thanking you for your condolence
about the Daly episode, that you mustn't take these miseries more
seriously than I do.   I have my plan & my armour of proof—& my
ultimate prospects.   I can't write enough to "explain" more—explanations have to be copious; but you are in error in thinking there
was anything *whatever* prescribed to me, with Daly, but the withdrawal
of my play.   Daly's "motive" was a season so utterly disastrous (the
smallest audiences I have *ever* seen in a London theatre—10 & 15 in
the stalls &c,) that he had but one idea—to *get out* of his contract to
produce a new & untried piece on which he should have to pay royalties—with old things of his repertory, costing him nothing, still to fall
back on.   So unable to *throw up* a play he had accepted as vigorously & rigorously as he had accepted mine he took the *biais* of treating me with an incivility which would lay upon *me* the initiative.   The
relations of manager & author, even in the most "initial" stages of
rehearsal afforded him perfect opportunity, by the violation of the
plainest usages.   He is an utter cad & Ada Rehan is the same.   They
simply kicked me between them (& all in *one* "rehearsal") out of the
theatre.   How can one rehearse with people who are dying to get rid

of you—& what sort of collaboration is that?   I simply walked off—
to their great joy—with my MS. in my pocket.   Such things are unspeakably injurious to ones faith & one's patience & one's purpose—
but *au fond,* it isn't these débris & sickenings that are fatal (if one
knows what one's about:) what is heartbreaking is the having to *tell*
them and talk about them & answer people's questions (I don't say
this for *you!*) mostly indiscreet & idle.   *That,* only, is the real giving
one's self away.   There is *no* answer to be given, or information supplied, in relation to *any* situation one is in with a theatre or a manager.
Silence, till production takes place, if it is ever to, is the only thing
that meets the dangers & covers the abysses.   Please *know* nothing if
any one asks you about my affairs.   I say nothing myself whatever.
I only do my business and go my way.   My situation with Alexander
is an example.   The intervening Jones will probably *have* to come
on—a contract of 2 years ago that Jones holds him too (after asking
for a delay which would have permitted *my* appearance;) and as the
still more intervening Mrs. Tanqueray gives signs of probably running
till next summer, *my* advent is apparently much relegated.   I don't
say this in Woe—but merely as a specimen.   I can *meet* these horrors,
in a word, I think (for another year,) but I can't *talk* about them, &
shall say nothing more till I have something worthwhile to tell you.

Much love: ever your   Henry

---

*Constance Fenimore Woolson fell from a second-story window in
Venice and died on 24 January 1894. She was sick and delirious
at the time of her fall, but it was generally believed that she had
committed suicide. The harsh death of someone for whom he had
a deep affection overwhelmed Henry. He made arrangements to
travel to Rome to stand by "that most unhappy woman's grave,"
but after reading a newspaper account of the death he "utterly
collapsed" and was unable to go. He set out for Italy at last in
the middle of March, ostensibly to get away from London and its
distractions but perhaps also drawn by memories of his friend since
he arranged to stay in the Casa Biondette in Venice, an apartment
she had stayed in some years before her death. The depth of Henry's
grief can be gauged from his letter to William of 24 March from
Genoa, not reprinted in this selection.*

In March 1894 Henry, who dreaded reporters and newspaper

publicity, faced the prospect of a public scandal. Katharine Loring, to whom Alice had entrusted her diary, had four copies privately printed in early 1894, one for herself and one each for the three surviving brothers. William, who had read the diary, suggested to Henry in a letter written on 24 March that eventual publication would add a "leaf to the family laurel crown." But Henry dreaded the prospect that copies might fall into the hands of reporters because he had gossiped a great deal on his visits to Alice, and she had faithfully recorded his candid comments on literary greats and social acquaintances.

From Henry James

Grand Hotel, Rome. | May 28ᵗʰ 1894.
My dear William—my dear Alice.———I wrote you a scrappy note from Ravenna a few days since—but I must follow it up, without delay, with something better. I came on here an hour afterwards, & shall remain till June 1ˢᵗ or 2ᵈ. I find Rome deliciously cool & empty & still very pleasing in spite of the "ruining" which has been going on so long & of which one has heard so much—i.e. the redemption & cocknefication of the ruins. It is "changed" immensely—as everyone says; but I find myself, I am afraid, so much *more* changed—since I first knew & rhapsodised over it, than I am bound in justice to hold Rome the less criminal of the two. I am thinking a little about going down—if the coolness lasts, for 3 or 4 days to Naples; but I haven't decided. I feel rather hard & heartless to be prattling about these touristries to you, with the sad picture I have had these last weeks of your—William's—state of suffering. But it is only a way of saying that that state makes me feel it to be the greater duty for me to be as well as I can. Absit omen! Your so interesting letter of the 6ᵗʰ, dictated to Alice speaks of the possibility of your abscess continuing not to heal—but I trust the event has long ere this reassured, comforted & liberated you. Meanwhile may Alice have smoothed your pillow as even she has never smoothed it before. I turn quite sick when I hear from you that on top of this tribulation you have had to undergo another of Bob's fits of madness. This time it seems to me really a little too strong & too cruel—& I don't know what to say or to do to help you. Is the state produced in him by a difficulty in re-investing his capital? What else had he before him, for months, but this question of the *suites* of his with-

drawal? Alas, alas, I bleed. Apropos of these things I have just received from Warner (from London,) the legal paper to have executed
in regard to my participation in the Wykoff compromise—he asking
me to do this before a U.S. consul.[1] But the paper is all drawn explicitly up to be put through before the consul in *London*—so that I
am afraid I must wait till I get back there to have the thing done.
Warner's note makes no allusion to this point—from which I judge
he takes for granted I will do it simply on my return. I will go to
see the consul here or in Florence & ask him if *he* can be substituted
for the London one, but I am afraid he will say no—so that, as I
have been desiring not to get back to De Vere Gardens before Aug.
1ˢᵗ, I fear I may entail on you & Bob the wait of these intervening
weeks—unless I go home sooner. Such delay as I may inflict upon
you (making you *tarder* to come into your share of the $3000,) I beg
you both to forgive me. You speak of the question of the sending
of the 4ᵗʰ copy of Alice's Diary to Bob (in his present profane state,)
as if it were a matter still under discussion—whereas I have been
assuming that action was taken by Katherine in the sense in which I
immediately wrote you that I had written her (in the 1ˢᵗ days of April,)
on hearing from you that the book had *not* been sent, & on hearing
from Katherine that you judged it ought to be. I had instantly
judged likewise, & as Katherine had written to me that she was only
waiting for my voice in the matter, I immediately expressed to her
that I begged her without delay to transmit the copy to Bob. This
seemed to me the only safe, & normal course the only one putting
us *à l'abri* from some violent resentment on his part. But it shows
what "safety" is in dealing with a madman—that *now* the danger, the
resentment, may be in his *having* it. At any rate is not his having it
a *fait accompli*? I don't know for sure—for I haven't heard from
Katherine since then. When I wrote to her (to send the book,) I
hadn't yet received my copy—delayed in London; & it only came a
few days later—on which I wrote her again a letter which (discreet—
on the subject of her editing—as it was,) she may not have liked—
perhaps; though this idea may be groundless on my part. At any
rate I havent as yet heard from her again—& am therefore in the
dark as to Bob's possession or non-possession. As soon as I had *seen*
the Diary the question began greatly to worry me—though I still
hold that—given the fact that it *exists*, in the (to me!) regrettable form
it does—the only thing that didn't put us (practically) too much in
the wrong was to make him an equal inheritor of it with us. In
other words—as I mentioned to you in my note from Ravenna—the

printedness-*en-toutes-lettres* of so many names, personalities, hearsay, (usually, on Alice's part, through *me!*) about people &c, has, through making me intensely nervous & almost sick with terror about possible publicity, possible accidents, reverberations &c, poisoned as yet a good deal my *enjoyment* of the wonderful character of the thing— though it has not in the least dimmed my perception of that character.   This has been above all really why (in addition to a peculiar pressure of occupation,) I haven't written to you sooner on the subject.   I was too depressed to *face* it!   The other day, in Venice, Miss Wormeley, who is with the Curtises, said to me, as if she knew all about it, "I hear your sister's *letters* have just been published, & are so delightful:" which made me almost jump out of my skin.   It will probably seem to you that I exaggerate; in fact I am sure it will, as neither of your letters makes any allusion to this disturbing feature— which to me was almost all (as it were,) that I could FIRST see.   At any rate what I am *now* full of, as regards Bob's possession of the book is the possible angry, irresponsible *communication* of it in his hands—or the equally irresponsible well-meaning but very dreadful- to-me-to-think-of adventures it may have in those of the 2 Marys.[2]   I seem to see them showing it about Concord—& talking about it— with the fearful American newspaper lying in wait for every whisper, every echo.   I take this side of the matter hard, as you see—but I bow my head to fate, & am prepared for the worst.   *All* my sense of danger would have been averted if Katherine had only had a little more—had in about *20 places* put blanks or initials for names.   When I see that *I* say that Augustin Birrell has a self-satisfied smirk after he speaks—& see that Katherine felt no prompting to exercise a discretion about the name I feel very unhappy, & wonder at the strangeness of destiny.   I used to say everything to Alice (on system,) that could *égayer* her bedside & many things in utter confidence.   I didn't dream she wrote them down—but this wouldn't have mattered—the idea of her doing so wd. only have interested me.   It is the printing of these privacies *telles-quelles*, that distresses me, when a very few merely superficial discriminations (leaving her *text* sacredly, really untouched,) wd. have made all the difference!   It is a "surprise" that is too much of a surprise, though meant so well.   My observations about Birrell ("coloured" a little too to divert Alice!) were for instance made at a dining-club of which we both are members & about which I gossiped to the sister—on my principle of always bringing in the world to her & telling her in her sick solitude everything I could scrape together.—As regards the life, the power, the temper, the humour & beauty & expressiveness of the Diary in itself—these things were partly "discounted" to me in advance by so much of Alice's talk during her last years—& my constant association with her—which led me often to reflect about her extraordinary force of mind & character, her whole way of taking life—& death—in very much the manner in which the book does. I find in its pages, for instance, many things I heard her say. None the less I have been immensely impressed with the thing as a revelation & a moral & personal picture. It is heroic in its individuality, its independence—its face-to-face with the universe for-&-by herself—& the beauty & eloquence with which she often expresses this, let alone the rich irony & humour, constitute (I wholly agree with you,) a new claim for the family renown. This last element—her style, her power to write—are indeed to me a delight—for I never had many letters from her. Also it brings back to me all sorts of things I am glad to keep—I mean things that happened, hours, occasions, conversations—brings them back with a strange, living richness. But it also puts before me what I was tremendously conscious of in her lifetime—that the extraordinary intensity of her will & personality really would have made the equal, the reciprocal life of a "well" person—in the usual world—almost impossible to her—so that her disastrous, her tragic health was in a manner the only solution for her of the practical problem of life—as it suppressed the element of equality, reciprocity &c. The violence of her reaction against her British *ambiente*, against everything English, engenders some of her most admirable & delightful passages—but I feel in reading them, as I always felt in talking with her, that inevitably she simplified too much, shut up in her sick room, exercised her wondrous vigour of judgment on too small a scrap of what really surrounded her. It would have been modified in many ways if she had *lived* with them (the English) more—seen more of the men, &c. But doubtless it is fortunate for the fun & humour of the thing that it wasn't modified—as surely the critical emotion (about them,) the essence of much of their nature, was never more beautifully expressed. As for her allusions to H.—they fill me with tears & cover me with blushes. What I should LIKE to do *en temps et lieu* would be* to *edit* the volume with a few eliminations of text & dissimulations of names, give it to the world & then carefully burn with fire our own 4 copies. I find an immense eloquence in her passionate "radicalism"—her most distinguishing feature almost—which, in her, was absolutely direct & original (like everything that was in her;) unreflected, un-caught from entourage or example. It would really have made her, had she lived in the world, a feminine "political force." But had she lived in the world & seen things nearer she would have had disgusts & disillusions. However, what comes out in the book—as it came out to me in fact—is that she was really an Irishwoman!—transplanted, transfigured—but none the less fundamentally national—in spite of her so much larger & finer than Irish intelligence. She felt the Home Rule question absolutely as only an Irishwoman (not anglicised) could. It was a tremendous emotion with her—inexplicable in any other way—& perfectly explicable by "atavism." What a pity she wasn't born there—& had her health for it. She would have been (if, always, she had not fallen a victim to disgust—a large "if"!) a national glory!—But I am writing too much—& my late hindrances have left me with tremendous arrears of correspondence. I thank you, dear Alice, *caramente,* for your sweet letter received 2 or 3 weeks before William's. I crudely hope you won't let your house—so as to have it to go in the summer. Otherwise what will become of you. I dig my nose into the fleshiest parts of the young Francis. Tell Peggy I cling to her—& Harry too, & Billy not less.—Thanks for the allusion to the Jones-Alexander situation. I judge, in fact, however, it is *not* a fiasco (*The Masqueraders*) but a success with a certain quantity of run in it—that will take it through the summer. The question of the rehearsals of my piece will probably loom before me early in the autumn. However I know nothing till I get back—& the unspeakable Jones, even for one of his minor achievements, may have months & months *dans le ventre.*—I haven't sent you "The Yellow Book"—on purpose; & indeed I have been weeks and weeks receiving a copy of it myself. I say on purpose because although my little tale which ushers it in ("The Death of the Lion") appears to have had, for a thing of mine, an unusual success, I hate too much the horrid aspect & company of the whole publication.[3] And yet I am again to be intimately—conspicuously—associated with the 2d number.[4] It is for gold & to oblige the worshipful Harland (the editor.) Wait & read the 2 tales in a volume—with 2 or 3 others. Above all be *debout,* & forgive the long reticence of your affectionate

Henry.

*Should no catastrophe meanwhile occur—or even if it should!

[1] Henry Albert Wyckoff's will, from which the Jameses were to benefit, had been contested in the courts, and now the disputants were approaching a compromise settlement.

[2] The "2 Marys" are probably Mary Holton James and her daughter, Mary Walsh James.

[3] HJ, "The Death of the Lion," *Yellow Book* 1 (April 1894): 7–52; reprinted in *Terminations* (1895).

[4] A sketch of HJ appeared in the *Yellow Book* 2 (July 1894): 193. The same issue contained HJ's "Coxon Fund."

From Henry James

Casa Biondette | Venice. | June 29th [1894]

Dearest brother & sister.

I have very lately had a letter from each of you; yours, dear Alice, from Chocorua, enclosing 2 of William's notes; Eliot's letter[1] & Tweedy's; & yours, William, from Newport (you don't say what you were doing there;) but so nearly *all* my time when I am away from London (to get hold of some of that time!) goes in answering letters, notes &c, & explaining that I *am* away—that I will, for the moment, thank you as briefly as tenderly. You had, on writing, just got my short scrawl from Ravenna—but you will very soon afterwards have received my very long letter from Rome—written very few days later. I came back here these 6 days agone, (3 of which have gone in a visit to Mrs Bronson at the exquisitely lovely Asolo—a 3 or 4 hours journey from here;) back I mean from my visit to Rome & Florence. I spent a week with Baldwin—who goes to America for a few weeks on July 5th. I took occasion while under his roof to have my annual little summer brush of influenza—but he cured me up very brilliantly—& I was but 2 days in bed. I couldn't have been unfortunate more fortunately. I am now staying on here from day to day because it is still cool, & I don't know exactly where to go till July 25th, when I return to England. Also, I fear, because I am demoralized & my spirit broken by the most disastrous three months' attempt I have *ever* made to come "abroad" for privacy & quiet. I am sickened by all the precious time that has been filched from me & feel as if the loss were almost beyond repair. Florence & Rome were social traps. One thing has followed another, till one hasn't known where to turn. All Boston has been in Venice & much of it still is here. Mary Felton & Lily Norton are lodged under my very feet, five Walshes—2 of New York & 3 of Stamford—are at the hotel opposite, & notes from them just come in—in short the game goes bravely on. Besides this there are endless other embroilments with "people" which I won't even glance at. But I shall recover—& say farewell to Venice, alas, forever. That's the sad part of it—that all this closes the gates of Italy for the future; for every year it grows worse. However, I shall recover—& keep away. I too must have my Chocorua—must discover some twopenny cottag<e>, in some intensely out-of-the-way part of England, & rush down there when I want to get away from London—for these 3 months have been simple hell! Excuse this explosion of ill-humour; it is simple, direct, literal "demoralization." In 4 or 5 days I shall get off to some lone Swiss hillside & then I shall be better. I am very glad you are not banished from Chocorua— even though your 4-footed companions are.[2] I hope you won't miss them too much—& will be cool & happy there on a simple rustic basis. If you're tempted to repine thank your stars you are not here. May the North Carolina mountains also have bowed down to meet you.[3] I hope dear little Billy has exhaled his blood poisoning on your hilltops. I thank you greatly, dear Alice, for copying for me the president's letter—which, though a trifle wooden, portends, I hope, much profit to William. I am bewildered by his W[m's.] saying that "nothing has been done as yet," as regards the matter of Alice's Diary & Bob—for reasons that my letter from Rome will have made you understand. Does this mean that William knows *from Katherine* that in spite of my very affirmative answer to her letter telling me that she but waited for my assent to do it, she *didn't* send the volume to Bob? She has written me no word since a note I wrote her (shortly later than that,) *after* reading the Diary; which I hadn't received when I first said "Oh yes, *please* send it to him!" So I don't know at all what action she may have taken. But I judge that you do—& that the book hasn't gone. I am troubled about it every way. I don't mind Bob's so much reading it (though I fear his possible indiscretions) but I dislike it's going to the 2 Marys—that I quite hate.[4] None the less it seems to me still the *less* dangerous thing for Bob to have it (under entreaties of secrecy,) than to learn that he has been deprived of it by a distinction that he may insanely resent as unjustly invidious. At the same time, I must add, I don't see what intrinsic impossibility there is for *us* in keeping the publication *to* us an absolute & utter secret. It has only—the secret—to *be* really kept. But if Mrs. Whitman already knows—![5] You announce Mrs. W.'s advent to a man well nigh insane with "social claims," or social accidents— but I will try to do what I can for her short of staying in London in August & September to amuse her if other considerations, on my return, make it best for me to be away. *That,* oh William, I can't do!

But those are just the months those ladies expect one to be there! I *can't*. When *is* she to be in London? But I shall see. I shall write you less rabidly the next time; & affectionately both of yours

Henry James

[1] WJ had sent Charles Eliot a message of congratulations on the occasion of his twenty-fifth anniversary as president of Harvard. Eliot had replied on 20 May 1894, taking special notice of the fact that WJ had praised him for his "devotion to ideals." Having spent so much effort on land, buildings, and money, Eliot sometimes feared that he "should appear as nothing but a successful Philistine" to future generations (Harvard University Archives). AGJ made a copy of Eliot's letter and sent it to HJ.

[2] As an economy measure, WJ planned to have neither a horse nor a cow at Chocorua during the summer of 1894.

[3] WJ vacationed in the North Carolina mountains in June 1894.

[4] See letter of 28 May 1894, note 2.

[5] WJ sent a copy to Sarah Wyman Whitman in May 1894.

To Henry James

Chocorua, N.H. | July 10. 94

Dear Henry,

I have been up here for 10 days, revelling in the deliciousness of the country, dressed in a single layer of flannel, shirt, breeches and long stockings, exercising my arms as well as my legs several hours a day, and already feeling that bodily and spiritual freshness that comes of health, and of which no other good on earth is worthy to unlatch the shoe. We get on famously without a man or a horse, and I suspect that this will on the whole be the most salubrious summer we have spent here yet. Our three *Welschen* are perfectly happy, we have a charming young tutor, and were on the whole never more harmoniously situated in our lives. The Salters are on their own hill-top, Mrs. Gibbens in Cambridge, and Margaret in Keene Valley. Moreover a certain wealthy citizen of Boston may possibly rent the place from us for September and October, which will not only set Alice and me free for a little journeying (if it comes to pass) but insure our pecuniary solvency for the year. This latter consummation seems almost too good to be true, for the breaking up of the Gibbens partnership has of course made our housekeeping less economical than it was.—I enclose to you a receipt from Brown, Bros. & Co. This is composed of $262.50, being your quarter of the half-yearly mortgage interest from the McCarthys, and $133.33, your share of the May rents. The June rents haven't yet come in. The rents vary on account of occasional repairs. In May and June there was Insurance to pay out.   I shall try so far as possible to equalize them through out the year, by keeping back something on extra fat months.   I shall remit to Brown Brothers, each month for your account.   The Syracuse Building is going on.   It will cost us some 3500 dollars, and your share will be much more than covered by the Wyckoff money, now soon due.   You have already over 800 dollars to pay with, being your share of a "sinking fund" for such emergencies which I established some years ago.

I saw K.P.L. on the train last week.   To me the danger is now only that of Bob getting wind of the Diary and feeling legitimately "hurt." I don't see the *slightest* danger of any extracts from it floating about and reaching the ears of the Birrel's, Kingsley's & Co.[1]   If you see Mrs. Whitman, it will be well to impress upon her once more the idea that the *existence* of it is what must now be kept secret.   She is, so far, the only person to whom it has been shown, by us, though Alice recently informed her mother of its existence.   Mrs. G. will never tell.

I hope that Italy wears well.   To have physical health *and* Italy is the summum bonum.   But as between one *or* the other, give me the former; and I can only enjoy it in the bosom of nature, and in nonitalian air.   The purity of *this* life is simply divine, especially at the beginning and end of the day.

Your "Theatricals" came duly and were eagerly read—I regret to say with a certain tinge of disappointment* by most of us.   The last one is entirely for acting purposes—I suppose it is the one you made for Daly's company—and I should think it might be effective enough with Mrs. Jasper embodied in Rehan flesh and dimples;[2] but for reading, the *matter* is so slight, that my only wonder is that you could have carried it through with such verve, being on the whole in a line so unlike the spontaneous bent of your genius.   "Tenants" has more body, and well acted would I think be very effective indeed.   But Mrs. Vibbert does n't show her inside nature enough, and her relation to Lurcher is too positive a thing to be left merely indicated.[3]   In other words, the stuff is of too weighty a nature to be so sketchily treated, and a curious unsympathetic and uncanny impression remains on the reader.—But these are my first crude personal reactions.   You know the real defects and merits more than I ever can; and meanwhile I can't enough admire the transposition, so complete, of your composing attitude, to the requirements of the orchestra stalls and away from those of the library.   It *must* bear fruit sometime, only give up everything for *emotionality and breadth,* and make your repartees turn less on the verbal suggestions of the previous sentence!

Alice has for the past week been reading aloud at bed-time a batch of old letters to sister Alice which Katherine L. sent me. They are very sweet things, those from dear old Mother especially. Have you seen them? If not I will send them over.—I have just read Tess of the Durbervilles and the little minister, both with great upliftings, although the Tess-book does go to pieces so utterly in its last third.[4] But two such splendid examples of the contrast between the English genius and the Scotch!

Good bye! Be happy in your continental emancipation! Love from us both—To the children too "Uncle Harry" seems a very important personage.

Your affectionate | Wm

[*]Alice denies disappointment on her part, having (as I can personally testify) devoured the book instantly—By "we" I mean Boott, Margaret Gibbens and myself.

[1] Kingsley was not identified.

[2] The second play in HJ's *Theatricals* (1894) was *Disengaged*, intended for Augustin Daly. Daly's star Ada Rehan was to perform the part of Mrs. Jasper.

[3] In *Tenants*, the first play in *Theatricals*, Captain Lurcher is the evil schemer trying to frustrate Mrs. Vibert's plans for her children.

[4] Thomas Hardy (1840–1928), British novelist, *Tess of the D'Urbervilles* (1891); Sir James Matthew Barrie (1860–1937), British playwright and novelist, *The Little Minister* (1891).

From Henry James

34, DE VERE GARDENS. W. Dec. 8th. [1894]

My dear William.

I am just in time to catch today's post to thank you for your letter of Nov. 30th—telling me of Theo. S.'s return, the presence of the Emmet girls, your Thanksgiving, &c; & announcing the advent of a "financial" letter, which will be very welcome. I echo very heartily indeed your wish that I might have been in your midst, & that of all that *jeunesse*, at the merry Thanksgiving tide. I wish I could see the sweet young daughters of Elly. I long for the presence of more of the jeunesse that more or less belongs to one than I seem destined to get. If Harry is so rapidly turning into a man, I wish he might come out & see me before that transformation completely befalls. We must arrange this in the not too distant future. Apropos of Emmets, &c, I don't think I mentioned that Kitty E.'s eldest boy, "Willie" came out—for a week only—a couple of months ago, & was 2 or 3 times with me.   I found him rather saddish & sallow—or at least grave & vague; but decidedly "sympathique" & intelligent—a very nice young fellow.   He wrote me very gracefully on his return.   I grieve for Theodora's sea-miseries—please tell her so with my love & all my sympathy.   I feared them—foresaw them, for her, when I saw her take a dreary Boston Cunarder (or didn't she?) in the midst of a most tempestuous autumn.   My play is produced—or to be so—on Saturday night Jan. 5th—4 weeks from today.[1]   It was read yesterday to the company—but I had to delegate the office to Alexander: I had a sore throat & wasn't up to the physical effort.   On Monday 10th (day after tomorrow,) rehearsals begin with great violence & continue hard for the month.   The play is small & simple—only 3 acts—but pretty, I think, interesting, & distinctly "emotional"; a little romantic story in an old-time (last century,) setting.   I have endeavoured to make it both very artful & very human—and it will not, at any rate, be a disgraceful work.   It will be quite exquisitely mounted, dressed, &c & as well acted as London can act.   My only anxiety is as to how Alexander will carry the weight of his own part—which is a very beautiful & interesting one.   So awfully, fearfully much depends on him.   Keep praying for me at any rate.   Beyond all belief to you wd. be the *time* that the effort toward perfection, & to adjustment to the hard conditions, in a dramatic production, keeps continuing in an *endless* ordeal, to demand, day after day & week after week, from the moment the practical stage or period is entered upon.   One bothers a whole day over 3 words.   But pazienza—& all love.

Ever your   Henry.

[1] HJ's *Guy Domville*.

1895–1896

It is well known that Henry James's books were critical but not financial successes. He lived well because magazines paid well for serialization in contrast to the small royalties on sales of books. For whatever reasons, Henry did not write for a large public and, at least in his later years, was unwilling to compromise for the sake of popularity. But he approached writing for the theater with mercenary motives, dwelling with hopeful pleasure in his letters on the wealth accrued by popular playwrights. And here he was willing to compromise. Thus, following its unsuccessful run, he rewrote the fourth act of The American *to gratify the "British thickwittedness" of his audiences. The failure of* Guy Domville *shattered his dreams of making a fortune in the theater. On opening night, he was much too terrified to wait for reports in a nearby pub and decided to see another play, Oscar Wilde's* Ideal Husband.

From Henry James

34, DE VERE GARDENS. W. Saturday January 5th [1895] | 5.45. p.m.
Dear William & Alice.

I stick this florid "poster" into an envelope this tremulous afternoon, to help to beguile the hours until 8.30—& to bring my trepidation home to you. I am counting on some Psychical intervention from you—this is really the time to show your stuff. I shall possibly cable tomorrow a.m. The omens, thank God, are decently good. But what are omens? Domine in manus tuas—! This is a time when a man wants a religion. But Alexander told me yesterday that "the Libraries" had taken in advance £1600 worth of seats![1] But my hand shakes & I can only write that I am your plucky, but, all the same, lonely & terrified

Henry.

[1] Libraries were theater ticket agencies.

To Henry James

Cambr. Jan. 8. 95

Beloved Heinrich,

We prayed on the bended knees of our souls all day saturday for the play, but as no telegram with "invest" on it, or any other kind of telegram, arrived I began to fear on Sunday evening that the success had not been so brilliant. On Monday Mr. Boott called and said the advertizer had contained a cablegram from London saying the play had "proved a failure." I have looked through the N.Y papers, but can find nothing, though a short despatch may have escaped me. I am now all eagerness to get exact accounts of what did happen, and I hope you will have sent papers, whatever they may contain. If failure it was, of course many a first night's failure has proved a success later. But in any case the blow to you will have been a hard one, and a bitter Sunday you must have passed. I can't quite understand anything like *failure* direct and palpable in a play of yours, though I can conceive of lack of flagrant success. After your 5 years of devotion to this problem, the disappointment must be tremendous and lasting. I only hope however that you won't take it tragically from the social point of view, if it be a case of bad failure, or conceive yourself to be humiliated in the eyes of public and friends, because public and friends never do or can look on such things with the dead serious eye. It will be rather regarded as a larky kind of thing, and a joke, to have tried your hand and failed at that sort of job, and I profoundly recommend *je m'en fich-isme* to you as the only really sane and adequate philosophy for the occasion. A bad element in the case, if a hopeless one, is the pecuniary *zero*. I can now send you fortunately the January rents & mortgage-interest, of which the former got here to day. I have just sent a check for $362.50 to Brown Bros. & Co, to be transferred to B. S. & Co of London. Of course the 86 dollars go *mit*, and are not invested. This is only a line to express most heartfelt sympathy. Poor Mrs Gibbens'es face looks almost ravaged by the news, and Margaret also takes it indignantly. It shows how many points there are in plays!

All well here. Alice still in Philadelphia.

Your loving brother | Wm.

From Henry James

34, DE VERE GARDENS. W. Jan. 9th 1895

My dear William.

I never cabled to you on Sunday 6<u>th</u> (about the 1st night of my play,) because, as I daresay you will have gathered from some despatches to newspapers (if there have been any, & you have seen them,) the case was too complicated.   Even now it's a sore trial to me to have to write about it—weary, bruised, sickened, disgusted as one is left by the intense, the cruel ordeal of a 1<u>st</u> night that—after the immense labour of preparation & the unspeakable tension of suspense—has, in a few brutal moments, not gone well.   In three words the delicate, picturesque, extremely human & extremely artistic little play, was taken profanely by a brutal & ill-disposed gallery which had shown signs of malice prepense from the 1<u>st</u> & which, held in hand till the end, kicked up an infernal row at the fall of the curtain.   There followed an abominable ¼ of an hour during wh. all the forces of civilization in the house waged a battle of the most gallant, prolonged & sustained applause with the hoots & jeers & catcalls of the roughs, whose *roars* (like those of a cage of beasts at some infernal "Zoo") were only exacerbated (as it were!) by the conflict.[1]   It was a char[m]ling scene, as you may imagine, for a nervous, sensitive, exhausted author to face— and you must spare my going over again the horrid hour, or those of disappointment & depression that have followed it; from which last, however, I am rapidly & resolutely, thank God, emerging.   The "papers" have into the bargain, been mainly ill-natured & densely stupid & vulgar; but the only 2 dramatic critics* who count have done one mere justice.   Meanwhile all *private* opinion is apparently one of extreme admiration—I have been flooded with letters of the warmest protest & assurance.   The horridest thing about the odious scene was that Alexander lost his head & made a speech of a dozen words in which (in his nervous bewilderment,) he had the air of deferring to the rumpus as to the "opinion of the public", an accident that excited, outside of the obstreperous gallery, universal reprobation & of which he has since been, I think, signally ashamed.   It is what Archer alludes to in the provisional few words in the *World,* which with Clement's Scott's article in the *Telegraph* I send you by this post.[2]   I add 2 or 3 letters that will show you the "key" of the aforesaid "private" opinion.   Every one who was there has either written to me or come to see me—I mean every one I know & many people

I don't.   Obviously the little play, which I strove to make as broad, as gross, as simple, as clear, as British, in a word, as possible, is over the heads of the *usual* vulgar theatre-going London public—& the chance of its going for a while (which it is too early to measure,) will depend wholly on its holding on long enough to attract the *unusual.* I was there the 2$^{\underline{d}}$ night (Monday, 7$^{\underline{th}}$) when, before a full house—a remarkably good "money" house Alexander told me—it went singularly well.   But it's soon to see or to say, & I'm prepared for the worst. The thing fills me with horror for the abysmal vulgarity & brutality of the theatre & its regular public*—which God knows I have had intensely even when working, (from motives as "pure" as pecuniary motives *can* be,) against it; & I feel as if the simple freedom of mind thus begotten to return to one's legitimate form would be simply by itself a divine solace for everything.   Don't worry about me: I'm a Rock.   If the play has no life on the stage I shall publish it: it's altogether the best thing I've done.   You would understand better the elements of the case if you had seen the thing it followed (*The Masqueraders*) & the thing that is now succeeding at the Haymarket—the thing of Oscar Wilde's.[3]   On the basis of *their* being plays, or successes, my thing is necessarily neither.   Doubtless, moreover, the want of a roaring actuality, simplified to a few big *familiar* effects, in my subject—an episode in the history of an old English Catholic family in the last century, militates against it, with all *usual* theatrical people, who don't want plays (from variety & nimbleness of fancy) of different *kinds*, like books & stories, but only of *one* kind, which their stiff, rudimentary, clumsily-working vision recognizes as the kind they've had before.   And yet I had tried so to meet them!   But you can't make a sow's ear out of a silk purse.—I can't write more—& don't ask for more details.   This week will probably determine the fate of the piece.   If there is increased advance-booking it will go on. If there isn't, it will be withdrawn, & with it all my little hopes of profit.   The time one has given to such an affair from the very 1$^{\underline{st}}$ to the very last represents in all—so inconceivably great, to the uni[ni]tiated, is the amount—a pitiful, tragic bankruptcy of hours that might have been rendered retroactively golden.   But I am not plangent— one must take the thick with the thin—& I have such possibilities of another & better sort before me.   I am only sorry for your & Alice's having to be so sorry for yours forever

Henry.

   P.S.   I can't find the letter I wanted most to send you—it was so singularly eloquent & strong; from (on the part of her husband too,)

Mrs. Frank Hill, wife of the ex-editor of the *Daily News*—both very old friends of mine. I have stupidly lost it somehow. But I stick in a little one from the dramatic critic of the *St. James's Gazette*. Clement Scott's article in the *Telegraph*—is the work of a man usually awfully vulgar & Philistine—but I only mention it to show how he has been "drawn." But their standard of "subtlety"!—God help us! With one's i's all dotted as with pumpkins!—

P.S. I wish very much you would send this letter to Katherine Loring, to whom I can't as yet write as I promised on acct. of the infinity of notes I have to answer.

*W. Archer & Clement Scott. I will send you A.'s next week notice.

*I mean as represented by most of the Newspaper people—a really squalid crew.

[1] The London *Times*, 7 January 1895, reported that the play was a failure and the audience very indulgent. The reviewer thought Alexander's apology appropriate and suggested that others should do likewise, while the "chorus of popular dissent" was provoked by HJ's applauding friends.

[2] The Harvard Theater Collection preserves a clipping of an unsigned review in the *Telegraph*, 7 January 1895. The reviewer wrote: "But it should not surely be the policy of an English audience to discourage and dishearten one of the most gifted of American novelists who as yet has not quite mastered stage effect."

[3] Oscar Wilde, *An Ideal Husband*.

To Henry James

Camb. Jan. 15. 95.

Dear Old Harry,

We have thought a great deal about you and the play etc. and hoped for a letter before now. But I suppose you are hoping by waiting to give a more favorable account. I enclose a couple of scraps from Sundays N. Y. times, one "Harold Frederics" letter, the other editorial.[1] I suppose at any rate that its success is not going to be brilliant, and I pity you very much indeed for the tremendous disappointment it will be. Hereafter write plays for the ideal world, not for definite companies—there may be more stage success. Your Daisy Miller play is certainly better as a play than the Ada Rehan one in the first volume—better, I mean, to act.[2] Julia Marlowe is acting Browning's Colombe's Birthday now in Boston;[3] and if you obey your purely poetic muse and trust to posterity to do the acting you probably won't fail of anything but the "royalties"—I don't mean to disparage them, and I am almost as sorry as you can be that they are not likely to fall in very fast.—No news!   This is only a word of sympathy and good-will, in which Alice joins.

Yours lovingly | W.J.

[1] The *New York Times* reviewed *Guy Domville* on 13 January 1895.   According to Harold Frederic, HJ received "ruffianly" treatment, but the play was drawing good houses and "intelligent people who go speak highly of it."

[2] HJ, *Daisy Miller: A Comedy* (1883).   The Ada Rehan play was *Disengaged*. HJ's *Theatricals* was followed by *Theatricals: Second Series* (1894).

[3] Robert Browning, *Colombe's Birthday* (1844).

To Henry James

Cambr. Jan. 19. 95

Dear Harry

Your letters of the afternoon of the 5th, and of the 9th came this P.M. and caused both of us an immense relief. No newspapers, and no letter on the 14th day, had made me begin to suspect that you were very hard hit, and I had worried a good deal about you.   But your letter shows the situation to be an essentially sound one, and it shows moreover that your nerves and spirit are sound, so I have the very best hopes and trust that you will send us a bulletin at intervals of not longer than a week, so that we may keep the run of things. Archer's and Clement Scott's articles haven't appeared.   I have no doubt the play was exquisite and will in any case have had a success d'estime.   If it emboldens you to write in your own fashion it will be a fruitful experience.   I must say that your heroic experiment in the way of writing a play for the Daly Company seemed to me to be a step astray in which you sold your natural soul to the Devil and didn't get the devil's guerdon after all.   Alice is out at some private theatricals. Willy Emmet has come on to see his brother Grenville and is sitting by the fire smoking, with Rosina and a student-visitor all chatting away like old times.   W.E. is a fine fellow I imagine, s'thing very good about him.   I called this afternoon at Wendell Holmes's.   I wanted primarily to thank fanny for having sent out to me the poor old doctor's dress-suit and shirts to give away to some poor student or other, a feat which I had successfully accomplished, though after some delay.   The first man to whom I offered the dress coat, a Russian jewish exile and political prisoner over there, but a fine sort of spinozistic character, very intense, told me he had *made himself* a dress suit during the summer vacation!   That man will succeed.   Fanny was "engaged." Wendell took me up to his remote den at top of house where he was playing solitaire, that seeming to have become the recreation of his old age.(!) He was solicitous about you, and I was able to give him this reassuring account. He said he thought your tragic muse a tip-top thing, but doubted whether you could write a big play, and was urgent I should give you his love. I have got an impression of the absence of sentiment towards his father— desire to wipe out all relics, and change the house into his own etc, etc.—not amiable exactly. Boston truthfulness combined with a possible individual's selfishness produce sometimes queer results from the Old world point of view. E.g. in the paper last night there was a letter from wendell to the Pittsfield library giving it 1000 volumes from his father's collection, and prefaced by a statement, that he "did not exactly like to sell" his father's books, so sent some of them as a gift to this Library.[1] If the preamble had not been expressed, the gift would have been more graceful.

Willy Emmet says that the Trilby furore has led to the formation of Trilby Clubs, of which there is one at New Rochelle.[2] They seem to be the homologues on a lower level of intellect of the Browning Societies, and to belong to them satisfies the aspirations to "Culture" of the stratum concerned. W.E. says that they have evenings devoted to the various aspects—he recollects as subjects reported on and discussed "The french in Trilby"—the musical "aspect of Trilby" "The Character of Taffy," ["]The personality of Du Maurier," ["]The Art of du Maurier." The history of the ballad au clair de la lune, etc etc. Pray tell Du Maurier of this—it will make him laugh—unless he knows of it already from some enthusiast. It is a sweet world, in the interstices of its bedevilment & brutality.

Your ever loving   Wm James

You say nothing of my returning the letters you send—one I have destroyed—so I don't send them back. But will if you are keeping them. I will send yours to K.P.L. after having read it or parts of it, to Grace Norton.

[1] The *Boston Evening Transcript*, 17 January 1895, contained a brief report of the gift, quoting from Holmes's letter to the Berkshire Athenaeum: "I did not like to sell my father's books, and it is very pleasant to me to send them to a place which my father loved and which I love also."

[2] George Du Maurier, *Trilby* (1894).

To Henry James

Cambridge, March 17. 95

Dear Henry,   You have been showering letter after letter upon us, revealing the very groundwork of your soul as the waves of popular spite and of approval of the Best swept alternately over it in rê Guy Domville, and the silence of a dumb brute has been my return.   I was also stirred to the groun[d]work by sympathy and admiration, and touched by your devotion in writing at such length.   The day your big yellow letter of Feb 2nd came with all its enclosures, I sat down and began a reply but someone came in and spoilt the evening before I had written a page, and then it got too late. After that what always happens happened—not an hour till now in which to sit down. The letters were treated as you desired—the compromising enclosures about Alexander burnt (what absolutely satisfactory tributes to the play they were!), the letters sent to K.P.L. and afterwards read with certain omissions to Boott and Grace N.   Of course it is all ancient history for you now.   I only hope you're happy at the calm, and at your creative tasks again, with a future play not far away from execution that may hit the galleries as well as the stalls.   Meanwhile I should think it would do you good to drop dramatic composition for a while so as to go at it with fresh hunger.   We keep well, in spite of grip all round us, our Billy being the only internal victim.   March is here with its bright hard light and snow and wind and everything, giving the actual rigor of winter with all the potentiality of winter's death.   I must say I love it, erratic though such affection be.   I sent you the Syracuse dividend for this month the other day as per enclosed receipt.   I also wrapt up yesterday the letters given me by K.P.L. from Alice.   Mother's are especially touching with their cheerful vivacity of tone, living in the bright affections of the day.   The few that go of Wilky's are delightfully characteristic, especially the boyish ones—so richly genial.   They must be given eventually to his children.   There are a lot of your own which may call up memories of the writing of them.   I also packed up for you as a bit of local colour 2 photogs., of my house, and one of Mrs Gibbens's, taken by my colleague Edward Cummings who lives opposite, and a woodcut view of Chocorua, drawn and engraved by one Cleaves.[1]   It might be taken from our hillside, above our house, the latter eclipsed by trees in the hollow between the foreground and the lake.   It looks a little more tropical than Nature does there, but it makes a pretty effect, and I tho't you might add it to your wall decorations.   The whole goes by Sally & Rupert Norton, March 26th., I believe.—I have done my town-lectures all,[2] and in ten days shall have dropped three college hours a week, leaving only 8, under which I can go comfortably till the end of the year.—I went into Boston this P.M to see some folks. Mrs. Dorr had the grip. I spent an hour with Mrs. Crafts, good creature, talking chiefly about you. Then, finding Jim Putnam not home, I went to Mary Peabodys whom I hadn't seen for a year, and who her own tea being finished, had up some beef-steak and a bottle of beer for me. I have no news of any kind. Rosina and Alice have just gone to bed. The former shows her limitations, as who does not when house pent with you for a year. They are in the line of selfishness and egotism—but she has a fine slap dash hit or miss perceptive intellect, and I find her a most agreeable companion. The College is to give a Ben Jonson play "the Epicoene" in the Sanders Theatre this week, and Kitty's Elizabeth comes on to see it and stay here. Boott is indefatigable—has got us drilled in a new "National Anthem" he has recently composed—8 voices, and makes our house pianist middleton play all his pieces now. Good night, & God bless you.

Your loving brother Wm.

I dined the other night along with Mrs. Wagniére and her husband. I understand they have lost everything. They are staying with Fanny (greenough) Blake at Brookline.

[1] Cleaves was not identified.

[2] WJ gave three lectures on abnormal mental states, concluding on 26 February.

In the early 1890s Harvard University became concerned with the education of teachers and to that end established a department of pedagogy. William James gave a series of ten lectures there in 1891–92 on "Topics in Psychology of Interest to Teachers," published eventually and after extensive revision as Talks to Teachers on Psychology and to Students on Some of Life's Ideals *(1899). In 1895 he gave eight lectures on the topic at the Harvard Summer School, three in Norwich, Conn., and eight at Colorado College in Colorado Springs.*

The Colorado trip in early August was as much a vacation as a money-making venture. On the train for some seventy hours, William enjoyed good sleep, good breakfasts, and good landscapes, the last providing an "exhibition of space *the like of which I never saw," as he wrote his wife on the morning of 1 August, three hours away from his destination. Only her absence spoiled an otherwise ideal journey. By now all of his children were old enough to receive letters, and he informed his youngest that he was staying in a house with a big dog who was afraid of thunder, while to his son William he wrote that the mother and sister of famous western bandits had been pointed out to him by a porter on the train. Supposedly, the women were armed and dangerous.*

From Henry James

34, DE VERE GARDENS. W. Aug. 20ᵗʰ '95.

My dear William.

Very thrilling & touching your letter from Colorado Springs. I rejoice for you & with you that you can see so much that's strange & striking & see it in the way of business. Somehow I don't envy you, at all; but your fame & fortune delight me. I suppose the fortune is pretty meagre; but I hope it more than pays expenses. Thanks for the promise of the $150 from Syracuse; I shall doubtless soon be apprised of its arrival. I feel almost ashamed to show you that I'm in town again—but I hope it isn't for long; for longer than till Sept 1ˢᵗ. I was obliged to come up from Torquay a week ago to attend to some matters here—but it is my project to return there for September & probably October. I wrote you from there towards the end of July; but you appear not (by Aug 6ᵗʰ) to have received my letter—which, however, must have come to Chocorua after you had started West. I'm sorry all the populations of the Earth may listen to your honeyed accents and yet never your brother. Let us hope his day will come. Mea[n]while I hope all the West is under the charm. Much do I echo your sentiment, in the face of the American Deserts, about either staying abroad or staying at home—i.e. in one's American milieu; & more & more heartily am I impelled to practice the same. My abroad has become my at home, & I am, thank God, losing every last rag of the disposition to travel. I am extremely & finally weary of overmuch London—& absolutely determined, in order to save what remains to me of life, to break with the fatal flaw of spending in it more than 5 or 6 months of the year—i.e. the months of pure autumn & winter—i.e. from November to March–April. The great difficulty however is that one can't conveniently spend so many months out of one's home unless one has a regular second home—an alternative cottage. It's too long a time for English lodgings & inns, year after year, or foreign ones either—especially when, as regards the latter, my desire for foreign prowls has left me almost completely. I shld. be sorry to think I never shld. see Italy again— but, apart from that, only want to keep *still* here, somewhere, & do the immense future work I nourish the plan of. I delight in Devonshire & if I could find at the sweet & sympathetic Torquay a modest asylum, a small house with a small garden, something at £50 or £60 a year (a very good price thereabouts,) I would close with it on the spot, keeping this for the London months & easily making my rent by the simple & inevitable economy—saving—of not being ½ the year, in town. Another consideration that pushes to this is the fact that in long or frequent absences one's idle servants go utterly to pieces—*rot*, simply, in unfilled time. I'm sorry to say the Smiths show the effects, more & more, of the little I give them to do—in my simple & single & deadly regular life. It's the universal consequence here that they decay (the domestics in "easy" places—& with bachelors,) & d——k. There is nothing for it but to await it & pass through cataclysms & finally lose them.—But enough of this too domestic prattle. London seems very empty, thank God—though Barrett Wendell writes me from round the corner that he wishes to come & see me & is coming tomorrow. Perhaps he will give me some recent news of all of yez.—The bicycle at Torquay encounters obstacles in the perpetual & precipitous hills—so I haven't done very much as I find the upgoing not very congenial to my weakish heart—nor the downgoing to my weakish nerves. It is the only fault of the place—& is the fault of all Devonshire. I hope Alice & the infantry are having a fine pastoral period. I saw the other day the 2 R. Kiplings just before they sailed for Brattleboro. They were immensely friendly but he strikes me as strangely *ungrowing*. His feeling about America utterly arid, & his living there, under the circumstances, so poor. But what he has is pure operative genius, with nothing left over. Lebe wohl!

I embrace you all & am ever your fondest Henry
P.S. The P. Bourgets, now in Scotland, will probably descend upon me in September at Torquay.

From Henry James

34, DE VERE GARDENS. | W. Wednesday Dec. 18ᵗʰ 1895
My dear William.

I have let a terrible time elapse since the receipt of your last remittance—owing to a press of letters, work & everything else. Likewise your letter, (Nov. 8ᵗʰ) with Brown Bros.' receipt (for £30.12.3) was brief & burdened—I mean showed you so over-weighted with immediate cares that it seemed better not to let loose at you a fresh projectile. All thanks, none the less, for the last money. I am hoping, I confess, that you will already have found it possible to send me *this* month's remittance—as the season of one's heaviest annual drain approaches. So I am watching the post, rather. But je me range du côté de votre sagesse. I am sorry indeed that your load, this winter, is such as you stagger under. Well, one staggers, but one stands, & I pray strength be vouchsafed you. I have settled down, for the winter, to the good & evil of the London squash—which, I am happy to say, I now suffer to squash me less & less (I have found out *how,*) so that the good pretty well predominates. I am in a very good current of work & health (absit omen!) of which the results will be duly & cumulatively visible to you. But you must, for this, partake of my own patience. No *secousse*, thank heaven, lately, until this very a.m. when the papers came out with Cleveland's startling message on the Venezuela question & the action of the U.S. &c.[1] It is much of an explosion & is so taken here: though the papers are very quiet & decent about it. Their tone almost makes one feel that any country *must* be in the right which can show such decency as against such intemperance as Smalley in his admirable despatches from N.Y to the *Times* (& which make it a blessing—a luxury to one's self—he is now their American correspondent,) gives numerous specimens of from the said N.Y. press. Cleveland's demand that England shall let the matter be réglée by *his* Commission seems of course a very large order here. What poor old congested, but still not quite paralysed England will *do* is beyond one's present prophecy: one must hope that sanity & civilization, in both countries, will prevail. But the lurid light the American newspapers seem to project on the quantity of resident Anglophobia in the U.S.—the absolute war-hunger as against this country—is a thing to darken one's meditations. Whence, why does it, to-day, explode in such immense volume—in such apparent preponderance, & whither does it tend? It stupefies me—seems to me horribly inferior & vulgar—& I shall never go with it. I had rather my bones were ground into British powder! But all this is doubtless a surface-thing, a part of hideous political games; with deeper decencies & sanities & possibilities of reflection underneath. It will clear,—it is too hateful & hideous.—We are having a grey, mild, moist December & the stillness of Xmas is at hand: a time I love in London—with almost all the hurlyburly transported to the country. Save for a Xmas dinner or two, one really gets time. May the reverse of the medal not stare you too much in the face. *I*, at least, don't complicate your Xmas. with the importunity of my offerings. The 2 letters you last enclosed, from New Rochelle—are touching—about the poor vanished Kitty. How striking an example not of the "irony," but of the sympathy of "fate" that the picture you so irresponsibly painted of her so many years ago, should now matter to so many people! I should feel, in your place, quite proud of it—especially as the portrait, the "art," is so good. I hear of Carrie & her children (indirectly) in Rome. I've never been able to write to her since I heard from you that Cary had been a month in Cambridge without coming near you. Mrs. Cuyler, Mary's (Bob's Mary's) sister told me the other day (she has a daughter married here,) that, having lately been at Concord, she had found their house most pleasant & successful. She spoke of it with much commendation. But I gather that you scarcely see them. If you *could*, read M. Arnold's *Letters*, for the loveability of them—of him. Very little specific epistolary *talent*—no pencil or brush or colour, but a very valuable picture of an English life & nature. Apropos of beautiful things I never yet have thanked you for your splendid paper in the October Ethical Review.[2] I find it a pearl of wisdom & art. I embrace you all tenderly; & yours over & over

Henry.

[1] The protracted dispute between Great Britain and Venezuela over the boundaries of British Guiana was brought to a crisis by Cleveland's message to Congress of 17 December 1895, widely regarded as a threat of war should Britain refuse to settle the dispute by arbitration.

[2] WJ, "Is Life Worth Living?" *International Journal of Ethics* 6 (October 1895): 1–24; reprinted in *The Will to Believe* (1897).

The Venezuela crisis marks the beginning of William James's involvement in the American public debate. In a letter to the Harvard Crimson of 9 January 1896 he commented on remarks by

Theodore Roosevelt, a Harvard graduate and a former student of his, that anyone opposing Cleveland's policy was a "betrayer." On the contrary, William wrote, true patriots will refuse to be hypnotized by "sacramental phrases," will consult their "reason," and will exert themselves "as citizens" with all their might. Roosevelt, he continued, uses the crisis to argue for a bigger navy, thereby proposing a "novel national career" that upsets the national ideals Americans have cultivated hitherto. Roosevelt was again the target of his letters to editors several years later, when William joined the mugwumps in opposition to American imperialism in the Philippines.

To Henry James

[Cambridge] Dec 23. [1895]

Dear H—Altho done to death and made really sick by it, I can't help writing you a syllable about the 'ape and tiger' delirium we have been going through—the most disheartening thing I have ever witnessed. Boston seems to be the only place in the country that has completely kept its head. The good name for being a *safe* country that 80 years has gained for us is squandered in 3 days and we are now as *dangerous* to the world as anything since Bonaparte's time. Cleveland's action is absolutely enigmatical and irreconcileable with his previous character. There have been some few splendid newspaper articles, and yesterday I imagine, a lot of fine sermons, one magnificent one last night by Frank Peabody in the College Chapel in favor of civilization, but the naked savages have had for the most part the floor. Truly the era of insipid safety hasn't yet come over the world and there is eno' for a man to live for in dealing with his country's enemies inside the walls. But the best way out of it will leave our Executive a buffoon, and the effects we shall reap for 50 years.

Good night, and if not a merry, yet a firm hearted christmas.

W.J.

To Henry James

Address: Cambridge Mass | Philadelphia | Dec 26. [1895]

Dear H.

I wrote to you the other night in a very excited mood about the country, and of course it is difficult to exaggerate the evil that has been done.   Yet, as in the case of many evils, the good that grows out of repairing it may possibly be better than the good of never having had it.   The wanton jingo talk that for a couple of years past has been used as an insincere club to whack Cleveland with has been indeed diabolical, but the great popular jingoism of response to his proclamation has a very good side.   It shows that in spite of all our party-frenzy we are still a unit when it comes to a question of obedience to the executive, and that is the root of all national safety and greatness.   It is true that it then presupposes that the executive should not habitually be insane!

This time the executive has been absolutely insane in handing over to the uninstructed people at large, a question of whose merits it could know nothing except that here was a case in which it might have to fight for the right side.   The right side was assumed of course to be the Venezuela side, for what conception has our people of England except the nursery bugaboo one of the bully-coward power that is steadily bent on occupying all the possible remote corners of the world?   This irrational anglophobia is a national calamity.   And in the long campaign of education that is now before us that has got to be one of the items.   I wish I might go and make a speech at Edinburgh this April—they have voted me a doctor's degree, and are only waiting for me to come and claim it—But by April the scare will probably have blown over, and the Eastern war have begun.   If we could ourselves be putting in some licks for Armenia it would be good.[1]

I am here for the Am. Psychol. Ass[n].[2]—I hope you are keeping as happy as may be.   Your roll of papers for Peggy came duly, and she will thank you.   She is developing into a "natural sweetheart" as Mr. Battell of the Breadloaf inn said.

Farewell!— | W.J.

I enclose a fragment from the report of a peace-meeting in N.Y. on Monday.   Nothing like *l'esprit du peuple!*   I hope it may make you laugh as it did me.[3]

[1] The gradual collapse of the Ottoman Empire created opportunities for great-power rivalries, especially between Russia and Britain, with the accompanying dangers of war.   From 1894 to 1915 Armenians living under the Ottoman Empire were subjected to waves of persecution and massacre.

[2] The American Psychological Association met on 27–28 December 1895 at the University of Pennsylvania in Philadelphia.   WJ was a participant in a discussion "On Consciousness and Evolution."

[3] The Single Tax Movement of Henry George held a peace meeting on 23 December 1895.   The *New York Times* reported the next day that a majority at the meeting

cheered the "chief executive" and that Cleveland's critics were accused of treason. The meeting turned into a near riot.

To Henry James

Newport, Jan 26. 96

Dear old Henry—I have been shamefully silent towards you in these days that try men's souls.[1] There has been so much to say that one couldn't say it well briefly, and so much all the while to do that one couldn't write at length, so one didn't write at all. Your second letter since the war broke out[2] (that of the 3rd) came and was duly appreciated. Things seem at last in a better way. The Senate Committee on foreign affairs is overreaching itself with its jingo resolution,[3] and if England should get another war on its hands we shall assuredly stop all our swagger and devote ourselves to seeing fair play. (I hope that Russia *will* outwit England in the East however, for England deliberately sold herself to the devil in the Disraeli Salisbury policy there and ought to reap the divine vengeance.)[4] The anglophobic spirit, indeed the whole war spirit, is not as bad as it looks at a distance. There is much that is idealistic about it, however abstract and rotten practically the ideals may be. Cleveland (so far as appears) was moved to his appeal by the ponderosity of his coarse but essentially moral nature (not so Olney, I fear)[5] and there is no European people that wouldn't have gone twice as fighting mad as we if their ruler had spoken to them in similar tones. In *every* war-excitement the same old sacred phrases and feelings that have done service in all the previous struggles of humanity against oppression have to fire the heart and do service again, and when the wolf once gets fairly going there is no limit to the crimes of which he sincerely believes that his oppressor down-stream the lamb is guilty. That accounts for much of our anglophobia. Some of it also is a genuine reprobation of England's land grabbing instincts, an ideal objection to the conquest-policy which is the heirloom of great nations, felt by persons who are near enough to England to *feel* her, and who dont feel the remoter nations at all, or realize that the whole pack of them are *absolutely* cynical internationally, and that England's so-called hypocrisy is only the sign of a conscience that has begun to doubt, and of a potentially regenerate soul. The worst thing here is the insincerity, levity, and utter *irresponsibility* of the newspapers. It is french; and even ultra-french, in spite of splendid exceptions, as, e.g., the Boston Herald. It makes one despair of civilization, until one turns to the spectacle of the English journals throughout all this trouble, and sees thereby that civilization does mean something.   The phrase "trained-good-humour" in your letter cuts very deep.   I shouldn't wonder if this spectacle were really (though quite unconsciously) the very finest achievement that civilization has in this world of ours yet had to show. A great precedent to found future habits upon!   We have a long fight here to wage, but when one sees what good human creatures are on the other side with their turbid and simple emotions (the emotions that all the great deeds of history have been done with) one doesn't feel as if the fight were against Satan pure and simple, but only against evils incidental to certain forms of political relation.   Still that war-threat was the devil's own work, and fifty years won't weed its effects out of our history.   What we really need, I suppose, is a licking like that given to the French by the Germans, to teach us that there is a God in Israel, and that Man can't live by swagger alone, not even by ignorance and swagger in partnership!   Roosevelt believes in war as an ideal function, neccessary from time to time for national health. With such frank jingoes one can argue comfortably.   What Lodge believes in God only knows—I fear he may *not* be temperamentally predestinated to jingoism as Roosevelt is.   Did you see Lodge in England?—Well, enough of public affairs, it makes the newspapers more entertaining than all the various Kritiks of Em. Kant.

We are doing finely, except that I left harry in his bedroom with the grippe.   It is plain this year that Naturwissenschaft will not be his *fach*, and I only wish I could believe that literature in some way was to be so.   His *character* would conform best to some kind of a literary life, if only *talent* would develope in that line.   Who knows? *You* showed no presage of your present genius at his age!

I am through the 1st half year's work, and although it has been heavy, I find myself in prime condition.   I leave off, now, 6 hours a week of lecturing to the girls at Radcliffe.[6]   They are a sweet consolation to one's declining years.   My salary is raised to $4500, also.   I am here, finding Tweedy very little changed, for 36 hours only.   I lectured yesterday (on demoniacal possession!) to the Brooklyn Institute of that ilk (a course of 6 for $300),[7] to morrow I return home and make an "address" in the evening at the female College at Wellesley, next Friday, I read presidential address to S.P.R. in Boston, on Saturday in N.Y., and thereupon repeat my female College address at Bryn Mawr near Philadelphia.   All these public appearances help to make me known even if they don't enrich me.   I don't suppose they got you to read my address to the S.P.R. in London, as they did once before.[8]

Affectionately thine, W.J.

[1] WJ is quoting the opening words of *The Crisis*, no. 1, by Thomas Paine (1737–1809), English-born American political radical and writer.

[2] In late December 1895 Sir Leander Starr Jameson led a British attack on the Boer state of Transvaal, in present-day South Africa. The raid was reported in the United States on 2 January 1896.

[3] On 20 January 1896 the Foreign Relations Committee of the United States Senate presented for consideration by the Senate a resolution, often called the Davis Resolution, proposing a stronger version of the Monroe Doctrine.

[4] The defeat of Turkey by Russia in 1877 led to the Treaty of San Stefano, which Britain viewed as too favorable to Russia. British pressure resulted in the Treaty of Berlin of 1878 that tried to resolve the problem of former Turkish possessions in Europe and block Russian expansion to the Mediterranean. Salisbury was Britain's chief delegate in the Berlin negotiations, while Benjamin Disraeli (1804–1881) was prime minister.

[5] Richard Olney was secretary of state at the time.

[6] In the first half of the 1895–96 academic year, WJ taught two courses at Radcliffe, Philosophy 2a: Psychology and Philosophy 3: Philosophy of Nature, to a total of about thirty-five students.

[7] The course before the Brooklyn Institute of Arts and Sciences was titled "Recent Researches into Exceptional Mental Phenomena."

[8] WJ lectured on 27 January 1896 at Wellesley College on "Psychology and Relaxation." The lecture, repeated at Bryn Mawr College on 8 February, was later published as "The Gospel of Relaxation" in *Talks to Teachers*. HJ had read WJ's contribution to "A Record of Observations of Certain Phenomena of Trance" but did not read his presidential address. The latter was read by Myers on 31 January 1896. WJ delivered it in Boston on the same day and on 1 February in New York. It was reprinted as "Address of the President before the Society for Psychical Research," in *EPR*.

From Henry James

34, DE VERE GARDENS. | W. February 21st 1896.

My dear William.

I have delightful letters both from Alice & you, & I must ask Alice to whom I send tender love, to accept & share in this synthetic rejoinder as a provisional acknowledgment of her bounty. Her letter—of January 9th—was long & liberal & it was, please tell her, an immense pleasure to me to get it. Yours have been from Newport & from Philadelphia respectively—the latter accompanying Brown Bros.' receipt of your remittance of £34.16.0, news of the arrival of which I just have from B. S. & Co, & for which all thanks. It's a happy thought that our rents may, after a little, be uplifted. Meanwhile let us be thankful for present mercies. *I* am. I am thankful too, for the dazzlement of your enumeration of your lectures & of your wondrous pilgrimages & performances in delivering them. It is a very proud record, in my eyes, & I shld. think you would swell with a sense of your greatness. How much of American life it must be showing you—to bound thus from one local centre to another, & come in contact with all sorts & sexes of people. It makes me rue all the more that all this while I have never heard you orate. Cela me manque affreusement, & I don't see the remedy till you come out here—on a professional tour—to crown your success. The nearest approach to my doing so was to go the other day (more than a fortnight since,) to hear your valedictory to the S.P.R. read by Fred Myers—extremely well & with great gusto & point—to a room densely packed. (I went with poor Mrs. Mahlon Sands—a great Psychist & devotee of yours.) I thought your address admirably interesting & effective; it had great success; & Myers spoke *of* it—as well as spoke it—with enthusiasm. But it is your treatment of those other fascinating subjects that I want to hear. How worked & strained & overladen you must feel & how pitiful must seem to you my slow, small dribble of production. I hope with all my heart that you will, another year, get the laboratory off your back. But your powers seem equal to anything.—Our winter here goes on from one mild month to another—a season of unequalled & excessive blandness. I like something sharper—this moist mildness makes me more & more drop; but it would have been, with other good elements (a tolerably quiet & private existence,) an enjoyable season if it were not for the dark Venezuela cloud. Your letter from Newport was full of suggestion & instruction to me about the state of feeling in the U.S. &c. I enter into all you say—there is always more in things than first meets the eye. Smalley's letters to the *Times* continue to be extraordinarily good & luminous—they reflect admirably the whole evolution of feeling in America. Only the whole business *drags* so—& seems, in dragging, to *gather* mass & bulk rather than to lose it. I am as much struck as ever with the absence of irritation—of passion—here—& if the Liberals were in power one would feel that a settlement could be counted on; though of course it's partly because they're in opposition that they are particularly articulate *for* a settlement. The Government is persistently dumb—but every day, at the point things have reached, may make a difference. God grant it be a difference for the better. If we pull through peaceably I really think it will be one of the biggest of all the victories of civilization. Of course, here, one has the sense of there being many things in the air besides—but that makes really for the absence of exacerbation. Jameson & his Traansval fellow-raiders arrive in a day or two as prisoners to take their trial, & the plot will thicken as soon as they get here.[1] Millions of idiots will want to glorify & banquet them—& though the latter tribute will be for the moment impossible there will be asininity & contention & rumpus enough. Whatever their trial may be their penalty will be small. It is midnight, with a nasty warm rain outside, & I sit scribbling to you under my electric lamp—which, with its companions, has become, since I installed it, one of the consolations & cleanlinesses of existence. I had been reading, before sitting down to this, since dinner a volume of tales ("The Youth of Parnassus" &c) which young Logan Pearsall Smith, whom you put into relation with me some time ago, has just sent me.[2] There are much better things than I should have expected of his great simplicity—& he tells me it's the "study of *me*" that has made them so! Fortunately, therefore, I can encourage him for them.—I see no one of particular interest, thank heaven!—& have my time less compromised by the world than, in London, it has ever been. I have a great deal of started work on hand, & the omens are good for the results being so. On May 1$\underline{\text{st}}$, to a day, I flee to the country—not to Torquay again, however, but to some cottage somewhere else, where my life can go forward on a basis of Smiths. The place is still to find; but I am going down next month to look at something—which sounds very promising—I am told about near Rye in Sussex. (Rye is a few miles from Hastings.) I shall not, at any rate go abroad—to breast the tide of compatriots. It's a horrid thing to have to forswear Italy—but Italy is fatally infested. Such is our deadly age—or at least mine. Apropos of Italy & compatriots, not to say of deadliness, I have heard from Carrie that Cary has been lying ill of malarial fever in Rome—seized when they were on the point of starting for Egypt. But they *have* started now—he being better (after a long bout,) & a change of climate prescribed. She'll find it too hot there to stay long—& I have a terror of her turning up here later in the Season. But I shall have left town when she does, & that will restrict intercourse.—You interest me in what you say of Harry at college, but are rather vague & ambiguous—so that I don't quite understand how you mean to characterise him. You intimate that he doesn't care for Science—but *does* he care for Letters? I hope so, poor chiel. I should watch for him & over him to my fullest opportunity. Bob's Edward sends me 2 tales of his *façon* in the Harvard magazine for which he also tells me I am responsible—indirectly: at which I wince a little.[3] They are pert & thin—but show a notion of writing. Will Peggy, too, be a writress? I hope Billy & Francis will be mere athletes—or at most men of the world. But midnight is long passed, & my lids begin to flop.

Yours & everyone's always Henry James

[1] Since they acted without orders, Sir Leander Starr Jameson and other leaders of the raid were taken to England for trial. They reached England on 24 February and in July were tried and found guilty. Jameson's sentence was fifteen months at hard labor. On his way to the trial, he was greeted by cheering crowds. Jameson returned to the Cape Colony and eventually became prime minister.

[2] Logan Pearsall Smith, *The Youth of Parnassus, and Other Stories* (1895).

[3] Edward Holton James, "Tangent," *Harvard Monthly* 21 (December 1895): 107–17; "Cloistered," *Harvard Monthly* 21 (January 1896): 151–63.

From Henry James

34, DE VERE GARDENS. | W. May 29th [1896]

Dearest William & Alice.

A letter from you of May 17th (the one in wh: you mention the tragic death of your neighbour, Mr. Turner,) fills up to overflowing the measure of your late great generosity in writing to me. I have heard several times from both of you; & you, my dear Alice, have been particularly beautiful & brave.

Your letters lie before me now, & I blush with the sense of my own silence. It has in fact been systematic—the result of my having got into such a fearful funk about some overdue "serial" work (for the Illust: London News—beginning July 4th, but *à peine* started in MS.)[1] that after getting down into the country (end of April) I inexorably forbore to give an hour to anything but the need of catching up—which I have now almost done. I get under those exceptional circumstances nervous & exhausted, & my correspondence lies in ruins. No line of it can I touch. It won't really recover till another month or so. I am in town, as it happens, through this Whitsuntide week through *obligation*, from the 1st, to surrender my cottage for the 8 days to my landlord—who is now, oddly, occupying it for 3 days more with the Smiths. But I go back on June 2[d] to stay (alas only) till Aug 1st; & I have already had almost a clear month of it: enough to make me "care for" the little place so tenderly that I only wish I could clutch it as a permanent resource. But it is unclutchable: though the price cld. be managed if the *owner* could. Meanwhile however it is delightfully quiet & quaint & simple & salubrious, & the bliss of the rural solitude & peace & beauty are a balm to my spirit.   I shall in one way or another keep away from London till November 1ˢᵗ. Even this stealthy week of it is more than enough.   These few days have been enriched by the presence of the amiable "Carrie" & her children, & that of Bob's little Mary, with her aunt Mrs. Robertson.[2] She goes with Carrie to Norway.   I have had a couple of quiet hours with Mary, talking of Bob &c; & have been struck with her intelligence & maturity.   She hopes for little from B.'s catholicism; but on the other hand thinks his health & life very precarious—thinks they have become very much so during the last year.   She strikes me as such a lucid little person that there may be something in that.   I've seen no more of Carrie than I can decently help—she being, for her, quite demonstrative.   They have, she & her children, "improved" since I saw them two years ago, & Alice who has become very pretty— as pretty as her overdressed state permits—impresses me as a nice & civilizable little creature, the making of a "sweet & attractive woman" if one could only get at her & detach her.   But one can't.   Cary is *nothing* but a 3ᵈ-rate Wilkie.   They appear to be richer & richer— spend an immense lot of money & have many mysterious rich American friends.   But they are Nothing—& I can't write of them or think of them.—I enter very affectionately into everything you both tell me of your own troubles & interests—especially as the former never seem altogether to fall from you.   It must seem to you that offspring never exhaust the circle of the maladies.   But you, dear Alice, I pity most for your eternal household problems & servant-worries.   W. tells me that you can't get domestics for the country.   Mine, I am sorry to say, through insufficient occupation (engendered by my simplicity of life) & native poverty of stuff, are *rotting* more or less on my hands, but if the demon of drink—that lies in wait for *every* British creature, doesn't ride them to death meanwhile they may go on for a year or two longer.   It is a curious and perfectly established phenomenon in this country that *all* servants of bachelors *n'ont qu'un temps,* go eventually to the bad & that there is no help for it whatever. So, in the presence of some symptoms I am philosophically waiting. But meanwhile they share my hermitage—share it even with my landlord.   I rejoiced in the photos. of Billy & Francis & Peggy— though they were coarse, rather (as "technique") & unflattering.   But they show me how the originals ripen.   I wish I could watch them on the parent tree.   Everything that you tell me of Harry (his letter from Pelham &c) makes my heart warm to him.   Sara Darwin, whom

I saw a day or two ago, spoke to me enthusiastically of all your children & gave me a particularly sympathetic account of Peggy. You seem a good deal deluged with Emmets, whom I don't at all discriminate—& I hope they give half as much as they take. I seem to gather that Elly's (the elder's) marriage-*fiasco* is complete—& that she is past even pitying—if one could indeed *ever* pity such a voluntary little person. But there is one of them—Rosina?—from whom you seem to me to have suffered a good bit. You are angels & my continual wonder & admiration. One of William's letters was from the Virginia Springs—which *sound* so pretty, whether they be or no—& spoke of Ripleys, Helen Masons[3] &c, &c.—the rather dismal drama of one's faded relationships. It's good of you to keep so "in touch" with them! I hear with elation of the Lowell lectures[4]—as much elation as I can bring to bear on anything which only renews my far-off sense of disinheritedness. You, William, don't even allude to the possibility of your coming out for your Edinburgh degree, which you, Alice, speak of as apparently probable.[5] If you see your way to it it will be a delight to behold you. I shld. say I shld. think it would tempt you if I could say that of anything involving 2 voyages close together. But give me an inkling—in advance—I want to be in a good place to receive you. If I can only still be at Rye that will be perfection. Young Putnam sent me your introductory note to Point Hill & I wrote him a very courteous letter of which he has taken no notice whatever.[6] Les jeunes! I rejoice in the prospect of your collective book—which will have an awfully good title.[7] May it quickly come forth. The small *Life W. Living* is a precious possession & a delicious re-perusal.[8] What melancholy, what terrible duties *vous incombent* when your neighbours are destroyed. And telling that poor man's wife—! Life *is* heroic—however we "fix" it! Even as I write these words the St. Louis horror bursts in upon me in the evening paper.[9] Inconceivable—I can't try; & I *won't*. Strange how practically *all* one's sense of news from the U.S. here is huge Horrors & Catastrophes. It's a terrible country *not* to live in. I embrace you both & feel shabby at writing to you thus economically bracketed. But bear with me a little longer, & you, dear Alice in particular, shall have a glowing individual tribute from your all-affectionate

Henry James

[1] HJ, "The Other House" appeared in the *Illustrated London News* from 4 July to 26 September 1896 (vol. 109).

[2] Mrs. Robertson was not identified.

[3] Helen Mason Wood.

⁴WJ delivered eight lectures before the Lowell Institute in Boston on "Recent Researches into Exceptional Mental States" in October and November 1896.   WJ had proposed the course in April 1896.

⁵WJ received an honorary doctorate from Edinburgh in 1902.

⁶Putnam was not identified.

⁷WJ, *The Will to Believe and Other Essays in Popular Philosophy* (1897).

⁸WJ's *Is Life Worth Living?* was published as a small book in 1896.

⁹A tornado killed hundreds in St. Louis on 27 May 1896.

To Henry James

Chocorua, June 11. 1896

Dear Heinrich,

Your long letter of Whitsuntide week in London came yesterday evening, and was read by me aloud to Alice and Harry as we sat at tea in the kitchen window to get the last rays of the sunday.¹ You have too much feeling of duty about corresponding with us, and, I imagine with everyone. I think you have behaved most handsomely of late—and always, and though your letters are the great *fête* of our lives, I wont be "on your mind" for worlds. Your general feeling of unfulfilled obligations is one that runs in the family—I at least am often afflicted by it—but it is "morbid." The horrors of *not* living in America, as you so well put it, are not shared by those who do live here. All that the telegraph imparts are the shocks, the "happy homes," good husbands and fathers, fine weather honest business men, neat new houses, punctual meetings of engagements, &c., of which the country mainly consists, are neer cabled over. Of course the Saint Louis disaster is dreadful, but it will very likely end by "improving" the city. The really bad thing here is the silly wave that has gone over the public mind—protection humbug, silver, jingoism etc. It is a case of "mob-psychology." Any country is liable to it if circumstances conspire, and our circumstances having conspired, it is very hard to get them out of the rut. It *may* take another financial crash to get them out—which of course will be an expensive method. It is no more foolish and considerably less damnable than the Russo-phobia of England which would seem to have been responsible for the Armenian massacres. *That* to me is the biggest indictment "of our boasted civilization["]!!! It *requires* England I say nothing of the other powers to maintain the Turks at that business. We have let our little place, our tenant arrives the day after to morrow, and Alice and I & Tweedycle have been here a week enjoying it and cleaning house and place. She has worked like a beaver. I had two days spoiled by a psychological Experiment with *mescal*, an intoxicant used by some of our S. Western indians in there religious ceremonies, a sort of cactus bud, of which the U.S. government had distributed a supply to certain medical men including Weir Mitchell who sent me some to try. He had himself been "in fairyland." It gives the most glorious visions of colour—every object thought of appears in a jeweled splendor unknown to the natural world. It disturbs the stomach somewhat but that, according to W.M., was a cheap price, etc. I took one bud 3 days ago, vomited and spattered for 24 hours and had no other symptom whatever except that and the Katzenjammer the following day. I will take the visions on trust. We have had three days of delicious rain—it all soaks into the sandy soil here and leaves no mud whatever. The little place is the most curious mixture of sadness with delight. The sadness of *things*—things everyone of which was done either by our hands or by our planning, old furniture renovated, there isnt an object in the house that isn't associated with past life, old summers, dead people, people who will never come again etc, and the way it catches you round the heart when you first come and open the house from its long winter sleep is most extraordinary. I have been reading Bourget's Idylle tragique which he very kindly sent me,[2] and since then have been reading in Tolstoi's War and Peace, which I never read before, strange to say. I must say that T. rather kills B., for my mind. B's moral atmosphere is anyhow so foreign to me, a lewdness so *obligatory* that it hardly seems as if it were part of a moral *donné* at all, and then his overlabored descriptions, and excessive explanations. But with it all an earnestness and enthusiasm for getting it said as well as possible, a richness of ep[i]thet, and a warmth of heart that make you like him, in spite of the unmanliness of all the things he writes about. I suppose there is a stratum in france to whom it is all manly and ideal, but he and I are, as Rosina says, a bad combination. In spite of which I suppose I must write to him, like a frenchman, some flattering words.

Tolstoi is immense!

I am glad *you* are in a writing vein again, to go still higher up the scale! I have abstained on principle from the atlantic serial, wishing to get it all at once.[3] I am not going abroad, I can't afford it, I have a chance to give $500 worth of summer-lectures here, which won't recur, I have a heavy year of work next year, and shall very likely *need* to go the following summer, which will anyhow be after a more becoming interval than this; so, *somme toute*, it is postponed. If I went

I should certainly enjoy seeing you at Rye more than in London, which I confess tempts me little now. I love to *see* it, but staying there doesn't seem to agree with me, and only suggests constraint and money-spending, apart from seeing you. I wish you could see how comfortable our Cambridge house has got at last to be. Alice who is up stairs sewing "valences" on to toilet tables whilst I write below by the lamp—a great wood fire hissing in the fireplace, sings out her thanks and love to you. I will send you the Syracuse remittance as soon as I get back to Cambridge. I am glad you have established such good relations with Bob's Mary. Ned is a bright fellow who seems to impress people. What will come of his literary talent I don't know. He copies you too much now, but he has words of his own. He is pretty cruel to his father, I imagine. Thank God, the College year is practically over. I have to take good care of myself this vacation to embark on next year. Harry got here last night, after his last exam[n]. I enclose you a letter. He will have better times next year with analytic geometry and physics out of his life. He is very satisfactory on the whole, though I wish he were less silent. His pacific disposition reminds one of you.

Affect[ly]. Wm.

[1] Perhaps a slip for 'sun' or 'day's sun'. The reference is not to the day of the week, since HJ's letter arrived on 10 June, a Wednesday.

[2] Paul Bourget, *Une Idylle tragique* (1896).

[3] HJ, "The Old Things," *Atlantic Monthly*, April–October 1896 (vols. 77–78); published in book form as *The Spoils of Poynton* (1897).

To Henry James

Cambridge, Mass., Oct. 17, 1896.

Dear Henry:

I hope you will not be too offended at this typewritten letter to read it. Obeying the spirit of the age I find it impossible to carry on my correspondence without the help of a stenographer and typewriter. I wish you would do the same; you will find it incredibly relieves the burden of existence. I have received two letters from you since my last and have written to the executors at Albany about Grandma's portrait, which you will undoubtedly receive. Young Haughton has not yet turned up; he shall be welcomed when he does so. It was not necessary for you to make such elaborate apologies for handing him over to us. Students are easy enough to take care of. It is British travelers, whom one has to invite persons to meet,

that make one curse God and die. Yesterday we had J. M. Barrie
and his wife and one Dr. Nichol, apparently his owner, and invited a
roomful of our fellow citizens to see them. Small was the reward we
got in their presence, since Barrie neither smiled nor spoke, in spite
of the fact that he, as it were, demanded the invitation and is one of
the most exquisite writers of the age. We have got back to work and
life is "full." But I am in better spirits than I have been for a long
time, because I have sloughed off the laboratory, which veritably had
become a nightmare. Your pretty volume of "the Other House" arrived last week, and I am reading it the last thing at night and to
prepare me for my nap in the afternoon.[1] It opens splendidly, and
I fancy I shall not make any restrictions concerning it when I write
you about it again. I will send you a photograph of poor Child in a
day or two; the family are bearing their loss very well indeed, and I
judge are not going to suffer badly from the diminution of income,
though of course they will be somewhat straitened. Poor Mrs. Child
is really an angelic woman, and I care for few friends as I do for her.
I enclose a letter from Ned about Bob, a sad tale. I will try to see
him and get him, if possible, into a hospital. I enclose Brown's Syracuse remittance for September and October. The taxes are heavy
and the October dividend was $50. short. No more to-day,

From yours affectionately, | W.J.

[1] HJ, *The Other House* (1896). WJ received the one-volume American edition.

1897–1898

Several years before her death, the sister Alice had suggested that Robertson's degeneration was the effect and not the cause of the drinking that had begun in his army days. By 1897 Robertson and Mary James had been married twenty-five years; still, his life was unstable. During this period he spent a number of years in an asylum in Dansville, N.Y., seeking a cure for alcoholism in a regimen of baths and electrical treatments. In March 1897 he made a brief visit to England, meeting Henry for several hours of what Henry termed "studiously superficial talk." Upon his return, he embarrassed Henry by telling Mary that Henry had encouraged him to divorce her. Their son, Edward Holton James, had completed Harvard College and in 1896–97 was in graduate school. Relations between father and son were difficult.

Also difficult were the relations between the rest of the Jameses and the family of Garth Wilkinson James. Several years earlier in a letter to Henry, Alice Gibbens James had described William's "touching" attempts to get acquainted with the children—attempts that would have made Henry "groan in spirit." But some progress was eventually made in these relationships; in May 1903 Joseph Cary James called on William in Cambridge and made a pleasant impression.

The sad destiny of Garth Wilkinson was on William's mind early in 1897 when he was preparing his oration for the unveiling of the Saint-Gaudens memorial to Robert Gould Shaw on Boston Common on 31 May 1897. Shaw, the commander of the 54th Massachusetts Regiment composed of black troops and white officers including Garth Wilkinson, had been killed in the famous charge on Fort Wagner in July 1863. Booker T. Washington was also one of the speakers at the dedication. William invited him to be his house guest, but Washington declined because of other engagements.

That same spring William agreed to deliver the Gifford Lectures at the University of Edinburgh after having rejected a similar invitation from the University of Aberdeen. The lectures became The Varieties of Religious Experience *and in many ways extend and complete his involvement with the study of extraordinary mental states. Also that spring he successfully offered his services as a lecturer to the University of California for the summer of 1898.*

For Henry James 1897 was marked by the publication of two major books, The Spoils of Poynton *and* What Maisie Knew, *and by the signing in September of a long-term lease for Lamb House in Rye, a house that he would buy several years later. In the fall, he wrote the ghost story* The Turn of the Screw, *which he variously described as a "shameless pot-boiler" and a "fairy-tale pure and simple."*

To Henry James

Dictated

Irving St. Cambridge | Feb 7$\underline{\text{th}}$ 1897

Dear Harry,

Arriving home last evening from New York I found your letter of the 27$\underline{\text{th}}$ about Bob, the Emmets, Myers and your going to Italy.[1] As the season advances you will doubtless be quite safe from Bob in Italy as he would naturally then keep further north. Moreover I doubt if he goes at all as things now are with him. He is in poor condition physically, drinks every now and then, and may procrastinate indefinitely his departure. I had a much pleasanter interview with him 10 days ago.

I am just back from a lecture to a Medical Society at New York, and to Vassar College at Poughkeepsie, spending 3 days with Tweedy on the way.[2] The quiet of Newport did me good but the social gadding at New York, apart from Howells at whose hotel I staid, quite the reverse. Howells is the dearest, simplest, kindest soul in the world. He claims nothing, is resigned to living in a naked hotel room with not a thing of his own in it, and goes to the theatre and is grateful for the acting he gets, however poor, as it was the night we went together. He spoke of you, as always, with great interest and affection.

Honours have been cast in my path with unusual frequency since I wrote you. I have been invited to give the address at the unveiling of the St Gaudens monument to Robert Shaw[,] Wilkie's Colonel, and have accepted. It's a strange freak of the whirligig of fortune that finds me haranguing the multitude on Boston Common, and I hesitated a good deal what to do. But one ought not to be too ready to funk an honour and the problem is really a very simple one, there being only three or four things which any possible orator would on that occasion have to say.   It resolves itself really into the labor of making one's phrases impressive.   It comes off on Decoration Day, the 31$^{\underline{st}}$ of May.   The monument is really a glorious work of art, simple and realistic, and worthy of comparison with the very best modern work.   Don't bruit this abroad as it won't get into the papers, I hope, for some time.—I have also been nominated for the Gifford lectureship at Aberdeen; whether elected or not I don't yet know. But even if elected I shall decline because I am reasonably sure of a nomination later at Edinborough and the date there, as well as the emoluments and the greatness of the University, make it more of a prize.   These are 20 lectures on "Natural Theology", 10 one year and 10 the next, paid at the rate of some £60. a lecture, and most honorably filled hitherto.   I shall have to do my best possible work, and need long leisure with the subject which lies largely outside of my college teaching.   The Aberdeen chance begins in 1899, the Edinborough one in 1901, and the two additional years are what have chiefly moved my decision.

I have also just been offered 1500 dollars worth of lecturing in California either this summer or the following one, and have accepted for the latter.   So you see that *tout vient à point à qui sait attendre*.   All this means hard labor and is inseparable from a social jigging which is rank poison to my nature.   But when one is in a profession one must be ready to meet all its challenges and opportunities, tho' one's elementary faculties (memory &c) are on the wane, as mine distinctly are.   Don't speak of these Gifford aspirations of mine.   They are quite confidential and are not known to anyone here.   I shall feel quite proud if I ever get the Edinborough appointment.   But enough of Egotism!

Kate Gourlay's estate will be divided in a few days now and you will then know the disposition of the portrait.[3]   Cousin Lydia Mason died a month ago and Katharine Loring's father is dead.   I saw Marie Costa in New York whose youngest daughter is being married to one Alfred Schemerhorn and is immediately going abroad.[4]   Lilla Walsh is down with a rather serious trouble in one of her eyes.   She is a fine and good girl.

We are making new leases at Syracuse at a net advance of 900 dollars, which will give us 300 dollars apiece more per annum.   For the first year however the gain will be only half felt on account of improvements.

(12th) Bessie Andrew died 2 days ago.

I have had a raging toothache for 48 hours which leaves me very seedy. I have been this P.M to Concord to see Mary about Bob. Found her & Ned in a really charming "home" with a beautiful view spread out before them. I'm afraid that Bob won't do anything reasonable. They fear that there is another woman in the case, and it is not unlikely. He is degenerating fast, and I don't believe he can live many years longer at this rate.

I don't find Brown Bros. receipt for the Feb. $150.00, but they have transferred my draft to your London account.

Good bye! Love from us both.

W.J.

[1] HJ did not travel to Italy in the spring of 1897.

[2] WJ lectured on demoniacal possession before the New York Neurological Society at the New York Academy of Medicine on 2 February 1897. His lecture on "Psychology and Relaxation," given at Vassar College on 5 February 1897, was included in *Talks to Teachers* (1899).

[3] The portrait is that of their grandmother, Catharine Barber James. HJ was prepared to pay as much as £60.

[4] Although AGJ wrote 'Costa', the reference is to Marie Bay James Coster.

From Henry James

(Dictated)—to a Scotch Amanuensis—an Aberdeen & Edinburgh man—hence superficiality!

34, DE VERE GARDENS. | W. 25th February, 1897.

My dear William,

I had no sooner posted to Alice yesterday the letter which will reach her by the same steamer as this than I came in again to find your deeply interesting one of the 7th; which I must briefly thank you for in spite of my previous outpouring. This is because I can't delay to let you know that your news raises me to a state of the highest beatitude. It is more money in my pocket and more feathers in my cap than any pelf or plumage of my own could give me the sense of carrying. In short, I rejoice with all my heart, and my bosom swells with conscious pride. I like so much to think what pleasure it must also give to Alice that I regret having lost, by a few hours, the chance of overflowing to her about it. It comes back, indeed, as regards the first matter, to the old story of feeling only the more that I am out of it; but I seek the compensation of thinking that I shall neglect no endeavour to be in it if the episode of the foreign university does come to pass. Heaven speed that and smooth every approach. We shall have time to talk more of it; meanwhile I vibrate intensely to the 31st May. I don't know what I wouldn't give to be there. But even poor dear, dead Wilkie will be more there than I. He will be very much there—he will be all there, poor boy; and I can't help figuring it as a sort of beautiful, poetic justice to him. I rejoice to know that the monument is really eminent, and I intensely hope you will be able after the unveiling to send me a good photograph or two. If it were possible to have them before, that would help me to see you and hear you. But of course it isn't possible. I jubilate, in fine, that you accepted; and I jubilate, above all with the conviction that you will be triumphantly uplifted. Glory to the Highest! I told Alice yesterday how beautiful I thought your Agassiz address—perfect in every particular.[1] I hope it had high success. F. R. Morse wrote me, indeed, the other day that it has had the very highest. Bravo, as well, to the California University! I should think, indeed, all these peregrinations would tend to smother you in their social and epistolary train; but it is a gruesome part of the battle of life that victory is so much more compromising, so much more inconvenient, than defeat. Continue, all the same, victorious and forgive so many words about it. Yours, my dear William, more than ever,

Henry James

[1] WJ spoke on Louis Agassiz at the reception of the American Society of Naturalists held on 30 December 1896. His address is reprinted in *ECR*.

To Henry James

Cambridge, Mass., June 5, 1897.

Dear H.:

Alice wrote you (I think) a brief word after the crisis of last Monday.[1] It took it out of me nervously a good deal, for it came at the end of the month of May, when I am always fagged to death; and for a week previous I had almost lost my voice with hoarseness. At nine o'clock the night before I ran in to a laryngologist in Boston, who sprayed and cauterized and otherwise tuned up my throat, giving me pellets to suck all the morning. By a sort of miracle I spoke for three-quarters of an hour without becoming perceptibly hoarse. But it is a curious kind of physical effort to fill a hall as large as Boston Music Hall, unless you are trained to the work. You have to shout and bellow, and you seem to yourself wholly unnatural. The day was an extraordinary occasion for sentiment. The streets were thronged with people, and I was toted around for two hours in a barouche at the tail end of the procession. There were seven such carriages in all, and I had the great pleasure of being with St. Gaudens, who is a most charming and modest man. The weather was cool and the skies were weeping, but not enough to cause any serious discomfort. They simply formed a harmonious background to the pathetic sentiment that reigned over the day. It was very peculiar, and people have been speaking about it ever since—the last wave of the war breaking over Boston, everything softened and made poetic and unreal by distance, poor little Robert Shaw erected into a great symbol of deeper things than he ever realized himself—"the tender grace of a day that is dead"—etc.[2] We shall never have anything like it again. The monument is really superb, certainly one of the finest things of this century. Read the darkey Washington's speech, a model of elevation and brevity. The thing that struck me most in the day was the faces of the old 54th soldiers, of which there were perhaps about thirty or forty present, with such respectable old darkey faces, the heavy animal look entirely absent, and in its place the wrinkled, patient, good old darkey citizen.[3]

As for myself, I will never accept such a job again. It is entirely outside of my legitimate line of business, although my speech seems to have been a great success, if I can judge by the encomiums which are pouring in upon me on every hand. I brought in some mugwumpery at the end, but it was very difficult to manage it.

I haven't the least idea of where you may be, but am hoping to have news of you soon. I am curious to know whether you saw the Emmet girls at Paris, and how they struck you there.[4] I have not heard from them for a long time. Their mother, I am afraid, has dished herself completely.[5] I send this off in advance of Brown Bros.' receipt. The funds will come in a couple of days. I do not know that these receipts are of any consequence to you after all. We go to Chocorua next week.

Always affectionately yours, | Wm. James

[1] The Shaw monument was dedicated on Monday, 31 May 1897.

[2] The line, quoted in WJ's oration, is from Tennyson's "To E. L., on His Travels in Greece."

[3] Survivors of the regiment sat on the platform during the ceremonies.

[4] Ellen Gertrude Emmet Rand was in Paris studying art. Several of her sisters were with her.

[5] WJ is referring to Ellen James Temple Emmet Hunter. According to reports, her marriage with George Hunter was not a happy one.

To Henry James

Cambridge, April 10 98

Dear Henry,

A good long letter from you arrived a week ago—the silence having been long on both sides. I am right glad to hear you speak so enthusiastically of your prospects at Rye, for to me the country is the ideal, though for you as a bachelor I should think it might grow pretty lonesome if indulged in for too many months in the year. Otherwise you might do a fine economical stroke by giving up your London apartment altogether and resorting to lodgings and a club when you come up. I trust you may let De Vere Gardens for the season, for I have finance very much on the brain. Every writer must look to the day when he gets démodé and make provision for a shrinkage of income after sixty from his current work. I am looking towards a gradual withdrawing from teaching within the next ten years. I have managed to put by 2000 a year for the past five—I have put 500 into my house mortgage within a month, and altho the work is hard and the family very costly, it keeps balancing on the right side. I am practically spending at the rate of 10,000 a year.—a fearful thing of which the only *extravagant* item is *education*. The boys don't seem in the least to be spendthrifts, and never need pocket money.

Next year I shall earn a 1000 less by stopping outside lectures and instruction at Radcliffe (the Harvard female Annex) which latter I hate to do, for I much enjoy it, but it overworks me, and the Gifford preparation will be arduous. I got notice yesterday of my election as "correspondant de l'Institut" (Acad. des Sciences morales et Politiques), a considerable "honour" as such absurd things go.[1] But they come to a man the more senile and idiotic he grows. What with this, California next summer, Edinbro in a year, and Germany ditto, I begin to feel like Pascal's *infini* defined as a cercle dont le centre est partout et la circonférence nulle part.[2] My centre seems partout, and though it carries a certain exhilaration, I don't think it exactly healthy, for I should like better to sit in one centre and make steady definite progress in a quiet way. Your abhorrence of London is, I fancy, based on a longing to simplify and concentrate your consciousness. When my brain gets fatigued, as at this season, the mere complication of life drives me wild—everything inhibits everything else, and I do nothing to speak of, but my needful lectures and the answering of notes. It is very unwholesome. We have Elizabeth Emmet (Kitty's) in the house & young Miller from Bryn Mawr.

But why do I talk of myself so when the country is quivering on
the edge of earthquake. We eat, drink and sleep War.[3] It is a altogether new phenomenon, ascribable I suspect for the most part to
deliberate newspaper criminality. The abominations of the press
have literally passed all belief, and the word WAR in enormous capitals repeated for two months past on every front page of the "great
dailies" has at last produced its suggestive effect. It must come, to
relieve the tension. The "people" are really crazy for it, now, for its
own sake, demanding it as the parisian populace did before 1870.
Congress, living also by "suggestion" of what the people requires, is
in an equal state of craze, and McKinley who has done magnificently
so far, seems (if one can trust the last reports) to be on the point of
yielding. It is a heart-sickening business to all thinking men. The
war-howlers have no words foul enough to denounce McKinley's tur-
pitude in seeking delay "in order to avert war." To morrow, however,
his message to Congress is finally expected; and it may be that much
of the talk of the last few days is mere bluff meant to put pressure
on Spain. We may still hope for that. If war comes, what we *shall*
do with Cuba, no one knows. At any rate it commits us more and
more to the hideous old international ornière of the European countries, based on hatred and rapacity, and the only bright element in
it, is the slight platonic rapprochement between us and England
which the months seem to be bringing, but which may fade out as
fast as it came.

The worst of it is the complete destruction of the old belief in the
vox populi. There is no doubt of collective attacks of genuine madness sweeping over peoples and stampeding them. And liberalism
must slowly & sadly go to work against the possibility of them. The
worst of these recent attacks is that the leaders in them are *absolutely
insincere* villains, I mean the editors. Those of the new york *Journal*
(a Harvard graduate millionaire named Hearst) and *World* ought to
be hung higher than any criminals, and yet there isn't so far a law
that can touch them.[4] But enough! it is a sickening affair. The
bright feature is that an American president still proves to be a good
man. McKinley was not credited with such back bone as he has shown
or such fighting tenacity, though his admirable diplomatic powers
and temper were always recognized. He has had a *fearful* strain to
bear.—Well, you will read this retrospectively, to the sound of the
cannon perhaps.—I enclose two receipts from Brown Bros. Mrs.
Gibbens and I would like to lay by rather more of the Syracuse income, restricting it say to $1800 a year, (150 a month clear) so as to

increase our sinking fund, which now amounts to only a few hundred dollars. Our 35,000 of mortgage of which the interest comes in in Jan & July draws 6% & will be paid up in 10 years. It can never be reinvested at that rate, so we ought to try to prevent the shrinkage in income then, by adding from year to year a little to the principal. Do you agree to that? I hope so. I have been distributing rather more than 1800 a year during the past couple of years.

Affectionately yours, Wm James

The[y] talked of Swap at Syracuse, if it could have been effected with but 45,000 dollars cash, or still better 40,000, would have been ultimately to our great advantage, giving us a much better estate on a *corner* across the street. But Alice and Mrs. Gibbens had a genuinely feminine dread of any change, and as the *immediate* advantage was but small, I let the thing drop. If I had been alone in the matter I should not have hesitated a moment. Make no allusion to this explanation when you write.

W.J.

T. S. Perry & family are going to Japan for three years. He has just been appointed Professor of English in one of the Tokio Universities, and is in great glee over the expected fun.

Tip top news all the time from Bob.

[1] The Académie des Sciences Morales et Politiques was one of five academies comprising the Institut de France.

[2] WJ did not lecture in Germany.

[3] When rebellion against Spanish rule broke out in Cuba in 1895, American public opinion demanded that the United States support the rebels. Passions were aroused by the sinking in Havana Harbor on 15 February 1898 of the American battleship *Maine,* with the loss of 260 men. President McKinley delivered his message to Congress on 11 April, asking for the use of force to establish peace and a stable government. Congressional critics claimed that the message was weak and on 19 April approved a joint resolution requiring the use of force for the liberation of Cuba. On 21 April, McKinley sent an ultimatum to the Spanish government. On 24 April, Spain replied with a declaration of war.

[4] William Randolph Hearst (1863–1951), American newspaper publisher, owner of the *New York Herald;* Joseph Pulitzer (1847–1911), Hungarian-born newspaper publisher, owner of the *New York World.*

From Henry James

34, DE VERE GARDENS, W. 20 April, 1898.

My dear William,

There are all sorts of *intimes* and confidential things I want to say to you in acknowledgement of your so deeply interesting letter—of

April 10th—received yesterday; but I must break the back of my response at least with this mechanical energy; not having much of any other—by which I mean simply too many odd moments—at my disposal just now. I do answer you, alas, almost to the foul music of the cannon. It is this morning precisely that one feels the fat to be at last fairly in the fire. I confess that the blaze about to come leaves me woefully cold, thrilling with no glorious thrill or holy blood-thirst whatever. I see nothing but the madness, the passion, the hideous clumsiness of rage, of mechanical reverberation; and I echo with all my heart your denouncement of the foul criminality of the screeching newspapers. They have long since become, for me, the danger that overtops all others. That became clear to one, even here, two years ago, in the Venezuela time;[1] when one felt that with a week of simple, enforced silence everything could be saved. If things *were* then saved without it, it is simply that they hadn't at that time got so bad as they now are in the U.S. My sympathy with you all is intense—the whole horror must so mix itself with all your consciousness. I am near enough here to hate it, without being, as you are, near enough in some degree, perhaps, to understand. I am leading at present so quiet a life that I don't measure much the sentiment, the general attitude around me. Much of it can't possibly help being Spanish— and from the "European" standpoint in general Spain *must* appear savagely assaulted. She is so quiet—publicly and politically—so decent and picturesque and harmless a member of the European family that I am bound to say it argues an extraordinary illumination and a very predetermined radicalism not to admire her pluck and pride. But publicly, of course, England will do nothing whatever that is not more or less—negatively—for our benefit. I scarcely know what the newspapers say—beyond the Times, which I look at all for Smalley's cables: so systematic is my moral and intellectual need of ignoring them.[2] One must save one's life if one can. The next weeks will, however, in this particular, probably not a little break me down. I must at least read the Bombardment of Boston. May you but scantly suffer from it!

I have just come back from that monstrous rarity for *me,* a visit of three or four days in the country—to G. O. Trevelyan, who is extraordinarily rich and much-housed, and spends Easter at his huge (or rather his wife's) modern mansion of Welcombe, near Stratford-on-Avon. The Eastertide has been lovely; that country was full of spring and of Shakspeare, besides its intrinsic sweetness; and I suppose I ought to have been happy. But I wasn't—I hate too much such a lavishment of precious time.   Fortunately I've got, through protracted and infernal cunning, almost altogether out of it.   There was no one there—they live only in a furnished wing of the huge, hereditary white elephant of a house—but the Speaker and Speakeress of the House of Commons, who are very amiable folk.[3]   Also deadly commemorative Shakspeare trilogies at the Stratford theatre, to which we were haled for two nights.[4]   Basta!

I rejoice with intense rejoicing in everything you tell me of your own situation, plans, arrangements, honours, prospects—into all of which I enter with an intimacy of participation.   Your election to the *Institut* has, for me, a surpassing charm—I simply revel and, as it were, wallow in it.   Je m'y vautre.   But oh, if it could only have come soon enough for poor Alice to have known it—such a happy little nip as it would have given her; or for the dear old susceptible Dad! But things come as they can—and I am, in general, lost in the daily miracle of their coming at all: I mean so many of them—few as that many may be: and I speak above all for myself.   I am lost, moreover, just now, in the wonder of what effect on American affairs, of every kind, the shock of battle will have.   Luckily it's of my nature—though not of my pocket—always to be prepared for the worst and to expect the least.   Like you, with all my heart, I have "finance on the brain." At least I try to have it—with a woeful lack of natural talent for the same.   It is none too soon.   But one arrives at dates, periods, corners of one's life: great changes, deep operations are begotten.   This has more portée than I can fully go into.   I shall certainly do my best to let my flat when I am ready to leave town; the difficulty, this year, however, will be that the time for "season" letting begins now, and that I can't depart for at least another month.   Things are not ready at Rye, and won't be till then, with the limited local energy at work that I have very wisely contented myself with turning on there.   It has been the right and much the best way in the long run, and for one's good little relations there; only the run has been a little longer. The remnant of the season here may be difficult to dispose of—to a sublessee; and my books—only a part of which I can house at Rye, are a complication.   However, I shall do what I can this year; and for subsequent absences, so long as my present lease of De Vere Gardens runs I shall have the matter on a smooth, organised, working basis.   I mean to arrange myself always to let—being, as such places go, distinctly lettable.   And for my declining years I have already put my name down for one of the invaluable south-looking, Carlton-

Gardens-sweeping bedrooms at the Reform Club, which are let by the year and are of admirable and convenient (with all the other resources of the place at one's elbow) *general* habitability.   The only thing is they are so in demand that one has sometimes a long time to await one's turn.   On the other hand there are accidents—"occasions."   Then—with this flat suppressed—I shall, with Lamb House but £70 a year & the Reform room but £50, I shall, in respect to *loyer*, have taken in a great deal of pecuniary sale.[5]   This business of making Lamb House sanitary & comfortable & very modestly furnishing is of course, as it came very suddenly, a considerable strain on my resources; but I shall securely outweather it—& this year, & next, thank heaven, my income will have been much larger than for any year of my existence.   My main drawback will be my sacrifice, on going to Rye, of my excellent Scotch amanuensis[6]—whom I can't take with me, without too great an expense in making up to him the loss of his other—afternoon & evening—engagements here.   Moreover he is not a desirable inmate—I couldn't again, as I did for 8 weeks last summer, undertake his living with me.   My pressing want is some sound, sane, irreproachable young type-writing & bicycling "secretary-companion", the expense of whom wd. be practically a 100-fold made up by increase & facilitation of paying work.   But though I consider the post enviable it is difficult to fill.   The young typists are mainly barbarians—& the civilized, here, are not typists.   But patience.   I don't go into the Bob-question more than to jubilate devoutly in yr. good news of him. I don't *understand*, I fear, very clearly, your inquiry as to my assent (that is the question itself,) to your new Syracuse idea; but I *give*, that assent, freely to what you think best— judging it to be in the interest of conservatism & prudence.   I hope War will make no difference in the advent of Harry & M.G.[7]   I shall be ready for H. by the mid-June.   I embrace you all—Alice longer than the rest—& am, with much actuality of emotion,

                                                  Ever your   Henry

Address: William James, Esq., | Membre Correspondant de l'Institut de France, | (Académie des Sciences Morales et Politiques) | 95, Irving Street, | Cambridge, Mass., U.S.A.[8]

Postmarks: KENSINGTON W AP 20 98   NEW YORK N.Y. APR 27 1898   BOSTON MASS. APR 28 1898

[1] For WJ's view of the Venezuela crisis see *Correspondence*, 2:384, 385, 387–88.

[2] In his report in the London *Times* of 19 April 1898, George Washburn Smalley described in detail the congressional action that led to the war.

[3] William Court Gully (1835–1909) served as speaker of the House of Commons

from 1895 to 1905.   His wife was Elizabeth Anne Walford Gully (d. 1906).

[4] The Shakespeare Memorial Theatre in Stratford-on-Avon staged annual festivals in honor of Shakespeare's birthday.   In 1898 the festival opened on 14 April with a new production of *Antony and Cleopatra*.   The birthday performance was on 23 April.

[5] A slip for 'sail'.

[6] William MacAlpine.

[7] Margaret Merrill Gibbens Gregor.

[8] Below the address, WJ wrote 'War with spain'.

From Henry James

34, DE VERE GARDENS, W. April 22ᵈ [1898]

Dearest William & Alice & All.

I wrote to you by the last American post—but what these couple of days have brought forth fills me with a kind of horror that makes me want to get near you again—haunted as I am with all sorts of glooms & anxieties.   However, why do I talk to you of mine when your own are probably as much as you find pertinent?   This is only— tonight, a clock-ticking midnight—to show you how fondly I think of you—depressed & disgusted as you must be.   I feel utterly over-darkened—but I shall shake it off by intensity of work.   I wish I might have a word from you as to how Boston feels & "acts." I have the sense—it blights for the time everything for me here—of being miserably far away & not bearing my share of your pressure.   But I *do* bear it & tonight it's heavy on me.   There *is* a certain comfort in the attitude of this country—it is very agreeable to one here; & the absolute fury of much of the Continental press (the French papers showing their usual mastery of insult,) emphasises it and seems to make it a reality.   I wish the *occasion* had been a better one (for the drawing-together) but occasions come as they can.—I have a sort of dread of poor dear old Tweedy at Sea-girt Bellevue Court being "shelled"!   But I have—for the rest—no glimmer nor light of any kind upon defences and resources.   I'm mainly glad Harvard College isn't—nor Irving St—the thing nearest Boston Bay.   *Any* word as to how things strike you on the spot will be a benediction—from any of you—to yours, all, ever so tenderly—

Henry James

To Henry James

Cambridge, May 3. 98

Dear H.,

Your letters of April 20 & 23rd. have come duly, and I write a line in the midst of great "pressure" to reassure you about the war, which seemed by April 23 to be squeezing your feelings very hard.   First, there is *absolutely* no fear of our coast being raided.   Second, we are getting used to the situation—and all the states, I believe, have immediately raised their required number of volunteers.   The real trouble is to come hereafter when Spain shall have left Cuba, and left us responsible for order there.   The whole thing is very mixed; and like all human things, is mixed of ideal and unideal elements.   The ideal fact is that we are making an absolutely *disinterested* war.   Not a soul thinks of conquest or wishes it.   The popular mind has been wrought up towards its final excitement simply by pictures of the suffering inflicted on non-combatants in Cuba.   It is Armenia over-again with a nobler termination on the part of the "Power."   (That our first act should be to exacerbate still more the said sufferings by our blockade is one of those inconsistencies that infest all "Great" things.)   The great unideal element is the forcing of the president to war when things were going on so swimmingly by the mere threat of it.   That was pure mob-excitement; but it is the sort of thing that can happen anywhere when war has been talked enough.   It was none the less abominable, as it took place, in its brutality.   In favor of it as a policy it is to be said that any experiment of leaving Spain in nominal possession of an "autonomous" Cuba would have been so unlikely to run smoothly, that we should have had to intervene after 5 years of friction—so why not now, & save the five years?   The cry of vengeance for the Maine was also abominable, as our knowledge of the facts stood.   But what remains for us, now that the die is cast, is to rescue what ideal elements we can from the situation and make them, as much as possible, the *maasgebend* ones.   Once for all it diversifies our affairs, and in a great country that is important.   Once for all it mixes us with Europe and will force us to become more responsible-feeling. It will probably in the end tend to increase reforms here, for with these foreign responsibilities we *must* put in our best men.   It approximates us in feeling to England—an enormous gain.   McKinley couldn't do otherwise than yield to Congress.   They had the constitutional right to say whether or no there should be war, and he had to execute their bidding or lose all hold whatever of the situation, in the state of feeling that then reigned.   The whole thing is an object lesson as to the forces that make history.   The blind instinct of masterfulness has been here the main thing.   It would not have got under way but for a sort of philanthropy; but it did the work.   On it all the great nations are based; and we evidently have *that* much of a great nation in us.   It remains to be seen whether the other requisite—the ability successfully to rise to the responsibilities of masterfulness, shall be with us too.   These big movements are always too coarse in their elements to bear much scrutiny—it is the gross results that prove whether on the whole they are worthy of applause or condemnation—and who lives long enough, will see.

We have just let Chocorua.   Billy has to day taken ether & had his wrist bone set,—a fall off a bicycle.   He is in fine shape—captain of his school crew on the river, and very unhappy at his accident.   Love from all of us.   Don't agonize over us *at all*.

In July, William began his train trip to California, choosing the most scenic route. On 29 July he was in Montreal and on 2 August in Banff, in what is now Alberta. After spending several days there, he reached Seattle on the fifth, Portland on the sixth, and, traveling south on the Southern Pacific Railroad, a route completed in 1887 and famous for its scenery, arrived in San Francisco on the tenth. Many trains on this line had open observation cars. The train probably stopped near Mount Shasta so that passengers could sample the mineral waters.

In addition to the series of lectures to teachers, he delivered a lecture on "Philosophical Conceptions and Practical Results" to the Philosophical Union of the University of California, in which he introduced pragmatism and initiated the controversy over meaning and truth that dominated American philosophical discussion for about a decade. On 13 August he departed for a camping trip in the Sierra Nevada that involved a five-day excursion by mule, unaware that he had damaged his heart by overexertion in early July while hiking in the Adirondacks. His letters to his wife about the excursion, some of which she sent to Henry, contain his most detailed descriptions of scenery.

That summer his nineteen-year-old son, Henry, went to England where he visited his uncle. William warned his brother that young

Henry was unlike other Jameses, that he was taciturn and might easily bore him, being a poor scholar with a poor memory. Nevertheless, William was very pleased with his son, who had "excellent clear ideas of what he grasps at all." The bachelor uncle Henry's letters about the visit are lost, but everything seems to have gone very well since William found his brother's letters on the subject a "real blessing."

To Henry James

On the train, 3 hours from Boston, | Sept. 22. 98
Dear H.—This is the sixth day of it (with the only stop one of 10 hours at Salt Lake City on Sunday to worship at the Mormon tabernacle, which was much like D͏ͬ McElroys at N.Y.) and I am right glad of the prospect of seeing alice and the dear old home so soon. One acquires a disgust for one's clothes on such a journey, and after six nights of berth and Pullman wash room longs for bed and bath tub. But that is selbstverständlich. The main thing is that the trip has done me a world of good, morally and intellectually, & made me see this world's affairs—I think also a bit the next world's—in a simpler broader light. These magnificent railroads & new settlements bring home to one the fact that all life rests so on the physical courage of common man. It trims the best of one's conceptions. California is *wonderful,* but I won't pretend to descant on it. Alice sent me a letter from you to her—I haven't noted the date (Aug 24)—it must have been very recent—in which you spoke of letters to her which she sent to Harry & which you had read. I hope she sent lots. It was my confidence that through him you would hear from me more or less directly that made me not write to you on the journey, which now sinks into the infinite azure of the past, leaving so good a memory, but not likely to be repeated. My last 4 days I lectured 2-ce a day to audiences of from 500 to 800, and ended in a blaze of glory, with many thanks for having emancipated the school teachers' souls. Poor things they are so servile in their natures as to furnish the most promising of all preys for systematic mystification and pedantification on the part of the paedogogic authorities who write books for them, and when one talks plain common sense with no technical terms, they regard it as a sort of revelation. It does my soul good to hear you speak so well of Harry who is indeed an extremely long headed, and fair-judging youth, with a great instinct for perceiving the truth

in human affairs.   In his peacable and tactful disposition, which is by no means a yielding one, he reminds me much of you, and will I am sure match some kind of success in life.   He is so charmed with the way you're "fixed," as to redouble my desire to get to Rye to see you.   I suppose he's on the water now.—A former student on the train has lent me Cyrano de B——c, and I have just read it, with more complete and satisfying organic feelings of delight than I have had for a long time.[1]   What absolutely delectable stuff it is, and how delicious to see the french language flexibilizing itself more and more by dipping into the older springs.   I wish that Stevenson had been alive to translate it for the English stage—if possible! the swagger is so much in his own vein.   Rabelais, Moliere, & V. Hugo, all meet in it.   I have also been reading one of the vols of Michelets history of France—never read one before.[2]   There is a *wonderful* style for you again—I had no idea of his absolutely free genius as a writer.   As free as Carlyle, granted the neccessary limits.—I wrote a letter to Rosina from the Hotel del Monte (one of the most finished and exqui-site places in the world, in a country only 50 years old!) and sent it to you to forward, not knowing her address.   Oddly enough a couple of days later came your announcem! of her visit to you.   She's a gifted girl, with a great capacity for seeing truth, but a curious hostility to aught that savors of discipline, being all for sport and strong sensa-tion, like a true aristocrat.   Heaven knows what is to become of her. With my family, I can make no pecuniary contributions, and I dare say you have made abundant ones already.   Bay & Leslie seem to have all the dutiful virtues which she lacks, and yet there is something very fine and large about Rosina—a capacity for impersonal views very rare in women.   If she comes home, we shall entertain her for a while and then pass her over to the Emmets.—*What* a time to live in!   I should think a cruel fate to have to leave this world before the Dreyfuss mystery is cleared up.   There is a fatal weakness in the french nature.   England and Germany come out by contrast.   As for America, qui vivra verra.   I hope for nothing good from the Republi-can politicians.   Public opinion seems to be getting less and less im-perialistic, which considering our administrative impossibilities, is an encouraging sign.   Our soldiers of whom I saw a lot in California, are really a magnificent body of youths, such firm good serious & intelligent faces.   Of course they underwent a rigorous surgical selec-tion.   But the moral expression is splendid; and Tommy Atkins may hang his head in comparison.   To day comes news that the medical commission to study the causes of disease at the camps reports *flies* as the spreaders of typhoid poison—a very plausible idea.[3]—I will stop here and add a PS. as to how I find things "at home" after I get there. I haven't done a stroke of work yet on my Edinb. lectures. It will, I fear be a big sort of ordeal, both the composition of them & the 5 or 6 weeks of starring it, which disagrees with my nerves so thoroughly, though I like it will[4] enough per se, and for a very few days at a time. I must keep myself in prime condition this winter to advance the work, and have dropt my usual Radcliffe course in order to lighten the burden.

Sept. 25. Am in my old socket again as if it had not been! California gleams as though a diorama or any optical contrivance that intensifies and illuminates by isolating and framing in darkness. A goodly country. I find Alice in tip top condition the house charming, and nothing happened of account, to anyone in the neighborhood. Grace Norton I have seen this evening, very cheery and well, full of a visit to Newport to see Mrs. Bullard, and incidentally visited a splendid collection of pictures belonging to one Theodore Davis who seems to be a sort of eccentric grand Seigneur. Harry on the Ocean, Billy & Tweedy at the Salters still. Much to do, before term opens, I hope to finish by Tuesday the writing out of my "Talks to Teachers on Psychology" which will doubtless have a successful sale and a useful function, and best of all let me out forever from the possibility of repeating them.[5] My Will to Believe is in its fourth 1000, and I have just rec'd from Longmans a check for nearly $900 above the four hundred which I paid for the plates—I consider that fine for that kind of book. Alice sends her best love and gratitude for your kindness to and liking for, our Harry

Yours ever, W.J.

This extract from a letter from Mrs. Whitman ought to please you—it is a sort of judgment of posterity on that early 'piece.'

[1] WJ is referring to the play *Cyrano de Bergerac* (1897) by Edmond Rostand, a romantic, unhistorical portrayal of Savinien Cyrano de Bergerac (1619–1655), French writer.

[2] Jules Michelet, *Histoire de France* (1833–67).

[3] In the Spanish-American War, as in many others, typhoid fever was a major cause of death.

[4] A slip for 'well'.

[5] *Talks to Teachers* was published in April 1899.

From Henry James

LAMB HOUSE, | RYE. Oct. 11$\underline{\text{th}}$ 1898

My dear William.

I am overwhelmed with the sense of my arrears à votre égard—so overwhelmed that I'm almost paralysed. I waited—in intention—first, till your return from California; & then—but since then—these last 2 or 3 weeks—I *haven't* waited; only been defeated, from day to day & hour to hour, in the act of trying to write. I have made the rather ominous discovery that a rather copious current of friends "staying" sets toward my door—now that that door opens into—what it *does;* & I have struggled of late, in particular, with many interruptions—but of this side of the situation more at some other time. On my side I've never been so copiously supplied with news of you nor felt so *en rapport;* for I had the benefit of all of Harry's budgets from Alice—for all the weeks he was in England—he most kindly having let me see whatever he received from his mother. So I lived your life & tracked your adventurous steps in the Adirondacks as well as in California—& all with wonder and bedazzlement—so furiously contrasted has the turn of your existence, this summer, been to the turn of mine & so withering a light your ideal of movement & mountaineering seemed to me to shed on my mere state of being fenced in & propped up with old furniture & brick-work. The whole record has been interesting to me in the highest degree—& your letters themselves endlessly wonderful to me & delightful. Alice has kindly sent me 2 or 3 of the very last, on the eve of your return; beside which I have yours to myself straight, from the train on your way back. (Please say to Alice with my love & thanks, that I will speedily, in writing to her, return her those she sent me.) Since the one on the train, finished after your arrival, I have one from you of Sept. 29$\underline{\text{th}}$, after Harry's arrival, about your mistake in sending me twice over certain Syracuse money—I'm very sorry you've had trouble about this—& concur wholly, of course in your rectifying the matter by suppressing, as you propose, the remittance you would otherwise make this month. I am easily vague about the circumstances of these remittances—& moreover there are others, as yet unacknowledged by me—as having been made by you from the wilderness—where I didn't wish to pursue you; the Gourlay money being in the number. But enough of that. Awfully interesting the time you must have had—a deluge of impressions & sensations; & yet with a total—& indeed a circumstantial effect, for me, of *not* kindling my desire to wander in your wake or dream of ever tackling those immensities. Mon siège est fait & my fate is other—for which I console myself— as to the vision of the globe itself by the sense—or suspicion, some- how, of the *no*-loss when you mention the human & social "factors"— pulling me up, e.g., with the bewilderment of the idea of the Diblee family[1] (constructed, I confess from the poor child always with the Emmets & whose very speech defies comprehension) as an oasis in the personal desert. However, such mystifications are doubtless more or less explicable, & I am deeply depressed that I can't talk with you, hear you or profit by you before everything evaporates & fades. It will have become, to you, by next summer, a tale stale with the staleness of the ten-times told. Harry will have answered all your questions about *me*—& I have tried to anticipate yours about *him*. Tell him, with my love, that I like to think of him—& that I count upon him in the if not "great," small, hereafter. I hope he will find that his time in England has girded him for the labour of the *Crim-son*—in which I can't help wishing there were more profit visible to the outsider. I confess, & with relief, since you mention it, that *I* didn't understand why he spent so much time with the Clarks[2]— periods in which—since he *didn't* move about much—I should have been delighted to have him, rather, here. But I didn't like to reflect to him on it, lest I should seem to undermine friends of yours & Alice's—who yet didn't seem to me worth his sacrifices. However, things happen as they can—& when he comes to put in a couple of years at Oxford & take this place for his home of the period (as he will, I trust have told you that I greatly desire him to do—*both*,) he will, I hope, be more Clarkless. I grieve that he had a rough passage home—& I deplored, in advance, his long one. He will have told you about Rosina—whom you speak of as more remarkable, more "important," I think, than she quite strikes me in this ("European") light. I am, somehow, strangely sorry for her—she is so *incurably* crude & her present situation does so little for her, keeps her only with inferior people (save her sister Bay,) & makes her non-profit of Paris a painful sort of thing. She is pathetic, in spite of her high pitch, & I don't see her future. I am not, however, obliged to. I haven't, as yet, been obliged to "contribute" anything. They appear to have, the girls, some Gourlay money as yet unexpended—to count on it to see them through this winter. Their mother appears to me [to] have, even through Hunter & Hunter's whiskey position, almost nothing. What a lack we have of brilliant relations!—I expect to remain here late—till some time in December. I should *like* then to go abroad, & will do so if possible. The effect of this place is *already* to make me desire to shake off the complications & expense of De Vere Gardens (more fundamentally, I mean, than simply by letting them furnished,) & I shall probably do so at no distant date. I renewed my lease—not foreseeing these events—not long ago; but that will probably not prevent, as my proprietors can get, on a new tenant, by letting me off, a rise. I am on the other hand very desirous not to give up 5 or 6 winter months of London in the year—they are very important to me—& I love my admirable flat. But the case will right itself—the solution arrive. I shall write at a very early day to Alice—& as it's now past midnight I will knock off. My letter is stupid & void—but I really can't *write*—I've unlearned it, & I can't express myself really with the pen's embarrassing aid. I would have dictated this—but for reasons. I say nothing of all the huge public affairs. Dreyfus *is*—I agree with you—a dénoûment to live for. But it looks to me dark for France. The U.S. remote colonies run by bosses will also be charming.[3] The *neatest* thing of all is the English Soudan success—& on the whole the cleanest, as the Dervishes are, I believe, bloody demons.[4] Good-night—good night! I embrace you all. If Harry can find time to write me 3 lines so much the better—but he mustn't worry about it. My love to Margaret Gibbens, whom it was a great pleasure to see, & who so sweetly recalled Alice! I hope your winter will be right free of everything but the command of your time for next year.

Ever your Henry.

[1] HJ probably misspelled the name. The Dibblee family was not identified.

[2] HJ is referring to the family of Joseph Thacher Clarke.

[3] The United States entered the war with Spain without any policy concerning the future of Cuba, Puerto Rico, and the Philippines, but by the fall of 1898 it was clear that the United States planned to rule the islands as colonies.

[4] The Muslim revolt in the Anglo-Egyptian Sudan, which began in 1881, was drawing to a close by 1898. The Muslims were defeated at Omdurman in September 1898. HJ's description of the Dervishes as "demons" echoes newspaper reports.

1899

Henry James's Awkward Age *appeared in serial form in 1898–99 and was published in book form in April 1899. Although not a success with the public, Henry thought it his best work thus far. In February 1899 he was working on an idea that became* The Sacred Fount, *a short novel. He was to have departed for Paris and eventually Italy on 27 February 1899, but the fire at Lamb House described in the next letter delayed his departure.*

Williams's plans for the summer were uncertain. He was due a sabbatical in 1899–1900 and toyed with the idea of spending the year and the summer before it in Europe. But he had done little work on the Gifford Lectures—the exact date of delivery was still under negotiation—and thought that his library at home would be the best place to work. The condition of his heart, however, forced his hand. In November 1898 he learned that he had a vulvular lesion and by May 1899 had decided to go to Europe and take the baths at Nauheim, a recognized center at that time for the treatment of heart disease. The heart trouble did not keep him away from another Adirondack hike in late June when he became lost and aggravated his heart symptoms.

From Henry James

LAMB HOUSE, | RYE. Thursday | March 2ᵈ 1899.
My dear William.

A most interesting letter from you to-day, enclosing one from the Newburgh Walshes, & above all the beautiful, innocent ghostly one from Father's 19ᵗʰ year.[1] How lovely & touching the latter—& how strange & antediluvian! What a beautiful hand & admirable style! I remember his telling me once in long-past years (when we were in Ashburton Place, I think,) that he had "lived" once—when very young—in a certain house in Hancock St; but he didn't mention the occasion of it, nor do I make that out now very clearly—save as an episode of the time when he had quarreled with, or seceded from, his father—on clerical or anti-clerical grounds—& had undertaken to shift for himself.   My impression is that the Hancock St time was of very brief duration.   But it's all as quaint & dim as an old faded steel-engraving, & the document is intensely precious, sacred & to be treasured.   I return it for the deepest drawer of the archives.

Your little sealed letter given me before you last returned to the U.S. is in a very private receptacle in De Vere Gardens—where I can't put my hand on it till I again have ingress there, after my "let" is up.[2]   My tenant shows signs of wanting to renew (after June,) & I shall probably assent to it (though I *might* get better terms;) therefore I don't quite [k]now when I *can* go in.   But as soon as I do you shall have the little unbroken packet.

I was at last to have started for Folkestone (but an hour hence) last Monday—to sleep there & cross the channel next day; & was to that end sitting up into the small hours of Sunday night—2 a.m.—to write some procrastinated letters.   But, alas, a *sniffing* that had engaged me in a but dimly-uneasy way for the previous hour became suddenly more intense, & I perceived smoke issuing from the crevices of the floor of the upstairs green room (Harry will know it) in which I was sitting & in which I had had a fire daily for 3 months.   I roused the sleeping Smith, & we pried & chopped up some planks—near the fireplace—to find the place on fire underneath & behind, the hearth, grate &c.   But, we got the little local fire-brigade—quickly, & they dealt with the matter discreetly & competently, not flooding me with premature water, & in fact sparing me all real damage *by* water.   But they were here till almost morning—& no wink we slept that night. It was one of the lurking tricks & traps that old houses may play you when, by a singularly exceptional omission an old hearth (on re-arranging the *rest* of a whole chimney-angle) has not been stirred on acct. of its pretty & pleasant last-century type.   That was the case in that room alone—woefully; for close beneath it were infamous old floor beams of a hundred–200-years ago, on which the hot stove *sat*—& which had not combusted before only by reason of generations of parsimonious firelessness.   The whole place had got ig-nited—but they got *at* it—mainly through the wall of the diningroom beneath, which had to be hacked open—for the fire burnt only down-ward.   The dénoûment left me with 2 rooms only partly disfigured, but wholly & fully insured.   But it was a great escape & a great warn-ing—an escape above all through the blessing of my late vigil.   Had I gone to bed in another room (where I was sleeping,) & been with my head under the bedclothes, the thing would have got a sickening start.   As it was, it was a scare & a mortal bore—but above all an

admonition—& cheaply got.   I have already arranged for repa-
rations,—reconstruction—of the most absolutely & ideally safety-
making & scientific type.   Edward Warren came down on Tuesday &
went in to the whole matter, & his London builders' foreman comes
down tomorrow to put the thing in hand.   And every other fireplace & its environment in the house is to be gone again into search-
ingly—though that is the only one that suffered, originally, an over-
sight.   The admirable new slow-combustion grate put into it—&
resting *on* the very floor almost—was, given the reckless old conditions, so long *impune,* just the fatal new wine in old bottles.   But I'm
telling you too long a story—only lest you should hear of my flurry
otherwise & take it for more serious.   I shall get off, I firmly believe,
on the 7th, leaving the work confined to the 2 rooms & in excellent
hands.   Meanwhile the season here goes on absurdly springlike,
balmy & flowery.   I pray there be no trick or trap in *this.*

But it's late again—past midnight—& I fear to confirm your oddly-
extravagant notion that I am "raining" letters right & left.   You almost too much deprecate, I think, the few I do manage—usually
after very long absolutely dumb intervals of months together—to despatch a little *bunch* of, by giving up a few mornings to arrears & with
secretarial aid.   You thus hear of several at once—but you overesti-
mate the quantity.   I write to Boott twice a year at most—to G.N.
about once in 2 years, to Charles once in 4.[3]   I'm very sorry I seem
to you to chaff Boott too much—it doesn't *appear* to me, as I write,
that I *do;* & in truth it is difficult to see what I can write him about
very austerely.   But I must try again, if possible, while I'm away (I
have a new letter from him,) & be more guarded.   More & more
doubtless, with prolonged separation, do false notes & cross-purposes
multiply—& no amount of "earnestness" avails to avert them: it's a
part of the "irony of fate!"

This makes me regret all the more that you appear to doubt of the
likelihood or desirability of coming over next summer.   Heaven
knows I understand the hugging, under every circumstance, one's
foyer—but I hoped—imagined—you were in the launched *stage.*   I
don't yet grasp—am mystified & mixed as to—*when* you give your 1st
Gifford course. Won't you let me definitely know when you next
write?   And when—by which I mean as *soon* as—it does become at
all clear whether you sail or abide (this summer) I shall also be very
glad to know.   It may make some difference in my own movements—
the time I stay abroad &c.   But I intensely desire to be back betimes; & I shall pray for your advent, unless you see very vivid reasons

against it: which unfortunately—with the recollection of your last time's *épreuves*—I can more or less imagine. Only you'll have a haven *here* that you didn't have then.

I'm sorry to say I *do*—most deplorably see "people" looming up at every step of a fresh Italiänische Reise—the bane, the curse, now, of that never more to be indefendably tasted land—adulterated at present in every mouthful. These 2 last months of sovereign solitude that I've enjoyed here! But abroad it's all a battle—from the waylaying Emmets in Paris, and the waylaying Bourgets at Costebelle, onwards. Well, I must fight—! Goodnight—12.45, & all's well! I wrote longfully to Harry the other day. I re-embrace you all & am your constant

Henry

P.S. Your non-allusion to Bob gives me peace—& I hope stands for the same for *you*.

¹ The letter, dated 13 January 1830, is addressed to Isaac Wilber Jackson (1804–1877), professor of physical sciences at Union College, and describes the senior Henry's brief period in Boston at the age of eighteen. He had dropped out of Union College for a time in a conflict with his father over money.

² In 1892 before departing for home, WJ had left his will in HJ's care.

³ Grace Norton and Charles Eliot Norton.

To Henry James

Cambr. March 19. 99

Dear H.—

Your long letter telling of the fire came a few days since. What an escape you had! and how providential that you hadn't gone to bed. I am very sorry, all the same, for the annoyance, which must be very great. It makes one tremble for ones own house, wooden as it is. But we *thought* we had every source of exposure from hearths, chimneys and furnace pipes, secured. Our Syracuse premises had a small fire this winter—I forget whether I told you—from which after putting things in *better* condition than they were before, we still had 96 dollars surplus from the insurance money. I hope your fire may be equally profitable. The Windsor Hotel in N.Y. a very handsome structure, to which Alice and I went when we were married, was burnt yesterday, in *half an hour,* with great loss of life, and injury.—I suppose you are already on the Continent, and I can only urge incognito and brutal *disregard* of all your social duties. It is the only way of safety. Simply cut people. Solitude is a vital neccessity at certain times. I wish *I* had a good holiday, to visit the small towns of Italy in the Springtime, all alone.* But I doubt if it ever comes!

You ask about our definite plans, sabbatical, Gifford, and the like.

Harry & Billy are going to spend the summer in the Rocky Mountains or rather the Oly[m]pic Range farther west, in Oregon chiefly, I imagine, as hirelings at $300 a year of the U.S. forestry commission. A charming fellow named Fisher, who spent last year in the Californian Sierras on the Biological Survey got them into it, and they will probably be in a very good gang. I wish that Bill might develope professionally into a forester or landscape gardener. This will be a coup d'essai for him. Harry takes it for the 'culture' involved. It will be monotonous—a *census* of the trees; but awfully wholesome to the soul and body to be always in those wonderful woods, and I'm sure it is incomparably the finest possible way for them to spend their vacation. Also patriotic.

They being removed, we have offered our Chocorua place to let; and with the younger children with the Salters there, Alice and I will spend most of the summer here in Cambridge, drudging away at the Gifford work. I get no time to do anything at it these weeks. The interruptions are interminable. *Plaise a Dieu* that I get the job finished by October! It requires wide-ranging use of books, so I must be near my own Library and that of the College. What I aim at is to leave, with the lectures finished, by Oct. 1st., immediately proceed to give them at Edinburgh, (2 a week, making a 5 weeks job), then proceed, to Munich probably, to pass the winter, and write up the next years course, with books that I take along, I can do it more out of my own head than the first course The ideal thing would be to come back to England in August, letting Alice & the children return in September, whilst I should stay on till Christmas in Scotland giving my lectures, and paying a substitute for that part of my year's work at home. But I don't know yet whether the Harvard authorities will allow *dergleichen;* and this whole scheme, localities and all, is liable to be modified in all sorts of ways by the course of events.—The house here in Cambridge is offered to rent, we retaining occupation till the fall; and the idea is, if we go abroad, to take Bill, Peg, & Tweedy, while Harry stays in the Graduate school here, making up his mind what next to do. I should *rather* stay at home for the lecture-writing business—I dread the inconveniences and possible lack of books abroad. But our social existence here is so time-robbing and complicating, and withal gives so much responsible hard work to poor Alice, that it is our duty to go, whatever accrues to me. Moreover at a place like Munich, the children will not only get German, but Peggy & Tweedy can start horseback riding, swimming etc., & have music teaching cheap.   Peg is already at the piano with some success.

The Gifford money will make me feel comparatively easy.   And I wish that I might get, the second summer, a little wholly irresponsible travelling, which does me so much good.   You've no idea of the good memories of that Californian trip.

The great excitement *here* is the war upon the Filipinos; though I am sorry to say that the rest of the country seems perfectly stolid under the infamy.   The old human instincts of war-making and conquest sweep all principles away before them.   The present state of things is due simply to abominable stupidity and bungling on the part of those in charge of affairs, both in Washington and on the spot.   No experience, and consequently no imagination.   If the magnificent little Aguinaldo escapes and holds out all summer, there's a chance that the country's consciousness will become enlightened and the loathsome republican machine ultimately driven out of power.   I think I sent you a letter of mine to the Transcript.   Herein follow a couple more.[1]   Also Bob's only signs of life for several months.   His mind is evidently weakening.   But what a caricature of father he is beginning to be; and how poor father would writhe at the spectacle.

Ed. Rod has just finished a course of lectures here, and gone.   To us not attractive!   He may be "shy"—but at any rate he's the dullest, most inferior companion, for a frenchman, or would-be frenchman, that I ever saw.   He bro't an invitation to me to give a "Conférence" next winter at Paris, which naturally I declined.

The blessed month of March is here, with its strange inner movement of dissolution and gestation, its wintry present and security of better hope.   I love it above all times, for the soul seems to want outlook and potentiality more than aught else, and March gives that.—I am putting through the press a little vol of popular lectures on psychol. &c., which I manufacture at my own expense, & give to Holt on commission, and which I hope to sell by the hundred outright to the english Longmans.   I am curious to see what the result will be on receipts.   The initial outlay is considerable, for I have to *give away* 3 or 4 hundred copies.[2]   Good bye, dear brother.   Do enjoy yourself on the Continent, especially in Italy.   Of course when we get abroad we expect to pay you a good long visit at Rye.   But apart from that, I imagine that the Continent will be our better abode.

There is a sense of responsibility and a heaviness in England that weigh on my vacation desiring soul.

Affectionately thine   W.J.

[*]Would I might do it for a while with *you!*

[1] After some hesitation, President McKinley, a Republican, became an advocate of the policy of annexation.   On 1 March 1899 WJ published a letter to the editor in the *Boston Evening Transcript* on "The Philippine Tangle."   A second letter was published on 4 March and another one, in the *New York Evening Post,* on 10 March. These letters and other anti-imperialist writings are reprinted in *ECR*.

[2] In an effort to increase his income, WJ published *Talks to Teachers on Psychology* himself, using Henry Holt & Co. only as a distributor.

Henry James's visit to his friends Paul and Minnie Bourget at Hyères on the French Riviera proved awkward. Paul Bourget had converted to Catholicism—a conversion that Henry thought was more a matter of social position than of sincere faith. And the two men differed in their opinions about the Alfred Dreyfus affair, Henry very sympathetic with the defenders of Dreyfus, while Paul Bourget, who was suspected of being anti-Semitic, believed Dreyfus guilty.

From Henry James

LE PLANTIER | COSTEBELLE | HYÈRES. April 2ᵈ 1899.

Dearest William,

I greatly appreciate the lucidity & liberality of your so interesting letter of the 19ᵗʰ telling me of your views & prospects for next summer &c—of all of which I am now able to make the most intimate profit.   I enter fully into your reasons for wanting to put in the summer quietly & concentratedly in Cambridge—so much that with work unfinished and a spacious house & library of your "very own" to contain you, I ask myself how you can be expected to do anything less.   Only it all seems to mean that I shall see you all but scantly & remotely.   However, I shall wring from it when the time comes every concession that can be snatched, & shall meanwhile watch your signs & symptoms with my biggest opera-glass (the beautiful one, one of the treasures of my life,) que je vous dois.

Nothing you tell me gives me greater pleasure than what you say of the arrangements made for Harry & Billy in the forest prime-val—& the vision of their drawing therefrom experiences of a sort that I too miserably lacked (poor Father!) in my own too casual youth. What I most of all feel, & in the light of it conjure you to keep doing for them, is their being *à même* to contract local saturations & attachments in respect to their *own* great & glorious country, to learn, & strike roots into, its infinite beauty, as I suppose, & variety. *Then* they won't, as I do now, have to assimilate but half-heartedly the alien splendours—inferior ones too, as I believe,—of the indigestible Midi of Bourget & the Vicomte Melchior de Vogüe, kindest of hosts & most brilliant of *commensaux* as I am in the act of finding both these personages. The beauty here is, after my long stop-at-home, admirable & exquisite; but make the boys, none the less, stick fast & sink up to their necks in everything their *own* countries & climates can give de pareil & de supérieur. Its being that "own" will double their *use* of it.—I at last got away from home & spent 16 days in Paris, where I was "very, very kind" (& easily & comfortably so,) to Leslie & Rosina E.,—Bay being (then,) still in England, where success will be eventually, I think, quite within her grasp. I breakfasted, dined, theatre'd, museumed; walked & talked them (sans compter constant tea & little cakes,) & left them a souvenir on my departure (what I, for the moment, *could*.) I've been here a week & depart tomorrow or next day. It has been rather a tension—so utterly inapt have I become for staying with any one for more than 24 hours; but my year-by-year repeated postponements, the preparations & (material) conciliations, the loveliness of the place &c have made it the very least I could do. Both B. & his wife have been profusely kind & considerate. Their *train de vie* is a wondrous mark of prosperity & success (beyond even what I understand,) & this little estate (—2 houses—near together—in a 25-acre walled "parc" of dense pine & cedar, along a terraced mountain-side, with exquisite views inland & to sea,) is a precious & enviable acquisition. The walks are innumerable, the pleasant "wildness["] of the land (universally accessible) only another form of sweetness, & the light, the air, the noble, graceful lines &c, all of the 1st order. It's classic—Claude—Virgil. Vogüe, the only other guest (working almost all day, however, for dear life, at the serial novel he is running—almost ended—in the *Revue*)[1] is an interesting & very "consummate" specimen of the gentilhomme français turned journalist, novelist &c. All the same, they make me homesick. I treat the "Affaire" as none of my business (as it isn't,) but *its* power to make one homesick in France, & the French air, every hour & everywhere to-day, is not small.   It *is* a country en décadence. Once one *feels* that, nothing—on the spot—corrects the impression. However, I must glide—I can't go into details—& I seem to have spent all of *every* precious a.m. since I left Rye in writing letters.   I all the more, again, bless *your* sacrifice of time as per your last.   I expect to get to Genoa on the 4th or 5th April & there to make up my mind as to how I can best spend the following 8 weeks, in Italy, in evasion & seclusion.   Unhappily I *must* go to Rome & Rome is infernal.   But I shall make short work of it.   My nostalgia for Lamb House is already such as to make me capable de tout.   *Never* again will I leave it!   I don't take you up on the Philippines—I admire you & agree with you too much.   You have an admirable eloquence. But the age is *all* to the vulgar!   Bob's letters most curious, yet rather comforting, if it be not cynical to say so, as an indication of shrinkage (with the weakening mind) of his terrible "personality."   Blessed is his long stay at Dansville.   Farewell, with a wide embrace,

Ever your   Henry.

[1] *Les Morts qui parlent* by Eugène Marie Melchior, vicomte de Vogüé, appeared in the *Revue des Deux Mondes* in six installments from 1 February to 15 April 1899.

To Henry James

Chocorua, May 12 '99[1]

Dear Henry,

Your letter congratulating the boys on their Western trip was a benediction and an exquisite piece of literature, to receive a prominent place in your posthumous "remains."   I should have thanked you for it at the moment, but had so many other things to say, notably about our european plans that I have stored it up until now.   On our total situation, there is much to say.   I had such queer cardiac symptoms last summer, that in November I had my heart examined. It was rather a shock to find a murmur that revealed a slight valvular lesion.   I have grown no worse all winter, and was examined anew last week with the result of showing no progress.   It is also ausgemacht to my satisfaction that I *need* expect no progressive deterioration in a case as slight as this.   Very likely the heart has accommodated itself already to the valvular insufficiency, and there will be an end of the "organic" sysptoms, equilibrium having been reached. Certainly I have no symptoms of impaired circulation; and the symptoms which I do have are all those of nervous perturbation, ascribable to fatigue and overstrain of the organ. I may live as long with this as without it, so my spirits, which from the first were curiously little affected (the family being fairly well provided for in case of my sublation) are now entirely in equilibrium. I wrote you that our provisional plan was to spend the summer doing Gifford work in Cambridge. The later scheme, not to be fully determined on till the end of next week, is to leave on July 15th. for Nauheim a german bath place (in Hesse, I think) whose specialty is heart trouble, and spend a few weeks there. I confess I rather dread the continuous labor here, and it is just as well that I should be informed as early as possible of the regimen which a place like Nauheim uses in cases like my own. I am certainly not going to become hipped about the organ— or alter any of my ways of life unneccessarily, but perhaps for the very reason of emboldening me, I ought to know betimes the dodges and opinions of such a place.

After that, say Sept. 1. I shall have one year in which to have written 2 courses and delivered one course of Gifford lectures—2 vols of 300 pp. each. It will be a tight squeeze, at my rate of work, and I must not waste any time at all in shilly-shallying or indecision, but determine where to settle and get into working equilibrium and stay. There is Munich, there is Weimar there is Mecklenburg. I ought by rights to be near a library. Were it not for the social responsibilities of every sort inevitable in case we went to England, I confess I should feel strongly tempted to settle in some country place there. But I do shrink most awfully from them, from either accepting or having to decline invitations from strangers. Its a white man's burden— whereas in Germany all seems light, passive, and purely refreshing. I can't well express what that stodgy lack of "lift" is, that rubbing in of an old dull stupid heavy and tyrannical order, which I associate with everything english, from the common people upwards. The continental common people are a gift from heaven! What I should like to do anyhow would be to repair straight from Nauheim (in case we went there) to your house for two or three weeks (Alice and I) the children being still at Vevey, and settle in England (largely by your advice) till the 1st course be delivered (January or February) *then* go to the Continent, for good. Send any suggestions or comments that occur to you! I will let you know as soon as our decision is irrevocably made.—We are up here getting the house ready for the summer, altho by this time it is unlikely that any tenant will offer to come. All sorts of heavy and expensive repairs. I go down on

Monday (this is Saturday) Alice will have to stay ten days. Your account of Bourget's place was luminous and wonderful. I hope the home sickness for Rye has faded away. Love from Alice.

Ever thine W.J.

[1] The date may be wrong since WJ states that he is writing the letter on Saturday, which was 13 May.

From Henry James

Hotel d'Europe | Rome | June 3^d. [1899]

Dearest William & dearest Alice: never more dear!

I am tremendously moved by both your letters—following each other at 48 hours' interval (though one is of May 12—Chocorua, & the other of the 21st) & I indeed literally vibrate too much to your situation to respond with quite requisite command of my nerves & my ideas. These find however an immediate *sfogo* in the immense desire practically to help you. Over William's revealed delicacy—or symptom, or whatever one may most luminously call it—I find myself interested & even agitated to the depths. But it's a question of care & of taking account—& blessed & precious are all such—for they dispose in their own high way of so many others! They are the aids & conveniences & reinforcements of life. Oh, how I want to assist in the reinforcement that this one will bring you! Every scrap of your place & every articulation of your needs preoccupies, interests, animates me. If you're uncertain about the autumn & early winter—the time after you've been to Nauheim & to Rye (thank God for Nauheim, & thank God still more for Rye!) won't it help you a little to decide & feel easy, won't it weigh a little in the balance, that 34 De Vere Gardens is, after July 5th, when my tenant goes out, wholly at your service, yearning for you & aching for you, so that you've only to consider it a convenient, commodious, excellent resting-place & refuge for the interval before Edinburgh & eke for all intervals after. It will be servantless—the Smiths being at Rye with me—but *that*, in London, is easily remedied. It would give me such a joy that you shld. be there & without the cost of a penny to you, save for the servants you take. There is no question of *letting* it for the autumn—it's an impossible time; & even if there were—! If my actual tenant shld. desire it again, the flat, it would only be from January—& he has given as yet no sign; also, I wd. only let to him on a rise of rent. Therefore see if *having* De Vere Gardens free, doesn't weigh with you as to the question of your autumn & winter whereabouts. Excuse me for leaping so straight at this material detail—I do it only in my desire to show some concrete form for my yearning to succour you. I feel for you both a tenderness that would fairly *se démêner* in your service if it could. But there won't be any need of that. To have you at Lamb House as soon as ever you can come—that will be the first thing to look forward to. I get back there the 30th of this month & am woefully homesick for the day. Italy has been again a thoroughly delightful experience, but my capacity for the wastefulness & *trimballage* of travel shrinks year by year, & after a few weeks I long again for my small regularities & privacies. I've been a month—a beautiful month in this place—I was 3 weeks in Venice &c, &c. I've done what I wanted here, perfectly—& I must put in 10 or 12 days in Florence to supplement it. "People," people, alas, are in spite of every precaution the eternal enemy: I say this under the weight of the fact that Marion Crawford has just besieged me in such force that I have capitulated & promised to go down 2 or 3 days hence, & spend 2 or 3 with him at his wondrous Sorrento. It will be probably a rare vision, of many things, & I've thought it, for once in my life, foolish not to take it; but it is the social trap once more, & the social trap is *everywhere*. Then, at any rate I hurry back to Florence, to Paris & to home. There has been much restorative & above all remedial & ameliorative *work* going on at L.H., every brick of it an improvement, & it will not be quite over till toward the end of the month. But a joy it will be to welcome & detain you there in the great late-summer pleasantness of the place! May all move straight & swift & smooth for you in all the coming weeks! I can't tell you, dearest William, how delicately I want to help all the future to handle you! I've heard much of Nauheim & all as a blessed source of benefit: especially last summer from the ubiquitous Bourgets (she bad as to heart & immensely strengthened,) & from Baldwin of Florence (now of Rome, but actually not here,)—besides Sydney Colvin & many of the English. Draw it mild, take in sail, in every way, till you *go*. Your last letter on Roosevelt & the Philippines (enclosed in your envelope,) commands all my admiration & sympathy. I agree with you no end—we have ceased to be, among the big nations, the one great thing that made up for our so many crudities, & made us above all superior & unique—the only one with clean hands & no record of across-the-seas murder & theft. *Terminato—terminato!* One would like to be a Swiss or a Montenegrian now. I applaud with all my heart the courage & "scathing"ness with which you drive it home.—and Margaret, dearest Alice, is to be married—which, oh, I *feel* it for you—& almost for myself. I send her my ghostly greeting on it—but oh, oh, oh! I greet your mother with real compassion. How many things you have going on! But come to me quickly & we'll manage them together. I close this to get it off without another hour for the delay that must be see[m]ing to you so great—the time taken—for my response. Splendid *this* mention of Harry & Billy. I hunger for the sight of Peggy & Francis. *Do* find a moment to write me 3 lines, even, before you sail.

> Ever your *tenerissimo*   Henry James

To Henry James

> Adirondack Lodge, June 21. 99

Dearest Henry,   Your heartbreakingly beautiful and loving letter from Rome of the 3rd came to me yesterday, forwarded by Alice, who had opened and read it. And I, who through all these years have "claimed" that the Jameses were deficient in simple family affection, and that celtic doubleness of nature and XIXth century "critical spirit" had warped us far away from those anchorages! We live and learn; and even I live as if a slave to family affections! Local affections I have too, and patriotic ones, though the latter now-a-days have bitter bread to eat. I thank you for your echo on the Philippine adventure. "Terminata, terminata," indeed is our ancient national soul! It was verily something of a fiction always, but one of those fictions which, once ingrained in tradition, grow into habits and realities. I never thought it would crumble without *an instant's* hesitation. The *shallowness* of public feeling in the matter is the incredible thing. One's best friends, whom one always supposed suckled on the same ideals with ones self, are ruthless and determined advocates of conquest at any price. "We *can't* go back" etc. These passions of pride and war and mastery are the deepest thing in the race! As for me, it drives away my sleep at night to think of the relapse into savagery of this country, that was so safely out of the inheritance of its traditions. All we have done so far to "elevate" the natives has been (apparently) to open some three hundred "saloons" in Manila. But *basta così!* When I got on this subject I can't stop. It is like the Dreyfuss case—one cannot mention it in general company, but it works all the worse within.

My ridiculous cardiac weakness seems to have opened all the

sluices of pathos in your nature.   Dont take it seriously—it doesn't
menace either longevity or life—it only checks me in too rapid moun-
tain-climbing—a bad check to my personal self-consciousness, to be
sure, for that resource hitherto has been my main hold on primeval
sanity and health of soul.   I undoubtedly strained my heart in racing
with those greyhounds of Goldmarks last summer, and afterwards in
the Sierras.   But I'm glad I had the experience, even at that price!
The subjective symptoms have almost disappeared this spring; and
now I am back in this sweet-aired sanctuary, all alone in the hotel,
taking the old walks through the forest, very slowly, and with no
discernable effects save good ones.   My going to Nauheim is only to
get "points"—not that I need any present treatment; and I am so
refreshed already with my ten days vacation that it *may* be we shall
decide to stay and work in Chocorua till the fall and then sail straight
for England.   The Gifford business, it cannot be denied is a *very*
heavy job for my powers to put through in one year; though if I but
had the time, I have little doubt of my ability to write the couple of
volumes required, and inject into them a good deal of variety and
vitality.   But the time is fearfully short.   Yet I couldn't have got at it
a day earlier.   The offer of de Vere Gardens is a great insurance in
case of shipwreck, but we shall only repair to it as a last resort, if
everything else fails.   London is (as G. Meredith says) to me "instead
of a sky a ceiling," and all the indoor comfort fails to compensate for
the out of door *banalité,* of which the enormous *scale* is so oppressive.
Moreover the climate seems profoundly to disagree with me.   I must
erst get acclimated.   I fatally shrink also from society, and feel as if
some country place, not too far away from access to a city, were the
desideratum.   Alice too will be happy enough in the country.

I am right glad to hear that your trip to Italy this time has been
more prosperous from the social (or rather anti-social) point of view
than your last one was.   I wish that I might look forward next spring
to a real tour through italian cities—to be let loose on a new one
after brkfst. is one of the good things that life affords.   It *may* be
possible yet.   I hope your visit to Crawford was remunerative.   I
haven't yet read one of his novels!   I have just finished Meredith's
amazing marriage[1]—an experience of real *torture* for his *abominable*
perversities and crudities of manner and diction—and yet one must
go on on for the sake of the heroic moral atmosphere and personages,
none less than seven feet high.   But the hideous subjectivity and jolt-
ingness and zigzagging perversity and artificiality of it, throws one
into the arms of the latin genius again.   A propos of which I will

send you a truly mellow and marrowy poem entitled Lucifer by my colleague George Santayana.[2]   I think it a most distinguished work of art.   Item I send my own last volume, for the sake of the *last three* "talks" it contains—not the psychology part.[3]   Good bye, and a 1,000,000 thanks for your letter and offers of service.   Harry should have left last night for the Pacific slope.   Billy follows on the 30th. I enclose a letter from Dick Fisher, the head of the boy's gang, who accompanied Peggy to spend a few weeks at his mothers small boarding school in Berkshire.   It gives a pleasant touch both as to Dick and Peg.

Your loving   W.J.

You are not likely to cross a party of young woman containing the Goldmark girls.   If you do, make up to the latter.   Pauline is the best girl I know in this low world, though ultra simple in mind.

[1] George Meredith, *The Amazing Marriage* (1895).

[2] George Santayana, *Lucifer: A Theological Tragedy* (1899).

[3] WJ is referring to the three talks to students that he added to *Talks to Teachers* (1899).

In the short time Henry James had lived in Lamb House, he had become strongly attached to his country home and in the summer of 1899 eagerly seized the opportunity to buy it. It is hard to understand the motives behind William's cool response, unless he really thought that Henry was engaging in a risky financial speculation. William's reply clearly opened some of Henry's old wounds and the exchange over Lamb House is among the most animated in the whole correspondence.

From Henry James

LAMB HOUSE, | RYE. July 31st 1899.

My dear William.

I am living from day to day in the hope of hearing from you at Nauheim & getting thereby an *address*—& meantime I launch this into the vague of *posterestante* as I launched a few lines (with an enclosure of a letter that had come for you,) a few days since.   In that letter I told you of Baldwin being at Nauheim (for himself) & already

on the lookout for you.   Within the last couple of days I have wished
you were nearer to you,[1] that I might consult with you a little as to
a material matter touching me nearly that has suddenly come up—
but with separation & time (or rather loss of time) interfering I shall
have to shift for myself & act on my own lights—& this I can easily
do.   I don't mean—don't be alarmed—that I've received a proposal
of marriage!   I only mean that Arthur Bellingham, my landlord, has
suddenly died, in S. Africa, & his widow inheriting this house has,
without delay—*from* S. Africa, where she is & belongs—offered to *sell*
it to me—with the studio—for £2000.   It is a rapid & *inespéré* realization of what I hoped for, for my peace of mind, from the 1$\underline{st}$ moment
I knew, as a tenant, the place.   Of the absolute felicity (i.e. desirability,) & urgency of my seizing the opportunity there is not the dimmest
shadow of a doubt.   It fixes me, in security, *ideal* suitability & safety,
for life, in a blessed little *home*, which I've tried & tested now *à fond*, &
of which nothing could possibly exceed the congruity with my needs,
actual & future, my purse & my desires.   It relieves me of change &
barter of landlords over my head, of nervousness, uncertainty, South
African second husbands, sales & other dangers.   *And* it's of a (given
the little place as I now find & love it,) DIVINE reasonableness & modi-
city as to terms.   The only thing is that I haven't *got* £2000, to pay
down, *disponibles*, & I must borrow the money.   I'm so *outside* of every
business contrivance & proceeding that, were you at hand I should
ask you for a wrinkle or two on this head.   But there is a perfectly
simple & convenient course open to me, I judge—which is to go to
Brown Shipley & Co. who have been my bankers ever since I came
abroad with Aunt Kate & Alice in 1872 (save during the 1874–75 that
I spent in America) to this moment, & with whom my relations have
uninterruptedly been of the most genial & unclouded nature—I
never having by a penny overdrawn my account, & never done anything but distinctly *underdraw* it, &c.   I shall propose to them the
transaction:—to lend me the money that I require, on the security
of the house itself—banks here do that here by one's depositing with
them the title-deeds.   I shall probably not have to borrow the full
sum—I have at hand *some* ready money—& I shall be able to pay it
off, on my present blessed basis of operative quiet & comfort, very
steadily & not at all slowly. I feel that you would agree with me that
this [is] a better way to do the thing—much—than any other—, and
when I *have* done it I shall feel a peace that passeth understanding.
If I then (next January—early next year or so) arrange to definitely
get *rid* of the remainder of my lease of De Vere Gardens (as I've made

up my mind to do—I don't want to keep them on 5 or 6 years more to live in only 3 or 4 months of the year—my certain future *maximum* for London,) I shall be on a footing of which the idealism brings, as I reflect on it, the tears to my eyes.   They are indeed just now predominantly tears of joy at the thought of acquiring this blessed little house so promptly & so cheaply.   The Bellinghams (for Arthur B. will have—I have reason to know—arranged the matter with his wife before his death,) are treating me with excellent consideration & respect—& the occasion is presenting itself exactly as it was my dream that it should.   *So vogue la galère.*   I go up to London for 48 hours day after tomorrow (if not tomorrow p.m.) & I will let you know of future developments.   Meanwhile I languish for your own news; & am full of impatience to hear your overland-journey is achieved & your situation at Nauheim defined.   Don't let me languish to[o] long, & give my love to Baldwin over & above Alice & Peggotty.

Ever your affectionate   Henry

[1] A slip for 'me'.

To Henry James

Villa Luise, Nauheim | Aug. 2nd. 1899
Dear H.—Your letter rê the purchase of Lamb House, has just arrived.   Don't be in a hurry—no one will gobble it—till you have consulted some business friend—I don't mean as to the buying, which I suppose wise anyhow, but as to the price and terms.   Sellers of houses are invariably willing for the sake of a prompt sale, to take less than they first ask.   What they ask is what they hope for, not what they expect.   As for raising the cash, do you know that they want it "down"?   May they not let some of it go on mortgage?   If they want all the cash down, you can raise part of it doubtless on a mortgage from Brown Shipley & Co., and you can raise the rest on a mortgage on your Syracuse share, or the whole of it on that, if need be.   B., S., & Co. are probably looking for better interest than the regular mortgage interest in England is, and a Savings bank would be a better source to apply to.   These latter lend most of their money on mortgages, but never lend more than ⅔ of the value of the property.   You can't possibly raise the full amount with only the house as security, except at some exorbitant rate of interest.   In Boston 4% mortgages can be got.   In Cambridge 5%.   At Syracuse 4½%.   Provision can be made for gradual payment of the money borrowed, & to have this

to do is a great incentive to economy. I have paid all but $1100 of the $8000 I raised on my Cambridge house to buy out my portion of Bob's share. I should try first to reduce the price by offering £1500 or £1600. *Don't be afraid!* Then find if they want all cash down or are willing that some of the price should be secured by a mortgage on the house. If all cash, find out what the best terms are which a local savings bank will give (as to amount loaned, interest, and facility of repayment)—and get the rest from Syracuse. As some of it will in any case have to come from Syracuse, and as, the estate being undivided, we are each severally responsible for the full money to be raised, in case of foreclosure, the quicker the machinery for that is set in motion the better. We might both send Mrs. Gibbens, who now receives the rents a power of attorney to sign for us. You ought then to pay in the principal at the rate of $1000 or more a year.—I rejoice heartily with you in this windfall of a chance.—It is getting very dark on the Balcony where I write this, so I only say that Alice should have arrived yesterday at the Ceresoles at Vevay. I am in for a regular "Kur"—how I *loathe* the name, but the conditions of life are agreeable in material respects. Baldwin is a great comfort—how he worships *you!*—and since our hearts have to stop anyhow altogether, I don't know why one should take a gradual renunciation of service on their part so ill. Nevertheless this whole "Curwesen" is a vile thing for me to feel myself again so unexpectedly part & parcel of.—Consult some business friend. You must have some!

Lovingly yours   W.J.

To Henry James

[Nauheim] Aug. 2nd. [1899] | 2nd letter

Dear H.

Baldwin has just dropt in and I have communicated to him the contents of your letter. He thinks 2000 a very extravagant price for that house in view of the fact that you told him the present proprietors paid not very long ago 1200 for it. It *cannot* have increased in value. You see, the best way is to compute on a basis of *rent*. At a 2000 pound price (= 10,000 dollars) you would be paying $500 of mortgage interest (at 5%); and the taxes on the place, besides insurance, repairs, etc. (Perhaps you pay the latter now.) Certainly from $700 to 800 would be your rental. I don't know what the place costs you annually now, but it is probably a good deal less than that. Hasn't your lease a good many years yet to run? And is such a place *promptly* saleable, or lettable, in case you should ever wish, or be obliged, to give it up?

You ought to consult some wary business friend in England before you in any way commit yourself. You may depend on it that they are counting on an ideally maximum price from you when they ask you 2000 pounds.

In haste W.J.

From Henry James

LAMB HOUSE, | RYE. Aug 4$^{\underline{th}}$ 1899.

Dear William.

Your two letters make me feel that I have disquieted you more than I meant & drawn upon myself & my project a colder blast than I could apprehend. But I beg you to be reassured. I do, strange as it may appear to you, in this matter, know more or less what I'm about. I didn't mean at all to leave any question about the wisdom of my buying this house, & buying it for every reason of peace of mind, absence of worry as to what may become of it over my head in a place where property is steadily increasing in value, & where *not* to have anything in the air or in the background of a nature possibly compromising to one's *basis*, is for me an absolutely necessary condition of fruitful work. Besides I think I am not unreasonable in letting it count for something that I am intensely, piously *fond* of it—so fond of it that to own it will be a direct operative good, a source of nourishing & fertilizing pleasure to me. At my age it should surely be something that one *wants*, simply, so much to do a thing—for I am not yet wholly senile. Let me earnestly beg of you not to discuss the matter with Baldwin, who was here but one night, and whose judgment of the value of the house I can't for a moment accept as in any way qualified. He knows *nothing* of the place, the conditions, the situation of Rye (as regards houses, demand, the *extreme* opposite for everything here,) & he scarcely appeared to me to appreciate the place at all. His pronouncement that £2000 is a "very extravagant price" would be grotesque if it were not perfectly ignorant. (For God's sake do not repeat to him *this;* but, PLEASE, drop the subject altogether—with him. I *hate* its being talked of with any one but Alice.) The sum in question is in fact, so far from being excessive,

as to be, as things stand to-day at Rye, extremely reasonable. The
house *was* bought some 15 years ago for £1200 (I *believe*—though I
only know it on mere hearsay—it may have been for more: I know
it was thought an extraordinary bargain.) This was in the last years
just before Rye had begun to be a great golfing-place, before the
small "craze" about its being pretty & picturesque & just the place to
have—to get—an old house &c., had set in. Since that time everything has gone up; there are 50 applications to the principal real-
estate agent (for old—for *any*—houses) for one that he is able in any
way to meet, & "picturesque["] building is breaking out all over. A
few years after buying the house my late landlord bought the studio
which abuts on the garden & more or less commands it. This is a
little *old* Wesleyan chapel (not at all ugly,) which he heard the Catho-
lics *and* (or) the Salvationist army people were in treaty for (the little
Catholic community here have tried since to sub-hire it;) on which
he pounced in & acquired it. I don't know how much more he paid
for it; the possession was vital to the privacy of the garden & it must
have cost a certain number of hundred pounds. He afterwards
spent money on arranging it as a studio, putting in big north-light
&c. It is the house *and* the studio that are offered me for £2000—&
I assure you that no one here thinks the proposal excessive—by
which I mean rather (for no one knows it here,) none of *my* friends
who have seen it & with whom I have spoken of it, *would* think it
so. With one of them, my very excellent friend & architect Edward
Warren I have discussed & consulted at every step, of the way. He
knows, by profession, experience, taste &c, the whole matter of
houses, all over England, as no one I know does—they are the very
stuff in which he labours, & he is full of soundness, thrift reason &
sense. I have again & again spoken with him of the contingency of
purchase on just this basis & with his fullest approval. Now that it
has come he wrote me yesterday: "As to Lamb House, this is great &
good news—brave news indeed. Putting house & studio together at
£100 (a very modest rent indeed—they'd fetch from £120 to £130, I
should think) £2000 is only 20 years purchase, & 25 is what is almost
always thought reasonable. It is of a piece with the admirable mod-
eration of the Bellingham-Dawes (Dawes = solicitor) combination, as
shown in the first instance, that it doesn't seek to exploit this occasion.
I am immensely happy to think you will buy—& buy well in all senses.
As a mere commercial investment you will do, I think, extremely
well." Warren himself would have taken the house like a shot, on
the chance of eventual purchase, if I hadn't. He came down here

with me to look at it when I first came & practically arranged the whole matter for me.   And he is utterly disinterested, practical & wise.   I allow no weight whatever to Baldwin's judgment as against his.   I don't think Baldwin really *saw* the house.

Aug. 5th—I could write no more last night—I had been to town for 2 days & was very tired; & meanwhile this a.m. comes Alice's letter with your postscript.   Please tell Alice that I thank her a hundred thousand times & will write to her the very 1st moment I can.   I am too busy with interrupted work, due for near dates, to make up for, & can't here express myself to her fully.   On the question of her admirable offer, please say to her meanwhile that she needn't give it—nor you either, *any* such question, the ghost of a thought.   I find on going into the matter, that I shall not have to raise or borrow a *penny*.   I have no payments whatever to make till February 3^{d} 1900, & then only of a sum of money which I have already & have had for some time in B. S. & Co's hands, (besides another balance at the Rye bank,) & which, 6 months hence, will be but a fraction of my cash funds.   These £800 (I have with B. S & Co £900) are the *only* purchase payment I shall have to make.   The other £1200 are in a mortgage on the house at 4 percent, in most respectable hands here, & which is eminently content to remain, as I shall let it.   I can easily— *sans me vanter*—pay it off in a year.   But that is a separate matter, which I can't go into now, & as to which—in short, enough: surely at my age, with full possession of one's facts & one's *data*, & with no burden of precipitate or foolish acquisition (of *any* acquisition,) compromising one's past, one may ask to be quietly trusted.   I have *accepted* (I accepted after 3 days of earnest meditation,) Mrs. B.'s offer. I was all advised & matured about it in advance.   After I heard of A. Bellingham's death I expected the step, from his widow, & wrote of it to E. Warren.   He came down here 3 or 4 days afterwards—10 days ago—& I had one more, as I had already had fifty, talks with him.   But my acceptance was in truth only the effect of *all* the extreme desire I had had for three years, ever since I 1st laid eyes on the house while at Point Hill, to see myself in it as my *home* for the rest of my days.   This achieved sense will be inestimably precious to me—will *do* far more for me than anything else *can*. There is no solid sense of home without it, & nothing could have possibly been more mature & more accumulated than this long vision—for I nourished it all the year *before* I could take the house.   *No* competent person would say that I don't get the realisation of it on easy terms.   I am stupefied, since you again, in your p.s. to Alice's letter again quote

him, at Baldwin's *acharnement* (as to the "bad speculation any way")
against the place.   I can only say that if that was his impression it
was wholly different from that of *every* other person who has seen it—
so different that I can only believe he had no intelligent or informed
impression at all.   I was in fact struck with his giving no positive sign
of it (one is fairly *used* to it in visitors & quite misses the absence; &
I attributed it to his want of English terms of comparison &c.)   I
repeated to him with no *responsible* intention—only picturesquely, as
it were—the £1200 legend, which came to me in some vague &
roundabout way—while I was at Point Hill—that I have forgotten, &
I have never heard a word about the matter since.   It *may* be true (I
don't know who knows) or quite incorrect.   I only *do* remember—as
I said above—hearing *then* that, thanks to the indifference & eccen-
tricity of old Davies Lamb, the then owner,[1] the thing was thought
extraordinarily cheap.   As the best house in Rye, it has even a small
element of "fancy" value.   If it will reassure you at all I will ask Edward Warren to write to you—but I daresay this longwindedness of
mine will prove for you a sufficient dose.   I meant to ask you—to
convey that I did so—to please take the wisdom of the *intention* of
purchase on my part for granted—as carrying with it, on my behalf,
various presumptions sufficient.   *You,* after all, have bought & built
&c, & I have never wanted faith!   I *may,* of course, have made a
mistake—any one, every one, always may: but all I can say is that if,
feeling as I have felt, consistently, from the first, I had let this present
opportunity pass instead of *acting,*—for the very joy of it—I should
have had to sit down, in utter depression, as without faith in myself
or *any* courage for *any* act.   My joy has shrivelled under your very
lucid warnings, but it will re-bloom.   My misfortune, & it's a great
one for occasions like this, is that, as an individual of imagination
(& "nerves") all compact,[2] (& more & more the older I grow,) I am
temporarily accessible, in an extreme degree, to "suggestion"—from
any quarter that supervenes, or intervenes, with the remotest assurance or emphasis, & that, though all the while, in the background,
my own judgment waits in limited—partial—eclipse, absolutely certain to reappear, the other influence launches me on a sea—a torment—of sickening nervosity, in which work, attention, sleep, alas
peace, perish for the time & in which I can only wait for them to come
back, as they do, after a while, with a bound.   It is only a question of
patience & prayer.   I couldn't have *afforded* to invite you to challenge
my *datum* the other day—I know myself, alas, too well.   It's such a
rare boon for me to want anything so simply & singly as I've wanted

L.H. that, for myself, it seemed (the nature of the want,) just a rare bird to be caught. Never to catch it means a life without *any* joy!—But enough of this interminable talk. It's all but a tribute to the seriousness of your participation & the generosity of your offer of help. You will rue the day I mentioned the business at all.—During 2 days just spent in town I feel that I've practically got rid of De Vere Gdns. I hadn't—uncertain, & with practical botherations in the way of the material move, &c—really sounded my proprietors there before; but on *being* definitely sounded, they immediately responded & give me every reason to hope they will, this term, (within 2 or 3 months) take my flat (by *letting* the 6-years remainder of my lease,) off my hands. It is worth much more to them than when they let to me 16 years ago.—Tell Alice I *have* Peggie's education-scheme in perfect form for her. But je n'en peux plus,* not a word!

Ever your | Henry.

P.S. *It's a day, here, of torrid, exhausting heat.—I do heartily rejoice in the promise of Nauheim for you—though understanding your repulsion.

[1] Lamb House was completed in 1723 by James Lamb. No information about Davies Lamb was found.

[2] The allusion is to Shakespeare's *Midsummer Night's Dream*, act 5, sc. 1, lines 7–8: "The lunatic, the lover, and the poet are of imagination all compact." 'Compact' here means composed.

To Henry James

Villa Luise, Bad-Nauheim, | Aug 8. 1899

Beloved H'ry

It has filled this home with grief to find that our letters about the purchase "rubbed you the wrong way." You took them far too seriously—but I know just how you felt! Somehow I got from your first letter the impression that you were quite *rathlos* and wanted someone to talk the thing over with. I didn't gather that you had had business-advice, or know any of the facts you now tell about the rising market in Rye. Now both appear above the horizon, and of course there is nothing more to be said than "bravo" to the undertaking. Half the estate already on a mortgage, and the other half of it in cash in your own hands, too! How different a picture. Alice is only sorry she can't in any way hold out her helping hand. When one is asked for counsel—& I tho't you were asking for that—what is more appropriate than to show all the lions in the path? The other fellow's eagerness does the opposite part of the work. Baldwin's opinion was a purely financial one of one rent against the other: and he supposed, as I did, that Rye was an old stagnant place where property couldn't rise. Of the total advisability of your buying he expressed no opinion whatever. The opinion I express now is that it is the best possible thing for you to do; and I trust that it is already done irrevocably. So both Alice and I beg your pardon profoundly for giving you so bad a night, with our petty store of maxims preaching down a daughter's heart.[1] Forgive and forget! I should have told you that you have some $1200 in the Syracuse sinking fund, which *in case of need* could be taken out. Only in case of need would it be best, for at present the s.f. remains undivided, and for alterations, improvements or accidents, it is much better to have it kept so. In case you do want any money let me manage it, for a second mortgage on Lamb House would doubtless be disadvantageous.—I have now had six baths, and feel as if they were beginning to take hold. In June I got lost in the Adirondacks and converted what was to have been a "walk" into a 13-hours scramble without food and with anxiety. The result was a very much worse condition of the cardiac organ, with entirely new symptoms; so I came here in the nick of time. The life is *ultra* sedative, and the first consequence depression of spirits. But everybody here gets well & so shall I. It is painful to come to Germany again, and find ones self so much a foreigner. I have lost all my security with the language, and every body seems to speak english. A truly cultivated folk!—Will you please order a daily paper sent to me as above? The german papers give so little news. I leave the choice to you, merely saying that I get an occasional Standard from a lady in this house.[2]—I will pay the bill when I arrive.—I met Canon McColl last night—he said he knew you. Alice sends love and contrition.

Ever your affectionate | Wm.

[1] From Tennyson's *Locksley Hall,* line 94.
[2] The *Standard* was a newspaper published in London.

From Henry James

LAMB HOUSE, | RYE. August 9th [1899]
Dearest William & dearest Alice.

I have your 2 excellent letters of successive days, & indeed *yours,* dear Alice, your beautiful *first,* with its noble offer of help &c, I

haven't even yet properly acknowledged. None the less I have still
to ask you to let me make this poor scrawl serve for both of you, as
I seem to flow over into considerable lengths & am, after my long &
rather "reposeful" absence, & with time lost in London &c, since,
very much pressed with work, now that I have got back to it. Thank
heaven it is fully profitable. I am much affected by your gentle recognition of the elements of the situation here which I tried to sketch
for you, & which if you had only *been* here, would make all sketching
superfluous. I wish indeed you could only see L.H. *now*—at the
prettiest moment of the summer, with the garden in quite—its
most—profuse "herbaceous" & other bloom & looking quite charming; the purple clusters of grapes heavy in the greenhouse, the splendid bignonia throwing out its rich red flowers all up & down the
south (house) wall, the big purple clematis flushing à l'envi, & the
wisteria heavily, or, rather, lightly, draping the porch of my study.
Peace, (quite apart from these superficial influences,) has come back
to me—because it inevitably *had* to. My disposition in respect to the
house has had these 2 full years (that is since September '97) to solidify—therefore it isn't a light matter. This place is of a singular &
infallible lettability & saleability (I could sell it 3 days after completing
purchase to Edward Warren, e.g., who knows his subject *à fond* &
wd. pounce on it—or to three or four other persons happily known
to me.) But that has, thank God, NOTHING to do with the matter.
It is exactly & intensely NOT as a "speculation"—bad or good—that
I have accepted Mrs. Bellingham's offer—but because on the contrary the place is a house of rest out of which I pray heaven I may
never shift far all the rest of my days. *That* outlook is the very bribe
of bribes—the relief & rest of the "last long home." The extraordinary congruity of the little place with all my needs, conveniences,
tastes, limitations (& even extensions,) with every sort of security, sa-
lubrity & economy—& a congruity not general & approximate, but
stretching into every detail & ramification—this fact presented itself
to me as making a kind of timorous epilepsy of the idea of *passing*
her offer & committing myself afresh to the unrest of having everything thrown again into question, with my peace of mind at the mercy
of every wind of rumour that blows in this gossiping little town—as
to what they are doing—*going* to do, with L.H. (a perpetual worry &
indignity) & with the enraging sense that everything I have done to
it, & may yet inevitably do, is all done—& to *be* done—for mysterious,
contingent, unpleasant & inferior parties other than myself. Mrs. B.
is a 4ᵗʰ rate (though I believe very decent) S. African *theatrical* person,

of a hand to mouth situation, & of in every way inferior contacts & possibilities—& it's no way in the interest of one's "dignity," of the decency of one's position or one's credit here, that one should positively *elect* to "keep on" with her when one has, on such uncommonly easy terms, the chance to keep on only with one's *self.* My whole being cries out aloud for something that I can call my own—& when I look round me at the splendour of so many of the "literary" fry my confrères (M. Crawfords, P. Bourgets, Humfry Wards, Hodgson Burnetts, W. D. Howellses &c,) & I feel that I may strike the world as still, at 56, with my long labour & my genius, reckless, presumptuous & unwarranted in curling up (for more assured peaceful production,) in a poor little $10,000 shelter—once for all & for all time— *then* I do feel the bitterness of humiliation, the iron enters into my soul, & (I blush to confess it,) I *weep!* But enough, enough, enough! I am on firm ground again, & back at work, & the way is clear.   I thank you & Alice more than I can say for your offers of advances. There is not any appearance of probability *whatever* that I shall have to ask you for any of the Syracuse sinking fund. I have only to have 5 or 6 months of normal work to float comfortably over everything—& those I *shall* have.   I am touched to tears (you will think me very lachrymose!) by *your,* dearest Alice, writing to your mother to keep some of your inheritance for me. *Do,* kindly, now, write to her *not* to—before she set me down as a sponge & a failure. But it was lovely of you to have this inspiration.—You will say, doubtless:— "Why the deuce then did you write to us in an—as it were—*appealing,* consultative way at *all?*" It was the impulse to *fraternize*—put in that way—with you, over the pleasure of my purchase, & to see you glow with pride in *my* pride of possession &c.   I did so immediately— before I had seen Dawes or found out anything: which was idiotic, but gushing.   And I reckoned, alas, without Baldwin.—I have your pencil-note from Harry, in which his situation sounds rough, but his humour happy & his tone admirable.   I had, lately, a very cheering letter from him from Tacoma—which I shall answer before long, & when I have an address.   But I hope *you,* Alice, are not worrying about him.   They are evidently a very social community & paternally—not to say—maternally, governed.—I take joy in every hour of William's regimen & reaction.   He must go back next year.   His boxes have all safely come & are safely set apart.   I subscribe tomorrow to the *Chronicle* for him.   (This almost intolerable suspense of Dreyfus!)—I have Peggy's educatrix all drawn up for you—but I won't (it's too long) attempt to go into details till I see you. Mademoiselle Souvestre, a very good friend of mine, and a most distinguished & admirable woman (of 65 to-day)—daughter of the celebrated Emile—has had for many years a very highly esteemed school for girls at high, breezy Wimbledon, near London (an admirable situation)—where she has formed the daughters of many of the very good English *advanced Liberal* political & professional connection during these latter times. She is a very fine, interesting person, her school holds a very particular place (all Joe Chamberlain's daughters were there & they adore her,) & I must tell you more of her. She wd. be excellent for Peggy's French. The whole subject, in fact, demands *extreme* threshing out. She (Mlle. S.) is a special friend of the Ribots in Paris—they form her *foyer* there. But good night again— it's past midnight, & I am your doubly affectionate

Henry.

To Henry James

Villa Luise, Bad-Nauheim | Aug. 11 1899
Beloved H.—Your long and heart-melting letter of the 9th. arrives this evening, making us feel better, for the tears were not all on your side, Alice having shed some on receiving your first reply, and needing all the example of my well known fortitude to keep her from shedding many more and cursing God and dying, that very night. Even before your letter came, she had been full of regrets and misgivings lest you should interpret what she wrote as officious meddling. But you, even now seem to be melodiously imploring us to let you have something in the world, beside the memory of your childhood's happiness, that you may still call your own. Whereas we (especially Alice) were simply rapturously overflowing at the thought of your finally owning Lamb House, and *all* we wanted was to help you to get it cheaper. With the supposed data which we had, how could we avoid making the suggestions we did? I vaguely seemed to remember that the rent was less than $400 and that you had a 21 years lease. The rest followed as a matter of simple logic.—*Now,* all I can say, for both of us, is that it is an excessively tickling thought to have a brother become a sort of english squire, and that for your own sake we fairly revel in sympathetic feelings of ownership and assured possession. It will make it 10 times as interesting to us when we visit

you, to feel you as the owner of the eternal rock on which the place is rooted—even down to the fiery centre of the terrene globe—for I am sure the Bellinghams don't reserve any "mineral rights," as the man who sold me my last Adirondack patch did.   It is a great and good and holy and eke a most prudent and financially sagacious thing, dear Harry, and I am proud of you for having already done it.   Once more, forgive, forget!

I thank you for the Souvestre information.   Evidently that is to be looked after.   What Peggy most wants is a kind of hardening.   A year with lots of lawn-tennis, etc.; and I have an idea that in Scotland there are splendid schools, possibly more genuine than any foreign transplantation.   I shall write to Scotland for advice, and also to Mrs. Henry Sidgwick, and when we get to Lamb House we will combine our information.

I am getting more wonted to this life and am able to walk more without bringing on the symptoms.   But I am apparently a slow case, and may have to be here eight weeks, which is not very good for the completion of my Gifford lectures by Jan. 15.[1]—Luckily I can postpone the first course; and if the worse should come to the worst, I can doubtless postpone the second course also, getting certain exemptions from the College at home, my excuse being such a good one.   Good night, dear landed proprietor! Squireen.

Your loving   W.J.

The paper of your long envelopes wears its edge quite through in coming even this distance.   It is unsafe.

Address: Henry James Esq | Lamb House | Rye | Sussex | England
Postmarks: BAD-NAUHEIM 12.8.99.   <   > STATION. AU 14 99

[1] WJ's course on "The Psychology of Religious Experience" was to begin on 15 January 1900.   Because of postponements, the first lecture of the first course was delivered on 16 May 1901.

At Nauheim, William skimmed, as he put it, numerous books describing extraordinary religious experiences in preparation for the Gifford Lectures. By September his physical condition had sufficiently improved to allow him to stop the baths. With a sense of freedom and release he departed for Switzerland on 21 September to pick up his daughter, who had been staying in a pastor's home near Geneva. After a stopover in Paris, where they did some shop-

ping, William, Alice, and Peggy crossed the stormy English Chan-
nel in early October, staying briefly in Rye, before going to London,
where they established themselves in Henry's apartment.

To Henry James

[London October 9, 1899]
Dear H.[1]—It is now that I indeed ought to wish that I had never left
America! The luxury, the beauty, the perfectly *charming* greeting of
this place which we are to treat now as our own, when it opened
its sunny chambers to us, the spaciousness, the books, the taste and
character make the whole experience one of the most memorable
and dreamlike of our lives. On Peggy it will doubtless stamp a lasting record. I didn't remember how charming the place was, and
that we should now, as it were, possess it, is one of those things which
it is a pity should not have been foreseen, so that the previous years
might have been let up by the confidence. It means safety, space,
everything to us, just now. What a contrast to the single small bedroom in which we lived at Nauheim. Good night and heaven bless
you.

Your loving W.J.

[1] WJ's note is on the same paper as a note from AGJ to HJ. AGJ writes that she,
WJ, and Margaret Mary James are very happy at 34 De Vere Gardens and are
settling in.

1900

There is little doubt that William's homeless condition during this period contributed to the decline of his health. The three months in Henry's London apartment ended on 13 January 1900 when he and Alice, leaving Peggy behind with a friend, departed for the French Riviera and the château of Charles Robert Richet, a French psychologist and fellow psychical researcher. There they found a seriously ill Frederic Myers with his family and Rosalie Thompson, a psychic. The Jameses' stay could not have been restful since they became involved in bizarre quarrels among Myers, his wife, and Rosalie Thompson, one of which ended in the Jameses' room when the trio rushed in and Myers ordered his wife to kiss the medium and to be nice to her. In William's view, Henry, who was in Rye, was missing out on a great deal of material useful in his "line of business."

In late April, William decided that he craved "transalpine air" and they were once more on the move, this time for Geneva, where Alice ordered some dresses from a dressmaker. By this time William had written three lectures and sent them to Henry to be typed by William MacAlpine, Henry's secretary. From Geneva it was back to Nauheim, where it was found that he was suffering not only from his heart condition but also from a fever and bleeding, then to Heidelberg where a doctor told him that Nauheim was useless, then back to Geneva, and from there to Luzern. In late July the Jameses went to Paris to consult a heart specialist where after scenes of "fearful recrimination" with his wife William made an "ass of himself." Alice had received good reports about a faith healer and at her urging he allowed the healer to treat him. The result was a severe case of boils that broke out when they reached Ostend on their way to London to see yet another heart specialist.

Throughout all this, Henry was planted in Lamb House, except for a short visit to London in March when he met his thirteen-year-old niece and took her to a cinema that was showing pictures of the Boer War. In August he acknowledged the receipt of £225 for The Sacred Fount; *at the time he was at Lamb House working on an international "tale of terror," which he never finished.*

To Henry James

Dictated

Hotel du Littoral. Ostend | Aug 8ᵗʰ 1900

Dear Henry,

Your letter of the 5ᵗʰ forwarded from the Hotel Previtali has just gladdened our hearts. I am still confined to bed and shall almost certainly be so tomorrow, so Alice has just wired to Brown, Shipley to forward our 10 days accumulation of mail hither, so we shall get your other letter in the morning. The foolish hope that the boils would advance fast enough for us to move forward on each morrow has kept us from ordering letters until now. Boils are surely the most slowly evolving things in nature—Christian doctrine is nothing to them. But the superintending, observing, re-observing, covering and uncovering, poking and pressing of them is perhaps the occupation most deeply adequate to our human faculties, such as they are, and being by itself enough to fill a day with quivering interest, goes far to neutralize the other inconveniences (and they are great) of being afflicted with them.

We are amused but not astonished at your reaction upon our adventure with the healer, and easily promise you silence on the subject. If your discretion remains as great as ours, neither of us will be compromised. It has been a good example of the way in which a suggestion to do almost anything, coming at the nick of time when one is entirely at a loss *what* to do, will be acted on. Alice had a certain amount of hope. I never for an instant took the cure aspect of it seriously but accepted, in addition to the collateral reasons I gave you yesterday, only in order to "lay" the subject and to add the case of this healer to my anthropological collection. In this latter respect I have been richly rewarded. She is a rank type, unlike anything I ever saw. Of course I never thought of boils, or any danger from the imposition of her hands.

Thorne leaves Paris on Friday and unless I can get off with comfort tomorrow we shall give up this attempt at meeting him and proceed to London Friday or Saturday. Will let you know from day to day how things turn out.

The wind must have whistled round the Rye chimney pots to your heart's content during these last days. It seems to be starting up here afresh this morning. We have had little but storm all these 10 days.

Affectionately yours | W.J.

On 14 August 1900 William saw Dr. Thorne, who ordered him back to Nauheim immediately. Although William thought the baths might be "another expensive sham," he believed that he had no alternative but to obey. By 23 August he was back in Nauheim to resume the "solemn mockery" of the bathing regimen under the supervision of Theodor Schott, his Nauheim doctor, who scolded him for going to the damp climate of England the previous year against his advice. While William was unsure of the success of the Nauheim treatment, he believed that it sometimes helped in lowering his blood pressure. At this time he considered taking injections, under the direction of William Wilberforce Baldwin, of Roberts-Hawley "animal extract," which had produced "astonishing rejuvenations." Schott, however, opposed the scheme, especially as the injections could not be given at Nauheim.

Unable to write the Gifford Lectures while at Nauheim, William read and conversed with Dickinson Sergeant Miller, a Harvard graduate student in philosophy. On 2 September he reached a low point and, after deciding that he should not exert himself by walking, hired a wheelchair to take him to dinner. During this period Alice was in England trying to arrange passage for a visit to America. William's letters to her alternate between complaints of loneliness and assurances that he can get along without her. The complicated misunderstandings and explanations between them ended with the arrival of his "bride" at Nauheim in late September.

The following month the Jameses were on the move again, arriving in Rome in late October after a fatiguing journey, relieved that there would be no more traveling for a while.

To Henry James

Villa Luise, Monday Sept 23. [1900][1]

Dearest Henry

The bride arrived yesterday afternoon in good shape, and looking very well. Journey comfortable. Deck not cold. Only one other young bride in the Railway compartment, and fair sleep. How can I ever thank you enough for all your brotherliness and kindness to her in her perplexities? As a reward I give you free leave to put her into a novel! Human hearts are frail constructions; and the amount of subjective perplexity she seems to have got out of my objective perplexity during these weeks as to whether I should face the next couple of months without her, or put an extinguisher on her noble plan of return, is, by her present confiding revelation of it to me, a marvel. I am glad she made you her confidant during the period, and glad you so steadily supported and helped her. As for myself, it has been a curious example of the way in which a subconscious certainty of one sort—viz. that she must *not* go—and a conscious conviction of another—viz. that she ought to go and that it would be shameful for me to play the baby and stop her—will coexist for a long time, and no equilibrium be reached. It wasn't till the morning after I learned of her first decision to stay that I knew what the sum total of me wished. However, all is now cleared up, and we look forward to many years of unclouded happiness together! Poor little Peggy must have had her perplexities as well.

I am getting on very well in the way of present comfort. The best sign is the heartier internal state of hope and ambition. The baths will certainly do no harm, in the manner in which I am now taking them, and they will probably do a small amount of (impermanent) good. The only serious hope of real betterment lies in Baldwin's injections, on which unfortunately I can't begin till November. But even now I am fumbling over the lecture MS. and as soon as I can do even two pp. a day of work on that, I shall, with Alice restored and helping along in every way, be absolutely happy. The next months seem short. I am hoping that Rome will prove so good that we shan't need to think of Egypt. But if Egypt *is* indicated, it will be magnificent if you and we can go conjointly. The sight of you in Rome will be pleasant enough, but I can well understand your preference for the smaller cities. I hope that the Brookes will take D.V.G. for the full year and that not London, but Italy, will be your way of spending the high winter. I feel very sorry that poor McAlpine should have lost sleep over my MS. Tell him he must make light of such things—I could easily have restored a few pages. I suppose the copy will shortly come—you storing the original MS. with that of the lectures I sent you in the winter. Good bye! Take a vacation now, and don't have any of us on your mind any more till cries for succour shall again be raised from our quarter. We are in safe keeping.

Your loving & grateful W.J.

[1] Monday was 24 September 1900.

To Henry James

Nauheim, Oct. 4. 1900

Dear Henry,

My heartiest congratulations on your being Lord of Lamb House.[1]
May it never sour on you or you on it, but may you both grow into
an ever intimater union and attachment. The correct thing for you
now is to join the Tory party, and if possible, get returned for Parliament. Don't let it lead you into a penny more of expense until the
mortgage is entirely paid off! It seems to be in first rate repair at
present. I wish it might always be an appurtenance of the James
family, but I fear there is little chance of that, with all the younger
generation immersed in American activities, unless indeed you succeed in re-creating some of them after yr. own image. As for the
egyptian business, to tell the truth I feel relieved at what you write
of your own probable impediments. Heaven knows *I* don't want to
go dangling about there myself if I can help it, prolonging the unreal-
ity, and having chambermaids and waiters for my almost exclusive
companions. Nothing but dire continuation of illness would induce
me to continue that weary existence a month longer than is neccessary. I need, for cheerfulness, either to be again an active life on my
own account or to be among people themselves active, with whom I
can sympathize. What a pathetic "commentary," that foreign cities,
so rapturous to be let loose upon, when one is well and beginning a
vacation, should be so nauseous a dose when the vacation month
after month is forced upon one! But I still live: *E pur si muove.* The
5th lecture has, since I have been here, reached its 30th page, and
from now onwards I think no day will pass without at least one or
two pages accomplished. I have resigned irrevocably from the second course, which under no circumstances, however favorable, could
I in the time now left hope to get ready by the limit of date appointed.[2] It is a great relief to be rid of that responsibility. The last
bath, probably, was ta'en this morning. In a fortnight I shall be able
to report results. At present they are imperceptible.

I am glad you found the "boots," and thank you much for sending
them. They doubtless will arrive to morrow. Alice says she gave you
a pair of woolen gloves of mine to give away. As they are as good as
new, and were my salvation last winter, (my manual circulation being
very imperfect) I should like, if you should still by accident have kept
hold of them, to have them sent on also—but this time to the Hotel
Sᵗ Gotthardt, Luzern. If bestowed, all the better for their new

wearer. The loss of MacA.'s copy is queer—I can't help suspecting he may have forgotten to stamp it. *Most* fortunately, he has the duplicate copy, which I didn't suppose he was going to take—or at any rate had forgotten. Fine weather here on the whole continues. 1000 blessings on your head, and on your house's!

Your loving & grateful William

I have sent a "scientific instrument" to your care, to be harbored. It is part of a measurer of arterial tension, that I dont wish to carry about with me.

Address: Henry James Esq. | Lamb House | Rye | Sussex | England
Postmarks: BAD-NAUHEIM 5. 10 00   RYE OC 7 00   ASHFORD STATION OC 7 00

[1] HJ signed the legal documents giving him ownership of Lamb House on 1 October 1900.
[2] WJ delivered the second course of Gifford Lectures beginning on 13 May 1902.

To Henry James

Hotel Hassler, Rome, Nov 13. 1900

Dear H.,

Your letter received two days ago and sent on by Alice to Harry in Washington rejoiced us both exceedingly by the splendid news it contained of the falling in to you of the room at the reform Club. Lord of Lamb House, and perpetual tenant of that room, it seems to me that you could not have the shelter of your earthly tenement in snugger or better shape. I have often thought of it as the ideal thing for you, and wished it might not be too long delayed, and here it is already. How big is the apartment anyhow? And does it get the sun well?

The Scribner came also, and Alice read the Tone of Time aloud the same night and we both enjoyed [it] greatly.[1] It is a charming and interestingly wrought out bit of fancy. The days here slip by, the only trouble, paradoxical as it may appear, being that there is *too little time!* Invalidism breaks the day into so many segments that they crowd out more real life. My two injections make holes of 20 minutes at 10 & 6. Baldwin always spends at least half an hour during his visit. I come back to lunch at one, wherever I may be. From 2 to 3. I lie on my back & nap if I can. At 5 I practice Schott's widerstand's gymnastik,[2] and so it goes. This is the eighth day of the injections, and I cannot doubt that they are taking hold. Many symptoms show it; and although the days vary very much, I have not been so

free from aortic distress any week for many months past.   I have
actually begun to prowl through the streets a little as in old times.
The dignity of Rome, in its shabby shirt sleeved unpretentiousness
grows on me more and more.   Were I in walking trim I think I
should spend hours daily in just rambling the streets.

I finisht my 5th lecture yesterday all but a couple of pp. about
J. Bunyan for which I need his life, and am 8 pp. into lecture VI.   I
hate to do it, but I find I must ask you to send me hither the books
without delay.   Of course you will have got my last letter of instructions.   If you get a new box made, have the cover screwed, not
nailed; and send the whole thing by FAST freight.

Please ask Macalpine to send me his bill for copying.   I wish you
would mail me the second copy, which you have in your possession,
of the lecture.   There were certain type written portions of the original which he was not to copy but of which most fortunately he said
he kept a stenographic copy.   Can he out of that supply those pp. in
this copy which you send?   I can't imagine *how* that great big envelope came to be lost.   You had better register this one.   I find the
process of getting a registered letter is not impossibly vexatious here.
Glorious sunset to night.   I have been up on the roof.

Mrs. J. Bancroft was here this P.M.—an old brown woman, the ghost
of her former self.   How I hate to have to do with doctors!

Sleep calmly and well now, as one who has arrived in port and
whom the storms can no longer trouble, with your London & your
country habitation.

Peg seems to get along very well—she does n't write to you for fear
of infecting.[3]

Love from us both,   W.J.

Did Macalpine ever inquire at Hastings about its loss.   I asked him
to, but I have as yet got no reply.

P.S.   Do you remember some pads of writing paper which you
ordered made for me at Partridge & Cooper's?   On leaving you last
January I offered you two or three which you accepted rather reluctantly as if you had no use for them.   If you still have them, I will
ask you to disgorge them into the book boxes, for my use here.   It
is good paper, & the pad form very convenient for my writing on my
lap as I still must, and I shall soon be out of paper.   If you haven't
them, or have forgotten & can't find them, dont give them a thought.
I shall surely be able to get good paper here.

[1] HJ, "The Tone of Time," *Scribner's Magazine* 28 (November 1900): 624–34; reprinted in *The Better Sort* (1903).

[2] Theodor Schott's Nauheim treatment included exercise, consisting of movements done slowly and against resistance.

[3] Margaret Mary James had the mumps.

To Henry James

Rome, Dec 22, 1900 | Hotel Primavera

Dearest H'ry,

I forgot to answer your questions about L' Stephen, from whom I received the 3 vols. which he sent me, and acknowledged them in a letter which by mistake I put into an envelope addressed to Myers.[1] Myers returned the letter, and with a postscript I sent it on to Stephen—this last 10 days ago. I suppose by this time that he has got everything. Isn't his address Hyde Park Gate?

I suppose that yesterday you and Peggy went down to Rye. I'm afraid you have dérangéd yourself for her sake—but I let everything happen and only pray that in some future you may get your reward. My memory has travelled back much of late to those dark days a year ago when Alice and I were with you, I so ill; and what comfort we enjoyed and how sociable, sympathetic & solicitous you were. I am rather grudging in expressing recognition, especially to members of the family, but you may be sure, my dear boy, that the blessings of your hospitable and loving *accueuil* were both appreciated and recorded in my heart as well as in Alice's, and that we are hoping some day to entertain you in kind, though not I trust as a victim of nervous prostration such as I was.

My organism is the meanest kind of trash. No doctor can touch me without getting bitten. Here are these injections. They have done what nothing hitherto known to medecine could have done to my arteries, and for a year past all the doctors here declared my arteries to be the fountain of all my other troubles. I wrote you that the nervous system failed to follow suit; but it has become evident in a week past that the nervous system has been falling back, so that, as sensations and activity go, I make no gains at all. Baldwin professes that he can't understand it; I'm sure *I* can't. But it's discouraging in a high degree to find things taking such an unexpected turn. I shall presently insist on stopping the injections entirely, and see what happens then.

Myers has arrived at Valescure (S! Rafael, Var) but is evidently in a bad way with *his* arteries. Perhaps he will come on here. We had a visit this a.m. from Geo. Putnam & his wife and daughter (our old

Quincy St. neighbors). They are the first home friends we have been with since our departure, if you except Mrs. John Bancroft who is here for Baldwin's treatment. We drove over the Janiculan with them. It is fine to see old Garibaldi's statue meditatively looking down upon S! Peter's and the Vatican from his height. Happy the hero who has such an enemy to triumph over, an enemy of whom not one ideal thing could be said, for Austria, the Vatican and Naples surely in that time represented putrescent human meanness and naught beside, and as against them every italian patriot seemed half divine. We passed the monument to Bruno—do you remember that perfectly superb inscription?—

A Bruno

Il secolo da lui divinato

Qui

Dove il rogo arse.

"Here, where the faggots burned!" Was there ever a finer one? Pray read it to Peggy!

I have heard from the Edinburgh authorities their official action, which is that I can lecture between May 1 & July 17th., with a preference expressed for as early a date as possible, so I shall hope for the 1st of May, and it will be desirable for several reasons that we should reach England by April 1st. It seems strange, but I am obliged to knock off touching the lectures again, having got only through one 3rd. of lecture VII. $3\frac{2}{3}$ more to do therefore. I hope in 10 days or a fortnight to touch them again, but after a few days, I seem to go to pieces.

I am about to recommence with electricity (which has always relieved the fag of College work at home towards spring) using a battery hired here. It may be, though, that we leave here earlier than has been foreseen, and that I may need a battery elsewhere. Would you therefore be so very kind as to take my little battery now in Lamb House, up to London, & to hold it subject to my order to send, or at least leave it in Smith's hands at Rye, ready to send, if needed, to me wherever I may ask. It is that heavily wrapped box————Alice tells me it was probably sent to Liverpool, so no matter! I should have asked her before I began to write.—Nevertheless in case it *should* not have gone to Liverpool, it was a box some 15 inches x 9 x 9 wrapt. in paper and a lot of silk covered wires with leathered pads on the ends of them to go with it. While I am speaking of "things," let me once more express a hope that Bill's watch is in a dry place.

I bother you enough, but you can't think how bothersome it is to have one's things so scattered.

The weather here keeps glorious, and Rome, in every one of its peculiarities, is a feast. I never go out without enthusiasm welling up in my heart for *every* feature of it—for the eyes, I mean, for to the reflective mind its history is a painful business. The very focus of the world's cruelty, baseness & corruption. Alice has been reading Tacitus—a good deal of it aloud, in english. Incredible horrors of cruelty. Thank Peg for her outline of Roman History which is just what we required.

I hope you will prove harmonious together, and that you may have fairly decent weather for the season. We send no presents! Difficulties enough. Peggy will go home with enough trousseau! and life here is very dear. How the Boers are going it! I must say I hope they'll keep it up. There is a queer rumor that McKinley is going back on his tracks in the Philippines, but I don't believe it. He *can't* do it, can't swallow his vomit like that.

Well, for me this is a long letter. Good bye dear Henry. Kiss Peggy for us, and take a merry Christmas from us both,

Your loving brother | Wm. J.

If you don't instantly find the battery, don't spend a minute in looking for it.

I suppose you will have paid McA. the 30 shillings.

If Peggy gets chilblains let her try *Tchthyol* ointment.[2] Surround it with absorbent cotton from Chymists

[1] Leslie Stephen, *English Utilitarians*, 3 vols. (1900).

[2] WJ clearly wrote 'Tchthyol'. Thyol and thymol are chemical compounds used medicinally.

1901

The Jameses were still in Rome when Frederic Myers and his family arrived there on 1 January 1901 to consult Baldwin. Within a short time, Myers was fatally ill with pneumonia. According to Axel Munthe, one of the physicians attending Myers in his last days, at the moment of Myers's death William was seated outside the chamber with a notebook ready to record any posthumous communications.

To Henry James

Dictated

Hotel Primavera | Rome. Jan 17. 1901 | 8.45 PM.

Dear H.

We are sitting in our bed-room.   I in front of the open stove, and Alice under the electric table-lamp, and I dictate these lines to you while poor Myers at the opposite end of the hallway lies dying.   For it has come to this.   Five or six days ago, after no special exposure, he was seized with double pneumonia; and of course, with the existing complication a non-recovery seemed a foregone conclusion.   I myself have not seen him since the pneumonia became pronounced till this afternoon when I was hastily summoned to administer some morphia.   Though the death process, so far as respiration goes, began before noon he has been kept comfortable by morphia and is now sound asleep and may last until the morning.   He has the most extraordinary cerebral vitality it is possible to conceive of.   He has talked rationally and with some eagerness until within two hours. This morning, with the death rattle almost begun and drugged with morphia he wanted to be read to, and was read to.   Yesterday he listened to a great deal of reading and read the paper himself though he could hardly hold it in his fingers.   His intense assurance of a future life gives him, and through his example has given the family, a curious serenity and superiority to the accidents of his illness which seems to have struck immensely both Baldwin and Munthe who has been in consultation.   The features of most of the sick rooms that doctors visit are apparently physical misery and moral suffering, un-

relieved by any intellectual manifestations. All this intellectual vitality and general moral superiority in Myers is in the grand style and
something decidedly exceptional.

Lady Stanley telegraphs that she will arrive Saturday morning.
No other member of the family appears to be coming and by Sunday
I suppose they will turn their faces homewards. Most of Myers'es
Magnum Opus is printed and the remainder of the matter, he says,
can adequately be put into shape by Hodgson.[1] It is much to be
regretted, however, that he could not live to finish it himself and at
least see it published. Of its "success" he in no case could be witness,
for that must be declared by the opinion of future years and not by
the immediate reviewer. My own impression is that it will probably
stand as epoch-making, and count in history as the first decisive foot-
mark made on a new pathway of science.

The children behave very well though Silvia has cried a great deal
today. Mrs. Myers in a state of extreme tension and strain to which
sound sleep will probably succeed when all is over. We are being
drawn upon in no way at all for aid. Our only regret is that we can
be so little useful.

Friday morning, 10. o'clock. Poor F.W.H.M. passed away at half
past 9 last night. The family are in a very normal state this morning.
I am helping with certain telegrams etc. & Baldwin is doing all the
practical about the body, etc. The whole thing winds up too soon
and is a warning that one must not leave one's work to the morrow.
Last year at Carqueiranne he was so well compared with me, that
when the medium Mrs. Thompson predicted his death within two
years and my recovery, it looked more as if the names had been substituted for one another.

Theodora is here, very "nice."

Your letter of last Monday has arrived. I am grieved that you
should have been so out of shape, especially with eczema, of which
I did not know you were a subject I have had an attack on my legs—
you do not name the seat of yours—almost every summer for years
past. It comes in not very large patches, and with me has always
been completely cured by just dabbing on and letting dry the following application given me long years ago by D.̲ White, "Boston's first
dermatologist":—I put it on another slip.—Just *shake* bottle, pour a
little into a saucer, moisten therewith a linen rag, slap it a couple of
times on the eczematous places, without rubbing—just to wet them.
Then let dry—the zinc oxide forms a white coating which in a week
cures me entirely. The operation should be repeated every 3 hours.

Of course you know that nothing woolen should touch an eczema place.

We read your Article on Thackeray & Winchelsea with much pleasure—thanks for sending the magazine.[2]

Off now, sending telegrams for the poor M's.

Hamilton Aidé just arrived.

Love! W.J.

[1] Frederic William Henry Myers, *Human Personality and Its Survival of Bodily Death* (1903).

[2] HJ, "Winchelsea, Rye, and *Denis Duval*," *Scribner's Magazine* 29 (January 1901): 44–53.

From Henry James

THE REFORM CLUB Jan. 24 1901

My dear William.

A laggard in response you & Alice will indeed feel that I have become. I've had for 3 or 4 days your so interesting & relieving letter dictated to Alice at the hour of poor Myers's death, & though it greatly eased me off (as to my fears that the whole thing would have worn you out,) yet till this moment my hand has been stayed. I wrote you very briefly, moreoer, as soon as the papers here gave the news. Blessed seems it to have been that everything round about Myers was so sane & comfortable; the reasonableness & serenity of his wife & children &c; not to speak of his own high philosophy—which it must have been fine to see in operation.   But I hope the sequel hasn't been prolonged, & have been supposing that, by the necessary quick departure of his "party," you will have left independent again & not too exhausted.   We here, on our side, have been gathering close round the poor old dying & dead queen, & are plunged in universal mourning tokens—which accounts for my black-edged paper.[1]   It has really been, the Event, most moving, interesting & picturesque. I have felt *more* moved, much, than I should have expected (such is *community* of sentiment,) & one has realized all sorts of things about the brave old woman's beneficent duration & holding-together virtue. The thing has been journalistically overdone, of course—greatly; but the people have appeared to advantage—serious & sincere & decent—*really* caring.   Meanwhile the drama of the accession, new reign &c, has its lively spectacular interest—even with the P. of W.

for hero.[2] I dined last night in company with some Privy Councillors who had met him ceremonially, in the a.m., & they said (John Morley in particular said,) that he had made a very good impression. Speriamo! I find London answering very well, but with so much more crowdedness on one's hours & minutes than in the country, that I shall be glad indeed when the end comes. Meanwhile, however, work proceeds, Mcalpine adheres, & interest suffices. I go out to see Peggy on Sunday next. Clarke has just started on a fresh foreign journey; Italy &c. He may go to Rome? Personal & private news have I none; but it occurs to me to ask you how—*should* I WANT, after a while, a certain sum of $1000 which you told me (Alice I think spoke of it, last) is with Lee Higginson &c as my share of set-aside Syracuse money—can I get *at* the same, have it conveyed to me? I may not require it at all, but it is a convenience to know. The war has *doubled* the income tax here: it is hideous.

Ever tenderly your Henry.

[1] Queen Victoria died on 22 January 1901.

[2] Albert Edward (1841–1910), Prince of Wales, ascended the throne as Edward VII on 22 January 1901.

In her share of a letter written jointly with William on 25 January 1901 in Rome, Alice Gibbens James reported to Henry that Myers's death had adversely affected William's condition: "He is down again, nerves and sleep deplorable, aortic pain returned." According to Alice, Myers's widow depended upon William and tired him "most of all" by constantly talking about her dead husband. At the same time the deadline for the several-times-postponed Gifford Lectures was rapidly approaching. In his portion of the letter William announced that he had completed eight lectures, enough for ten hours of reading, but that he still needed three chapters for the book. The Jameses lingered in Rome for another month or so, William enjoying good working days during the second half of February. The last two weeks, he wrote Henry on 24 February, were the "best yet." Meanwhile in London Henry was suffering from a "visitation of violent lumbago." In a letter written on 6 March he advised William and Alice not to come to England in early April lest they fall "into the whirlpool of Easter" and the bank holiday that followed. William and Alice arrived at Lamb

House on 15 April and were eventually joined there by their son Henry. After nearly a month in England, the trio departed on 14 May for Edinburgh and the Gifford ordeal.

To Henry James

20 Charlotte Square | Edinburgh, May 16. [1901]

Dear H.

Glorious weather, and an audience of between 2 & 3 hundred which filled the room—more than seemed to be expected. Half a dozen of the Professors, and the Principal (Muir author of the life of Mohammed) met in the Senate room & we robed ourselves, and preceded by a beadle with a mace, traversed the court to a lecture room where according to Alice & H. the students, about one third of the audience, had been whistling, singing & stamping for some time. Muir introduced me with some stammering & tottering remarks, and I stood up & read my material. The audience were very attentive & sympathetic and gave protracted and solid applause at the end, the like of which they give at Harvard, and which one gets from no other sort of audience known to me. In sum, the plunge is made, the chill over & the warm reaction set in. I feel, of course some pectoral perturbation, but it will rest off, and there will be less of it next time, I'm sure. We moved into these lodgings at 4 P.M. & have been driving round Arthur's Seat, till now.[1] The lodgings are splendidly situated in a house with *large* rooms & lofty ceilings and we have three on the 1st floor, one small and two in the top story for 3 guineas a week, ordering our own meals, the landlady being cook. It augurs great peace and well being. Edinb. is magnificent, the noblest looking city in the world I imagine, but there is an east wind, and it is very cold out of the sun—the people call it "hot."(!!!). One needs a fire.

Altogether you see that God is very good to us! I write just this word to let you know it on my own authority. Will send you the Scotsman tomorrow, with its report.[2] Alice is in high feather & sends you love & gratitude. Harry is a great help.

Ever fondly | W.J.

[1] Arthur's Seat is a hill near Edinburgh.

[2] The Edinburgh newspaper *Scotsman* published a report of each of the lectures, the first appearing on 17 May 1900. For the *Scotsman's* description of the proceedings, see *VRE*, 540–41.

From Henry James

LAMB HOUSE, | RYE. May 27th 1901.

Dearest William.

Your letter of May 24th has been a great joy & has set at rest my uncertainties & questions. Followed by your *second* & deeply interesting Scotsman it has placed me quite by your side & in your midst. May you boom bravely along now. It must be indeed a fine feeling & a recovery of life. I was sure that Edinburgh wd. be a strong impression for you—& you make me quite yearn to rebehold it. Yet the prospect of going hence on Wednesday (till Saturday) to Welcombe makes me almost cry with reluctance.[1] However, one is always glad afterwards—if only for the joy of getting home. The beauty of this place at this moment, in blossom, colour, general exuberance of natural life, is so exquisite that I am sorry you are losing it. However, much will remain for your return. Nothing, thank God, happens— beyond such emotions as that Miss Weld proves decidedly a bijou, that Nick is *en pension* at a sheep farm,[2] that McAlpine (visiting some friends here for his Whitsuntide) came in to-day to luncheon, & that I hear from Theodora S. that the hapless Godkins *are* on the point of arriving. They have, thank heaven, a Doctor (Draper—a young one,) with them;[3] but a house ("in Devonshire" &c,) still to find. It's quite terrible to me, pressed with occupation, to think of having to peregrinate so far as that to see them *sous peine* of heartlessness. And Mrs. Bancroft demanding the same of me from London! *You* & Alice are well out of it all. If you *can* send me still the 2 or 3 other Scotsmen (for you will have delivered tomorrow 5 lectures, I suppose,) I shall be very grateful. Much love to Alice & Harry.

Ever your   Henry

[1] Welcombe, near Stratford-on-Avon, was the mansion of George Otto Trevelyan.
[2] Nick was a terrier.
[3] Draper was not identified.

The first of the Edinburgh ordeals was over on 17 June 1901. Following another stay at Nauheim, the Jameses were back in the United States on 9 September after a smooth voyage for everyone except Peggy, who was very seasick. American customs proved a simple matter and they had to pay only forty dollars for all of

their "truck." William had written the first of his several letters of
resignation in Rome on 8 December 1900, asking that after his
retirement his name be included in the philosophy department list-
ings as someone willing to give "informal private aid and advice
to students of philosophy." His resignation was not accepted, and
for a number of years he remained on the faculty with reduced
teaching responsibilities. In 1901–2 he taught only one course in
the first semester: "The Psychological Elements of the Religious
Life." Still ahead, of course, was the second course of Gifford Lec-
tures.

To Henry James

Silver Lake, N.H. Sept. 21. 1901

Dearest Henry,

I write this at 8.30 A.M. on the grass in front of the Salter's little
"Hill top" house, with my back against a stone, a fragrant South-wind
blowing in my face, and the spacious "view" bathed in warmest hazi-
est light, hills melting beyond hills in vapory succession, whilst the
foreground plunges into a vast sea of intervening woods, just
trembling on the verge of the autumnal "turn." It is very lovely, and
I wish you could see it, by being transported hither instantaneously
at this moment. I have been here now 12 days, having arrived rather
seedy. I am much better; and I am convinced that for my needs
there is nothing like this sort of environmental condition—living *terre*
à terre right on the level of nature, in a country like this, to which my
education has adapted me, & which I know how to live with and
enjoy. It looked terribly penurious & poverty-stricken when I first
came, after the robustiousness of all the places we had been in in
Europe, but it has an insidious charm in its asperity & austerity, and
the old sense of immediate contact with it has come back. The
woods are reasserting their empire every where. Old stone walls in
the midst of them marking the boundaries of ancient fields, and old
cellars surprising you, showing where ancient farm houses & their
barns once stood. Unkempt, confused, without dignity, is the new
growth, but the plants are endless in variety and the fragrance unlike
anything we have been in contact with in Europe. Nevertheless, I
don't advise you ever to come. When one is once adapted to an
environment the thing is to stay there and not revolutionize one's
insides. Where one *is* ought to remain one's Absolute, and one's

motto should be "dwell deep." One can't do that in more than one country, so *stay* where you are. More than ever do I feel now that the crudity of America, once left behind, would do nothing but shock you. Your delightful letter of the 10th. has surprised me, ere I got off this. It sounds very sweet—your september light over that cheerful land; and your list of visits does n't sound so formidable. My mss. have all apparently arrived, so I'm safe in that way. Alice has been re-papering our Salon, & Harry says our pictures look well— he has been *here* for a couple of days. I suppose you remembered my 10 s to Miss Weld, and I count on you to send me shortly an account of my indebtedness, as per my memorandum. I dined a couple of days ago at our little lakeside place. The tenants seem enthusiastic about it, and much disappointed that we can't extend their lease to another couple of years. It looked very harmonious & sweet. The country has apparently gone hysteric mad over McKinley's assassination. There is apparently as much popular sentiment of loyalty towards our president *as such* (whoever he may be) as towards any european monarch—which although irrational & often idiotic in both cases, is a magnificent conservative force in a nation. Roosevelt has some splendid qualities & instincts, and may do well. His jingoism is of course his foible. Its lucky in some respects that McK. is out of the way, but his example, apotheosized as now, may be worse than his presence, and after all he ought to have lived to experience the inevitable "reaction"—he stood for absolutely nothing but "success," and could no more have survived failure than a napoleon.*[1]—I haven't written a line since I've been here, but expect to start up again when in Cambridge. My condition is a nasty puzzle. I shall stay here till the 27th or 28th. And meet my students on Tuesday Oct 1st.

Gratitude to you-ward still gushes from my heart.

Lovingly, Wm James

[1] Although the asterisk appears to be WJ's, no footnote was written.

From Henry James

LAMB HOUSE, | RYE, SUSSEX. November 1st 1901

Dearest Alice, dearest William.

I have been, you will have felt, systematically silent, & now I have before, unacknowledged, but not uncherished, no less than *4* letters from you—2 from each, beginning with your beautiful one, William, in pencil, written out of doors at Chocorua, with your back against a stone, & exquisitely consoling when it arrived, on the whole, as a proof that the *pieces* of you were all there, smashed as you might be by the concussions of your return.   Then there have been 2 brave ones from Alice, the 1ˢᵗ with a postscript from you, & liberal & copious from the midst of your early turmoil & the "last ditch" of your sheets—so easily conceived by *me!* the 2ᵈ giving news of poor old Tweedy's death & telling me of her meaning to go on to his obsequies. (Besides these 2, there has been a most valued one from Harry, for which tell him with my love that he shall have separate thanks.)   I've held off from writing, through real promptings of mercy—feeling so far every separate & distinct (so far as individually distinguishable) convulsion of your reconstruction that I wanted to simplify by with-olding *any* addition to your overburdened consciousness.   At least you were not to have words of mine accumulating, with a responsibil-ity to them, in your ears.—And now I've been with you, dear Alice, in thought, all over your queer lonely pilgrimage to Newport, even though knowing that while I hang about the vision it is all past & gone.   A grey & gruesome vision to me, somehow—about which I can't—save for you in it, all loose and lost, feel very intimate or tender.   Newport, unlike other things of the far-away, has become sort of disintimatized with time.   Yet I was was there, of *old,* much more than William.   But these are vain & trackless things.   I shall more—if I haven't, unberufen, *less*—from you to go upon!—Little is there to tell, thank goodness, on the whole, of the "make-up," re-cent & actual, of my autumn days here.   The season, the aspects, the picture, the garden &c, on the whole admirable, & *peace,* from day to day, as my portion, to a degree that has made me feel almost dis-loyal to *your* distracted home with it.   It has been rather a cold *unfed* peace, for the ebbing tidal wave of the Smith-business more & more left my position defined for the present as high & dry.[1]   However, the stillness has been sweet, the complications *nil,* the tinned tongue, from Jarreti's, regularly renewed, & Mrs. Bourne, otherwise, a nurs-ing mother to me.   Besides, I *am* reconstructing—Alice Skinner, whom you will remember, being back as rather vague & limp parlour-maid (she will improve,) & a cook-housekeeper, rejoicing in the admi-rable name of Mrs. Paddington, to come on the 11ᵗʰ.   (I've had to wait five weeks for her—she seeming, however, worth it.   It's a long story, but she was invented for me by the admirable Lomas, the God-kins' butler, & has spent most of her life in 2 excellent places, one 19, the other 10 years—& the latter a single gent's., in the country;

I've been up to town & seen her, & liked her; she *wants*, much, to come, & is prodigiously recommended: so the omens are good—which is all one can ask. And I pay her £3. a month, tout compris.) Little Weld & the young Nicholas,[2] the main features of my daily scene, are meanwhile all I could ask of them; work goes on with steady strides, to speak without presumption, & I shld. like to think I haven't to budge till about Jan. 10ᵗʰ, when I hope to go [to] town with a book finished.[3] But the poor irrepressible Godkins, housed, at last, at Torquay, after prolonged difficulties (yet he no flagrantly worse) appeal to me so not to *put off* coming to them there that I expect to do so, fearfully à contre coeur,—for 3 or 4 days—about the 20ᵗʰ of this month; & then to go again, for a week or two, after I get up to town. Such is my simple story. The days shorten, & my little lonely walk becomes more meagre; but the air colours, the fireside glows, the book multiplies, & the sun, in the garden, still so hangs about that it's a little feast, each morning, to breakfast with my window wide open to it. I had lately, with George, a feverish carnival—the putting in off *107* new roses;[4] as to which we hope the assured comfort will be for the rest of our days. They provide, at a swoop, for much of the annual garden question. But don't let me seem to be pelting you with roses in the midst of your sterner stuff! I do hope with all my heart it is all running clearer. I thoroughly believe, dear William, that you *will* work in, work back, work up, if you make it a life-&-death question to give up everything but your own needs *for* it. I am ravished when—whenever—I hear of your going to bed rather than receive the assault—e.g.—of Paulina. Go to bed, systematically, scientifically, rather than receive *quoi que ce soit* from *qui que ce soit*, if not something meeting your "real" need. Full of wisdom & truth—& "pathos"!—your beautiful letter (about the hemispheric non-mixing &c,) from the aching Chocorua. Yet little needed by the monotonous *me* as counsel, in truth—who have felt in my bones, for years, all you say, & whose existence has been one intense conformity to it on the "dwelling deep" lines. To stick where I am & nurse what I have happened to get from the sticking, has been *all* my life-saving instinct. I've lost as well as gained, by my thin straight line, but gained more than I've lost. But little Nick (who is getting extremely to resemble Smith in face!) turns, & tosses in deep slumber, from his chair at elbow, & reminds me that it's, as ever, over my letters, much more than midnight. I've *yearned*, dearest Alice over everything to[5] you tell me of the young existences round you, & I hold tight, tell Peggy, the silver cord that binds *her* here & that I seem to feel we agreed she shld. leave, practicably, trailing in her wake. But Billy, Francis—these indeed I wish I could get into closer relation with. They must be full of savour. However, c'est du pain sur la planche of my future. I don't worry you with vain *voeux* about *your* service-question but only pray for you, hard, all the time, and it *is* 1.30 a.m!

Always your   Henry.

P.S.   I am forgetting to tell you that Marie Léon's[6] poor photographs have only *now,* at last, at the end of 9 weeks, come: 2 portraits having been selected by me as *the least impossible* (as a COMBINATION) out of all her proofs. W^m is excellent, *beautiful,* in both: in one *more* beautiful than in any of his photos. ever, I think. But I am fearfully sacrificed in each, and the value of the thing as a *double* thing thereby much impaired. If we had only had singles of each! Yours, W^m, at any rate, is as happy as mine is disagreeable. Or perhaps mine is only "*true,*" & my truth naturally lurid as yours is irrespressibly bland. But the point is I don't see, yet, how to send you a number together of the heavy, rather clumsy cards, & I shall have to despatch 3 or 4 to begin with, separately & individually. But I shant be able to get even the 1st of these off by this week's post. It's too late   But they will come—by the next—& the *original* of the Lecture of which I sent you just after your departure Miss Weld's copy.

[1] The "Smith-business" refers to the dismissal of the Smiths for drunkenness.
[2] HJ is apparently referring to his dog.
[3] HJ, *The Wings of the Dove* (1902).
[4] HJ meant to write 'the putting in of'. George was George Gammon.
[5] The word 'to' is a false start.
[6] Marie Léon was not identified.

1902

Late at night in January 1902 at Lamb House, while listening to the wind howling around his "old house," with servants asleep, and with his "wire-haired fox terrier of celestial breed" dozing in an armchair nearby, Henry James wrote to William Dean Howells, the only English-writing novelist he read with "concentrated passion," that he had had a working fall and early winter, finishing The Wings of the Dove, *which he described as a "love-story" of "romantic tinge, and touching and conciliatory tone." Unsure of its publication, he was already "panting" to move on to the next "two or three" subjects. He had, among other things, promised to write a memorial volume about William Wetmore Story and had to examine Story's letters and diaries. Also on the horizon, but not mentioned in the letter to Howells, was what he considered his best novel,* The Ambassadors, *which began serial publication in January 1903. On 27 January he visited London where several days later he was stricken with "inflammation of the bowels" that eventually sent him "howling" back to Lamb House and to bed for a "dozen wretched days."*

William was in Cambridge rushing to complete the second course of Gifford Lectures for delivery at Edinburgh. Although the course did not begin until 13 May, he had to be in Edinburgh by 11 April to receive an honorary degree. Since The Varieties of Religious Experience *was scheduled for publication in June 1902 to coincide with the delivery of the final lecture, he was busy with proofs and indexes before his departure for Scotland on 1 April.*

To Henry James

Cambridge, March 11. [1902]

Dearest Henry,

Your three letters relating your illness have come in succession, making one realize that it must have been a very serious thing. I have not written to you, because from one day to another I lived in the throes of 'finishing' my lecture MS. and being badly fagged was unfitted for any other act.   The thing has trailed itself along till now, when only some final retouches to the last chapter (in proof) are required, and the making of an Index.   So I breathe freely, but I 'feel the strain'.   You don't tell exactly what the matter was, beyond its being "abdominal"—keep it now till you can pour it into my private ear!   Our arrival mustn't take you back to Rye too early, we shall go as soon as possible and stay as long as possible at the Godkins, from whom an invitation has come, and take care of ourselves, either in London or in the country, until your own natural date for Rye arrives.   I count immensely on enjoying the sweetness and repose of Rye in a way more athletic and normal than I could before.   I am sure you will notice a great difference of "tone."   I hope to heaven you will have no more illness—you must have had an extremely lonely life for a month or more, and the visit to Godkins will undoubtedly do a lot of good.   Farewell and *Gesundheit!*—

Your loving, | W.J.

I long to see Rye under the Paddington régime.

William James's second Edinburgh course of lectures was over on 9 June 1902. The next day he and Alice boarded the Ivernia *at Liverpool and were back in Boston on 19 June. On this somewhat hurried visit, they still managed to do some shopping in London and spend about a week with Henry at Lamb House. Henry was concerned to clear out his De Vere Gardens apartment and packed furniture and pictures for shipment to Irving Street.*

To Henry James

Cambr. Oct 25. 1902

Dearest Henry,

I have been an unpardonably long time without writing to you, & within the past week a letter from Billy at Lamb House and one from you to Harry have arrived, making you feel very near.[1]   You have felt near enough—through the "sphere" of your beautiful furniture which curiously drops into place everywhere in this house, just as if created for it and converts a certain previous spareness and roominess into a comfortable plenitude and abundance.   You remember that I swore (against your impatient protest) that we should pay the market value—the invoice price was too *spottbillig*, so guessing as nearly as we can, I send you about 150 dollars in two drafts on London, which will also cover (if you stretch it enough in your imagination) some of those arrears of disbursement of yours on our account which we left behind (doctor's bills, type writing etc, etc) when we went away two years ago. Now, dear Henry, don't shake your head at this, which is only plain *honesty* on my part, but get the checks cashed, and if you wish in any way to respond, do so by getting the money you took from the Syracuse sinking fund paid in at as early a day as you can. I wrote not earlier, partly because I was waiting to make report about this furniture (God bless it) and partly because I was *floundering* so in the matter of health. I ran down a good deal during September, but as soon as I got back here I recommenced the "Lymph," and from the very first day, my system responded just as it did last year. Day by day a diminution of fatigue symptoms, which, sooth to say, when I first came here were pretty bad. I shall probably have that now to fall back on as a permanent resource. I am lecturing 3ce a week, but I cannot say I do it with any pleasure[2]—I've grown away from the job in these three years, and one can do so much more justice to one's self by writing, with so very much smaller relative expenditure of energy for the result obtained. I somehow "kind o' feel" that this is my last year. The coal strike is broken, thank Heaven, but there is probably trouble ahead, for the thing has got into politics, and socialism of some sort has made a bigger stride than ever before. The mine owners have disgusted the public by their arrogant tone. Meanwhile the rulers of the sky have been most kind—the warmest loveliest october known, furnaces not to be thought of and a fire in the grate only need[ed] two or three times so far. We have ordered a lot of wood from Chocorua, and shall probably end by getting all the furnace and kitchen anthracite we need, as the need successively falls due.

Yesterday came the news of poor Sara Sedgwick's death. Darwin will probably feel it very much, and so will Theodora. I am glad the latter got there before the end. As for Sara, I always feel that when after 60 one grazes death, it is better not to come back and have to do it over again—these late lingering illnesses of decay are so much worse than premature snatching off. Poor old Boott is, I am afraid, breaking down, much rheumatic pain, stiffness and weakness, yet he insists on walking out regularly twice a day, and his house is very hard to warm. I foresee trouble ahead. Chas. Norton seems shaky too, and altogether immortality here is not the lot of man. Grace N. is very unchanged although I think the death of Prof. Bôcher has made a great difference in her life. She used to ride out with him a great deal, and lately I have taken his place, driving from 2 to 4 hours, and seeing some beautiful environing country which I never saw before.—I have read the Wings of the Dove (for which all thanks!) but what shall I say of a book constructed on a method which so belies everything that *I* acknowledge as law? You've reversed every traditional canon of story-telling (especially the fundamental one of *telling* the story, wh. you carefully avoid) and have created a new *genre littéraire* which I can't help thinking perverse, but in which you nevertheless *succeed,* for I read with interest to the end (many pages, and innumerable sentences twice over to see what the dickens they could possibly mean) and all with unflagging curiosity to know what the upshot might become. Its very *distingué* in its way, there are touches unique and inimitable, but its a "rum" way; and the worst of it is that I don't know whether it's fatal and inevitable with you, or deliberate and possible to put off and on. At any rate it is your own, and no one can drive you out or supplant you, so pray send along everything else you do, whether in this line or not, and it will add great solace to our lives.*—This is an exquisite warm day, 4.30 P.M. and we are momentarily awaiting the advent of a coach and four belonging to W. R. Warren of N.Y., Keene Valley and Lincoln, to pick us up, Alice & I, and take us out to the latter place 15 miles away, to spend the Sabbath. The warrens are at the football game, where Harry also is, having escorted Philip Burne Jones (staying with the Nortons interminably) thither. The english visitor is getting to be *the* nuisance of Cambridge. I have to give a dinner to Prof Edgeworth of Oxford this week. Our two German maids, who knew *nothing,* are getting into shape, and Alice feels encouraged. Its a pleasure to see smiling faces and to hear good voices as we now do. Billy seems to have been enraptured with Rye, and I am glad he made so good an impression. He ought this very day to be arriving in Geneva, where I hope he will soon become adapted. But the coach is overdue and I will now stop. With lots of love and gratitude (I wish you could see the furniture) in which Alice joins, I am ever affectionately yours,

W.J.

[*]"In its way" the book is most *beautiful*—the queer thing is the way—I went fizzling about concerning it, and expressing my wonder all the while I was reading it.

[1] WJ's son William spent about two weeks at Lamb House on his way to Geneva, where he was to spend the winter.

[2] In 1902–3 WJ taught Philosophy 3: The Philosophy of Nature.

From Henry James

LAMB HOUSE, | RYE, | SUSSEX. November 11th 1902

Dearest William.

I just have your good letter enclosing two cheques, to the amount of £30, on the terrible matter of the expedited furniture, which makes me still bleed, in thought, as costing you, at this rate, the eyes of your head. I accept the money, since you so scrupulously send it, then, with thanks, as the greater part of it will cover the 2 bills I paid—Harrod's Stores, in Town, & Wright & Pankhurst's here, for packing, boxing, delivering at ship. Of these Harrod's was of course much the larger & amounted to £*13.10.* That for the pieces *here* was, with the rail charges hence to ship at Albert Docks on the Thames, £*8,9,11.* If these sums seem large, remember that the cases were also large & very numerous, & that, apparently (as I figure, that is, from what Alice wrote on their arrival,) everything was very safely & solidly & thoroughly packed. Your remittance not only discharges this in full (the *whole* packing bill amounting to but £*22,* short of a penny,) but leaves me thus in your debt to the amount of about £*8.* As, however, you press this further amount upon me, I am willing gratefully to take it as representing handsome payment for the few extra articles of furniture that I chucked in at the last (all of *minime* value,) consular fees & any small matters by you were previously owing me. These things are all completely wiped out by it; you don't owe me a farthing more on anything whatever; & if you should ever attempt to send the same I notify you that I will mildly but inexorably return it on your hands. I rejoice greatly in your account of the happy intermarriage of your rooms & the alien articles. How I wish I could see the latter in place. This house has also much gained by *my* comparatively few spoils of De Vere Gdns: comparatively few, but all it will hold. I feel that all this time I have expressed to you & particularly to Alice, dreadfully little of the delightful interest I felt in the too brief possession of Billy & in the general benediction of his presence. But I tried to say something of it to Harry. I rejoiced in him in every way; he was an ornament to my life; & our harmony was without a cloud. He will of course have written you everything about his start at Geneva, whence I have had from him a cheerful & above all a *settled* letter. Flournoy appears to have been, for his matriculation, or whatever, a real benediction & an indispensable aid. I count upon B. for next summer—yet fear that the Alps &c, at the end of his semester (July, early,) will do me a very natural & inevitable *tort*. But there is time to talk of that.— It does me a world of good to hear of your having recovered, since your return to C., any physical tone lost before that. And if you know why & how, all blessings upon the process. Also upon the state of feeling you speak of in respect to your lecturing. I should think indeed the bloom might have faded from that. If you are of the same disposition next year I hope with all my heart that you may see your way to a final chuck. The night grows old—or rather the a.m. grows young (it's past midnight in the little green room so well known of you both;) otherwise there would be much your letter puts under my pen. Your reflections on the *W. of the D.*, e.g. greatly interest me; yet, after all, I don't know that I can very explicitly *meet* them. Or rather, really, there is too much to say. One writes as one *can*—& also as one sees, judges, feels, thinks. And I feel & think so much on the ignoble state to which in this age of every cheapness, I see the novel, as a form, reduced, that there is doubtless greatly, with me, the element of what I would as well as of what I "can." At any rate my stuff, such as it is, is inevitable—for *me*. Of that there is no doubt. But I should think you might well fail of joy in it—for I certainly feel that it is, in its way, more & more, positive. Don't despair, however, even yet, for I feel that in its way, as I say, there may be still other variations of way that will more or less *donner le change*. And it's *1.20* a.m. What you tell me of F.B. much moves me. I am on the very edge of writing him a most tender letter. Also to Grace Norton— *tenderissima*. All my love to Alice, who must not think of writing me this winter, while she has her so added correspondence with Billy on her hands. I have very positive hope of repaying, conveniently, the sinking fund £200, early in 1903.

Ever your Henry.

1903

With the Gifford Lectures out of the way and with reduced teaching responsibilities, William James turned his thoughts to writing a book of philosophy that would set out his own vision of reality. He had been a professor of philosophy since 1897, when his title had been changed from that of professor of psychology, and was sharply aware of the fact that he had contributed little to his subject apart from scattered and mostly popular essays. He was also concerned that because of his heart condition he might die before he had presented his radical empiricism to the public. In July 1903 he wrote the first sentence of his book: "Philosophy is a queer thing, at once the most sublime and the most contemptible of human occupations." He expected this beginning to be followed by a torrent of words, but few came and by the end of the 1903–4 academic year he had written a grand total of thirty-two manuscript pages instead of the 400 or 500 he had hoped for, not "brilliant" for a year's work. This never-completed book was to have been titled "The Many and the One."

Henry's proposal to visit the United States received a cool response from William for reasons that remain a matter for guesswork and psychological probing, unless one accepts at face value William's stated fear of exposing the aristocratic Henry to the crudities of American life. Henry made his visit in 1904–5 in spite of William's cautionary words.

From Henry James

LAMB HOUSE, | RYE, | SUSSEX. April 10th 1903

Dearest William.

I have all this winter most infamously treated you—at least since the New Year—or rather, no—much before it; being in receipt of 3 or 4 admirable letters from you that have till this hour languished unanswered. The one small spark of decency that I have been capable of was writing some month ago a poor stopgap letter to Peggy—sending you a message trying to attenuate my silence or

promising you some better satisfaction.   Yet even now I find it is 11
o clk. at night & the influences rather adverse!   I rise tomorrow
a.m.—Easter Saturday—to get over to Brighton & spend there, with
some old friends, the 2 or 3 days of this (as ever) most East-windy
(especially *here*) Eastertide.   I came down here from London (where
I have been since the mid-January,) 2 days ago, & I go back from
Brighton *to* town again, till the 10ᵗʰ May (about.)   It is not till then
that the vernal Rye is at all pleasant or that I desire ever to be here.
It (*This*) is the most *raw* time of the year.   London, on the other hand,
has been this winter very agreeable & salutary—the more that I had
been there so little for so long.   It has always its old faults—that if
you go in for *any* society you have, before you know it, inconveniently,
fatiguingly much.   But I try to go in for as little as is rigidly inevitable, & I am happy to say rigid regularity of work hasn't in the least
suffered.   I've seen a few old friends, but, thank God, I haven't made
any new to speak of!   Billy & I exchanged flurries over your intimat-
edly probable arrival—& then, when you didn't arrive, wisely rejoiced
that you hadn't partaken of so very qualified a joy.   It would have
been delightful to see you—if one could have been sure of seeing
you not finding yourself more the worse than the better.   As the
months go on I miss Bill the more—I mean as to the small prospect
of my doing more than have a very mean little glimpse of him at the
summer's end.   He is excellent about writing, better than I, & I seem
to get the sense that his "personal charm" smooths his path through
life, & that he incurs general good will.   I took leave of Theodora S.
3 days since (how poor Wᵐ D. *will* miss her!)[1] & she will give you the
latest about my appearance & conversation.   She will tell you that
the desire to go "home" for 6 months (not less,) daily grows in me &
that I particularly wish it before senile decay sets in.   But she will
also tell you that I don't see my way to anything of the sort within
any calculable number of months—or years.   And my dilemma is
rather tragic. It is all economic.   It is more & more important I
should go, to look after my material (literary) interests in person, &
quicken & improve them, after so endless an absence—of that I am
authentically assured, & *see* it, above all, for myself.   But the *process
itself* is so damnably expensive—6 mos. of American hotels (for I can't
stay with people—it's utterly impossible,) that I move, as it were, in
a vicious circle.   I say 6 months because I want & need the material &
impressions that only that time would give me.   I should wish to
write a *book* of "impressions["] (for much money) & to that end get

quite away from Boston & New York—really *see* the country at large. On the other hand I don't see myself prowling alone in western cities & hotels, or finding my way about by myself, & it is all darksome & tangled.   Some light may break—but meanwhile next Wednesday (awful fact,) is my 60ᵗʰ birthday.————I have had *here* the last 6 weeks (which doesn't make it any easier,) a tiresome little episode, one of the sorrows of a proprietor.   I have had to *buy* a large piece of the Garden next my own from J. H. Gasson, the blatant tradesman & scourge of Rye, in order to protect myself from his power to build (at *west* end of mine) & overlook or otherwise annoy me.   It had been for sale, unbeknown to me, & he had pounced on it & purchased—to threaten me, under the guise of offering it to me—*considerately*—at an of course excessive rate.   The danger poisoned my rest, & wd. have ruined my one view & all my little place, practically—so that there was nothing to do but to buy—& save the situation.   I have done so, & the (*this*) property is proportionately improved & defended, forever; but I have had to build a wall round most of the acquired piece, in order to *let* it to my neighbour Stonham, & the whole business has taken the £200, which I had set apart to repay into our Syracuse "sinking fund."   However, I have every reason to believe that I shall still be able to do that within this year. The incident has been a great bore.   Still, Lamb House is a much better place for the now *acquired* safety—which (the safety) has hitherto been but a thing of hazard.   I don't want to annex the new piece to my own garden—for the added trouble & expense of cultivating it—my own is so all-sufficient, & I have let it to Stonham for 7, 14 or 21 years (terminable by either.)   Of course I've a very poor rent, but that doesn't matter.   The benefit is secured & the place is off my hands & in very good ones.   Pardon this long dull story, & this sordid & prosaic letter.   I will really write you a better one when I come back here in May.   London is as bad for writing (letters other than local notes,) as for reading; which is saying much.   I think with joy of your better health, & I embrace tenderly the noble Alice & the 3 so interesting others.

Always & ever yours, & Alice's,   Henry.

[1] William Erasmus Darwin.

To Henry James

Cambridge, May 3. 1903

Dearest Heinrich,

Your long and *inhaltsvoll* letter of April 10th. arrived duly, and constituted, as usual, an "event."   Theodora had already given us your
message of an intended visit to these shores; and your letter made
Alice positively overflow with joyous anticipations.   On my part they
are less unmixed, for I feel more keenly a good many of the désagré-
ments to which you will inevitably be subjected, and imagine the sort
of physical loathing with which many features of our national life will
inspire you.   It takes a long time to notice such things no longer.
One thing, for example, which would reconcile *me* most easily to
abandoning my native country forever would be the certainty of immunity, when travelling, from the sight of my fellow beings at hotels
and dining-cars having their boiled eggs bro't to them, broken by a
negro, two in a cup, and eaten with butter.   How irrational this dislike is, is proved both by logic, and by the pleasure taken in the custom by the élite of mankind over here.   For instance, when I ventilated this dislike 3 or 4 evenings ago at President Eliot's, I found that
the 3 people who heard me, Mrs. Eliot, President Pritchett of the
Institute of Technology, and Mrs. George Baker, a very refined person whose equally gentlemanly husband is one of our professors of
English literature, never wanted *their* eggs in any other way.   Yet of
such irrational sympathies and aversions (quite conventional for the
most part) does our pleasure in a country depend, and in your case
far more than in that of most men.   The *vocalization* of our coun-
trymen is really, and not conventionally, so ignobly awful that the
process of hardening oneself thereto is very slow, and would in your
case be impossible.   It is simply *incredibly* loathsome.   I should hate
to have you come, and as a result feel that you had now *done* with
America forever, even in an ideal and imaginative sense, which after
a fashion you can still indulge in.   As far as your copyright interests
go, couldn't they be even more effectually and just as cheaply or more
cheaply attended to, by your hiring a duplicate *Pinker* over here?
Alice foresees Lowell lectures; but lectures have such an awful side
(when not academic) that I myself have foresworn them—it is a sort
of prostitution of one's person.   This is rather a throwing of cold
water; but it is well to realize both sides, and I think I can realize
certain things for you better than the sanguine and hospitable Alice
does.   Now for the other side, there are things in the American out

of door nature, as well as comforts indoors that can't be beat, and from which *I* get infinite pleasure. If you avoided the *banalité* of the Eastern cities, and traveled far and wide, to the South, to Colorado, over the Canadian Pacific to that coast, possibly to the Hawaian Islands, etc., you would get some reward, at the expense, it is true, of a considerable amount of cash. I think you ought to come in March or April and stay till the end of October or into November. The hot summer months you could pass in an absolutely quiet way—if you wished to,—at Chocorua with us, where you could do as much writing as you liked, continuous, and undisturbed, & would (I am sure) grow fond of, as you grew more and more intimate with, the sweet rough country there. After June 1904 *I* shall be free, to go and come as I like, for I have fully decided to resign, and nothing would please me so well (if I found then that I could afford it) as to do some of that proposed travelling along with you. I could take you into certain places that perhaps you would not see alone. Don't come therefore, if you do come, before the Spring of 1904!

I have been doing nothing in the way of work of late, and consequently have kept my fatigue somewhat at bay. The reading of the divine Emerson, volume after volume, has done me a lot of good, and, strange to say has thrown a strong practical light on my own path. The incorruptible way in which he followed his own vocation, of seeing such truths as the Universal Soul vouchsafed to him from day to day and month to month, and reporting them in the right literary form, and thereafter kept his limits absolutely, refusing to be entangled with irrelevancies however urging and tempting, knowing both his strength and its limits, and clinging unchangeably to the rural environment which he once for all found to be most propitious, seems to me a moral lesson to all men who have any genius, however small, to foster. I see now with absolute clearness, that greatly as I have been helped & enlarged by my University business hitherto, the time has come when the remnant of my life must be passed in a different manner, contemplatively namely, and with leisure and simplification for the one remaining thing, which is to report in one book, at least, such impression as my own intellect has received from the Universe. This I mean to stick to, and am only sorry that I am obliged to stay in the University one other year. It is giving up the inessentials which have grown beyond one's powers, for the sake of the duties which after all are most essentially imposed on one by the nature of one's powers.—Emerson is exquisite! I think I told you that I have to hold forth in praise of him at Concord on the 25th—

in company with Senator Hoar, T. W. Higginson, & Chas Norton— quite a *vieille garde* to which I now seem to belong.[1] You too have been leading an Emersonian life—though the environment differs to suit the needs of the different psychophysical organism which you present.

I have but little other news to tell you. Chas. Peirce is lecturing here—queer being, with his pathetic little old alsatian wife. Boott is in good spirits, and as sociable as ever. Grace Norton ditto. I breakfasted this Sunday morning, as of yore, with Theodora, who had a bad voyage in length but not in quality, though she lay in her berth the whole time. I can hardly conceive of being willing to travel under such conditions. Otherwise we are well enough, except Peggy, whose poor condition I imagine to result from influenza. Aleck has been regenerated through & through by "bird-lore," happy as the day is long, and growing acquainted with the country all about Boston. All in consequence of a neighboring boy on the street, Earl Stafford by name, 14 years old, and an ornithological genius, having taken him under his protection. Yesterday all day long in the open air, from seven to seven, at Wayland, spying and listening to birds, counting them, & writing down their names! I shall go off to morrow or next day to the country again, by myself, joining Henry Higginson and a colleague at the end of the week, and returning by the 14th for PhD. examinations which I hate profoundly. H.H has bo't some 5 miles of the shore of lake Champlain adjo[in]ing his own place there, and thinks of handing it over to the University for the surveying, engineering, forestry & mining school. He is as liberal hearted a man as the Lord ever walloped entrails into. His portrait by Sargent, a vast thing, destined for the "Union" building which he gave to the College, is esteemed a bad failure—I haven't seen it. *En revanche,* my own portrait has just been taken (one more sitting due) by Mrs. Whitman. She is always sure of a good snap-shot likeness, and I fancy that this will be one of her best. It is spirited—and flattering! Alice thinks it very good. I must not forget to say that Cary James called here for a very short time a few days ago and made an *extremely* good impression, manner, voice, everything, manly and good. I have written a letter to Carrie in consequence. He has joined a broker's firm (Tracy & Co) in N.Y. and expects to have to travel a good deal for a year or two. Rosina Emmet has just left us. I never saw a girl who had more definitely chosen the better and not the worser potentialities which her nature offered. I think her "splendid" now, & so does Alice. Bob we don't see. He is still at

Concord. The Marys have gone, I understand, to Seattle, to be with Edward, whose marriage every witness reports to be a great success.

What a devil of a bore your forced purchase of the unneccessary neighboring land must have been. *I* am just buying 150 acres more at Chocorua, to round off our second estate there. Keep well & prolific—everyone speaks praise of your better sort, which I am keeping for the country.[2] Alice is in bed with another headache, tho' they are much rarer since she has given up meat. She would send all her love. I *do* send all of mine.

Your   W.J.

[1] WJ delivered an address at the celebration of the centenary of the birth of Ralph Waldo Emerson on 25 May 1903. The address is reprinted in *ERM.*

[2] HJ, *The Better Sort* (1903).

From Henry James

Lamb House, | Rye, | Sussex. | May 24th, 1903.
Dearest William.

How much I feel in arrears with you let this gross machinery testify—which I shamelessly use to help to haul myself into line.[1] However, you have most beneficently, from of old, given me free licence for it. Other benefits, unacknowledged as yet, have I continued to receive from you: I think I've been silent even since *before* your so cheering (about yourself) letter from Ashville, followed, a few days before I left town (which I did five days ago) by your still more interesting and "important" one (of May 3rd.) in answer to mine dealing (so tentatively!) with the question of my making my plans, so far as is complicatedly and remotely possible for going over to you for 6 or 8 months. There is—and there *was* when I wrote—no conceivability of my doing this for at least a year to come—before August 1904, at nearest; but it kind of eases my mind to thresh the idea out sufficiently to have a direction to *tend* to meanwhile, and an aim to work at. It is in fact a practical necessity for me, *dès maintenant,* to know whether or no I absolutely want to go if, and when, I *can:* such a difference, in many ways (more than I need undertake to explain) do the prospect of going and the prospect of *not* going make. Luckily, for myself, I do already (as I feel) quite adequately remain convinced that I *shall* want to whenever I can: that is unless I don't put it off for much *more* than a year—after which period I certainly shall *lose* the impulse to return to my birthplace under the mere blight of incip-

ient senile decay.   If I go at all I must go before I'm too old, and,
above all, before I mind being older.   You are very dissuasive—even
more than I expected; but I think it comes from your understanding
even less than I expected the motives, considerations, advisabilities
etc. that have gradually, cumulatively, and under much study of the
question, much carefully invoked *light* on it, been acting upon me.
I won't undertake just now to tell you what all these reasons are, and
how they show to me—for there is still plenty of time to do that. Only
I *may* even at present say that I don't despair of bringing you round,
in the interval (if what is beyond the interval *can* realise itself) to a
better perception of my situation.   It is roughly—and you will perhaps think too cryptically—speaking, a situation for which 6 or 8
months in my native land shine before me as a very possible and
profitable remedy: and I don't speak *not* by book.   Simply and su-
pinely to shrink—on mere grounds of general fear and encouraged
shockability has to me all the air of giving up, chucking away without
a struggle, the one chance that remains to me in life of anything that
can be called a *movement:* my one little ewe-lamb of possible exotic
experience, such experience as may convert itself, through the senses,
through observation, imagination and reflection now at their maturity, into vivid and solid *material,* into a general renovation of one's
too monotonised grab-bag.   You speak of the whole matter rather, it
seems to me, "à votre aise"; you make, comparatively, and have always
made, so *many* movements; you have travelled and gone to and fro—
always comparatively!—so often and so much.   I have practically
never travelled at all—having never been economically able to; I've
only gone, for short periods, a few times—so much fewer than I've
wanted—to Italy: never anywhere else that I've seen everyone about
me here (who *is,* or was, anyone) perpetually making for.   These visions I've had, one by one, all to give up—Spain, Greece, Sicily, any
glimpse of the East, or in fact of anything; even to the extent of
rummaging about in France; even to the extent of trudging about, a
little, in Switzerland.   Counting out my few dips into Italy, there has
been no time at which *any* "abroad" was financially convenient or
possible.   And now, more and more, all such adventures present
themselves in the light of mere agreeable *luxuries,* expensive and su-
pererogatory, inasmuch as *not* resolving themselves into new material
or assimilating with my little acquired stock, my accumulated capital
of (for convenience) "international" items and properties.   There's
nothing to be done, by me, any more, in the way of writing, *de chic*
little worthless, superficial, *poncif* articles about Spain, Greece or

Egypt. They are the sort of thing that doesn't work in at all to what now most interests me: which is human Anglo-Saxondom, with the American extension, or opportunity for it, so far as it may be given me still to work the same. If I *shouldn't,* in other words, bring off going to the U.S., it would simply mean giving up, for the remainder of my days, all chance of such experience as is represented by interesting "travel"—and which in this special case of my own would be much more than so represented (granting the travel to be American.) I should settle down to a mere mean oscillation from here to London and from London here—with nothing (to speak of) left, more, to happen to me in life in the way of (the poetry of) motion. That spreads before me as for mind, imagination, special, "professional" labour, a thin, starved, lonely, defeated, *beaten,* prospect: in comparison with which your own circumgyrations have been as the adventures of Marco Polo or H. M. Stanley. I *should* like to think of going once or twice more again, for a sufficient number of months, to Italy, where I know my ground sufficiently to be able to plan for such quiet work there as might be needfully involved. But the day is past when I can "write stories" about Italy with a mind otherwise pre-occupied. My native land, which time, absence and change have, in a funny sort of way, made almost as romantic to me as "Europe", in dreams or in my earlier time here, used to be—the actual bristling (as fearfully bristling as you like) U.S.A. have the merit and the precious property that they meet and fit into my ("creative") preoccupations; and that the period there which should represent the poetry of motion, the one big taste of travel not supremely missed, would carry with it also possibilities of the prose of *production* (that is of the production of prose) such as no other mere bought, paid for, sceptically and half-heartedly worried-through adventure, by land or sea, would be able to give me. My primary idea in the matter is absolutely economic— and on a basis that I can't make clear to you now, though I probably shall be able to later on if you demand it: that is if you also are accessible to the impression of my having *any* "professional standing" là-bas big enough to be improved on. I am not thinking (I'm sure) vaguely or blindly (but recognizing direct intimations) when I take for granted some such Chance as my personal presence there *would* conduce to improve: I don't mean by its beauty or brilliancy, but simply by the benefit of my managing for once in my life not to fail to be on the spot. Your allusion to an American Pinker as all sufficient for any purpose I could entertain doesn't, for me, begin to cover the ground—which is antecedent to that altogether. It isn't in the least a question of my trying to make old copyrights pay better or look into arrangements actually existing; it's a question—well, of too much more than I can go into the detail of now (or, much rather, into the general and comprehensive truth of) or even that I can ever do so long as I only have from you that you Doubt. What you say of the Eggs(!!!) of the Vocalisation, of the Shocks in general, and of everything else, is utterly beside the mark—it being absolutely *for* all that class of phenomena, and every other class, that I nurse my infatuation. I want to see them, I want to see everything, I want to See the Country (scarcely a bit New York and Boston, but intensely the Middle and Far West and California and the South)—in *cadres* as complete, and immeasurably more mature, than those of the celebrated Taine when he went, early in the sixties, to Italy, for six weeks, in order to write his big book.[2] Moreover, besides the general "professional" I have thus a conception of, have really in definite view, there hangs before me a very special other probability—which, however, I must ask you to take on trust, if you can, as it would be a mistake for me to bruit it at all abroad as yet. To make anything of this last-mentioned business I must be on the spot—I mean not only to carry the business out, of course, but to arrange in advance its indispensable basis. It would be the last of follies for me to attempt to do *that* from here—I should simply spoil my chance. So you see what it all comes to, roughly stated—that the 6 or 8 months in question are all I have to look to unless I give up the prospect of ever stirring again. They are the only "stir" I shall ever be able to afford, because, though they will cost something, cost even a good bit, they will bring in a great deal more, in proportion, than they will cost. Anything else (other than a mere repeated and too aridly Anglo-American winter in Florence, perhaps, say) would almost only cost. But enough of all this—I am saying, *have* said, much more than I meant to say at the present date. Let it, at any rate, simmer in your mind, if your mind has any room for it, and take *time*, above all, if there is any danger of your still again replying adversely. Let me add this word more, however, that I mention August 1904 very advisedly. If I want (and it's half the battle) to go to the West and the South, and even, dreamably, to Mexico, I can only do these things during the winter months; it wouldn't do for me to put in all that part of the summer during which (besides feeling, I fear, very ill from the heat) I should have simply to sit still. On the other hand I should like immensely not to fail of coming in for the *whole* American autumn, and like hugely, in especial, to arrive in time for the last three

or four weeks of your stay at Chocorua—which I suppose I should do if I quitted this by *about* mid-August. Then I should have the music of *toute la lyre,* coming away after, say, three or four Spring weeks at Washington, the next April or May. But I *must* stop. These castles in Spain all hang by the thread of my finding myself in fact economically able, 14 months hence, to *face* the music. If I am not, the whole thing must drop. All I can do meanwhile is to try and arrange that I *shall* be. I am scared, rather—well in advance—by the vision of American expenses. But the "special" possibility that shines before me has the virtue of covering (potentially) all that. One thing is very certain—I shall not be able to hoard by "staying" with people. This will be impossible to me (though I *will,* assuredly, by a rich and rare exception, dedicate to you and Alice as many days as you will take me in for, whether in country or town. Basta!)———
I talk of your having room in your mind, but you must be having at the present moment little enough for anything save your Emerson speech, which you are perhaps now, for all I know, in the very act of delivering. This morning's Times has, in its American despatch, an account of the beginning, either imminent or actual, of the Commemoration—and I suppose your speech is to be uttered at Concord. Would to God I could sit there entranced by your accents—side by side, I suppose, with the genial Bob! May you be floated grandly over your cataract—by which I don't mean have any manner of *fall,* but only be a Niagara of eloquence, all continuously, whether above or below the rapids. You will send me, I devoutly hope, some report of the whole thing. It affects me much even at this distance and in this so grossly alien air—this overt dedication of dear old E. to his immortality. I hope all the attendant circumstances will be graceful and beautiful (and *not* with either Ellen or Edward for the centre of the fire-wheel.) I came back hither, as I believe I have mentioned, some six days ago, after some 18 weeks in London, which went, this time, very well, and were very easy, on my present extremely convenient basis, to manage. The Spring here, till within a week, has been backward and blighted; but Summer has arrived at last with a beautiful jump, and Rye is quite adorable in its outbreak of greenery and blossom. I never saw it more lovely than yesterday, a supreme summer (early-summer) Sunday. The dear little charm of the place at such times consoles one for the sordid vandalisms that are rapidly disfiguring, and that I fear will soon quite destroy, it. Another scare for me just now is the threatened destruction of the two little charmingly-antique silver-grey cottages on the right of the little vista

that stretches from my door to the church—the two that you may remember just beyond my garden wall, and in one of which my gardener has been lately living. They will be replaced, if destroyed, by a pair of hideous cheap modern workingmen's cottages—a horrid inhuman stab at the very heart of old Rye. There is a chance it may be still averted—but only just a bare chance. One would buy them, in a moment, to save them and to save ones little prospect; but one is, naturally, quite helpless for that, and the price asked is impudently outrageous, quite of the black-mailing order. On the other hand, let me add, I'm gradually consoling myself now for having been black-mailed in respect to purchase of the neighbouring garden I wrote you of. Now that I have got it and feel the value of the protection, my greater peace seems almost worth the imposition. This, however, is all my news—except that I have just acquired by purchase a very beautiful and valuable little Dachshund pup of the "red" species, who has been promising to be the joy of my life up to a few hours since— when he began to develop a mysterious and increasing tumifaction of one side of his face, about which I must immediately have advice. The things my dogs have, and the worries I have in consequence! I already see this one settled beneath monumental alabaster in the little cemetery in the angle of my garden, where he will make the fifth. I have heard, most happily, from Harry at Marburg; he seems to fall everywhere blessedly on his feet. But you will know as much, and more, about him than I. I am already notching off the days till I may hope to have him here in August. I count on his then staying through September. But good-bye, with every fond *voeu.* I delight in the news of Aleck's free wild life—and also of Peggy's (which the accounts of her festivities, feathers and frills, in a manner reproduce for me). Tender love to Alice. I embrace you all and am always yours

Henry James.

[1] HJ is referring to the fact that the letter is typed.
[2] Hippolyte-Adolphe Taine, *Voyage en Italie* (1866).

To Henry James

Chocorua, June 6. '03

Dearest Henry,
    Your long and excitingly interesting type-written letter about coming hither arrived yesterday, and I hasten to retract all my dampening

remarks, now that I understand the motives fully. The only ones I had imagined, blindling that I am, were fraternal piety and patriotic duty. Against those I thought I ought to proffer the thought of "eggs" and other shocks, so that when they came I might be able to say that you went not unwarned. But the moment it appears that what you crave is millions of just such shocks & that a new lease of artistic life, with the lamp of genius fed by the oil of twentieth century American life is to be the end and aim of the voyage, all my stingy doubts wither, and are replaced by enthusiasm that you are still so young-feeling, receptive, and hungry for more raw material and experience. It cheers me immensely, and makes me feel more so myself. It is pathetic to hear you talk so about your career and its going to seed without the contact of new material; but feeling as you do about the new material, I augur a great revival of energy and internal effervescence from the execution of your project. Drop your english ideas & take America and Americans as they take themselves, and you will certainly experience a rejuvenation. This is all I have to say *to day*—merely to let you see how the prospect exhilarates us.

August, 1904, will be an excellent time to begin. I should like to go South with you—& possibly to Cuba—but as for California, I fear the expense. I am sending you a decidedly moving book by a mulatto ex-student of mine, Du Bois, professor [of] history at Atlanta (Georgia) negro College.[1] Read Chapters VII to XI for local colour, etc.

We have been up here for 10 days, the physical luxury of the simplification is something that money can't buy. Every breath is a pleasure—this in spite of the fact that the whole country is drying up and burning up—it makes one ashamed that one can be so happy. The smoke here [h]as been so thick for 5 days past that the opposite shore is hidden. We have a first rate hired man, a good cow, nice horse, dog, cook, second-girl etc. Come up and see us in August 1904!

Your ever loving | W.J.

Poor Helen Child who was married a year ago to one Sargent a botanist, died a week ago after a fortnights illness, stupor due to a tumor on the brain. Innocent, unworldly, optimistic child of 40, with invalid habits, whose future happiness was not certain, so 'tis just as well. Poor Mrs. Child's mind is enfeebling, but her bodily health excellent I saw a good deal of Bob on the 25th. at Concord. He was well dressed and seemed to be in very good shape. He is living in one of his own small houses, alone, & getting his meals at the Hotel. Their large house is let, and the two Marys at Seattle.

[1] William Edward Burghardt Du Bois, *The Souls of Black Folk* (1903).

In his letter of 26 November 1903, not reproduced here, Henry wrote that his decision as to whether to visit America would be based largely on economic considerations. At issue was the rental of Lamb House for the duration of the visit and Alice's offer to help find suitable tenants for it. Henry's novel The Ambassadors *was published in November 1903 and he wanted to make certain that William received a copy from the publishers.*

To Henry James

Cambr. Dec 16. '03

Dearest H., Yours of the 2nd comes this A.M., as a longer one came about a week ago. The latter was "pathetic." That lack of means should make you hesitate to revisit your native land—that were indeed the limit! Since it is for purposes of production you would be justified in borrowing (mortgaging Lamb House, e.g.)—and I can see you through with a thousand. I should think that you might let Lamb House here from say August 1st onwards. We will do what we can towards it. The Ambassadors came 4 days ago, and opens finely. The illiberal H. M. & Co., after promising to send a copy of Story have found it convenient to forget their promise, but DON'T *you send a copy!*[1] Alice has read it in Boott's copy, and I, when the time comes round, will do the same or buy one. I am glad you liked my Germanic Museum speech, which brightened up a somewhat heavy occasion.[2] I forged it with endless labor-pangs, and in my condition that pure phrase-making business doesn't pay. I refuse almost daily some invitation or other to make an address. I hope you will be relishing Bill's article on Athletics in the Graduates Magazine.[3] I helped him out a little bit, but the thing is his all through, and being just what hundreds of persons are waiting to hear some *young* man say, is exciting much favorable comment. I enclose my last public utterance—autant en emporte le vent!—but being asked, I felt it was my duty to stand by the little band.[4] I am out of bed for the morning, for the first time in 5 days, having been having an attack of tonsillitis, which will leave me 'sick' for a week to come. Alice is just back from a week at Montreal with the Gregors—very pleasant. I have just sent in my resignation for good, of my Professorship, & am really pining to feel free.[5] Somehow the end of a chain which I still drag seems to be as irksome as the full amount would be.

There is no other news. Alice, and all (to whom your letter was just read at the bkfst. table) send love. Rye must be overlonely just now; I should think it would lead you to fag your brain too much. Thats why I fear the country as a winter residence.

Your ever affectionate, | W.J.

[1] HJ's *William Wetmore Story and His Friends* (1903) was published in the United States by Houghton, Mifflin & Co.

[2] WJ, "Dedication of the Germanic Museum," *Harvard Illustrated Magazine* 5 (November 1903): 48–50, reprinted in *ECR*.

[3] William James, "Sport or Business?" *Harvard Graduates' Magazine* 12 (December 1903): 225–29.

[4] WJ is probably referring to his address on the Philippine question delivered at the Twentieth Century Club in Boston on 30 November 1903; reprinted in *ECR*.

[5] WJ finally resigned in 1907.

From Henry James

Lamb House, | Rye, | Sussex. | Dec. 29th, 1903.
Dearest William.

A good letter from you and another from Bill are beneficently with me; yours of the 16th enclosing your noble political speech, and Bill's transmitting me his scarce inferior Athletics article. They find me sitting as tight, here, as I can, through the inevitable little complications and oppressions of this so supposedly festive season—so much being made of that here; and not fortunately, as yet, having had to fight any bad assault of the temperature and the elements. It is fine weather, for me, in this place, at least in winter, when a wild gale doesn't blow; and we have lately had mild and windless days and nights which have let us sleep on both ears. Your two letters seem to paint a moment of some domestic depression—I mean with Alice's absence, poor little Aleck's goggles and your tonsillitis; but I hope all these are now troubles well past—in addition to which they are intimate notes that have made me the more yearn for you. I have broken down under the postal avalanche of the season, reinforced by the presence of my remarkable little friend Jonathan Sturges, of whom you have heard me speak, and who, being infirm and delicate, requires during his visits a good deal of personal attention. There-fore I am shamelessly working off in this fashion every letter I can, and really desiring to take any correspondential resentment of it for the sign of a relation (by letter at least) ended. I am disgusted to learn that H. and M. have never had the grace to send you the Story vols; which but adds to the meanness of their not having addressed *me* (all I should have expected) a single complimentary copy. Apro-pos of which I have it at heart to rectify a statement I made some weeks ago in writing to C.E.N., to whom I owed recognition of his having let me use a few of Story's letters to him: to rectify, I mean, on the possibility of his having repeated to you my remark. I men-tioned that up to the moment of writing to him I had received, in acknowledgement of the book no word of amiability from the Story offspring—and I hadn't; but immediately afterwards I did receive from them all very pleasant and evidently very sincere gratulation— the delay of which had proceeded from their scatteredness over the Continent and nonreceipt, till they got home, of the copies addressed them. So, as I wish to lave their memory, kindly mention this to C.N. in case you remember. But enough of a most closed incident. I am touched by your finding "pathetic" what I told you of a particu-lar consideration that had to weigh with me in the matter of a pil-grimage next summer, and I do not proudly resent it, for I think that, all things considered, at this end of time, the circumstance in itself *is* slightly pathetic. But don't take too much that view of it, for I shall then feel that I may have represented my anxieties as more squalid than I need have done. It isn't that one wouldn't, with some decent ease, be able to "go" at all, and even stay for a sufficiently graceful number of weeks. I sounded the note in respect to which you respond, because what I have been having in mind has loomed before me as a rather positively expensive programme: Six or eight months all of hotels and travelling expenses, with production, and thereby remuneration, meanwhile much interrupted (and when I say much I mean entirely.) It's so long—beyond all counting—since production has been interrupted with me *at all* (save by some bout of illness) that I've grown to regard such a vision as a kind of mon-strosity of extravagance. Attribute to *that* special cause the pusilla-nimity of any want of confidence that I may have expressed. There are really, I think, quite sufficient grounds for my confidence being excellent, and many signs and symptoms that urge it to become so. Moreover it comes over me strongly that I shall go quite melancholy mad if, during any such period, I *don't* manage, to some degree or other, to relapse into work; so necessary is that consciousness to my common, from-day-to-day *bienêtre*. A quiet corner somewhere, (only not in Cambridge or Boston!) is all I shall require for that indispensable sanitation; and I suppose some such are not wholly unthinkable even at the local hotel. So think of me as really coming, and don't, I beseech you, breathe a word of the reason I last gave you for my possible reserves. Of all of which enough for the present. I am "carried away" by your Anti-imperialist discourse, as I am by all your discourses; only I fear it will be a long day before we do really revomit the Philippines. I shall write to Bill directly, to thank him for *his* charming contribution to the family eloquence. May it indeed resound and rebound. Tell Alice that I am joyful over her flight to Montreal—I mean over her not having unlearned how to strike occasionally for freedom. But I mustn't let this sprawl—I intended but a page of it. I take my visitor back to town myself a day or two hence, and spend three or four there; then I return hither to sit as tight as I may again till about Feb. 1st. I am trying to as nearly as possible finish by that time a long novel, which, but for its length, should have been finished a month ago. I had agreed to deliver it in time for publication on May 1st; but I have got it transferred to August, which will be better.[1] Meantime I am counting on having finished still another (begun a couple of years ago) before the date of my "embarcation": so that I shan't, at least, not have tried to qualify myself. If I go to town, for a stretch, a month hence, it will be but for February and March. I shall have been here then, (by Feb. 1st.) nine months on end; but these late weeks of autumn have had their merits—great merits of tranquility and of uninterruptedness for working and reading: also for solitary meditation when these processes, transcending one's modest range, exhaust. Much love to all, and in particular to Alice—to whom I shall write when I *next* write.

Yours all and always | Henry James

[1] HJ, *The Golden Bowl* (1904). The American edition was published by Charles Scribner's Sons on 10 November 1904; the English edition, by Methuen & Co., on 10 February 1905.

1904

In the letter that follows, William mentions Horace Fletcher and his book on the advantages of the thorough chewing of food. Horace Fletcher was in his mid-fifties, independently wealthy and philanthropically minded, when he worked out several simple rules for proper eating, which he promoted by writing, lecturing, and performing feats of endurance. According to Fletcher, one should eat only when hungry and chew each mouthful until it becomes nearly liquid and can be swallowed without effort. Among other benefits, Fletcherism, as the practice came to be called, was to result in loss of weight. The portly Henry, who at times worried about his weight, adopted Fletcherism, to his eventual regret.

To Henry James

Cambridge, Mass., Jan. 1, 1904.

Dear H.,—

A long and charming letter from you to Grace Norton came in to us yesterday, and made me feel like writing to you immediately. I have been cooped up in the house with a poisonous influenzal catarrh for three weeks, and my mental and physical strength have seemed entirely abolished. To vary the business, and live up to your example, after I had had it a week I broke out with acute inflammation in the joints of my left foot. Whether we call it gout or rheumatism the doctor says depends upon the previous habits of the patient. You call yours gout, so I will do the same. It has subsided now almost entirely, after a fortnight, but it gave me for two or three days an idea of how sensitive to pain a part of one's organism could become.

Three weeks ago a letter came from you, still dallying with the question of coming to America. Alice took it to Montreal with her and I thought that she had answered it there. It appears, on inquiry just now, that she has not answered it. It represented you in a rather pathetic light. Alice went in to a luncheon club two days ago and ventilated Lamb House. It is possible that an advertisement in the Nation next spring might help, and I should think that between English and American sources you could hardly fail of getting a good tenant. If you come I shall be ready to accompany you on any moderate tour which you may propose to make. I shall be very free next year, having offered my resignation to the Corporation. Eliot made a long call on Alice the other day when I was too ill to see him, and said that for certain reasons they did not want me to go on the retired list, but that I could draw pay equivalent to retiring allowance on the Gurney foundation, and take it out in writing and not in teaching.[1] This of course would be a very fine arrangement; but to understand it fully I must have a personal interview with the President, and there is no hurry about that. Peggy is now in Montreal, having apparently a very good time. She is in fine condition this year, seeming quite free from the morbidness which to a certain extent last year afflicted her, and is altogether rather a big souled and large minded pattern of humanity. Harry takes his bar examinations to-morrow, and is already negotiating his entrance into one of the big offices in Boston. Billy works away at the Medical School, just as if he had never had his first year of study already. When I compare his work with the kind of work I used to do, it is Hyperion to a Satyr. I can hardly imagine a greater contrast. Nevertheless I don't at all definitely see him in my mind's eye as a future practitioner of medicine. Alec is big and gracious in disposition. I think he will turn out all right also. I have been leading a life almost entirely constituted of interruptions, reading manuscripts, making speeches, interviewing students, all trifling things but in the end so entirely consuming my time that I feel as if something surgical would have to be performed to enable me to get at my own business, instead of other people's, and I am going to be energetic from now onward and say no to every one that comes along.

Poor old Boott is, I fancy, in a somewhat critical situation, confined to his room with a tendency to pneumonia of an indolent sort. The doctor has not wished to alarm him, so he doesn't understand his own situation and is rather impatient. I doubt whether he outlives this winter. I am sending you a book by Horace Fletcher, with certain passages marked for you to read.[2] Every word is true about it. You are in a very favorable situation for learning his art of chewing, which he says it takes a good three months for a man to acquire automatically. It may make a great revolution in your whole economy, however, and I advise you to give it your most respectful attention. I am quite sure that it meets my case to a T, and I am going to try to become a muncher, as he is. He is a very charming man, has made a fortune at business, and owns a palazzo on the Grand

Canal in Venice, where he keeps his family.   We have not yet read your "Ambassadors," my head has been unable to stand any consecutive reading.   The Story Book seems to be a great success, but appears to have been very badly managed by Houghton, Mifflin & Company.   At Alice's lunch club several ladies said they had wished to give it for a Christmas present, but no copies were to be had in Boston.   There is a tide in the affairs of books which ought to be taken at the flood; I fear that in this case H. M. & Co. are letting that tide go by.

The Airedale terrier has turned out splendidly.   The only trouble is that, occupied as we are, it is very difficult to give him and his comrade sufficient exercise.

Good-bye, dear Henry, I am dictating off a lot of New Year's letters and you must take this as one of them.   I shall write you with greater richness and fulness when I regain possession of my wits, eyes, etc. A happy New Year to you from your loving

W.J.

Poor Jenny Higginson and young George's boy of 10, & Jenny's "companion,["] were victims of the awful Chicago theatre-fire.[3]

[1] WJ agreed not to resign and to offer Philosophy 9: Metaphysics for the first half of 1904–5.

[2] Horace Fletcher, *The New Glutton or Epicure* (1903).

[3] The fire at the Iroquois Theater in Chicago, which broke out during a holiday matinee on 30 December 1903 when the theater was packed with women and children, killed about 570 people.   Among the victims were Jeannette B. Higginson (b. 1869), daughter of George Higginson and Elizabeth Hazard Barker Higginson of Stockbridge, Mass., and her young nephew, Roger Griswold Higginson (b. 1894) of Winnetka, Ill., son of "young George" Higginson, who was a son of the Stockbridge Higginsons.

To Henry James

THE JEFFERSON, | RICHMOND, VIRGINIA. Feb. 8 1904
Dearest H'ry,

I received here yesterday from Alice your letter from Rye, explaining as how you had felt obliged to decline the Lowell Lecture course.   This takes a load off my own mind; for although Alice, with that love which women have of seeing their men folks cut an appearance in the public eye, had invoked with many *voeux*, your acceptance of the invitation, I could see nothing desirable in it.   The whole lecture-business now-a-days, save where there is a stereopticon, or exhibition of facts not presentable as "reading-matter," or where the lecturer is an artist in his line and speaks without notes, is doomed to second-rateness, and from the point of view of the relations of the audience to the lecturer, is even a degradation to the latter. I have felt this strongly, in my own brief experience; and nothing save the direst pecuniary pressure would make me consent to appear before a miscellaneous and simply curious audience again—even if I had the health & strength requisite for doing so without strain. In point of fact I have now regularly to decline about 4 invitations a week to make "addresses" or "talks" or lectures, all over the country. "Women's Clubs" are the great inviters. In your case particularly there would be a large audience, there simply to see your person, and hear your voice, and gossip about your peculiarities afterwards, with no sympathetic intent, and almost no interest in the matter of your discourse. It would be only a some what more solid equivalent for the publication of your portrait in the newspaper with a gossippy breezy article adjoined, about you. Add to this, that a *read* lecture is doomed to inferiority—To really succeed the lecturer must *speak*, & *command* his audience—and you are well out of the scrape, and I hope will stay so.

How you are working! And gout into the bargain too. Mine was much mitigated and abbreviated, I think, by Driver's treatment, of compresses, renewed only twice daily, of fl. extr. of opium in bicarbonate of soda-solution, and *aspirin* taken internally. It was a small affair, severely painful for only two days, & I walked in a week, though my great toe-joint is still tender. I am taking piperazin, of the loathsome taste, still.

I left home 16 days ago and am on my way back. On the whole the result has been to make me doubt the wisdom of my rash promise to accompany you on a Southern tour. I went with Edw. Emerson,* his wife & daughter, to Tallehassee, staying only 24 hours on the way, at Magnolia on the S! Johns River. Loathsome Hotel at T., but pretty country. Total impression of alienation & never wishing to return. The vile speech of the commercial travellers & general Human inferiority depressed my soul. At Savannah, charming Hotel, and city with many elements of refinement, and old time suggestiveness— somewhat like the vicinity of washington Square and lower fifth Avenue in our youth. Charleston a painful case of death in life and self-survival, never at best more than a village, morally, Richmond an active thriving northern-like city, with as splendid a blood-soaked environment as any thing in the world. Four years of successfully holding the US. at bay, and battles only a few miles off all the while. I get home gladly: The objects and impressions that feed one's mental interests are too rare in this land to make it worth while to strain them from the ocean of ugliness and commoness which holds them in suspension. One can't get at the *country*, so as to make use of its resources, and when one does so, the hotel-crowd is displeasing—I speak of some of the N. & S. Carolina winter "resorts." Naturally, I have thought much of how you could stand all this, and I have quaked with apprehension, lest you shd. throw all up and scurry back in a fit of disgust. The only thing in America is to get among good private people, and suffer their hospitality, which is *overdone*. You would have, I think, to single out a few spots where you could settle for a fortnight at least, and work. Asheville might be one. Some S.C. winter country resort another. Savannah might do for a 3rd. You ought to see some of the big Florida Coast resorts (Palm Beach or Miami) as specimens of the multimillionaire paradise. Then New Orleans, probably. And finally, Colorado Springs or Denver, Chicago, Saint Louis, California, & Seattle. It will cost you $8.00 a day throughout, possibly 10—say 2000 dollars as a maximum for 200 days of it, including voyages. The thing is to make good nature & human tolerance your mission, remembering that God made these people and Christ died for them, and that the business-ideals, and ideas of personal comfort which animate them are also part of His plan, as much as your ideals are! *I* feel no call to assimilate them, even for purposes of the imagination, as you will, for my constructive work lies in so altogether different a sphere of being. Simplicity and rurality are what my outer life aspires to hereafter, and undergoing these hotel conditions merely to get away from home for a while makes me ask "is it worth it?" The background of *everything* is too irredeemably crude in our country, and the speech of our people too horrible, if you once let your self get sensitive to it.

I am forgetting that in *Washington* you will probably find united the best conditions for a long stay in the winter.

Good bye! In an hour my train leaves! Plenty of news this A.M. War in the East apparently inevitable, and likely, either way, to be a turning point in the world's history.[1] Awful fire in Baltimore yesterday—here the day was as peaceful as early spring. Get well of your gout!

Your loving   W.J.

[*]Sweet natured fellow, for all his boyish prejudices!

[1] The *New York Times*, 8 February 1904, reported that Japan and Russia had broken off diplomatic relations on the sixth. On the eighth Japan attacked the Russian fleet at Port Arthur.

From Henry James

Lamb House, | Rye, | Sussex. | Feb. 23rd, 1904.

Dearest W.

I have had these several days your so interesting letter from Richmond Va. which came to me in town, but which I have now before me here, as the partial consolation of a parenthetic dash home determined, I am sorry to say, by a slight renewed visitation of gout. I ought perhaps to speak of this last rather with joy than bitterness, as it has been very brief, was a moderate and merciful, not a huge and enraged inflamation, and is permitting me already to plan, after but one day in bed, and the rest of the time hobbling about my room, for a return to London this p.m. If I achieve the latter a few hours hence I hope to go on there for another period of six weeks or so without further molestation. Your letter meanwhile sustains and refreshes me from many points of view: especially as to your golden words about the Lowell lectures, which fall in wholly with my own deepest convictions. I have had a second letter from Lowell, asking me to contract on the basis of a year's postponement (from *next* winter;) but this also I have not agreed to, though I haven't absolutely said Nay. I have told him I can agree to nothing, that the presence of other work makes it impossible I should calculate, and that my hope is small of being able to assent even when I see him personally next autumn. So it's as good as a refusal, and to the idea of refusal I shall more and more "freeze". I want, most exactly, to have gone to the U.S. *not* to lecture, or otherwise "produce" myself; instead of having gone vulgarly and gregariously to do it. I repeat that your appraisement of the business is absolutely just—there's no other word to be said. It would be an odious business even if the pecuniary bribe were great; so that for a small bribe it's simply unthinkable. Basta. Your sad-coloured reflections on your impressions of travel interest but don't appal me: I feel myself solicited on grounds as to which the whole "liking" question is so irrelevant and imponderable. I don't think I go much by likings, anyhow, as I grow older, and should be at a loss to-day, here or anywhere, to say very much what I *do* like—or too utterly don't. I hope that by this time, at any rate, you will have found your journey to have rid you of peccant humours or whatever other sources of depression. Your account of the long, hard, iron-bound frost does a little terrify me—though, when I think of it, as between that and these last two years of eternal diluvian damp, *our* perpetual portion, the advantage seems to me all in favour of the dry bright medium. I want much to see at any rate if it won't do me a good turn. And apropos of good turns let me tell you that I have found only on coming down here Horace Fletcher's extraordinary little volume which you mentioned some weeks back that you were sending me. You mentioned it with such approval that I missed, in town, its not coming, and meant to write you for news of it. It has simply awaited me here, I having forgot that I don't have books forwarded; and I put my hand on it only last evening (that is had the spirit to pull it out of its cover:) when a mere dip into it made me sit up so straight that I failed, under the consequent excitement, almost entirely of my night's sleep. I don't know who H.F. is, and I never heard of him in Venice; but his treatise somehow speaks to me on the spot, and I have been breakfasting this morning wholly in the light of it. This single experiment has seemed to me illuminating—but I'm fairly afraid to commit myself to rash hope. I have all the same a sneaking confidence, engendered in these few hours. I've read the book already almost twice over, and I shall certainly give its doctrine the most patient and resolute trial. I seem to suspect in it secret affinities with my own poor organism—and if so most blessed ones. I shall at any rate give them every chance to declare themselves, and shall inform you of results—I'm so sure you'll be interested—as I go. But I can't help wishing meanwhile that you would do me this great favour—to send me one or two of this delightful creature's other books. That is I mean mainly, one other copy of "The New Glutton", and one of the "A.B.–Z of Our Own Nutrition".[1] I'm sure I shall have good use for them. His sentimental and rose-coloured side is a bit against him—but my present feel is that to have eaten one meal, one only, *really* according to his rites, is to be disposed to swallow *him* at least whole—without mastication. Please say to Peggy that I receive here a lovely letter from her, all about Montreal and her beautiful Ball-Dance at home—at which I only wish I might ponderously have figured. It is a delight to hear from her, but I'm not sure I shall be able to reply till I get back here to stay. It has become my habit, of necessity, to write my letters in the evening, and when my evenings are much broken into as they are during limited London periods, the letters inevitably wait. I hope with all my heart that you are better than earlier in the winter, and that you all hang together in peace and cheer. I am still rather down with my tiresome ailment—otherwise I would tick out more; but I am on the rise again and will do better next time. Love all round.

Yours always affectionately | Henry James

[1] Horace Fletcher, *The A.B.–Z of Our Nutrition* (1903).

To Henry James

Dictated

Irving St. March 14ᵗʰ [1904]

Dear H,

Since writing to you I have been swimming in deep seas of influenza, gout and Erysipelas of the face. The two latter enemies are in full retreat but the poisonous catarrh still reigns, and sooth to say I am extremely weak. It has been a rather luckless winter for me and today Billy, who has been ailing, has fully-developed influenza symptoms. But March and the high sun and the general growth of things toward Spring atone for everything. Alice has just mailed you a Boston Advertiser.[1] It would appear from a Probate notice which I get from Arthur Lyman that I am mentioned as well as you in the will. It seems to be an extraordinarily beautiful document. Evidently Boott was rich enough to give reign to the pure instinct of friendliness in a large way. I didn't realize the amount of sentiment which the dear old boy possessed, and feel stricken at my own hardness of judgment towards him, not that I have anything to reproach myself in the way of hardness of conduct.

15ᵗʰ 10 a.m. It is snowing without but I've had a splendid night and feel as if I had made a big step towards convalescence. To go back to the interrupted thread: Who would have thought of Boott expiring surrounded by this perfume of sentiment. Evidently he had grown much richer in the last few years than any of us suspected. I have no idea what the residuum is which goes to Franky D.[2]

I wish he were back for an hour—that we might congratulate him on the will and hear his laugh over our appreciation. In fact I wish he were back for several hours of more tender and sympathetic communion than life yielded although life yielded plenty that was intimate enough. But the sense of shortcomings seems an inevitable companion of death and makes me resolve that you and I shall hereafter abound and super-abound in every form of flattery and affectionate demonstration, blind to evil, seeing nothing but good, giving credit for ten times more than we see and laying aside that grudging, carping and critical attitude which Alice says is the moral keynote of the James family, [I never did! A.] in spite of other merits which she acknowledges. [adores! A.]

Bootts 500 to you will decidedly lubricate your travels here, and a similar sum to me would make it easy for me to accompany you to California.

I sent another copy of Fletcher's Glutton and also his A.B.Z. book to you the other day.   I hope your work of mastication goes bravely on.   I find it impossible to acquire the habit duely, but I find also that every step in that direction works improvement.

We haven't seen Bob for some weeks.   When he was last here he made on Alice an excellent impression.   He spoke kindly of his wife and seemed to be and to have been sober.

No farther news from Leslie Clarke.[3]   Elly Hunter cannot leave her farm to pay us her promised visit in March.

Good bye, dear H.   I hope your gout does n't leave lameness between the attacks.

Your ever loving   W.J. (by A.H.J.)

[1] Written vertically in the left margin of the first page is a note from AGJ: 'Dear H. I sent the Advertiser to Lamb House. AHJ.'

[2] Francis Boott Duveneck.

[3] Leslie Pell-Clarke was dying.

Henry James disliked and feared journalists as invaders of his privacy. Some months before his visit to America, William became aware of newspaper reports stating that Henry was in love and engaged to be married. William reported the rumor in a lost letter to Henry. The supposed object of Henry's affections was Emilie Busbey Grigsby (d. 1964), described in her obituary as a hostess who led a flamboyant life of entertaining writers and artists. She was the ward, or mistress, of a notorious banking and street-railway tycoon who showered her with jewelry, mansions, and art collections. She had met Henry in 1903 and claimed that the character of Milly Theale in The Wings of the Dove *was based upon her.*

From Henry James

LAMB HOUSE, | RYE, | SUSSEX. May 6ᵗʰ 1904.

Dearest William.

Your "Grigsby" letter, which has just come in, would be worthy of the world-laughter of the Homeric Gods, if it didn't rather too much depress me with the sense of the mere inane silliness of this so vulgarly chattering & so cheaply-fabricating age—the bricks of whose mendacity are made without even as many wisps of straw as would go into the mad Ophilia's hair. My engagement to *any one* is—as a "rumour"—exactly as fantastic & gratuitous a folly as would be the "ringing" report that Peggy, say, is engaged to Booker Washington, *veuf,* or that Aleck is engaged to Grace Norton. There *is* a Miss Grigsby whom I barely know—to speak of—who has been in London 2 or 3 Junes or July's (a friend of the H. Harlands & of Marie Meredith (Sturgis,) G.M.'s daughter,) whom I have seen, in *all,* 5 or 6 times, in the company of a dozen people—& *once* alone, for 10 minutes, when in consequence of 3 or 4 DECLINED invitations from her I called on her at the Savoy Hotel. She is, I believe, a Catholic, a millionaire & a Kentuckian, & gives out that she is the original of the "Milly" of my fiction *The Wings of the Dove,* published before I had ever heard of her apparently extremely silly existence. I have never written her so much as 3 words save 2 or 3 times, at most, to tell her I wouldn't come up from Rye to lunch or dine with her (I've *never* done it!) & I hadn't till your letter (entailing these so burdensome denegations—for a busy pen & a minding-one's-own-business-spirit,) so much as been conscious of the breath of her name for practically a year—since about last June, that is, when I met her once at dinner in London (being there for a few days,) & *never* afterwards beheld her or communicated with her in any fashion whatever. *She* must have put about the "rumour" which, though I thought her silly, I didn't suppose her silly *enough* for. But who—of her set & species—isn't silly enough for *anything,* in this nightmare world of insane bavardage? It's appalling that such winds may be started to blow, about one, by not so much as the ghost of an exhalation of one's own, & it terrifies & sickens me for the prospect of my visit to your strange great continent of puerile *cancans.* Who & what, then, is safe? When you *"deny,"* deny not simply by my authority, please, but with my explicit derision & disgust. The friends I cross (I suppose—still!) to N.Y., from Southampton with, are poor Mrs. Benedict & her daughter, C. Fenimore Woolson's sister & niece, whom I have known these 25 years or so (having a house at Cooperstown & originally introduced to me by Henrietta Pell-C.)   They come regularly, & have always come, to all the Bayreuth festivals, & *always* by the N. G. Lloyd boats, of which they know every officer, servant, nook and cranny.   They go back from Bayreuth, as usual, this year (have been in Germany all winter,) & wrote some time ago, begging me to let them make all arrangements for me on their ship—*exactly* my projected date; so that I should have nothing to do but to come aboard at Southampton, & find them, dès Bremen, having prepared place at table & everything else for me.   As a lone & inexpert man I simply & naturally *assented* to that very kind proposal—as saving me all research & giving me peace of mind—so that if all goes well I shall probably be extremely glad to have done so.   But that is the only witchcraft I am using. And I deplore having, in such haste, to write you about such rubbish, when there are "real" things to write about, such as they are, for which I have just now too little time.   One of them is, precisely, that I must hurry down to the Station in a few moments, to meet Howells, who comes over from Folkestone to spend 2 or 3 days with me— leaving his daughter there—because, apparently, eternally & interferingly "tired."   They are out here without Mrs. H., who comes out with John later—for the summer & autumn, & were in London for 3 weeks before I came back here (Howells very pleasant indeed again to commune with, & the girl charming in her way,)—which I did a few days ago.   I brought my three months in London to a close with the liveliest sense of the good part they had played in attenuating— always—my big annual dose of Rye; but now it's a blessing to be here again, sticking as fast as possible till I "sail."   There are some links still missing in the prospective sailing process—but they will in one way or another supply themselves, & it is my conviction that nothing but the jealousy of the gods in the form of some grave accident will keep me—*can* keep me—from embarking.   So I am treating the matter as a prayed-for certainty.   The great link missing is the question of any "let" of the house.   *That* presumably is not to be, but even over that, even over its possibly costing me the services of Mrs. Paddington (she *hates* to be left here alone—I mean workless & masterless for long periods—which comes from her being so good a servant,) I shall not worry.   And I *may* be able to LEND the house to one or other of 2 or 3 possible subjects of benificence—though I shall choose them very carefully.   But this is all for today.   I continue to found my life on Fletcher.   He is immense—thanks to which I am getting much less so.   I hope (& gather) with all my heart that Billy is restored to

comfort & beauty.   I embrace you straight round & am always your
hopelessly celibate even though sexagenarian

Henry

To Henry James

Cambridge, June 28. 1904

Dear H.—I came down from Chocorua yesterday A.M. to go to—

Mrs. Whitman's funeral!   She had lost ground steadily during the
winter.   The last time I saw her was 5 weeks ago, when at noon I
went up to her studio thinking she might be there.   I found her in
a ball dress, sitting in front of a very bad portrait of herself which a
Philadelphia painter named Alexander, had just finished for Radcliffe
College (the Harvard "Annex"[)] of which she was one of the gover-
nors.   She was gasping for breath, looking as if hunted, spots of white
and lividity were coming and going in her cheeks, and I saw that she
ought to speak to no one, so I left immediately.   Her door had been
left open to Grant Lafarge, and when I entered she tho't it was he.
He followed on my heels and staid to talk some business.   She told
me that she was to go on the following day to the Mass. General
Hospital, for a cure of rest & seclusion.   There she died last Friday
evening, having improved in her cardiac symptoms, but pneumonia
supervening a week ago.   It's a great mercy that the end was so unexpectedly quick.   What I had feared was a slow deterioration for a
year or more to come, with all the nameless misery—peculiarly so in
her case—of death by heart disease.   As it was, she may be said to
have died standing, a thing she always wished to do. She went to
every dinner party and evening party last winter, had an extension,
a sort of ball room, built to her Mount Vernon house etc.   The funeral was beautiful both in trinity church and at the grave in M.
Auburn.   I was one of the eight pall-bearers—the others of whom
you would hardly know. The flowers & greenery had been arranged
in absolutely Whitman-ian style by Mrs. Jack Gardner, Mrs Henry
Parkman, and Sally Fairchild, the Scene at the grave was *beautiful*,
she had no blood relatives, & all Boston—I mean the few whom we
know—had gone out, and seemed swayed by an overpowering emotion which abolished all estrangement & self-consciousness.   It was
the sort of ending that would please her, could she know of it.   An
extraordinary and indefinable creature!   I used often to feel coldly
towards her on account of her way of taking people as a great society

"business" proceeding, but now that her agitated life of tip-toe reaching in so many directions, of genuinest amiability, is over, pure tenderness asserts its own. Against that dark background of natural annihilation she seems to have been a pathetic little slender worm writhing and curving blindly through its little day, expending such intensities of consciousness to terminate in that small grave.

She was a most peculiar person. I wish that you had known her whole life here more intimately, and understood its significance. You might then write a worthy article about her. For me, it is impossible to define her. She leaves a dreadful vacuum in Boston. I have often wondered whether I should survive her—and here it has come in the night, without the sound of a footstep, and the same world is here—but without her as its witness.

Enough! Now that I am down here, I shall stay for Commencement which is to morrow, & for Phi Beta Kappa day, which is the day after. To-day Secretary Taft gives an address to the Law School Association in Sanders Theatre.

I left them all very well in the country—well myself, for my two weeks of it. There is a fearful drouth, and the dust in the road just beside our windows is six inches deep. We live in it. So be prepared for the worst, when you come in September. What I advise is that you should stop at Salisbury on your way from N.Y. and see *them* & *that* country, and then proceed there Northward for a longer stay in New Hampshire.

There is only one thing that I wish you might do for me, that is purchase at Partridge & Coopers, from 4 to 6 blank books—"large letter" size. They used to make them, containing about 100 sheets, bluish gray paper, soft leather back, flexible board size—superior to anything they make here.

I sent you 150 dollars this month from Syracuse and am now sending you your July dividend of 300. I hope that you are well, and not afraid of the American ordeal.

Lovingly | W.J

From Henry James

Lamb House, | Rye, | Sussex. | July 9th, 1904.
Dearest W.

I am thrice indebted to you all—for a beautiful letter from Bill, for a glorious one from Peg, and now for your own, to-day, in which you tell me of poor Mrs. Whitman's death, so interestingly and touchingly, and which was accompanied by your enclosure from the *impayable* Fletcher. I take you first, out of your order, sending love and benedictions to Peg and Bill, whom I am not forgetting, but only keeping over till I am out of a very tight squeeze of belated, overdue work. I must write to *you*, if only—and it isn't only!—to respond on the subject of dear Mrs. W, your news of whom is somehow a shock quite out of proportion to the quantity of my acquaintance with her. When she was last in London, however—two years ago—I saw a good deal of her, and of the feverish, overactive, over-doing and overdone state she was in, and, though I thought her equilibrium sadly menaced, I looked forward with real pleasure to seeing her at home, and we parted with many mutual vows and as the best of friends. I can well imagine that in Boston she *counted* much—much more than she could have ever done here; and thereby, easily, how much you must miss and mourn her. I find myself quite painfully sorry to have to do the former. It is a breath of the too great future darkness! But I shall come, doubtless, on many of her "tracks" with you, and even that will interest me. I'm glad her entombment was so great a demonstration, and can easily imagine what it may have been.

Fletcher's long-winded screed affects me, I confess, like a lot of waste paper—so rebarbative do I find all his humanitarian gush *over and beyond* the point of his precious little definite munching message; for which I go on not ceasing to bless him. It is disappointing to be thus in communication with him and only have (or almost only) so much *dont on n'a que faire*, instead of three or four definite answers to three or four definite things that one would like to ask him. He does his cause an injury, to my sense, by *overstatement*—overstatement of the reduction of quantity of food that one can get on with treated in his way. His way does reduce most blessedly the quantity, but leaves it still much above the point, the very low limit, that he gives his own example for, gives without in the least notifying that he is exceptional. He *must* be, and it engenders mistakes, disappointments and deceptions for others to struggle toward a standard positively not realiseable, or realiseable only with damage. I am a small eater, and I now eat (without damage by degree of reduction) much less than of old; but the method is still far from enabling me to get on with his miraculous paucity. About this, and two or three other matters, I greatly yearn to question him, and would do anything to see him for a quarter-of-an-hour and tap him for information. I don't grow thin, alas, either—though I *have* very distinctly ceased growing stouter at the rate I was following when the revelation descended on me.   For the first few weeks I in fact felt I *was* thinning, but this consciousness, so enchanting, has since then sadly dropped. The truth is that the method, though a priceless boon, encounters difficulties of application that require absolutely unbroken vigilance. It doesn't do itself; you must do it *your*self, actively, consciously, in the most intimate detail, all the while.   This is nothing, truly, to pay for all it does for you; but you have inevitably to reckon with the two dangers (or at least *I* have) that are always in wait.   One is the fact that *all* feeding with others is insidiously against it, through begetting accidents, inattentions and compromises.   The other is that eating alone lays also its traps in the way of inadvertences, *other* accidents, tendencies absentmindedly to relapse, through the wool-gathering effect of the act of mastication itself (which always excites my imagination and makes me think *away* from it; so that I have too prematurely swallowed, often, while following a remote train.)   Reading at table, to make one slower, tends, in the same way, to make one bolt in proportion as one is interested and has become thereby oblivious.   So you see the question isn't simple!   However it is simple enough to have made me, since I have been giving attention to it distinctly better (and at dreadful 62!) *than I ever have been in my life.*   Rien que ça! That is something.   Tell the good Fletcher when you have a chance; but tell him also, please, that I yearn for pleading speech of him.

I still nurse the superstition that I embark for N.Y. on Aug. 24th— though much is darkness still betwixt now and then.   *I believe* I shall get off, and shall make for it the boldest push of which I am capable; it is in fact too thoroughly important for me not to be stoutly put through.   I am rather blighted, for one thing, by seeing no real prospect, at all, I fear, of letting this house; on which I have been building a good deal, and the non-let of which will make something of a difference to me.   I have had in fact but one audible inquiry, on the part of two young, but competent and independent and solvent American sisters (Miss Horstmans, of Washington,)[1] who came down from town yesterday, with the "lady-friend" (of mine) who had mentioned it to them, and who lunched, inspected and raved.   (They have a golfing brother, and were thinking of something "quiet and comfortable" in England for the autumn and winter.)   But on my going over to Hastings with them in the p.m, to put them into their London express, they struck me, at the last, as opening the back door so very wide for retreat, and for almost indefinite postponement of decision, that I felt them to be, immediately, broken reeds, and have ceased at all to build on them. I sought to bribe them too with terms, as they admitted, quite abjectly low. I really think their sole use for the idea had been to get the excursion, the lunching here, the seeing—what they did see—out of it. Such is the immorality of women!

I note carefully what you say of your country drought and dust, but I really feel, assuming my arrival, that in spite of these *fléaux,* if they are still prevailing at the end of August, I must get up to your protection with as little delay, after landing, as possible. I can pay no visit to Salisbury Conn. as soon as I arrive—that really will be impossible to me; and I will resort to any subterfuge to avoid it. The very head and front of my coming is that I am to pay no "staying" visit at all save to your sole selves. This must be fundamental—it's the very basis. So I shall project myself upon you straight, at any cost, and will lurk in the woods all day, or sit up to my neck in the Lake or lie flat on my face on Chocorua-top, if the elements, by the roadside, are too much against me. We are having great heat and prolonged dryness here—no rain to speak of for many weeks. But it all means a grand sense of summer, after nearly two years of rain previously, two summers practically quite missed. This garden and the Rye cobbles are, thank heaven, practically dustless, and one's walks abroad are all across the grassy acres of the marsh and the fields, or on the cool sea-sands.—But I am too interminably keeping this up. All too without a word about yourself, or the selves of any of you; save that you know you have my constant prayers. It sounds tough—all you had come down from the country for; but I hope you have been, since then, reabsorbed into the breast of Nature. I will write again soon, as my road straightens—as I quite count on its doing, tenants or no tenants. The tenants are a detail, a drop in the bucket. I bless you all, I renew my vows to Peg at least, and I am yours affectionately always

Henry James

P.S. On reading over these last words, of last night, they strike me as unaccommodating and ungracious; whereby I correct them to the tune of saying that oh yes, certainly, I will proceed with pleasure from N.Y. to Salisbury Conn, if at the time of my arrival the conditions *chez vous* don't appear as favourable as they may be slightly later. I reflect that I shall probably not be able to get off, really, without two or three days with E^2 —which may as well come then as afterward. And I am also forgetting that George B. Harvey, the head of the Harpers, with whom I have much business already definitely arranged and more still probably arrangeable, has a fortnight ago written to express to me the hope that I shall be able to go down, on disembarking, straight to *him,* somewhere on Long Island, or in New Jersey (Elberon???) for a short stay in the interest (partly) of said arrangements. So you see there are open doors—which we shall have time still either to open further or to close.—I am much obliged to you for the July remittance, the figure of which makes it particularly welcome at this complicated moment. I hope that doesn't mean that it impinges on the August; and the August, I may add, will also be very welcome to me if I may receive it before starting. Last of all, I didn't send special love yesterday to Alice—which I make up now with interest.

H.J.

[1] Louise Horstmann Boit leased Lamb House while HJ was in America.
[2] Ellen James Temple Emmet Hunter was living in Salisbury, Conn.

1905

William James permitted himself too many distractions to make progress on his great work, "The Many and the One"; still, he is known in the history of philosophy primarily for what he did accomplish in the last five years of his life. From September 1904 to May 1905 he published six essays developing radical empiricism, his most technically developed philosophical writing. In October 1904 he published, in defense of his friends F. C. S. Schiller and John Dewey, the first of a series of essays on the subject of humanism. The controversy over humanism, or pragmatism as it became known, led him to deliver the lectures that were published as Pragmatism *(1907) and to write a number of papers, mostly short and polemical, on the pragmatic conception of truth. This collection of essays was published under the title* The Meaning of Truth *(1909). Two works, more systematic and constructive, completed his philosophical outburst,* A Pluralistic Universe *(1909) and the unfinished introduction to philosophy published posthumously as* Some Problems of Philosophy *(1911).*

During 1905 William traveled extensively. On 11 March he sailed for Europe, visiting Greece and Italy, returning home on 11 June. From 30 June to 7 July he was in Chicago, lecturing on "Characteristics of an Individualistic Philosophy."

In 1904 Henry James was at a new stage in his career. In August he committed the care of his servants and of his dachshund, Max, to the charity and humanity of the temporary occupants of Lamb House and left for a visit to America, landing in the United States on 30 August, where he was met by his nephew, Henry James, and George B. Harvey, president of Harper and Brothers. He visited with William and toured the United States extensively, meeting with friends in Philadelphia and Washington and traveling to Florida with stopovers in Richmond, Asheville, and Charleston. Continuing to California and Vancouver, he stopped along the way in St. Louis and Chicago. In several cities he delivered one or the other of his two stock lectures, "The Question of Our Speech" and "The Lesson of Balzac."

During his stay in the United States, Henry had considerable trouble with his teeth, and some of his correspondence is devoted to the scheduling of dental appointments in Boston. Late in his stay he visited Edith Wharton in Lenox, Mass., where in her company and in her car he enjoyed a tour of the Berkshires, on one occasion covering "an easy circuit of 80 miles" between lunch and a late dinner.

Henry embarked for the return voyage on 5 July 1905 but before his departure took the trouble to inform a poor scholar, who had asked for his help in compiling a Henry James bibliography, that an author deserved the "blessed shelter of obscurity" for his "early aberrations" and that the prospect of having his early unsigned pieces identified filled him with the "bitterness of woe." Having published the last of his major novels, The Golden Bowl, *in February 1905, Henry now became an elder statesman of the literary world, devoting much time to collected editions of his novels and tales, to volumes of criticism, and to his autobiography.*

From Henry James

Butler Place | Thursday [January 26, 1905]

Dearest William.

I have had good letters & postcards from you on the matter of my coming up to Roberts—or, much more fortunately, my *not* coming up; & I have only been waiting, amid this fury of the elements, & in this dreadful deathtrap, (almost,) of cold & wind & blizzarded helplessness & desolation, to be able to write you intelligently & intelligibly, & above all to thank you for your beneficent intervention. I am only too delighted *not* to have to make that dreary dental journey, & I was to have gone into Phila. to-day (at *this* very a.m. hour,) to see a Dentist there whom I have got into relation with. The storm has however blocked me helplessly in (the snow is a foot deep on my *window-sill,* & you may therefore imagine the temperature of the room I write in). The trolleys don't run; I can't get to the station; high drifts & a polar hurricane bar the way. But I hope to escape hence on Saturday a.m.—I mean from this well-meant but fatally (& oh, so "complacently"!) uncomfortable house. But for the Dentist, whom I can't get to *till* then, I must spend Saturday & Sunday in Philadelphia—probably at the Rittenhouse Club. My poor right-hand upper front tooth has come out, & I look like a "fright," but I am cynical, indifferent, desparate—I don't mind it. All this business of "kind" platitudinous, promiscuous Philadelphia has been a fearsome ordeal

(how had you gathered that I was finding it "so satisfying," *juste ciel?*) & I shall just have escaped from it with my life—which I am yearning unspeakably to do.   I *hope* to get off on Monday a.m. to *Richmond,* & to be there a couple of days,—or 3, if I can't get clothes washed, at the *Jefferson* Hotel.   My plan is to go thence straight to Biltmore, to which I am at last definitely & renewedly committed (*personally,* again to the Vanderbilts who were on a visit to Washington, & who return to B. on the 31st & wish me to "join" them on the way—a thing probably, however, not possible.)   No mention comes from you of my (*your* little) *trunk,* comitted to Alice's charity to be filled with my lighter clothing, having reached you safely—but I assume that it has done so, with my letter containing key, & that the blessed A. will have found my instructions lucid enough to be able to find & put up in it the things I enumerated.   I have been waiting to judge where it can [be] most safely & wisely expressed to me, & Biltmore, evidently *will* be safest & wisest   Will you, or will the blessed A., *on receipt of this* kindly have it go to:
————c/o George Vanderbilt Esq.
    Biltmore House
        Biltmore
            North Carolina
————enclosing me the key & the Express company's receipt in a letter?   Oh, it will be a holy service; & it would have been a holier one (from me to myself) if I had only *kept* some of the warmer things (for this accursed place) that I too prematurely, to get rid of the travelling *trouble* of them, shipped back.   However, the Southern sun, for which I fairly *sicken,* will *re*-create me—if once I can get to it, & if I want to be *met* by 3 or 4 things for re-entering New England, perhaps I can get you *then* to send them to me—especially that thick overcoat, for which I now languish.   (From Richmond I shan't miss it.)   And as to this re-entering New England it is very important I should get you to secure 3 days, for Roberts, before I go to Chicago St. Louis & California.   I must *come back from Fla.,* & start afresh from Boston for that—I shall then be too nervous about my teeth (assuming that I can successfully go even *till* then,) to have courage, or folly, to start westward without this dealing with them.   (I tremble, as it is, from day to day—for more loosenings & comings out.   Still, I am very carefully, & I must either risk it, or risk losing the South—& the "Book"-money of the South.)   The dates he gave you for me become now too *early* for me (Feb. 14 & 15th) as I can't do my stint of travel, even at the least, & get back to Boston in time.   On the other hand

I have got my St. Louis lecture postponed to about March 7ᵗʰ (from Feb. 21ˢᵗ)—& can make my Chicago one, as yet unfixed as to date about a week before therefore. Will you telephone Roberts to know if he can keep me 2 or 3 séances (if he thinks 3 most prudent,[)] for Feb. 23, 24, 25? This will give me about, or a little less than 25 days in the South—sufficient & perhaps more, I ween, enabling me to get to you on Feb. 22ᵈ p.m.—But I must stop scribbling—with no time for anything more but love & blessings. Tell A. I hang over her tenderly—& over you all. I congratulate you on freedom & California. But I "hear," somehow, you are "thinking of going abroad." Don't *dream* of it—without *me!!*—J. Wᵐ White is 1ˢᵗ Phila. SURGEON, great friend of Sargent, Abbey, & Sir Fdk. Treves (the king's Surgeon;) whom I *"got into"* Reform Club (he is often in London) a year ago, A. & T., his godfathers, not being able to attend at ballot. Hence his *pounce* on your

Henry.

From Henry James

BILTMORE HOUSE, | BILTMORE, NORTH CAROLINA. Sunday [February 5, 1905]

Dearest William.

Your note of the 3ᵈ just comes in, telling me of your having taken your passage for Naples, &c. Well, may you not rue it—that's all! Which means nothing else than receive my most prayerful blessing on it. But I do hope you don't go *alone*. It makes me at any rate indeed rejoice that I am to get *at* you—though all too little—before you sail. *Discount* my wail of discomfort sent from here just after arrival—yesterday & say nothing of it (no more than of my Butler Place repinings;)[1] my disconcertedness was aggravated by this tiresomely horrid & mistimed little outbreak of gout, which is slightly better today (I can leave my room;—but not, probably the house while I'm here.) It *is* deadly bleak & cold & too impractically spacious—but I have got the service better organized in my room, where I practically spent all day yesterday, & the latter *does* begin to get a little warmer toward 3 or 4 p.m. I am cutting my days in Charleston down to 2, & any *other* mad thought has been simply the fruit of a complication with poor Owen Wister, "nervously" ill, with a medical attendant, at Camden S.C., & saying he would *like* to join me at C. (for the purpose of introducing old lingering Southern social types to me well known to *him*) if I could give him 4 or 5 days. But I must cut the southern types, along of my d——d teeth; besides I want to get *on*.

Please begin & forward letters to c/o Mary (Bob's) "the Bennett, Daytona, Fla." You talk of my doing many things there—but my days will be extremely numbered. However, the thing is to get away from here, on my 2 feet, first. I hang over Harry—tell him—*with* Alice—tell *her*. I rejoice in all your helpful facts (Chocorua, McClure[2] &c,[)] & am yours ever

Henry.

[1] HJ is referring to the Philadelphia home of Sarah Butler Wister.

[2] In WJ's letter, now lost, he probably mentioned his article on Thomas Davidson, "A Knight-Errant of the Intellectual Life," *McClure's Magazine* 25 (May 1905): 3–11; reprinted in *ECR*.

To Henry James

95 Irving St. | June 28. 1905 | 5 P.M.

Dear H.—

The key arrived duly. This has been the best commencement day I remember, and the only fault of it has been that they did n't make you & Howells stand up side by side for an LLD.—not on your accounts for that means nothing, but because they missed the best spectacular point they could possibly have made. Hartwell & his son have been here, and have but just now gone.

If correcting your proof on language why not add a word about "vurry," ["]Amur̄rca," ["]tullugram," Phulladulphia etc. Also twundy[1] for twenty.[2]

Well, my dear boy, here we part again, after having scarcely met, at least at this end of the term. I can imagine your peace when you first reach Lamb House, and get to uninterrupted work again. The N. Am. articles are very exquisite[3]—I hope (and expect) that you will find new fruitage from the new impressions and the stirring up. I want to take your Golden Bowl to read on the train to Chicago, but it is *lent* beyond recovery.

Lovingly yours, Wm James

[1] WJ originally wrote 'twunny', then inserted a 'd' between the two 'n's and circled the three letters. Whether he intended the word to be read as 'twunny', 'twundny', or 'twundy' is not clear.

[2] WJ is probably referring to HJ's lecture "The Question of Our Speech"; reprinted in *The Question of Our Speech. The Lesson of Balzac. Two Lectures* (1905).

³ HJ's trip resulted in a series of essays published as *The American Scene* (1907). WJ is referring to the first of the essays, "New England: An Autumn Impression," *North American Review* 180 (April 1905): 481–501; (May 1905): 641–60; (June 1905): 800–816.

From Henry James

95 Irving Street, | Cambridge, Mass., July 2, 1905.

Dearest W:

I am ticking this out at you for reasons of convenience that will be even greater for yourself, I think, than for me. I am putting in this quiet cool Sunday morning with my blessed friend Buckner's aid—putting it in over as many belated little last letter-jobs as possible: all of which won't prevent my finding a mountain of the *really* postponed awaiting me at L.H. from the moment I arrive. But let me at any rate give you, if only for five minutes, a little of the breath of this peaceful Cambridge hour, shared here with Alice, Bill and Aleck only, or rather conferred essentially *by* them. Your good letter of farewell reached me at Lenox, from which I returned but last evening—to learn, however, from A., every circumstance of your departure and of your condition, as known up to date. The grim grey Chicago will now be your daily medium, but will put forth for you, I trust, every such flower of amenity as it is capable of growing. May you not regret, at any point, having gone so far to meet its queer appetites. Alice tells me that you are to go almost straight thence (though with a little interval here, as I sympathetically understand,) to the Adirondacks:¹ where I hope for you as big a bath of impersonal Nature as possible, with the tub as little tainted, that is, by the soapsuds of *personal:* in other words, all the "board" you need, but no boarders. I seem greatly to mislike, not to say deeply to mistrust, the Adirondack boarder. Apropos of whom, by the way, Charles Norton, whom I saw three days ago, very pleasantly, at the really sweet Ashfield, spoke to me ever so genially of your McClure article on Davidson; saying that his enjoyment and admiration of it had made it of no consequence at all that the man had always so displeased him. He didn't care, the article, the picture, was so fine! Which was very good for Charles. (I heard you give it that evening at P.BH.,² but am taking the magazine with me to read it over, in some blessed stillness, I hope, of the Ivernia deck.) Let my report meanwhile be beautiful of everything here. Alice more utterly invaluable and beneficent than ever; Aleck back from Chocorua in excellent handsome cheerful form—his mother and Bill and I all equally struck with it; and going off to-morrow A.M., I believe, to his seaside camp; with an outfit of wonderful toggery that he is already sporting about the house. I saw Bay Emmet at Stockbridge, where she has painted, for Miss Tuckerman, an extremely clever and successful oval portrait of Susie Sedgwick, which delights Miss T., but which has, like all B's portraits of women, a more conventional and subordinate quality than her renderings of men—she does the latter so much more freely and fearlessly. But the point is that she told me she was going straight back to Salisbury, *really* to stay, in a very good new studio she has just had made there, and that she counts on Billy's returning and working with her. She appears distinctly to want him and to promise help and profit for him. So I think he is hopefully going. I greatly enjoyed the whole Lenox countryside, seeing it as I did by the aid of the Whartons' big strong commodious new motor, which has fairly converted me to the sense of all the thing may do for one and one may get from it. The potent way it deals with a country large enough for it not to *rudoyer,* but to rope in, in big free hauls, a huge netful of impressions at once—this came home to me beautifully, convincing me that if I were rich I shouldn't hesitate to take up with it. A great transformer of life and of the future! All that country charmed me; we spent the night at Ashfield and motored back the next day, after a morning there, by an easy circuit of 80 miles between luncheon and a late dinner; a circuit easily and comfortably prolonged for the sake of good roads. This was very wonderful. Dear old C.E.N. was at his best in every way; but the impression of the poor girls there, in the dull unpeopled void, out of which the years have taken all interest for them, was saddening exceedingly, especially in respect to Sally. But I mustn't rattle on. I have still innumerable last things to do. But the portents are all propitious—*absit* any ill consequence of this fatuity! I am living, at Alice's instance, mainly on huge watermelon, dug out in spadefuls, yet light to carry. But good bye now. Your last hint[s] for the "Speech" are much to the point, and I will try even thus late to stick them in. May every comfort attend you!

Ever yours, | Henry James

[1] Between 28 July and 3 August 1905, WJ lectured at the Summer School of the Cultural Sciences at Glenmore in Keene Valley.

[2] WJ's appreciation of Davidson was written in about October 1903. No information was found concerning the reading mentioned by HJ.

To Henry James

Cambridge, July 12. '03[1]

Dearest Henry

I imagine you as having arrived yesterday P.M. or this A.M.   May the voyage have been "restful," and not too insomnic, though the Ivernia, as I recollect her, had pretty poor berths.   It must be a delight to your poor starved eyes to see the english faces, and hear the solid english speech again, but I'm thinking that your backward vision of all our makeshift way of being will fructify within a year in ways you at present don't realize, and give you a distinct backward shove towards youngness.   To have discovered the new faculty of popular orator in yourself is a great arrest to the senescent process. "Emily" Higginson did nothing but talk of you, *most* intelligently & lovingly chiefly for your intimate adoption of George.   She was considerable chastened from two winters ago; and quoted, as did everyone else the most extravagant opinions about the charm of your lectures.   *There's* a new profession for you, any day, if you can stand it!— and me, who warned you that you never cd. do it!   I've had some experience of the sort myself at Chicago, where instead of the humdrum philosophy class of 40 which I expected, I found a "chapel" full of 800 people.   It appalled me, not being prepared.   500 remained faithful, however, and at my last lecture I hooked them all and felt them pulling at my line like one fish—a fine kind of experience, which shows that "parts," at any rate, of the matter that I present, are susceptible of popular treatment, which is a comfort, in view of the possible Sorbonne.[2]   The summer term at Chicago U. is quite inspiring.   Great hulking rustics from prairie farms, with thick hands, teachers mainly, and tall womankind to match, aged well over 25, all of them, and earnest and absorbent in a way unknown to Harvard.   The weather was comfortable, and the social time very simple, and pleasant enough.   The Higginsons were living in their new stable, much handsomer and more convenient than any usual house, under the circumstances, and are going to spend the summer getting the place in order and starting the house-foundation etc.   He was handsome & "sweet," and she much less egotistic than before.   I came back with a venemous cold, but am better to day.   No one at home but Harry, now, who goes into his new Office next week.   The tranquillity is very pleasant, and yesterday & to day are cool.   First rate letters from Peg, & Aleck.   Alice says you showed her the jewellery of your mouth.[3]   I was on the point of asking for a sight of it, but refrained think[ing] it might seem indelicate. Between no-scruples & over scruples the path is hard for such as me. Good bye!—I imagine you fairly wallowing in Lamb House, and in Anglicanism in general—perhaps joining the Church. Alice sends all her love,

Yours fondly   W.J.

[1] The letter was misdated. The correct date is 12 July 1905.
[2] WJ did not teach at the Sorbonne.
[3] HJ's dental work.

From Henry James

Lamb House. | July 24th 1905.

Dearest William.

Your beautiful & admirable letter on your return to Irving St from Chicago fills me with rejoicing—by the vividness of the impression it gives me of the success of your performance there (through your so happy "wording" of the same.) Most uplifting such quantity & quality of attention must have been to you, & making of the thing comparatively little of a *corvée*. Charming to me too your mention of the echoes still in the air of *my* so much shorter & less edifying episode—which seems (now & here,) to belong, as I knew it quickly would, to some land of dreams or related romance. "Romance," yes!—so odd is that that cast is already stealing over the whole "performing" element (in especial,) of my American time & making its now lost & past character quite, or almost, a source of lachrymal reflection. Perverse & strange is life—that the opportunity in question should be snatched from me, as it really is, just when I had (rather "poetically") discovered it. But it does perhaps in fact hang there as a kind of ideal resource—a theoretic if not an actual support. I find myself back here, for that matter, only to take the measure of the engagements to other work that build me in & round, & that will give me a superabundance to think of for a good while to come. I have been taking here 10 days of practically complete privacy & rest & solitude (with servants—save Mrs. P.[1] & George Gammon—scattered to the winds &c;) so that the transition to peace & protection has been utter, & all helped of course by the rich prettiness, the perfection of the English summer—splendid weather till within a day or two—spread over these lawns & bowers. L.H. justifies itself (& me,) down to the ground; nothing could conceivably "wear" better—unless it be George Gammon himself, whose perfect care of the garden, & general constancy, trustiness & cheer (unlimited obligingness in other ways &c)—steadily enhance his value. He has made the garden over to me now in far better condition than it has ever known. I wrote to Alice a couple of days ago in accents that she will have found querulous, I fear—through my having been (as a kind of cold douche to my so auspicious home-coming) met by a broken-down & overdone Mrs. P., desirous only to depart. That spectre has been exorcised— she has revived & rallied—& we have lived here, alone & other-servantless, these several days, in a simplified state that we have both enjoyed & that I wish could only go on. We haven't even tried to re-"mount" the house, & don't seem to want to. She only seems, alas, considerably—a good deal—older than when I left; but her financial thrift has partaken of genius, & instead of my having to "fork out" to her (on liabilities incurred,) she has restored to me gold & silver economised on what I had allowed her. Add to this that I am already in much better physical case & condition than I had fallen into in all the American abnormalism of (my) life, & you will see that there are consolations even for the lapse of "romance" & the forfeiture (above all,) of the warm & rich human element of your house. I began to "Fletcherise" the day I got back & have been doing it with consistent intensity, without interruption; whereby promptly *se constate* a drop, a cessation, of the hovering & haunting gout I had had *all* the while I was in America (after the 1ᵘ month,) & which, all the later times, was so chronic as to be kept at bay only by perpetual aspirin; together with other marked improvements; steadily *more* marked. (I didn't take asperin at sea, by the way, but to the extent of 4 or 5 tabloids, but I blessed your *trional* gift, which gave me such nights as I had *never* had on shipboard before. Yet shipboard simply, bitterly poisons me, at the best.) I really believe (àpropos of this renewed observation of Fletcherism—on resumption,) that I *should* be able to go to the States to lecture again if I could succeed in eating *always* & without exception, like the Jacksons, *alone*—that is accepting no invitations whatever.[2] I could so keep myself well. But the thing would be impossible—& that way madness lies!—All this while I write you are all probably grilling with heat of the most furious sort (reported by the papers here.) And yet I hope not *now*—that is that you have by this time had a "let-up." Heaven send it. But I am tenderly confluent with you all.

Ever your Henry.

[1] Mrs. Paddington.
[2] The unsociable Jacksons were not identified.

To Henry James

95 Irving S! | Oct 22. 1905

Dear H.—The wheel of life seems to be whirling for each of us in such wise that we "don't write." Since College began on the 28th. of September the routine here has been perfect—I with 6 lectures a week, (3 of them to 250 men, ended for good two days ago)[1] Harry at the office, Bill at the Art School,[2] Aleck at Brown & Nicholls's,[3] Mary Salter and Jack[4] a member of our family, and Margaret & her Rosamond of Mrs. Gibbens's, Peggy having endless dress-making, and Alice playing the part of Providence over all, no company, no breaks no excitements,—how should letter writing slip in? Our "grippes" are over, and we are normal again, Alice & I, and she has been very free from headache since her bad time in August. We have decided, whatever else we do, to spend next summer at Chocorua, and that to me is a great relief. It always agrees with me there, and last summer was not a success. I have written nothing since last March, and expect to do no writing this winter, so I shan't be in a state to lecture in France next winter, even if appointed, and sooth to say I more than doubt whether I ought to at all. *Writing* is the genuine way for me to work off my energy, and lecturing brings that to a stop. I went to our Friday Club dinner a fortnight ago. Howells was there, for a wonder, and very nice, speaking of you with great relish. T.S.P. & his family (minus one daughter just married) have gone to France to stay 2 or 3 years. I read your Golden Bowl a month or more ago, and it put me, as most of your recenter long stories have put me, in a very puzzled state of mind. I don't enjoy the kind of "problem," especially when as in this case it is treated as problematic (viz. the adulterous relations betw. Ch. & the P.),[5] and the method of narration by interminable elaboration of suggestive reference (I dont know what to call it, but you know what I mean) goes agin the grain of all my own impulses in writing; and yet in spite of it all, there is a brilliancy and cleanness of effect, and in this book especially a high toned social atmosphere that are unique and extraordinary. Your methods & my ideals seem the reverse, the one of the other—and yet I have to admit your extreme success in this book. But why won't you, just to please Brother, sit down and write a new book, with no twilight or mustiness in the plot, with great vigor and decisiveness in the action, no fencing in the dialogue, no psychological commentaries, and absolute straightness in the style? Publish it in my name, I will acknowledge it, and give you half the proceeds. Seriously, I wish you *would,* for you *can;* and I should think it would tempt you, to embark on a "fourth manner." You of course know these feelings of mine without my writing them down but I'm "nothing if not" outspoken. Meanwhile you can despise me and fall back on such opposite emotions as Howells's who seems to admire you without restriction, as well as on the records of the sale of the book. How does the Collected edition get on. And are you now at work on "America" or on the prefaces to that? Of our neighborhood, there's no news to relate. Grace N. has miss Irwin living with her for a couple of months. I, as usual on Sundays, have bkfstd. with Theodora, this AM. finding Eliots wife & baby there.[6] Geo. Ashburner has been here. Yesterday we had to dinner the Mrs. Booth of Liverpool whom I told you of having met at Athens, she being one Lydia Butler whom we used to play with at fort Hamilton.[7] A very cultivated person, & her husband an important ship-owner. We've had an extraordinarily beautiful autumn, warm and radiant with colour, and almost no rain. I have about got my strength back; but I look forward with some apprehension to the long pull in California which will begin in January. I think I lecture much better than I ever did; but I seem to be pretty unfit for all unwonted forms of exertion. No intercourse whatever with Bob since last spring. I started for concord one P.M. a month ago, but the trolley broke down and I never got there, and have had no opportunity since. Some new and extensive bridge-work on my teeth! I hope that yours are all stable and your roots insensible! England seems very goodly—both place and people, from this present time & place. Make the most of them! Alice sends her love & wants me to tell you how much she was touched by the affectionate solicitude of your last letter. Peggy has had much travail of soul over her 'coming out,' & she and alice have decided that it shall not be with a bang, but by almost imperceptible degrees. Keep well and believe me your ever loving

W.J.

[1] In 1905–6 WJ taught a part of Philosophy 1: General Introduction to Philosophy and the first half of Philosophy 9: Metaphysics.

[2] William James studied at the School of the Museum of Fine Arts, Boston.

[3] Alexander Robertson James attended the Browne and Nichols School for Boys at 20 Garden St., Cambridge, which was run by two Harvard graduates, George Henry Browne and Edgar Hamilton Nichols.

[4] Jack was not identified.

[5] Among the central characters of HJ's *Golden Bowl* are Prince Amerigo, his wife Maggie, and Charlotte Stant, who marries Maggie's father. Charlotte was the Prince's

mistress before his marriage; she and the Prince resume their affair after the marriage.

[6] Eliot Norton.

[7] Fort Hamilton is on Long Island. When the James family was living in New York City in the years from 1847 to 1855, WJ and HJ often went to Fort Hamilton in the summers. Several sons of Charles Booth, a merchant in Liverpool, were in the shipping business and owned Alfred Booth & Co. and Booth Steam Ship Co. Lydia Butler Booth was probably married to one of the sons.

From Henry James

LAMB HOUSE, | RYE, | SUSSEX. November 23$\underline{d}$ 1905.

Dearest William.

I wrote not many days since to Aleck, & not very, very many before to Peggy—but I can't tonight hideously further postpone acknowledging your so liberal letter of Oct 22$\underline{d}$ (the one in which you enclosed me Aleck's sweet one,) albeit I have been in the house all day without an outing, & very continuously writing, & it is now 11. p.m. & I am rather fagged: my claustration being the result 1$\underline{st}$, of a day of incessant bad weather, & 2$\underline{d}$ of the fact that Grenville Emmet & his Indian bride spent yesterday & last night here, much breaking into my time, & 3$\underline{d}$ that I go tomorrow up to town, to proceed thence, under extreme & cogent pressure, to pay a 36 hours' visit, in the country, to the Humphry Wards. She & Humphry go to America after the New Year, & I think she wants me greatly to indoctrinate & *avertir* her. She will in sooth be lionized limb from limb. But don't you & A. think it necessary to lift a finger. *I* am not in any degree "beholden" to them—I regard it quite as the other way round; & she, amiable & culture-crammed woman as she is, is strangely stupid. (*Burn* & repeat not this—such reverberations—of imbecillity—of[1] come back to me from the U.S.!) Grenville's Squaw is much better than I thought she wd. be—facially ugly, but vocally & intelligently good & civilized, & with a certain "air"; & he (in addition to being in his way a "dear",) is, for a lawyer, almost fabulously ingenuous. One gets such strange *bouffées,* from those young people, of the general blankness of the homes over which the Kitty T. of our youth later presided. I am having a very good & peaceful autumn—(the best one I have ever had here, with *enormous* profit from Fletcher,) & shall prolong my present phase till February 1$\underline{st}$, going then up to town till (probably) May. I am working off my American book very steadily (absit omen!)—or rather the stuff which is taking, irresistibly & inevitably, the form of 2 moderately-long books (separate, of course, not 2 vols; which wouldn't at all do, but a sort of First & Second Series, with an interval between, the 1ˢᵗ winding up with Philadelphia & Washington & the 2ᵈ beginning with 2 papers on the South & going on with all the rest of my so unaccountably-garnered matter.)² I have practically *done* the 1ˢᵗ, & serial publication of it begins in December.³ I shall be mightily glad to have tapped it all off, for the effort of *holding rather factitiously on* to its (after all virtual) insubstantiality just only to convert it into some sort of paying literature is a very great tension & effort. It would all so melt away, of itself, were it not for this artificial clutch! But I am hoping to have made the whole thing, really, a short job (for the way it will have been done.) You tell me what is good of yourself & your more or less disposed-of College lectures, & of your probably not going to France next year ('faudra voir!) but you say nothing about California, & I am much puzzled by a mystery & ambiguity in all your sequences—Peg's admission to Bryn Mawr, mixed up with her simu[l]taneous social début & your California absence &c. When do you go there, anyhow, & when does she go to B.M., & does she go to California with you, & if she doesn't who takes her out, at home & with whom does she abide? However, I shall write to Alice for information—all the more that I deeply owe that dear eternal Heroine a letter. I am not "satisfied about her," please tell her with my tender love, & should have testified to this otherwise than by my long cold silence if only I hadn't been, for stress of composition, putting myself on very limited contribution to the post. The worst of these bad manners are now over, & please tell Alice that my very next letter shall be to her. Only *she* mustn't put pen to paper for me, nor so much as dream of it, before she hears from me. I take a deep, a rich & brooding comfort in the thought of how splendidly you are all "turning out," all the while— especially Harry & Bill & especially Peg, &, above all, Aleck—in addition to Alice & you. I turn you over (in my spiritual pocket,) collectively & in[di]vidually, & make you chink & rattle & ring; getting from you the sense of a great, though too-much (for my use) tied-up fortune. I have great joy (tell him with my love,) of the news of Bill's so superior work, & yearn to have some sort of a squint at it. Tell him, at any rate, how I await him, for his holidays, out here—on this spot. And I wish I realized more richly Harry's present conditions. But I am probably in*capa*ble of doing it—& he must judge me so. I await him here not less.———I mean (in response to what you write me of your having read the *Golden B.*) to try to produce some uncanny form of thing, in fiction, that will gratify you, as Brother—but let me say, dear William, that I shall greatly be humiliated if you *do* like it, & thereby lump it, in your affection, with things, of the current age, that I have heard you express admiration for & that I would sooner descend to a dishonoured grave than have written. Still, I *will* write you your book, on that two-& two-make-four system on which all the awful truck that surrounds us is produced & *then* descend to my dishonoured grave—taking up the art of the slate pencil instead of, longer, the art of the brush (vide my lecture on Balzac.) But it's, seriously, too late at night, & I am too tired, for me to express myself on this question—beyond saying that I'm always sorry when I hear of your reading anything of mine, & always hope you won't—you seem to me so constitutionally unable to "enjoy" it, & so condemned to look at it from a point of view remotely alien to mine in writing it, & to the conditions out of which, *as* mine, it has inevitably sprung—so that all the intuitions that have been its main reason for being (with *me*,) appear never to have reached you at all—& you appear even to assume that the life, the elements, forming its subject-matter deviate from felicity in not having an impossible analogy with the life of Cambridge. I see nowhere about me done or dreamed of the things that alone for me constitute the *interest* of the doing of the novel—& yet it is in a sacrifice of them on their very own ground that the thing you suggest to me evidently consists. It shows how far apart & to what different ends we have had to work out, (very naturally & properly!) our respective intellectual lives. And yet I can read *you* with rapture—having 3 weeks ago spent 3 or 4 days with Manton Marble at Brighton & found in his hands ever so many of your recent papers & discourses, which having margins of mornings in my room, through both breakfasting & lunching there (by the habit of the house,) I found time to read several of—with the effect of asking you, earnestly, to address me some of those that I so often, in Irving St. saw you address to others who were not your brother. I had no *time* to read them there. Philosophically, in short, I am "with" you, almost completely, & you ought to take account of this & get me over altogether.—There are 2 books by the way (one fictive) that I permit you to *raffoler* about as much as you like, for I have been doing so myself—H. G. Wells's *Utopia* & his *Kipps*.[4] The *Utopia* seems to me even more remarkable for other things than for his characteristic cheek, & *Kipps* is quite magnificent. Read them both if you haven't—certainly read Kipps.—There's also another subject I'm too full of not to mention the good thing I've done for myself—that is for Lamb House & my garden—by moving the greenhouse away from the high old wall near the house (into the back garden—setting it up better against the *street* wall) & thereby throwing the liberated space into the front garden to its immense apparent extension & beautification.   The high recaptured wall is alone worth the job—though the latter has been proving far more abysmal & long-drawn than I intended.   But hot-water pipes & a radiator fed from the new greenhouse stove, or boiler, pass straight into the garden room now & warm & dry it beautifully & restore it to winter use.   But oh, fondly, goodnight!

Ever yr   Henry.

[1] The word 'of' is an undeleted false start.

[2] HJ published only one book of observations of America, *The American Scene* (1907).

[3] The first installment of the serial publication, "New York and the Hudson: A Spring Impression," appeared in the *North American Review* 181 (December 1905): 801–33.

[4] Herbert George Wells, *A Modern Utopia* (1905) and *Kipps; the Story of a Simple Soul* (1905).

1906

William James's prolonged negotiations with David Starr Jordan, president of the newly founded Stanford University in Palo Alto, California, concluded with James teaching at Stanford in the spring of 1906. The remuneration of $5,000 that he received for teaching one course was very generous by the standards of the time. He departed for the long journey to California on 29 December 1905, suffering from the bad air on the train because, as he noted in his diary, "women refuse to have ventilators open." After stopping for two nights at the Grand Canyon, he reached Palo Alto on 8 January 1906 and two days later gave his first lecture to about 200 students and 200 visitors. In his diary he noted, "Funk is over! it went all right."

To Henry James

STANFORD UNIVERSITY, CALIFORNIA Feb. 1st. 1906
Beloved Heinrich—Verily 'tis long since I have written to thee, but I have had many and mighty things to do, and lately many business letters to write, so I came not at it. Your last was your delightful reply to my remarks about your "third manner," wherein you said that you would consider your bald head dishonored if you ever came to pleasing *me* by what you wrote, so shocking was my taste. Well! only write *for* me, & leave the question of pleasing open! I have to admit that in the Golden Bowl & the W. of the D., you have succeeded in *getting there* after a fashion, in spite of the perversity of the method and its *longueurs*, which I am not the only one to deplore. But enough! let me tell you of my own fortunes! I got here (after 5 pestilentially close aired days in the train, and one entrancing one off at the Grand Canyon of the Colorado) on the 8th., and have now given 9 lectures, to 300 enrolled students & about 150 visitors, partly colleagues. I take great pains, prepare a printed syllabus, very full; and really feel for the first time in my life, as if I were lecturing *well*.[1] High time, after 30 years of practice! It earns me $5000, if I can keep it up till May 27th.; but apart from that, I think it a bad way of expending energy. I ought to be writing my everlastingly postponed

book, which this job again absolutely adjourns.   I can't write a line
of it while doing this other thing. [A propos to which, I got a telegram
from Eliot this AM. asking if I would be Harvard Professor for the 1st
half of next year at the University of Berlin.   I had no difficulty in
declining that, but I probably shall not decline *Paris,* if they offer it
to me year after next.]   I am expecting Alice to arrive in a fortnight.[2]
I have got a very decent little second story, just enough for the two
of us, or rather amply enough, sunny, good fire place, bathroom,
little kitchen etc, on one of the three residential streets of the University land, and with a boarding house for meals just opposite, we shall
have a sort of honeymoon picnic time.   And, sooth to say, Alice must
need the simplification.   Fortunately she need n't bring Peg.   The
latter went sheer out of her mind at the beginning of the year over
her "coming-out" condition.   It was a revelation to me of the feminine nature as something wholly different from that of man.   Every
other thought absent save the thought of being a "success," and such
unhappiness and such heroism, and such resolve to accept every invitation, often 3 a day, and to get all there were in the air.   It was like
the puberty-ordeals of savage tribes.   Alice who had to bear all the
expense of it, quite went to smash under the strain.   But she writes
now that the frenzy is over, Peggy thinking of other things, and reasonable and getting round to something like her natural self, or what
we always supposed to be such.   No word of this when you write
home!   It has been a bad thing all round.   And of all the rotten
ideals I know, this that our young girls have, of the momentous consequences of their coming "out" with "success," is the rottenest.   Basta!
You've seen this wonderful spot so I need n't describe it.   It is really
a miracle; & so simple the life and so benign the elements, that for
a young ambitious professor who wishes to leave his mark on Pacific
Civilization while it is most plastic, or for *any one* who wants to teach
and work under the most perfect conditions for 8 or 9 months, *and
who is able to get to the East or Europe for the remaining three,* I can't
imagine anything finer.   It is utopian.   Perfection of weather.   Cold
nights, though above freezing.   Fire pleasant until 10 o'clock A.M.
then unpleasant.   In short "the simple life" with all the essential
higher elements thrown in as communal possessions.   The drawback
is, of course, the great surrounding human vacuum—the historic silence fairly rings in your ears when you listen—and the social insipid-
ity.   I'm glad I came, and with God's blessing I may pull through.
One calendar month is over, anyway.   Do you know aught of G. K.

Chesterton? I've just read his "Heretics." A tremendously strong writer and true thinker, despite his mannerism of paradox. Wells's Kipps is good. Good bye. Of course your breathing the fog of London while I am bathed in warmest lucency. Keep well.

Your loving W.J.

[1] At Stanford WJ offered his introduction to philosophy course.

[2] AGJ reached Stanford on 14 February 1906 and found WJ on crutches because of gout.

In April 1906 Henry James was in his rooms at the Reform Club in London, planning a "pleasing itinerary" of a motoring trip through Kent and Sussex with Edith Wharton that was to begin on 26 April in Dover and include a pause for lunch at Lamb House on the first day. On 19 April the London Times *carried reports of the earthquake that had shaken San Francisco the day before, with headlines noting great loss of life and widespread devastation. Henry could not have been reassured by the reports that followed, filled as they were with news of fires, looting, fallen telegraph lines, martial law, and the plight of 200,000 homeless people facing starvation. Since no news was being received from neighboring towns, Henry knew nothing about the fate of William and Alice in Palo Alto until 28 April when he received a cable from the Jameses' oldest son, Henry, informing his uncle as well as his brother William, who was in England en route to France to study art, that William and Alice were safe. William had written a letter to Henry on 22 April, but the letter did not reach him until well into May.*

Two days after the earthquake, on 20 April, William learned that there would be no more work at Stanford University that year. In his diary he greeted the news with a "Hurrah!" Since he was not to leave for home until 27 April, he indulged himself during his week of enforced idleness with an automobile drive in search of the old Gibbens ranch and with several "very jolly" dinners.

From Henry James

THE ATHENÆUM, | PALL MALL. S.W. May 1ˢᵗ 1906.
Dearest—beloved Ones!

I am writing you very briefly—because verily, now that for the 1ˢᵗ
time a really reassuring word has reached me, I feel that I have collapsed, simply, with the tension of all these dismal days without it.
You will perhaps find a smile still, after your horrors (as I can't *but*
suppose them,) for *my* appealing to you on *my* situation—so I *don't!*
But one's public, "social" newslessness here has been (after the 1ˢᵗ few
days) hideous—& I am (just yet) quite powerless to speak—now that
Harry has been able to cable that an uplifting (more or less) letter
from you is on the way to us (Bill having been with me (1ˢᵗ at Liverpool) since the 28ᵗʰ p.m.) When that comes I *shall* be able to write
you—I am, before it, as limp & spent as if I had been hanging 14
days by my heels. I should tell you that I have shared every pulse
of your nightmare with you if I didn't hold you quite capable of telling me that it hasn't *been* a nightmare. I haven't a *donnée* about you
(save that of your being alive) so that in default of a nightmare I can't
conceive *what* it can have been. It is only in nightmare terms, in
short, that I write you even thus much. I embrace you with the last
tenderness & devotion & hang over you with incoherent *howls* & yelps
of relief—a human Ryeley much more than a literary brother.[1] I
don't attempt the presumption of detail—only clinging to a dim vision & conviction that it will all be intellectually & "psychologically"
"blest" to you. But you yourselves can tell the how & whence &
why of this better than I! Heaven grant your'e not bodily (i.e.
"nervously") blighted by it. And now, though it's only noon,
I want to go to bed! Bill is of course writing. I send this into
space—not knowing if you are yet homeward & still wondering why
your'e not.

Your ever tenerissimo   Henry.

[1] Ryelie was a dog.

To Henry James

Cambr. May 9. 1906

Dearest Brother & Son—

Your cablegram of response was duly received, and we have been
also "joyous" in the tho't of your being together. I knew of course,
Henry, that you would be solicitous about us in the earthquake, but

didn't reckon at all on the extremity of your anguish as evinced by your frequent cablegrams home, and finally by the letter to Harry which arrived a couple of days ago and told how you were unable to settle down to any other occupation, the thought of our mangled forms, hollow eyes, starving bodies, minds insane with fear, haunting you so. We never reckoned on this extremity of anxiety on your part, I say, and so never thought of cabling you direct as we might well have done from Oakland on the day we left, namely April 27th. I much regret this callousness on our part. For *all* the anguish was yours; and in general this experience only rubs in what I have always known, that in battles, sieges & other great calamities, the pathos & agony is in general solely felt by those at a distance, and although physical pain is suffered most by its immediate victims, those at the *scene of action* have no *sentimental* suffering whatever. Everyone at san francisco seemed in a good hearty frame of mind, there was work for every moment of the day and a kind of uplift in the sense of a "common lot" that took away the sense of loneliness that (I imagine) gives the sharpest edge to the more usual kind of misfortune that may befall a man. But it was a queer sight, on our journey through the City on the 26th (8 days after the disaster) to see the inmates of the houses of the quarter left standing, all cooking their dinners at little brick camp-fires in the middle of the streets, the chimneys being condemned. If such a disaster had to happen, somehow, it couldn't have chosen a better place than San Francisco (where everyone knew about camping, and was familiar with the creation of civilizations out of the bare ground) and at 5.30 in the morning when few fires were lighted & every one, after a good sleep, was in bed. Later, there would have been great loss of life in the streets, and the more numerous foci of conflagration wd have burned the City in one day instead of in 4, and made things vastly worse.

In general you may be sure that when any disaster befalls our country it will be *you* only who are wringing of hands, and we who are smiling with "interest," or laughing with gleeful excitement. I didn't hear one pathetic word uttered at the scene of disaster, though of course the crop of "nervous wrecks" is very likely to come in in a month or two.

Although we have been home 6 days, such has been the stream of broken occupation, people to see, and small urgent jobs to attend to, that I have written no letter till now. To-day, one sees more clearly and begins to rest. "Home" looks extraordinarily pleasent, and though damp & chilly, it is the divine budding moment of the year.

Not, however, the lustrous light & sky of Stanford U.—No nibble yet at the Chocorua places.—Piddington is here and the S.P.R. winding up seems to promise to run sufficiently smoothly.[1]   The Hodgson control is panning out extremely plausibly—something occurred yesterday regarding an old conversation between H. & me, that brings the notion of his ghost being there closer to me than I have ever felt it before.[2]—I have just read your paper on Boston in the N.A.R.[3]   I am glad you threw away the scabbard and made your critical remarks so straight.   What you say about "pay" here being the easily won "salve" for privations, in view of wh. we cease to "mind" them is as true as it is strikingly pat.   *Les intellectuels* here, wedged between the millionaires and the han[d]workers are the really pinched class here. They feel the frustrations and they can't get the salve.   *My* attainment of so much of pay in the past few years brings home to me what a all-benumbing salve it is.   That whole article is of your best.   We long to hear from W. jr.   No word yet.

Your ever loving,   W.J.

[1] From 1890 the Society for Psychical Research in the United States had been the American Branch of the Society for Psychical Research in England.   The death of Richard Hodgson in 1905, secretary-treasurer of the branch, led to its dissolution, and John George Piddington was sent from England to wind up its affairs.   Some records were sent to England and others to New York, where James Hervey Hyslop was organizing an independent group for the conduct of psychical research in America.

[2] Many psychical researchers made arrangements to communicate after death. For the history of the attempts to communicate with Richard Hodgson and WJ's conclusions, see his "Report on Mrs. Piper's Hodgson-Control" (1909); reprinted in *EPR*.

[3] HJ, "Boston," *North American Review* 182 (March 1906): 333–55; reprinted in *The American Scene* (1907).

From Henry James

THE ATHENÆUM, | PALL MALL. S.W. May 11th 1906

Dearest William.

To day at last reach me (an hour ago,) your blest letter to myself of April 19th & Alice's not less sublime one (or a type copy of the same,) addressed to Irving St & forwarded by dear Peg, to whom all thanks.   I have just sent them on to Bill in Paris, together with one from his mother to himself (of postmark—25th—so interestingly later) addressed to my care & which I have had to exercise an heroic delicacy not to open.   But Bill, I fondly trust, will send it back to me, & I have asked him to hand on the 2 others, for brief perusal & return, to the good Rodgerses, who have been assiduous in their yearnings after you since our 1st news. I have written to Harry a good deal from the 1st, & to your dear selves last week, & you will know how wide open the mouth of my desire stands to learn from you everything & anything you can chuck into it. Most vivid & pathetic these so surprisingly lucid pictures dashed down—or rather so calmly committed to paper—by both of you in the very midst of the crash, & what a hell of a time you must have had altogether! What a noble act your taking your Miss Martin to the blazing & bursting S.F.—& what a devil of a day of anxiety it must have given to the sublime Alice. Dearest sublime Alice, your details of feeding the hungry & sleeping in the backyard bring tears to my eyes. I hope all the later experience didn't turn to *worse* dreariness & weariness— it was probably kept human & "vivid" by the whole associated elements of drama. Yet how differently I read it all from knowing you now restored to your liberal home & lovely brood—where I hope you are guest-receiving & housekeeping as little as possible. How your mother must have folded you in! I kept thinking of her, for days, please tell her, almost more than of you! It's hideous to want to condemn you to *write* on top of everything else—yet I sneakingly hope for more; though indeed it wouldn't take much to make me sail straight home—just to talk with you for a week. You will know how everything has gone with respect to Bill—& how quickly he has got settled at Julian's (for these next weeks & till he can look round further,) in Paris.[1] I think he is in an excellent state of mind, & apparently of body. I return to Rye on the 16th, with rapture—after too long a tangle of delays here. However, it is no more than the right moment for adequate charm of season, drop (unberufen!) of last wind &c.—But why do I talk of these trifles when what I am after all really full of is the hope that they have been crowning you both with laurels & smothering you with flowers at Cambridge. Also, greedily (for you) with the hope that you didn't come away *minus* any lecture-money due to you. I trust you had pretty well had it all before the Quake. Bill has told me of the improved Syracuse arrangement that the incomparable Harry has virtually completed & if it really corresponds to what he appeared to consider definite I am of course devoutly grateful. In relation to which I seem to have gathered that it is *this* month you are able to recommence my remittances again? You will of course tell me if the Syracuse increase becomes an *assured* prospect—though I infer (through Bill,) that it will be

some time before the new leases take effect.   But good-bye for now—
with ever so tender love.

Ever your | Henry.

P.S.   Perhaps you loathe the name (word)—but I do hope you
are going to "write something" about the whole thing, & to get
a Big Price for it.[2]   I seem to think of you as much overclouded &
invaded by the S.F. miseries after that 1ˢᵗ day or two.   *And* your fell
journey—!

[1] The Académie Julian, founded in 1868 in Paris by Rodolphe Julian, attracted
many American art students.

[2] WJ described his earthquake experiences in "On Some Mental Effects of the
Earthquake," *Youth's Companion* 8 (7 June 1906): 283–84; reprinted in *EPs*.

To Henry James

Cambr. May 20. 06

Dearest H.,

Yours from the Athenaeum Club of the 11th. comes this A.M. and
prompts a word of reply, tho I am too much on the jump for more
than a word.   *All* the earthquake anguish has been *yours*.   Taking it
so lightly ourselves, how could we suppose that you would take it so
hard?   But the sensibility and affectionateness of your nature (in
spite of all its squeamishness!) has by this earthquake been blazoned
in the eternal roll-call of such things, and shall never be forgotten—
by us at any rate.   Do you remember, some years ago, my saying that
the Jameses had little or no *affection*.   I was thinking of the Webbs,
by contrast, when I spoke, and of Mrs. Gibbens's way of feeling chronically about each relative just as most people feel the hour after their
death.   I take it all back: The Jameses, with you as their representative and type-setter, beat the Webbs out of the field!   I am *ému* in the
extreme by the way in which your feelings have been harrowed by
our imaginary fate.   I wish now that you would make an Earthquake
the centre of your next novel—'twould go far to restore the average,
for *action*, in your *Oeuvre!*   Strange that you should have divined, as
it were, my writing for the Youth's Companion.   I send you in another cover, a proof.

Pray send this on to Billy, whose letter from the Hotel Sᵗ James etc
(excellently writ) I duly received.   You say he is at Julian's—that fetid
pestilential place.   Not a word about McMonnies—didn't he go to
him?.   At any rate he seems to have lost no *time*, and I suppose that

Sargent's letting him see him paint was out of the question. I should think that what wd. help him most just now would be to see someone else who had big eyes, and not afraid to use them, *paint*. We live in hope, however, of something developing in Paris. He ought to exercise there, not succumb to the temptations, and keep his health. His earnestness will surely bear its fruit.

Very busy here! The "Hodgson-control" impresses me very much in the records, and I am making myself responsible for a report on this particular Piper-phase. To-morrow Alice & I go out, I for the first time, to have a sitting, when it may appear. I am curious to see what impression it will make.

Harry goes to Warners and his 3 weeks of vacation between offices have begun. He has been to Chocorua for 4 days. Neither place let. Peg seems in prime condition. I am sleeping again, after 4 months of disuse of that function, but very busy here just now. Have just bo't a type-writer—new model Smith. Am sending $800 of my California money to relieve suffering there—the very least I could decently do. I will send you probably in two days the May rents you ask for. The new lease doesn't begin till May 1907. Be economical, for God's sake, if not for your own. Bob luncht here to day (Sunday). Queer! Much love! Great haste.

Your & Bill's W.J.

From Henry James

THE REFORM CLUB November 17th 1906

Dearest William.

I had a few days ago a very interesting & valuable letter from [you]—written even though you pleaded in fatigue & fag—& I scrawl this acknowledgment at the end of a rather darksome & drenching 24 hours spent in town, under a particular necessity whence I go back to Rye a couple of hours hence accompanied by T. S. Perry (for 3 or 4 days;) he having come over a week ago from France, & I having put him up here at the Athenaeum & introduced him at the British Museum Lib:, all, I think, to his great delectation. We dined together last p.m. at the Athenaeum, & my principal impressions of him (for I saw him practically but once in America) bear on the extraordinarily small change in his mind, nature & above all expression, since our juvenile days—& on the premature antiquity of appearance which so belies his inward youth—as also so happily for him, his still

remarkable physical hardness & vigour.   But he is very genial and
amusing—& told me last night that honorary members of the Athenaeum being made but for "distinction," the hall porter on his com-
ing-in, was always asking him for what he was distinguished: to which
he had had to only reply—"For my appetite."   He has seen a good
deal of Bill at Giverny &c, & speaks of him with great kindness &
affection.   Your letter breathed as to yourself a certain exhaustion—
which on the part of so great & heroic a lecture-maker I will understand; but it gave me the news of your having retreated from the
Paris undertaking; which has quenched in me rather a haunting anxiety.   I didn't, I couldn't believe in that essentially bristling & bus-
tling—that in every way formidable & arduous, business for you—&
I really hoped that time would bring a revision of your judgment.
It wouldn't have led to *my*—as far as Paris is concerned—seeing much
of you, for Paris has become to me, with time, a place of terror, almost—in fact almost every other place than L.H. has!   But since
you've cast the terror of Paris *from* you, you must take up instead
with the peace of L.H. & come over with Alice & put in a part of the
time that was to have been there.———Nov. 18th.   I broke off this,
for interruption, yesterday, & an hour or two later came back *here* (to
Lamb House) accompanied by T.S.P., who sits down by the draw-
ingroom fire amply content with books while, as it's drearily & dis-
mally wet, I drive this retarded & (so far as this paper is concerned,)
embarrassed, pen.   T.S.P. is very genial, pleasant & talkative (immensely "improved")—a very easy inmate to entertain.   But we have
been living here for 3 weeks in a deluge—paying for our long beautiful rainless summer, that lasted from the end of May to the end of
October.   Yesterday after your letter comes one from Bill enclosing
me one from his mother to him & thereby giving me later news of
you (Nov. 5th,) of your sleeping better & of your Lowell Lectures
about to begin.[1]   May a huge retentissement attend these & promote
the same for the sale of the Book afterwards.   But invent a vulgar
(comparatively) & mercenary name for it, & don't, oh don't, spell it
heartbreakingly.   You speak of Harry as "stern" & of Aleck as tall &
taciturn & of Alice as also comparatively bereft of speech, & the picture somehow as making for righteousness; that is for repose & for
the social minor key—that is for the benefit of your nerves, the tranquillity & unity of your house & the possession of your powers &
hours.   Peggy has written me an interesting, touching perhaps just
slightly agitated & overwrought letter; not, however, breathing depression—only suggesting that she may become sated with that me-

dium before she has done all her time there. But even then she will, clearly, have got a good deal out of it—she gets a good deal—so much—out of everything she comes in contact with. I can give her (I immediately wrote to her,) very little interesting history from this dull (thank God!) house just now—where I hope to prolong the dulness till the end of January. Some time in February I shall go over to Paris, without fail to see Bill. In the note from him accompanying your letter, dearest Alice, last night, he says he finds in his work at Juliens "more interest & more fun than ever." Also that he is staying on at his little hotel for the present, & that Loulie Hooper has left for Switzerland (she was also staying there.) So he won't marry *her!*—at any rate just yet. But you will know of these things more than I. I yearn meanwhile over Aleck meanwhile, please tell him, with my love, & over the noble sacrificed Ryley (though understanding the sacrifice) & even over the cool young Sidney Lovett his friend, so vividly remembered for his high urbanity. I seem to gather (in another connection) that Mrs. Piper comes out—*has* perhaps actually come out, to England & wish I could learn, dear Alice,—what people or circle she comes *to* & where she is to be, for ever since that message you sent me in the Spring I've had such a desire for the possibility of something further—even to the degree of an obsession?[2] Will the Cambridge people have hold of her?[3] Mrs. Verrall, Mrs. Myers &c? Can you in any way help me to her—wholly out of all the psychical connection as I am here.—save perhaps by those two women. But I judge Mrs Myers *néfaste*. This is all for now. Have you read H. G. Wells's American ("Future") book?[4] I find it full of interest, though shouted as through a gramophone by a man who was there— with that large order (the Future!) but 5 weeks, about; full of ideas & refreshing freedoms, ironies, & of a colossal but delectable "cheek"— of the extraordinary rude force & passion that make him the only one of the younger "literary" generation here except Lowes Dickenson & to some extent the too tricky & journalistic Chesterton (who has reduced to a science the putting of everything à rebours) presenting any interest whatever. But I must go down & look after my guest—& another who comes to dinner. My hot water pipes (excellently installed, now that all the dire upheaval is over) prove the most blessed success. They will really make me here a most blessed little winter climate & minister thereby to my whole prosperity, save me in fires & add to the value of the property.

Your all-loving Henry.

P.S. You can stay here now, William, perfectly at any season.

[1] WJ gave the Lowell Institute lectures on pragmatism from 14 November to 8 December 1906.   The lectures were published as *Pragmatism* (1907).

[2] In a lost letter AGJ had reported to HJ that Mrs. Piper had given her messages purporting to come from HJ's mother.   HJ was much impressed by them and searched for ways to pursue the matter.

[3] HJ is probably referring to Eleanor Mildred Sidgwick who, after the deaths of Henry Sidgwick and Frederic William Henry Myers, was the leading figure of the Society for Psychical Research in England.

[4] Herbert George Wells, *The Future in America: A Search after Realities* (1906).

1907

After several attempts to resign from teaching, William James fi-
nally succeeded, giving his last class at Harvard in Philosophy D:
General Problems of Philosophy on 22 January 1907. He con-
cluded his lectures on pragmatism before the Lowell Institute in
Boston on 8 December 1906, repeating them at Columbia Univer-
sity in New York City from 29 January to 8 February 1907. Be-
sides being much impressed by the city, he encountered a new Amer-
ican academic generation, many of whom held doctorates from his
own program at Harvard. One wonders if he, an announced critic
of the Ph.D. octopus, was struck by the fact that it was now impos-
sible for others to do what he himself had done, become a full
professor without a baccalaureate degree.

To Henry James

Cambr. Feb. 14. 1907

Dear Brother & Son—

I dare say that you will be together in Paris when you get this, but
I address it to Lamb House all the same.   You twain are more
"blessed" than I, in the way of correspondance this winter, for you
give more than you receive, Bill's letters being as remarkable for wit &
humor as Henry's are for copiousness, considering that the market
value of what he either writes or types is so many shillings a word.
When *I* write other things, I find it almost impossible to write letters.
I've been at it *stiddy*, however, for three days, since my return from
New York, finding as I did, a great stack of correspondence to attend
to.   The first impression of N.Y., if you stay there not more than 36
hours, which has been my limit for 20 years past, is one of repulsion
at the clangor, disorder, and permanent earthquake conditions.   But
this time, installed as I was at the Harvard Club (44th. St) in the
centre of the cyclone, I caught the pulse of the machine, took up the
rhythm, and vibrated *mit*, & found it simply magnificent.   I'm surprised at you, Henry, not having been more enthusiastic, but perhaps
that superbly powerful and beautiful subway was not opened when
you were there.   It is an *entirely* new N.Y., in soul as well as in body,

from the old one, which looks like a village in retrospect. The courage, the heaven scaling audacity of it all, and the *lightness* withal, as if there was nothing that was not easy, & the great pulses and bounds of progress in so many directions all simultaneous that the co-ordination is indefinitely future, give a kind of *drumming background* of life that I never felt before. I'm sure that once *in* that movement, and at home, all other places would seem insipid. I observe that your book—the Scene in America, dear H., is just out. I must get it and devour again the chapters relative to N.Y. On my last night, I dined with Norman Hapgood, along with men who were successfully and happily in the vibration. H., & his most winning-faced young partner, Collier, Jerome, Peter Dunne, F. M. Colby, & Mark Twain. (The latter, poor man, is only good for monolog, in his old age, or for dialog at best, but he's a dear little genius all the same.) I got such an impression of easy efficiency in the midst of their bewildering conditions of speed and complexity of adjustment. Jerome, particularly, with the world's eyes on his court room, in the very crux of the Thaw trial, as if he had nothing serious to do.[1] Balzac ought to come to life again. His Rastignac imagination sketcht the possibility of it long ago. I luncht, dined, & s'ts bkfstd., out, every day of my stay, vibrated between 44th. St., seldom going lower and 149th. with Columbia University at 116 as my chief relay station, the magnificent space-devouring Subway roaring me back and forth, lecturing to a thousand daily, and having four separate dinners at the Columbia faculty club, where colleagues severally compassed me about, many of them being old students of mine, wagged their tongues at me and made me explain. It was certainly the high tide of my existence, so far as *energizing* and being "recognized" were concerned, but I took it all very "easy" and am hardly a bit tired. Total abstinence from every stimulant whatever is the one condition of living at a rapid pace. I am now going whack at the writing of the rest of the lectures, which will be more original and (I believe) important than my previous works. I saw much of Miller, Bill,[2] in N.Y. Columbia has made him a full Professor at last, diminishing his work, but not yet raising his pay. They have a *very* strong philosophic team—to be ranked by some, no doubt, more highly than our Harvard team, and the finances of Harvard unluckily do not permit of a new appointment being made in my place. How large the Harvard world is and how small a part I have played in it of late, is illustrated by the fact that during two weeks at the Harvard Club, I saw hundreds of graduates going & coming, and was spoken to by only one man, Dick Derby, till the last day, when I recognized Gordon Bell. I am almost un-known to the younger men, in these years.—[An hour later] I have just drest myself and had bkfst., and some conversation with your mother and Harry about the possibility of taking Aleck to Switzerland this summer. He seems to be at rather a dead point at school, and with the worry of exam⁵, and his inability to get ahead with french, etc., his poor memory etc., it looks as if a radical change, which would at the same time consolidate his "preparation" from the in many respects spurious and deadly conventional obligation of being a Harvard graduate might be in order.[3] There are many future adjust-ments to be considered, but the immediate practical hypothesis is that of either sending him for Billy to take to Switzerland and locate (for a year probably), or for your mother to take him and do the same, leaving me at home. If your mother should go it might be well for Peggy to go with her, how would Henry like to keep her at Lamb House for a few weeks? It would do *her* good. The whole thing is in the air just now, and we may relapse into the ordinary Chocorua program forthwith. It would be contingent, in fact, on our renting that place. Aleck's future has I think got to be in some artistic line. Sensibility is his key-note, and on that line he may suc-ceed. He's very slow in intellectual development. I must now go to a "department meeting." Farewell! blessings on you both!

W.J.

[1] On 25 June 1906 Harry Kendall Thaw (1871–1947), of a prominent and wealthy family, killed Stanford White. Thaw believed that his wife was unfaithful and was involved with White. William Travers Jerome was the prosecutor in the sensational and protracted case to which newspapers devoted hundreds of stories. Eventually Thaw was found innocent by reason of insanity.

[2] WJ is indicating that the remarks which follow are addressed to his son, who knew Miller from an earlier time.

[3] Alexander Robertson James, who was dyslexic, failed the Harvard entrance exam-inations several times and by the summer of 1906 had made up his mind to study painting.

To Henry James

Salisbury, May 4th. '07

Dearest H.—I've been here a week "resting," and finding it exactly what I require, sleeping like a hippopotamus, and between walking and driving, getting all the fresh air there is going—*cold* air, however, and to day a frigid rain, which promotes indoor pursuits, inclusive of this letter. It is 10 a.m., and I've been talking for 2 hours with the incomparably healthy-minded and intelligent Rosina about all the members of the family, going deep into their respective psychologies. The crisis of *their* life is the return to night from six months at a private "sanatorium" of poor Leslie, of whom they seem to be in a sort of terror for she has developed into a full-blown ner[v]ous invalid of late, the organic point of weakness being gastric, but the nerves all gone to smash. I doubt whether she has been in the wisest medical hands. The Doctor, Quintard, who owns the establishment, has kept her there (at *150 dollars a week!!!*) for six months—I believe Henrietta has footed the bill—and she is now in a week or so to go abroad for as long as it works, with Mary Foote, to be joined later by Bay. I think they will go first to the Continent, but on their way home I suppose you may have to get ready for a visit from them at Rye. Alice has sent me a letter from you to Harry describing your automobile tour with the Wharton's and the charm of your Faubourg S.! Germain existence—the whole thing must have been great for you and extremely nourishing, in such intelligent and sympathetic company as hers; and I am *so* ultra glad that you are to visit poor little Venice once more. You speak of then ending your days within the walls of the Rye garden—but you *wont*. Among other things you'll come to America again. I've been so overwhelmed with work, and the mountain of the *Unread* has piled up so, that only in these days here have I really been able to settle down to your "Scene in America," which in its peculiar way seems to me *supremely great*. You know how opposed your whole "third manner" of execution is to the literary ideals which animate my crude and Orson-like breast, mine being to say a thing in one sentence as straight and explicit as it can be made, and then to drop it for ever; yours being to avoid naming it straight, but by dint of breathing and sighing all round and round it, to arouse in the reader who may have had a similar perception already (Heaven help him if he hasn't!) the illusion of a solid object, made (like the "ghost" at the Polytechnic) wholly out of impa[l]pable materials, air, and the prismatic interferences of light, ingeniously focused by mirrors upon empty space. But you *do* it, that's the queerness! And the complication of inuendo and associative reference on the enormous scale to which you give way to it, does so *build out* the matter for the reader that the result is to solidify by the mere bulk of the process, the like perception from which *he* has to start. As air, by dint of its volume, will weigh like a corporeal body; so his own poor little initial perception, swathed in this gigantic envelopment of suggestive atmosphere, grows like a germ into something vastly bigger and more substantial. But it's the rummest method!—for one to employ systematically as you do now adays; and you employ it at your peril. In this crowded and hurried reading age, pages that require such close attention remain unread & neglected. You can't skip a word if you are to get the effect, and 19 out of 20 worthy readers grow intolerant. The method seems perverse: "Say it *out*, for God's sake,["] they cry, "and have done with it." And so I say now, Give us *one* thing in your older directer manner, just to show that, in spite of your paradoxical success in this unheard of method, you *can* still write according to accepted canons. Give us that interlude; and then continue like the "curiosity of literature" which you have become. For gleams and inuendoes and felicitous verbal insinuations you are unapproachable, but the *core* of literature is solid. Give it to us *once* again! The bare perfume of things will not support existence, and the effect of solidity you reach is but perfume & simulacrum. For God's sake don't *answer* these remarks, which (as Uncle Howard used to say of Father's writings) are but the peristaltic belchings of my own crabbed organism. For one thing, your account of america is largely one of its omissions, silences, vacancies. You work them up like solids, for those readers who already germinally perceive them [to others you are *totally* incomprehensible]. I said to myself over and over in reading: "How much greater the triumph, if instead of dwelling thus only upon America's vacuities, he could make positive suggestion of what in "Europe" or Asia may exist to fill them." That would be nutritious to so many american readers whose souls are only too ready to leap to suggestion, but who are now too inexperienced to know what is meant by the contrast-effect from which alone your book is written. If you could supply the background which is the foil, in terms more full and positive! At present it is supplied only by the abstract geographic term "Europe." But of course anything of that kind is excessively difficult; and you will probably say that you *are* supplying it all along by your novels. Well, the verve and animal spirits with which you can keep your method going, first on one place then on another, through all those tightly printed pages is something marvellous. and there are pages surely doomed to be immortal, those on the "drummers" e.g. at the beginning of Florida. They are in the best sense rabelaisian.—But a truce, a truce! I had no idea, when I sat down, of pouring such a bath of my own subjectivity over you. Forgive! forgive! and don't reply, don't at any rate in the sense of defending yourself, but only in that of attacking *me*, if you feel so

minded. I have just finisht the proofs of a little book called "pragmatism" which even you *may* enjoy reading. It is a very "sincere" and
from the point of view of ordinary philosophy-professional manners,
a very unconventional utterance, not particularly original at any one
point, yet in the midst of the literature of the way of thinking which
it represents, with just that amount of squeak or shrillness in the
voice that enables one book to *tell*, when others don't, to supersede
its brethren, and be treated later as "representative." I shouldn't be
su[r]prised if 10 years hence it should be rated as "epoch-making,"
for of the definitive triumph of that general way of thinking I can
entertain no doubt whatever—I believe it to be something quite like
the protestant reformation. You can't tell how happy I am at having
thrown off the nightmare of my "professorship." As a "professor" I
always felt myself a sham, with its chief duties of being a walking
encyclopedia of erudition. I am now at liberty to be a *reality*, and
the comfort is unspeakable—literally unspeakable, to be my own
man, after 35 years of being owned by others. I can now live for
truth pure and simple, instead of for truth accommo[da]ted to the
most unheard-of requirements set by others. Bill writes the most
splendid letters home; but I'm all in the dark about his artistic prow-
ess, and wish that you could have given some more positive hint of
it. Of course under studio condition it has to be modest. I only
hope that some day the fruits of the training will break out suddenly
from the hull. One thing is sure, that with the taste and sensibility
and artistic intelligence he has, he never will do anything positively
bad. But the main thing is that he keeps so devoted to it, and so
happy at it.—Well, I'll wind up. I pray you, enjoy Venice! Rosina
just arrives from the station, dripping, with the sweetest little mare
for Bay, sent to her from Virginia by her friend Mr. Hanna. You
have doubtless heard that our Chocorua place is let for the summer,
to the Goldmarks, nice people, for 400 dollars. I mean to keep away
from Cambridge all I can, for when there I stay too much in doors,
and it doesn't quite agree with me. Tell Bill that there isn't the slightest chance of my going over to the Amsterdam Congress of alienists.
I can't imagine what for a brief moment made me feel tempted by
the prospect enough to put down my name. I want above all things
now to keep myself in decent order for writing, and if possible making
a little money by it. The thing that is worst for me is dinner parties,
and as they do Alice good, it is inconvenient.

    —Lunch has been eaten, and my momentum is spent, so I'll close
and go and take my nap. This outing will have done you a lot of

good, and I like to think of the same. But I'm entirely in the dark about your literary occupations especially about the Collective edition, of which I say nothing—Wait! I am forgetting the papers in Harper's bazaar—strange vehicle & channel![1]—yet young women are so quick to catch on to that sort of a thing that among the readers they will be a few who will conceive and bring forth fruit.

Your affectionate W.J.

Elly & Rosina send much love.

[1] HJ, "The Manners of American Women," *Harper's Bazaar* 41 (April 1907): 355–59; (May 1907): 453–58; (June 1907): 537–41; (July 1907): 646–51.

To Henry James

Stonehurst, Intervale | Oct 6. '07

Dearest Brother—I write this at the Bryce's, who have taken the Merriman's House for the summer, and whither I came the day before yesterday, after closing our Chocorua House, and seeing Alice leave for home. We had been there a fortnight, trying to get some work done, and having to do most of it with our own hands, or rather with Alice's heroic hands, for mine are worth almost nothing in these degenerate days. It is enough to make your heart break to see the scarcity of "labor," and the whole country tells the same story. Our future at Chocorua is a somewhat problematic one, tho I think we shall manage to pass next summer there and get it into better shape for good renting thereafter, at any cost—(—not the renting but the shaping.) After that what *I* want is a free foot, and the children are now not dependent on a family summer any longer. Bill has been with us, little changed by Paris, and evidently booked for a very simple and concentrated life. I like his simplicity and earnestness very much, and it is evident that he is embarked now on a life rather of deepening than of expansion, in which his essential character will remain unchanged. Peggy got off to Bryn Mawr safely and reports arrival. She has had a wholesome summer, and is much better in health than when she came back in the spring. Alice is more *vaillante* than ever, and has kept surprisingly serene and well. I spent the 1st 3 weeks of Sept—warm ones—in my beloved & exquisite Keene Valley, where I was able to do a good deal of uphill walking, with good rather than bad effects, much to my joy. Yesterday I took a 3 hours walk here, ¾ of an hour of it up hill. I have to go alone, and slowly; but its none the worse for that and makes me feel like old times. I leave this P.M. for 2 more days at Chocorua—at the hotel.   The Fall is late, but the woods are beginning to redden beautifully.   With the sun behind them some maples look like stained glass windows.   But the penury of the human part of this region is depressing, and I begin to have an appetite for Europe again.   Alice too!   To be at Cambridge with no lecturing, and no students to nurse along with their thesis-work, is an almost incredibly delightful prospect.   I am going to settle down to the composition of another small book, more original and ground-breaking than anything I have yet put forth(!) which I expect to print by the spring, after which I can lie back and write at leisure more routine things for the rest of my days.[1]

The Bryce's are wholly unchanged, excellent friends & hosts, and I like her as much as him.   The trouble with him is that his insatiable love of information makes him try to pump *you* all the time instead of letting you pump *him*, and I have let my own tongue wag so, that when gone, I shall feel like a fool, and remember all kinds of things that I have forgotten to ask him.   I have just been reading to Mrs. B., with great gusto on her part and renewed gusto on mine, the first few pp. of your chapter on Florida in the American Scene.   *Köstlich* stuff!   I had just been reading to myself almost 50 pp. of the New England part of the book, and fairly melting with delight over the Chocorua portion.   Evidently that book will last, and bear reading over and over again,—few pp. at a time, wh. is the right way for "literature" fitly so called.   It all makes me wish that we had you here again, and you will doubtless soon come.   I mustn't forget to thank you for the gold pencil-case souvenir.   I have had a plated silver one for a year past, now worn-thru, and experienced what a "comfort" they are.   Good by, and Heaven bless you.

Your loving   W.J.

[1] Perhaps WJ has in mind the posthumously published *Some Problems of Philosophy* (1911).

From Henry James

LAMB HOUSE, | RYE, | SUSSEX. October 17th 1907.

Dearest William!

Your liberality, the way you have lately (& for so long past) written to me *sans compter*, you & Alice & Harry & all of you, your munificence, I say, is celestial; for this evening comes in your blessing of 8 pages from under the Bryce's Intervale roof—at the very time of my being most bowed down under the long shame of all my accumulated (though somehow these many months practically *insurmountable*) silence. It's late at night, but I seize my pen to at least begin a letter to you & tell you how all summer—& from my time in Paris, even, last March-April &c, & in Italy through May-June, your so meanly acknowledged, & scarce acknowledged at all, out-pourings have enriched & delighted me. And I had a *divine* letter from Alice, the other day only, still unanswered, & one just now, a joy to me, from Aleck; & though I owe also, now, responses to *him* & Peg & Harry & Bill, all urgently, I let everything slide till I've been a bit decent to *you*. I seem to have followed your summer rather well & intimately & rejoicingly, thanks to Bill's imparting up to the time he left me & to the beautiful direct copious news aforesaid from yourself & from Alice, & I make out that I may deem things well with you when I see you so mobile & so mobilizable (so emancipated & unchained for being so) as well as so fecund & so still overflowing. Your annual go at Keene Valley (wh: I'm never to have so much as beheld) & the nature of your references to it—as this one tonight—fill me with pangs & yearnings, I mean the bitterness, almost, of envy: there is so little of the Keene Valley side of things in my life. But I went up to Scotland a month ago, for 5 days at John Cadwalader's (of N.Y.) vast "shooting" in Forfarshire (let to him out of Lord Dalhousie's real principality,)[1] & there, in absolutely exquisite weather, had a brief but deep draught of the glory of moor & mountain as that air, & ten-mile trudges through the heather & by the braeside (to lunch with the shooters,) delightfully give it. It was an exquisite experience. But those things are over, & I am "settled in" here, D.V., for a good quiet time of urgent work (during the Season here that on the whole I love best, for it makes for *concentration*—& il n'y a que ça—for *me!*) which will float me, I trust, till the end of February: when I shall simply go up to London till the mid-May. No more "abroad" for me within any calculable time, heaven grant! Why the devil I didn't write to you after reading your *Pragmatism*—how I kept from it—I can't now explain save by the very fact of the spell itself (of interest & enthrallment) that the book cast upon me: I simply sank down, under it, into such depths of submission & assimilation that *any* reaction, very nearly, even that of acknowledgement, would have had almost the taint of dissent or escape. Then I was lost in the wonder of the extent to which all my life I have (like M. Jourdain) unconsciously pragmatised. You are immensely & universally *right*, & [I] have been absorbing a number more of your followings-up of the matter in the

American (Journal of Psychology?)² which your devouring devotee Manton Marble, of Brighton (whom I was capable of re-spending 2 days with lately—difficult to face as is the *drench* of talk which his opulent chosen isolation makes him discharge on one from pent-up sources) plied, & always on invitation does ply, me with. I feel the reading of the book, at all events, to have been really the event of my summer.   In which connection (that of "books,") I am infinitely touched by your speaking of having read parts of my American Scene (of which I hope Bill has safely delivered you the copy of the English edition) to Mrs. Bryce—paying them the tribute of that test of their value.   Indeed the tribute of your calling the whole thing "*Köstlich* stuff" & saying it will remain to *be* read so & really gauged, gives me more pleasure than I can say, & quickens my regret & pain at the way the Fates have been all against (all finally & definitively now,) my having been able to carry out my plan & do a second instalment, embodying more & complementary impressions.   Of course I *had* a plan—& the 2ᵈ vol. would have attacked the subject (& my general mass of impression) at various *other* angles, thrown off various other pictures, in short *contributed* much more.   But the thing was not to be.   My Western journey was (through the complication of my having to get back to N.Y. remuneratedly to "lecture" & that of the mere scrap of time left for it by the then so devilish & now so life-giving Roberts) too brief & breathless for an extended impression or an abiding saturation, a sufficient *accumulation* of notes; & though even this wouldn't have prevented my doing something could I have got at that part of my scheme *quickly,* the earlier mass of the same delayed me till so much time had elapsed that here, & at a distance, & utterly out of actual touch, the whole thing had faded, melted for me too much to *trust* it as I should have needed to.   I shld. have to go back for 6 mos., & embark on impossible *renewals,* to do that second vol. And yet without it the 1ˢᵗ affects me as a mere rather melancholy lopsided fragment, infinitely awkward without its mate!   But I must go to bed & finish tomorrow!

October 18ᵗʰ   A melancholy, dreary diluvian day, & succession of days altogether, so that much confinement to the house—beyond the limit of what makes for righteousness & continuity of application— prepares for you a correspondent congested & oppressed.   (A *bad* autumn & winter here—or anywhere in the country—are rather fatal.   But it remains to be seen if these shall be *too* bad.)   I am having a good deal of decent quiet & independence, without invasions from London & a new excellent amanuensis from thence, a young, boyish

Miss Bosanquet, who is worth all the other (females) that I have had put together, & who confirms me in the perception, afresh—after eight months without such an agent—that for certain, for most, kinds of diligence & production, the intervention of the agent is, to *my* perverse constitution, an intense aid & a true economy. There is no *comparison!* I am very busy, though it doesn't outwardly show much—but I won't reveal the secrets of the prison-house more than to say that it will be an immense relief to me when the famous Edition is off my hands. You must wonder what has become, or is becoming, of it; but it is very much to the fore of my consciousness, with the very great application that the very copious amount of minute revision & beautification I have gone in for has taken & is taking even yet, & the very great deal of time devoured by the proof-reading of 23 (amended) volumes, & the writing for 17 vols. of 17 Prefaces of the most brilliant character & of 7000 (seven thousand) words each. (Some of the books of course—6 of them—appear in two vols.) The prefaces are very difficult to make *right*, absolutely & utterly, as they supremely have to be; but they are so right, so far, that the Scribners, pleased with them to the extent quite—for publishers—of giving themselves away—pronounce them "absolutely unique"! Their (the Scribners') deliberation is in their very just desire to have almost all the volumes in hand & ready—to avoid any possible *after* hitch or delay—before they begin to publish at all. *Then* they will issue them rapidly, as I understand, & *coup sur coup;* at the rate of 2 books a month—really handsome ones, I make out.[3] What I am doing in the way of revision is equally "unique"—but overwhelmingly enlightened, inevitable & interesting: any judgement *a priori* (or even subsequently) to the contrary being simply fifteenth-rate!—Reading over your last nights' letter again, in its beautiful charity, makes me participate to intensity in the divine difference your reprieve from immemorial college-labour must mean for your days & nights & all your goings & comings, & throw myself into all the questions of your life as so modified & embellished. Otium cum dignitate—putting independent labour, as comparatively otiose, for dependent. And your dignitas now so immense & so consummately earned, every particle of it so paid for over the counter!—it thus ought to be a very good period of life for you, your palpable essential youth & mobility backing all the rest up. I haven't dignitas & I haven't otium, but on the other hand I have Fletcher, who is fully worth, I feel, *both,* & who helps me to a luxurious *im*mobility (*à peu près*) which is almost as good as Youth! How Alice must profit too by your emancipation—profit

I mean "sympathetically", & in spite of having you more thereby on her hands (unless by an increase of your mobility she has you *less;* in which case she won't have gained so much, for she'll have you more on her mind, & her mind, like all fine minds, is a more restless seat of occupation, & even of anxiety, than her hands.) You are very interesting & "pathetic" about the receding and unpeopled Chocorua, with its irremediable *desertion* of hands, but I can't help hoping that in spite of everything, all changes, I mean, you will still be able to hold on to it & *sufficiently* exploit it—so much did my all too brief vision of it seem to have to say to *me!* Brief, brief & all too frustrated & fragmentary (partly through being so Roberts-ridden, though he *was* to be such a "blessing in disguise") does almost all my American time affect me now as having been; all consisting of baffled snatches & prevented chances & stinted indulgences & divided claims—in proportion to what I *wanted* to get out of it. Perhaps I wanted too much—I certainly did in proportion to my powers of dealing with it: for it seems after all, in retrospect, *formidable* more than aught else (I mean contacts & efforts & relations—not *relatives*—seem,) & the whole thing couldn't doubtless have been other than it was! Besides, I am in possession of unused & yet usable material from it still.———But it's into the status of your children that I throw myself most, & into all that it must say to you & to Alice to have them so interesting & so valuable. It says indeed almost as much to *me* as it can to you both! What you speak of as to Bill as you find him on his return is most truly felt: he strikes me as essentially & intensely *entire.* And it's all right to be entire if it doesn't mean you're prematurely concluded. He has visibly great power of growth. Harry is a blessing to me "all the time"—of Harry I can't trust myself to speak. And will you tell Aleck that I am hovering on the very brink of answering a Delicious Letter I've just had from *him?* I owe one, as I have said, to Peg as well, but hers shall go straight to Bryn Mawr. *She* sounds most handsome & precious. Also I've been overjoyed at your reports & at Alice's, of your happy impression of Bob. It brings tears to my eyes to think of him at last in quiet waters—if they *be* waters unadulterated. Heaven grant he be truly a spent volcano. Apropos of whom Bill will have told you of the presence of Ned *here,* with him, 2 or 3 times—& will probably have left me nothing to add. I hope I don't do him—poor Ned—injustice, but he strikes me as irremediably without form & void—as he is strangely & unhappily without attraction & breeding. I don't know what impression he makes, about, as he goes—I can't think a very pleasing or helpful (to himself) one; though on the other hand I judge him really amiable & without harshness or tortuosity. But he is untutored & untutorable—& is now in Paris (as yet alone, in the Latin quarter) "studying sociology", for the winter. Louisa, I believe, is to go over, but they evidently don't "stay together" more than they can help—& she *dégage*, to my sense, no feeblest, faintest ray of magnetism. But I am writing on too far into the dead unhappy night, while the rain is on the roof—& the wind in the chimneys. Oh your windless (gale-less) Cambridge! *Choyez-le!* Tell Alice that all this is "for her too", but she shall also soon hear further(!!) from yours & hers, all & always,

Henry.

[1] The estates were probably those of Arthur George Maule, 14th earl of Dalhousie (1878–1928).

[2] WJ published a number of short papers in the *Journal of Philosophy* in defense of pragmatism. These papers and some others were published in *The Meaning of Truth* (1909). There was an *American Journal of Psychology,* but WJ published nothing in it during this period.

[3] The first two volumes of *The Novels and Tales of Henry James* were published in the New York Edition by Charles Scribner's Sons on 14 December 1907.

From Henry James

LAMB HOUSE, | RYE, | SUSSEX. Nov: 13: 1907

Dearest William!

This is a small scrap of a sign; partly because I wrote you at rather inordinate length no long time since, and partly because I have designs, immediate and intense, on each other of les votres; though, thanks to a mountain or[1] "correspondential" arrears, which flings its dark shade over the otherwise smiling (unberufen!) champaign field of my present state, I shall have to tick-out my love on this so public-looking system—which I am returning to, for general labour, after eight month's severance from it, with deep and particular appreciation. What I am really wanting to say to-day is what I might have said two or three weeks ago, viz: that a man I don't particularly know, though I have known him a little for some years, one C. Lewis Hind, a London journalist, ex-editor of The Academy and one thing or another has written to tell me that you are the person in America he wants utterly most to see during a short stay he is just beginning there, and that he will take it gratefully if I say a good word to you for him in advance, in case he shall be able to approach you during his days in Boston. He doesn't ask me for a letter, and I wouldn't give it to him if he did, for I used to think him rather a donkey and am under no obligation to him whatever—he rather to me. But he is a perfectly decent, respectable, and I believe amiable man; "interested in Philosophy" and, I infer, supremely in Pragmatism; so that if he comes along and makes you a sign, please understand that I have written you this explanatory, but not urgent nor insistent word.

And there is another like matter—only much more interesting. Do you remember my old (though not aged) and remarkable friend Elizabeth Robins, formerly on the stage, and whom you must have met when with me at the initial time of "The American" play-business? She is more remarkable than ever, and in every way eminent and intelligent, really distinguished; whereby, having naturally, some years since, utterly cast off the theatre and all its works, she has gone in for literature, Female Suffrage, the Colour Question in the U.S. (she springs from Louisville Ky.) and various other activities. She writes me confidentially that she has just taken an engagement to do a Book on said Colour Question, and that she leaves for America almost immediately to prepare it; with plenty of openings on the Southern view—having, among other things, a winter pied-à-terre in Florida—but with a lack of good chances of *renseignement* in the North. She asks me if I could put her in contact with any good source of Inspiration on the subject there; and I have simply ventured to suggest You as the best source of Inspiration I know upon anything. Therefore I shall give her a note to you, just that you may tell her a few things; which I wouldn't dream of doing did I fear to launch her at you the least as a Bore or a Bother. She won't be in the slightest degree one or the other; but is really so interesting, charming and accomplished a person that she will pay her way with you abundantly by the interest and pleasure of talking with her. She has lately hurled herself with ardent conviction into the Suffragette agitation, but not in the obstreperous, police-prodding or umbrella-thumping way of many others, and is, I believe, their most valued platform oratress, swaying multitudes like a heroine of Ibsen. All of which is just to tell you that I'm giving her a little letter. She asked me if I could put her up to Jerome of N.Y.; but, besides that I never saw him but once, I don't know that he would be particularly helpful to her; and at any rate you can tell her about this.

But I overflow too far; especially as, between sentences, I this morning dash out to tree-planting in the garden which, tell him with all my love, I wish Harry were here to have a finger in: as my principal small exploit has been, within half an hour, to get in a small but very good-looking Walnut tree: in place of that fourth-rate tall balsaam-poplar, in the studio-angle of the lawn, that has been for the last two years sickening, decaying, dying, and poisoning by fabulously big and ugly roots, an incredible complicated wilderness of them, all the surrounding surface. The rest of you will, I trust, see the slow and sturdy walnut develope (I have reacted against quick trees) but I shall only see it started. This is all just now—save that I go on the 23rd. to Liverpool to meet poor Lawrence Godkin, who arrives there with dear little Katherine G's cold ashes for interment near E.L.G. at Hazelbeach, the so oddly, so perversely fixed little out-of-the-way Northamptonshire churchyard in which their father and husband was (as I feel) so erratically laid after his death near Torquay several years ago. You will doubtless have heard of poor Katherine's long, wretched struggle for life, these last months, and of her death a week ago. L. was, had become, as time went on, exceedingly attached to her; and now comes out all alone on this melancholy and already wintry mission; and has cabled to me practically to ask if I won't meet him and see him through: to which I have unreservedly responded. Fortunately Alice and Betty Lyon, her devoted friends, are here, and will have been of great utility. But it is all dreary—and, as an "arrangement" so strangely "felt".[2] I hope you are having a glorious late autumn; it has been on the whole very decent here, and everything about us never so handsome. But good-bye

Ever yours | Henry James

[1] A slip for 'of'.

[2] Catharine Buckley Sands Godkin died on 8 November 1907 in New York. Her ashes were transported for burial in England, where services were held on 25 November. HJ was one of the mourners.

1908

It is difficult to tell how much William James himself sought out the distractions that kept him from carrying out his announced projects. Having announced that all he really wanted was the possibility of writing another book on philosophy and after insisting that he loathed lecturing and the socializing that went with it, he nevertheless agreed to lecture at Hibbert College, Oxford, on "The Present Situation in Philosophy," his stated reasons being the money—£200—and the fact that it would do "good to Alice." He accepted the offer on 29 November 1907. Since the lectures were to start on 4 May 1908, he had very little time for preparation. He sailed for England with Alice and Peggy on 21 April. The trip provided an opportunity for touring and sightseeing, especially in Holland and Belgium, where he found Bruges a "picturesk little town" and was delighted by the Hans Memling pictures. The Jameses were back in Boston by 16 October. The Hibbert lectures were published as A Pluralistic Universe *(1909) and included a chapter of intellectual autobiography under the title "The Compounding of Consciousness."*

To Henry James

95 IRVING ST. | CAMBRIDGE, MASS. Feb 4. 08

Dearest H.—Just a scribble to inform you of the situation here. I meant to write 3 weeks ago but have been a victim of a most virulent attack of grippe, just beginning to be able to understand what I read, if it is serious. Aleck is now in his 6th week—I in my 4th.—of the same affliction. Of course it has knocked out all power of work on Oxford lectures, and will for at least a fortnight night more. No use trying *that* sort of thing unless one is swinging forward physically! The lectures seem therefore more problematic than ever. Fortunately Alice was in Montreal for a fortnight of it and didn't know, so she escaped the strain. In the midst of it, a couple of weeks ago came the 1st 4 vols. of your Collected N. & T., for which all possible thanks. On the whole they are *handsome!*—I read Roderick H. which I hadn't lookt at since it first appeared. My brain could hardly understand anything, much less *enjoy,* but it bro't back the old charm. What a colossal worker you are, to have gone all over it verbally again! I am not sure either, that in *that* case at all events, it was not labor lost, or that the simpler and more naive phrasing of the original edition does n't keep a better harmony. But what astounds me is your power of steady *work!* Bill is splendid, so cheerful, serviceable, and gentlemanly in every relation. I have yet to become acquainted with his work!!! He makes a splendid combination with Aleck. I may say that he is now trying Chocorua (our summer-fashioned house) with a friend, to "paint out of doors." The thermometer was 0° this A.M. here—probably 30° below, there! Harry seems well, but solid & stern—hates needless words. Has been very busy over some private theatricals in Boston, of wh. he was stage manager. Peg gives good accounts of herself. Alice is OK. I hope you are and that the hard times won't cut down *your* profits on your N. & T.

Much love, W.J.

At some point while he was in England, William decided that the best thing for the academically deficient Alexander Robertson would be to have him tutored at Oxford. He arranged for his son to come to England and met him at the dock upon his arrival in September 1908.

To Henry James

At Salter's, Oct 21. 08

Dear Henry,

Alice will probably have written to you already of our stormy passage with Peggy in bed for 8 days, but Alice & I not at all sick. We got thru, however, paying only $120 at the Custom house, and found the "home" looking very sweet. The weather was hot indian summer, & early the next morning I came straight up here to get in a last short taste of the country's sweetness. No use comparing American scenery with english—they have no common denominator. So quickly does one take the tune of the english thing that this N.H. autumn seemed to me almost heartbreaking in its sentimentality. The smoky haze, the windless heat, the litter of the leaves on the ground in their rich colours, with enough remaining on the trees to make the whole scene red and yellow, the penury & shabbiness of everything human, the delicate emaciated morbidness, and feminine secretness of all nature's effects was so pathetic!   No sound, no people, earth & sky both empty, and almost alarming in their emptiness.   The elaborateness of english scenery, the simplicity of American,—its hard to be torn so both ways by one's admirations, and the best policy is to think as little as possible about the contrast.   The Salters have dismist their hired man & girl, and are doing their own work right Tolstoyanly.   I have been down to our own house a couple of times—it looks very nice, & the tenants have had it beautifully cleaned up.   I shall stay out my week, hindered by one of my poisonous catarrhs having come upon me instantaneously.   By the time I get back, Alice will doubtless have distributed her new acquisitions thru the house, and I shall settle down to some steady work.

Aleck wrote us a couple of heart-rending homesick letters—It may last for a couple of weeks, but I am sure that in 3 weeks time he will be accommodated to the colder social climate which surrounds him.

It is queer to think of our english summer, erst so real, now an insubstantial pageant faded.   Yet the Lamb House garden still smiles & enfolds *you!*   I hope the work is going off slick—by this time the play may have been produced at the S! James, and you may believe that I hope it will be a great success.   I shall, now that I am removed from the vividness of your presence, begin to read the prefaces in due order.   Good bye.

Your loving | W.J.

From Henry James

LAMB HOUSE, | RYE, | SUSSEX. Nov: 2: 1908.

Dearest William.

It was delightful to get your letter from the languid Chocorua country with its wondrous characterization of that languor—even though it also told of your horrid overdone voyage & dear Peg's long martyrdom.   For God's sake give up the cultivation of slow ships & avail yourselves of the conveniences of your age.   During all those days we had exquisite golden *breathless* weather here—& that same still goes on: an immaculate exquisite warm & fireless October.   Before Alice's renewed custom-house gallantry I bow down in admiration—wondrous & unspeakable to me the glory of her achievements & the spectacle of her genius. Some day at her full leisure I shall beseech her to tell me a little how all the importations range themselves & "tell." Of course dear little Aleck has sent me *his* letter & postcards from you—& he & I do what we can to exchange tidings. I don't dream of hearing from him much (his letters must all be to *you;*) but I guess he is getting into the phase of accommodation—& it's a good sign that my lately offering to go & see him soon, he wrote that he really thought our meeting had better wait till Xmas—as to which he is probably quite right. If he were still very *sore* (with homesickness) he would have been likely, I think, to desire to see me. So I shall have him here in a few weeks. What you told him of Bill's work (in your absence)—your characterization of it—fills me with joy—tell him I long for the sight of him & his "touch"; & count on it for no distant date.———I have received from Jae Walsh's wife a cable—as you probably have a telegram—announcing poor little Dick W's death in New York (which I didn't suppose him, when here, so much on the way to.) What a pathetic little dénouement, figure & remembrance—of that impression of him here. But the point is that I have no shadow of an *address* to acknowledge her civility in cabling to—& am therefore enclosing a letter herein that I have written her—& can't send otherwise, to ask you to address it somehow if you possibly can—& get it to her hands. You will probably (if she did telegraph you) be—have *been*—writing her yourself.———I don't speak of Charles Norton's extinction—it leaves somehow at once too much & too little to say—& I have written to Sally & to Grace. It has been, as it were, discounted; but I shall be very much interested in all the *sequelae*, which in one way & another, will be many. I daresay you are back in Cambridge now to a pacified & richly embellished house. I think you must even have come to C.E.N.'s funeral. I hope with all my heart that Peggot thrives again in spite of her horrid sea-change, & I hang over her, tell her, as I do over her Mother, with endless interest & solicitude. The Season here, as I say, has been admirable—but I am sorry to say I am too much invaded, approached & beset by people—Emily Cochran & her 2 daughters (e.g.) rather *hovering* at me in London—after other recent descents & assaults; but I can't possibly have them here (I but gave her the wide berth in America) & have asked them to lunch with me in town next week. But of the challenges from London the end seems never. Mrs. Wharton arrives on the 5ᵗʰ—& that circumstances looms large.   What looms incredibly large to me is the modern insane, incoherent globe-life.   People *recur*—from the antipodes—at the end of three months (I don't say that for *her,* whom I shall be very glad to see, but for every one.[)] I embrace you all—I wish *you* would recur; & am ever your universal

Henry.

P.S.   Mrs. Paddington doesn't *tarir* on Alice—"she's so domesticated!"

Robertson James at last found some peace in his last years. In Concord he painted, enjoyed the visits of his grandchildren, and dabbled in psychical research. At some point in 1909 he received William's Meaning of Truth *and, after explaining to his brother where he, William, had gone wrong, added that William should not even think of replying since "I am too busy painting pictures in Walden Woods to notice you." William was dealing with logical truth, a "dead thing" in Robertson's view, and not the truth that "makes people happy and brings content." In a reminiscent mood, he recalled their early wanderings and the truth they had in those times, which came from the "generous sweet and trusting love of those departed ones," their parents and Alice and Wilkie.*

Henry James was having "pectoral" trouble, a variety of symptoms that he decided were due to fletcherizing. In February he cabled William that he had stopped the practice and was practically well. William replied with some concern that the news might hurt Horace Fletcher, to whom he showed Henry's telegram. Since William, too, was suffering various symptoms connected with his heart and receiving treatments from a "quackish" physician, the correspondence for the early months of 1909 is rich in medical lore.

From Henry James

LAMB HOUSE, | RYE, | SUSSEX. February 3$^{\underline{d}}$ 1909.
My dear William.

I am making up my mind to tell you, with every precaution, that my "pectoral" trouble has of late been giving out some rather worrying *heart-symptoms*—for which I have been seeing Skinner, who has given me *digitalis,* as a matter of course, & strichagen (or strychnine!) & who hasn't, up to now (I've only been seeing him a few—10—days) *alarmed* me in the least.   It was only 11 or 12 days ago that my consciousness—rather uncomfortable, ever since you left England—became rather suddenly aggravated, in respect to panting, gasping, getting generally out of breath in respect to minor efforts &c, & it was only *then* I sent for him & got temporary relief.   I have got it greatly by a resumption of walking (very mildly & carefully, but regularly,) after an almost motionless autumn; & in fact the 1ˢᵗ diagnosis of my condition appeared to be, that with the extraordinary oddity of its developing thus in the very lap & bosom of the best period of health I have had in all my life—the past 6 years of Fletcherization—with no shadow of *strain* or overdoing—it was in a manner the result of my gradual but more & more increasing cessation of "exercise." From my 1ˢᵗ great profits from Fletcherism—& more completely since my 1ˢᵗ consciousness of "thoracic" queerness—I have "gone out" less & less—& never in my life so little as these last 4 or 5 months, with the enormous luxury (in itself) of feeling how Fletcherism & its effects have permitted that lapse—from the *goad* of motion—with that impunity (to all the rest of my feelings.) Directly I began to act on the assumption that my heart would [be] the better for discreetly resumed locomotion the effect was apparently prompt—almost magical—I began to feel ever so markedly better. I have felt less well the last 3 or 4 days—but it's too soon to say, & in short I am—have been to day—a little solitarily worried & depressed. What I find myself desirous of is to get some authoritative *London* judgment—Skinner is careful & kind, but not, I think, other than very moderately *intelligent* & perceptive. I don't *know* in the least whom to turn to—& have a horror of Besley Thorn? Is there any one *you* can indicate to me?—or cause to be indicated to me by any one else you can suggest? I am thinking of writing to Osler* to ask— but have felt a need today to open myself to you. Don't, you & Alice, take me hard; I can't believe that the extraordinary *gain* of health (what I've never *fully* detailed & expressed to you) that has been my portion for so long has only suddenly, perversely, eccentrically, led up to & *flowered into* a GRAVE trouble! But it consoles me to talk to you a little even thus—& makes me want, too, to say more.———— However, I will only say now (three or four hours later) that Skinner has been with me this afternoon & found me exceedingly normal & right save for the results of "long & protracted (systematic) under-exercise & *under-feeding*"—the latter especially for the last 4 or 5 months. He sent me immediately out for an hour (slow & by myself,) & I felt immensely better by the time I got in. Everything points to this being the true history of the matter—the more I go over it; but I can't expatiate thus.—Aleck will do beautifully since your 3 letters, yours Alice's & Harry's—all incomparable & divine.

Yours all devotedly Henry James
*if he can name me the right man.

From Henry James

LAMB HOUSE, | RYE, | SUSSEX. [February 5, 1909]
Dearest William.

I am feeling so infinitely & promptly *better* that I blush for the slightly depressed letter that I wrote you on Tuesday last—& if I had waited 24 hours longer probably wouldn't have sent it. I was simply sickined for 48 hours by Skinner's *drugs*—"tonics," whiskeys, liquor-brandies & the like (which he doesn't in the least mind one's not taking however[)]—& I have quite cleared it up with him that I take *nothing;* besides which he will have the scantest further occasion to come. For our Diagnosis is triumphant—my queer feelings are *completely* yielding to the return at last, after an interval deplorably long & fallacious, to a due amount of reasonable exercise & a due amount of food FOR the same. I have walked about 4 miles (taken in 2 hours) for the last 3 or 4 days, *with* more food than at any time for too many months, alas, & with the consequence that my sensations are absolutely ceasing to be distinguishable from the normal. In short the last fortnight (counting out the *stomachically-spoiled* 2 days on which I wrote you,) have completely cleared up—in the sense, I mean, of having enlightened—my whole backward view of this history. But I can't tell it you properly—because, as I said to you in my last letter—it wd. be impossible save in a long *talk* to make you understand a little how & why the blest—& why, 1st of all, *so* extra-blest—Fletcherism lulled me, charmed me, beguiled *from the first* into the luxury & the convenience of not having to drag myself out to eternal walking. One must have been through what it relieved me from to know *how not suffering from one's food all the while, & having suffered all one's life, & at last finding it intermit & cease & vanish,* could make one joyously & extravagantly relegate all out of doors motion to a more & more casual & negligeable importance. In short I can't put it veraciously without being too physiological & unfit for the family circle. *To have at last bowels that would act*—without the hell-goad of trying to *walk-up* an action—THAT made the time one could take for reading & in-door pursuits (& for doing my *Edition!*) a delicious, insidious bribe. So more & more I gave up locomotion—at last almost completely. *Then* a year & ½ ago began the 1st thoracic worry, in spurts, bang out of the heart of my gained perfection of all other health. Walking *seemed* to make that worse—only tested by short spurts. So I thought non-walking more & more the remedy, & applied it more & more, & ate less & less, naturally—& this autumn began to gasp & pant; after a settled immobility of long duration really—& a perfection, as I say, of other health. On the other hand I hadn't for a long time *read* so much!   My heart was really disgusted—all the while—with my having ceased to call on it—which I have begun to do again, in the most prudent, reasonable manner, & with the most luminous response.   I am better the 2ᵈ ½ hour of my walk than the 1ˢᵗ; & better the 3ᵈ than the 2ᵈ & ready to *skip* during all the latter part.   Skinner is delighted with me, & will come in future, occasionally, only to feel my pulse.   But this hasty scrawl must go off by the waiting Burgess, to catch the American post of tomorrow. And all this time I am not mentioning your splendid 6 pages-letter of the 24ᵗʰ (speaking of my Ch. Norton article so charmingly!)[1]—& to which I can't do justice tonight.   Aleck will go on beautifully— serenely: he is the young angel of adolescent *reason*.   I am to see him on the 18ᵗʰ in town on the occasion the enclosed tawdry little card specifies—I have of course asked him to come up for the 1ˢᵗ afternoon, & he will tell you all about it.   I am to go up on the 13ᵗʰ or 15ᵗʰ, for a couple of renewed rehearsals, *goings-over* of the little play, which, announced but for 5 consecutive matinées will go on if the box-office "speaks."[2]   It's a proof for you of how much better I feel that I look forward to that little term of mild motion (mild, note you, not wild) as positively attractive & favourable to me.   But you shall [have] more good news of everything & I am hurriedly yours all

Henry James

[1] HJ, "An American Art Scholar: Charles Eliot Norton," *Burlington Magazine* 14 (January 1909): 201–4; reprinted in *Notes on Novelists* (1914).

[2] HJ's play *The High Bid* was first performed on 26 March 1908 and played several times in London in 1909.

To Henry James

95 IRVING ST. | CAMBRIDGE, MASS. Feb. 13. 09

Dear Henry,

I won't say that your letter of the 3rd, which came yesterday, was a bolt "from a clear sky," for I had been imagining, ever since I left, that some exacerbation of your symptoms might be any day possible and break your stoical reserve.   I am cabling you this morning to try Dr. James McKenzie, of 17 Bentinck St., Cavendish Square, whom Dr Pratt, the best heart man in Boston recommends to me as THE man to go to.   Should he be away, Sir T. Lauder Brunton, who has just publisht a book on the therapeutics of the circulation is your man.[1]

He is a *sommité*, and, I believe, a charming man. Evidently the innervation of your heart has got deranged, and the gasping, etc., may mean nothing but an intermittent pulse, which is not in itself alarming. There is probably also a fatty element involved. But its no use speculating thus at long range! My own idea is that, whatever the state of your organs may be, a couple of months at Nauheim next year is your best chance. I'm thinking seriously of it again for myself, and it would be jolly for us to meet there on neutral ground. Moorfield Storey was there last summer with his wife and is going again, and tells me (she was in bed most of last winter with her heart & arteries) that she hasn't been as well for years. Don't fail to write all that McKenzie (or whoever) tells you. You can hardly conceive of my sympathy or interest in your lot. If walking helps you, and so promptly too, it must be that the heart element is not very bad. But moderate your efforts in other ways! Write little *eigenhändig*, and write shorter letters than you habitually do! No need of writing at all to younger members of this family. *I* find the act of writing to be a great tax.

I am pursuing treatment of a quackish sort here, the result of which, up to date, is to debilitate me very much. Qui vivra verra! Our plans are *very* unsettled—there are grounds for wishing to spend the summer and next winter on the Continent but we ought then to rent both places, and nothing yet is in sight. Mo[r]eover the problem with Aleck is urgent, and we await palpitatingly his answer to the various family letters which he seems to have sent to you.

No more to day, dearest H. from your loving brother,

W.

The Nation says that your play is definitely announced—at last![2] May it be a prosperous one.

[1] Thomas Lauder Brunton, *Therapeutics of the Circulation* (1908).

[2] The *Nation* 88 (11 February 1909): 149, in a review of the London Afternoon Theater, noted that HJ's new play is "an event of no small literary and dramatic importance."

From Henry James

LAMB HOUSE, | RYE, | SUSSEX. July 18. [1909]

Dearest William.

Horribly silent have I too long been in spite of two most generous letters from you—the first from Salisbury Conn., as long ago (hideous for me to relate,) as the end of May, & the 2ᵈ from Silver Lake, N.H., of comparatively the other day.   I received both of them in town, from which I lately returned after a stay of a couple of months; a stay on from week to week (for it seemed good for me) during which I kept promising myself to write as soon as ever I should get back to these more peaceful shades—remarkably dense just now as an effect of too long a term of cold & torrential rain (which made also for my hanging on in town, where the weather can more or less be flouted.) But you spoil me—that is the real truth—by your unreckoning munificence.   Now that I *am* back here dear little old L.H. reasserts its value & its charm as almost never before; the garden is thick & blooming—& withal (thanks to inveterate George) beautifully neat; to day is a delightfully mild & soft sun-dappled, shade-flickering, west-windy Sunday, full of rustle & colour; & I have just tried to express to Harry how "unhandsome" (as Father used to say) it is that I should be piggishly keeping, or at least having, it all to myself—to the exclusion of my near & dear.   Nurse at least & keep firm on its feet the project of your *all* coming out to me next summer.   The years fearfully lapse & it won't do to miss another.   Yet I am counting on Bill for September—& *all* September—at furthest, if so be it he can't come sooner.   I am, however, immediately writing him about this.   I am really better—ever so much better—than I have been at any time since I began to grow too fat & move too little; my clothes hang loose upon me, & I must soon begin to have some of them "taken in"; a delicious prospect after years of letting out.   In short I am *easy*, & will say no more about it—save that I feel myself to have profitted enormously by getting renewedly into touch with dear Horace Fletcher, during a few days he spent with me in town.   His physiology is priceless to me, & his example ditto—though I have no use for his general bland & boresome idealisms & christian endeavourings—on which, however, we don't have to touch at all—having a most beautiful & successful relation without it.   I feel that physiologically & on *that* Fletcherizing basis he knows *absolutely* where he is; & we threshed things out together in a way that will have really been of great use to me for the rest of my days—of this I am confident. I don't despair of returning to & leaning on dear Mother Nature even to within almost measurable distance of dear—of almost *as* dear—H.F. himself, who visibly before me, during ten days, partook of one very simple dish (& of only about a 3$^{\underline{d}}$ of that—frequently a Welsh Rabbit!) not more than once in 48 hours—& with the effect of remain[i]ng but the MORE *frais & dispos* & active all the while.   I see now—with the effects (*local doctor-produced*) of my 1ˢᵗ bewilderment of some months ago cleared up—effects of "more *meat* & really a glass of good port-wine after dinner," eventuating 1ˢᵗ in a bilious attack here & then, in town, in the 1ˢᵗ fit of gout, in my *right* foot this time, for years—with those consequences intelligently outlived, & forever, I say, I am more full of resource, on a more intimately understood Fletcher basis, for the rest of my days, than ever before. But enough of that—which may be summed up, as I say, in the statement that I am *easier* than for a long time past, & that I know, I feel, a great deal more than I had done before, about remaining so. Also I have lots of interesting work before me—two jobs that are for the moment a little conflicting. I am having at last to come to the point of doing for the Macmillans the "London"—more or less impressionistic & with drawings by Joseph Pennell—that I long ago contracted with them for & that it has been ever since convenient, & necessary, for me to hold off from (the agreement as to *time* I having made from the 1ˢᵗ an easy one.) I shall enjoy doing it when once I buckle down, & the terms being very good, & the possibility of tourist &c sale big, the profit *may* be very great. Only meanwhile the Theatre has been loudly knocking in my door, & my reasons both intrinsic & extrinsic for listening to it exceedingly strong & valid & urgent. Therefore as the New "Repertory" Theatre (Haymarket—in the person of Herbert Trench,) & the later-to-be-opened one in the person of Frohmann—but acting (on *me*) through J. M. Barrie—have both applied to me for plays at an early date, I am for this summer pegging away for *them*, all the more that from Trench I have already received my advance of money "down".[1] All of which facts, however, are *only* for family consumption. I hang about you all in imagination & wonder, & hope, ardently, that you are most—save the heroic Harry, I fear—to whom I have just written—among your various woods & lakes & orchards & piazzas, & above all that Alice & Peggy to whom I send my tenderest love, haven't too monstrous a social situation to face. When I image *those* resources of yours in their large romanticism, I look out of my window at my so rosy & so mulberried & so swarded garden with a more consoled sense of its small contractedness—that is of its snugness combined with its emptiness—in respect to your presence; & heaven send that you be all making in your various ways a successful & manageable summer of it. Your own movements—through space—seem to me to testify for you; as for myself, "better" as I am, *déplacements* less & less appeal—save the always interesting one (after sufficient intervals,) of going hence up to town & reverting back here again. That oscillation will simply suffice me for the remainder of my life—but of course it is a very good one. Also it has "come my way" to motor—or rather to be motored—a good deal these last weeks, & that, when not overdone, & in this admirable county of Sussex in particular—or for that matter anywhere in England—I find, if *contemplatively* done (& only then,) immensely suggestive, interesting & inspiring. Mrs. Wharton has been these 2 months in & near London, with an admirably conceived & guided Panhard[2]—& was *here,* just after my return, for 3 or 4 days; during all of which, fine weather occasionally favouring, she whirled me admirably about—notably from London down to Dorsetshire (to Frampton, the Sheridans', near Dorchester, where we spent the night;) & the other day hence to the west extremity of the County—Chichester—& then the next day otherwise back through absolute enchantments of scenery & association. I find I get a good deal out of it.———All this time I'm not thanking you in the competent way for your "Pluralistic" volume—which now I can effusively do. I read it, while in town, with a more thrilled interest than I can say; with enchantment, with pride, & almost with comprehension. It may sustain & inspire you a little to know that I'm *with* you, all along the line—& can conceive of no sense in any philosophy that is not yours! As an artist & a "creator" I can catch on, hold on, to pragmatism, & can work in the light of it & apply it; finding, in comparison everything else (so far as I know the same!) utterly irrelevant & useless—vainly & coldly parallel! Sydney Waterlow told me a day or two ago that he had had a very interesting & beautiful letter from you—the spirit of which he seemed greatly—immensely—to appreciate. Awfully interesting what you tell me of Plutarch—whom I reopened—with extreme interest, to the extent of 3 or 4 Greek Lives—a year or two ago; not having looked into him since old Newport days. But I can for this year only go on reading *London* books—of which there are far too many. But the best interest me. I pray for Aleck & embrace you all.

Ever your fond Henry.

[1] This was HJ's last venture into the theater, resulting in *The Outcry.* The play was not produced.

[2] Panhard was Wharton's automobile.

To Henry James

Chocorua, Aug 2nd. '09

Dearest Henry—Your delightful letter of July 18th from Rye comes just as I am about to write to you to report progress. Hurrah for the London job, & hurrahissimo for the theatrical jobs—if only the latter turn out well! as they ought to. We have been here for a month, with — —

Aug 6th.

with a good deal of company for a fortnight past, which has now abated, tho' Alice & I leave to morrow for a couple of days with the Merrimans at Intervale. Bill, who has just gone to Salisbury, has been making a very good portrait of me. I feel sure that he will eventually "find himself" and do tip-top work, subtle as well as broad—of late the quality of 'breadth' is all that has been aimed at by Boston artists. Hunt's influence in that way was far from good, unless complemented by successors. I think there is no doubt of B. staying most of the winter in the Boston Art School which now is in a way to do him more good than ever. Our summer has been very dry, though on the whole not hot, and the "lawn" is parched. Likewise a strange caterpillar pest, which began last summer has *sévi* and defoliated innumerable trees, sparing so far however our own little elms. Alice works a great deal over the place, but I shirk every duty and decision, being in a phase of existence where I need all my energy for my own tasks. My "thoracic symptom" is about what it was last summer—no worse. I get a second wind, but it takes a long time, so I don't enjoy the freedom of the country as I once did. But no matter, circumstances are such that all care is taken off my shoulders by Alice & Harry, and the income holds out. Peggy was never in better shape than she is in this summer, both physically & morally. It is a pleasure to see her sun browned face. I think I shall probably leave for the Adirondacks by the 15th. but I don't know for sure yet, it will depend on how enterprising I feel. Aleck having passed only in french, is back in hot Cambridge with his tutor. How long, oh lord, how long?

I am over-delighted that you have at last graduated from the interminable Scribner proofs,[1] & that newer horizons, even theatrical horizons, beckon. Love from us all, & *augurii* of the best.

Your loving. WJ.

[1] WJ is referring to *The Novels and Tales of Henry James,* completed in July 1909.

From Henry James

                    LAMB HOUSE, | RYE, | SUSSEX. October 31ˢᵗ 1909.
Dearest William.

I have beautiful communications from you all too long unacknowledged & unrequited—though I shall speak for the present but of two
most prized letters from you (from Cambridge & Chocorua respectively—not counting quaint sequels from Franconia, "autumn-tint"
postcards &c, a few days ago, or thereabouts, & leaving aside altogether, but only for later fond treatment, please assure them, an admirable one from Harry & an exquisite from Bill.) To these I add
the arrival still more recently of your brave new book, which I fell
upon immediately & have quite passionately absorbed—to within 50
pages of the end;[1] a great number previous to which I have read this
evening—which makes me late to begin this.   I find it of thrilling
interest, triumphant & brilliant, & am lost in admiration of your
wealth & power.   I palpitate as you make out your case, (since it
seems to me you so utterly do,) as I under no romantic spell ever
palpitate now; & into that case I enter intensely, unreservedly, & I
think you would allow almost intelligently.   I find you nowhere as
difficult as you surely make everything for your critics.   Clearly you
are winning a great battle & great will be your fame.   Your letters
seem to me to reflect a happy & easy summer achieved—& I recognise in them with rapture, & I trust not fallaciously, a comparative
immunity from the horrid human *incubi*, the awful "people" fallacy,
of the past, & your ruinous sacrifices to that bloody Moloch.   May
this luminous exemption but grow & grow! & with it your personal &
physical peace & sufficiency, your profitable possession of yourself.
Amen, amen—over which I hope dear Alice hasn't *lieu* to smile!   I
came back here a month ago from a month's absence, & should have,
especially for this last month, a pretty fair account of myself to give
weren't it for the curse of our abominable season, a summer & autumn of the most blighting, the most cruel, inclemency.   This whole
October has capped the climax with diluvian & unceasing rains
(they've been going on since May;) horrible roaring tempest & brutal
polar cold!   One doesn't know how one "is" in such conditions—one
is simply beaten & laid low by the elements.   And still it goes on.
This blessed old house helps me to endure—is, if possible, even a
growing boon to me, with its singular little secret of being favourable
to life, & in respect to my heart-trouble of upwards a year ago (as to
its bad *crisis*) I am very distinctly & confirmedly better & better; in

spite of anginal tendencies (which lapse, practically, even as they come—& which I can in a measure control or accommodate myself to.) Movement, ambulation & circulation, continue as markedly good for me as Mackenzie guaranteed, & it is a question, only, of getting, conveniently *enough* of them; which I do better in London than here, unfortunately, during these oncoming days of waning light & increasing mud. I haven't felt the need to see Mackenzie again—that fact will give you by itself a good deal, the measure. There are other things, or mainly *one* other—which I might sum up as being at last, again, *definitely & unmistakeably,* the finally proved *cul de sac* or defeat of literal Fletcherism—might so sum up if I could go at all into the difficult & obscure subject by letter. I *can't* do so— though I will return to it on some future writing, & after more results from my of late—that is these last 3 months' very trying experience— which has abated since queer lights (*on* too prolonged Fletcherism) have more & more distinctly & relievingly come to me. But mean- while communicate nothing distressful to poor dear H.F. if he is in America—his malady of motion, a perfect St. Vitus's Dance of the déplacement-mania, make me never know *where* he is. I am wor- rying out my salvation—very interesting work & prospects, I think, much aiding—& "going into" the whole fearsome history intelligibly *this* way is an effort from which I recoil.

November 1st I broke this off last night & went to bed—& now add a few remarks after a grey soft windless & miraculously rainless day (under a most rainful sky,) which has had a rather a sad hole made in it by a visitation from a young person from New York, addressed to be[2] by poor Ida Smalley there as her bosom friend (Helen Fiske by name, daughter of vice-president of Metropolitan Insurance Com- pany)[3] who, arriving from town at 1.30, to luncheon, remained New Yorkily conversing till 6.30, when I got her off to Hastings, where she was—& I trust *is*—to sleep. She stole from me the hour or two before my small evening feed in which I hoped to finish "The Mean- ing of Truth"; but I have done much toward this since that repast, & with a renewed eagerness of inglutition. You surely make philoso- phy more interesting & living than any one has *ever* made it before, & by a real creative & undemolishable making; whereby all you write plays into *my* poor "creative" consciousness & artistic vision & pretension with the most extraordinary suggestiveness & force of application & inspiration. Thank the powers—that is thank *yours!*—for a relevant & assimilable & *referable* philosophy, which is related to the rest of one's intellectual life otherwise & more conve-

niently than a fowl is related to a fish.   In short, dearest William, the
effect of these collected papers of your present volume—which I had
read all individually before—seems to me exquisitely & adorably cu-
mulative &, so to speak, consecrating; so that I, for my part, feel
Pragmatic invulnerability constituted.   Much will this *suffrage* help
the cause!———Not less inspiring to me, for that matter is the account you give, in your beautiful letter of Oct 6ᵗʰ, from Chocorua, of
Alice & the offspring, Bill & Peggot in particular, confirming so richly
all my precious observations of the son & letting in such rich further
lights upon the Daughter.   I shall write soon to Bill & tell him all
I believe of him & count on from him; & I languish for the sequel
of the Medea-performance plan & for further news of Peg's connection with it.   I wd. almost cross the wintry ocean to see my gifted
niece in the "title rôle."   But I mean really & truly, soon to write her
straight & supplicate her for a letter.   Poor dear Aleck—his "parts"
have evidently to grow more successively than simultaneously, & each
as a distinct & independent proposition; but I am convinced that they
will still, together make a fair, coherent & beautiful sentence.   But
we mustn't try too much to hurry it up—to the risk of loss of part of
the good meaning.   I send him his faithful old Uncle's love.   And
àpropos of Uncles, though not so much of love, I had Bob's Ned here
again for a day 3 weeks ago, on his way back from London to Paris—
impressed as to manners & even appearance & the general tinge,
faint though it be, as of civilization; but so indescribably *Naught,* as
regards anything like content or character or value or possession of
anything to give, or perception of anything to take, that the result is
almost uncanny.*   I got oddly enough at the same time a short letter
from Bob—tacked on to one of Mary's; the 1ˢᵗ word I have had from
him for years & which I immediately & rejoicingly answered.   Humorous & fairly friendly, but queer & latently vicious or invidious—
all, however, in a harmless & sad & imaginable way (as out of the
bitter depths of a consciousness of comparative failure & obscurity—
comparative to you & me, with our "literary talent" &c!) which moves
me to nothing but tender & unexpressible (not quite *in*expressible!)
compassion for the image of narrowed-down savourless life that he
presents.   Little has he too reduced himself to having either to give
or to take! Another thing which just lately made a grudged hole in
a couple of days was my having consented at the gentle Florence
Pertz's instance to read the voluminous type-copy of a Life of J. J. G.
Wilkinson—done by a cousin, a Dr. Clement Wilkinson of Wind-
sor⁴—but done so drearily & artlessly & impossibly, & on a subject

really most thankless & arid & dead, that I had no hesitation in saying that publication is wholly hopeless & unprocurable—a verdict in which she entirely concurs; so that, visibly, the thing will blush unseen—after the poor cousin's most well-meaning & uninspired & unreadable toil. But good-night again—as my thoughts flutter despairingly (of attainment) toward your farawayness, under the hope that the Cambridge autumn is handsome & wholesome about you. I yearn over Alice to the point of wondering if some day before Xmas she *may* find a scrap of a moment to testify to me a little about the situation with her now too unfamiliar pen. Oh if you only *can*, next summer come out for 2 years! This house shall be your fortress & temple & headquarters as never, never, ever, before. I embrace you all—I send my express love to Mrs. Gibbens—& am your fondest of brothers

Henry James

P.S. I have read both your Hodgson report & your Am. Magazine article—thanks![5] The former depressing; the latter most interesting & uplifting!

*He has the merit, on the other hand of being wholly un-importunate & un-boring, & of certain practical discretion in relations—or non-relations

[1] WJ, *The Meaning of Truth* (1909).

[2] A slip for 'me'.

[3] Helen Fiske Evans.

[4] Clement John Wilkinson, *James John Garth Wilkinson* (1911).

[5] WJ, "The Confidences of a 'Psychical Researcher,'" *American Magazine* 68 (October 1909): 580–89; reprinted in *EPR*.

1910

On 4 February 1910 William James received a letter from Henry's doctor stating that there was no cause for anxiety about Henry's condition. Since he had not been aware that Henry was ill, William immediately cabled the doctor for news and received a reassuring reply. On 9 February Henry himself cabled that he was making an "excellent recovery." This flurry of cables and letters caused enough anxiety and suspicion about the true state of Henry's condition that William's son Henry departed for England. On 13 March, William received a letter from his brother that he described as "very pathetic" and immediately decided to go to him. A letter from son Henry received on 19 March describing the "bad nervous condition of H.J." added to his worries. He and Alice departed on 29 March for England, reaching Lamb House on 7 April at 1:30 in the afternoon, where they found Henry in bed and in poor condition.

On 5 May, somewhat reassured about Henry's progress, William left Alice to look after his brother and set off for Paris to consult a heart specialist about his own symptoms. There, in spite of high blood pressure and "awful" days, he had a "delightful lunch" with Henri Bergson on 15 May. The next day he bought a first-class ticket for Nauheim and left Paris on 17 May. He was examined by doctors in Nauheim on the eighteenth and two days later had a radiogram taken of his heart that showed the "aorta enlarged and drawn down by heart's weight." When later X rays showed a better condition, he dismissed the new result, writing in his diary that "errors of observation may cover the amount." Still alone at Nauheim, he continued to inquire with concern and anxiety about Henry.

From Henry James

Lamb House Feb. 8th 1910.

Dearest William & Alice & All!

I intend to cable to you cheeringly tomorrow, but meanwhile it is high time this should go off to you by the next American post (which

is tomorrow,) & I am preparing it as you see by this rude medium which is for the moment easier to me than still a bit shaky ink-
slinging. I have waited till I could write you *firmly* & emphatically
that I am on my way to real valour, or at least validity, again—& that
has had to come little by little. But I am very steadily & smoothly
getting the last dismal six weeks well behind me—& such is the manner in which I was hoping to go on before speaking of them at all.
I mean my wish was all to be able to delay speaking of them at all
till I could refer to them absolutely in the past tense. Well, that is
indeed what is now quite conveniently & cheeringly happening.
Skinner, who has been excellent & devoted, told me a few days since
of his having had your cable & answered it very reassuringly & also
written you—which is why I have put off these signals of my own for
a lapse of days numerous enough to be more cheering & reassuring
still. I am getting well again without a break or a flaw & am already
quite lustily & ably convalescent. The blest Skinner took me out for
the third time, this a.m., in his motor-car for an hour & ½—his wide
round of the country side, & I sat at farm house & cottage & other
doors while he made his calls—to my immense refreshment & sus-
tainment. The weather is still & always of the meanest—yet everything in the way of outer air works straight for my good, & my
strength is excellently coming back. I *eat* steadily a little more &
more—& with *that* the blest process of recovery works. For I have
had, really, a pretty dismal & dreary time, or *had* had, till a few days
since (of more confirmed improvement) from 3 or 4 days after Xmas.
It has all been, frankly & briefly, the last rude remainder of the heri-
tage of woe of too-prolonged & too-consistent Fletcherism—a final &
conclusive (I trust) debt of suffering to that fond excess to be paid
off. I think it will *all* have been paid off this time—& I can't give
you my reasons in this 1ˢᵗ rather faltering scrawl. But my diagnosis
is, to myself, crystal clear—& would be in the last degree demonstra-
ble if I could linger more. What happened was that I found myself
at a given moment more & more beginning to fail of power to eat
through the daily more marked increase of a strange & most persistent & depressing stomachic crisis: the condition of more & more
sickishly *loathing* food. This weakened & undermined & "lowered"
me, naturally, more & more—& finally scared me through rapid &
extreme loss of flesh & increase of weakness & emptiness—failure of
nourishment. I struggled in the wilderness, with occasional & delu-
sive flickers of improvement (of a few hours) for many days—& with
Skinner co-operating most kindly—& then 18 days ago I collapsed &

went to bed & he instantly sent in an excellent Nurse (who is still with me for a few days more;) whereby the worst of the burden was lifted & the worry & anxiety soothed & the fairly dismal "lonesomeness" assuaged. I had some rather depressing discouragements for a fortnight—11 or 12 days—but no complications of any sort; nothing but a slow gradual & successful struggle to be able to want food enough to swallow it, & on that basis I have got better—& shall know how to remain so. But it has all been a queer & indescribable history—that is a 'rum' & strange consciousness in the light of my Fletcheristic & "thoro[u]gh mouth-treatment" past. *I hadn't intermitted that jealously & intently & intensely* ENOUGH *after the mortal warnings of last (the later) summer & the autumn that I wrote you of—& a greater vigilance—of intermission & violation was all the while insidiously required. Failing it,* came the angry & at 1ˢᵗ most obscure crisis. But at the darkest hour in bed light broke—"more artfully & more scientifically & more grimly *dis*Fletcherise & you'll get well;" & that has been the basis on which I began visibly, sensibly, traceably, regularly to do so. I make this queer egotistic & possibly incoherent statement for the benefit of your certain curiosity & wonderment & tenderness; but I mustn't write any more now. I have been sitting up all day—that is from 10 a.m. to this 9 a.m.[1]—& Nurse reminds me of bedtime. She will stay 4 or 5 days more—then I shall cease to need her at all. Skinner has been devoted, Mrs Paddington perfect, & this house equally perfect as a "nursing home." I only pray now for weather. But I will write you more & better in a very few days. Have no fear nor anxious thought for me now. I have yearned over you—but was silent from poor writing power without alarming you. I mean I feared to by my shaky scrawl or statement. And I cudgel my brain to know how you knew—enough to cable Skinner. You will tell me. Oh for a letter! If my so admirable friends the Protheros are with or near you will you explain to *them*—for she has beautifully written me 2 or 3 times I write her most *soon*. And I send you all such love!

Ever your restored   Henry.

[1] A slip for '9 p.m.'

From Henry James

Garlant's Hotel. March 15th [1910]

Dearest William & Alice.

You will have got a good deal of our news by cable these last days—& this afternoon early I despatched you a long message in reply to William's about sailing on the 19th or the 29th. This probably will bring us some response tomorrow—& meanwhile I want these still rather pale & ineffectual symbols to get off to you by tomorrow's post. I am still flushed with the sad consciousness of the pretty wild wail I addressed you from Rye on the 3^d or 4th (after Harry had been with me 4 or 5 days.) The *spirit* of that fairly demoralized appeal abides with me, I confess—even after what has happened these last days—I mean by reason of my great yearning to see you. For I have been very ill—& even though now better, & here in town, & with my interview (a very good one) with Osler over, I feel still the eminently uphill nature of the journey my poor vitiated stomach has got to take, with a grim patience, back to any functional felicity—& how sad & heavy my digestive consciousness must be for, I am afraid, a good while to come. This makes so for a very peculiar black depression that I reach out—as my last lachrymose letter said—to such aid & comfort & companionship (of *les miens,* whom I so crudely clutch at!) as I can, however grossly, invoke. Well, Harry has gone out to a play, & I am alone here till my early bedtime & I just scratch this along to get beforehand with it for prompt posting tomorrow. I made the journey up from L.H. on Saturday last 12th very much better than I feared during a long series of bad days before & after Harry's arrival. The breaking of the long dire spell & vicious circle there is something—much—to have done—even though I still feel that much of my remaining convalescence must be slow. I had a decent & quiet & amended Sunday—& then yesterday a.m a long & most genial & most thorough overhauling from Osler, whom Skinner came up to meet. (But Skinner, save for his great good will is negligeable.) Osler *entirely* & absolutely enters into & concurs in the crystal clear view of my physiological & stomachic history—that my 6 years of passionate & intimate Fletcherism had, after the first long, & excellent period of benefit, bedevilled my digestion to within an inch of its life. But I can't go again into this glaring, staring truth of my whole physical consciousness now: it is enough that he wholly recognises that my obstinate *mal* is exactly what I felt it from the 1st (1st of the so difficultly achieved effort to *dis*Fletcherize, & which at last only took *preponderant* effect toward the end of last year—during December,) the pain & rebellion & anguish of the 6-year-long disused & dishabitated stomach to *function,* to accommodated itself to the introduction of food in anything but the guise of absolute formless "mouth-treated" (or mouth-treating) saliva. The Devil & the Deep Sea! He has nothing to recommend or promise me but the gradual effect of this return to more normal feeding—*taking* of my food— but for this final effect he absolutely engages, as the stomach hasn't been "organically" disfigured or perverted in the least. Also as the result of an extremely thorough & undressed examination of me, Skinner present & further testifying, he gives me a singularly uplifting, in fact a quite inspiring *general* account of myself—finding me even "splendid" for my age of (finishing) 66; *excellent* state of heart arteries lungs, & machine generally ("pulse of a boy!") & of how he should have *expected* to find my stomach dislocated &c, after its prolonged adventure, in a way of which it gives no sign whatever. (All *anginal* symptoms have quite left me since beginning to disFletcherize!) He has asked Harry & me to come down from Saturday to Monday to them at Oxford, & great as is the effort to me of the idea of being a guest in my still sick condition, I shall make an heroic point of it in order that he shall see me *more* & more closely & that I shall get perhaps some good benefit of it. We cabled you today that Harry is planning to sail by the Empress of Britain on the 25th—& I planning, at least, to hang on here at Garlant's in order to have him with me if I do so. I have bad days & hours, mixed with better ones—but am believing more in these latter, & so if by the 25th I haven't found the London basis wholly break down I shall *try* my powers at my club room. I confess I am an arrant coward now over the solitude of Lamb House in anything of a prolongation of depressed sickness. This was of the essence of the abject craven wail of my last letter. But the ineffable blessing that Harry's goodness & greatness & patience & wisdom have been to me—well, remains ineffable! He is the most perfect human being surely now in operation on this planet—& the *sense*, & the rightness & the infallibility of him!—Even now, as I write, all too seedily, your letter of the 6th,— just on arrival of Boutroux's—dearest William, is brought in to me, & gives me the joyous sense that you at least I may see soon—if you decide, on the *whole* showing, to come out about April 1st. I marvel at your courage in being able to think of such heroics without the support of Alice—while I, who have no right to her, whine for her like a babe. But it will do me unutterable good to see you & have you with me—& every benefit I can lavish upon you I will lavish to the *comble*. Your letter contains 2 or 3 fallacies, however, about my condition which I can't but *relever* however rudely. My illness had no more to do with a "nervous breakdown" than with Halley's comet: I *had* no nervous break-down whatever—& no reason to have one. It came from the rebellion of my intensely enfeebled & perverted stomach under the shock of the antidote that had become vitally imperative in the way of the resumption of normal mastication &c again—& which, the vitiation having the deep-seatedness of so many years, has had to be mortally slow to ebb. It had, & needed, no other genesis whatever. I *became* agitatedly nervous (like our poor Alice of other years, a little!) under the depression & discouragement of relapses & sufferings & of Skinner's well meaning bunglements—but they were another & superficial affair. Likewise my play (of the Repertory Theatre) isn't *yet* produced at all—& won't be, thank God, till May. No play *can* be with the author utterly stricken out, by illness, of rehearsals! Therefore no performance

March 16<u>th</u> I just finish this scrawl this a.m.; not in very brilliant case, having had a poor night after a poor day—but determined to hang on here at least long enough to see Osler again—as above, & hoping for you dearest William to fill up the aching void left for me by Harry's departure. I *dream* of the companionship of Alice—but all that is infinitely difficult for you, & I am your poor clinging old Brother always

Henry James

Henry and Alice reached Nauheim on 8 June. On 23 June the threesome left for Switzerland, where Alice wanted to do some shopping. In the meantime, in Concord on 3 July Robertson James suffered what was probably a heart attack and died the same day. The news reached Geneva by 9 July, prompting William to exclaim, "What a triumph to skip out like that!"

They left Switzerland for London on 12 July and reached Rye on the twenty-third, with William having some good days and some bad ones when he suffered from "atrocious weakness & bad breathing." On 11 August he made the last entry in his diary and with his wife and brother left Rye for Liverpool to board the Empress of Britain *for Quebec, from where they traveled by train to Chocorua. According to Alice, 24 August was "a terrible day of suffering," with William remarking that "it has come so rapidly, rapidly." Treated with digitalis and morphine he lingered until 2:30 P.M. Friday, 26 August, when he died in the arms of his wife.*

Henry James experienced the death of his older brother as a "mutilation" of himself. He remained in the United States for almost a year, departing for home on 30 July 1911. There, as the lone survivor, he busied himself with his autobiographical A Small Boy and Others *(1913) and* Notes of a Son and Brother *(1914). After suffering several strokes, Henry James died in London on 28 February 1916.*

Biographical Register
Index

Biographical Register

Abbey, Edwin Austin (1852–1911), painter, illustrator, muralist, born in Philadelphia, in later years lived in England.

About, Edmond-François-Valentin (1828–1885), French writer, editor of *Le XIXe Siècle*.

Acland, Henry Wentworth (1815–1900), Regius Professor of Medicine at Oxford.

Adamowiz, Anna, an unidentified woman whom WJ met in Berlin in 1868.

Adams, Miss, an unidentified woman whom WJ met in Berlin in 1867.

Adams, Henry (1838–1918), American historian.

Adams, Marian (Clover) Hooper (1843–1885), wife of Henry Adams.

Agassiz, Louis (1807–1873), Swiss naturalist.

Aguinaldo, Emilio (1869–1964), Philippine statesman, leader of the revolt against Spain.

Ahlborn, Dr., an otherwise unidentified homeopathic physician who attended Henry James, Sr.

Äidé, Hamilton (1826–1906), British novelist and poet.

Albee, John (1833–1915), American author, WJ's neighbor at Chocorua.

Aldrich, Thomas Bailey (1836–1907), American author, editor of the *Atlantic Monthly*.

Alexander, Sir George (George Alexander Gibb Samson) (1858–1918), British theatrical producer and actor, manager from 1891 of St. James's Theatre in London.

Alexander, John White (1856–1915), American painter.

Allen, Charles Grant Blairfindie (1848–1899), Canadian-born naturalist and writer.

Allston, Washington (1779–1843), American artist.

Ames, Frederick Lothrop (1835–1893), Boston businessman, member of the Harvard Corporation.

Anderson, Frank Eustace (1844–1880), American classical scholar who taught at Harvard.

Andrew, Elizabeth Loring (1852–1897), daughter of John Albion Andrew who was governor of Massachusetts during the Civil War.

Archer, William (1856–1924), British drama critic and author.

Arnold, Matthew (1822–1888), English poet and critic.

Arthur. *See* Sedgwick, Arthur George

Ashburner, Anne (1807–1894), sister of Grace Ashburner and aunt of Theodora Sedgwick, Arthur George Sedgwick, Sara Sedgwick Darwin, and Susan Ridley Sedgwick Norton.

Ashburner, George, a relative of WJ's friends Anne Ashburner and Grace Ashburner.

Ashburner, Grace (1814–1893), sister of Anne Ashburner. She and Anne lived
together in Stockbridge, Mass., and after 1860 in Cambridge. A third sister,
Sarah Ashburner Sedgwick, was the mother of Arthur George Sedgwick,
Sara Ashburner Sedgwick Darwin, Susan Ridley Sedgwick Norton, and
Theodora Sedgwick. The Sedgwick children lived with Grace and Anne
Ashburner after the death of their parents. When WJ mentions visits to the
Ashburners, he probably has in mind Grace and Anne.

Atkinson, Charles Follen (d. 1915), attended the Lawrence Scientific School in
1861–65, later was a businessman in Boston.

Augier, Émile (1820–1889), French playwright.

Austen, Jane (1775–1817), British novelist.

Babinet, an unidentified public figure.

Baker, Christina Hopkins, wife of George Peirce Baker.

Baker, George Peirce (1866–1935), professor of English at Harvard.

Baldwin, William Wilberforce (1850–1910), American physician and author who
resided mostly in Florence, Italy.

Balfour, Arthur James Balfour, 1st earl of (1848–1930), British statesman and
philosopher.

Balls, Miss, HJ's landlady at Bolton St.

Balzac, Honoré de (1799–1850), French novelist.

Bancroft, Hester Jones, second wife of John Chandler Bancroft (1835–1901),
American businessman.

Barrie, Sir James Matthew (1860–1937), British playwright and novelist. In 1894
he married Mary Ansell.

Bateman, Virginia Frances (1853–1940), American-born actress, wife of Edward
Compton.

Battell, Joseph (b. 1839), a Vermont "character" who in 1866 built the Bread Loaf
Inn, near Middlebury, Vt.

Beach, Henry Harris Aubrey (1843–1910), Boston physician who treated AJ and
other members of the family.

Beesly, Edward Spencer (1831–1915), British scholar and writer.

Bell, Gordon Knox (d. 1955), a lawyer in New York, graduated from Harvard
in 1893.

Bellingham, Mrs., owner of Lamb House, who was either the mother or the
widow of Arthur Bellingham.

Bellingham, Arthur, owner of Lamb House and thus HJ's landlord. When he died
suddenly in 1899, HJ purchased the house from his estate.

Benedict, Clara Woolson (d. 1923), sister of Constance Fenimore Woolson.

Benedict, Clare, a writer, daughter of Clara Woolson Benedict.

Benson, Eugene (1839–1908), American painter and critic who lived primarily
in Italy.

Bentley, George (1828–1895), British editor of *Temple Bar.*

Bernard, Claude (1813–1878), French physiologist.

Biddle, Elizabeth Le Roy Emmet (b. 1874), daughter of Katharine Temple Emmet and wife of Nicholas Biddle.

Birrell, Augustine (1850–1933), English essayist and politician.

Blake, Frances Greenough, widow of Arthur W. Blake, a Boston banker. Frances
  Blake was related to Francis Boott. She was about ninety-six when she died,
  probably in 1939.
Blake, William (1757–1827), British poet and engraver.
Bob (Bobby). *See* James, Robertson
Bôcher, Ferdinand (1832–1902), professor of modern languages at Harvard. His
  wife was Caroline Little Bôcher (d. 1894).
Boit, Edward Darley (1840–1915), American artist, established studios in Paris
  and Rome.
Boit, Mary Louisa Cushing, wife of Edward Darley Boit.
Booth, Edwin (1833–1893), American actor. Booth portrayed Hamlet in New
  York City on many occasions, most notably in the fall of 1864.
Boott, Francis (1813–1904), American composer, father of Elizabeth Boott Du-
  veneck. After the death of his wife in 1847, he lived with his daughter,
  mostly in Italy.
Boott, Lizzie. *See* Duveneck, Elizabeth Boott
Bornemann, an unidentified young woman whom WJ met in Berlin in 1867–68. At
  the time her parents were dead, and she was living with her brother, a lawyer.
Bosanquet, Theodora, HJ's secretary from 10 October 1907. She became a writer
  after HJ's death.
Bourget, Minnie David, wife of Paul Bourget whom she married in 1890.
Bourget, Paul-Charles-Joseph (1852–1935), French writer and journalist.
Bourne, Mrs., a member of HJ's household staff at Lamb House.
Boutroux, Émile (1845–1921), French philosopher.
Bowditch, Henry Pickering (1840–1911), American physiologist, professor at the
  Harvard Medical School.
Bowen, Francis (1811–1890), American philosopher, professor at Harvard.
Bradford, George Partridge (d. 1890), a friend and contemporary of Emerson's
  who operated a school in Newport.
Brewster, Henry Bennet (1850–1908), philosophical writer.
Brimmer, Martin (1829–1896), for many years president of the Museum of Fine
  Arts in Boston.
Brimmer, Mary Ann Timmins, wife of Martin Brimmer and aunt of Gemma
  Timmins.
Brodrick, George Charles (1831–1903), British journalist, later warden of Merton
  College, Oxford, son of William John Brodrick (1798–1870), 7th Viscount
  Middleton.
Broglie, Jacques-Victor-Albert, duc de (1821–1901), French politician and his-
  torian.
Bronson, Arthur, husband of Katherine De Kay Bronson.
Bronson, Katherine De Kay (d. 1901), socialite and hostess. In the late 1850s she
  and her husband, Arthur Bronson, owned a villa in Newport and later a
  home in Venice called Casa Alvisi.
Brooke, Helen Ellis, wife of Stopford Wentworth William Brooke.
Brooke, Stopford Augustus (1832–1916), Irish-born English clergyman and man
  of letters.
Brooke, Stopford Wentworth William (1859–1938), English-born Unitarian clergyman, husband of Helen Ellis Brooke and son of Stopford Augustus

Brooke. The younger Brooke served as a minister in Boston before returning to England.

Broughton, Rhoda (1840–1920), English novelist.

Brown, Gertrude Mason (1842–1888), daughter of Lydia Lush James Mason and granddaugher of Robert James who was WJ's father's brother.

Browne, George Henry (1857–1931), one of the founders of the Browne and Nichols School for Boys in Cambridge.

Brownell, William Crary (1851–1928), American author.

Brunton, Sir Thomas Lauder (1844–1916), British physician.

Bryce, James, Viscount Bryce (1838–1922), British historian and politician.

Bryce, Marion Ashton, Lady Bryce, wife of James Bryce.

Buckner, an unidentified American friend of HJ.

Bullard, Louisa Norton (b. 1823), Grace Norton's sister.

Bunyan, John (1628–1688), English religious writer.

Burne-Jones, Edward Coley (1833–1898), British artist.

Burne-Jones, Sir Philip (1861–1926), British author and painter, son of the painter Edward Burne-Jones.

Burnett, Frances Hodgson (1849–1924), English-born writer of children's novels.

Bushnell, Horace (1802–1876), American clergyman.

Butler, Joseph (1692–1752), English bishop and moralist.

Cadwalader, John Lambert (1837–1914), American lawyer.

Caine, Sir Hall (1853–1931), English novelist and dramatist.

Cambon, Pierre-Paul (1843–1924), French diplomat.

Carnes, Lewis Mortimer (1837–1893), husband of Serena Mason Carnes.

Carnes, Mason (b. 1870), son of Serena Mason Carnes.

Carnes, Serena Mason (1847–1891), daughter of Lydia Lush James Mason and Henry Mason and wife of Lewis Mortimer Carnes (1837–1893).

Carr, Joseph William Comyns (1849–1916), British critic, dramatist, and producer.

Carrie (Carry). *See* James, Caroline Eames Cary

Cary, Joseph, father of Caroline Eames Cary James.

Cecil, Robert Arthur Talbot Gascoyne, 3d marquis of Salisbury (1830–1903), British Conservative statesman.

Cellini, Benvenuto (1500–1571), Italian sculptor.

Cérésole, Alfred, a pastor who lived near Vevey, Switzerland, and who with his wife took in boarders.

Chamberlain, Joseph (1836–1914), British statesman.

Channing, Henrietta A. S. (d. 1888), widow of Edward Tyrrell Channing (1790–1856) who had been professor of oratory and rhetoric at Harvard.

Charmes, François-Xavier (1848–1916), former editor of the *Revue des Deux Mondes*.

Cherbuliez, Victor (1829–1899), French novelist.

Chesney, George Tomkyns (1830–1895), military officer and writer.

Chesterton, Gilbert Keith (1874–1936), English author.

Child, Francis James (1825–1896), professor of English at Harvard, fellow boarder with WJ at Miss Upham's in 1861. He married Elizabeth Ellery Sedgwick in 1860. The Childs had three daughters, Helen, Susan, and Henrietta, and a son, Francis.

Child, Susan Sedgwick (b. 1866), daughter of Francis James Child.

Childe, Blanche de Triquiti, wife of Edward Lee Childe.

Childe, Edward Lee (1836–1911), and his wife, Blanche de Triquiti Childe, entertained HJ frequently at their château near Montargis, France.

Clark, Andrew (1826–1893), British physician.

Clarke, Miss. In the first half of 1894 there are many references in WJ's letters to a healer named Miss Clarke, whose name he sometimes spelled Clark; her first name is not given. Boston directories for the period list an Ada C. Clark, a magnetic healer, at 1453 Washington St.

Clarke, Joseph Thacher, American-born writer on archaeology who lived in Harrow, England. He was a friend of AGJ who met Clarke in 1868 in Dresden when she lived there with her mother and sisters.

Clarke, Mary Temple Rose, daughter of Lady Rose and wife of Sir Stanley de Astel Clarke (1837–1911), British military officer.

Clary, O. Ware, a tenant of the Jameses at 211 S. Salina St., Syracuse, and a dealer in rubber goods.

Claude Lorrain (1600–1682), French landscape painter.

Cleveland, Grover (1837–1908), president of the United States in 1885–89 and 1893–97.

Clifford, William Kingdon (1845–1879), British mathematician and philosopher.

Cochran, Emilie Belden Walsh (1844–1924), daughter of Alexander Robertson Walsh, who was WJ's mother's brother, and wife of Thomas Cochran, Jr.

Colby, Frederick Myron (b. 1848), American author.

Coleridge, Bernard John Seymour, 2d Baron (1851–1927), British jurist.

Collier, Robert Joseph (1876–1918), American editor and publisher, editor of *Collier's Weekly*.

Colvin, Sidney (1845–1927), British critic, keeper of prints and drawings at the British Museum.

Compton, Edward (1854–1918), British actor, manager of the Compton Comedy Company.

Compton, Mrs. Edward. *See* Bateman, Virginia Frances

Coster, Marie Bay James (1841–1904), daughter of Augustus James, who was WJ's father's brother, and wife of Charles Robert Coster.

Cowper, Henry (1836–1887), member of Parliament.

Crafts, Clémence Haggerty, wife of James Mason Crafts.

Crafts, James Mason (1839–1917), American chemist, president of the Massachusetts Institute of Technology from 1898 to 1900. His wife was Clémence Haggerty Crafts.

Cranch, Christopher Pearse (1813–1892), American artist and poet.

Crawford, Francis Marion (1854–1909), American novelist who resided mostly in Italy.

Cummings, Edward (1861–1926), assistant professor of sociology at Harvard, lived at 104 Irving St. and was the father of Edward Estlin Cummings (1894–1962), American poet.

Curtis, Ariana Randolph Wormeley (1833–1922), American author, wife of Daniel Sargent Curtis and HJ's hostess in Venice.

Curtis, Daniel Sargent (1825–1908), HJ's host in Venice, husband of Ariana Curtis.

Cuyler, Alice Millard Holton, daughter of Edward Dwight Holton and sister of Mary Holton James. Her husband was James Wayne Cuyler; their daughter married Sir Philip Grey-Egerton.

Daly, Augustin (1838–1899), American playwright and theatrical producer.

Darwin, Sara Ashburner Sedgwick (1839–1902), sister of Theodora Sedgwick and Susan Ridley Sedgwick Norton, wife of William Erasmus Darwin.

Darwin, William Erasmus (1839–1914), English banker, eldest son of Charles Darwin, married Sara Ashburner Sedgwick in 1877.

Davidson, Thomas (1840–1900), Scottish-born writer.

Davis, Jefferson (1808–1889), president of the Confederacy.

Davis, Theodore M. (d. 1915), a resident of Newport. When he died at the age of seventy-eight, his obituary in the *New York Times* noted that he had excavated Egyptian tombs at his own expense.

Dawes, Walter, British solicitor representing the Bellingham estate in the sale of Lamb House to HJ.

Dawison, Bogumil (1818–1872), Polish-born actor, a member of the Dresden Court Theater from 1852 to 1864.

Dennett, John Richard (1838–1874), Canadian-born journalist.

De Quincey, Thomas (1785–1859), British essayist.

Derby, Hasket (1835–1914), American physician, lectured on cataract surgery.

Derby, Richard (1881–1963), American surgeon, graduated from Harvard in 1903, studied medicine at Columbia University.

Devrient, Emil (1803–1872), German actor.

Dickinson, Goldsworthy Lowes (1862–1932), English writer.

Dilke, Emilia Frances Strong Pattison (1840–1904), British art historian, widow of Mark Pattison, married Charles Wentworth Dilke in 1885.

Disraeli, Benjamin (1804–1881), British statesman.

Dixey, Ellen Sturgis Tappan (b. 1849), daughter of Caroline Sturgis Tappan, sister of Mary Aspinwall Tappan, and wife of Richard Cowell Dixey whom she married in 1875.

Dixwell, Epes Sargent (1807–1899), headmaster of the Dixwell School attended by many friends of WJ and HJ. His wife was Mary Ingersoll Bowditch Dixwell (d. 1893). They had six children, one of whom, Fanny Bowditch Dixwell, married Oliver Wendell Holmes, Jr.

Dixwell, Fanny Bowditch. *See* Holmes, Fanny Bowditch Dixwell

Doré, Gustave (1832–1883), French painter and book illustrator.

Dorr, Mary Gray Ward (c. 1820–1901), Boston hostess, had a summer home at Bar Harbor, Maine. She was the mother of George Bucknam Dorr and an aunt of Thomas Wren Ward, WJ's friend from their early years in Newport.

Doudan, Ximénès (1800–1872), French writer.

Dreyfus, Alfred (1859–1935), a French military officer. In 1894 Dreyfus, a Jew, was convicted of treason and imprisoned. The case provoked a bitter fight in France between the left and the right, with the left arguing that Dreyfus was a victim of anti-Semitism. He was finally exonerated in 1906.

Driver, Stephen William (b. 1834), a physician who lived in Cambridge.

Droz, Gustave (1832–1895), French writer.

Du Bois, William Edward Burghardt (1868–1963), American educator and author, professor at Atlanta University.

Dumas *fils*, Alexandre (1824–1895), French dramatist and novelist.

Du Maurier, George Louis Palmella Busson (1834–1896), British novelist and illustrator who drew cartoons for *Punch* and illustrated some of HJ's works.

Dunne, Finley Peter (1867–1936), American journalist and humorist.

Duveneck, Elizabeth Boott (1846–1888), daughter of Francis Boott, studied painting, and in 1886 married Frank Duveneck, one of her teachers.

Duveneck, Francis Boott (b. 1886), an engineer, son of Frank Duveneck and grandson of Francis Boott.

Duveneck, Frank (1848–1919), American painter, married Elizabeth Boott.

Dwight, John Sullivan (1813–1893), American music critic and editor.

Dwight, Thomas (1843–1911), completed Harvard Medical School in 1867, taught anatomy at Harvard from 1873.

Eardley-Wilmot, Robert, physician, author of *On the Natural Mineral Waters of Leamington* (1884).

Edgeworth, Francis Ysidro (1845–1926), Irish-born political economist.

Eliot, Charles William (1834–1926), in charge of the chemistry laboratory at the Lawrence Scientific School in 1861–63, president of Harvard from 1869.

Eliot, George, pseudonym of Marian Evans (1819–1880), English novelist.

Eliot, Grace Hopkinson (d. 1924), second wife of Charles William Eliot.

Elliot, Mary Lee Morse, sister of Frances Rollins Morse and wife of John Wheelock Elliot (d. 1925), Boston physician.

Emerson, Annie Shepard Keyes, wife of Edward Waldo Emerson.

Emerson, Edward Waldo (1844–1930), son of Ralph Waldo Emerson.

Emerson, Ellen Tucker (1839–1909), daughter of Ralph Waldo Emerson.

Emerson, Ralph Waldo (1803–1882), American author.

Emmet, Edith Leslie (b. 1877), daughter of Ellen James Temple Emmet Hunter.

Emmet, Elizabeth. *See* Biddle, Elizabeth Le Roy Emmet

Emmet, Grenville Temple (1877–1937), son of Katharine Temple Emmet and husband of Pauline Anne Ferguson Emmet, was a lawyer and diplomat.

Emmet, Katharine (Kitty) Temple (1843–1895), WJ's cousin, wife of Richard Stockton Emmet.

Emmet, Minnie. *See* Peabody, Mary Temple Emmet

Emmet, Rosina Hubley (b. 1873), daughter of Ellen James Temple Emmet Hunter.

Emmet, William (Willie) Temple (1869–1918), a lawyer, son of Katharine Temple Emmet.

Erckmann-Chatrian, pen name of two French authors, Alexandre Chatrian (1826–1890) and Émile Erckmann (1822–1899).

Ethel, Agnes (1852–1903), American actress.

Evans, Helen Fiske, daughter of Haley Fiske (1852–1929), American lawyer and insurance executive.

Everett, William (1839–1910), American teacher and writer, Harvard instructor in 1870–77.

Fairchild, Sally (b. 1869), daughter of Charles Fairchild (b. 1838), a lawyer and banker, and Elizabeth Nelson Fairchild.

Fay, Amy (Amelia Muller) (1844–1928), American pianist, sister of the first wife of Charles Sanders Peirce.

Felton, Cornelius Conway (1807–1862), American classical scholar, president of

Harvard at the time of his death. His second wife was Mary Louisa Cary, sister-in-law of Louis Agassiz. Felton had three daughters, who were in the same age group as WJ and HJ, and two younger sons.

Felton, Mary S. (d. 1896), daughter of Cornelius Conway Felton.

Fergusson, Sir William (1808–1877), British physician.

Ferrier, David (1843–1928), Scottish neurologist and physiologist.

Feydeau, Ernest-Aimé (1821–1873), French novelist.

Fischer, Paul David (1836–1920), German official and writer.

Fisher, Richard Thornton (1876–1934), American forester.

Fiske, John (1842–1901), American historian and philosopher of evolution.

Fiske, Maud (b. 1865), daughter of John Fiske.

Flaubert, Gustave (1821–1880), French novelist.

Fletcher, Horace (1849–1919), American writer and lecturer on health and dietetics.

Flint, Austin (1812–1886), American physician.

Flint, Austin, Jr. (1836–1915), American physician and physiologist, son of Austin Flint.

Flournoy, Marie-Hélène Burnier (d. 1909), wife of Théodore Flournoy.

Flournoy, Théodore (1854–1920), Swiss psychologist, husband of Marie-Hélène Burnier Flournoy.

Foote, Mary Hallock (1847–1938), American artist and author.

Frederic, Harold (1856–1898), American journalist and author, London correspondent for the *New York Times*.

Freund, Ellen Washburn (died c. 1877), wife of Maximilian Bernhard Freund and sister of Francis Tucker Washburn, William Tucker Washburn, Lucy Washburn Putnam, and Martha Washburn.

Freund, Maximilian Bernhard (b. 1835), German physician, husband of Ellen Washburn Freund.

Frohman, Charles (1860–1915), American-born theater manager.

Gainsborough, Thomas (1727–1788), British painter.

Gammon, George, HJ's gardener at Lamb House.

Gardner, Isabella Stewart (Mrs. Jack Gardner) (1840–1924), American socialite and patron of art.

Garrison, Wendell Phillips (1840–1907), literary editor of the *Nation* from July 1865.

Garrod, Sir Alfred Baring (1819–1907), British physician, author of works on gout and rheumatism.

Gaskell, Charles George Milnes (b. 1842), husband of Lady Catharine Henrietta Wallop Gaskell.

Gasson, Henry John, a dealer in china, earthenware, and marine supplies in Rye.

Gautier, Théophile (1811–1872), French critic, poet, and novelist.

Gibbens, Eliza Putnam Webb (1827–1917), WJ's mother-in-law.

Gibbens, Margaret. *See* Gregor, Margaret Merrill Gibbens

Gibbens, Mary. *See* Salter, Mary Sherwin Gibbens

Gilbert, Sir William Schwenck (1836–1911), British playwright.

Gladstone, William Ewart (1809–1898), British statesman.

Glaser, an unidentified German family whom WJ met in Teplitz in 1868.

Godkin, Edwin Lawrence (1831–1902), American journalist, co-founder of the *Nation* in 1865.

Godkin, Katharine Buckley Sands (d. 1907), second wife of Edwin Lawrence Godkin.

Godkin, Lawrence (1860–1929), a lawyer, son of Edwin Lawrence Godkin and his first wife, Frances Elizabeth Foote Godkin.

Goldmark, Pauline Dorothea (d. 1962), social worker and consumer advocate.

Goldoni, Carlo (1707–1793), Italian dramatist.

Got, François-Jules-Edmond (1822–1901), French actor.

Gourlay, Catharine (d. 1896), a paternal relative.

Gray, Asa (1810–1888), American botanist, professor at Harvard.

Gray, Horace (1828–1902), American jurist, appointed in 1882 as an associate justice of the United States Supreme Court; half-brother of John Chipman Gray.

Gray, John Chipman (1839–1915), American lawyer and educator, friend of Mary Temple.

Gray, Thomas (1716–1771), English poet.

Greeley, Horace (1811–1872), American journalist and politician.

Greene, Miss Elizabeth, an unidentified friend whom WJ met while vacationing on the Maine coast in 1872 and 1873.

Greenough, Henry (1807–1883), American architect, husband of Frances Boott, sister of Francis Boott.

Gregor, Leigh Richmond (1860–1912), professor of modern languages at McGill University, Montreal, Canada, husband of Margaret Gregor.

Gregor, Margaret Merrill Gibbens (1857–1927), sister of AGJ, wife of Leigh Richmond Gregor.

Gregor, Rosamond (b. 1900), daughter of Margaret Merrill Gibbens Gregor and Leigh Richmond Gregor.

Grey-Egerton, May Wayne Cuyler (d. 1959), daughter of Alice Millard Holton Cuyler and Maj. James Wayne Cuyler (d. 1883), married Sir Philip Henry Brian Grey-Egerton in 1893.

Grigsby, Emilie Busbey (d. 1964). See *Correspondence*, 3:271–72n.

Grimm, Gisela von Arnim (1827–1889), wife of Herman Friedrich Grimm.

Grimm, Herman Friedrich (1828–1901), German critic and author, married to Gisela von Arnim. In 1867 WJ had a letter of introduction to Grimm from Ralph Waldo Emerson and was a frequent visitor at the Grimm household.

Grogan, an unidentified person, a friend of Pratt.

Grousset, Paschal (1844–1909), French journalist and author.

Grymes, Mary Helen James (1840–1881), daughter of WJ's uncle John Barber James, married Charles Alfred Grymes (1829–1905), a New York physician whose mother was Suzette Bosch Grymes from New Orleans.

Grymes, Suzette Bosch, mother-in-law of Mary Helen James Grymes.

Gryzanovski, Ernst Georg Friedrich (1824–1888), Polish-born diplomat and writer.

Gurney, Edmund (1847–1888), British aesthetician and psychical researcher.

Gurney, Ellen Sturgis Hooper (1838–1887), sister of Edward William Hooper and Marian Hooper Adams and wife of Ephraim Whitman Gurney. She suffered periods of mental breakdown.

Gurney, Ephraim Whitman (1829–1886), professor of history at Harvard and dean of the faculty in 1870–75, married Ellen Sturgis Hooper on 3 October 1868.

Gurney, Kate Sara Sibley, married Edmund Gurney on 5 June 1877. After Gurney's death, she married Archibald Grove.

Hagen, Hermann August (1817–1893), German entomologist who came to Harvard in 1867 at the invitation of Louis Agassiz.

Hall, Frank (d. 1888), painter, probably English.

Hall, Granville Stanley (1844–1924), American psychologist, a graduate student at Harvard in 1876–78, president of Clark University, Worcester, Mass.

Hammond, William Alexander (1828–1900), American neurologist, founder of the *Quarterly Journal of Psychological Medicine and Medical Jurisprudence*.

Hanna, Mr., an unidentified friend of the Emmet family.

Hapgood, Norman (1868–1937), American author and editor.

Harcourt, Augustus George Vernon (1834–1919), British chemist.

Hare, Sir John (1844–1921), English actor and theatrical manager.

Harland, Henry (1861–1905), American-born novelist and editor, one of the founders and the editor of the *Yellow Book*. Harland sometimes used the pen name of Sidney Luska.

Harrison, Benjamin (1833–1901), American statesman, president in 1889–93.

Harrison, Frederic (1831–1923), British jurist, philosophical writer, editor.

Hartwell, Alfred Stedman (1836–1912), American military officer who rose to the rank of general in the Civil War. Hartwell moved to Hawaii and became an official in the Hawaiian judiciary, prior to the annexation of the islands by the United States.

Harvey, George Brinton McClellan (1846–1928), American editor and diplomat, editor of the *North American Review* from 1899, president of Harper and Brothers, publishers, from 1900.

Haughton, Richard (d. 1947), an insurance executive in Philadelphia who graduated from Harvard in 1900.

Hawthorne, Julian (1846–1934), American writer, son of Nathaniel Hawthorne.

Hawthorne, Nathaniel (1804–1864), American author.

Hay, John (1838–1905), American writer and diplomat.

Hayes, Rutherford B. (1822–1893), president of the United States in 1877–81.

Helmholtz, Hermann Ludwig Ferdinand von (1821–1894), German physiologist, physicist, and psychologist.

Heyse, Paul Johann Ludwig von (1830–1914), German author.

Higginson, Elizabeth (Lylie) Hazard Barker (1836–1901), wife of George Higginson and daughter of Jeannette James Barker, WJ's father's sister.

Higginson, Emily Wakem (b. 1864), the second wife of George Higginson.

Higginson, George (1833–1921), husband of Elizabeth Hazard Barker Higginson and brother of Henry Lee Higginson.

Higginson, George (b. 1864), son of George Higginson and Elizabeth Hazard Barker Higginson.

Higginson, Henry Lee (1834–1919), American banker, a partner in the firm Lee, Higginson and Co., and WJ's banker and financial adviser. He was a brother of George Higginson.

Higginson, Samuel Storrow (b. 1842), attended the Sanborn School in Concord with GWJ and RJ, studied at Harvard, served as a chaplain in a black regiment, in later life was a businessman.

Higginson, Thomas Wentworth (1823–1911), American abolitionist orator and author.

Hill, Jane Dalzell Finley, wife of Frank Harrison Hill (1830–1910), British journalist and editor of the *Daily News*.

Hillard, Katherine (d. 1915), author and Italian scholar. There are others with similar names and there is a possibility of confusion.

Hillebrand, Karl (1829–1884), German journalist and essayist.

Hind, Charles Lewis (1862–1927), British journalist and critic, editor of the *Academy*, an English monthly devoted to literature, science, and art.

Hoar, George Frisbie (1826–1904), United States senator from Massachusetts.

Hodgson, Richard (1855–1905), Australian-born psychical researcher, secretary of the American Society for Psychical Research in Boston.

Hodgson, Shadworth Hollway (1832–1912), British philosopher.

Holmes, Fanny Bowditch Dixwell, wife of Oliver Wendell Holmes, Jr. There is evidence that at one time WJ had a romantic interest in her.

Holmes, John (1812–1899), brother of Oliver Wendell Holmes, Sr.

Holmes, Oliver Wendell, Sr. (1809–1894), American author and physician, one of WJ's examiners in the Harvard Medical School.

Holmes, Oliver Wendell, Jr. (1841–1935), American jurist. According to his diary preserved in the Harvard Law School Library, Holmes visited either the James home or WJ and HJ nearly every week in late 1866 and 1867. On 17 June 1872 he married Fanny Dixwell. In later years relations between WJ and Holmes were cordial but more distant.

Holt, Henry (1840–1926), American author and publisher.

Holton, Edward Dwight (1815–1892), father of Mary Holton James, was a Milwaukee businessman, railroad executive, banker, and the Free Soil candidate for governor of Wisconsin in 1853.

Honey, George (1822–1880), British actor.

Hooper, Edward William (1839–1901), a lawyer in Boston, brother of Marian Hooper Adams and Ellen Sturgis Hooper Gurney.

Hooper, Louisa Chapin (b. 1874), niece of Henry Adams. Her husband was Ward Thoron.

Hopkins, Mrs., an unidentified woman whom WJ met in Berlin in 1867.

Hosmer, Burr Griswold, author of *Poems* (1868).

Hosmer, Edward Downer (1843–1912), graduated from Harvard in 1865, later practiced law in Chicago.

Houghton, Richard Monckton Milnes, 1st Baron (1809–1885), British politician and book collector.

Howells, Elinor Gertrude Mead (1837–1910), wife of William Dean Howells.

Howells, John Mead (1868–1959), an architect, son of William Dean Howells.

Howells, Mildred (1872–1966), an illustrator, daughter of William Dean Howells.

Howells, William Dean (1837–1920), American novelist.

Hunt, William Morris (1824–1879), American painter, opened a studio in Newport in 1856 and moved to Boston in 1862. WJ studied with Hunt in 1858–59 and 1860–61.

Hunter, Ellen (Elly) James Temple Emmet (1850–1920), one of WJ's six Temple cousins (*see* Temple, Mary). In 1869 Ellen Temple married Christopher Temple Emmet (1822–1884), a physician and lawyer, and moved to San Francisco. Their children were Mary Temple Emmet Peabody, Rosina Hubley Emmet, Ellen Gertrude (Bay) Emmet Rand, and Edith Leslie Emmet. On 1 September 1891 Ellen Temple Emmet married George Hunter. The Hunters had one child, George Grenville Hunter (b. 1892).

Hunter, George (1847–1914), of Glasgow, Scotland, second husband of Ellen James Temple Emmet Hunter.

Huxley, Thomas Henry (1825–1895), English biologist and anatomist.

Irving, Henry (1838–1905), British actor.

Irwin, Agnes (1841–1914), American educator, dean of Radcliffe College.

Jack, Mrs. *See* Gardner, Isabella Stewart

Jackson, Charles Loring (1847–1935), American chemist, taught at Harvard from 1871.

James, Alexander Robertson (1890–1946), WJ's son, a painter, initially named Francis Tweedy, which he disliked, later renamed Alexander Robertson.

James, Alice (1848–1892), WJ's sister, moved to Europe permanently in November 1884. For details of her life see *AJB*.

James, Alice Howe Gibbens (1849–1922), WJ's wife.

James, Caroline (Carrie) Eames Cary (b. 1851), wife of GWJ.

James, Catharine Barber (1782–1859), WJ's paternal grandmother.

James, Edith (1864–1892), daughter of Howard and Josephine James.

James, Edward (Ned) Holton (1873–1954), son of RJ, attended Harvard College in 1891–92 and 1893–96, the graduate school in 1896–97, married Mary Louisa Cushing on 27 December 1899.

James, Florence. *See* Rosse, Florence James

James, Francis (Frank) Burr (1859–1888), son of Howard James and his first wife.

James, Garth Wilkinson (Wilkie, Wilky) (1845–1883), WJ's brother, enlisted in the Union army, became an officer in a black regiment, and was severely wounded in July 1863 in the assault on Fort Wagner, Charleston, S.C. On 12 November 1873 he married Caroline Eames Cary in Milwaukee. Their first child, Joseph Cary James, was born on 4 October 1874; their second, Alice James (later Alice James Edgar) on 24 December 1875. For details see *BBF*.

James, Henry (1811–1882), WJ's father.

James, Henry (Harry) (1879–1947), WJ's son, a lawyer and biographer.

James, Herman (Humster) (1884–1885), WJ's son.

James, Howard (1828–1887), WJ's father's brother, husband of Josephine James.

James, Howard (1866–1920), WJ's cousin, son of WJ's father's brother Howard James and Josephine Worth James. At about the age of twenty he tried his luck in the theater but gave up the stage for medicine. In 1893 he completed his studies at the Georgetown medical school in Washington, D.C. In 1896, with WJ's help, he obtained a physician's post with the Boston Lunatic Hospital but was unable to keep it because of drunkenness. He was licensed to practice medicine in New York in 1917. For additional details see *Correspondence*, 2:432.

James, Joseph Cary (1874–1925), son of GWJ, a businessman in Milwaukee.

James, Josephine Worth (1831–1920), wife of Howard James, WJ's father's brother.

James, Margaret Mary. *See* Porter, Margaret Mary James

James, Mary Louisa Cushing (b. 1865), wife of Edward Holton James, usually referred to by her middle name.

James, Mary Lucinda Holton (1849–1922), wife of RJ.

James, Mary Robertson Walsh (1810–1882), WJ's mother.

James, Robertson (Bob, Bobby) (1846–1910), WJ's youngest brother, enlisted in the Union army and became an officer in a black regiment. He married Mary Holton on 18 November 1872 in Milwaukee. Their first child, Edward Holton James, was born on 18 November 1873; their second, Mary Walsh James (later Mary Walsh James Vaux) on 18 August 1875. For details see *BBF.*

James, William (Bill, Billy) (1882–1961), WJ's son, an artist.

Jameson, Sir Leander Starr (1853–1917), Scottish-born physician, in late December 1895 led an attack upon the Boer state of Transvaal.

Jenks, Henry Fitch (1842–1920) attended Harvard in 1859–63, later was a Unitarian minister.

Jerome, William Travers (1859–1934), American lawyer.

Jersey, Victor Albert George Child Villiers, 7th earl of (1845–1915), British colonial administrator.

J.L.F. *See* La Farge, John

Jones, Henry Arthur (1851–1929), British playwright.

Jordan, David Starr (1851–1931), American educator, president of Stanford University.

Joukofski, Paul, a Russian artist, son of Russian poet Vasili Andreyevich Zhukovsky (1783–1852).

Julian, Rodolphe (b. 1839), French painter and art teacher.

Jusserand, Jean-Adrien-Antoine-Jules (1855–1932), French diplomat and literary scholar.

Kate, Aunt. *See* Walsh, Catharine

Kemble, Frances Anne (Fanny, Mrs. Pierce Butler) (1809–1893), British actress, a friend of HJ.

King, Arthur, son of Charlotte Matthews King and C. W. King, a merchant in Canton, China. Arthur King's grandmother was Charlotte Walsh Matthews, a sister of WJ's maternal grandfather.

King, Charlotte Elizabeth Sleigh Matthews, widow of C. W. King, a merchant at Canton, China. Genealogical sources do not provide dates for her, but since her mother died in 1816, Charlotte King must have been about seventy in 1885. Her mother was a sister of James Walsh, WJ's grandfather.

Kipling, Caroline Starr Balestier (1862–1939), sister of Charles Wolcott Balestier and wife of Rudyard Kipling.

Kipling, Rudyard (1865–1936), English author.

Knowles, James Thomas (1831–1877), British editor who edited the *Contemporary Review* from 1870 to January 1877 and then the *Nineteenth Century.*

Kracht, Fräulein von, an unidentified woman whom WJ met in Germany in 1868.

Labiche, Eugène-Marin (1815–1888), French comic playwright.

La Farge, Christopher Grant (1862–1938), American architect and illustrator, son of John La Farge.

La Farge, John (1835–1910), American artist, an art student with WJ in Newport in 1860–61.

Lamar, Lucius Quintus Cincinnatus (1825–1893), secretary of the interior in 1885–88.

Lamb, Charles (1775–1834), British essayist.

Lang, Andrew (1844–1912), Scottish scholar.

Lecky, William Edward Hartpole (1838–1903), Irish historian and essayist.

Lee, Elizabeth Perkins. *See* Shattuck, Elizabeth Perkins Lee

Lee, Vernon. *See* Paget, Violet

Leopardi, Giacomo (1798–1837), Italian poet, known for his pessimism.

Lockwood, Florence Bayard (1842–1898), American-born author.

Lodge, Henry Cabot (1850–1924), American politician and author, United States senator from Massachusetts.

Lodge, Mary Greenwood (Mrs. James Lodge), associated with Sarah Wyman Whitman in a circle of literary women.

Lomas, butler to Edwin Lawrence Godkin in England.

Lombard, Mrs., an unidentified American who with her daughter Fanny often traveled in Europe.

Lombard, Fanny, daughter of Mrs. Lombard.

Longfellow, Ernest Wadsworth (1845–1921), American painter, son of Henry Wadsworth Longfellow.

Loring, Caleb William (1819–1897), a lawyer and businessman, father of Katharine Peabody Loring and Louisa Putnam Loring.

Loring, Francis William (1838–1905), American painter who lived in Europe for extended periods of time.

Loring, Katharine Peabody (1849–1943), AJ's companion.

Loring, Louisa Putnam (1854–1923), the younger sister of Katharine Peabody Loring, was a consumptive who was later engaged in charity work.

Loring, Susan Mason Lawrence, wife of William Caleb Loring.

Loring, William Caleb (1851–1930), American lawyer, brother of Katharine Peabody Loring.

Lothrop, Anne Maria Hooper (1835–1930), wife of Thornton Kirkland Lothrop.

Lothrop, Thornton Kirkland (1830–1913), a Boston lawyer.

Lovett, Sidney (d. 1979), American clergyman, chaplain at Yale University.

Lowell, Abbott Lawrence (1856–1943), American educator, president of Harvard.

Lowell, Frances Dunlap (d. 1885), second wife of James Russell Lowell.

Lowell, James Russell (1819–1891), American poet, editor, and diplomat. In 1857 he married Frances Dunlap, his second wife.

Ludwig, Karl Friedrich Wilhelm (1816–1895), German physiologist.

Lushington, Godfrey (1832–1907), British lawyer.

Lyman, Arthur (1861–1933), American lawyer.

Lyons (perhaps Lyon), Miss. There were three Miss Lyons, Fanny, Alice, and Betty, apparently sisters, friends of Katharine Buckley Sands Godkin. No other information about them was found.

MacAlpine, William, HJ's stenographer and typist from February 1897 to 1901.

MacColl, Malcolm (1831–1907), British clergyman and theological writer, from 1884 canon of Ripon.

McElroy, Dr., an unidentified clergyman from New York.

MacKenzie, Sir James (1853–1925), Scottish-born physician.

McKinley, William (1843–1901), president of the United States in 1897–1901.

Macmillan, Alexander (1813–1896), British publisher.

MacMonnies, Frederick William (1863–1937), American sculptor and painter.

Makart, Hans (1840–1884), Austrian painter.

Mallock, William Hurrell (1849–1923), British author.

Marble, Manton (1834–1917), an editor.

Marlowe, Julia (Julia Marlowe Taber) (1866–1950), English actress.

Martin, Lillien Jane (1851–1943), American psychologist.

Mason, Alice, widow of William Sturgis Hooper, married Charles Sumner in 1866. They were divorced several years later, after he suspected a liaison between her and Baron Friedrich von Holstein, a German diplomat. She later resumed her maiden name.

Mason, Henry (1819–1891), husband of Lydia Lush James Mason. The Masons lived in Europe; Henry Mason died in Paris.

Mason, Herbert Cowpland (1840–1884), a captain in the Union army, was wounded at Gettysburg on 3 July 1863. Identified in *NSB*, 126.

Mason, Lydia Lush James (1820–1897), daughter of Robert James who was WJ's father's brother, and mother of Serena Mason Carnes.

Mathews, Florence Wilkinson, daughter of James John Garth Wilkinson, wife of St. John Mathews.

Mathews, Mary James Wilkinson, daughter of James John Garth Wilkinson.

Maudsley, Henry (1835–1918), British physiologist and psychologist.

Mead, Larkin G. (1835–1910), American sculptor, brother of the wife of William Dean Howells.

Meredith, George (1828–1909), English writer.

Merriman, Daniel (1838–1912), American clergyman, husband of Helen Bigelow Merriman. The Merrimans spent their summers at Intervale, N.H., near Chocorua.

Merriman, Helen Bigelow (1844–1933), American author and artist, wife of Daniel Merriman.

Michelet, Jules (1798–1874), French historian and writer.

Middleton, Lamar (1872–1909), American journalist, tutor to WJ's family in 1894.

Miller, Catharine Barber Van Buren (b. 1849), daughter of Ellen King James Van Buren who was WJ's father's sister. She was separated from her husband, Peyton Farrell Miller, in about 1888 and remarried.

Miller, Dickinson Sergeant (1868–1963), American philosopher, instructor at Bryn Mawr College from 1893 to 1899, taught at Harvard from 1899 to 1904.

Millet, Elizabeth Greeley Merrill, wife of Francis Davis Millet.

Millet, Francis Davis (1846–1912), American painter and illustrator, in later years lived in England.

Millet, Jean-François (1814–1875), French painter.

Mitchell, Maggie (1832–1918), American actress.

Mitchell, Silas Weir (1829–1914), American neurologist and author.

Mohl, Julius (1800–1876), husband of Mary Clarke Mohl.

Mohl, Mary Clarke (1793–1883), British-born Parisian hostess.

Morison, James Augustus Cotter (1832–1888), British biographer and author.

Morley, John, Viscount Morley (1838–1923), British statesman and author, editor of the *Fortnightly Review* and other magazines.

Morris, Ellen James Van Buren (1844–1929), daughter of Ellen King James Van Buren (1823–1849), who was WJ's father's sister, and Smith Thomson Van Buren and wife of Dr. Stuyvesant Fish Morris (1843–1925).

Morse, Frances Rollins (1850–1928), a close friend of AJ and WJ.

Morse, Harriet Jackson Lee (b. 1852), mother of Frances Rollins Morse and Mary Lee Morse Elliot.

Morse, Mary. *See* Elliot, Mary Lee Morse

Morse, Samuel Torrey, husband of Harriet Jackson Lee Morse and father of Frances Rollins Morse and Mary Lee Morse Elliot.

Muir, William (1819–1905), British educator, author of *The Life of Mahomet and History of Islam.*

Müller, Friedrich Max (1823–1900), German-born philologist.

Munroe, Dr., a Boston physician who treated Catharine Walsh.

Munroe, Allen (1819–1884), business agent of the James family in Syracuse.

Münster, Alexandrine, Gräfin zu, the widowed Princess Dolgoruki, originally Princess Galitzin, former wife of Georg Herbert, Graf zu Münster-Ledenburg.

Münsterberg, Hugo (1863–1916), German-born psychologist, from 1892 WJ's colleague at Harvard.

Münster-Ledenburg, Georg Herbert, Graf zu (1820–1902), Hanoverian statesman. Münster's second wife was Harriet Elizabeth St. Clair-Erskine.

Münster-Ledenburg, Harriet Elizabeth (St. Clair-Erskine), Gräfin zu (1831–1867), British writer.

Munthe, Axel Martin Fredrik (1857–1949), Swedish physician and writer, author of *The Story of San Michelle.*

Musset, Alfred de (1810–1857), French poet whose plays were often adapted for opera.

Myers, Eveleen Tennant, wife of Frederic William Henry Myers.

Myers, Frederic William Henry (1843–1901), British essayist and psychical researcher.

Myers, Silvia, daughter of Frederic William Henry Myers and Eveleen Tennant Myers.

Ned. *See* James, Edward Holton

Neilson, Adelaide (1846–1880), English actress.

Nichols, Edgar Hamilton (1856–1910), author of mathematics textbooks, one of the founders of the Browne and Nichols School for Boys in Cambridge.

Nicoll, William Robertson (1851–1923), British journalist and editor, J. M. Barrie's supporter and publisher.

Noakes, Burgess (1887–1980), HJ's servant at Lamb House from 1901.

Norton, Charles Eliot (1827–1908), American art historian, editor of the *North American Review* (1864–68), and co-founder of the *Nation.* He was married to Susan Ridley Sedgwick Norton.

Norton, Eliot (1863–1932), son of Charles Eliot Norton and husband of Margaret Palmer Meyer Norton.

Norton, Elizabeth (Lily) Gaskell (d. 1958), daughter of Charles Eliot Norton.

Norton, Grace (1834–1926), sister of Charles Eliot Norton.

Norton, Jane (1824–1877), sister of Charles Eliot Norton and Grace Norton.

Norton, Rupert (1867–1914), American physician, son of Charles Eliot Norton.

Norton, Sara (Sally) (b. 1864), daughter of Charles Eliot Norton.

Norton, Susan Ridley Sedgwick (1838–1872), wife of Charles Eliot Norton.

Olney, Richard (1835–1917), American statesman.

Orr, Alexandra Leighton (Mrs. Sutherland Orr) (1828–1903), British biographer of Robert Browning.

Osgood, James Ripley (1836–1892), American publisher.

Osler, Sir William (1849–1919), Canadian-born physician, professor of medicine at Oxford.

Otway, Sir Arthur John (1822–1912), British politician.

Paddington, Mrs., HJ's cook and housekeeper at Lamb House.

Paget, Sir James (1814–1899), British physician.

Paget, Violet (1856–1935), British author living in Florence, wrote under the pseudonym Vernon Lee.

Paley, William (1743–1805), English theologian and philosopher.

Palgrave, Francis Turner (1824–1897), British poet and critic.

Palmer, Alice Elvira Freeman (1855–1902), American educator, wife of George Herbert Palmer.

Palmer, George Herbert (1842–1933), American philosopher, WJ's colleague at Harvard, husband of Alice Elvira Freeman Palmer.

Parkman, Mary Frances Parker (d. 1942), wife of Henry Parkman (1850–1924), Boston banker.

Parnell, Charles Stewart (1846–1891), Irish nationalist leader.

Pasteur, Louis (1822–1895), French chemist.

Pater, Walter Horatio (1839–1894), British essayist and critic.

Pattison, Emilia. *See* Dilke, Emilia Frances Strong Pattison

Pattison, Mark (1813–1884), British scholar, rector of Lincoln College, Oxford, first husband of Emilia Frances Strong Pattison.

Peabody, Elizabeth Palmer (1804–1894), American reformer, educator, editor.

Peabody, Francis Greenwood (1847–1936), professor of Christian morals at Harvard.

Peabody, Mary Codman, daughter of Margaret Russell Codman Peabody (1820–1893) and William Augustus Peabody (d. 1850), a clergyman. She lived in Brookline and later in Boston.

Peabody, Mary (Minny, Minnie) Temple Emmet (b. 1872), daughter of Ellen Temple Emmet Hunter, married Archibald Russell Peabody (1873–1908) on 23 August 1894.

Pearson, Charles Henry (1830–1894), British historian, fellow of Oriel College.

Peirce, Charles Sanders (1839–1914), American philosopher. In 1862 he married Harriet Melusina Fay; they separated in 1876. On 30 April 1883 he married Juliette Froissy. Peirce was an assistant at the Harvard College Observatory from October 1869 to December 1872. From 1861 he was an aide in the United States Coast and Geodesic Survey.

Peirce, Juliette Froissy, second wife of Charles Sanders Peirce.

Pell-Clarke, Henrietta Temple (1853–1934), one of WJ's six Temple cousins.

Pell-Clarke, Leslie (1853–1904), husband of Henrietta Temple Pell-Clarke.

Pennell, Joseph (1857–1926), American-born artist and author.

Perkins, Helen Rodgers Wyckoff (1807–1887), daughter of Mary Robertson Wyckoff and Albert Wyckoff, sister of Henry Albert Wyckoff, and wife of Leonard Perkins. Mary Robertson Wyckoff and WJ's maternal grandmother were sisters.

Perry, Lilla Cabot (1848–1933), American painter, wife of Thomas Sergeant Perry.

Perry, Thomas Sergeant (Sargy) (1845–1928), American literary scholar, for a time editor of the *North American Review,* husband of Lilla Cabot Perry.

Pertz, Florence, granddaughter of James John Garth Wilkinson.

Piddington, John George (1869–1952), British psychical researcher.

Pinker, James Brand (1863–1922), HJ's literary agent from 1898.

Piper, Leonora Evelina (1859–1950), American trance medium, probably the most intensely studied medium in the early years of the Society for Psychical Research.

Pollock, Sir Frederick (1845–1937), British jurist and philosophical writer.

Porter, Margaret Mary James (Peg, Peggy, Peggot, Peggotty) (1887–1952), WJ's daughter.

Post, Mary Ann King (1819–1892), daughter of Ellen James King, WJ's father's half-sister.

Pratt, an unidentified person whom WJ and HJ knew in Paris in 1856–57. Later in life he was a physician.

Pratt, Herbert James (b. 1841), a physician and traveler, graduated from Harvard in 1863, served as a military surgeon in the Civil War, and completed Harvard Medical School in 1868.

Pratt, Joseph Hersey (1872–1942), American physician.

Prince, Katharine (Kitty) Barber James (1834–1890), WJ's cousin, daughter of WJ's father's brother, William James, and wife of William Henry Prince.

Pritchett, Henry Smith (1857–1939), American astronomer, president of the Massachusetts Institute of Technology.

Prothero, Sir George Walter (1848–1922), British historian and editor, husband of Margaret Prothero.

Prothero, Margaret, wife of Sir George Walter Prothero.

Pumpelly, Raphael (1837–1923), American geologist, traveler, and writer.

Putnam, George (b. 1834), a lawyer in Boston, graduated from Harvard in 1854.

Putnam, Georgina Lowell, daughter of Mary Lowell Putnam and sister of James Russell Lowell.

Putnam, Harriet Lowell, wife of George Putnam.

Putnam, James Jackson (1846–1918), American neurologist.

Putnam, Marion Cabot (1857–1932), wife of James Jackson Putnam.

Quincy, Henry Parker (1838–1899), a physician and professor at Harvard, graduated from Harvard in 1862 and from the Harvard Medical School in 1867.

Quintard, Dr., an unidentified physician.

Rand, Ellen Gertrude (Bay) Emmet (1876–1941), an artist, daughter of Christopher Temple Emmet and Ellen James Temple Emmet Hunter.

Regnault, Henri-Alexandre-Georges (1843–1871), French painter.

Rehan, Ada C. (1860–1916), Irish-born actress, leading lady in Augustin Daly's theater company.

Renan, Joseph-Ernest (1823–1892), French historian and critic.

Reni, Guido (1575–1642), Italian painter.

Renouvier, Charles (1815–1903), French philosopher.

Reynolds, John Russell (1828–1896), British physician, often consulted by patients with nervous disorders.

Ribera, José (1588–1656), Spanish painter.

Ribot, Théodule-Armand (1839–1916), French psychologist.

Richards, Annie Ashburner, a relative of Anne and Grace Ashburner and a friend of AJ, married to Francis Gardner Richards.

Richardson, Henry Hobson (1838–1886), American architect, sketched plans in 1884 for a house for WJ.

Ripley, Helen, daughter of Catharine Walsh Andrews Ripley (1806–1865) and Joseph Ripley of Norwich, Conn. Catharine Ripley's mother was a sister of James Walsh, WJ's maternal grandfather.

Ritter, Charles (1838–1908), Swiss scholar whose friendship with WJ dated from the 1850s.

Roberts, an unidentified American dentist used by HJ in 1905.

Robertson, Alexander (1733–1816), endowed a school in New York in 1799 for the "education of children of parents belonging to the Scotch Presbyterian Church."

Robertson, George Croom (1842–1892), British philosopher, editor of *Mind*.

Robin, Charles-Philippe (1821–1885), French anatomist.

Robins, Elizabeth (1862–1952), American actress and novelist.

Robinson, Henry Crabb (1775–1867), British lawyer, diarist, and a friend of many German and English writers.

Rockefeller, John Davison (1839–1937), industrialist and philanthropist, organizer of the Standard Oil Company.

Rod, Édouard (1857–1910), Swiss-born novelist and critic.

Rodgers, Henrietta Dorrington (Nettie) (b. 1843), sister of Katharine Outram Rodgers and granddaughter of Helen Robertson Rodgers, WJ's maternal grandmother's sister.

Rodgers, Katharine Outram (Katie) (b. 1841), granddaughter of Helen Robertson Rodgers, WJ's maternal grandmother's sister. She lived in Europe for extended periods.

Roosevelt, Theodore (1858–1919), president of the United States from 1901 to 1909. While a student at Harvard, Roosevelt took courses from WJ.

Ropes, John Codman (1836–1899), American lawyer and military historian, completed Harvard Law School in 1861.

Rose, Charles Day (1847–1913), son of Charlotte Temple Rose who was Mary Temple Tweedy's sister.

Rose, Lady Charlotte Temple (d. 1883), sister of Mary Temple Tweedy, married Sir John Rose (1820–1888), a Canadian, in 1843. He was her second husband.

Rosebery, Archibald Philip Primrose, 5th earl of (1847–1929), British statesman and author.

Rosina. *See* Emmet, Rosina Hubley

Rosmini-Serbati, Antonio (1797–1855), Italian philosopher.

Rosse, Florence James (1862–1908), daughter of Howard James and wife of Irving Collins Rosse (1847–1901), a physician.

Rossetti, Dante Gabriel (1828–1882), London-born poet and painter.

Rowse, Samuel Worcester (1822–1901), American artist, illustrator.

Royce, Josiah (1855–1916), American philosopher, one of WJ's close personal friends.

Ruskin, John (1819–1900), British essayist and critic.

Rutson, Albert, a friend of Charles Eliot Norton and HJ's "neighbor above stairs" on Half-Moon St. (*HJL*, 1:91).

Sainte-Beuve, Charles-Augustin (1804–1869), French writer and critic.

Saint-Gaudens, Augustus (1848–1907), American sculptor.

Saintsbury, George Edward Bateman (1845–1933), English critic.

Salisbury, marquis of. *See* Cecil, Robert Arthur Talbot Gascoyne

Salter, Charles Christie (1839–1870), a divinity student at Harvard in 1863–64.

Salter, Mary Sherwin Gibbens (1851–1933), sister of AGJ and wife of William Mackintire Salter.

Salter, William Mackintire (1853–1931), husband of Mary Sherwin Gibbens Salter, a lecturer in the Society for Ethical Culture.

Sand, George (1804–1876), pseudonym of Amandine-Aurore-Lucie Dudevant, French novelist.

Sands, Mrs. Mahlon (d. 1896), American-born socialite who with her husband owned a villa in Newport in the late 1850s. She was a sister-in-law of the second wife of Edwin Lawrence Godkin.

Santayana, George (1863–1952), Spanish-born philosopher, WJ's colleague at Harvard.

Sardou, Victorien (1831–1908), French playwright.

Sargent, Amelia Jackson Holmes (1843–1889), sister of Oliver Wendell Holmes, Jr.

Sargent, Frederick Le Roy (1886–1928), American biologist and author, husband of Helen Maria Child Sargent.

Sargent, Helen Maria Child (d. 1903), daughter of Francis James Child and wife of Frederick Le Roy Sargent.

Sargent, John Singer (1856–1925), American painter.

Sargy. *See* Perry, Thomas Sergeant

Scherer, Edmond-Henri-Adolphe (1815–1889), French critic.

Schermerhorn, Alfred Egmont (1871–1932), a dealer in real estate and a member of one of the oldest families in New York, husband of Elizabeth Mary Coster Schermerhorn.

Schermerhorn, Elizabeth Mary Coster (1877–1946), daughter of Marie James Bay Coster and wife of Alfred Egmont Schermerhorn.

Schiller, Ferdinand Canning Scott (1864–1937), British philosopher.

Schiller, Johann Christoph Friedrich von (1759–1805), German poet and dramatist.

Schliemann, Heinrich (1822–1890), German archaeologist.

Schott, Theodor (1852–1921), German physician, specializing in the treatment of heart diseases by a combination of digitalis, exercise, and baths at Nauheim.

Scott, Clement William (1841–1904), British author and critic.

Scudder, Horace Elisha (1838–1902), American editor and writer, served as editor for the publishers of the *Atlantic Monthly*.

Sedgwick, Arthur George (1844–1915), American lawyer and journalist who from time to time was associated with the *Nation*. He was the son of Sarah Ashburner Sedgwick, who was the sister of Grace and Anne Ashburner, and the brother of Theodora Sedgwick, Susan Ridley Sedgwick Norton, and Sara Sedgwick Darwin.

Sedgwick, Sara. *See* Darwin, Sara Ashburner Sedgwick

Sedgwick, Susie, an unidentified person associated with Stockbridge, Mass.

Sedgwick, Theodora (also Marian Theodora) (1851–1916), sister of Arthur George Sedgwick, Susan Ridley Sedgwick Norton, and Sara Ashburner Sedgwick Darwin.

Sévigné, Marie de Rabutin-Chantal, marquise de (1626–1696), known primarily for her letters.

Shaler, Nathaniel Southgate (1841–1906), professor of geology at Harvard.

Shattuck, Elizabeth Perkins Lee, daughter of Henry Lee, married Frederick Cheever Shattuck (1847–1929), a physician, in the summer of 1877.

Shaw, Robert Gould (1837–1863), commanded the 54th Regiment of Massachusetts Volunteer Infantry, the first black regiment in the Union army, and was killed on 18 July 1863 during the assault on Fort Wagner, Charleston, S.C. GWJ served under Shaw.

Shepherd, Charles William, an English author whom WJ met in Teplitz in 1868.

Shinn, Earl (1837–1886), American art critic.

Sidgwick, Eleanor Mildred (1845–1936), British educator and psychical researcher, wife of Henry Sidgwick.

Sidgwick, Henry (1838–1900), British philosopher, president of the English Society for Psychical Research in 1882–84 and 1888–92. He was married to Eleanor Mildred Sidgwick.

Skinner, Alice, HJ's parlor maid at Lamb House.

Skinner, Ernest, HJ's physician at Rye.

Smalley, George Washburn (1833–1916), correspondent for the *New York Tribune*. His wife was Phœbe Gamant Smalley.

Smalley, Ida, daughter of George Washburn Smalley.

Smith, Goldwin (1823–1910), British controversialist, journalist, historian.

Smith, Logan Pearsall (1865–1946), American-born author, lived in England after 1888. He was the son of Hannah Whitall Smith whose writings on religion WJ admired.

Smith, Robert Pearsall (1827–1898), American Quaker preacher, father of Logan Pearsall Smith.

Smiths, husband and wife, HJ's servants from 1886 until 1901 when he had to dismiss them for drunkenness.

Souvestre, Émile (1806–1854), French writer.

Souvestre, Marie (d. 1905), French-born headmistress of Allenswood, a school for girls at Wimbledon.

Spangenberg, Johanna, keeper of a boarding house in Dresden where WJ stayed in 1868.

Spottiswoode, William (1825–1883), British mathematician and physicist.

Stanley, Dorothy (Dolly) Tennant (b. c. 1851), a painter, wife of Sir Henry Morton Stanley and sister of Eveleen Tennant Myers.

Stanley, Sir Henry Morton (1841–1904), British explorer of Africa.

Stephen, Julia Prinsep Duckworth, second wife of Leslie Stephen.

Stephen, Leslie (1832–1904), British essayist, editor, and critic. His first wife was Harriet Marian Thackeray (d. 1875), daughter of William Makepeace Thackeray. In 1878 he married Julia Prinsep Duckworth.

Stevenson, Frances Matilda Van de Grift Osbourne (b. 1840), wife of Robert Louis Stevenson, her second husband.

Stevenson, Robert Louis (1850–1894), British novelist.

Stickney, Albert (1839–1908), American lawyer, completed Harvard Law School in 1862.

Stillé, Alfred (1813–1900), American physician.

Stonham, Edgar Lewis, HJ's neighbor in Rye.

Storey, Gertrude Cutts, wife of Moorfield Storey.

Storey, Moorfield (1845–1929), American lawyer and author.

Story, William Wetmore (1819–1895), American lawyer, poet, and sculptor.

Sturges, Jonathan (1864–1911), American-born writer and translator, a victim of polio. He was admired by HJ whom he visited for extended periods at Lamb House.

Sturgis, Marie Eveleen Meredith (b. 1871), daughter of George Meredith.

Sullivan, Sir Arthur Seymour (1842–1900), British composer.

Sully, James (1842–1923), British psychologist and philosopher.

Swinburne, Algernon Charles (1837–1909), British poet and critic.

Symonds, John Addington (1840–1893), British author.

Taft, William Howard (1857–1930), president of the United States from 1909 to 1913.

Taine, Hippolyte-Adolphe (1828–1893), French philosopher, psychologist, and critic.

Tappan, Caroline Sturgis, wife of William Aspinwall Tappan, a friend of Ralph Waldo Emerson. The Tappans lived in Boston, spending their summers on the Tanglewood estate in Lenox, Mass.

Tappan, Ellen. *See* Dixey, Ellen Sturgis Tappan

Tappan, Mary Aspinwall (1852?–1941), daughter of Caroline Sturgis Tappan and sister of Ellen Sturgis Tappan Dixey.

Temple, Elly. *See* Hunter, Ellen James Temple Emmet

Temple, Mary (Minny) (1845–1870), daughter of Catharine Margaret James (1820–1854), WJ's father's sister, and Robert Emmet Temple (1808–1854). After the death of their parents, the six Temple children, Mary, Katharine, Henrietta, Ellen, Robert, and William James, were brought up by Edmund Tweedy and his wife, Mary Temple Tweedy.

Temple, Robert (b. 1840), WJ's cousin who led a troubled life and landed in jail in about 1885.

Temple, William James (1842–1863), one of six Temple children who were cousins of the Jameses, a student at Harvard for one year. A captain in the United States infantry, he was killed in the battle at Chancellorsville on 1 May 1863.

Tennyson, Lionel (1854–1886), son of the poet, married Eleanor Locker.

Thayer, James Bradley (1831–1902), American lawyer.

Theodora. *See* Sedgwick, Theodora

Thies, Clara, daughter of Louis Thies.

Thies, Louis (d. 1871), German pharmacist, curator of the Gray Collection of Engravings at Harvard University, husband of Clara Crowninshield Thies. When the Thies family traveled to Europe in 1866, they rented their house at 20 Quincy St., Cambridge, to the Jameses. Several years later the Jameses bought the house.

Thompson, Rosalie (Mrs. Edmond Thompson) (b. 1868), a trance medium studied by Myers.

Thorne, William Bezly (d. 1917), British physician who treated WJ for his heart condition. Thorne wrote about the treatment of heart disease according to the Schott method at Nauheim. Since library catalogues list a Leslie Thorne (b. 1868) who also specialized in the treatment of chronic diseases of the heart at Nauheim, there is some possibility of confusion. It has not been established whether two doctors named Thorne treated WJ.

Tilden, Samuel Jones (1814–1886), American politician, a presidential candidate in 1876.

Timmins, Gemma, the sister of Minna Timmins Chapman who was the wife of John Jay Chapman (1862–1933), American critic and essayist.

Tintoretto (1518–1594), Italian painter, whose real name was Jacopo Robusti.

Titian (c. 1490–1576), Venetian painter.

Toy, Crawford Howell (1836–1919), American Orientalist, began teaching at Harvard in 1880.

Trench, Herbert (1865–1923), Irish-born playwright, artistic director of the Haymarket Theatre in London.

Trevelyan, Caroline Philips, wife of Sir George Otto Trevelyan.

Trevelyan, Sir George Otto (1838–1928), British historian and politician.

Treves, Sir Frederick (1853–1923), British surgeon.

T.S.P. *See* Perry, Thomas Sergeant

Tuck, Henry (1842–1904), graduated from the Harvard Medical School in 1867, and in July of that year went to Europe for fourteen months. In later years he was a medical examiner for life insurance companies.

Tuckerman, Emily (d. 1924), a friend and correspondent of Edwin Lawrence Godkin.

Tuckey, Charles Lloyd (1885–1925), British physician.

Turgenev, Ivan Sergeevich (1818–1883), Russian writer. HJ met Turgenev in 1875 and corresponded with him extensively.

Turner, Joseph Mallord William (1775–1851), British artist, championed by John Ruskin who had a collection of Turner's work.

Turner, Samuel Epes (1846–1896), professor at Harvard.

Tweedy, Edmund (d. 1901), husband of Mary Temple Tweedy.

Tweedy, Mary Temple (Aunt Mary) (d. 1891), wife of Edmund Tweedy and sister of Robert Emmet Temple and hence an aunt of WJ's Temple cousins. She died at the age of eighty.

Tyndall, John (1820–1893), British scientist.

Van Buren, Elly. *See* Morris, Ellen James Van Buren

Van Buren, Kitty. *See* Miller, Catharine Barber Van Buren

Van Dyck (or Vandyke), Anthony (1599–1641), Flemish painter.

Vaux, Mary Walsh James (b. 1875), daughter of RJ, wife of George Vaux, Jr.

Verrall, Margaret de Gaudrion Merrifield (1859–1916), British psychical researcher.

Villari, Pasquale (1827–1917), Italian historian and politician.

Vogüé, Eugène-Marie Melchior, vicomte de (1848–1910), French novelist.

Voss, Johann Heinrich (1751–1826), translator of *The Odyssey* and *The Iliad*.

Wagniére, Laura Huntington, of Boston, was related to the Greenoughs and Huntingtons. She was married to a Swiss banker.

Walcott, Henry Pickering (1838–1932), American physician, acting president of Harvard in 1900–1901.

Walsh, Catharine (Aunt Kate) (1812–1889), WJ's mother's sister who lived with the Jameses. She died in New York City.

Walsh, Elizabeth Robertson (Lila, Lilla) (1850–1901), daughter of James William Walsh who was WJ's mother's brother, took care of Catharine Walsh (Aunt Kate) in New York City.

Walsh, Hugh (d. 1817), born in Ireland, one of the first inhabitants of Newburgh, N.Y.

Walsh, James William, Jr. (1852–1908), a New York stockbroker, son of James William Walsh, WJ's mother's brother.

Walsh, Louisa Corrin (b. 1849), daughter of Alexander Robertson Walsh, WJ's mother's brother.

Walsh, Richard Montgomery Lawrence (1848–1908), a stockbroker and amateur painter, a cousin of the Jameses.

Ward, Mary Augusta Arnold (Mrs. Humphrey Ward) (1851–1920), English novelist.

Ward, Thomas Humphrey (1845–1926), British art critic and editor.

Ward, Thomas Wren (1844–1940), a banker, graduated from Harvard in 1866, a member of the expedition to Brazil led by Louis Agassiz. He was the son of Samuel Gray Ward, American banker, and Anna Hazard Barker Ward. His mother was the sister of William H. Barker, who was the husband of Jeanette James, WJ's aunt. Thomas Wren Ward had two sisters: Elizabeth (Bessie) Ward de Schönberg and Lydia Ward von Hoffman.

Waring, Daisy, daughter of George Edwin Waring (1833–1898), American engineer who lived in Newport.

Warner, Joseph Bangs (1848–1923), WJ's attorney.

Warren, Edward Prioleau (1856–1937), British architect. Warren helped HJ to repair and furnish Lamb House.

Warren, William Ross (1860–1918), American businessman, member of the visiting committee for philosophy at Harvard.

Washburn, Francis Tucker (1843–1873), graduated from Harvard in 1864, attended Harvard Divinity School, and became a Unitarian clergyman.

Washburn, William Tucker (1841–1916), graduated from Harvard in 1862, a lawyer, author of *Fair Harvard* (1869), brother of Francis Tucker Washburn.

Washington, Booker Taliaferro (1856–1915), American educator.

Waterlow, Sydney Philip Perigal (1878–1944), English scholar and diplomat. Waterlow moved to Rye in 1907.

Watson, Mary Forbes (1836–1891), daughter of Robert Sedgwick Watson and Mary Hathaway Watson of Milton, Mass.

Webb, Susie, an otherwise unidentified relative of AGJ.

Wedmore, Frederick (1844–1921), British art critic.

Weld, Mary, HJ's secretary from 1901 to 1904.

Wells, Herbert George (1866–1946), English author.

Wendell. *See* Holmes, Oliver Wendell, Jr.

Wendell, Barrett (1855–1921), professor of English at Harvard.

Wharton, Edith Newbold Jones (1862–1937), American novelist.

White, James Clarke (1833–1916), American physician, specialist in dermatology.

White, James William (1850–1916), American surgeon.

Whitman, Sarah Wyman (Mrs. Henry Whitman) (d. 1904), Boston hostess and artist.

Whitwell, May, an unidentified friend of WJ. In his diary entry for 29 January 1908, WJ noted May Whitwell's death.

Wilde, Oscar (1854–1900), Irish-born playwright.

Wilkie (Wilky). *See* James, Garth Wilkinson

Wilkinson, Florence. *See* Mathews, Florence Wilkinson

Wilkinson, James John Garth (1812–1899), British homeopathic physician, writer, a Swedenborgian friend of Henry James, Sr. He was the father of Mary Wilkinson Mathews, Emma Wilkinson Pertz, and Florence Wilkinson Mathews.

Wilkinson, Mary. *See* Mathews, Mary James Wilkinson

Winsor, Justin (1831–1897), American historian and librarian.

Wister, Owen (1860–1938), American lawyer and writer.

Wister, Sarah Butler (1835–1908), daughter of Fanny Kemble and mother of Owen Wister.

Wood, Helen Mason (1841–1897), daughter of Lydia Lush James Mason and granddaughter of Robert James, WJ's father's brother.

Woolson, Constance Fenimore (1840–1894), American-born novelist and poet, lived in Europe from 1879.

Wormeley, Katharine Prescott (1830–1908), British-born author and translator, sister of Ariana Randolph Wormeley Curtis.

Wright, Chauncey (1830–1875), American philosopher, advocate of Darwinism, associated with WJ in several philosophy clubs in Cambridge.

Wyckoff, Albert (1840–c. 1899), son of Alexander Robertson Wyckoff and nephew of Henry Albert Wyckoff. He was married to Sarah J. Wyckoff.

Wyckoff, Henry Albert (1815–1890), son of Mary Robertson Wyckoff and Albert Wyckoff and brother of Helen Rodgers Wyckoff Perkins. Mary Wyckoff and WJ's maternal grandmother were sisters.

Wyckoff, Sarah J., wife of Albert Wyckoff.

Zola, Émile (1840–1902), French novelist.

Zouche of Haryngworth, Robert Nathaniel Cecil George, Lord (1851–1914), married Annie Mary Eleanor (b. 1857), daughter of 18th Lord Saltoun of Abernethy, on 15 July 1875. She left his house after three months.

Index

This index is a name and subject index, omitting more trivial references, for the text of the letters and the notes. Neither the Introduction by Professor McDermott nor the connecting passages added by the editors are indexed.